![Haynes THE BOOK logo]

Renault 19 Diesel
Service and Repair Manual

Steve Rendle

Models covered

(1946-264-1AF2)

All Renault 19 Diesel and Turbo Diesel models, including special/limited editions,
Hatchback and Saloon/Chamade
1870 cc Diesel engines

For petrol engine models, see manual number 1646

© Haynes Publishing 2002

ABCDE
FGHIJ
KLMN

Printed in the USA

A book in the **Haynes Service and Repair Manual Series**

ISBN **1 85010 935 X**

British Library Cataloguing in Publication Data
A catalogue record for this book is available from the British Library.

Haynes Publishing
Sparkford, Nr Yeovil, Somerset BA22 7JJ, England

Haynes North America, Inc
861 Lawrence Drive, Newbury Park, California 91320, USA

Editions Haynes S.A.
Tour Aurore - IBC 18 Place des Reflets,
92975 Paris La Defense 2, Cedex, France

Haynes Publishing Nordiska AB
Box 1504, 751 45 UPPSALA, Sverige

Contents

LIVING WITH YOUR RENAULT 19 DIESEL

Roadside repairs

MAINTENANCE

Routine maintenance and servicing

Contents

REPAIRS & OVERHAUL

Engine and associated systems

Transmission

Brakes and suspension

Body equipment

Wiring diagrams

REFERENCE

Index

The Renault 19 was first introduced in France, with both petrol and Diesel engines, in September 1988, in 5-door Hatchback form. It was in February 1989 that the Hatchback first became available in the UK.

Since introduction, the Diesel model range has expanded to include 3-door Hatchback (in September 1989), and 4-door Chamade (Saloon) models (in November 1989). Utility models based on the Hatchback are also available in some territories. In mid-1992, the "Phase 2" models were introduced, with revised body styling, and at the same time the Turbo Diesel engine was introduced to the range.

The car follows conventional front-wheel-drive design practice, with a transverse engine and transmission unit accommodated within a subframe.

The engine is of 4-cylinder, in-line overhead camshaft type and, with the exception of the fuel system, Turbo and non-Turbo engine components are similar. All models are fitted with a 5-speed manual gearbox.

The front suspension is of MacPherson type and the rear suspension is of either tubular (enclosed-bar) or four-bar (open-bar) type.

A wide range of standard and optional equipment is available across the model range, including power steering, anti-lock braking, electric windows, central locking, etc.

The car is quite conventional in design and the DIY home mechanic should find most work straightforward.

Renault 19 Chamade ("Phase 1")

Renault 19 Turbo DX ("Phase 1")

Your Renault 19 Diesel manual

The aim of this manual is to help you get the best value from your vehicle. It can do so in several ways. It can help you decide what work must be done (even should you choose to get it done by a garage). It will also provide information on routine maintenance and servicing, and give a logical course of action and diagnosis when random faults occur. However, it is hoped that you will use the manual by tackling the work yourself. On simpler jobs it may even be quicker than booking the car into a garage and going there twice, to leave and collect it. Perhaps most important, a lot of money can be saved by avoiding the costs a garage must charge to cover its labour and overheads.

The manual has drawings and descriptions to show the function of the various components so that their layout can be understood. Tasks are described and photographed in a clear step-by-step sequence.

Project vehicles

The main project vehicle used in the preparation of this manual, and appearing in many of the photographic sequences was a Renault 19 RT 1.9 Turbo D Hatchback. Additional work was carried out and photographed on a Renault 19 1.9 D Biarritz Hatchback.

Acknowledgements

Thanks are due to Champion Spark Plug, who supplied replacement component information. Certain other illustrations are the copyright of Renault (UK) Limited, and are used with their permission. Thanks are also due to Kings of Taunton Ltd, who provided technical assistance, Sykes-Pickavant Limited, who provided some of the workshop tools, and to all those people at Sparkford and Newbury Park who helped in the production of this manual.

This manual is not a direct reproduction of the vehicle manufacturers' data, and its publication should not be taken as implying any technical approval by the vehicle manufacturers or importers.

We take great pride in the accuracy of information given in this manual, but vehicle manufacturers make alterations and design changes during the production run of a particular vehicle of which they do not inform us. No liability can be accepted by the authors or publishers for loss, damage or injury caused by any errors in, or omissions from, the information given.

Working on your car can be dangerous. This page shows just some of the potential risks and hazards, with the aim of creating a safety-conscious attitude.

General hazards

Scalding

• Don't remove the radiator or expansion tank cap while the engine is hot.
• Engine oil, automatic transmission fluid or power steering fluid may also be dangerously hot if the engine has recently been running.

Burning

• Beware of burns from the exhaust system and from any part of the engine. Brake discs and drums can also be extremely hot immediately after use.

Crushing

• When working under or near a raised vehicle, always supplement the jack with axle stands, or use drive-on ramps. *Never venture under a car which is only supported by a jack.*
• Take care if loosening or tightening high-torque nuts when the vehicle is on stands. Initial loosening and final tightening should be done with the wheels on the ground.

Fire

• Fuel is highly flammable; fuel vapour is explosive.
• Don't let fuel spill onto a hot engine.
• Do not smoke or allow naked lights (including pilot lights) anywhere near a vehicle being worked on. Also beware of creating sparks (electrically or by use of tools).
• Fuel vapour is heavier than air, so don't work on the fuel system with the vehicle over an inspection pit.
• Another cause of fire is an electrical overload or short-circuit. Take care when repairing or modifying the vehicle wiring.
• Keep a fire extinguisher handy, of a type suitable for use on fuel and electrical fires.

Electric shock

• Ignition HT voltage can be dangerous, especially to people with heart problems or a pacemaker. Don't work on or near the ignition system with the engine running or the ignition switched on.

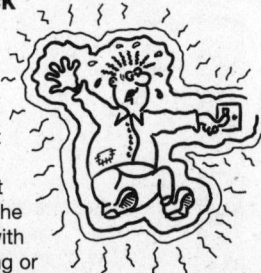

• Mains voltage is also dangerous. Make sure that any mains-operated equipment is correctly earthed. Mains power points should be protected by a residual current device (RCD) circuit breaker.

Fume or gas intoxication

• Exhaust fumes are poisonous; they often contain carbon monoxide, which is rapidly fatal if inhaled. Never run the engine in a confined space such as a garage with the doors shut.
• Fuel vapour is also poisonous, as are the vapours from some cleaning solvents and paint thinners.

Poisonous or irritant substances

• Avoid skin contact with battery acid and with any fuel, fluid or lubricant, especially antifreeze, brake hydraulic fluid and Diesel fuel. Don't syphon them by mouth. If such a substance is swallowed or gets into the eyes, seek medical advice.
• Prolonged contact with used engine oil can cause skin cancer. Wear gloves or use a barrier cream if necessary. Change out of oil-soaked clothes and do not keep oily rags in your pocket.
• Air conditioning refrigerant forms a poisonous gas if exposed to a naked flame (including a cigarette). It can also cause skin burns on contact.

Asbestos

• Asbestos dust can cause cancer if inhaled or swallowed. Asbestos may be found in gaskets and in brake and clutch linings. When dealing with such components it is safest to assume that they contain asbestos.

Special hazards

Hydrofluoric acid

• This extremely corrosive acid is formed when certain types of synthetic rubber, found in some O-rings, oil seals, fuel hoses etc, are exposed to temperatures above 400°C. The rubber changes into a charred or sticky substance containing the acid. *Once formed, the acid remains dangerous for years. If it gets onto the skin, it may be necessary to amputate the limb concerned.*
• When dealing with a vehicle which has suffered a fire, or with components salvaged from such a vehicle, wear protective gloves and discard them after use.

The battery

• Batteries contain sulphuric acid, which attacks clothing, eyes and skin. Take care when topping-up or carrying the battery.
• The hydrogen gas given off by the battery is highly explosive. Never cause a spark or allow a naked light nearby. Be careful when connecting and disconnecting battery chargers or jump leads.

Air bags

• Air bags can cause injury if they go off accidentally. Take care when removing the steering wheel and/or facia. Special storage instructions may apply.

Diesel injection equipment

• Diesel injection pumps supply fuel at very high pressure. Take care when working on the fuel injectors and fuel pipes.

⚠ *Warning: Never expose the hands, face or any other part of the body to injector spray; the fuel can penetrate the skin with potentially fatal results.*

Remember...

DO

• Do use eye protection when using power tools, and when working under the vehicle.

• Do wear gloves or use barrier cream to protect your hands when necessary.

• Do get someone to check periodically that all is well when working alone on the vehicle.

• Do keep loose clothing and long hair well out of the way of moving mechanical parts.

• Do remove rings, wristwatch etc, before working on the vehicle – especially the electrical system.

• Do ensure that any lifting or jacking equipment has a safe working load rating adequate for the job.

DON'T

• Don't attempt to lift a heavy component which may be beyond your capability – get assistance.

• Don't rush to finish a job, or take unverified short cuts.

• Don't use ill-fitting tools which may slip and cause injury.

• Don't leave tools or parts lying around where someone can trip over them. Mop up oil and fuel spills at once.

• Don't allow children or pets to play in or near a vehicle being worked on.

Jump starting

When jump-starting a car using a booster battery, observe the following precautions:

✔ Before connecting the booster battery, make sure that the ignition is switched off.

✔ Ensure that all electrical equipment (lights, heater, wipers, etc) is switched off.

✔ Make sure that the booster battery is the same voltage as the discharged one in the vehicle.

✔ If the battery is being jump-started from the battery in another vehicle, the two vehcles MUST NOT TOUCH each other.

✔ Make sure that the transmission is in neutral (or PARK, in the case of automatic transmission).

HAYNES HiNT

Jump starting will get you out of trouble, but you must correct whatever made the battery go flat in the first place. There are three possibilities:

1 *The battery has been drained by repeated attempts to start, or by leaving the lights on.*

2 *The charging system is not working properly (alternator drivebelt slack or broken, alternator wiring fault or alternator itself faulty).*

3 *The battery itself is at fault (electrolyte low, or battery worn out).*

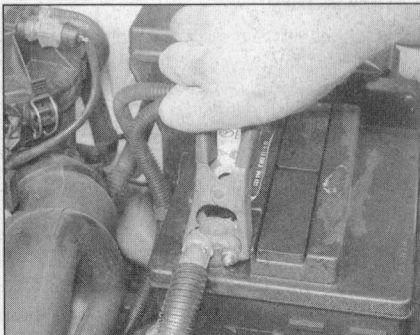

1 Connect one end of the red jump lead to the positive (+) terminal of the flat battery

2 Connect the other end of the red lead to the positive (+) terminal of the booster battery.

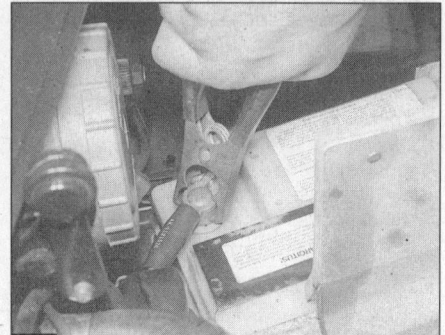

3 Connect one end of the black jump lead to the negative (-) terminal of the booster battery

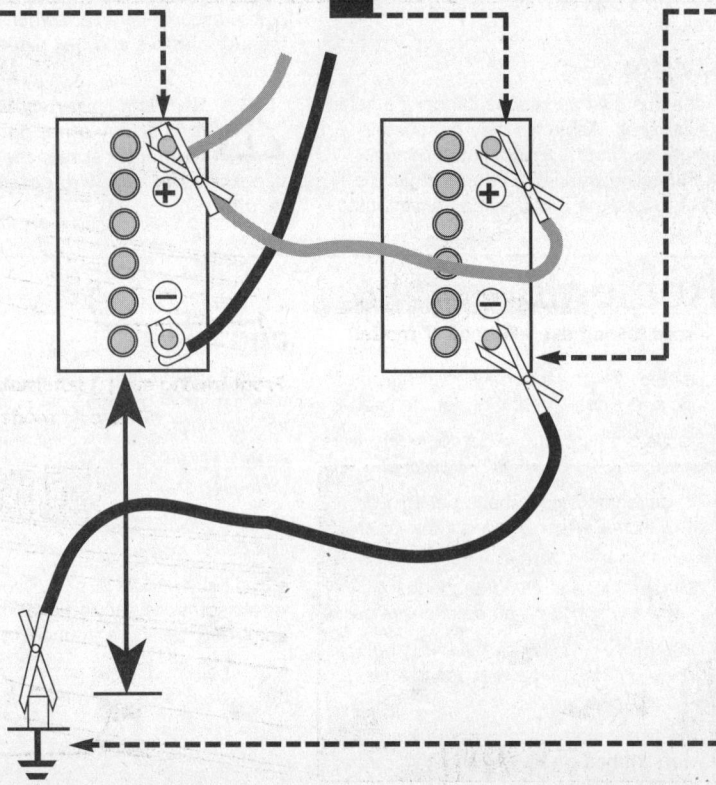

4 Connect the other end of the black jump lead to a bolt or bracket on the engine block, well away from the battery, on the vehicle to be started.

5 Make sure that the jump leads will not come into contact with the fan, drive-belts or other moving parts of the engine.

6 Start the engine using the booster battery, then with the engine running at idle speed, disconnect the jump leads in the reverse order of connection.

Wheel changing

The spare wheel is located in a cradle under the rear of the vehicle. The cradle is lowered by turning the cradle retaining screw, located at the rear of the luggage compartment near the tailgate/boot lid lock striker. The cradle retaining screw can be turned by engaging the end of the wheel brace (located in clips on the side of the luggage compartment) with the slot in the screw. Lift the cradle to release the retaining catch, then lower for access to the spare wheel. The jack is located in clips on the side of the luggage compartment (see illustrations).

To change a wheel, remove the spare wheel and jack (as described previously), apply the handbrake and place chocks at the front and rear of the wheel diagonally opposite the one to be changed. Select first or reverse gear. Make sure that the vehicle is located on firm level ground and then slightly loosen the wheel bolts with the brace provided (where applicable remove the trim first). Locate the jack head in the jacking point on the relevant side of the vehicle to be raised, and raise the jack by turning the screw using the wheel brace (see illustration).

When the wheel is clear of the ground remove the bolts and lift off the wheel. Fit the spare wheel and moderately tighten the bolts. Lower the vehicle and then tighten the bolts fully. Refit the trim where applicable. If possible, check the tyre pressure on the spare wheel. Remove the chocks and stow the jack, tools, and the damaged wheel. Have the damaged tyre or wheel repaired, or renew it as soon as possible.

Using the wheel brace to lower the spare wheel

Jack location in the luggage compartment

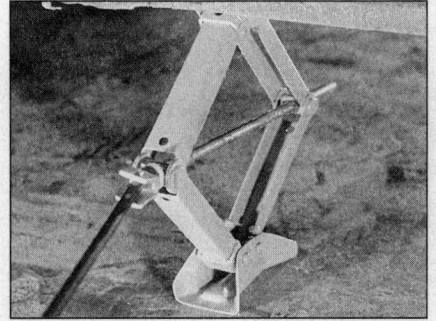

Jack correctly located in the jacking point

Towing

Towing eyes are fitted to the front and rear of the vehicle for attachment of a tow rope. The towing eyes can be accessed through slots in the bumpers (see illustrations). Always turn the ignition key to position "M" when the vehicle is being towed, so that the steering lock is released and the direction indicator and brake lights are operational.

Before being towed, release the handbrake and place the gear lever in neutral. Note that greater than usual pedal pressure will be required to operate the brakes, since the vacuum servo unit is only operational with the engine running. Similarly, on models with power steering, greater than usual steering effort will be required.

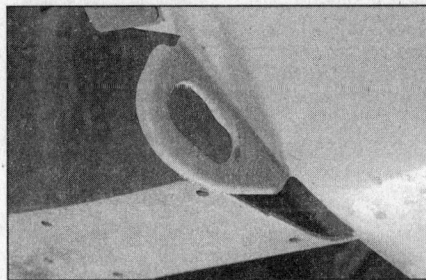

Front towing eye - "Phase 1" model

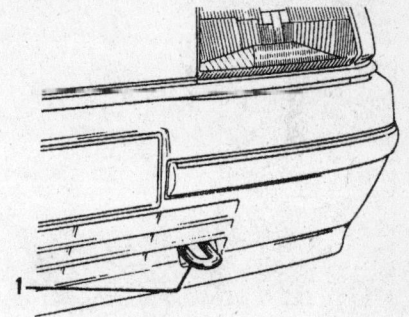

Front towing eye (1) (alternative location) - "Phase 1" model

Front towing eye (1) - "Phase 2" model

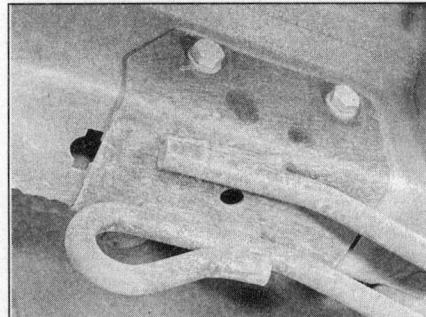

Rear towing eye

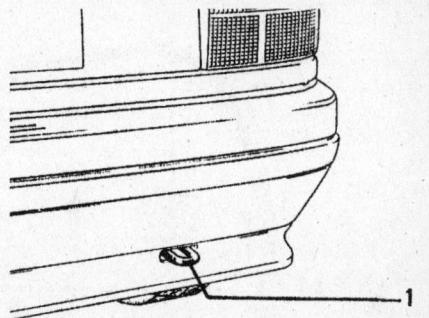

Rear towing eye (1) - alternative location

Identifying leaks

Puddles on the garage floor or drive, or obvious wetness under the bonnet or underneath the car, suggest a leak that needs investigating. It can sometimes be difficult to decide where the leak is coming from, especially if the engine bay is very dirty already. Leaking oil or fluid can also be blown rearwards by the passage of air under the car, giving a false impression of where the problem lies.

⚠️ **Warning: Most automotive oils and fluids are poisonous. Wash them off skin, and change out of contaminated clothing, without delay.**

HAYNES HiNT *The smell of a fluid leaking from the car may provide a clue to what's leaking. Some fluids are distinctively coloured. It may help to clean the car carefully and to park it over some clean paper overnight as an aid to locating the source of the leak.*

Remember that some leaks may only occur while the engine is running.

Sump oil

Engine oil may leak from the drain plug...

Oil from filter

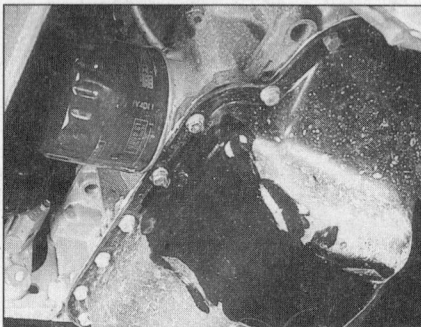

...or from the base of the oil filter.

Gearbox oil

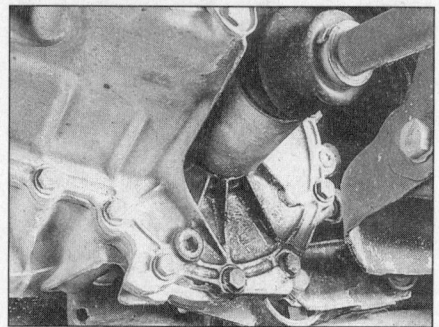

Gearbox oil can leak from the seals at the inboard ends of the driveshafts.

Antifreeze

Leaking antifreeze often leaves a crystalline deposit like this.

Brake fluid

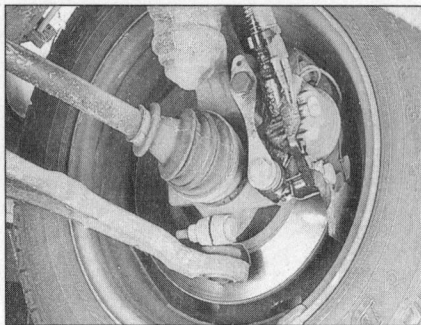

A leak occurring at a wheel is almost certainly brake fluid.

Power steering fluid

Power steering fluid may leak from the pipe connectors on the steering rack.

Chapter 1
Routine maintenance and servicing

Contents

Degrees of difficulty

| Easy, suitable for novice with little experience | | Fairly easy, suitable for beginner with some experience | | Fairly difficult, suitable for competent DIY mechanic | | Difficult, suitable for experienced DIY mechanic | | Very difficult, suitable for expert DIY or professional | |

Engine

Oil filter type (Champion recommendation) .... Champion F105

Cooling system

Air conditioning compressor drivebelt tension	See Section 11 of this Chapter	
Antifreeze mixtures:	**Antifreeze**	**Water**
Protection to -23°C	35%	65%
Protection to -40°C	50%	50%

Fuel system

Air filter type (Champion recommendation):
    Non-Turbo models .... Champion W212
    Turbo models .... No information at time of writing
Fuel filter type (Champion recommendation) .... Champion L131 or L137
Idle speed:
    Non-Turbo engines except F8Q 706 .... 825 ± 25 rpm
    F8Q 706 engine .... 800 ± 50 rpm
    Turbo engines .... 825 ± 50 rpm
Fast idle speed:
    Bosch injection pump .... 1000 ± 50 rpm
    Lucas injection pump .... Not adjustable (factory set)
Anti-stall speed:
    Non-Turbo models (with 4 mm shim - see text) .... 1350 ± 50 rpm
    Turbo models (with 4 mm shim - see text) .... 1250 ± 50 rpm

Brakes

Minimum front brake disc pad thickness (including backplate) .... 6.0 mm
Minimum rear brake disc pad thickness (including backplate) .... 5.0 mm
Minimum rear brake shoe lining thickness (including shoe) .... 2.5 mm

Suspension and steering

Power steering pump drivebelt tension	See Section 11 of this Chapter	
	Front	**Rear**
Tyre pressures (tyres cold)	2.2 bars	2.2 bars

Note: *Recommended tyre pressures are marked on a label attached to the driver's door edge or frame. Pressures apply only to original equipment tyres, and may vary if any other make or type of tyre is fitted; check with the tyre manufacturer or supplier for correct pressures if necessary.*

Electrical system

Alternator drivebelt tension .... See Section 11 of this Chapter
Wiper blade type (Champion recommendation):
    Windscreen .... Champion X-5103
    Rear window .... Champion X-4503

Torque wrench settings

	Nm	lbf ft
Engine sump drain plug	15 to 25	11 to 18
Roadwheel bolts	90	66

The maintenance intervals in this manual are provided with the assumption that you, not the dealer, will be carrying out the work. These are the minimum maintenance intervals recommended by the manufacturer for vehicles driven daily. If you wish to keep your vehicle in peak condition at all times, you may wish to perform some of these procedures more often. We encourage frequent maintenance because it enhances the efficiency, performance and resale value of your vehicle. If the vehicle is driven in dusty areas, used to tow a trailer, or driven frequently at slow speeds (idling in traffic) or on short journeys, more frequent maintenance intervals are recommended.

When the vehicle is new, it should be serviced by a factory-authorised dealer service department in order to preserve the factory warranty.

Every 250 miles (400 km) or weekly

- ☐ Check the engine oil level (Section 3)
- ☐ Check the engine coolant level (Section 3)
- ☐ Check the brake fluid level (Section 3)
- ☐ Check the screen washer fluid level (Section 3)
- ☐ Check the condition of the battery (Section 4)
- ☐ Visually examine the tyres for tread depth, and wear or damage (Section 5)
- ☐ Check and if necessary adjust the tyre pressures (Section 5)

Every 5000 miles (8000 km)

In addition to all the items listed previously, carry out the following:

- ☐ Renew the engine oil (Section 6)
- ☐ Renew the engine oil filter (Section 6)
- ☐ Drain any water from the fuel filter (Section 7)
- ☐ Check the turbocharger pipe and hose connections for security and leakage - where applicable (Section 8)
- ☐ Check the power steering fluid level, where applicable (Section 9)
- ☐ Check all underbonnet components and hoses for fluid leaks (Section 10)
- ☐ Check the condition of the auxiliary drivebelt(s), and renew if necessary (Section 11)
- ☐ Check the operation of the clutch mechanism, where applicable (Section 12)
- ☐ Check the operation of the horn, all lamps, and the wipers and washers (Sections 13)
- ☐ Check the operation of the heating and (where applicable) the air conditioning system (Section 14)
- ☐ Check the condition of the air conditioning system refrigerant - where applicable (see Section 14)
- ☐ Check the headlamp beam alignment (Section 15)
- ☐ Check the condition of the wiper blades (Section 16)
- ☐ Check the condition of the front brake pads and renew if necessary (Section 17)
- ☐ Check the suspension and steering components for condition and security (Section 18)
- ☐ Check the condition of the driveshafts (Section 19)
- ☐ Check the bodywork and underframe for damage and corrosion (Section 20)
- ☐ Check the condition of the exhaust system components (Section 21)

Every 10 000 miles (16000 km)

In addition to all the items listed previously, carry out the following:

- ☐ Renew the air filter (Section 22)
- ☐ Renew the fuel filter (Section 23)
- ☐ Carry out a road test (Section 24)
- ☐ Check the manual gearbox oil level (Section 25)

Every 15 000 miles (24 000 km)

In addition to all the items listed for the 5000 miles interval, carry out the following:

- ☐ Check and if necessary adjust the idle speed (Section 26)

Every 40 000 miles (64 000 km)

In addition to all the items listed for the 5000 and 10 000 miles intervals, carry out the following:

- ☐ Check the operation of the handbrake mechanism, and adjust if necessary (Section 27)
- ☐ Check the condition of the rear brake shoes and renew if necessary - rear drum brake models (Section 28)
- ☐ Check the condition of the rear disc brake pads and renew if necessary - rear disc brake models (Section 29)
- ☐ Renew the brake fluid (Section 30)
- ☐ Check the front wheel alignment, and adjust if necessary (Section 31)

Every 70 000 miles (112 000 km)

In addition to all the items listed previously, carry out the following:

- ☐ Renew the timing belt (Chapter 2A)

Every 2 years

In addition to all the items listed previously, carry out the following:

- ☐ Renew the coolant (Section 33)

Note: *Renault do not specify renewal intervals for the antifreeze mixture, as the mixture used to fill the system when the vehicle is new is designed to last the lifetime of the vehicle. However, it is strongly recommended that the coolant is renewed at the intervals specified in the "Maintenance schedule", as a precaution against possible engine corrosion problems. This is particularly advisable if the coolant has been renewed previously, using an antifreeze other than that specified by Renault. With many antifreeze types, the corrosion inhibitors become progressively less effective with age. It is up to the individual owner whether or not to follow this advice.*

1

Underbonnet view of a Renault 19 Turbo Diesel

1 Washer fluid reservoir
2 Suspension strut top mounting
3 Brake fluid reservoir
4 Engine oil filler cap
5 Preheating system control unit
6 Brake vacuum pump
7 Coolant expansion tank
8 Auxiliary fuse/relay box
9 Intercooler
10 Air cleaner
11 Thermostat housing

12 Cooling fan
13 Engine oil level dipstick
14 Engine oil filter
15 Power steering fluid reservoir
16 Alternator
17 Fuel filter
18 Fuel system priming plunger
19 Right-hand engine mounting cover
20 Fuel injection pump
21 Accelerator cable

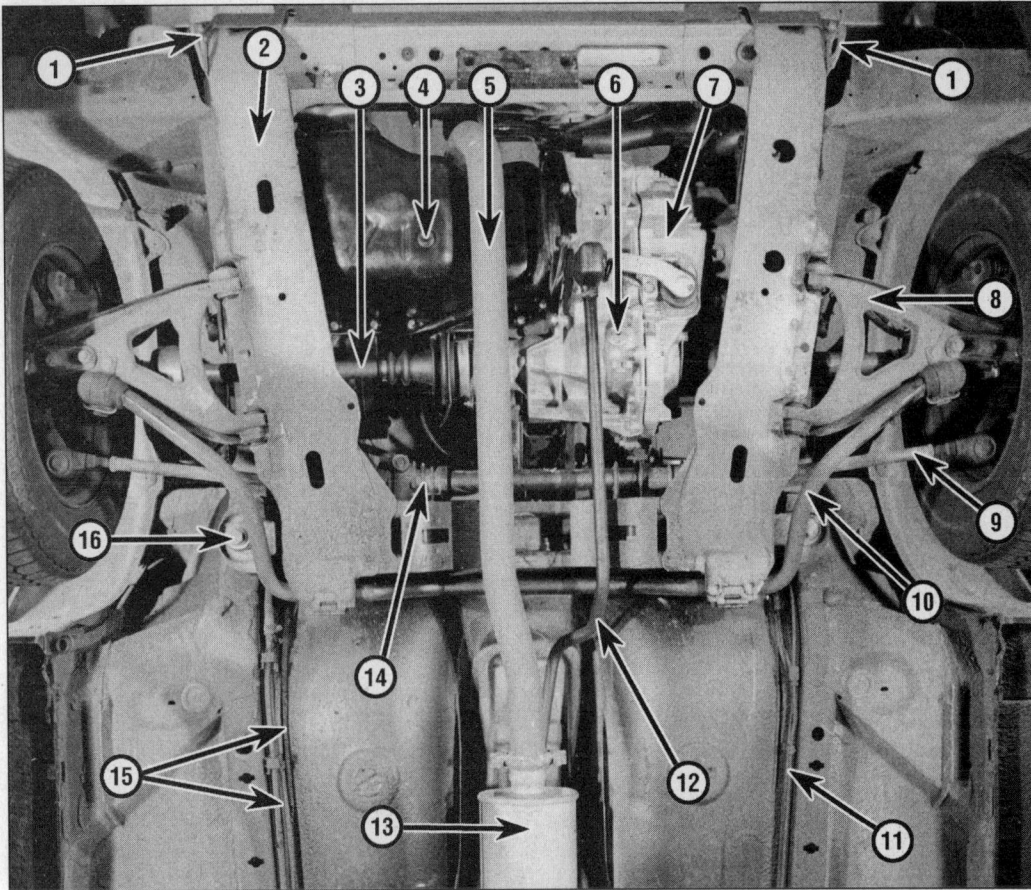

View of the front underside

1 Front towing eyes
2 Subframe
3 Driveshaft
4 Engine oil drain plug
5 Exhaust front section
6 Gearbox oil drain plug
7 Gearbox
8 Front suspension lower arm
9 Steering track rod
10 Front anti-roll bar
11 Brake fluid pipes
12 Gearchange link rod
13 Front silencer
14 Steering rack
15 Fuel pipes
16 Engine support cross-member

1

View of the rear underside

1 Fuel tank filler pipe
2 Fuel tank
3 Brake fluid pipes
4 Fuel pipes
5 Handbrake cables
6 Exhaust expansion box
7 Rear axle side mounting bracket
8 Rear axle
9 Rear shock absorber
10 Exhaust silencer
11 Spare wheel

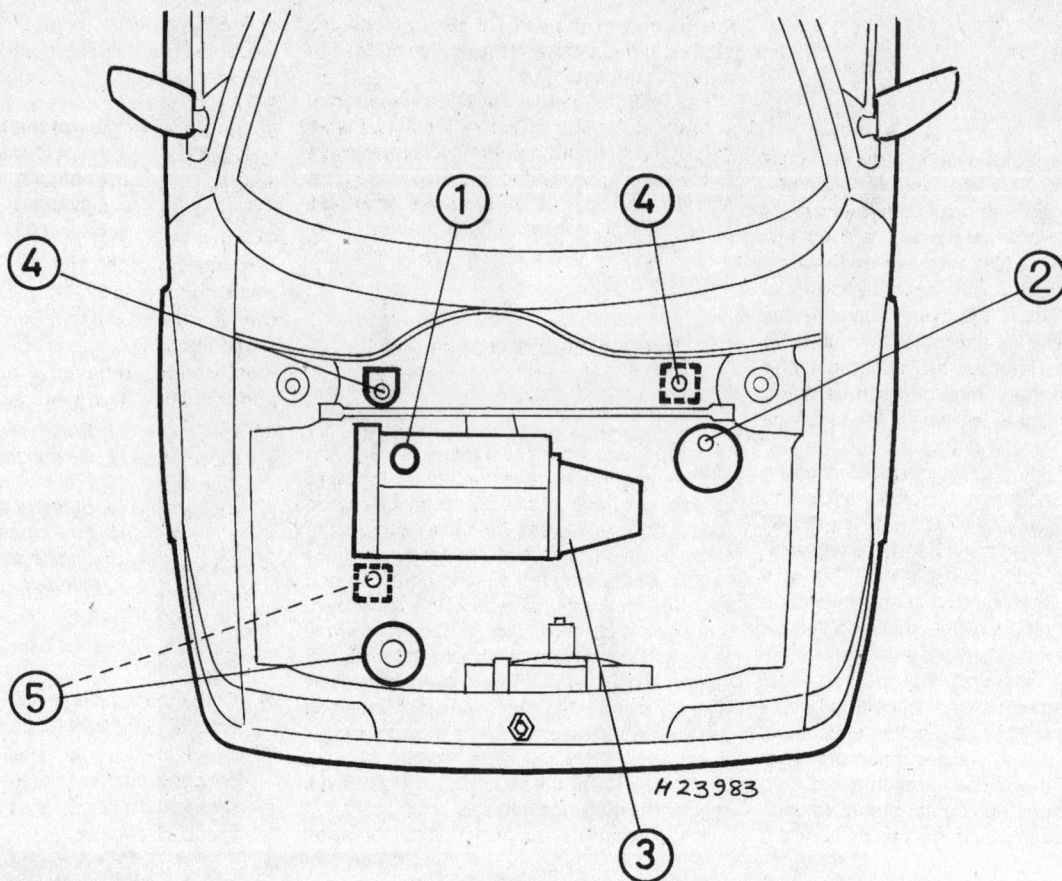

H 23983

Lubricants and fluids

Component or system	Lubricant type/specification
1 Engine	Multigrade engine oil, viscosity SAE 10W/30 to 15W/40, to CCMC-PD2, API CD, or better
2 Cooling system	Ethylene glycol-based antifreeze
3 Manual gearbox	Tranself TRX 80W
4 Brake fluid reservoir	Hydraulic fluid to SAE J1703F, DOT 3 or DOT 4
5 Power steering fluid reservoir . .	Elf Renaultmatic D2, Dexron type ATF
Fuel	Commercial diesel fuel for road vehicles (DERV)

Capacities

Engine oil

Sump capacity (for oil change, including filter)	5.5 litres
Oil filter	0.5 litre
Difference between "MAX" and "MIN" dipstick marks	2.0 litres

Cooling system
Coolant (approximate capacities):

Non-Turbo engines	6.8 litres
Turbo engines	7.1 litres

Manual gearbox

JB3-type	3.4 litres
JC5-type	3.1 litres

Fuel tank

All models	55.0 litres

Maintenance procedures

1 Introduction

This Chapter is designed to help the home mechanic maintain his/her vehicle for safety, economy, long life and peak performance.

The Chapter contains a master maintenance schedule, followed by Sections dealing specifically with each task on the schedule. Visual checks, adjustments, component renewal and other helpful items are included. Refer to the accompanying illustrations of the engine compartment and the underside of the vehicle for the locations of the various components.

Servicing of your vehicle in accordance with the mileage/time maintenance schedule and the following Sections will provide a planned maintenance program, which should result in a long and reliable service life. This is a comprehensive plan, so maintaining some items but not others at the specified service intervals will not produce the same results.

As you service your vehicle, you will discover that many of the procedures can - and should - be grouped together because of the particular procedure being performed, or because of the close proximity of two otherwise unrelated components to one another. For example, if the vehicle is raised for any reason, the exhaust can be inspected at the same time as the suspension and steering components.

The first step in this maintenance program is to prepare yourself before the actual work begins. Read through all the Sections relevant to the work to be carried out, then make a list and gather together all the parts and tools required. If a problem is encountered, seek advice from a parts specialist, or a dealer service department.

2 Intensive maintenance

If, from the time the vehicle is new, the routine maintenance schedule is followed closely and frequent checks are made of fluid levels and high wear items, as suggested throughout this manual, the engine will be kept in relatively good running condition and the need for additional work will be minimised.

It is possible that there will be times when the engine is running poorly due to the lack of regular maintenance. This is even more likely if a used vehicle, which has not received regular and frequent maintenance checks, is purchased. In such cases, additional work may need to be carried out, outside of the regular maintenance intervals.

If engine wear is suspected, a compression or leakdown test (Chapter 2A) will provide valuable information regarding the overall performance of the main internal components. Such a test can be used as a basis to decide on the extent of the work to be carried out. If for example a compression or leakdown test indicates serious internal engine wear, conventional maintenance as described in this Chapter will not greatly improve the performance of the engine, and may prove a waste of time and money, unless extensive overhaul work (Chapter 2B) is carried out first.

The following series of operations are those most often required to improve the performance of a generally poor-running engine.

a) Clean, inspect and test the battery (Section 4)
b) Check the levels of all the engine related fluids (Section 3)
c) Check the condition and tension of the alternator drivebelt (Section 11)
d) Check the fuel filter - drain off any water and renew the filter if necessary (Sections 7 and 23)
e) Check the condition of the air filter, and renew if necessary (Section 22)
f) Check the condition of all hoses and check for fluid leaks (Section 10)
g) Check and if necessary adjust the idle speed (Section 26)

Weekly checks

3 Fluid level checks

Engine oil

1 The engine oil level is checked with a dipstick that extends through a tube and into the sump at the bottom of the engine. The dipstick is located towards the front of the engine **(see illustration)**. On models equipped with an oil level gauge, the check can be made by switching on the ignition - the upper and lower limits on the gauge correspond to the upper and lower marks on the dipstick.
2 The oil level should be checked with the vehicle standing on level ground and before it is driven, or at least 5 minutes after the engine has been switched off.
3 Withdraw the dipstick from the tube and wipe all the oil from the end with a clean rag or paper towel. Insert the clean dipstick back into the tube as far as it will go, then withdraw it once more. Check that the oil level is between the upper ("MAX") and lower ("MIN") marks/notches on the dipstick. If the level is towards the lower ("MIN") mark/notch, unscrew the oil filler cap on the valve cover and add fresh oil until the level is on the upper ("MAX") mark/notch **(see illustrations)**. Note that the difference between the minimum and maximum marks/notches on the dipstick corresponds to 2 litres.
4 Always maintain the level between the two

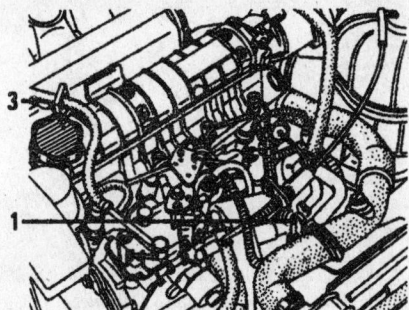

3.1 Location of engine oil level dipstick (1) and oil filler cap (3)

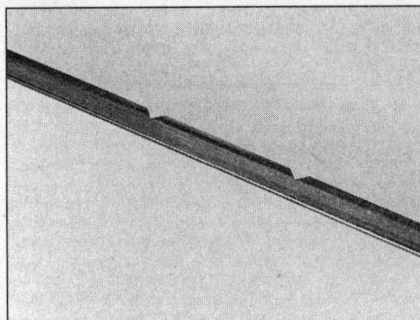

3.3a Engine oil level dipstick "MIN" and "MAX" level notches

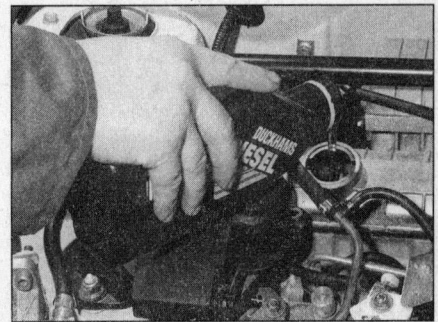

3.3b Oil is added through the filler on the valve cover

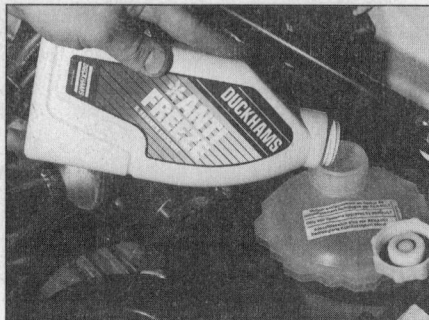

3.9 Adding coolant to the expansion tank

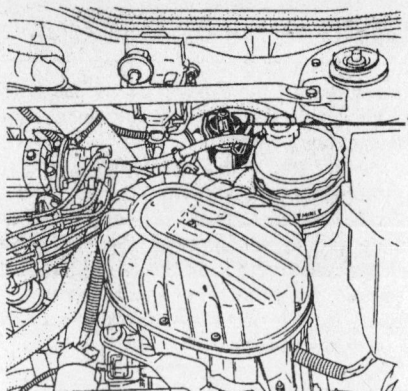

3.11a Brake fluid reservoir location (1) - left-hand-drive non-ABS model (some right-hand-drive models have a remotely-mounted reservoir in the same location)

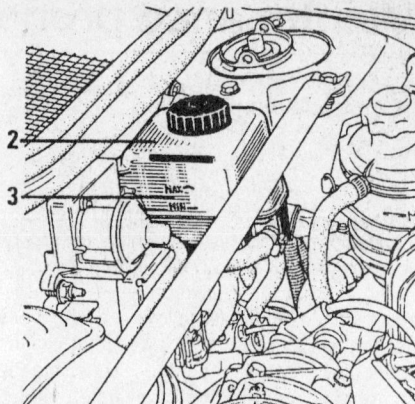

3.11b Brake fluid reservoir location (2) and level markings (3) - left-hand-drive ABS model

dipstick marks/notches. If the level is allowed to fall below the lower mark/notch, oil starvation may result which could lead to severe engine damage. If the engine is overfilled by adding too much oil, this may result in oil leaks or oil seal failures.

5 An oil can spout or funnel may help to reduce spillage when adding oil to the engine. Always use the correct grade and type of oil as shown in *"Lubricants, fluids and capacities"*.

Coolant

⚠️ *Warning: DO NOT attempt to remove the expansion tank pressure cap when the engine is hot, as there is a very great risk of scalding. Do not allow antifreeze to come in contact with your skin, or with the painted surfaces of the vehicle. Rinse off spills immediately with plenty of water. Never leave antifreeze lying around in an open container, or in a puddle on the floor. Children and pets are attracted by its sweet smell, but antifreeze can be fatal if ingested.*

6 All vehicles covered by this manual are equipped with a pressurised cooling system. An expansion tank is located on the left-hand side of the engine compartment. The expansion tank has a continual flow of coolant passing through it in order to purge air from the cooling system.

7 The coolant level in the expansion tank should be checked regularly. The level in the tank varies with the temperature of the engine. When the engine is cold, the coolant level should be up to the maximum ("MAX") level mark on the side of the tank. When the engine is hot, the level will be slightly above the mark.

8 If topping up is necessary, wait until the engine is cold, then slowly unscrew the pressure cap on the expansion tank. Allow any remaining pressure to escape then fully unscrew the cap.

9 Add a mixture of water and antifreeze (see below) through the expansion tank filler neck until the coolant is up to the maximum ("MAX") level mark **(see illustration)**. Refit and tighten the pressure cap.

10 With a sealed type cooling system, the addition of coolant should only be necessary at very infrequent intervals. If frequent topping up is required, it is likely there is a leak in the

system. Check the radiator, all hoses and joint faces for any sign of staining or actual wetness, and rectify as necessary. If no leaks can be found, it is advisable to have the pressure cap and the entire system pressure tested by a dealer or suitably equipped garage as this will often show up a small leak not previously visible.

Brake fluid

⚠️ *Warning: Hydraulic fluid is poisonous; wash off immediately and thoroughly in the case of skin contact, and seek immediate medical advice if any fluid is swallowed or gets into the eyes. Certain types of hydraulic fluid are inflammable, and may ignite when allowed into contact with hot components; when servicing any hydraulic system, it is safest to assume that the fluid is inflammable, and to take precautions against the risk of fire as though it is petrol that is being handled Finally, it is hygroscopic (it absorbs moisture from the air) - old fluid may be contaminated and unfit for further use. When topping-up or renewing the fluid, always use the recommended type (see "Recommended lubricants and fluids"), and ensure that it comes from a freshly-opened, previously-sealed container.*

HAYNES HINT *Hydraulic fluid is an effective paint stripper, and will attack plastics; if any is spilt, it should be washed off immediately using copious quantities of fresh water.*

11 The location of the brake fluid reservoir varies according to model. On models without ABS, the brake fluid reservoir is located on the top of the brake master cylinder which is attached to the front of the vacuum servo unit. Alternatively, on certain models, the reservoir may be remotely-mounted on the bulkhead, with hoses supplying the master cylinder. On

models with ABS the brake fluid reservoir is located on top of the ABS hydraulic unit attached to the bulkhead. The maximum and minimum marks are indicated on the side of the reservoir and the fluid level should be maintained between these marks at all times **(see illustrations)**.

12 On models with ABS, first switch on the ignition, then depress the brake pedal several times in order to activate the electric hydraulic pump on the ABS unit. Leave the ignition switched on during the check.

13 The brake fluid inside the reservoir is readily visible. With the car on level ground the level should be above the ("MIN") (Danger) mark and preferably on or near the ("MAX") mark. Note that wear of the brake pads or brake shoe linings causes the level of the brake fluid to gradually fall, so that when the brake pads are renewed, the original level of the fluid is restored. It is not therefore necessary to top up the level to compensate for this minimal drop, however the level must never be allowed to fall below the minimum mark.

14 If topping-up is necessary, first wipe the area around the filler cap with a clean rag before removing the cap. When adding fluid, pour it carefully into the reservoir to avoid spilling it on surrounding painted surfaces **(see illustration)**. Be sure to use only the

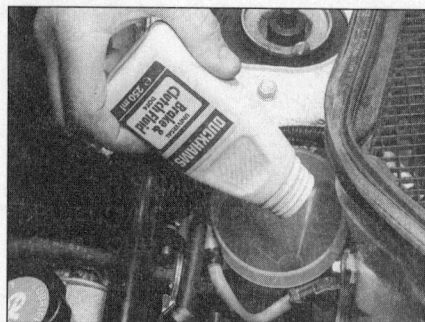

3.14 Topping up the brake fluid level using a funnel and hose - right-hand-drive non-ABS model shown

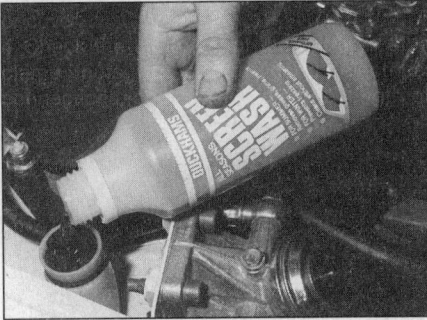

3.19 Topping up the washer fluid level

4.2 Lifting the cover for access to the battery

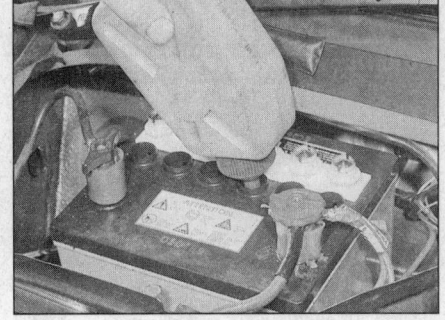

4.13 Topping up the battery electrolyte level

specified brake hydraulic fluid since mixing different types of fluid can cause damage to the system. See *"Lubricants, fluids and capacities"* at the beginning of this Chapter.

15 When adding fluid it is a good idea to inspect the reservoir for contamination. The system should be drained and refilled if deposits, dirt particles or contamination are seen in the fluid.

16 After filling the reservoir to the proper level, make sure that the cap is refitted securely to avoid leaks and the entry of foreign matter. On models with ABS switch off the ignition.

17 If the reservoir requires repeated replenishing to maintain the proper level, this is an indication of a hydraulic leak somewhere in the system which should be investigated immediately.

Washer fluid

18 The windscreen/tailgate/headlamp washer fluid reservoir is located at the right-hand front corner of the engine compartment.

19 Check that the fluid level is at least up to the bottom of the filler neck, and top up if necessary **(see illustration)**. When topping up the reservoir, a screen wash should be added in the recommended quantities.

4 Battery check

Caution: Before carrying out any work on the vehicle battery, read through the precautions given in "Safety first!" at the beginning of this manual.

1 The battery is located on the right-hand side of the engine compartment, on the bulkhead.

2 Prise up the plastic battery cover for access to the top of the battery **(see illustration)**.

3 The exterior of the battery should be inspected for damage such as a cracked case or cover.

4 Check the tightness of the battery cable clamp nuts to ensure good electrical connections, and check the entire length of

each cable for cracks and frayed conductors.

5 If corrosion (visible as white, fluffy deposits) is evident, remove the cables from the battery terminals, clean them with a small wire brush, then refit them. Corrosion can be kept to a minimum by applying a thin layer of petroleum jelly to the clamps and terminals after they have been reconnected.

6 Make sure that the battery tray is in good condition, and that the retaining clamp is tight.

7 Corrosion on the tray, retaining clamp and the battery itself can be removed with a solution of water and baking soda. Thoroughly rinse all cleaned areas with plain water. Dry the battery and its surroundings with rags or tissues, which should then be discarded.

8 Any metal parts damaged by corrosion should be covered with a zinc-based primer, then painted.

9 Most models are fitted with a "maintenance-free" battery which does not require topping-up. If this is the case, the battery will be sealed, and it will not be possible to remove the cell covers.

10 On models fitted with a low-maintenance or a conventional battery, the electrolyte level should be checked periodically as follows.

11 Pull out the cell covers from the top of the battery.

12 Check that the level of electrolyte is approximately 15 mm above the tops of the cell plates.

13 If necessary top-up the level, using only

distilled or demineralised water **(see illustration)**.

14 Refit the cell covers.

15 Information on the battery, charging and jump-starting can be found in Chapter 5 and in the preliminary Sections of this manual.

5 Tyre checks

1 The original tyres on this car are equipped with tread wear safety bands which will appear when the tread depth reaches approximately 1.6 mm (0.063 in). Tread wear can be monitored with a simple, inexpensive device known as a tread depth indicator gauge **(see illustration)**.

2 Wheels and tyres should give no real problems in use provided that a close eye is kept on them with regard to excessive wear or damage. To this end, the following points should be noted.

3 Ensure that tyre pressures are checked regularly and maintained correctly. Checking should be carried out with the tyres cold and not immediately after the vehicle has been in use **(see illustration)**. If the pressures are checked with the tyres hot, an apparently high reading will be obtained owing to heat expansion. Under no circumstances should an attempt be made to reduce the pressures to the quoted cold reading in this instance, or effective underinflation will result.

5.1 Checking the tyre tread depth with an indicator gauge

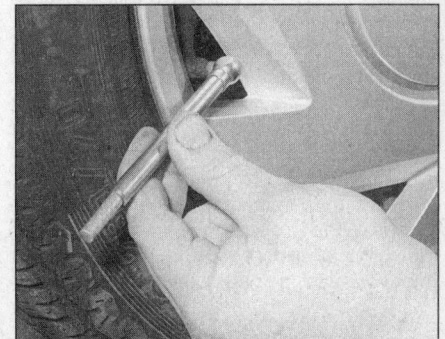

5.3 Checking the tyre pressures with a tyre pressure gauge

Tyre Tread Wear Patterns

Shoulder Wear

**Underinflation
(wear on both sides)**
Check and adjust pressures

**Incorrect wheel camber
(wear on one side)**
*Repair or renew suspension
parts*

Hard cornering
Reduce speed!

Centre Wear

Overinflation
Check and adjust pressures

*If you sometimes have to inflate
your car's tyres to the higher
pressures specified for maximum
load or sustained high speed,
don't forget to reduce the pressures to normal afterwards.*

Toe Wear

Incorrect toe setting
Adjust front wheel alignment

Note: The feathered edge of
the tread which characterises
toe wear is best checked by
feel.

Uneven Wear

Incorrect camber or castor
*Repair or renew suspension
parts*

Malfunctioning suspension
*Repair or renew suspension
parts*

Unbalanced wheel
Balance tyres

Out-of-round brake disc/drum
Machine or renew

4 Note any abnormal tread wear **(see
illustration)**. Tread pattern irregularities such
as feathering, flat spots and more wear on
one side than the other are indications of front
wheel alignment and/or balance problems. If
any of these conditions are noted, they should
be rectified as soon as possible.

5 Underinflation will cause overheating of the
tyre owing to excessive flexing of the casing,
and the tread will not sit correctly on the road
surface. This will cause a consequent loss of
adhesion and excessive wear, not to mention
the danger of sudden tyre failure due to heat
build-up.

6 Overinflation will cause rapid wear of the
centre part of the tyre tread coupled with
reduced adhesion, harsher ride, and the
danger of shock damage occurring in the tyre
casing.

7 Regularly check the tyres for damage in the
form of cuts or bulges, especially in the
sidewalls. Remove any nails or stones
embedded in the tread before they penetrate
the tyre to cause deflation. If removal of a nail
reveals that the tyre has been punctured, refit
the nail so that its point of penetration is
marked. Then immediately change the wheel
and have the tyre repaired by a tyre dealer. Do
not drive on a tyre in such a condition. In
many cases a puncture can be simply

repaired by the use of an inner tube of the
correct size and type, although make sure that
the item which caused the puncture is
removed first. If in any doubt as to the
possible consequences of any damage found,
consult your local tyre dealer for advice.

8 Periodically remove the wheels and clean
any dirt or mud from the inside and outside
surfaces. Examine the wheel rims for signs of
rusting, corrosion or other damage. Light alloy
wheels are easily damaged by "kerbing"
whilst parking, and similarly steel wheels may
become dented or buckled. Renewal of the
wheel is very often the only course of remedial
action possible.

9 The balance of each wheel and tyre
assembly should be maintained to avoid
excessive wear, not only to the tyres but also to
the steering and suspension components.
Wheel imbalance is normally signified by
vibration through the vehicle's bodyshell,
although in many cases it is particularly
noticeable through the steering wheel.
Conversely, it should be noted that wear or
damage in suspension or steering components
may cause excessive tyre wear. Out-of-round
or out-of-true tyres, damaged wheels and
wheel bearing wear/mal-adjustment also fall
into this category. Balancing will not usually
cure vibration caused by such wear.

10 Wheel balancing may be carried out with
the wheel either on or off the vehicle. If
balanced on the vehicle, ensure that the
wheel-to-hub relationship is marked in some
way prior to subsequent wheel removal so
that it may be refitted in its original position.

11 General tyre wear is influenced to a large
degree by driving style - harsh braking and
acceleration or fast cornering will all produce
more rapid tyre wear. Interchanging of tyres
may result in more even wear, however it is
worth bearing in mind that if this is completely
effective, the added expense is incurred of
replacing simultaneously a complete set of
tyres, which may prove financially restrictive
for many owners.

12 Front tyres may wear unevenly as a result
of wheel misalignment. The front wheels
should always be correctly aligned according
to the settings specified by the vehicle
manufacturer.

13 Legal restrictions apply to many aspects
of tyre fitting and usage and in the UK this
information is contained in the Motor Vehicle
Construction and Use Regulations. It is
suggested that a copy of these regulations is
obtained from your local police if in doubt as
to current legal requirements with regard to
tyre type and condition, minimum tread depth,
etc.

Every 5000 miles

6 Engine oil and filter renewal

1 Frequent oil and filter changes are the most important preventative maintenance procedures that can be undertaken by the DIY owner. As engine oil ages, it becomes diluted and contaminated, which leads to premature engine wear.

2 Before starting this procedure, gather together all the necessary tools and materials **(see illustration)**. Also make sure that you have plenty of clean rags and newspapers handy to mop up any spills. Ideally, the engine oil should be warm, as it will drain better and more built-up sludge will be removed with it. Take care, however, not to touch the exhaust or any other hot parts of the engine when working under the vehicle. To avoid any possibility of scalding, and to protect yourself from possible skin irritants and other harmful contaminants in used engine oils, it is advisable to wear rubber gloves when carrying out this work. Access to the underside of the vehicle will be greatly improved if it can be raised on a lift, driven onto ramps or jacked up and supported on axle stands (see *"Jacking, towing and wheel changing"*). Whichever method is chosen, make sure that the car remains as level as possible, to enable the oil to drain fully.

3 Remove the oil filler cap from the valve cover, then position a suitable container beneath the sump. Where applicable, remove the cover from the engine/gearbox splash shield, then clean the drain plug and the area around it, then slacken it half a turn using a special drain plug key (8 mm square) **(see illustrations)**. If possible, try to keep the plug pressed into the sump while unscrewing it by hand the last couple of turns. As the plug releases from the threads, move it away sharply so the stream of oil issuing from the sump runs into the container, not up your sleeve!

4 Allow some time for the old oil to drain, noting that it may be necessary to reposition the container as the oil flow slows to a trickle.

5 After all the oil has drained, wipe off the drain plug with a clean rag and renew its sealing washer. Clean the area around the drain plug opening, then refit and tighten the plug to the specified torque setting. Where applicable refit the cover to the engine/gearbox splash shield.

6 Move the container into position under the oil filter, located on the front of the cylinder block (a small container will be required to fit under the filter if an engine/gearbox splash shield is fitted).

7 Using an oil filter removal tool, slacken the filter initially **(see illustration)**. Loosely wrap some rags around the oil filter, then unscrew it and immediately position it with its open end uppermost to prevent further spillage of oil. Remove the oil filter from the engine compartment and empty the oil into the container.

8 Use a clean rag to remove all oil, dirt and sludge from the filter sealing area on the engine. Check the old filter to make sure that the rubber sealing ring hasn't stuck to the engine. If it has, carefully remove it.

9 Apply a light coating of clean oil to the sealing ring on the new filter, then screw it into position on the engine **(see illustration)**. Tighten the filter firmly by hand only - do not use any tools. Wipe clean the exterior of the oil filter.

10 Remove the old oil and all tools from under the car, then (if applicable) lower the car to the ground.

11 Fill the engine with the specified quantity and grade of oil, as described earlier in this Section. Pour the oil in slowly, otherwise it may overflow from the top of the valve cover. Check that the oil level is up to the maximum mark on the dipstick, then refit and tighten the oil filler cap.

12 Note that when the engine is first started, there will be a delay of a few seconds before the oil pressure warning light goes out while the new filter fills with oil (this does not apply to Turbo models, for which the procedure described in the following paragraph should be followed). Do not race the engine while the warning light is on.

13 On Turbo models, the following procedure must be observed before starting the engine.

a) *Disconnect the wiring from the stop solenoid on the injection pump, and insulate the connector.*

b) *Crank the engine on the starter motor until the oil pressure warning light goes out (this may take several seconds).*

c) *Reconnect the wiring to the stop solenoid, then start the engine using the normal procedure.*

d) *Run the engine at idle speed, and check the turbocharger oil and coolant unions for leakage. Rectify any problems without delay.*

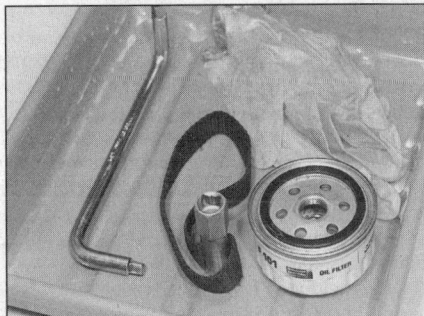

6.2 Tools and materials necessary for engine oil change and filter renewal

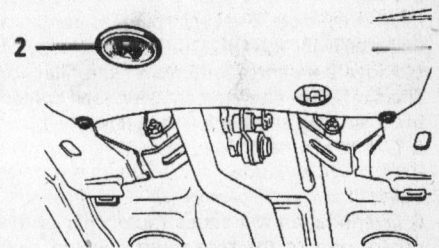

6.3a Sump drain plug cover (2) - not fitted to all models

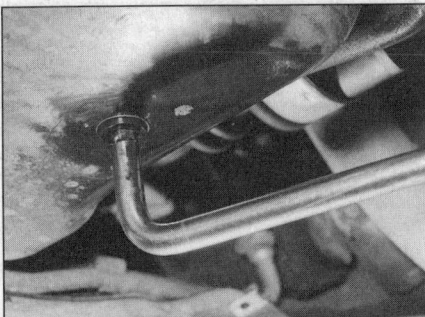

6.3b Using the special drain plug key to unscrew the sump drain plug

6.7 Using an oil filter removal tool to slacken the filter

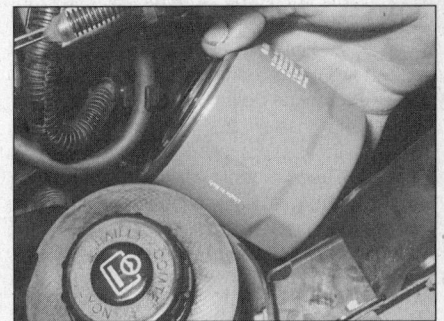

6.9 Screw the new filter into position by hand

1

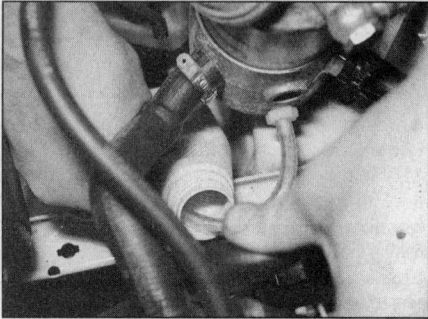

7.2 Tubing attached to drain plug at base of fuel filter housing

14 Run the engine for a few minutes, and check that there are no leaks around the oil filter seal and the sump drain plug.

15 Switch off the engine and wait a few minutes for the oil to settle in the sump once more. With the new oil circulated and the filter now completely full, recheck the level on the dipstick and add more oil if necessary.

16 Dispose of the used engine oil safely with reference to *"General repair procedures"* in the reference Sections of this manual.

7 Fuel filter water draining

1 A water drain plug is provided at the base of the fuel filter housing.

2 Place a suitable container beneath the plug. To make draining easier, a suitable length of tubing can be attached to the outlet on the plug to direct the fuel flow **(see illustration)**.

3 Loosen the fuel inlet union on the filter head, then open the drain plug by turning it anti-clockwise **(see illustration)**.

4 Allow the entire contents of the filter (or filters) to drain into the container, then tighten the drain plug and the fuel inlet union.

5 Dispose of the drained fuel safely.

7.3 Loosening the fuel inlet union on the filter head

6 Prime and bleed the fuel system as described in Chapter 4.

8 Turbocharger check

1 Check all hose and pipe connections (oil, coolant and boost pressure) for security and leaks.

2 Rectify any problems without delay.

9 Power steering fluid level check

1 The power steering fluid reservoir may be located at the front of the engine compartment, or attached to the power steering pump, depending on model **(see illustrations)**.

2 For the check, the front wheels should be pointing straight-ahead and the engine should be stopped and cold. The car should be positioned on level ground.

3 Level markings vary according to model. On models fitted with a remotely-mounted reservoir, there are two types of reservoir

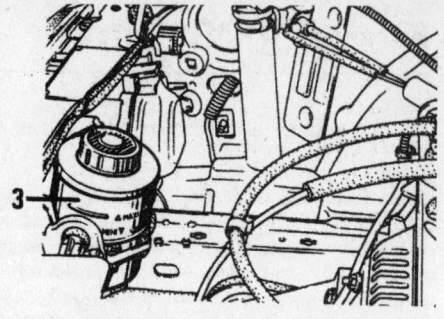

9.1a Remotely-mounted power steering fluid reservoir (3)

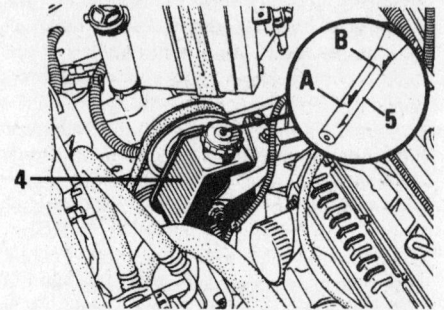

9.1b Pump-mounted power steering fluid reservoir (4)

5 Dipstick
A and B Level markings

fitted. On the first type the fluid should be on the shoulder of the filter screen, and on the later type the fluid should be between the "MIN" and "MAX" level marks **(see illustrations)**. On models with a reservoir mounted on the power steering pump, the level should be between the maximum and minimum marks on the dipstick.

4 Before removing the filler cap use a clean rag to wipe the cap and the surrounding area to prevent any foreign matter from entering the reservoir. Unscrew and remove the filler cap.

5 Top up if necessary with the specified grade of automatic transmission fluid **(see illustration)**. Be careful not to introduce dirt into the system, and do not overfill. Frequent topping up indicates a leak which should be investigated.

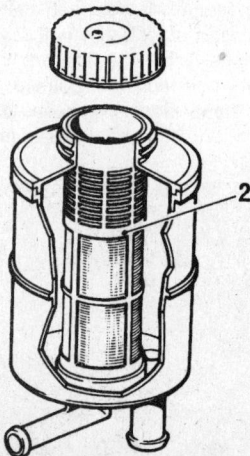

9.3a Early type power steering fluid reservoir showing level shoulder (2) on filler neck

9.3b Later type power steering fluid reservoir

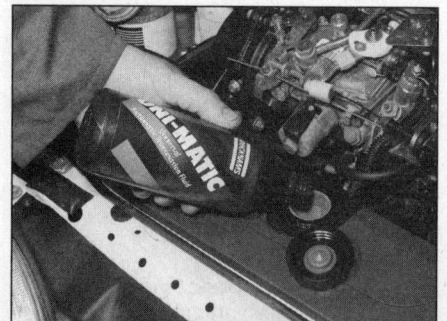

9.5 Topping up the power steering fluid reservoir

10 Hose and fluid leak check

1 Visually inspect the engine joint faces, gaskets and seals for any signs of water or oil leaks. Pay particular attention to the areas around the valve cover, cylinder head, oil filter and sump joint faces. Bear in mind that over a period of time some very slight seepage from these areas is to be expected but what you are really looking for is any indication of a serious leak. Should a leak be found, renew the offending gasket or oil seal by referring to the appropriate Chapter(s) in this manual.

2 Also check the security and condition of all the engine related pipes and hoses. Ensure that all cable ties or securing clips are in place and in good condition. Clips which are broken or missing can lead to chafing of the hoses, pipes or wiring which could cause more serious problems in the future.

3 Carefully check the radiator hoses and heater hoses along their entire length. Renew any hose which is cracked, swollen or deteriorated. Cracks will show up better if the hose is squeezed. Pay attention to the hose clips that secure the hoses to the cooling system components. Hose clips can pinch and puncture hoses, resulting in leaks. If wire type hose clips are used, it may be a good idea to replace them with screw-type clips.

4 Inspect all the cooling system components (hoses, joint faces etc.) for leaks. A leak in the cooling system will usually show up as white or rust coloured deposits on the area adjoining the leak. Where any problems are found on system components, renew the component or gasket, referring to Chapter 3.

5 With the vehicle raised, inspect the fuel tank and filler neck for punctures, cracks and other damage. The connection between the filler neck and tank is especially critical. Sometimes a rubber filler neck or connecting hose will leak due to loose retaining clamps or deteriorated rubber.

6 Similarly, inspect all brake hoses and metal pipes. If any damage or deterioration is discovered, do not drive the vehicle until the necessary repair work has been carried out. Renew any damaged sections of hose or pipe.

7 Carefully check all rubber hoses and metal fuel lines leading away from the petrol tank. Check for loose connections, deteriorated hoses, crimped lines and other damage. Pay particular attention to the vent pipes and hoses which often loop up around the filler neck and can become blocked or crimped. Follow the lines to the front of the vehicle carefully inspecting them all the way. Renew damaged sections as necessary.

8 From within the engine bay, check the security of all fuel hose attachments and pipe unions, and inspect the fuel hoses and vacuum hoses for kinks, chafing and damage.

9 Where applicable, check the condition of the power steering fluid hoses and pipes.

11 Auxiliary drivebelt checking and renewal

Checking

1 The auxiliary drivebelt is located on the front right-hand side of the engine.

2 The configuration of the drivebelt and auxiliary units varies depending on model, and whether the model is equipped with power steering and/or air conditioning.

3 Due to their function and material makeup, drivebelts are prone to failure after a period of time and should therefore be inspected, and if necessary adjusted periodically.

4 Since the drivebelt is located close to the right-hand side of the engine compartment, it is possible to gain better access by raising the front of the vehicle and removing the right-hand wheel, then removing the splash

11.4 Removing the lower timing belt cover for access to the auxiliary drivebelt

shield from inside the wheelarch. On certain models it will also be necessary to remove the lower timing belt cover (see illustration).

5 With the engine switched off, inspect the full length of the drivebelt for cracks and separation of the belt plies. It will be necessary to turn the crankshaft (using a socket or spanner on the crankshaft pulley bolt) in order to move the belt from the pulleys so that the full length of the belt can be inspected thoroughly. Twist the belt between the pulleys so that both sides can be viewed. Also check for fraying, and glazing which gives the belt a shiny appearance. Check the pulleys for nicks, cracks, distortion and corrosion.

Tensioning

6 The tension of the belt is checked by pushing midway between the pulleys at the point indicated (see illustrations). Renault technicians use a special spring-tensioned tool which applies a force of 30 N to the belt and then measures the deflection. An alternative arrangement can be made by using a straight-edge, steel rule and spring balance. Hold the straight edge across the two pulleys, then position the steel rule on the belt, apply the force with the spring balance, and measure the deflection.

7 If adjustment is necessary, loosen the alternator/power steering pump/air conditioning compressor pivot bolt first, then loosen the locknut and adjustment bolt (as applicable). Alternatively, on models equipped with a separate belt tensioner/adjuster mechanism, loosen the tensioner bolt(s) and move, or turn, the tensioner (as applicable) to relieve the tension in the belt (see illustration).

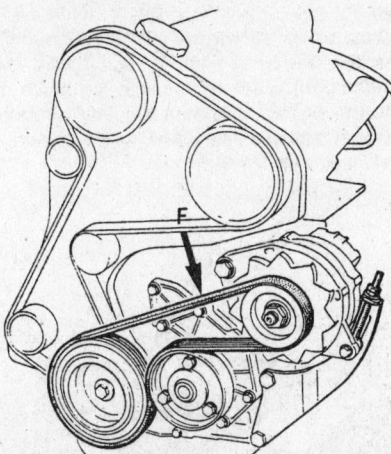

11.7 Loosening the auxiliary drivebelt tensioner bolt - model with power steering

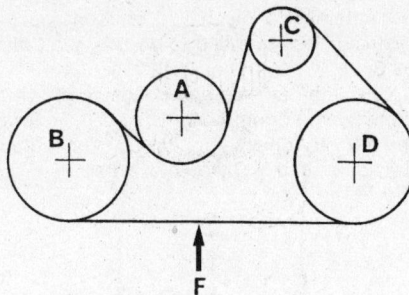

11.6a Auxiliary drivebelt tension checking point (F) - models without power steering or air conditioning

Deflection under a force of 30 N = 3. to 6. mm

11.6b Auxiliary drivebelt tension checking point (F) - models with power steering and air conditioning

A Water pump pulley
B Crankshaft pulley
C Alternator pulley
D Air conditioning compressor pulley
Deflection under a force of 30 N = 2.0 to 3.5 mm

11.11 Removing the auxiliary drivebelt - model with power steering

8 To apply tension to the belt, on models without a separate belt tensioner/adjuster mechanism, insert a lever between the pulley end of the alternator/power steering pump/air conditioning compressor (as applicable), and move the relevant component to tension the belt. Tighten the adjustment and pivot bolts.
9 To apply tension to the belt, on models with a separate belt tensioner/adjuster mechanism, turn or reposition the tensioner (as applicable) to achieve the correct belt tension. Where applicable, tighten the tensioner locknut on completion.
10 Run the engine for about 5 minutes, then recheck the tension.

Removal and refitting

11 To remove a belt, slacken the belt tension fully as described previously. Slip the belt off the pulleys, then fit the new belt ensuring that it is routed correctly **(see illustration)**.
12 With the belt in position, adjust the tension as previously described.

12 Clutch mechanism check

1 Check that the clutch pedal moves smoothly and easily through its full travel, and that the clutch itself functions correctly, with no trace of slip or drag. If the movement is uneven or stiff in places, check that the cable is routed correctly, with no sharp turns.
2 Inspect the ends of the clutch inner cable, both at the gearbox end and inside the vehicle, for signs of wear and fraying.

13 Electrical system check

1 Check the operation of all the electrical equipment, ie lamps, direction indicators, horn etc. Refer to the appropriate Sections of Chapter 12 for details if any of the circuits are found to be inoperative.
2 Note that stop light switch adjustment is described in Chapter 9.

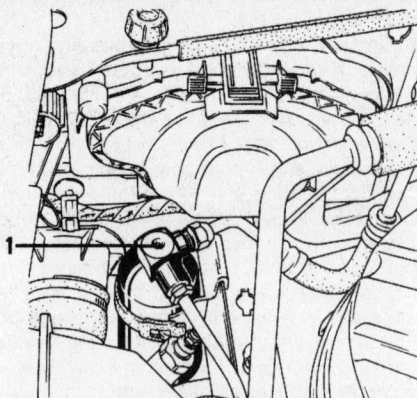

14.2 Air conditioning refrigerant sight glass (1) on top of dehydration unit

3 Visually check all accessible wiring connectors, harnesses and retaining clips for security and for signs of chafing or damage. Rectify any faults found.

14 Heating/air conditioning system check

⚠ **Warning: On models fitted with air conditioning, do not attempt to open the refrigerant circuit. Refer to the precautions given in Chapter 3.**

1 Check that the heating system operates correctly. See Chapter 3.
2 On models with air conditioning, check that the system operates correctly. Run the engine, and switch the air conditioning on to its maximum setting. After it has been operating for a few minutes, inspect the sight glass on top of the dehydration unit **(see illustration)**. If a continuous stream of bubbles is visible, the refrigerant level is low, and professional advice should be sought. **Do not** attempt to discharge or recharge the system unless qualified to do so - see Chapter 3.
3 Check the tension and condition of the air conditioning compressor drivebelt. Refer to the auxiliary drivebelt checking procedure in Section 11 of this Chapter for details.

15.1a Headlamp beam vertical (height) adjustment screw (arrowed) - "Phase 1" models

15.1b Headlamp beam horizontal adjustment screw (arrowed) - "Phase 1" models

4 During the Winter period, it is advisable to run the air conditioning system occasionally (for 10 minutes or so once a month) in order to ensure correct functioning of the compressor and distribution of the oil within the system.

15 Headlamp beam alignment check

1 Accurate adjustment of the headlamp beam is only possible using optical beam setting equipment, and this work should therefore be carried out by a Renault dealer or service station with the necessary facilities. For reference, the location of the beam adjusting screws are as shown **(see illustrations)**.
2 On all models it is possible to adjust the headlamp beam to compensate for the load

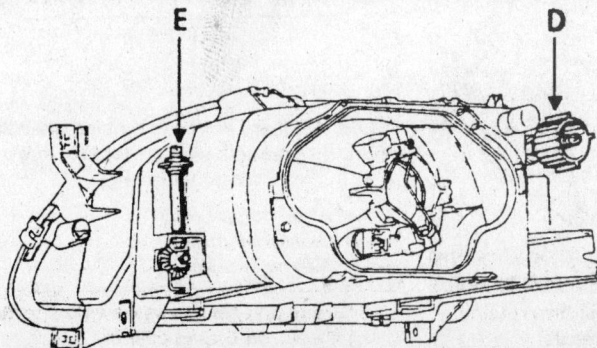

15.1c Headlamp beam adjustment screws - "Phase 2" models
D *Vertical (height) adjustment*
E *Horizontal adjustment*

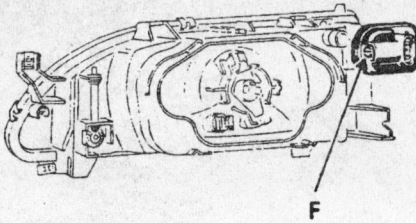

15.2 Headlamp beam vertical (height) adjustment screw (F) - "Phase 2" models with electrically-adjustable headlamps

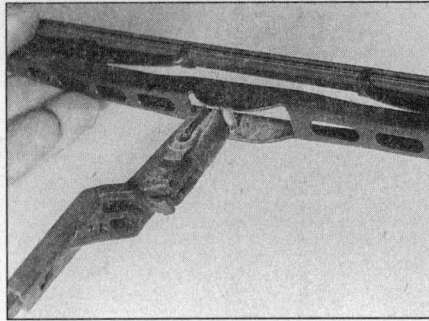

16.3 Removing a wiper blade from the arm fork

16.6 Hinged cover lifted on the tailgate wiper arm

being carried. An adjustment knob is located on the rear of each headlamp on some models, whereas on other models a five-position knob is located on the facia panel inside the car (which operates an electric motor to adjust the headlamps). In the latter case, position 0 should be selected for an unladen vehicle, and position 5 should be selected for maximum load. On models with electrically-adjustable headlamps, a screw is provided for manual adjustment on the rear of the motor (see illustration).

16 Wiper blade check

1 The wiper blades should be renewed when they are deteriorated, cracked, or no longer clean the windscreen or tailgate glass effectively.
2 Lift the wiper arm away from the glass.
3 Release the catch on the arm, turn the blade through 90° and withdraw the blade from the arm fork (see illustration).
4 Insert the new blade into the arm, making sure that it locates securely.
5 Check the wiper arms for worn hinges and weak springs, and renew as necessary.
6 If working on the rear window wiper, lift the hinged cover for access to the retaining nut (see illustration).
7 Make sure that the wiper is in its rest position, and note this position for correct refitting. If necessary, switch the wipers on

and off in order to allow them to return to the "park" position.
8 Unscrew the retaining nut and pull the arm from the spindle (see illustration). If necessary use a screwdriver to prise off the arm, being careful not to damage the paintwork. On the tailgate wiper it will help if the arm is moved to its fully raised position before removing it from the spindle.
9 Fit the new arm using a reversal of the removal procedure.
10 At the same time, take the opportunity to check the washer jets for blockages. Blockages can be removed with a pin, which can also be used to adjust the aim of the jets, if necessary.

17 Front brake disc pad check

⚠ Warning: The dust created by wear of the pads may contain asbestos, which is a health hazard. Never blow it out with compressed air and don't inhale any of it. An approved filtering mask should be worn when working on the brakes. DO NOT use petroleum based solvents to clean brake parts. Use brake cleaner or methylated spirit only.

1 Apply the handbrake, then jack up the front of the car and support on axle stands (see "Jacking, towing and wheel changing").

2 For better access to the front brake calipers, remove both front wheels.
3 Using a steel rule, check that the thickness of the brake pad linings and backing plates is not less than the minimum thickness given in the Specifications. On the Girling caliper it will only be possible to view the centre area of the pads through the small aperture (see illustration), but on the Bendix type all of the pad area is visible.
4 If any one pad thickness is less than the minimum amount, renew all the front pads with reference to Chapter 9.

18 Suspension and steering check

Front suspension and steering check

1 Raise the front of the vehicle and securely support it on axle stands (see "Jacking, towing and wheel changing").
2 Visually inspect the balljoint dust covers and the steering rack and pinion gaiters for splits, chafing or deterioration (see illustration). Any wear of these components will cause loss of lubricant together with dirt and water entry, resulting in rapid deterioration of the balljoints or steering gear.
3 On vehicles equipped with power-assisted steering, check the fluid hoses for chafing or deterioration, and the pipe and hose unions

1

16.8 Unscrewing the wiper arm retaining nut from the spindle

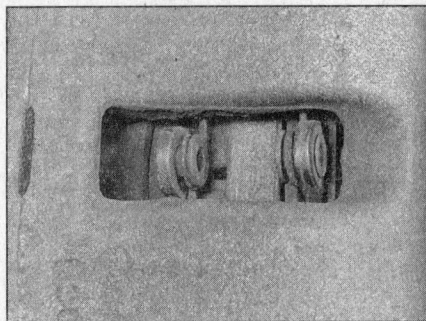

17.3 Brake pad thickness viewing aperture on Girling caliper

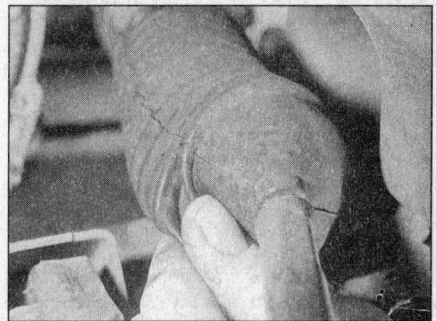

18.2 Checking the condition of a steering rack rubber gaiter

18.4 Checking for wear in the front suspension hub bearings

19.1 Check the condition of driveshaft constant velocity (CV) joint rubber gaiters

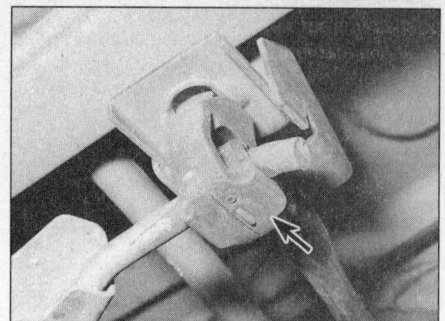

21.3 Exhaust rubber mounting (arrowed)

for fluid leaks. Also check for signs of fluid leakage under pressure from the steering gear rubber gaiters which would indicate failed fluid seals within the steering gear.

4 Grasp the roadwheel at the 12 o'clock and 6 o'clock positions and try to rock it **(see illustration)**. Very slight free play may be felt, but if the movement is appreciable, further investigation is necessary to determine the source. Continue rocking the wheel while an assistant depresses the footbrake. If the movement is now eliminated or significantly reduced, it is likely that the hub bearings are at fault. If the free play is still evident with the footbrake depressed, then there is wear in the suspension joints or mountings.

5 Now grasp the wheel at the 9 o'clock and 3 o'clock positions and try to rock it as before. Any movement felt now may again be caused by wear in the hub bearings or the steering track-rod balljoints. If the outer balljoint is worn the visual movement will be obvious. If the inner joint is suspect it can be felt by placing a hand over the rack and pinion rubber gaiter and gripping the track-rod. If the wheel is now rocked, movement will be felt at the inner joint if wear has taken place.

6 Using a large screwdriver or flat bar, check for wear in the suspension mounting bushes by levering between the relevant suspension component and its attachment point. Some movement is to be expected - the mountings are made of rubber - but excessive wear should be obvious. Also check the condition of any visible rubber bushes, looking for splits, cracks or contamination of the rubber.

7 With the car standing on its wheels, have an assistant turn the steering wheel back and forth about an eighth of a turn each way. There should be very little, if any, lost movement between the steering wheel and roadwheels. If this is not the case, closely observe the joints and mountings previously described, but in addition check the steering column universal joints for wear and also check the rack and pinion steering gear itself.

Rear suspension check

8 Chock the front wheels, then jack up the rear of the car and support it securely on axle stands (see *"Jacking, towing and wheel changing"*).

9 Working as described previously for the front suspension, check the rear hub bearings, the suspension bushes and the shock absorber mountings for wear.

19 Driveshaft check

1 With the vehicle raised and securely supported on stands (see *"Jacking, towing and wheel changing"*), turn the steering onto full lock, then slowly rotate the roadwheel. Inspect the condition of the outer constant velocity (CV) joint rubber gaiters while squeezing the gaiters to open out the folds **(see illustration)**. Check for cracking, splits or deterioration of the rubber which may allow the escape of grease and lead to the ingress of water and grit into the joint. Also check the security and condition of the retaining clips. Repeat these checks on the inner CV joints. If any damage or deterioration is found, the gaiters should be renewed (see Chapter 8).

2 At the same time, check the general condition of the outer CV joints themselves, by first holding the driveshaft and attempting to rotate the wheels. Repeat this check on the right-hand inner joint by holding the inner joint yoke and attempting to rotate the driveshaft. The left-hand inner joint is concealed by a rubber gaiter which is bolted to the transmission casing, and it is not possible to hold the joint since the yoke is an integral part of the differential sun wheel. However, one way to get round this problem is to have an assistant hold the right-hand wheel stationary with 4th gear selected, and then to attempt to rotate the left-hand driveshaft. If this method is used, don't confuse wear in the left-hand CV joint with general wear in the gearbox.

3 Any appreciable movement in the CV joint indicates wear in the joint, wear in the driveshaft splines or a loose driveshaft nut.

20 Bodywork and underframe check

1 With the car raised and supported on axle

stands or over an inspection pit, thoroughly inspect the underbody and wheelarches for signs of damage and corrosion. In particular examine the bottom of the side sills and concealed areas where mud can collect. Where corrosion and rust is evident, press firmly on the panel by hand and check for possible repairs. If the panel is not seriously corroded, clean away the rust and apply a new coating of underseal. Refer to the relevant Sections of Chapter 11 for further information on body repairs.

2 Check all external body panels for damage and rectify where necessary.

21 Exhaust system check

1 With the engine cold (at least an hour after the vehicle has been driven), check the complete exhaust system from the engine to the end of the tailpipe. Ideally the inspection should be carried out with the vehicle on a hoist to permit unrestricted access, but if a hoist is not available raise and support the vehicle safely on axle stands (see *"Jacking, towing and wheel changing"*).

2 Check the exhaust pipes and connections for evidence of leaks, severe corrosion and damage. Make sure that all brackets and mountings are in good condition and tight. Leakage at any of the joints or in other parts of the system will usually show up as a black sooty stain in the vicinity of the leak.

3 Rattles and other noises can often be traced to the exhaust system, especially the brackets and mountings **(see illustration)**. Try to move the pipes and silencers. If the components can come into contact with the body or suspension parts, secure the system with new mountings or if possible, separate the joints and twist the pipes as necessary to provide additional clearance.

4 Run the engine at idling speed then temporarily place a cloth rag over the rear end of the exhaust pipe and listen for any escape of exhaust gases that would indicate a leak.

5 On completion, carefully lower the car to the ground.

Every 10 000 miles

22 Air filter renewal

Non-Turbo models

1 Remove the securing screws (noting that one of the screws is located in the centre of the cover), and withdraw the air cleaner cover (see illustrations).
2 Lift the filter element from the air cleaner casing (see illustration).
3 Clean the inside of the air cleaner casing and the cover, and fit a new filter element.
4 Refit the cover using a reversal of the removal procedure.

Turbo models

5 Loosen the four captive securing bolts, and lift off the air cleaner cover.
6 Proceed as described in paragraphs 2 to 4 inclusive (see illustration).

23 Fuel filter renewal

Note: *Certain models are fitted with a dual-element filter assembly. On these models, only the inlet (fuel tank side) filter should be renewed at the normal specified interval. The outlet (injection pump) side filter should be renewed at every third inlet filter change.*
1 Drain the filter bowl (see Section 7).

2 Unscrew the through-bolt from the top of the filter head, then withdraw the bolt, whilst supporting the filter bowl (see illustration).
3 Lower the filter bowl, taking care not to strain the coolant hoses. Recover the lower seal, and lift out the element (see illustrations). (If desired, the filter bowl can be removed completely after disconnecting the coolant hoses.)
4 Recover the upper seals, noting their locations (see illustrations).
5 Clean out the filter bowl.
6 Fit a new element and new seals (supplied with the filter) to the bowl, making sure that the seals are correctly located.
7 Fit the element and the bowl to the filter head, with the drain plug positioned on the engine side of the bowl. Fit and tighten the through-bolt.

22.1a Unscrew the side . . .

22.1b . . . and centre air cleaner cover securing screws - non-Turbo model

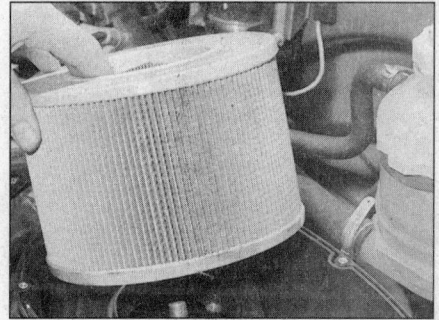
22.2 Lifting out the air filter element - non-Turbo model

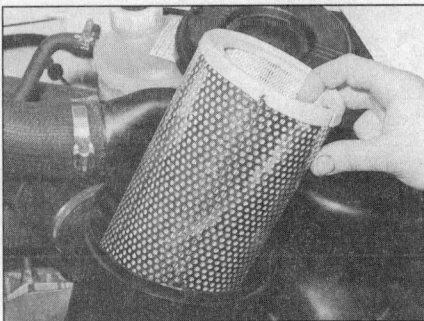
22.6 Lifting out the air filter element - Turbo model

23.2 Unscrew the fuel filter through-bolt and withdraw it, supporting the filter bowl

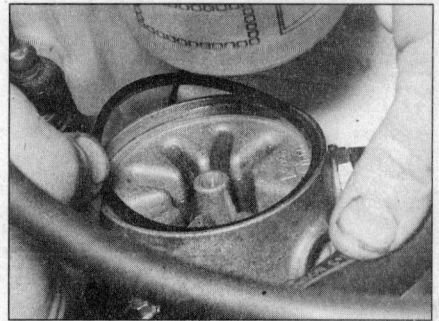
23.3a Recover the lower seal . . .

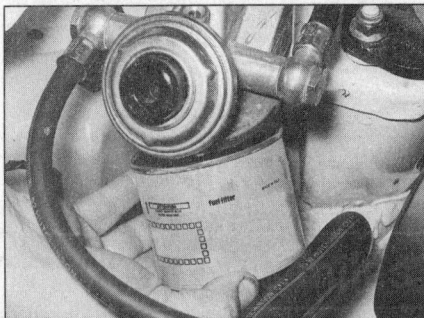
23.3b . . . and lift out the filter element

23.4a Recover the large . . .

23.4b . . . and the smaller upper seals

24 Road test

Instruments and electrical equipment

1 Check the operation of all instruments and electrical equipment.

2 Make sure that all instruments read correctly, and switch on all electrical equipment in turn to check that it functions properly.

Steering and suspension

3 Check for any abnormalities in the steering, suspension, handling or road feel

4 Drive the vehicle and check that there are no unusual vibrations or noises.

5 Check that the steering feels positive, with no excessive "sloppiness", or roughness, and check for any suspension noises when cornering and driving over bumps.

Drivetrain

6 Check the operation of the engine, clutch (where applicable), transmission and driveshafts.

7 Listen for any unusual noises from the engine, clutch and gearbox.

8 Make sure that the engine runs smoothly when idling, and that there is no hesitation when accelerating.

9 Check that the clutch action is smooth and progressive, that the drive is taken up smoothly, and that the pedal travel is not excessive. Also listen for any noises when the clutch pedal is depressed.

10 Check that all gears can be engaged smoothly without noise and that the gear lever action is not abnormally vague or "notchy".

11 Listen for a metallic clicking sound from the front of the vehicle as the vehicle is driven slowly in a circle with the steering on full lock. Carry out this check in both directions. If a clicking noise is heard, this indicates wear in a driveshaft joint, in which case renew the joint if necessary.

Check the braking system

12 Make sure that the vehicle does not pull to one side when braking, and that the wheels do not lock prematurely when braking hard.

13 Check that there is no vibration through the steering when braking.

14 Check that the handbrake operates

correctly without excessive movement of the lever, and that it holds the vehicle stationary on a slope.

15 Test the operation of the brake servo unit as follows. Depress the footbrake four or five times to exhaust the vacuum, then start the engine. As the engine starts there should be a noticeable "give" in the brake pedal as vacuum builds up. Allow the engine to run for at least two minutes and then switch it off. If the brake pedal is now depressed again, it should be possible to detect a hiss from the servo as the pedal is depressed. After four or five applications, no further hissing should be heard and the pedal should feel harder.

25 Manual gearbox oil level check

1 Position the car over an inspection pit, on car ramps, or jack it up (see *"Jacking, towing and wheel changing"*), but make sure that it is level. Where applicable remove the engine/gearbox splash shield.

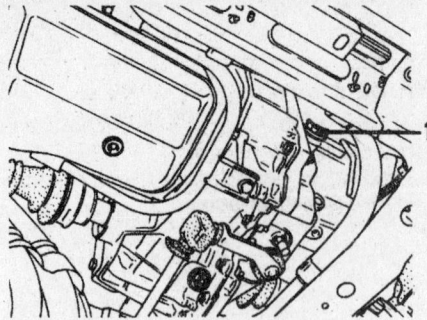

25.2 Manual gearbox filler plug location (1)

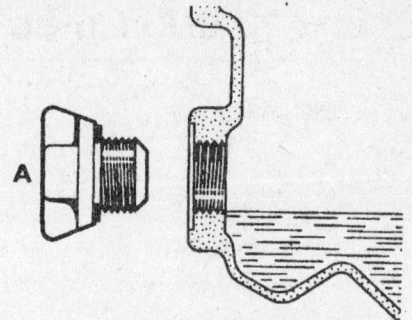

25.3 Manual gearbox filler plug (A) - correct oil level shown

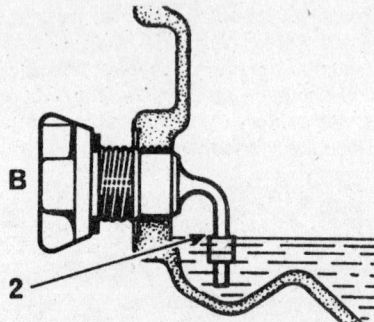

25.4 Alternative type of manual gearbox filler plug (B) and oil level collar (2)

25.5 Topping up the manual gearbox oil level

2 Unscrew the filler plug from the front-facing side of the gearbox **(see illustration)**.

3 Where a plain-type filler plug is fitted, the oil level should be up to the lower edge of the filler hole. Insert a finger to check the level **(see illustration)**.

4 Where a plug with integral dipstick is fitted, wipe clean the dipstick part of the plug then check the level by inserting the shouldered end of the plug through the hole without engaging the threads. Position the plug so that the outer arrow is pointing upwards and the inner dipstick is pointing downwards. On removal of the plug the level should be at the top of the collar on the dipstick. The bottom of the collar indicates the minimum level **(see illustration)**.

5 Where necessary top up the level using the correct grade of oil, then refit and tighten the filler plug **(see illustration)**.

6 If the gearbox requires frequent topping up, check it for leakage, especially around the driveshaft oil seals, and repair as necessary.

7 Where applicable, refit the engine/gearbox splash shield and lower the car to the ground.

Every 15 000 miles

6 Idle speed and anti-stall speed checking and adjustment

1 The usual type of tachometer (rev counter),

which works from ignition system pulses, cannot be used on diesel engines. A diagnostic socket is provided for the use of Renault test equipment, but this will not normally be available to the home mechanic. If it is not felt that adjusting the idle speed "by

ear" is satisfactory, one of the following alternatives may be used.

a) *Purchase or hire of an appropriate tachometer.*

b) *Delegation of the job to a Renault dealer or other specialist.*

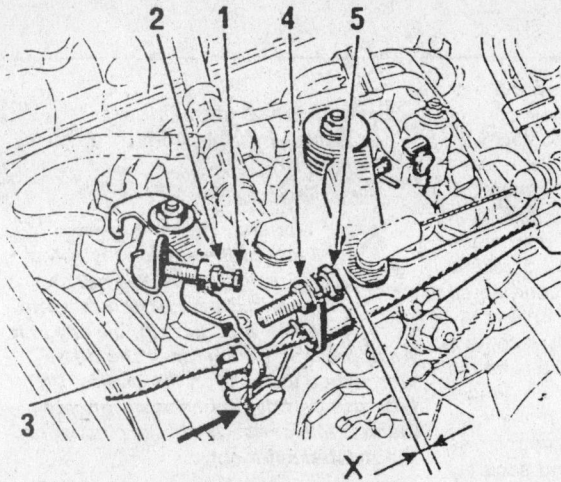

26.4 Idle speed and anti-stall speed adjustment points - Lucas injection pump

1 Idle speed adjustment screw
2 Locknut
3 Fast idle lever
4 Locknut
5 Anti-stall speed adjustment screw
X = Clearance between accelerator lever and anti-stall speed adjustment screw (see Specifications)

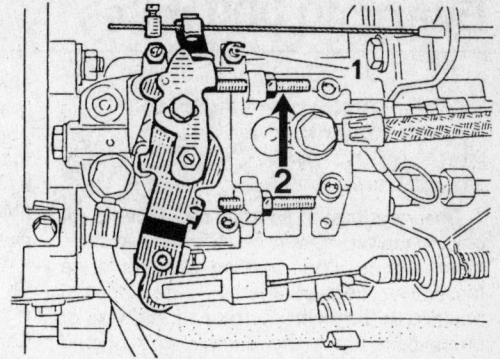

26.7 Idle speed adjustment screw (1) and anti-stall speed adjustment screw (2) - Bosch injection pump

c) Timing light (strobe) operated by a petrol engine running at the desired speed. If the timing light is pointed at a mark on the camshaft or injection pump sprocket, the mark will appear stationary when the two engines are running at the same speed (or multiples of that speed. The sprocket will be rotating at half the crankshaft speed but this will not affect the adjustment. (In practice it was found impossible to use this method on the crankshaft pulley due to the acute viewing angle.)

2 Before making adjustments warm up the engine to normal operating temperature. Make sure that the accelerator cable is correctly adjusted (see Chapter 4).

Idle speed checking and adjustment

3 With the accelerator lever resting against the idle stop, check that the engine idles at the specified speed. If necessary adjust as follows.

Lucas injection pump

4 Loosen the locknut on the idle speed adjustment screw. Turn the screw as required and retighten the locknut (see illustration).
5 Check the anti-stall adjustment as described later in this Section.
6 Stop the engine and disconnect the tachometer, where applicable.

Bosch injection pump

7 Loosen the locknut and unscrew the anti-stall adjustment screw until it is clear of the pump accelerator lever (see illustration).
8 Loosen the locknut and turn the idle speed adjustment screw as required, then retighten the locknut.
9 Make the anti-stall adjustment as described later in this Section.
10 Stop the engine and disconnect the tachometer, where applicable.

Anti-stall checking and adjustment

11 Make sure that the engine is at normal operating temperature, and idling at the specified speed, as described previously.

Lucas injection pump

12 Insert a shim or feeler blade, of the correct thickness (see Specifications), between the pump accelerator lever and the anti-stall adjustment screw.
13 The engine speed should increase to the specified anti-stall speed (see Specifications).
14 If adjustment is necessary, loosen the locknut, turn the anti-stall adjustment screw as required, then tighten the locknut (see illustration 26.4).
15 Remove the shim or feeler blade and check the idle speed as described previously.
16 Move the pump accelerator lever to increase the engine speed to approximately 3000 rpm, then quickly release the lever. The deceleration period should be approximately 2.5 to 3.5 seconds, and the engine speed should drop to approximately 50 rpm below idle.
17 If the deceleration is too fast and the engine stalls, unscrew the anti-stall adjustment screw 1/4 turn towards the accelerator lever. If the deceleration is too slow, resulting in poor engine braking, turn the screw 1/4 turn away from the lever.
18 Retighten the locknut after making an adjustment, then recheck the idle speed and adjust if necessary as described previously.
19 With the engine idling check the operation of the manual stop control by turning the stop lever clockwise (see Chapter 4, Section 1). The engine must stop instantly.
20 Where applicable, disconnect the tachometer on completion.

Bosch injection pump

21 Insert a shim or feeler blade of the correct thickness (see Specifications) between the pump accelerator lever and the anti-stall adjustment screw (see illustration).
22 The engine speed should be as specified for the anti-stall speed (see Specifications).
23 If adjustment is necessary, loosen the locknut and turn the anti-stall adjustment screw as required. Retighten the locknut.
24 Remove the shim or feeler blade and allow the engine to idle.
25 Move the fast idle lever fully towards the flywheel end of the engine and check that the engine speed increases to the specified fast idle speed. If necessary loosen the locknut and turn the fast idle adjusting screw as required, then retighten the locknut.
26 With the engine idling, check the operation of the manual stop control by turning the stop lever (see Chapter 4, Section 1). The engine must stop instantly.
27 Where applicable, disconnect the tachometer on completion.

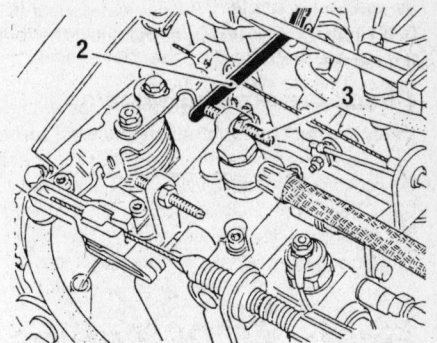

26.21 Checking the anti-stall speed adjustment - Bosch injection pump

2 Feeler blade
3 Anti-stall speed adjustment screw

1

Every 40 000 miles

27 Handbrake checking and adjustment

1 The handbrake should be capable of holding the parked vehicle stationary, even on steep slopes, when applied with moderate force. The mechanism should be firm and positive in feel, with no trace of stiffness or sponginess from the cables, and should release immediately the handbrake lever is released. If the mechanism is faulty in any of these respects, it must be checked immediately as follows. **Note:** *On models with rear drum brakes, if the handbrake is not functioning correctly or is incorrectly adjusted, the rear brake self-adjust mechanism will not function. This will lead to the brake pedal travel becoming excessive as the shoe linings wear. Under no circumstances should the handbrake cables be tightened in an attempt to compensate for excessive brake pedal travel.*

2 Chock the front wheels and release the handbrake. Jack up the rear of the vehicle and support it securely on axle stands (see *"Jacking, towing and wheel changing"*). On models with a catalytic converter, where applicable, undo the heat shield retaining nut(s) and lower the rear of the heat shield to gain access to the handbrake cable adjuster nut.

3 Slacken the locknut, then fully slacken the cable adjuster nut **(see illustration)**.

Models with rear drum brakes

4 Remove both the rear brake drums as described in Chapter 9.

5 Check that the knurled adjuster wheel on the adjuster strut is free to rotate in both directions. If it is seized, the brake shoes and strut must be removed and overhauled as described in Chapter 9.

6 If all is well, back off the adjuster wheel by five or six teeth so that the diameter of the brake shoes is slightly reduced.

7 Check that the handbrake cables slide freely by pulling on their front ends. Also

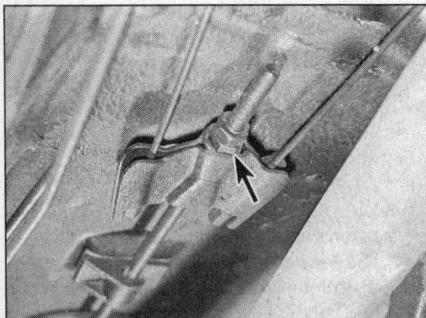

27.3 Handbrake cable adjuster locknut and adjuster nut (arrowed)

check that the operating levers on the rear brake trailing shoes return to their correct positions, with their stop-pegs in contact with the edge of the trailing shoe web.

8 With the aid of an assistant, tighten the adjuster nut on the handbrake lever operating rod so that the lever on each rear brake assembly starts to move as the handbrake is moved between the first and second notch (click) of its ratchet mechanism. This is the case when the stop-pegs are still in contact with the shoes when the handbrake is on the first notch of the ratchet, but no longer contact the shoes when the handbrake is on the second notch. Once the adjustment is correct, hold the adjuster nut and securely tighten the locknut. Where necessary, refit the catalytic converter heat shield retaining nuts.

9 Refit the brake drums as described in Chapter 9, then lower the vehicle to the ground.

10 With the vehicle standing on its wheels, repeatedly depress the footbrake to adjust the shoe-to-drum clearance. Whilst depressing the pedal, have an assistant listen to the rear drums to check that the adjuster strut mechanism is functioning; if this is so, a clicking sound will be heard from the adjuster strut as the pedal is depressed.

Models with rear disc brakes

⚠️ *Warning: The dust created by wear of the pads may contain asbestos, which is a health hazard. Never blow it out with compressed air and don't inhale any of it. An approved filtering mask should be worn when working on the brakes. DO NOT use petroleum based solvents to clean brake parts. Use brake cleaner or methylated spirit only.*

11 Check that the handbrake cables slide freely by pulling on their front ends, and check that the operating levers on the rear brake calipers move smoothly.

12 Move both of the caliper operating levers as far rearwards as possible, then tighten the adjuster nut on the handbrake lever operating rod until all free play is removed from both cables. With the aid of an assistant, from this point adjust the nut so that the operating lever on each rear brake caliper starts to move as the handbrake lever is moved between the first and second notch (click) of its ratchet mechanism. Once the handbrake adjustment is correct, hold the adjuster nut and securely tighten the locknut.

13 Refit the catalytic converter heat shield retaining nuts (where necessary), then lower the vehicle to the ground.

28 Rear brake shoe lining check - models with rear drum brakes

⚠️ *Warning: The dust created by wear of the shoes may contain asbestos, which is a health hazard. Never blow it out with compressed air and don't inhale any of it. An approved filtering mask should be worn when working on the brakes. DO NOT use petroleum based solvents to clean brake parts. Use brake cleaner or methylated spirit only.*

1 Remove the rear brake drums with reference to Chapter 9.

2 Check that each brake shoe lining thickness, including the shoe, is not less than that shown in the Specifications.

3 If any one lining thickness is less than the minimum amount, renew all of the rear brake shoes, as described in Chapter 9.

29 Rear brake disc pad check - models with rear disc brakes

⚠️ *Warning: The dust created by wear of the pads may contain asbestos, which is a health hazard. Never blow it out with compressed air and don't inhale any of it. An approved filtering mask should be worn when working on the brakes. DO NOT use petroleum based solvents to clean brake parts. Use brake cleaner or methylated spirit only.*

1 Chock the front wheels, then jack up the rear of the vehicle, and support securely on axle stands (see *"Jacking, towing and wheel changing"*).

2 For improved access to the rear brake calipers, remove both rear wheels.

3 Using a steel rule, check that the thickness of the brake pad linings and backing plate is not less than the minimum thickness given in the Specifications.

4 If any one pad thickness is less than the minimum amount, renew all the rear pads with reference to Chapter 9.

30 Brake fluid renewal

⚠️ *Warning: Hydraulic fluid is poisonous; wash off immediately and thoroughly in the case of skin contact, and seek immediate medical advice if any fluid is swallowed or gets into the eyes. Certain types of hydraulic fluid are inflammable, and may ignite when allowed to come into contact with hot components; when servicing any hydraulic system, it is safest to assume that the fluid is inflammable, and to take precautions against the risk of fire as though it is petrol that is being handled. Hydraulic fluid is also an effective paint stripper, and will attack plastics; if any is spilt, it should be washed off immediately using copious quantities of fresh water. Finally, it is hygroscopic (it absorbs moisture from the air) - old fluid may be contaminated and unfit for further use. When topping-up or renewing the fluid, always use the recommended type, and ensure that it comes from a freshly-opened, previously-sealed container.*

Note: *On models with ABS, before disconnecting any part of the hydraulic system, the system must be depressurised as* described in Chapter 9, Section 6. Failure to do so could result in personal injury.

1 The procedure is similar to that for the bleeding of the hydraulic system described in Chapter 9. Before starting, remove as much old brake fluid as possible from the reservoir by syphoning, using a clean poultry baster or similar.

2 Working as described in Chapter 9, open the first bleed nipple in the sequence, and pump the brake pedal gently until nearly all the old fluid has been emptied from the master cylinder reservoir. Top-up to the "MAX" level with new fluid, and continue pumping until only the new fluid remains in the reservoir and new fluid can be seen emerging from the bleed nipple. Tighten the nipple and top the reservoir level up to the "MAX" level line.

3 Old hydraulic fluid is invariably much darker in colour than the new, making it easy to distinguish the two.

4 Work through all the remaining nipples in sequence until new fluid can be seen coming from all of them. Be careful to keep the master cylinder reservoir topped-up to above the "MIN" level at all times, or air may enter the system and greatly increase the length of the task.

5 When the operation is complete, check that all nipples are securely tightened and that their dust caps are refitted. Wash off all traces of spilt fluid, and recheck the master cylinder reservoir fluid level.

6 Check the operation of the brakes before taking the vehicle on the road.

31 Front wheel alignment check

Refer to the information in Chapter 10.

Every 70 000 miles

32 Timing belt renewal

The procedure is described in Chapter 2A.

Every 2 years

33 Coolant renewal

⚠ **Warning: Wait until the engine is cold before starting this procedure. Do not allow antifreeze to come in contact with your skin, or with the painted surfaces of the vehicle. Rinse off spills immediately with plenty of water. Never leave antifreeze lying around in an open container, or in a puddle on the floor. Children and pets are attracted by its sweet smell, but antifreeze can be fatal if ingested.**

Coolant draining

1 If the engine is cold, unscrew and remove the pressure cap from the expansion tank. If it is not possible to wait until the engine is cold, place a cloth over the pressure cap of the expansion tank and **slowly** unscrew the cap. Wait until all pressure has escaped, then remove the cap.

2 Place a suitable container beneath the bottom hose connection to the radiator.

3 Loosen the clip, then disconnect the bottom hose and allow the coolant to drain into the container. The hose clips fitted as original equipment are released by squeezing the tags together with pliers.

4 Move the container beneath the cylinder block drain plug, located at the rear right-hand side of the cylinder block **(see illustration)**.

5 Unscrew the plug, and drain the coolant into the container.

6 Flush the system if necessary as described in the following paragraphs, then refit the drain plug and secure the bottom hose. Use a new hose clip if necessary. Refill the system as described later in this Section.

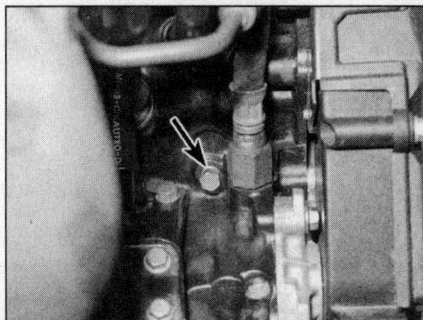

33.4 Coolant drain plug location (arrowed) on the rear of the cylinder block - viewed with engine removed

System flushing

7 With time, the cooling system may gradually lose its efficiency if the radiator matrix becomes choked with rust and scale deposits. If this is the case, the system must be flushed as follows. First drain the coolant as already described.

8 Loosen the clip and disconnect the top hose from the radiator. Insert a garden hose in the radiator top hose connection stub, and allow the water to circulate through the radiator until it runs clear from the bottom outlet.

9 To flush the engine and the remainder of the system, remove the thermostat as described in Chapter 3. Insert the garden hose, and allow the water to circulate through the engine until it runs clear from the bottom hose.

10 In severe cases of contamination, the radiator should be reverse-flushed. To do this, first remove it from the vehicle, as described in Chapter 3, invert it and insert a hose in the bottom outlet. Continue flushing until clear water runs from the top hose outlet.

11 If, after a reasonable period, the water still does not run clear, the radiator should be flushed with a good proprietary cleaning system.

12 Regular renewal of the specified

1

antifreeze mixture should prevent severe contamination of the system. Note that as the radiator is made of aluminium, it is important not to use caustic soda or alkaline compounds to clean it. See Chapter 3 for more details.

Coolant filling

13 Refit the cylinder block drain plug, radiator bottom hose and any other hoses removed if the system has just been flushed.

14 Open the coolant bleed screw, located at the top left-hand corner of the radiator **(see illustration)**.

15 Pour the appropriate mixture of water and antifreeze into the expansion tank, and close the bleed screw as soon as a continuous flow of bubble-free coolant can be seen flowing from it. Continue to fill the expansion tank until the coolant is at the maximum level.

16 Start the engine and run it at 1500 rpm (ie a fast idle speed) for approximately 4 minutes. Keep the expansion tank topped-up to the maximum level during this period.

17 Refit the pressure cap to the expansion tank, and run the engine at 1500 rpm for approximately 10 minutes until the electric cooling fan cuts in. During this period, the coolant will circulate around the engine and any remaining air will be purged to the expansion tank.

18 Switch off the engine and allow it to cool,

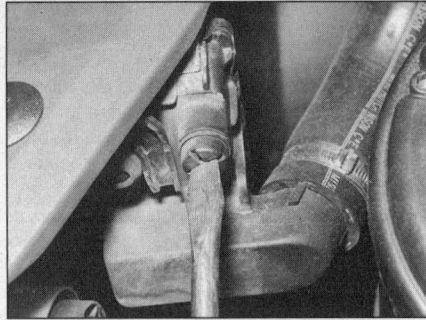

33.14 Loosening the coolant bleed screw in the radiator

then check the coolant level as described in Section 3 of this Chapter, and top-up if necessary.

Antifreeze mixture

Note: *Refer to the warning at the beginning of this Section. Renault do not specify renewal intervals for the antifreeze mixture, as the mixture used to fill the system when the vehicle is new is designed to last the lifetime of the vehicle. However, it is strongly recommended that the coolant is renewed at the intervals specified in the "Maintenance schedule", as a precaution against possible engine corrosion problems. This is particularly advisable if the coolant has been renewed*

previously, using an antifreeze other than that specified by Renault. With many antifreeze types, the corrosion inhibitors become progressively less effective with age. It is up to the individual owner whether or not to follow this advice.

19 It is advisable to renew the antifreeze mixture at the specified intervals. This is necessary not only to maintain the antifreeze properties, but also to prevent corrosion which would otherwise occur as the corrosion inhibitors become progressively less effective.

20 Always use an ethylene-glycol based antifreeze which is suitable for use in mixed-metal cooling systems. The proportion of antifreeze and levels of protection afforded are indicated in the Specifications.

21 Before adding antifreeze, the cooling system should be completely drained, preferably flushed, and all hoses checked for condition and security.

22 After filling with the correct water/antifreeze mixture, a label should be attached to the radiator or expansion tank stating the type and concentration of antifreeze used and the date installed. Any subsequent topping-up should be made with the same type and concentration of antifreeze.

23 Do not use engine antifreeze in the screen washer system, as it will cause damage to the vehicle paintwork.

Chapter 2 Part A:
Engine in-car repair procedures

Contents

Degrees of difficulty

| **Easy,** suitable for novice with little experience | 🔧 | **Fairly easy,** suitable for beginner with some experience | 🔧 | **Fairly difficult,** suitable for competent DIY mechanic | 🔧 | **Difficult,** suitable for experienced DIY mechanic | 🔧 | **Very difficult,** suitable for expert DIY or professional | 🔧 |

Specifications

General

Type	Four-cylinder, in-line, overhead camshaft
Designation:	
Non-Turbo engine	F8Q 706, F8Q 764, or F8Q 742
Turbo engine	F8Q 740 or F8Q 744
Capacity	1870 cc
Bore	80.0 mm
Stroke	93.0 mm
Firing order	1-3-4-2 (No 1 cylinder at flywheel end)
Direction of crankshaft rotation	Clockwise viewed from timing belt end
Compression ratio	21.5:1
Maximum power output (typical):	
Non-Turbo engines	47.0 kW (61 bhp) at 4500 rpm
Turbo engines	68.5 kW (89 bhp) at 4250 rpm
Maximum torque (typical):	
Non-Turbo engines	118 Nm (87 lbf ft) at 2250 rpm
Turbo engines	175 Nm (129 lbf ft) at 2250 rpm

Compression pressures (engine warm - 80°C)
Minimum pressure .... 20 bars
Maximum difference between cylinders .... 4 bars

Camshaft
Drive .... Toothed belt
Number of bearings 5
Camshaft endfloat .... 0.05 to 0.13 mm

Valve clearances
Inlet .... 0.20 mm
Exhaust .... 0.40 mm

Timing belt
Tension setting using Renault tool Ele. 364.04 (see text) .... 7.0 to 8.0 mm deflection under a load of 30 N

Lubrication system
System pressure (at 80° C):
  At 1000 rpm:
    Non-Turbo engines .... 2.0 bars
    Turbo engines .... 1.5 bars
  At 3000 rpm .... 3.5 bars
Oil pump type .... Two-gear
Oil pump clearances:
  Gear-to-body (minimum) .... 0.10 mm
  Gear-to-body (maximum) .... 0.24 mm
  Gear endfloat (minimum) .... 0.02 mm
  Gear endfloat (maximum) .... 0.085 mm

Torque wrench settings

	Nm	lbf ft
Camshaft sprocket	50	37
Camshaft bearing caps:		
8 mm diameter bolts	20	15
6 mm diameter bolts	10	7
Timing belt tensioner roller nut	50	37
Auxiliary shaft sprocket bolt	50	37
Injection pump sprocket securing nut	50	37
Crankshaft pulley bolt	90 to 100	66 to 74
Connecting rod (big-end) cap bolts	45 to 50	33 to 37
Sump bolts	12 to 15	9 to 11
Flywheel bolts*	50 to 55	37 to 41
Valve cover nuts/bolts	12	9
Main bearing caps	60 to 65	44 to 48
Cylinder head bolts (new bolts may be required - see Section 9):		
Non-Turbo engines with hexagon socket-head bolts:		
Stage 1	30	22
Stage 2	70	52
Stage 3	Wait for 3 minutes minimum	
Stage 4	Loosen all the bolts completely	
Stage 5	20	15
Stage 6	Angle-tighten a further 123° ± 2°	
Turbo engines, and non-Turbo engines with T55 Torx bolts:		
Stage 1	30	22
Stage 2	Angle-tighten a further 50° ± 4°	
Stage 3	Wait for 3 minutes minimum	
Stage 4	Loosen all the bolts completely	
Stage 5	25	18
Stage 6 (final stage for non-Turbo)	Angle-tighten a further 213° ± 7°	
Turbo engines only:		
Stage 7	Run engine until it reaches normal operating temperature (cooling fan cuts in), then allow the engine to cool for a minimum of 2 1/2 hours	
Stage 8	Angle-tighten a further 120° ± 7°	
Left-hand engine/gearbox mounting plate-to-body nuts	22	16
Left-hand engine/gearbox mounting bracket-to-body mounting nut	75	55
Lower engine steady bracket nuts	45	33
Right-hand engine mounting plate-to-body nuts	45	33

*Note: Use new bolts.

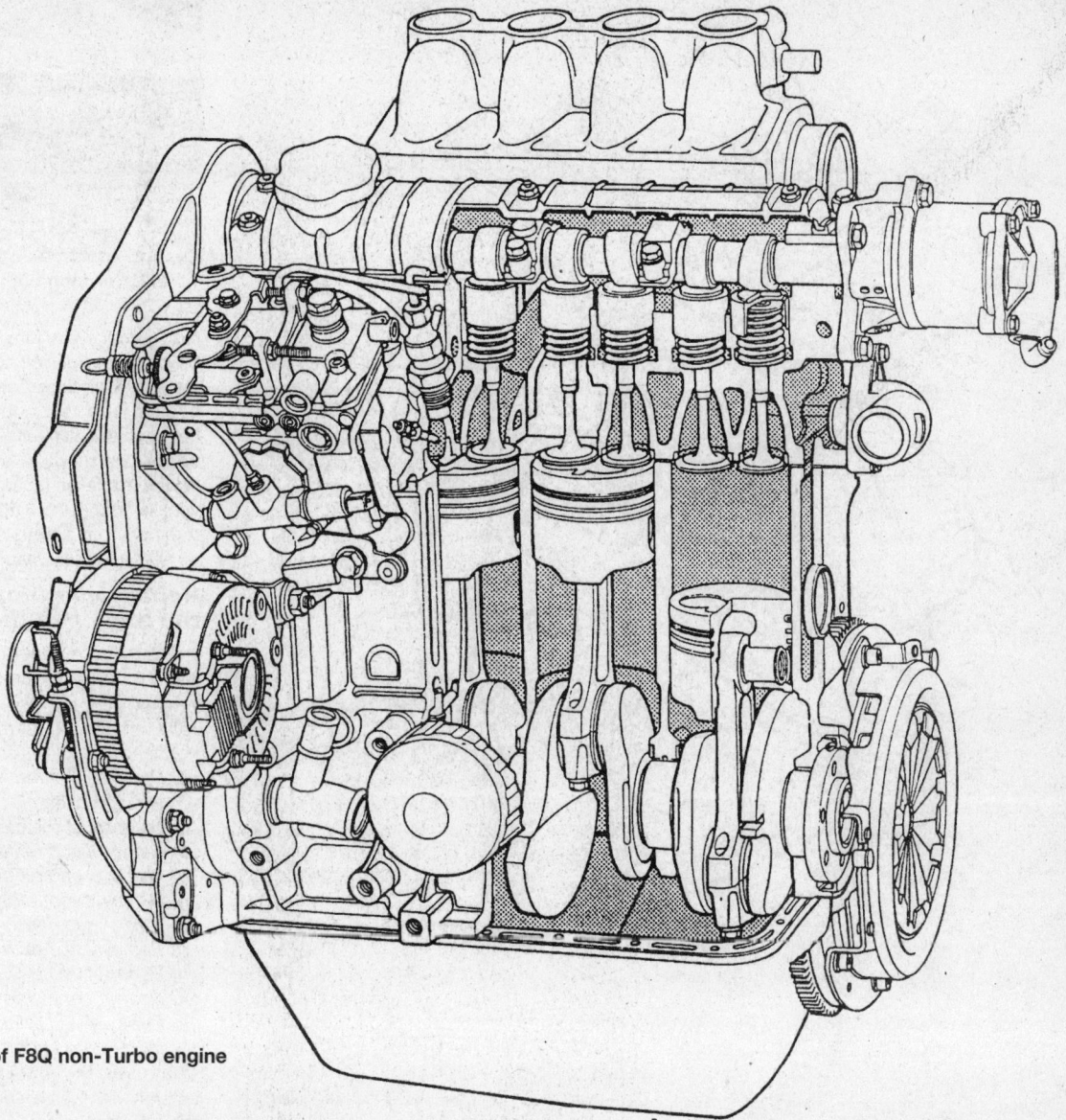

1.4 Cutaway view of F8Q non-Turbo engine

2A

1 General information

How to use this Chapter

This Part of Chapter 2 is devoted to in-car repair procedures. All procedures concerning engine removal and refitting, and engine block/cylinder head overhaul for all engine types can be found in Chapter 2B.

Refer to the *"Buying spare parts and vehicle identification numbers"* Section at the beginning of this manual for details of engine code locations.

Most of the operations included in Chapter 2A are based on the assumption that the engine is still installed in the car. Therefore, if this information is being used during a complete engine overhaul, with the engine already removed, many of the steps included here will not apply.

Engine description

The engine is of four-cylinder, in-line, single overhead camshaft type, mounted transversely at the front of the vehicle **(see illustration)**.

The crankshaft is supported in five shell-type main bearings. Thrust washers are fitted to No 2 main bearing to control crankshaft endfloat.

The connecting rods are attached to the crankshaft by horizontally split shell-type big-end bearings and to the pistons by gudgeon

pins. The gudgeon pins are fully floating and are retained by circlips. The aluminium alloy pistons are of the slipper type and are fitted with three piston rings, comprising two compression rings and a scraper-type oil control ring.

The single overhead camshaft is mounted directly in the cylinder head, and is driven by the crankshaft via a toothed timing belt.

The camshaft operates the valves via inverted bucket-type tappets, which operate in bores machined directly in the cylinder head. Valve clearance adjustment is by shims located externally between the tappet bucket and the cam lobe. The inlet and exhaust valves are mounted vertically in the cylinder head and are each closed by a single valve spring.

2.2 Carrying out a compression test

models, oil spray jets are fitted to the cylinder block to supply oil to the underside of the pistons. Certain models are fitted with an oil cooler. The oil cooler may be mounted between the oil filter and the cylinder block, or on certain models, a remotely-mounted oil cooler radiator is fitted at the front of the vehicle (in this case, the oil is fed to the cooler radiator from a housing located between the oil filter and the cylinder block).

Repair operations possible with the engine in the vehicle

The following operations can be carried out without having to remove the engine from the vehicle:

a) Removal and refitting of the cylinder head.
b) Removal and refitting of the timing belt and sprockets.
c) Renewal of the camshaft oil seals.
d) Removal and refitting of the camshaft.
e) Removal and refitting of the sump.
f) Removal and refitting of the connecting rods and pistons*.
g) Removal and refitting of the oil pump.
h) Renewal of the crankshaft oil seals.
i) Renewal of the engine mountings.
j) Removal and refitting of the flywheel (non-Turbo engines only).

*Although the operation marked with an asterisk can be carried out with the engine in the car after removal of the sump, it is better for the engine to be removed in the interests of cleanliness and improved access. For this reason, the procedure is described in Chapter 2B.

2 Compression and leakdown tests - description and interpretation

Compression test

Note: *A compression tester specifically designed for diesel engines must be used for this test.*

1 When engine performance is down, or if misfiring occurs which cannot be attributed to the ignition or fuel systems, a compression test can provide diagnostic clues as to the

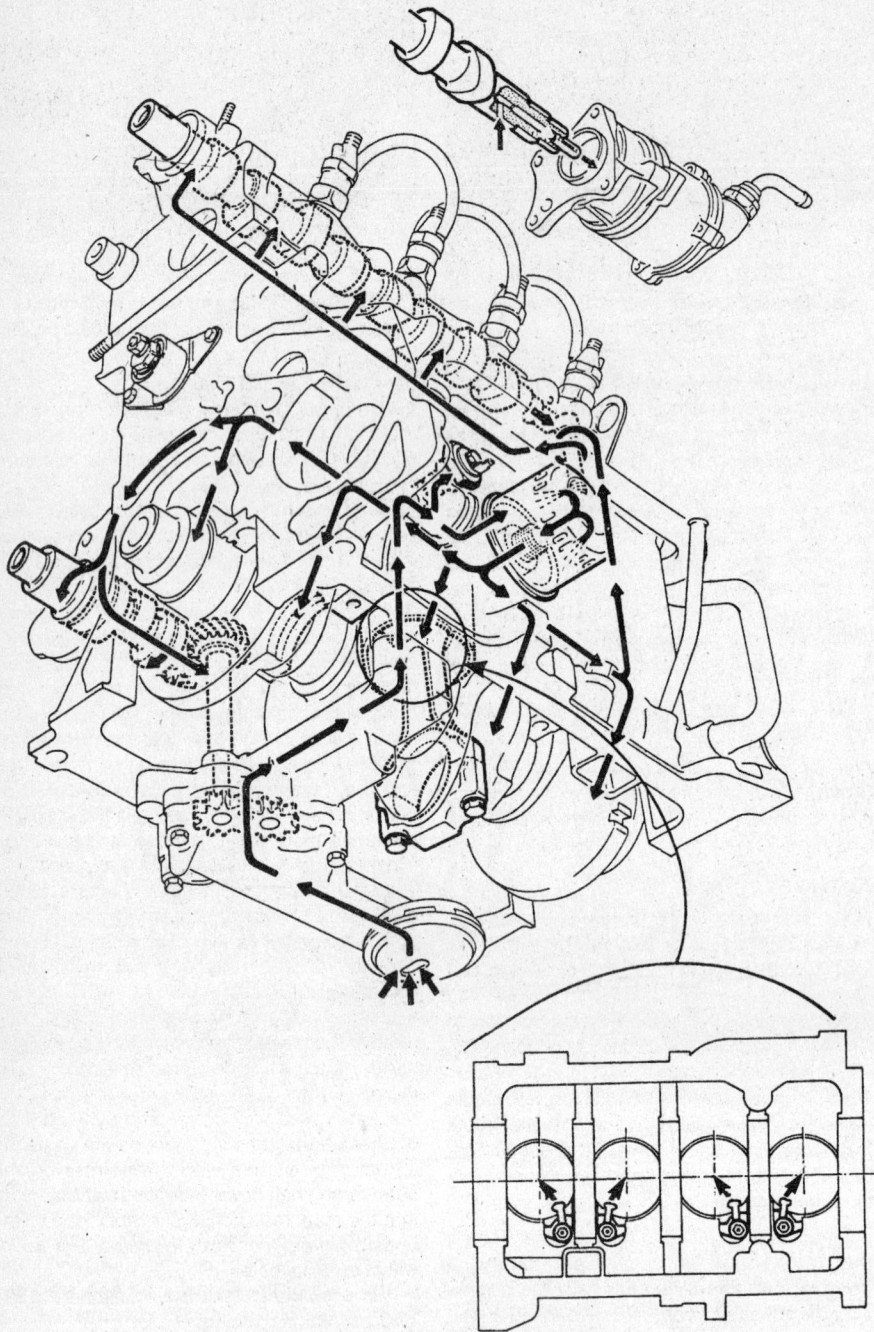

1.12 Engine lubrication circuit

An auxiliary shaft located alongside the crankshaft is also driven by the timing belt and actuates the oil pump via a skew gear.

The fuel injection pump is driven by the timing belt, and is described in further detail in Chapter 4.

A semi-closed crankcase ventilation system is employed, and crankcase fumes are drawn from an oil separator on the cylinder block and passed via a hose (and in certain cases, a second oil separator) to the inlet tract (see Chapter 4 for further details).

Engine lubrication is by pressure feed from a gear-type oil pump located beneath the crankshaft. Engine oil is fed through an externally-mounted oil filter to the main oil gallery feeding the crankshaft, auxiliary shaft and camshaft **(see illustration)**. On Turbo

3.4 Flywheel timing mark aligned with TDC (0°) mark on bellhousing

3.5 Removing the cover from the engine mounting bracket

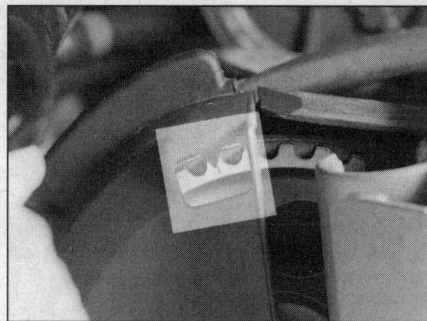

3.6 Camshaft sprocket timing mark aligned with pointer on timing belt cover

engine's condition. If the test is performed regularly it can give warning of trouble before any other symptoms become apparent.

2 A compression tester specifically intended for diesel engines must be used, because of the higher pressures involved. The tester is connected to an adaptor which screws into the glow plug or injector hole **(see illustration)**. It is unlikely to be worthwhile buying such a tester for occasional use, but it may be possible to borrow or hire one - if not, have the test performed by a garage.

3 Unless specific instructions to the contrary are supplied with the tester, observe the following points:

a) *The battery must be in a good state of charge, the air filter must be clean and the engine should be at normal operating temperature.*

b) *All the injectors or glow plugs should be removed before starting the test. If removing the injectors, also remove the fire seal washers (which must be renewed when the injectors are refilled - see Chapter 4), otherwise they may be blown out.*

c) *It is advisable to disconnect the stop solenoid on the pump to reduce the amount of fuel discharged as the engine is cranked.*

4 There is no need to hold the accelerator pedal down during the test because the diesel engine air inlet is not throttled.

5 The actual compression pressures measured are not so important as the balance between cylinders. Values are given in the Specifications.

6 The cause of poor compression is less easy to establish on a diesel engine than on a petrol one. The effect of introducing oil into the cylinders ("wet" testing) is not conclusive, because there is a risk that the oil will sit in the swirl chamber or in the recess on the piston crown instead of passing to the rings. However, the following can be used as a rough guide to diagnosis.

7 All cylinders should produce very similar pressures; any difference greater than that specified indicates the existence of a fault. Note that the compression should build up quickly in a healthy engine; low compression

on the first stroke, followed by gradually increasing pressure on successive strokes, indicates worn piston rings. A low compression reading on the first stroke, which does not build up during successive strokes, indicates leaking valves or a blown head gasket (a cracked head could also be the cause). Deposits on the undersides of the valve heads can also cause low compression.

8 A low reading from two adjacent cylinders is almost certainly due to the head gasket having blown between them; the presence of coolant in the engine oil will confirm this.

9 If the compression reading is unusually high, the cylinder head surfaces, valves and pistons are probably coated with carbon deposits. If this is the case, the cylinder head should be removed and decarbonised (see Chapter 2B, Section 7).

Leakdown test

10 A leakdown test measures the rate at which compressed air fed into the cylinder is lost. It is an alternative to a compression test and in many ways it is better, since the escaping air provides easy identification of where pressure loss is occurring (piston rings, valves or head gasket).

11 The equipment needed for leakdown testing is unlikely to be available to the home mechanic. If poor compression is suspected, have the test performed by a suitably equipped garage.

3 Top dead centre (TDC) for number one piston - locating

Note: *An 8 mm diameter rod or drill bit will be required if it is desired to lock the crankshaft in the TDC position.*

1 Top dead centre (TDC) is the highest point in the cylinder that each piston reaches as the crankshaft turns. Each piston reaches TDC at the end of the compression stroke and again at the end of the exhaust stroke; however, for the purpose of timing the engine, TDC refers to the position of No 1 piston at the end of its compression stroke. On all engines in this manual, No 1 piston (and cylinder) is at

the flywheel end of the engine.

2 When No 1 piston is at TDC, the timing mark on the camshaft sprocket should be aligned with the pointer on the outer timing belt cover (the sprocket mark can be viewed through the cut-out in the timing belt cover, below the pointer). Additionally, the timing mark on the flywheel should be aligned with the TDC mark on the gearbox bellhousing.

3 To align the timing marks, the crankshaft must be turned. This should be done by using a spanner on the crankshaft pulley bolt. Improved access to the pulley bolt can be obtained by jacking up the front right-hand corner of the vehicle (see *"Jacking, towing and wheel changing"*) and removing the roadwheel and the lower wheel arch cover (secured by plastic clips). If desired, to enable the engine to be turned more easily, remove the glow plugs (Chapter 5) or the fuel injectors (Chapter 4).

4 Look through the timing aperture in the gearbox bellhousing, and turn the crankshaft until the timing mark on the flywheel is aligned with the TDC (0°) mark on the bellhousing **(see illustration)**.

5 Unscrew the three securing bolts, and remove the plastic cover from the upper right-hand engine mounting bracket **(see illustration)**. Note the locations of any brackets which may be secured by the bolts.

6 Check that the timing mark on the camshaft sprocket is aligned with the pointer on the outer timing belt cover **(see illustration)**. Note that the mark may not align exactly due to the possible movement of the timing belt cover within its bolts holes.

7 It is possible to lock the crankshaft in the TDC position as follows.

8 Remove the plug on the lower front-facing side of the cylinder block, at the flywheel end, and obtain a metal rod which is a snug fit in the plug hole (8 mm diameter). Turn the crankshaft slightly if necessary to the TDC position, then push the rod through the hole to locate in the slot in the crankshaft web. Make sure that the crankshaft is exactly at TDC for No 1 piston (flywheel end) by aligning the timing mark on the flywheel with the TDC (0°) mark on the gearbox bellhousing as described previously. If the crankshaft is not positioned accurately, it is possible to engage the rod with a balance hole in the crankshaft

2A

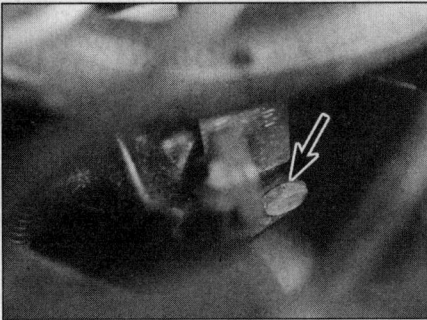

3.8a Remove the plug (arrowed) from the cylinder block . . .

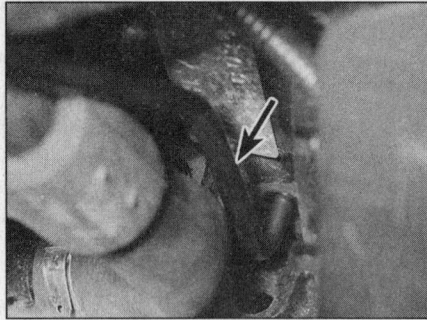

3.8b . . . and insert a suitable 8 mm rod (arrowed)

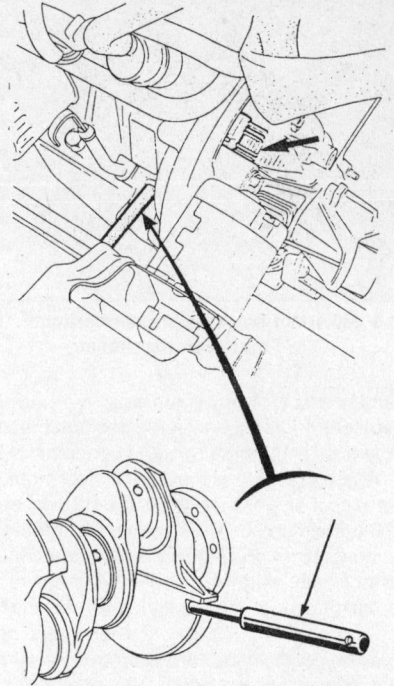

3.8c TDC mark on flywheel viewed through bellhousing aperture, and TDC locking tool engaged with crankshaft (arrowed)

web by mistake, instead of the TDC slot **(see illustrations)**.

4 Valve clearances - checking and adjustment

Note: *This operation is not part of the maintenance schedule. It should be undertaken if noise from the valvegear becomes evident, or if loss of performance gives cause to suspect that the clearances may be incorrect. A new valve cover gasket may be required on refitting.*

Checking

1 Where necessary for improved access, unclip any hoses or cables which are routed across the top of the valve cover, and move them to one side out of the way. If necessary, the accelerator cable can be disconnected with reference to Chapter 4. If fuel lines are disconnected, cover open unions to prevent dirt ingress.

4.3 Removing the valve cover

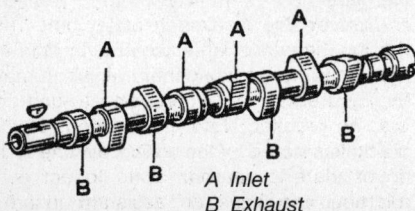

4.6 Cam lobe identification

A Inlet
B Exhaust

2 Where applicable, unscrew the securing bolts, and remove the upper timing belt/engine mounting cover. Note the locations of any brackets secured by the bolts.
3 Unscrew the nuts from the valve cover, and withdraw the cover from the engine **(see illustration)**. Recover the gasket.
4 During the following procedure, the crankshaft must be turned, using a spanner on the crankshaft pulley bolt. Improved access to the pulley bolt can be obtained by jacking up the front right-hand corner of the vehicle (see *"Jacking, towing and wheel changing"*) and removing the roadwheel and the lower wheel arch cover (secured by plastic clips).
5 If desired, to enable the crankshaft to be turned more easily, remove the glow plugs (Chapter 5) or the fuel injectors (Chapter 4).
6 Draw the valve positions on a piece of paper, numbering them 1 to 8 from the flywheel end of the engine. Identify them as inlet or exhaust (ie 1E, 2I, 3E, 4I, 5I, 6E, 7I, 8E) **(see illustration)**.
7 Turn the crankshaft until the valves of No 1 cylinder (flywheel end) are "rocking". The exhaust valve will be closing and the inlet valve will be opening. The piston of No 4 cylinder will be at the top of its compression stroke, with both valves fully closed. The clearances for both valves of No 4 cylinder may be checked at the same time.
8 Insert a feeler blade of the correct thickness (see Specifications) between the cam lobe and the shim on the top of the tappet bucket, and check that it is a firm sliding fit **(see illustration)**. If it is not, use the feeler blades to ascertain the exact clearance, and record this for use when calculating the new shim

thickness required. Note that the inlet and exhaust valve clearances are different (see Specifications).
9 With No 4 cylinder valve clearances checked, turn the engine through half a turn so that No 3 valves are "rocking", then check the valve clearances of No 2 cylinder in the same way. Similarly check the remaining valve clearances in the sequence shown **(see illustration)**.

4.8 Measuring a valve clearance

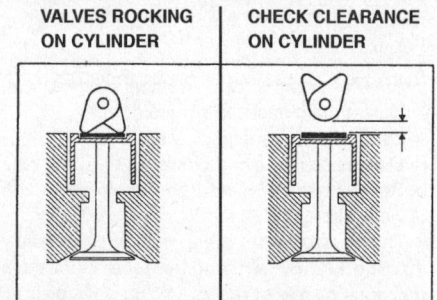

4.9 Valve clearance adjustment

VALVES ROCKING ON CYLINDER	CHECK CLEARANCE ON CYLINDER
1	4
3	2
4	1
2	3

4.10a Shim thickness engraved
on the underside

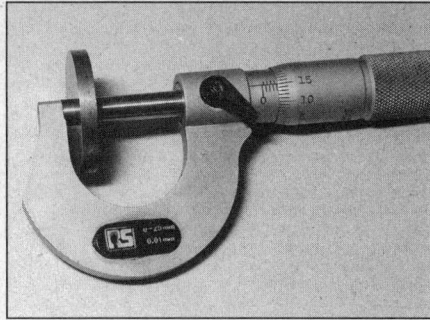

4.10b Measuring a shim using
a micrometer

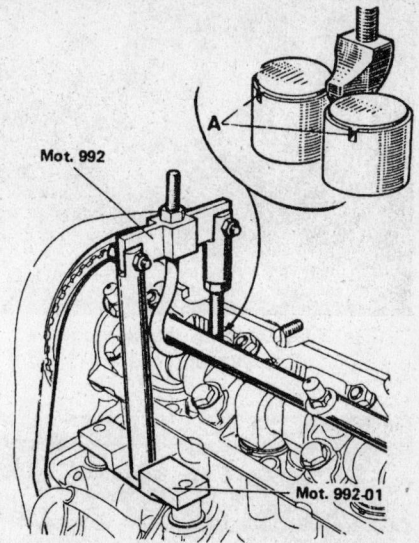

4.13 Renault tool for compressing tappet
buckets to change shims

*A Notches positioned at right-angles to
camshaft centre-line*

Adjustment

Note: *A micrometer will be required for this operation.*

10 Where a valve clearance differs from the specified value, then the shim for that valve must be replaced with a thinner or thicker shim accordingly. The shim size is stamped on the bottom face of the shim, but it is prudent to use a micrometer to measure the true thickness of any shim removed, as it may have been reduced by wear **(see illustrations)**.

11 The size of shim required is calculated as follows. If the measured clearance is less than specified, subtract the measured clearance from the specified clearance, and deduct the result from the thickness of the existing shim. For example:

Sample calculation - clearance too small

Clearance measured (A) = 0.15 mm
Desired clearance (B) = 0.20 mm
Difference (B - A) = 0.05 mm
Shim thickness fitted = 3.70 mm
Shim thickness required = 3.70 - 0.05 = 3.65 mm

12 If the measured clearance is greater than specified, subtract the specified clearance from the measured clearance, and add the result to the thickness of the existing shim. For example:

Sample calculation - clearance too big

Clearance measured (A) = 0.50 mm
Desired clearance (B) = 0.40 mm
Difference (A - B) = 0.10 mm
Shim thickness fitted = 3.45 mm
Shim thickness required = 3.45 + 0.10 = 3.55 mm

13 The shims can be removed from their locations on top of the tappet buckets without removing the camshaft if the Renault tool shown can be borrowed, or a suitable alternative fabricated **(see illustration)**.

14 To remove the shim, the tappet bucket has to be pressed down against valve spring pressure just far enough to allow the shim to be slid out. Theoretically, this could be done by levering against the camshaft between the cam lobes with a suitable screwdriver or similar tool to push the bucket down, but this is not recommended by the manufacturers. If

this method is to be used, take great care not to damage the camshaft, cylinder head, or tappet bucket **(see illustration)**.

15 An arrangement similar to the Renault tool can be made by bolting a bar to the camshaft bearing studs and levering down against this with a stout screwdriver. The contact pad should be a triangular-shaped metal block with a lip filed along each side to contact the edge of the buckets. Levering down against this will open the valve and allow the shim to be withdrawn.

16 Make sure that the cam lobe peaks are uppermost when depressing a tappet, and rotate the buckets so that the notches are at right-angles to the camshaft centre-line. When refitting the shims, ensure that the size markings face the tappet buckets (ie face downwards).

17 If the Renault tool cannot be borrowed or a suitable alternative improvised, then it will be necessary to remove the camshaft to gain access to the shims, as described in Section 8.

18 Remove the spanner from the crankshaft pulley bolt.

19 Refit the valve cover, using a new gasket where necessary.

20 Where applicable, refit the fuel injectors (as described in Chapter 4), or the glow plugs (see Chapter 5).

21 Refit/reconnect any hoses or cables which were moved for access. If the accelerator cable has been disconnected, reconnect it with reference to Chapter 4. If fuel lines were disconnected, reconnect them, then prime and bleed the fuel system as described in Chapter 4.

22 Where applicable, refit the upper timing belt/engine mounting cover.

5 Timing belt - removal, inspection and refitting

Caution: *If the timing belt breaks or slips in service, extensive engine damage may result. Renew the belt at the intervals specified in Chapter 1, or earlier if its condition is at all doubtful.*

Note: *A suitable tool will be required to check the timing belt tension on completion of*

4.14 Removing a shim from a tappet
bucket using screwdrivers

refitting - see text. A suitable puller may be required to remove the crankshaft pulley.

Removal

1 Disconnect the battery negative lead.

2 Jack up the front right-hand corner of the vehicle (see *"Jacking, towing and wheel changing"*) and remove the roadwheel and the lower wheel arch cover (secured by plastic clips).

3 If desired, to improve access, unbolt the strengthening bar from between the front suspension strut turrets.

4 Remove the auxiliary drivebelt as described in Chapter 1.

5 Unscrew the crankshaft pulley bolt while holding the crankshaft stationary. To hold the crankshaft, working under the vehicle, remove the flywheel cover plate/engine-to-gearbox bracing bracket. Note the locations of any brackets secured by the bolts. Refit one of the cover plate-to-gearbox bolts to act as a fulcrum, and have an assistant insert a screwdriver or similar tool in the starter ring gear teeth **(see illustrations)**.

2A

5.5a Unscrew the side . . .

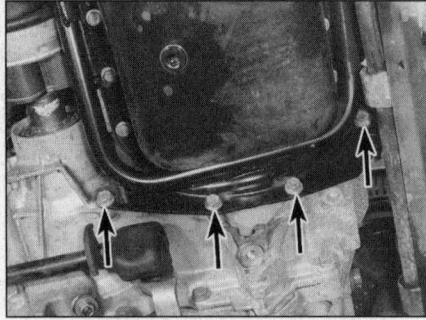

5.5b . . . and front securing bolts (arrowed) . . .

5.5c . . . and remove the flywheel cover plate/engine-to-gearbox bracing bracket (arrowed)

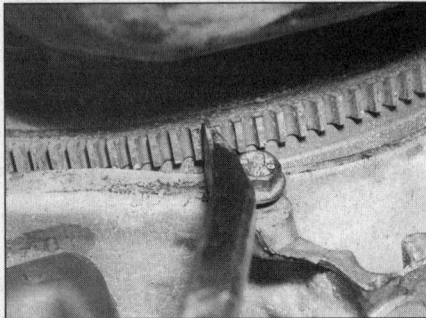

5.5d Insert a lever in the starter ring gear teeth

5.6a Remove the crankshaft pulley bolt . . .

5.6b . . . and the pulley

5.7 Unscrewing a fuel filter assembly securing bolt

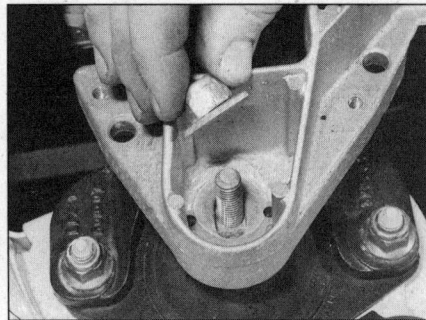

5.10 Remove the nut securing the upper engine mounting bracket to the mounting on the body

5.11a Unscrew the three securing bolts (arrowed) . . .

6 Remove the bolt and the pulley from the front of the crankshaft (see illustrations). Use a suitable puller if the pulley is tight.

7 To improve access, unscrew the two bolts securing the fuel filter assembly to the body panel, then unclip the filter hoses from the brackets on the engine (see illustration). The assembly can be moved to one side (on top of the engine) until completion of refitting.

8 Temporarily refit the crankshaft pulley bolt. Turn the crankshaft to position No 1 piston at TDC on the compression stoke, and lock the crankshaft in position, as described in Section 3.

9 The right-hand upper engine mounting bracket must be removed to enable the timing belt to be removed, therefore the engine must be supported. The assembly can be supported using a jack and a suitable block of wood to spread the load under the sump (in

5.11b . . . and withdraw the engine mounting bracket

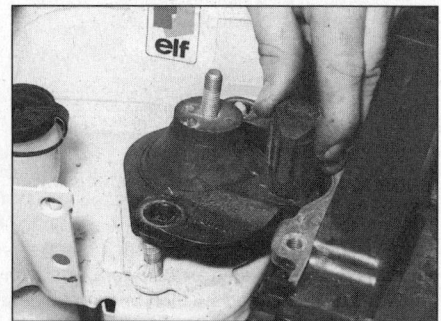

which case, remove the engine undershield, where applicable). Alternatively, connect a hoist and suitable lifting tackle to the engine

5.12 Remove the engine mounting rubber/movement limiter assembly

lifting brackets (in this case, the fuel return hose will have to be disconnected from the injection pump, and withdrawn from the hole

5.13 Removing the timing belt cover from the fuel injection pump sprocket

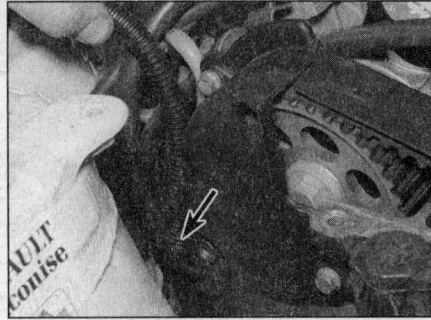

5.14a Note the location of any brackets (arrowed) secured by the bolts . . .

5.14b . . . and remove the timing belt cover from the camshaft sprocket

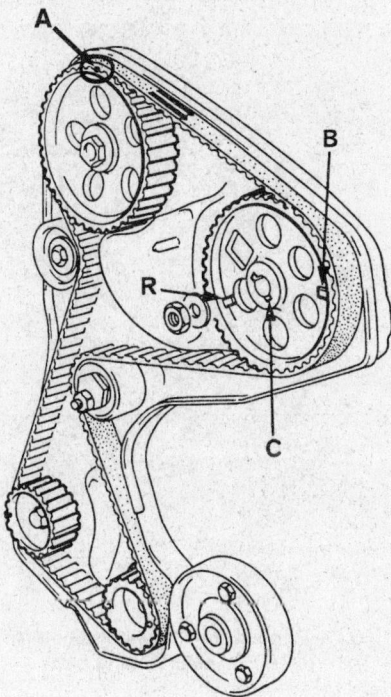

5.15c Fuel injection pump sprocket timing mark location with No 1 piston at TDC - Lucas injection pump

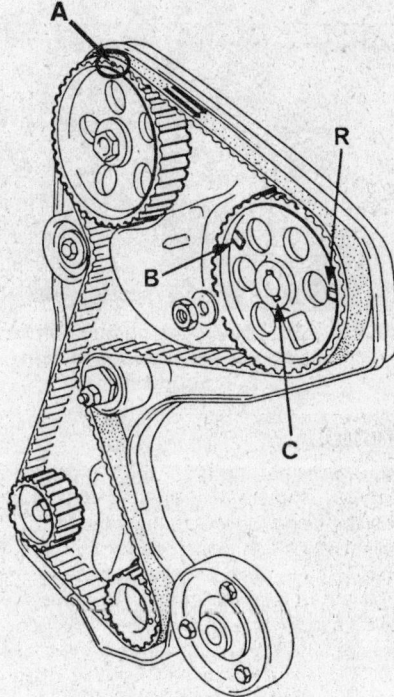

5.15a Camshaft sprocket and fuel injection pump sprocket timing mark positions with No 1 piston at TDC - models with one-piece fuel injection pump sprocket and Bosch injection pump

A *Camshaft sprocket mark (aligned with pointer on outer timing belt cover - cover removed in this view)*
B *Injection pump sprocket mark for use with Bosch pump*
C *Woodruff key*
R *Injection pump sprocket mark for use with Lucas pump*

in the rear engine lifting bracket).

10 Ensure that the engine/gearbox assembly is adequately supported, then unscrew the nut securing the upper mounting bracket to the mounting on the body **(see illustration)**. On certain models it is necessary to counterhold the mounting threaded rod using a suitable Allen key or hexagon bit, whilst loosening the nut with an open-ended spanner.

11 Unscrew the three bolts securing the

5.15b Camshaft sprocket and fuel injection pump sprocket timing mark positions with No 1 piston at TDC - models with one-piece fuel injection pump sprocket and Lucas injection pump

A *Camshaft sprocket mark (aligned with pointer on outer timing belt cover - cover removed in this view)*
B *Injection pump sprocket mark for use with Bosch pump*
C *Woodruff key*
R *Injection pump sprocket mark for use with Lucas pump*

upper mounting bracket to the engine, then withdraw the bracket **(see illustrations)**.

12 Unscrew the two nuts securing the engine mounting rubber/movement limiter assembly to the body, and withdraw the assembly **(see illustration)**.

13 Unscrew the securing bolts, and withdraw the timing belt cover which covers the fuel injection pump sprocket **(see illustration)**.

14 Unscrew the securing bolts, noting the

5.16 Running direction arrows on timing belt

locations of any brackets secured by the bolts, and remove the timing belt cover which covers the camshaft sprocket **(see illustrations)**.

15 With the crankshaft locked in position with No 1 piston at TDC (see paragraph 8), note the position of the timing mark on the fuel injection pump sprocket **(see illustrations)**. **Note:** *On models fitted with a two-piece adjustable injection pump sprocket, the sprocket timing mark may differ from those shown for the one-piece sprocket. If this is the case, take note of the type of mark found, and its location, for use when refitting.* Note that on models with a single-piece sprocket, there are two timing marks on the sprocket. The mark used depends on whether a Bosch or Lucas injection pump is fitted.

16 If the original belt is to be re-used, check if the belt is marked with arrows to indicate its running direction, and if necessary mark it **(see illustration)**. Similarly, make accurate

5.17 Loosen the timing belt tensioner adjuster nut

5.23a The running direction arrows on the belt must point clockwise

5.23b Align the timing marks on the belt with the crankshaft . . .

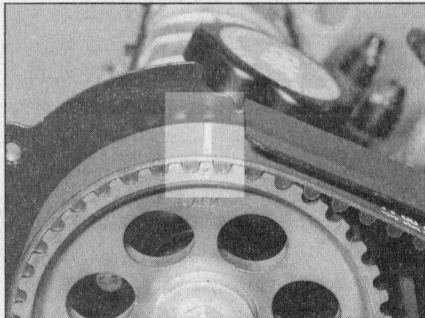

5.23c . . . camshaft . . .

5.23d . . . and injection pump sprocket marks (model with Lucas injection pump shown)

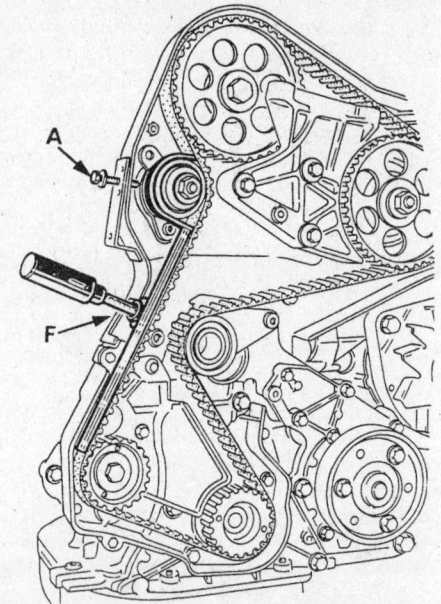

5.26 Renault tool (F) and M6 bolt (A) used to tension timing belt

alignment marks on the belt, corresponding to the timing marks on the camshaft, fuel injection pump and crankshaft sprockets.

17 Loosen the adjuster nut, and slide the timing belt tensioner back to relieve the tension from the belt **(see illustration)**. Re-tighten the nut.

18 Release the belt from the camshaft sprocket, fuel injection pump sprocket, idler wheel, crankshaft sprocket and auxiliary shaft sprocket, and remove it from the engine.

19 Do not turn the camshaft or the crankshaft whilst the timing belt is removed, as there is a risk of piston-to-valve contact. If it is necessary to turn the camshaft for any reason, remove the TDC locking tool from the cylinder block, before doing so, and turn the crankshaft anti-clockwise (viewed from the timing belt end of the engine) by a quarter turn to position all four pistons half way down their bores.

Inspection

20 Clean the sprockets, idler wheel and tensioner and wipe them dry, although do not apply excessive amounts of solvent to the idler and tensioner wheels otherwise the bearing lubricant may be contaminated. Also clean the rear timing belt cover, and the front of the cylinder head and block.

21 Examine the timing belt carefully for any signs of cracking, fraying or general wear, particularly at the roots of the teeth. Renew the belt if there is any sign of deterioration of this nature, or if there is any oil or grease contamination. The belt must, of course, be renewed if it has completed the mileage given in the maintenance schedule in Chapter 1.

Refitting

22 Check that the crankshaft is positioned with No 1 piston at TDC, and locked in position using the tool through the hole in the cylinder block as described previously. If the pistons have been positioned halfway down their bores (see paragraph 19), temporarily refit the outer timing belt cover which covers the camshaft sprocket, and check that the TDC mark on the camshaft sprocket is aligned with the pointer on the timing belt cover, then turn the crankshaft clockwise (viewed from the timing belt end of the engine) until the TDC locking tool can be refitted.

23 Align the timing marks on the belt with those on the crankshaft, camshaft and fuel injection pump sprockets, ensuring that the running direction arrows on the belt are pointing clockwise (viewed from the timing belt end of the engine). Note that the belt should be marked with lines across its width to act as timing marks **(see illustrations)**. If the original belt is to be refitted, and the timing marks have deteriorated (in which case, it is likely that the belt is in need of renewal in any case), use the alignment marks made on the belt before removal. Fit the timing belt over the crankshaft sprocket first, followed by the idler wheel, fuel injection pump sprocket, camshaft sprocket, tensioner, and auxiliary shaft sprocket.

24 Check that all the timing marks are still aligned.

25 The belt must now be tensioned as follows.

Adjustment using Renault special tool Ele. 346.04

Note: *The tension of the belt must be adjusted with the engine cold. The manufacturers specify the use of a special gauge, Renault tool Ele. 346.04 for checking the timing belt tension. If access to a suitable tool cannot be obtained, it is strongly recommended that the vehicle is taken to a Renault dealer to have the belt tension checked at the earliest opportunity.*

26 Fit the gauge to the engine, as shown **(see illustration)**.

27 Screw an M6 bolt through the threaded hole in the rear timing belt cover next to the tensioner. Loosen the tensioner nut, and tighten the bolt so that it pushes against the tensioner roller bracket to tension the belt **(see illustration)**.

28 Adjust the bolt pushing against the tensioner roller bracket to give the specified reading on the gauge (see illustration 5.26).

29 With the correct tension applied, re-tighten the tensioner nut to the specified

5.27 M6 bolt (arrowed) fitted to rear timing belt cover

5.45 Twisting the timing belt as an approximate tension check

6.2 Removing the crankshaft sprocket

6.8 Removing the auxiliary shaft sprocket

torque. This torque is critical, since if the nut were to come loose considerable engine damage would result. Loosen the bolt fitted to the rear timing belt cover so that it no longer rests on the tensioner roller bracket.

30 Remove the TDC locking tool from the cylinder block, then refit the crankshaft pulley and securing bolt. Prevent the crankshaft turning using the method described previously, and tighten the bolt to the specified torque. Refit the flywheel cover plate/engine-to-gearbox bracing bracket.

31 Check that the crankshaft is still positioned with No 1 piston at TDC (by temporarily refitting the locking tool to the cylinder block), then remove the TDC locking tool, and turn the crankshaft two complete turns in the normal direction of rotation, returning it to the TDC position again. Re-insert the TDC locking tool in the cylinder block.

32 Temporarily refit the timing belt cover which covers the camshaft sprocket, and check that the camshaft sprocket timing mark still aligns with the pointer on the cover, as noted before removal (see Section 3).

33 Re-check the belt tension as described previously. If the tension is incorrect, the setting and checking procedure must be repeated until the correct tension is achieved.

34 With the belt tensioned correctly, remove the M6 bolt from the rear timing belt cover, and remove the TDC locking tool from the cylinder block, if not already done. Refit the plug to the cylinder block TDC hole.

35 Check the fuel injection pump timing as described in Chapter 4.

36 Refit the upper timing belt covers, ensuring that any brackets secured by the bolts are in position as noted before removal.

37 Refit the engine mounting rubber/movement limiter assembly to the body, and refit the upper mounting bracket to the engine, as described in Section 14.

38 Refit the fuel filter assembly to the body, and clip the hoses into position.

39 Refit the auxiliary drivebelt as described in Chapter 1.

40 Refit the strengthening bar to the front suspension turrets.

41 Withdraw the jack, or the lifting tackle, as applicable, used to support the engine.

42 Refit the wheel arch cover and the

roadwheel, and lower the vehicle to the ground.

43 Reconnect the battery negative lead.

Approximate adjustment

44 Refer to the note at the beginning of paragraph 26 before proceeding.

45 If the special gauge is not available, the timing belt tension can be checked approximately by twisting the belt between the thumb and forefinger, at the centre of the run between the tensioner pulley and the auxiliary shaft pulley. It should be just possible to twist the belt through 90° using moderate pressure **(see illustration)**.

46 The checking, adjustment and final refitting procedures are as described previously in paragraphs 27 to 43, noting the following:

a) *Have the belt tension checked by a Renault dealer at the earliest opportunity.*

b) *If in doubt, err on the tight side when adjusting the tension, as if the belt is too slack, it may jump on the sprockets, which could result in serious engine damage.*

---

6 Timing belt sprockets, idler roller and tensioner - removal and refitting

Crankshaft sprocket

Note: *A suitable puller may be required for this operation.*

Removal

1 Remove the timing belt as described in Section 5.

2 It should be possible to simply pull the sprocket from the front of the crankshaft, however in some cases a puller may be required **(see illustration)**. It is a simple matter to make up a puller using two bolts, a metal bar and the existing crankshaft pulley bolt. By unscrewing the crankshaft pulley bolt, the sprocket is pulled from the end of the crankshaft.

3 Recover the Woodruff key if it is loose.

Refitting

4 Refitting is a reversal of removal. Note that the sprocket fits with the flange against the end

of the cylinder block/rear timing belt cover.

5 Refit the timing belt as described in Section 5.

Auxiliary shaft sprocket

Removal

6 Remove the timing belt as described in Section 5.

7 Hold the sprocket stationary using a suitable gear-holding tool. Alternatively, an old timing belt can be wrapped around the sprocket and held firmly with a pair of grips.

8 Unscrew the securing bolt, then pull the sprocket from the end of the shaft **(see illustration)**. If necessary, use two levers or screwdrivers to free the sprocket (if necessary, a puller can be used as described previously for the crankshaft sprocket).

Refitting

9 Refitting is a reversal of removal. Note that the sprocket fits with the hollow side against the cylinder block. Tighten the sprocket securing bolt to the specified torque.

10 Refit the timing belt as described in Section 5.

Fuel injection pump sprocket

Note: *A suitable puller will be required for this operation.*

Removal

11 Release the tension in the timing belt with reference to Section 5.

12 Hold the sprocket stationary using a suitable gear-holding tool. Alternatively, an old timing belt can be wrapped around the sprocket and held firmly with a pair of grips.

2A

6.13 Unscrewing the fuel injection pump sprocket nut

6.15 Using a puller to release the fuel injection pump sprocket

6.17a Make an alignment mark on the timing belt

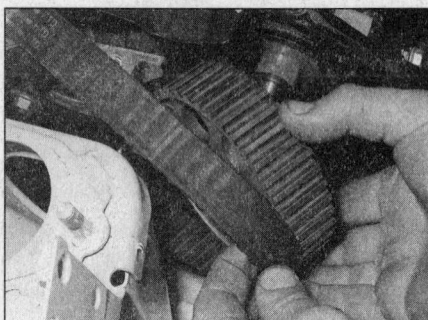
6.17b Disengage the sprocket from the timing belt

6.21 Remove the plastic alternator shield (arrowed)

6.23 Removing the alternator mounting bracket

13 Unscrew the sprocket securing nut, as far as the end of the pump shaft. Do not remove the nut at this stage **(see illustration)**. **Note:** *On models with a two-piece adjustable sprocket, do not loosen the three sprocket adjuster bolts, as this will alter the injection pump timing.*

14 On models with a single-piece sprocket, note the location of the Woodruff key in the end of the injection pump shaft. There are two key slots in the sprocket (for use with Bosch and Lucas injection pumps - see illustrations 5.15a and 5.15b). Mark the relevant key slot in the sprocket to ensure correct refitting.

15 Using a suitable puller, acting on the sprocket nut (not on the end of the pump shaft), release the sprocket from the taper on the pump shaft **(see illustration)**.

16 Remove the puller, then remove the sprocket securing nut, and recover the washer.

17 Make a mark on the timing belt corresponding to the location of the fuel injection pump sprocket timing mark (see illustrations 5.15a and 5.15b) to aid alignment when refitting. Disengage the sprocket from the timing belt, remove the sprocket, and recover the Woodruff key from the end of the pump shaft if it is loose **(see illustrations)**.

Refitting

18 Refitting is a reversal of removal, bearing in mind the following points.
a) *On models with a single-piece sprocket, ensure that the Woodruff key is engaged with the correct slot in the sprocket.*
b) *Tighten the sprocket securing nut to the specified torque.*
c) *Refit and tension the timing belt as described in Section 5.*
d) *Before refitting the timing belt cover over the injection pump sprocket, check the injection timing as described in Chapter 4.*

Camshaft sprocket - models with a rear timing belt cover which surrounds both the camshaft and fuel injection pump sprockets

Note: *This is an involved procedure due to the location of the upper engine mounting/fuel injection pump mounting bracket, which leaves insufficient clearance to remove the sprocket from the end of the camshaft. This means that the fuel injection pump and mounting bracket must be removed, as described in the following procedure. It is suggested that this procedure is read through thoroughly before beginning work.*

Removal

19 Disconnect the battery negative lead.
20 Remove the timing belt as described in Section 5.
21 Remove the plastic alternator shield **(see illustration)**.
22 Remove the alternator, with reference to Chapter 5.
23 Unbolt the alternator mounting bracket from the cylinder block **(see illustration)**.
24 Remove the fuel injection pump sprocket as described previously in this Section.
25 Remove the fuel injection pump with reference to Chapter 4.
26 Remove the bolt(s) securing the rear

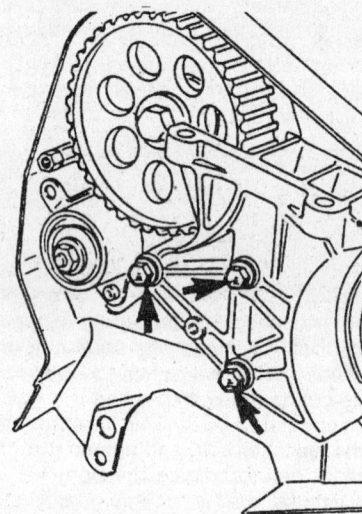
6.27 Fuel injection pump/engine mounting bracket-to-cylinder block bolts (arrowed)

timing belt cover to the fuel injection pump bracket.
27 Remove the three securing bolts, and withdraw the upper engine mounting/fuel injection pump mounting bracket from the engine **(see illustration)**. Note that it may not be possible to fully withdraw the upper two bolts from the bracket (due to limited clearance), in which case slide out the bracket with the bolts in position in their holes.
28 If not already done, remove the crankshaft TDC locking tool, and turn the engine a quarter of a turn anti-clockwise (viewed from

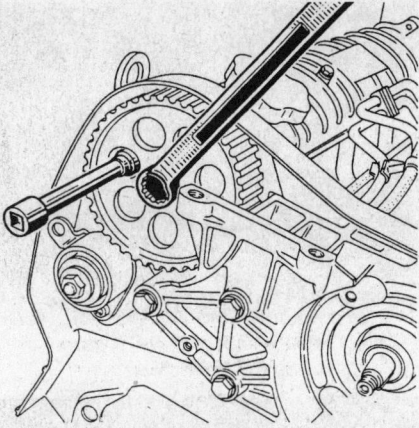

6.29 Using a socket and extension bar to counterhold the camshaft sprocket whilst unscrewing the sprocket bolt

6.30a Remove the bolt and washer . . .

6.30b . . . and the sprocket

6.31 Recover the Woodruff key from the end of the camshaft if it is loose

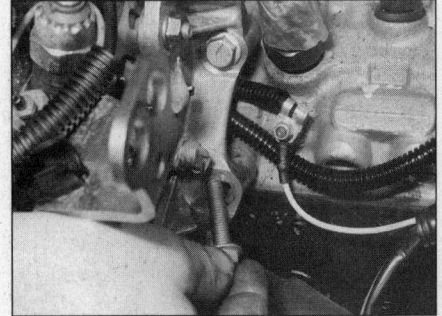

6.48 Removing one of the bolts securing the injection pump rear mounting bracket to the cylinder head

6.50 Remove the bolt (arrowed) securing the rear timing belt cover to the bracket

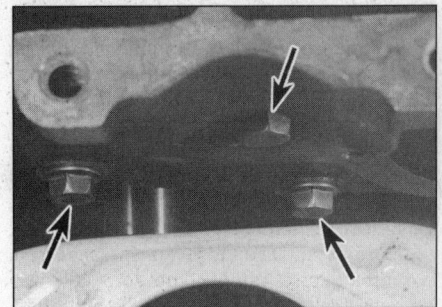

6.51a Unscrew the securing bolts (arrowed) . . .

the timing belt end of the engine) to position the pistons halfway down their bores. This is to avoid any possibility of piston-to-valve contact if the camshaft is inadvertently turned when loosening the sprocket bolt.

29 Unscrew the camshaft sprocket bolt. The sprocket can be held using a suitable socket and extension bar engaged with one of the rear timing belt cover securing bolts as shown **(see illustration)**. Alternatively, use an old timing belt wrapped around the sprocket. Recover the washer.

30 Remove the bolt and washer, and the sprocket from the front of the camshaft **(see illustrations)**. A suitable puller may be required, in which case ensure that the legs of the puller act on the holes in the sprocket, **not** on the sprocket teeth.

31 Recover the Woodruff key from the end of the camshaft if it is loose **(see illustration)**.

Refitting

32 Ensure that the Woodruff key is in place in the end of the camshaft, then refit the camshaft sprocket, noting that the projecting hub fits towards the cylinder head.

33 Ensure that the washer is in place, then refit the sprocket bolt, and tighten it to the specified torque, holding the sprocket as during removal.

34 Refit the upper engine mounting/fuel injection pump mounting bracket and tighten the securing bolts. Where applicable, refit the upper two bolts to the holes in the bracket before the bracket is refitted.

35 Refit the bolt(s) securing the rear timing belt cover to the upper engine mounting/fuel injection pump mounting bracket.

36 Refit the fuel injection pump with reference to Chapter 4.

37 Refit the fuel injection pump sprocket as described previously in this Section.

38 Refit the plastic alternator shield.

39 Refit the alternator mounting bracket to the cylinder block, and tighten the securing bolts.

40 Refit the alternator, with reference to Chapter 5.

41 Temporarily refit the outer timing belt cover which covers the camshaft sprocket, and check that the TDC mark on the camshaft sprocket is aligned with the pointer on the timing belt cover.

42 Turn the crankshaft clockwise (viewed from the timing belt end of the engine) until the crankshaft locking tool can be refitted (to position No 1 piston at TDC).

43 Refit and tension the timing belt, as described in Section 5.

44 Reconnect the battery negative lead.

45 Bleed the fuel system as described in Chapter 4.

Camshaft sprocket - models with a rear timing belt cover which surrounds the camshaft sprocket, but not the fuel injection pump sprocket

Note: Refer to the note at the beginning of the previous sub-Section before proceeding.

Removal

46 Proceed as described in paragraphs 19 to 23.

47 Disconnect all cables, hoses, pipes and wiring from the fuel injection pump, to facilitate removal, with reference to Chapter 4, Section 13.

48 Remove the bolts securing the injection pump rear mounting bracket to the cylinder head **(see illustration)**.

49 Remove the nuts securing the rear mounting bracket to the injection pump, then withdraw the bracket.

50 Remove the bolt securing the rear timing belt cover to the upper engine mounting/fuel injection pump mounting bracket **(see illustration)**.

51 Unscrew the three securing bolts, and remove the upper engine mounting/fuel injection pump mounting bracket, complete with the injection pump from the engine **(see illustrations)**. The assembly is removed by

2A

6.51b ... and withdraw the mounting bracket complete with the injection pump

7.3a Drill a small hole ...

7.3b ... and use a screw and pliers to pull out the seal

8.2 Withdraw the timing belt tensioner

8.3 Remove the bolts securing the timing belt cover to the cylinder head

sliding it out towards the front of the vehicle. Note that it may not be possible to fully withdraw the upper two bolts from the bracket (due to limited clearance), in which case slide out the assembly with the bolts in position in their holes.

52 Proceed as described in paragraphs 28 to 31.

Refitting

53 Proceed as described in paragraphs 32 and 33.

54 Refit the upper engine mounting/fuel injection pump mounting bracket, complete with the injection pump, and tighten the securing bolts. Where applicable, refit the upper two bolts to the holes in the bracket before the assembly is refitted.

55 Refit the bolt securing the rear timing belt cover to the upper engine mounting/fuel injection pump mounting bracket.

56 Refit the injection pump rear mounting bracket and tighten the securing bolts and nuts.

57 Reconnect all relevant cables, hoses, pipes and wiring to the fuel injection pump with reference to Chapter 4, Section 13.

58 Proceed as described in paragraphs 38 to 45.

Idler roller

Removal

59 Remove the timing belt as described in Section 5.

60 Unscrew the two securing bolts, and withdraw the idler roller assembly, manipulating it out from the rear timing belt covers.

Refitting

61 Refitting is a reversal of removal, but check that the roller turns freely without binding or excessive play.

62 Refit and tension the timing belt as described in Section 5.

Tensioner

Removal

63 Remove the timing belt as described in Section 5.

64 Remove the securing nut and the washer, and withdraw the tensioner assembly from the engine.

Refitting

65 Refitting is a reversal of removal, but check that the roller turns freely without binding or excessive play. Ensure that the peg on the cylinder block engages with the hole in the tensioner bracket.

66 Refit and tension the timing belt as described in Section 5.

---

7 Camshaft oil seals - renewal

Front (timing belt) end oil seal

1 Remove the camshaft sprocket as described in Section 6.

2 Remove the Woodruff key from the end of the camshaft, if not already done.

3 Using a small screwdriver, prise out the oil seal from the cylinder head, taking care not to damage the surface of the camshaft. Alternatively, the oil seal can be removed by drilling a small hole and inserting a self-tapping screw. A pair of grips can then be used to pull out the oil seal, by pulling on the screw **(see illustrations)**. If difficulty is experienced, insert two screws diagonally opposite each other. To ensure correct fitting, note the fitted position of the old oil seal.

4 Wipe clean the oil seal seating in the cylinder head, then dip the new seal in fresh engine oil, and locate it over the camshaft with its closed side facing outwards. Make sure that the oil seal lip is not damaged as it is located on the camshaft.

5 Using a tube of suitable diameter, drive the oil seal squarely into the housing to the previously noted depth. A block of wood cut to pass over the end of the camshaft may be used instead.

6 Refit the camshaft sprocket as described in Section 6.

Rear (flywheel end) oil seal

7 No oil seal is fitted to the flywheel end of the camshaft. The sealing is provided by a gasket between the cylinder head and the brake vacuum pump housing, and on certain models by an O-ring fitted between the pump and the housing. The gasket and the O-ring, where applicable, can be renewed after unbolting the pump from the cylinder head (see Chapter 9).

---

8 Camshaft and tappets - removal, inspection and refitting

Note: *A new camshaft front oil seal should be fitted, and a new valve cover gasket may be required on refitting. Suitable sealant will be required for the camshaft bearing caps and the bearing cap bolts.*

Removal

1 Remove the camshaft sprocket as described in Section 6.

2 Remove the securing nuts, and withdraw the timing belt tensioner roller from the engine **(see illustration)**.

3 Unscrew and remove the two bolts securing the upper rear timing belt cover to the cylinder head **(see illustration)**.

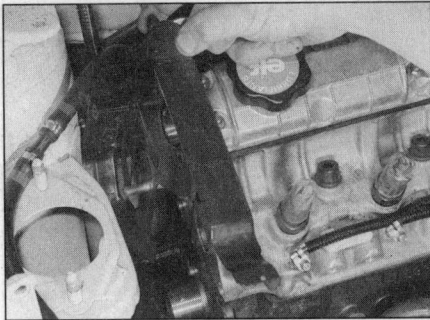

8.6 Withdrawing the timing belt cover from the engine

8.10 Measuring the camshaft endfloat using a dial gauge

8.12a Number the camshaft bearing caps from the flywheel end of the engine

8.12b Identification mark on No 3 . . .

8.12c . . . and No 5 camshaft bearing caps

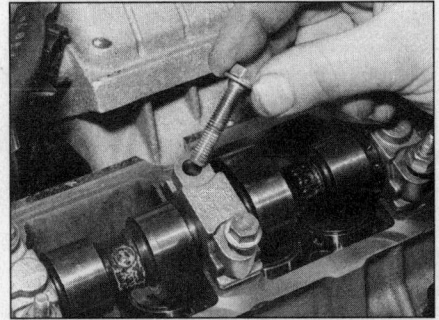

8.13a Removing a bearing cap bolt

8.13b Note that No 1 bearing cap is secured by 2 additional bolts

8.14 Lifting out the camshaft

8.15 Lift out the tappets

2A

4 Unscrew the lower bolt(s) securing the upper rear timing belt cover to the cylinder block.

5 Remove the timing belt idler pulley securing bolt which also passes through the rear timing belt cover.

6 Manipulate the rear timing belt cover from the front of the camshaft and, where possible, withdraw the cover from the engine (see illustration).

7 Remove the brake vacuum pump as described in Chapter 9.

8 Where necessary for improved access, unclip any hoses or cables which are routed across the top of the valve cover, and move them to one side out of the way. If necessary, the accelerator cable can be disconnected with reference to Chapter 4. If fuel lines are disconnected, cover open unions to prevent dirt ingress.

9 Unscrew the nuts from the valve cover, and withdraw the cover from the engine.

Recover the gasket.

10 Using a dial gauge, measure the camshaft endfloat, and compare with the value given in the Specifications (see illustration). This will give an indication of the amount of wear present on the thrust surfaces.

11 If the original camshaft is to be refitted, it is advisable to measure the valve clearances at this stage, as described in Section 4, so that any shims required can be obtained before the camshaft is refitted.

12 Check the camshaft bearing caps for identification marks, and if none are present, make identifying marks so that they can be refitted in their original positions and the same way round. Number the caps from the flywheel end of the engine (see illustrations).

13 Progressively slacken the bearing cap bolts and studs until the valve spring pressure is relieved. Remove the bolts and studs (noting their locations to ensure correct refitting), and the bearing caps themselves

(see illustrations). Note that No 1 bearing cap is secured by 2 studs and 2 additional bolts.

14 Lift out the camshaft together with the oil seal (see illustration).

15 Remove the tappets, keeping each with its shim (see illustration). Place them in a compartment box, or on a sheet of card marked into eight sections, so that they may be refitted to their original locations. Write down the shim thicknesses - they will be needed later if any of the valve clearances are incorrect. The shim size is stamped on the bottom face of the shim, but it is prudent to use a micrometer to measure the true thickness of any shim removed, as it may have been reduced by wear.

Inspection

16 Examine the camshaft bearing surfaces and cam lobes for wear ridges, pitting or scoring. Renew the camshaft if evident.

17 Renew the oil seal at the front end of the camshaft as a matter of course. Lubricate the lips of the new seal before fitting, and store the camshaft so that its weight is not resting on the seal.

18 Examine the camshaft bearing surfaces in the cylinder head and bearing caps. Deep scoring or other damage means that the cylinder head must be renewed.

19 Inspect the tappet buckets and shims for scoring, pitting and wear ridges. Renew as necessary.

Refitting

20 Ensure that the pistons are positioned half way down their bores, as described for sprocket removal in Section 6.

21 Oil the tappets and fit them to the bores from which they were removed. Fit the correct shim, numbered side downwards, to each tappet.

22 Oil the camshaft bearings. Place the camshaft with its oil seal onto the cylinder head. The oil seal must be positioned so that it is flush with the cylinder head face.

23 Apply sealant (CAF 4/60 THIXO, or equivalent) to the cylinder head mating faces of the front and rear camshaft bearing caps (Nos 1 and 5) **(see illustration)**.

24 Refit the camshaft bearing caps to their original locations, ensuring that the front oil seal is correctly located in the bearing cap.

25 Apply sealant to the threads of the bearing cap bolts and studs **(see illustration)**. Fit the bolts and studs, and tighten them progressively to the specified torque.

26 If a new camshaft has been fitted, measure the endfloat using a dial gauge, and check that it is within the specified limits.

27 Refit the brake vacuum pump with reference to Chapter 9.

28 Refit the rear timing belt cover, then refit and tighten the securing bolts.

29 Refit and tighten the bolt securing the timing belt idler pulley assembly.

30 Refit the timing belt tensioner roller, ensuring that the peg on the cylinder block engages with the hole in the tensioner roller bracket.

31 Refit the camshaft sprocket as described in Section 6, ignoring the reference to bleeding the fuel system at this stage.

32 Check the valve clearances as described in Section 4, and take any corrective action necessary.

33 Refit the valve cover, using a new gasket if necessary, and tighten the securing nuts.

34 Refit/reconnect any hoses or cables which were moved for access. If the accelerator cable has been disconnected, reconnect it with reference to Chapter 4.

35 Reconnect the battery negative lead.

36 Bleed the fuel system as described in Chapter 4.

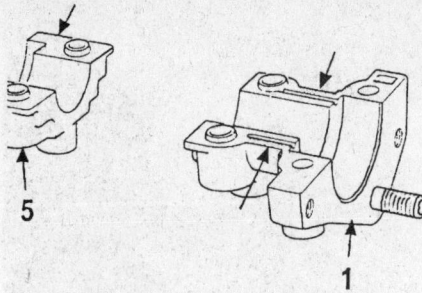

8.23 Apply sealant to the cylinder head mating faces (arrowed) of camshaft bearing caps Nos 1 and 5

9.6a Unscrewing the fuel supply pipe banjo union

9 Cylinder head - removal, inspection and refitting

Note: *A new cylinder head gasket must be fitted, and a new valve cover gasket and new cylinder head bolts may be required on refitting - see text.*

Removal

1 The following procedure describes removal and refitting of the cylinder head complete with manifolds and the fuel injection pump.

2 Disconnect the battery negative lead.

3 Drain the cooling system with reference to Chapter 1. Also drain the cylinder block by unscrewing the drain plug located on the right-hand rear face of the engine. Refit the plug after draining.

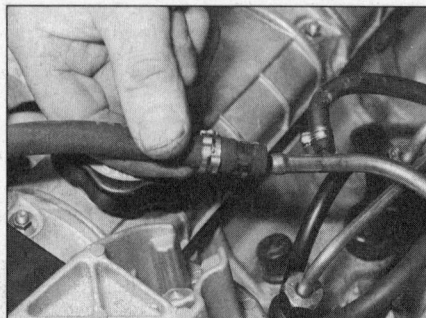

9.7a Disconnect the fuel return hose . . .

8.25 Apply sealant to the threads of the bearing cap bolts and studs

9.6b Cover the open end of the pipe and the opening in the injection pump

4 To improve access, unbolt the strengthening bar from between the front suspension strut turrets.

5 Disconnect the accelerator cable from the fuel injection pump, and move the cable clear of the engine, noting its routing, with reference to Chapter 4 if necessary.

6 Undo the banjo union and disconnect the fuel supply pipe from the injection pump. Recover the sealing washers from the banjo union. Cover the open end of the pipe, and plug the opening in the injection pump to keep dirt out (the banjo bolt can be refitted to the pump and covered) **(see illustrations)**.

7 Remove the securing clip, and disconnect the main fuel return hose from the pipe on the fuel injection pump. Feed the hose through the rear engine lifting bracket, located at the rear of the cylinder head, and move the hose clear of the engine **(see illustrations)**. Cover

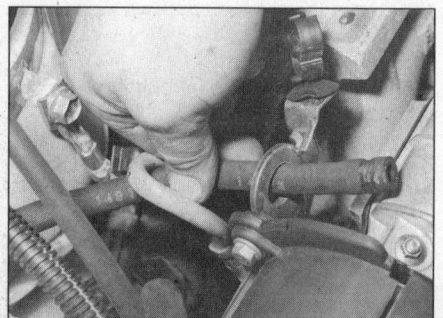

9.7b . . . and feed it through the engine lifting bracket

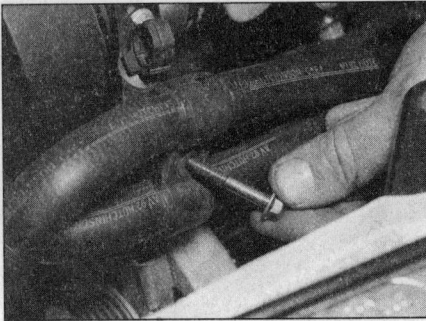

9.8 Unbolt the hose bracket from the injection pump mounting bracket

9.9 Disconnecting the breather hose from the oil separator - Turbo model shown

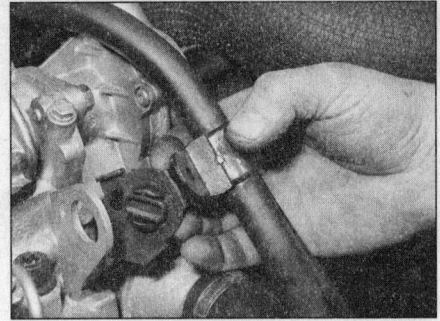

9.10 Unclip the hose bracket from the engine lifting bracket

9.12 Unbolt the thermostat housing and move it to one side - Turbo models

9.14 Removing the air cleaner-to-turbocharger air trunking - Turbo model

9.16 Disconnecting the coolant hose from the rear of the cylinder head

2A

the open ends of the pipe and the hose to prevent dirt ingress.

8 Unbolt the hose bracket from the front of the fuel injection pump mounting bracket, and move the hoses and bracket clear of the injection pump **(see illustration)**.

9 Disconnect the breather hose(s), from the crankcase oil separator(s), and where applicable (on Turbo models), disconnect the hose from the boost pressure fuel delivery corrector on the injection pump **(see illustration)**. Similarly, disconnect the corresponding ends of the hoses from the manifold.

10 Unclip the hose bracket from the front engine lifting bracket, unbolt the remaining hose bracket from the brake vacuum pump, and remove the hose assembly from the

engine **(see illustration)**.

11 On non-Turbo models, disconnect the coolant hose from the thermostat housing.

12 On Turbo models, unbolt the thermostat housing from the cylinder head, and move it to one side, leaving the hoses and sensor wiring connected **(see illustration)**.

13 On Turbo models, disconnect the air trunking running from the intercooler to the inlet manifold, and remove the trunking.

14 Disconnect the air trunking running from the air cleaner to the inlet manifold, or turbocharger, as applicable, and remove the trunking (note that, where applicable, the breather hoses which connect to the trunking will also have to be disconnected) **(see illustration)**.

15 On Turbo models, disconnect the air

trunking running from the intercooler to the turbocharger, and remove the trunking.

16 Disconnect the coolant hose from the left-hand rear corner of the cylinder head, and move the hose clear **(see illustration)**.

17 Disconnect the engine earth lead from the rear engine lifting bracket assembly **(see illustration)**.

18 Disconnect the vacuum hose from the brake vacuum pump **(see illustration)**.

19 Disconnect all relevant wiring from the fuel injection pump. Note that on certain pumps, this can be achieved by simply disconnecting the wiring connectors at the brackets on the pump. On some pumps it will be necessary to disconnect the wiring from the individual components (some connections may be protected by rubber covers). Label all connections to aid correct refitting.

20 Disconnect the electrical feed wires from the relevant glow plugs.

21 On non-Turbo models, disconnect the wiring plug from the temperature gauge/warning light sender unit, located at the left-hand front or rear of the cylinder head.

22 Disconnect all relevant pipes and hoses from the manifolds, and the turbocharger where applicable, with reference to the relevant Section(s) of Chapter 4. Label all pipes and hoses to aid correct refitting.

23 Where applicable, unbolt any hose brackets from the manifolds and surrounding area, and move the hoses to one side **(see illustration)**.

9.17 Disconnect the earth lead from the engine lifting bracket

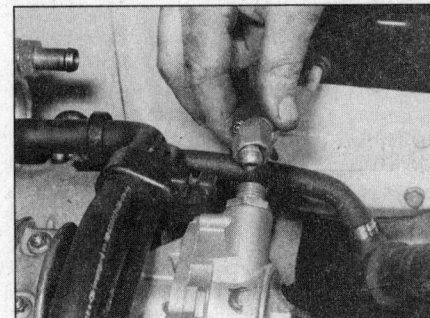

9.18 Disconnecting the brake vacuum pump hose

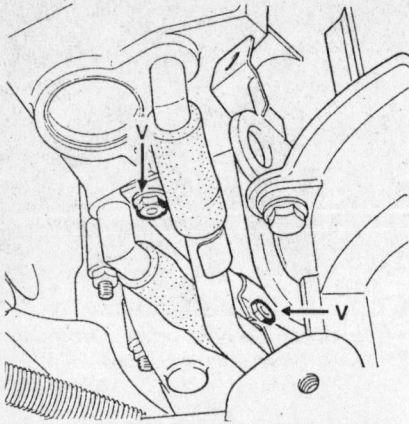

9.23 Hose bracket securing bolts (V) - Turbo models

9.24a Turbocharger inlet elbow-to-gearbox bracket bolts (arrowed)

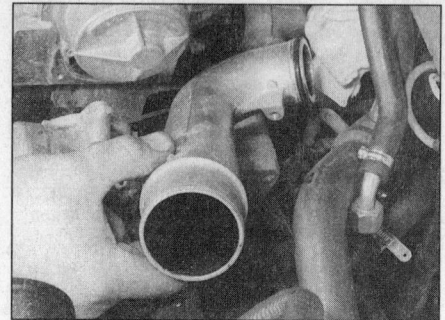

9.24b Removing the turbocharger inlet elbow

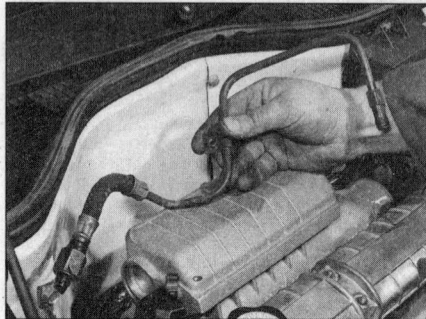

9.29 Removing the turbocharger oil feed pipe/hose assembly

9.32 Slackening a cylinder head bolt

24 On Turbo models, remove the two bolts securing the turbocharger inlet elbow to the bracket on the gearbox. Remove the nut and bolt securing the bracing bracket to the turbocharger and the inlet elbow, and remove the elbow **(see illustrations)**.

25 Remove the timing belt as described in Section 5.

26 Remove the bolt(s) securing the upper rear timing belt cover to the cylinder block.

27 Remove the timing belt idler pulley securing bolt which also passes through the rear timing belt cover.

28 Remove the exhaust front section as described in Chapter 4.

29 On Turbo models, unscrew the union nut securing the turbocharger oil feed pipe to the union on the cylinder block and remove the pipe/hose assembly **(see illustration)**.

30 On Turbo models, remove the bolts securing the turbocharger support bracket to the turbocharger and the engine, and remove the support bracket.

31 If not already done, remove the TDC locking tool from the cylinder block, and turn the crankshaft anti-clockwise (viewed from the timing belt end of the engine) by a quarter turn to position all four pistons half way down their bores.

32 Progressively slacken the cylinder head bolts in the reverse sequence to that shown in illustration 9.53 **(see illustration)**. When the tension has been relieved, remove all the bolts.

33 The cylinder head assembly complete with ancillaries is heavy, and it is advisable to attach a hoist and suitable lifting tackle to the lifting brackets on the cylinder head in order to lift it from the engine.

34 Lift the cylinder head (complete with manifolds, injection pump, and upper rear timing belt cover) upwards and off the cylinder block **(see illustration)**. If it is stuck, tap it upwards using a hammer and block of wood (taking care not to damage the fuel injection pump). **Do not** try to turn the cylinder head (it is located by two dowels), nor attempt to prise it free using a screwdriver inserted between the block and head faces.

9.34 Lifting the cylinder head assembly from the engine - Turbo model shown

35 If desired, the manifolds, turbocharger (where applicable) and fuel injection pump can be removed from the cylinder head with reference to the relevant Sections of Chapter 4.

Inspection

36 The mating faces of the cylinder head and block must be perfectly clean before refitting the head. Use a scraper to remove all traces of gasket and carbon, and also clean the tops of the pistons. Take particular care with the aluminium cylinder head, as the soft metal is damaged easily. Also, make sure that debris is not allowed to enter the oil and water channels - this is particularly important for the oil circuit, as carbon could block the oil supply to the camshaft or crankshaft bearings. Using adhesive tape and paper, seal the water, oil and bolt holes in the cylinder block. Clean the piston crowns in the same way.

> **HAYNES HiNT**
> To prevent carbon entering the gap between the pistons and bores, smear a little grease in the gap. After cleaning the piston, rotate the crankshaft so that the piston moves down the bore, then wipe out the grease and carbon with a cloth rag.

37 Check the block and head for nicks, deep scratches and other damage. If slight, they may be removed carefully with a file. More serious damage may be repaired by machining, but this is a specialist job.

38 If warpage of the cylinder head is suspected, use a straight-edge to check it for distortion. Refer to Chapter 2B if necessary.

39 Clean out the bolt holes in the block using a pipe cleaner, or a rag and screwdriver. Make sure that all oil is removed, otherwise there is a possibility of the block being cracked by hydraulic pressure when the bolts are tightened.

40 Examine the bolt threads and the threads in the cylinder block for damage. If necessary, use the correct-size tap to chase out the threads in the block, and use a die to clean the threads on the bolts.

Gasket selection

41 Turn the crankshaft to bring piston Nos 1 and 4 to just below the TDC position (just below the top face of the cylinder block). Position a dial test indicator (DTI) on the cylinder block and zero it on the block face. Transfer the probe to the centre of No 1 piston,

9.42 Measuring piston protrusion using a dial test indicator

9.44a Cylinder head gasket thickness identification marking location (R)

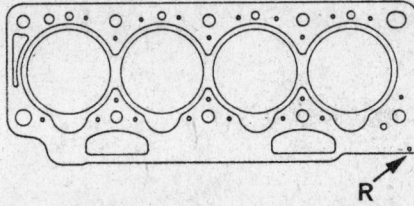

9.44b Cylinder head gasket thickness identification marking (arrowed) - "1 hole" type shown (ignore remaining holes - see text)

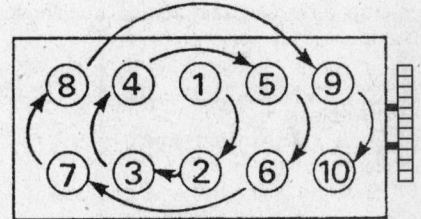

9.46 Measure the length (L) of the cylinder head bolts, to determine whether renewal is required

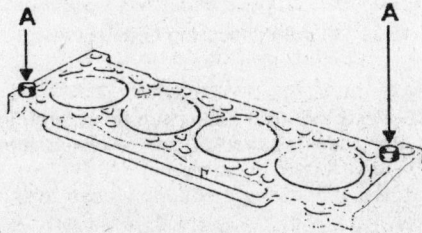

9.50 Cylinder head locating dowel locations (A)

illustrations). **Note:** *The gasket thickness identification holes are located in an area 25 mm from the flywheel end of the gasket. Do not take into account any other holes outside this area.*

Cylinder head bolt examination

45 On models fitted with T55 Torx cylinder head bolts, the manufacturers recommend that the bolts are measured to determine whether renewal is necessary, however some owners may wish to renew the bolts as a matter of course. The manufacturers do not specify checking or renewal for the hexagon socket-head-type bolts.

46 Where applicable, measure the length of each bolt from the base of the head (without a washer fitted) to the end of the shank **(see illustration)**.

47 If the length of any bolt exceeds 120.5 mm, all ten bolts **must** be renewed.

Refitting

48 Where applicable, refit the manifolds, turbocharger (where applicable) and fuel injection pump to the cylinder head, with reference to the relevant Sections of Chapter 4.

49 Turn the crankshaft clockwise (viewed from the timing belt end) until Nos 1 and 4 pistons pass bottom dead centre (BDC) and begin to rise, then position them halfway up their bores. Nos 2 and 3 pistons will also be at their mid-way positions, but descending their bores. Do not turn the crankshaft again until the timing belt is to be refitted (this is to prevent the possibility of piston-to-valve contact).

50 Ensure that the cylinder head locating dowels are fitted to the cylinder block, then fit the correct gasket the right way round on the cylinder block with the identification mark(s) at the front corner of the engine at the flywheel end **(see illustration)**.

then slowly turn the crankshaft back and forth past TDC, noting the highest reading produced on the indicator. Record this reading.

42 Repeat this measurement procedure on No 4 piston, then turn the crankshaft half a turn (180°) and repeat the procedure on Nos 2 and 3 pistons **(see illustration)**. Ensure that all measurements are taken along the longitudinal centreline of the crankshaft (this will eliminate errors due to piston slant).

43 If a dial test indicator is not available, piston protrusion may be measured using a straight-edge and feeler blades or vernier calipers. However, these methods are inevitably less accurate and cannot therefore be recommended.

44 Ascertain the greatest piston protrusion measurement and use this to determine the correct cylinder head gasket from the following table.

Piston protrusion	Gasket identification
Non-Turbo engines:	
Less than 0.868 mm	2 holes
0.868 to 1.000 mm	1 hole
More than 1.000 mm	3 holes
Turbo engines:	
Less than 0.073 mm	2 holes
0.073 to 0.206 mm	1 hole
More than 0.206 mm	3 holes

The identification holes are located at the front corner of the gasket, at the flywheel end **(see**

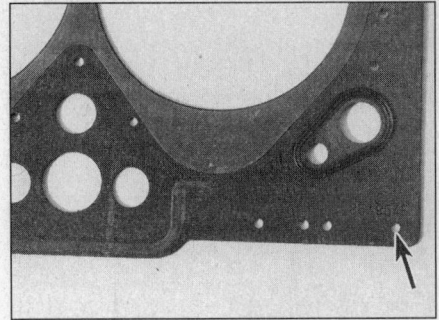

9.53 Cylinder head bolt tightening sequence

51 Lower the cylinder head onto the block. Ensure that the upper rear timing belt cover engages correctly with the lower rear timing belt cover on the cylinder block. Where applicable, disconnect the lifting tackle and hoist. Ensure that the swirl chambers do not drop out of their locations in the cylinder head as it is lowered into position.

52 Lubricate the cylinder head bolt threads, and the undersides of the bolt heads with a little engine oil, then insert them, together with their washers. Screw the bolts into their threads as far as possible by hand.

53 Tighten the bolts in the order shown, and in the stages given in the Specifications - ie, tighten all bolts in sequence to the Stage 1 torque, then tighten all bolts in sequence to the Stage 2 torque, and so on **(see illustration)**. Note that on Turbo models, the bolts must be tightened to the final stage after the engine has been run to normal operating temperature and allowed to cool (see Specifications).

⚠️ *Warning: On models with Torx type cylinder head bolts, the final tightening stages involve very high forces. Ensure that the tools used are in good condition. If the engine has been removed from the vehicle, it is recommended that tightening to the Stage 6 torque wrench setting (and beyond for Turbo models) is carried out with the engine refitted to the vehicle (it may be necessary to remove the right-hand upper engine mounting bracket for access to one of the bolts with the engine in the vehicle).*

2A

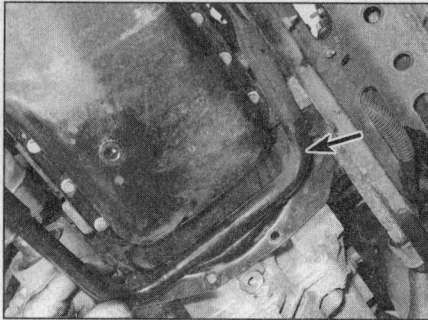

10.3 Removing the flywheel cover plate/engine-to-gearbox bracing bracket

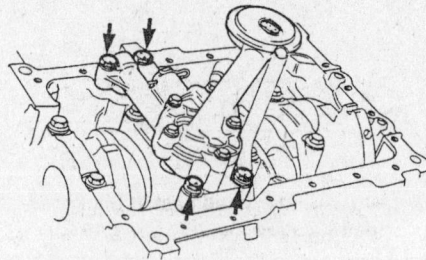

11.2a Oil pump securing bolts (arrowed)

11.2b Removing the oil pump

54 On Turbo models, refit the turbocharger-to-engine bracket, and tighten the securing bolts.

55 On Turbo models, refit the turbocharger oil feed pipe, and tighten the union to the cylinder block.

56 Refit the exhaust front section with reference to Chapter 4.

57 Refit the timing belt idler pulley securing bolt.

58 Refit the bolts securing the upper rear timing belt cover to the cylinder block.

59 Refit the timing belt as described in Section 5.

60 On Turbo models, examine the sealing ring in the turbocharger inlet elbow, and renew it if necessary. Refit the elbow and the bracing bracket.

61 Refit any hose brackets to the manifolds, as noted before removal.

62 Reconnect all relevant pipes and hoses to the manifolds, and the turbocharger where applicable, as noted before removal.

63 On non-Turbo models, reconnect the wiring plug to the temperature gauge/warning light sender unit.

64 Reconnect the feed wires to the relevant glow plugs.

65 Reconnect all wiring to the fuel injection pump.

66 Reconnect the engine earth lead to the rear engine lifting bracket.

67 Reconnect the coolant hose to the cylinder head.

68 Reconnect the air trunking between the air cleaner, inlet manifold, turbocharger and intercooler, as applicable. Ensure that any breather hoses are correctly reconnected.

69 On Turbo models, examine the sealing ring between the thermostat housing and the cylinder head, and renew it if necessary. Refit the thermostat housing to the cylinder head.

70 On non-Turbo models, reconnect the coolant hose to the thermostat housing.

71 Reconnect the crankcase breather hose(s), and on Turbo models the boost pressure fuel delivery corrector hose, and refit the brackets to the engine lifting bracket and the brake vacuum pump.

72 Refit the hose bracket to the fuel injection pump mounting bracket.

73 Feed the main fuel return hose through the engine lifting bracket, and reconnect it to the fuel injection pump pipe.

74 Reconnect the fuel supply hose to the injection pump.

75 Reconnect the accelerator cable with reference to Chapter 4.

76 Refit the strengthening bar to the front suspension strut turrets.

77 Refill and bleed the cooling system as described in Chapter 1.

78 Reconnect the battery negative lead.

79 Prime and bleed the fuel system as described in Chapter 4.

80 **On Turbo models, follow the procedure described in Chapter 4, Section 20, paragraph 25 (priming the turbocharger oil circuit) before starting the engine).**

81 On Turbo models, tighten the cylinder head bolts to the final stage after running the engine to normal operating temperature and allowing it to cool (see Specifications). It may be necessary to remove the right-hand upper engine mounting bracket, with reference to Section 14, for access to one of the bolts.

10 Sump - removal and refitting

Note: *A new sump gasket or suitable sealant (as applicable) must be used on refitting.*

Removal

1 Apply the handbrake, then jack up the front of the vehicle and support it securely on axle stands (see *"Jacking, towing and wheel changing"*). Remove the right-hand roadwheel and wheel arch cover. Where applicable, remove the engine undershield.

2 Drain the engine oil as described in Chapter 1, then refit and tighten the drain plug.

3 Unscrew the securing bolts, and remove the flywheel cover plate/engine-to-gearbox bracing bracket **(see illustration)**.

4 Unscrew and remove the bolts securing the sump to the cylinder block. Note that the bolts on the right-hand side of the sump are most easily reached working under the wheel arch. If necessary, tap the sump with a hide or plastic mallet to break the seal, then

remove the sump.

5 Remove the gasket where fitted.

Refitting

6 Clean all traces of gasket or sealing compound from the mating faces of the sump and cylinder block.

7 Where fitted, locate a new gasket on the sump, otherwise apply a bead of CAF 4/60 THIXO sealant (or equivalent) to the sump face.

8 If a gasket is not fitted, it is important that the sump is positioned correctly the first time and not moved around after the sealant has touched the cylinder block. Temporary long bolts or dowel rods may be used to help achieve this.

9 To prevent oil dripping from the oil pump and crankcase, wipe these areas clean before refitting the sump.

10 Lift the sump into position, then insert the bolts and tighten them progressively to the specified torque.

11 Refit the flywheel cover plate/engine-to-gearbox bracing bracket and tighten the securing bolts.

12 Refit the roadwheel, the wheel arch cover and, where applicable the engine undershield, and lower the vehicle to the ground.

13 Fill the engine with fresh oil with reference to Chapter 1.

11 Oil pump - removal, inspection and refitting

Removal

1 Remove the sump as described in Section 10.

2 Unscrew the four retaining bolts, and withdraw the pump from the cylinder block and drivegear **(see illustrations)**.

Inspection

3 Unscrew the retaining bolts and lift off the pump cover.

4 Withdraw the idler gear and the drivegear/shaft. Mark the idler gear before removal so that it can be refitted in its original position **(see illustration)**.

5 Extract the retaining clip, and remove the oil

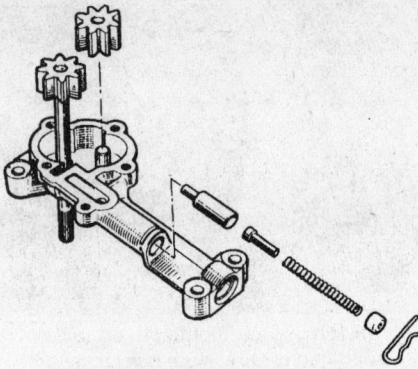

11.4 Oil pump components

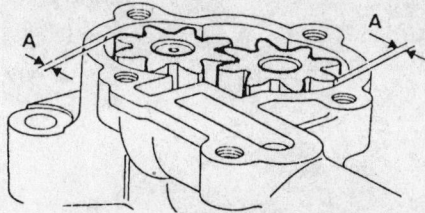

11.7c Oil pump gear endfloat measurement points (B)

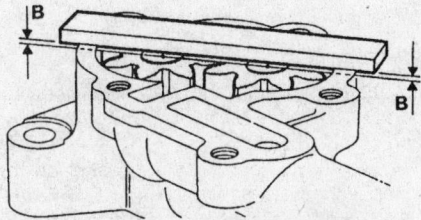

11.8a Tightening the oil pump cover bolts

11.7a Oil pump gear-to-body measurement points (A)

11.7d Measuring the oil pump gear endfloat

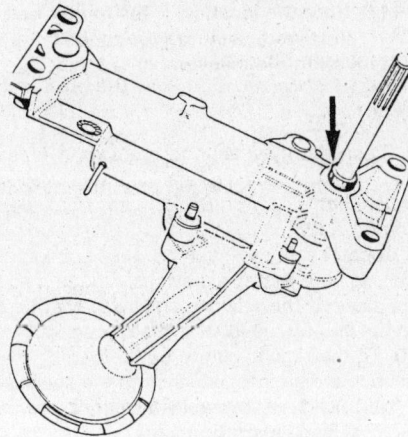

11.8b Dowel location (arrowed) in oil pump body

11.7b Measuring the oil pump-to-body clearance

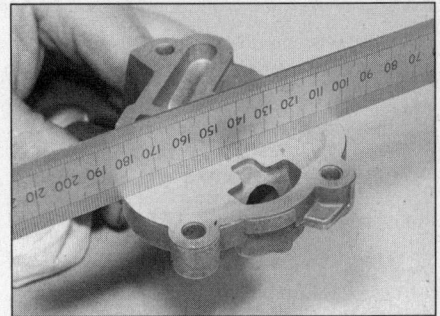

11.7e Checking the flatness of the oil pump cover

11.10 Tightening the oil pump securing bolts

2A

pressure relief valve spring retainer, spring, and plunger.

6 Clean the components, and carefully examine the gears, pump body and relief valve plunger for any signs of scoring or wear. Renew the complete pump assembly if excessive wear is evident (no spare parts are available).

7 If the components appear serviceable, measure the clearance between the pump body and the gears using feeler blades. Also measure the gear endfloat, and check the flatness of the end cover **(see illustrations)**. If the clearances exceed the specified tolerances, the pump must be renewed.

8 If the pump is satisfactory, reassemble the components in the reverse order of removal. Fill the pump with oil, then refit the cover and tighten the bolts securely. (A new pump should also be primed with oil.) Check that the locating dowel is in position where the driveshaft enters the oil pump body **(see illustrations)**.

Refitting

9 Wipe clean the mating faces of the oil pump and cylinder block.

10 Lift the oil pump into position, engaging the driveshaft with the drivegear. Insert and fully tighten the retaining bolts **(see illustration)**.

11 Refit the sump as described in Section 10.

12 Crankshaft oil seals - renewal

Front (timing belt) oil seal

1 Remove the crankshaft sprocket, as described in Section 6.

2 Prise out the old oil seal using a small screwdriver, taking care not to damage the surface of the crankshaft. Alternatively, the oil

seal can be removed by drilling two small holes diagonally opposite each other and inserting self-tapping screws in them. A pair of grips can then be used to pull out the oil seal, by pulling on each side in turn.

3 Inspect the seal rubbing surface on the crankshaft. If it is grooved or rough in the area where the old seal was fitted, the new seal should be fitted slightly less deeply, so that it rubs on an unworn part of the crankshaft surface.

4 Wipe clean the oil seal seating, then dip the new seal in fresh engine oil, and locate it over the crankshaft with its closed side facing outwards. Make sure that the oil seal lip is not damaged as it is located on the crankshaft.

5 Using a tube, or socket, of suitable diameter, drive the oil seal squarely into the housing until flush. A block of wood cut to pass over the end of the crankshaft may be used instead.

6 Refit the crankshaft sprocket as described in Section 6.

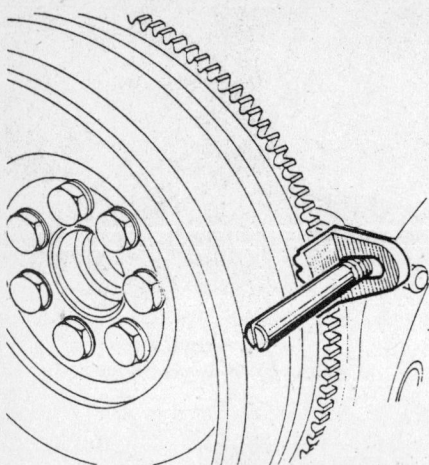

13.4 Tool bolted to cylinder block to hold flywheel stationary

13.10a Fit new flywheel bolts . . .

13.10b . . . and tighten them to the specified torque. Note bar (arrowed) used to hold flywheel stationary

14.6 Note the location of the longer bolt (arrowed) securing the rubber mounting/plate assembly to the body

14.8a Lower mounting bracket-to-gearbox bolt (arrowed)

Rear (flywheel end) oil seal

7 Remove the flywheel as described in Section 13.

8 Renew the oil seal as described in paragraphs 2 to 5 inclusive.

9 Refit the flywheel with reference to Section 13.

13 Flywheel - removal, inspection and refitting

Note: *On Turbo models, the engine and gearbox must be removed as an assembly (see Chapter 2B) before the flywheel can be removed. New flywheel bolts must be used on refitting.*

Removal

1 Remove the gearbox (non-Turbo models - see Chapter 7) or the engine/gearbox assembly (Turbo models - see Chapter 2B), as applicable.

2 Remove the clutch as described in Chapter 6.

3 Mark the flywheel in relation to the crankshaft to aid refitting.

4 The flywheel must now be held stationary while the securing bolts are loosened. To do this, locate a long bolt in one of the engine-to-gearbox mounting bolt holes and either insert a wide-bladed screwdriver or bar in the starter ring gear or use a suitable locking tool as shown **(see illustration)**.

5 Unscrew the securing bolts and withdraw the flywheel from the crankshaft.

Inspection

6 Examine the flywheel for scoring of the clutch face and for wear or chipping of the ring gear teeth. If the clutch face is scored, the flywheel may be machined until flat, but renewal is preferable.

7 If the ring gear teeth are worn or damaged, the flywheel must be renewed.

Refitting

8 Clean the flywheel and crankshaft faces, then coat the locating face on the crankshaft with Loctite Autoform, or an equivalent compound.

9 Locate the flywheel on the crankshaft making sure that the previously made marks are aligned. The securing bolt holes are offset, so the flywheel cannot be fitted incorrectly.

10 Fit the new securing bolts, then tighten them in a diagonal sequence to the specified torque. Hold the flywheel stationary as during removal **(see illustrations)**.

11 Refit the clutch as described in Chapter 6.

12 Refit the gearbox (Chapter 7) or the engine/gearbox assembly (Chapter 2B), as applicable.

14 Engine mountings - renewal

Left-hand engine/gearbox mounting

1 Connect a hoist and suitable lifting tackle to the engine lifting brackets to support the engine/gearbox assembly while the mounting is removed. Alternatively, the assembly can be supported using a jack and a suitable block of wood to spread the load under the sump.

2 For improved access, remove the air cleaner assembly, as described in Chapter 4. Additionally, on Turbo models, remove the air

ducting connecting the turbocharger and the inlet manifold to the intercooler.

3 Release the coolant expansion tank from its bracket, and move it to one side, clear of the engine/gearbox mounting.

4 Where applicable, remove the securing nuts, and withdraw the expansion tank mounting bracket from the engine/gearbox mounting assembly.

5 Ensure that the engine/gearbox assembly is adequately supported, then, working from underneath the mounting, unscrew the nut securing the mounting stud to the bracket on the gearbox. Note that it may be necessary to counterhold the stud on the flats under the mounting rubber as the nut is unscrewed.

6 Unscrew the two nuts and bolts securing the rubber mounting/plate assembly to the body bracket and withdraw the assembly. Where applicable, note the location of the longer bolt, which also secures the expansion tank mounting bracket **(see illustration)**.

7 The rubber mounting can be removed from the stud for renewal after removing the securing nut. Note that the rubber is a press-fit on the stud.

8 If desired, the mounting brackets can be removed from the body and the gearbox after removing the rubber mounting as described previously. Note that the bracket on the gearbox is secured by three bolts and a nut, and must be withdrawn vertically from the stud on the gearbox. Where applicable, note the location of the stud securing the bracket to the body, which also secures the expansion tank mounting bracket **(see illustrations)**.

14.8b Unscrewing a mounting bracket-to-gearbox bolt. Mounting stud arrowed

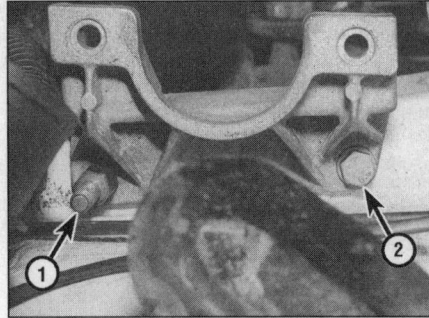

14.8c Mounting bracket-to-body stud (1) and bolt (2)

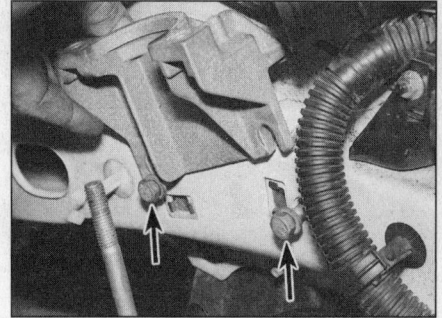

14.8d Removing the mounting bracket from the body - lower bolts arrowed

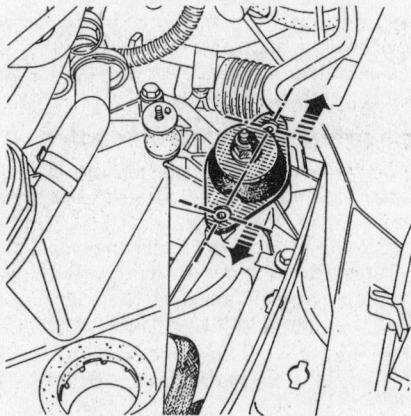

14.9 Position the mounting plate in the centre of the elongated holes in the body bracket - left-hand engine/gearbox mounting

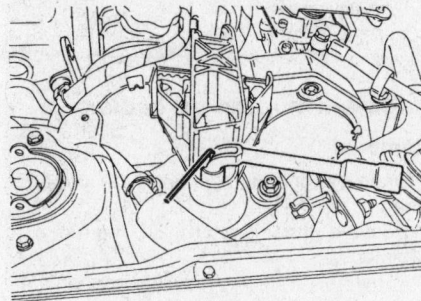

14.12 Counterholding the threaded rod whilst loosening the right-hand engine mounting nut

9 Refitting is a reversal of removal, but position the mounting plate in the centre of the elongated holes in the body bracket, and tighten all fixings to the specified torque **(see illustration)**.

Right-hand engine mounting

10 Proceed as described in paragraph 1.
11 Remove the securing screws, and remove the plastic cover from the upper engine mounting bracket. Note the location of any brackets secured by the bolts.
12 Ensure that the engine/gearbox assembly is adequately supported, then unscrew the nut securing the upper mounting bracket to the mounting on the body. On certain models it is necessary to counterhold the mounting threaded rod using a suitable Allen key or hexagon bit, whilst loosening the nut with an open-ended spanner **(see illustration)**.
13 Unscrew the three bolts securing the upper mounting bracket to the engine, then withdraw the bracket **(see illustration)**.
14 Unscrew the two nuts securing the mounting plate and the engine movement limiting rubber assembly to the body. Lift the movement limiting rubber assembly and the mounting plate from the body **(see illustration)**.
15 The engine mounting bracket is integral with the fuel injection pump mounting

bracket. Removal and refitting of this bracket is an involved procedure, and is described in Section 6 as part of the camshaft sprocket removal and refitting procedure.
16 Commence refitting by refitting the movement limiting rubber assembly and the mounting plate. Do not fully tighten the securing nuts at this stage.
17 Refit the upper mounting bracket, and tighten the bolts securing it to the engine. At this stage, do not fully tighten the nut securing the bracket to the mounting on the body.
18 Check that there is a clearance "X" between the end of the crankshaft pulley and the cut-away portion of the body side panel **(see illustration)**.
19 Tighten the nut securing the upper mounting bracket to the mounting on the body. If necessary, counterhold the threaded rod as during removal.
20 Working on the left-hand engine/gearbox mounting, check that the mounting plate is positioned in the centre of the elongated holes in the body bracket. If necessary loosen the nuts securing the mounting plate to the body bracket, and reposition mounting plate accordingly. Tighten the nuts to the specified torque.

2A

14.13 Withdrawing the right-hand upper mounting bracket

14.14 Withdrawing the right-hand engine mounting plate/movement limiting rubber assembly

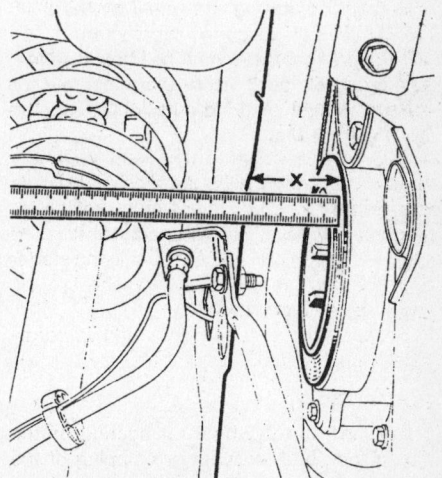

14.18 Ensure that there is clearance "X" between the end of the crankshaft pulley and the body side panel

$X = 50. \pm 5. \; mm$

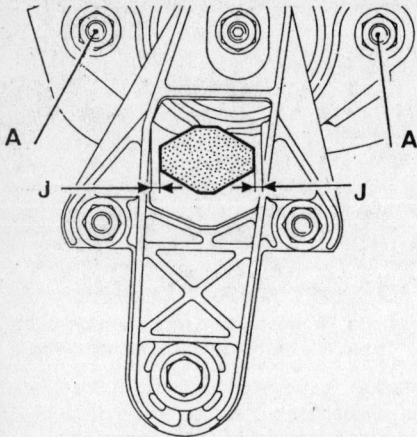

14.21 Position the movement limiting rubber in the centre of the hole in the right-hand upper engine mounting bracket

A Mounting plate/engine movement limiting rubber-to-body nuts
J = 2.5 mm

21 Working on the right-hand engine mounting, move the mounting plate as necessary to position the movement limiting rubber in the centre of the hole in the upper mounting bracket as shown **(see illustration)**.
22 Tighten the mounting plate/engine movement limiting rubber-to-body nuts to the specified torque.
23 Refit the cover to the upper engine mounting bracket.
24 Disconnect the hoist and lifting tackle, or remove the jack from under the sump, as applicable.

Lower engine steady bracket

25 For improved access, apply the handbrake, then jack up the front of the vehicle, and support securely on axle stands (see *"Jacking, towing and wheel changing"*).
26 Proceed as described in paragraph 1.
27 Ensure that the engine/gearbox assembly is adequately supported, then unscrew the steady bracket securing nuts, whilst counter-holding the bolts.

28 Remove the nuts, and withdraw the assembly, noting the locations of all rubbers, washers and spacers.
29 Refitting is a reversal of removal, bearing in mind the following points.
a) *Ensure that all rubbers, spacers and washers are positioned as noted before removal.*
b) *Ensure that the mounting nuts are positioned on the exhaust side of the bracket (see illustration).*
c) *Tighten the mounting nuts and bolts to the specified torque.*

15 Engine oil cooler - removal and refitting

Engine-mounted oil cooler

Removal

1 Drain the cooling system as described in Chapter 1.
2 Remove the oil filter with reference to Chapter 1.
3 Loosen the clips, and disconnect the coolant hoses from the oil cooler.
4 Unscrew the oil filter mounting stud, which also secures the oil cooler, and withdraw the oil cooler from the engine. Recover the sealing ring **(see illustrations)**.

Refitting

5 Refitting is a reversal of removal, but use a

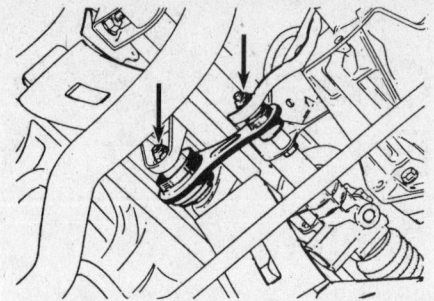

15.4a Remove the oil filter mounting stud . . .

14.29 Lower engine steady bracket nuts (arrowed) must be positioned on exhaust side of bracket

new sealing ring, and ensure that the oil cooler is fitted with the coolant inlet and outlet pointing vertically upwards.

Remotely-mounted oil cooler

6 On certain models, a remotely-mounted oil cooler assembly is fitted, located behind the front bumper. The cooler is connected to the engine via a housing located between the cylinder block and the oil filter (as described for the engine-mounted oil cooler). The oil passes via pipes to the oil cooler, where it is cooled by the airflow passing through the front of the vehicle, before returning to the engine.
7 At the time of writing, no details were available for the removal and refitting of the remotely-mounted oil cooler.

15.4b . . . then withdraw the oil cooler and recover the sealing ring

Chapter 2 Part B:
Engine removal and overhaul procedures

Contents

Degrees of difficulty

Easy, suitable for novice with little experience	**Fairly easy,** suitable for beginner with some experience	**Fairly difficult,** suitable for competent DIY mechanic	**Difficult,** suitable for experienced DIY mechanic	**Very difficult,** suitable for expert DIY or professional

Specifications

Lubrication system
Minimum oil pressure at 80°C:
  Non-Turbo engines:
    At 1000 rpm . . . .   2 bars
    At 3000 rpm . . . .   3.5 bars
  Turbo engines:
    At idle speed . . . .   1 bar
    At 3500 rpm . . . .   3 bars

Cylinder block
Material . . . .   Cast iron
Cylinder bore diameter:
  Class A or 1 . . . .   80.000 to 81.015 mm
  Class B or 2 . . . .   80.015 to 80.030 mm

Auxiliary shaft
Endfloat . . . .   0.07 to 0.15 mm

Crankshaft
Number of main bearings   5
Main bearing journal diameter:
  Standard . . . .   54.795 ± 0.01 mm
  Undersize . . . .   54.545 ± 0.01 mm
Main bearing running clearance . . . .   0.020 to 0.058 mm
Crankpin (big-end) journal diameter:
  Standard . . . .   48.00 mm
  Undersize . . . .   47.75 mm +0.02 mm - 0.00 mm
Big-end bearing running clearance . . . .   0.014 to 0.053 mm
Big-end cap side play . . . .   0.220 to 0.400 mm
Crankshaft endfloat . . . .   0.070 to 0.230 mm
Thrust washer thicknesses . . . .   2.30, 2.35, 2.40 and 2.45 mm

2B

Pistons and piston rings

Piston ring end gaps	Rings supplied pre-set
Piston ring thickness:	
Top compression ring:	
Non-Turbo engines	2.0 mm
Turbo engines	2.5 mm
Second compression ring	2.0 mm
Oil control ring	3.0 mm
Piston clearance in bore	0.015 to 0.030 mm (suggested values)

Connecting rods

Big-end side play	0.220 to 0.400 mm

Cylinder head

Material	Aluminium
Height	159.50 mm
Maximum acceptable gasket face distortion	0.05 mm
Swirl chamber protrusion	0.01 to 0.04 mm

	Inlet	Exhaust
Valve depth below cylinder head gasket face:		
Non-Turbo engines	0.85 ± 0.09 mm	0.97 ± 0.09 mm
Turbo engines	0.65 ± 0.09 mm	0.57 ± 0.09 mm
Valve seat angle . . . . , ...	120°	90°
Valve seat width	1.8 mm	
Valve guide bore	8.0 mm	
Valve guide outer diameter:		
Standard	13.00 mm	
Oversize	13.30 mm	

Valves

	Inlet	Exhaust
Head diameter:		
Non-Turbo engines:		
Conventional inlet valve seat	36.1 mm	31.5 mm
Stellite inlet valve seat*	36.35 mm	31.5 mm
Turbo engines	36.225 ± 0.125 mm	31.620 ± 0.120 mm
Stem diameter:		
Non-Turbo engines	8.0 mm	
Turbo engines	7.985 ± 0.04 mm	
Valve spring free length:		
Non-Turbo engines	43.41 mm	
Turbo engines	47.57 mm	

*Stellite valve seats are used with steel inlet valves

Torque wrench settings

Refer to Chapter 2A Specifications.

1 General information

Included in this part of Chapter 2 are the engine removal and general overhaul procedures for the cylinder head, cylinder block/crankcase and internal engine components (see illustrations).

The information ranges from advice concerning preparation for an overhaul and the purchase of replacement parts, to detailed step-by-step procedures covering removal, inspection, renovation and refitting of internal engine parts.

The following Sections have been compiled based on the assumption that the engine has been removed from the vehicle.

For information concerning in-vehicle engine repair, as well as the removal and refitting of the external components necessary for the overhaul, refer to Chapter 2A, and to Section 5 of this Part.

2 Engine overhaul - general information

It is not always easy to determine when, or if, an engine should be completely overhauled, as a number of factors must be considered.

High mileage is not necessarily an indication that an overhaul is needed, while low mileage does not preclude the need for an overhaul. Frequency of servicing is probably the most important consideration.

An engine which has had regular and frequent oil and filter changes, as well as other required maintenance, will most likely give many thousands of miles of reliable service. Conversely, a neglected engine may require an overhaul very early in its life.

Excessive oil consumption is an indication that piston rings, valve seals and/or valve guides are in need of attention. Make sure that oil leaks are not responsible before deciding that the rings and/or guides are bad. Perform a cylinder compression or leakdown check to determine the extent of the work required.

Check the oil pressure with a gauge fitted in place of the oil pressure sender, and compare it with the Specifications. If it is extremely low, the main and big-end bearings and/or the oil pump are probably worn out.

2B

1.1a Exploded view of cylinder head and associated components

1.1b Exploded view of lower engine components

Loss of power, rough running, knocking or metallic engine noises, excessive valve gear noise and high fuel consumption may also point to the need for an overhaul, especially if they are all present at the same time. If a tune-up does not remedy the situation, major mechanical work is the only solution.

An engine overhaul involves restoring the internal parts to the specifications of a new engine. During an overhaul, the pistons and rings are replaced and the cylinder bores are reconditioned. New main bearings, connecting rod bearings and camshaft bearings are generally fitted, and if necessary, the crankshaft may be reground to restore the journals. The valves are also serviced as well, since they are usually in less than perfect condition at this point. While the engine is being overhauled, other components, such as the starter and alternator, can be overhauled as well. The end result should be a like-new engine that will give many trouble-free miles. **Note:** *Critical cooling system components such as the hoses, thermostat and water pump MUST be renewed when an engine is overhauled. The radiator should be checked carefully to ensure that it is not clogged or leaking. Also it is a good idea to renew the oil pump whenever the engine is overhauled.*

Before beginning the engine overhaul, read through the entire procedure to familiarize yourself with the scope and requirements of the job. Overhauling an engine is not difficult if you follow all of the instructions carefully, have the necessary tools and equipment and pay close attention to all specifications; however, it can be time consuming. Plan on the vehicle being tied up for a minimum of two weeks, especially if parts must be taken to an engineering works for repair or reconditioning. Check on the availability of parts and make sure that any necessary special tools and equipment are obtained in advance. Most work can be done with typical hand tools, although a number of precision measuring tools are required for inspecting parts to determine if they must be renewed. Often the engineering works will handle the inspection of parts and offer advice concerning reconditioning and renewal. **Note:** *Always wait until the engine has been completely disassembled and all components, especially the engine block have been inspected before deciding what service and repair operations must be performed by an engineering works. Since the condition of the block will be the major factor to consider when determining whether to overhaul the original engine or buy a reconditioned unit, do not purchase parts or have overhaul work done on other components until the block has been thoroughly inspected. As a general rule, time is the primary cost of an overhaul, so it does not pay to fit worn or substandard parts.*

As a final note, to ensure maximum life and minimum trouble from a reconditioned engine, everything must be assembled with care in a spotlessly clean environment.

3 Engine removal - methods and precautions

If you have decided that an engine must be removed for overhaul or major repair work, several preliminary steps should be taken.

Locating a suitable place to work is extremely important. Adequate work space, along with storage space for the vehicle, will be needed. If a garage is not available, at the very least a flat, level, clean work surface is required.

Cleaning the engine compartment and engine before beginning the removal procedure will help keep tools clean and organized.

An engine hoist or A-frame will also be necessary. Make sure the equipment is rated in excess of the combined weight of the engine and gearbox. Safety is of primary importance, considering the potential hazards involved in lifting the engine out of the vehicle.

If the engine is being removed by a novice, an assistant should be available. Advice and aid from someone more experienced would also be helpful. There are many instances when one person cannot simultaneously perform all of the operations required when lifting the engine out of the vehicle.

Plan the operation ahead of time. Arrange for, or obtain, all of the tools and equipment you will need, prior to beginning the job. Some of the equipment necessary to perform engine removal and installation safely and with relative ease are (in addition to an engine hoist) a heavy duty floor jack, complete sets of spanners and sockets as described at the front of this manual, wooden blocks and plenty of rags and cleaning solvent for mopping up spilled oil, coolant and fuel. If the hoist must be hired, make sure that you arrange for it in advance, and perform all of the operations possible without it beforehand. This will save you money and time.

Plan for the vehicle to be out of use for quite a while. An engineering works will be required to perform some of the work which the do-it-yourselfer cannot accomplish without special equipment. These places often have a busy schedule, so it would be a good idea to consult them before removing

the engine in order to accurately estimate the amount of time required to rebuild or repair components that may need work.

Always be extremely careful when removing and refitting the engine. Serious injury can result from careless actions. Plan ahead, take your time and you will find that a job of this nature, although major, can be accomplished successfully.

The engine is most easily removed complete with the gearbox by lifting the assembly upwards from the engine compartment.

4 Engine - removal and refitting (with manual gearbox)

Note: *An engine hoist and suitable lifting tackle will be required for this operation. New roll pins and suitable sealant will be required when reconnecting the right-hand driveshaft.*

Removal

1 Disconnect both battery leads.
2 Drain the cooling system with reference to Chapter 1.
3 Drain the engine oil with reference to Chapter 1. Remove the drain plug and drain the gearbox oil, then refit and tighten the drain plug **(see illustration)**.
4 Remove the bonnet with reference to Chapter 11.
5 Unbolt and remove the strengthening bar from between the front suspension unit turrets.
6 Remove the radiator with reference to Chapter 3. Also disconnect the bottom hose from the cylinder block inlet elbow.
7 Apply the handbrake, then jack up the front of the vehicle and support it securely on axle stands (see *"Jacking, towing and wheel changing"*). Remove both front wheels. Where applicable, remove the engine undershield.
8 Working beneath the right-hand side of the vehicle, use a parallel pin punch to drive out the double roll pin securing the right-hand driveshaft to the gearbox differential sun wheel stub shaft **(see illustration)**.

2B

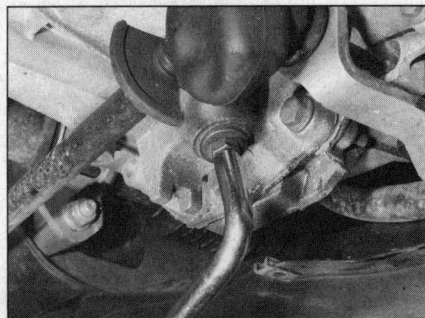

4.3 Unscrewing the gearbox oil drain plug

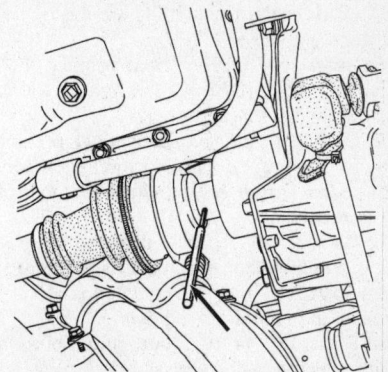

4.8 Using a pin punch (arrowed) to drive out the driveshaft roll pin

4.9 Remove the upper stub axle carrier-to-suspension strut nut and bolt

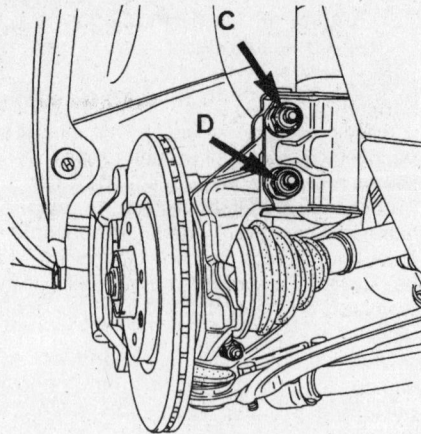

4.14 Stub axle carrier-to-suspension strut nuts (C and D)

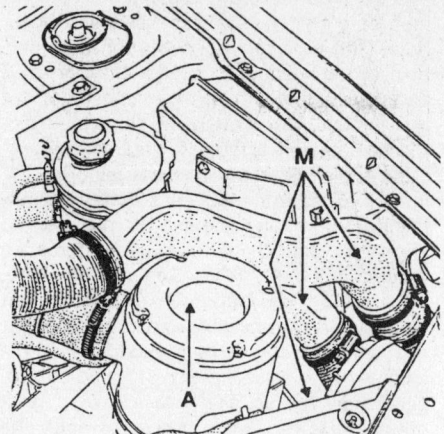

4.17 Remove the air cleaner (A) and the air ducting (M) - Turbo models

9 Loosen the two nuts and bolts securing the right-hand stub axle carrier to the suspension strut. Remove the upper nut and bolt, but leave the lower nut and bolt in position. Note that the nuts are on the rear side of the strut **(see illustration)**.

10 Pull the top of the stub axle carrier outwards until the inner end of the driveshaft is released from the stub shaft. Support the driveshaft using string or wire - do not allow it to hang under its own weight.

11 Working on the left-hand side, unbolt the front brake caliper with reference to Chapter 9, but leave the hydraulic hose connected. Tie the caliper to the front suspension coil spring, with wire or string, taking care not to strain the hose.

12 Disconnect the steering track rod end from the left-hand stub axle carrier with reference to Chapter 10.

13 Unscrew the three bolts securing the driveshaft rubber gaiter retaining plate to the left-hand side of the gearbox.

14 Unscrew and remove the two nuts and bolts securing the left-hand stub axle carrier to the suspension strut. Note that the nuts are on the rear side of the strut **(see illustration)**.

15 Pull the top of the left-hand stub axle carrier outwards until the inner end of the driveshaft is released from the yoke. There may be some loss of oil from the gearbox, so position a small container on the floor to catch it. If desired, the hub carrier can be disconnected from the lower arm as described in Chapter 10, and the stub axle carrier/driveshaft assembly can be removed completely.

16 Refer to Chapter 4 and remove the air cleaner unit, ducting and, where applicable, its mounting.

17 On Turbo models, disconnect and remove the air ducting connecting the intercooler to the turbocharger and the inlet manifold **(see illustration)**.

18 Disconnect the coolant and fuel hoses from the fuel filter assembly (be prepared for fuel spillage). Cover the open ends of the fuel unions to prevent dirt ingress.

19 Remove the two securing bolts, and withdraw the fuel filter assembly.

20 Disconnect the wiring from the preheating control unit on the engine compartment

bulkhead, labelling the connections to ensure correct refitting. Remove the securing nut, and withdraw the unit.

21 Disconnect all relevant coolant, vacuum and breather hoses from the engine, labelling each hose to avoid confusion when refitting. On Turbo models, ensure that the auxiliary water pump coolant hoses are disconnected (see Chapter 3).

22 Disconnect the fuel return hose from the pipe on the fuel injection pump, and where applicable, withdraw it from the brackets and clips on the engine, noting its routing. Cover the open ends of the pipe and hose to prevent dirt ingress.

23 Disconnect all relevant wiring from the sensors, switches and actuators on the engine, labelling all wires to aid refitting.

24 Disconnect the accelerator cable from the fuel injection pump, with reference to Chapter 4 if necessary, and withdraw the cable from the brackets on the engine.

25 Disconnect the speedometer cable with reference to Chapter 12.

26 Disconnect the engine earth strap from the rear engine lifting bracket, and disconnect the gearbox earthing strap from the end of the gearbox **(see illustration)**.

27 Disconnect the gearchange linkage from the gearbox with reference to Chapter 7.

28 Disconnect the clutch cable with

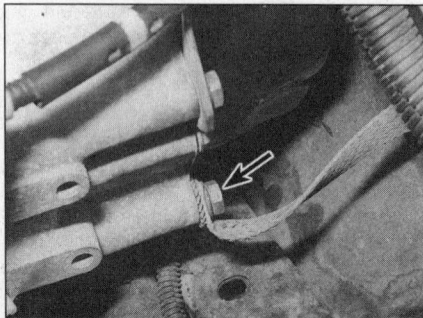

4.26 Gearbox earth strap securing bolt (arrowed)

reference to Chapter 6.

29 Remove the exhaust front section, as described in Chapter 4.

30 On models fitted with power-assisted steering, remove the power steering pump as described in Chapter 10.

31 On models fitted with air conditioning, have the system professionally discharged, then remove the compressor as described in Chapter 3.

⚠ *Warning: Under no circumstances attempt to open any of the connections or discharge the system without professional help.*

32 Make a final check to ensure that all relevant hoses and wires have been disconnected, and removed from any brackets or clips to facilitate engine removal.

33 Attach a suitable hoist to the engine lifting brackets, then raise the hoist to just take the weight of the engine.

34 Disconnect the left-hand engine/gearbox mounting, then unbolt the engine/gearbox mounting brackets from the gearbox and the body, and remove them completely. Refer to Chapter 2A for details.

35 Disconnect the right-hand engine mounting and the lower engine steady bracket with reference to Chapter 2A.

36 With the help of an assistant, slowly lift the engine/gearbox assembly from the engine compartment, manipulating it to clear surrounding components **(see illustrations)**. When high enough, lift it over the front body panel and lower the unit to the ground.

37 To separate the gearbox from the engine, proceed as follows.

38 Support the engine and gearbox on blocks of wood.

39 Remove the securing bolts, and remove the flywheel cover plate/engine-to-gearbox bracing bracket.

40 Unscrew and remove the engine-to-

4.36a Lift the engine/gearbox assembly from the engine compartment . . .

4.36b . . . manipulating it as necessary to clear surrounding components

4.40 Note the location of any wiring brackets (arrowed) secured by the engine-to-gearbox nuts and bolts

4.41 Separate the engine from the gearbox

gearbox nuts and bolts from around the gearbox and from the starter motor. There is no need to remove the starter motor. Note the locations of any brackets which may be secured by the bolts and nuts **(see illustration)**.

41 Ensure that the engine and gearbox are adequately supported, then carefully withdraw the gearbox from the engine, ensuring that the weight of the gearbox is not allowed to hang on the input shaft while it is engaged with the clutch friction disc **(see illustration)**.

Refitting

Note: *In order to correctly adjust the position of the engine/gearbox in the engine compartment when refitting the assembly, the crankshaft pulley must be fitted.*

42 Where applicable, reconnect the engine to the gearbox, noting the following points.
a) *Ensure that the clutch disc has been centralised as described in Chapter 6.*
b) *Apply a little high melting point grease to the splines of the gearbox input shaft. Do not apply too much grease, as it may contaminate the clutch.*
c) *Ensure that the weight of the gearbox is not allowed to hang on the input shaft as it is engaged with the clutch disc.*
d) *Make sure that any brackets noted before removal are in place on the engine-to-gearbox bolts, and tighten the bolts.*

43 Refit the flywheel cover plate/engine-to-gearbox bracing bracket, and tighten the securing bolts.

44 Suspend the engine/gearbox assembly from a hoist, as during removal, and lower the assembly into position in the engine compartment.

45 Refit and reconnect the left-hand engine/gearbox mounting, the right-hand engine mounting, and the lower engine steady bracket as described in Chapter 2A. Note the adjustment procedure for positioning the engine/gearbox assembly in the engine compartment.

46 Remove the hoist and lifting tackle.

47 Where applicable, refit the air conditioning compressor, with reference to Chapter 3, and have the system professionally recharged.

48 Where applicable, refit the power steering pump as described in Chapter 10.

49 Refit the exhaust front Section with reference to Chapter 4.

50 Reconnect the clutch cable as described in Chapter 6.

51 Reconnect the gear linkage to the gearbox as described in Chapter 7.

52 Reconnect the engine and gearbox earthing straps, as applicable.

53 Reconnect the speedometer cable with reference to Chapter 12.

54 Reconnect the accelerator cable with reference to Chapter 4.

55 Reconnect all relevant wiring, ensuring that it is routed through the brackets, where applicable, as noted before removal.

56 Reconnect the fuel return hose to the pipe on the fuel injection pump.

57 Reconnect all relevant coolant, vacuum, and breather hoses to the engine, ensuring that they are correctly routed as noted before removal. On Turbo models, make sure that the auxiliary water pump coolant hoses are correctly reconnected.

58 Refit the preheating system control unit, and reconnect the wiring.

59 Refit the fuel filter assembly, then reconnect the coolant and fuel hoses.

60 On Turbo models, reconnect the air ducting connecting the intercooler to the turbocharger and the inlet manifold.

61 Where applicable, refit the air cleaner mounting, then refit the air cleaner and the ducting.

62 Reconnect the left-hand driveshaft to the gearbox, then reconnect the stub axle carrier

to the suspension strut and, where applicable, the lower arm, with reference to Chapter 10. Note that the stub axle carrier-to-strut nuts must be positioned on the rear side of the strut.

63 Refit and tighten the bolts securing the driveshaft rubber gaiter retaining plate to the gearbox.

64 Reconnect the steering track rod end to the stub axle carrier, and tighten the nut to the specified torque (see Chapter 10).

65 Refit the brake caliper and tighten the bolts with reference to Chapter 9.

66 Reconnect the right-hand driveshaft to the differential, and secure using a new double roll pin **(see illustration)**.

67 Refit the upper nut and bolt securing the stub axle carrier to the suspension strut (note that the nut must be positioned on the rear side of the strut), and tighten the fixings to the specified torque (see Chapter 10).

68 Refit the radiator with reference to Chapter 3, and reconnect the bottom hose to the cylinder block inlet elbow.

69 Refit the strengthening bar to the front suspension unit turrets.

70 Refit the bonnet with reference to Chapter 11.

71 Refit the roadwheels and lower the vehicle to the ground.

72 Fit a new oil filter, and fill the engine with oil as described in Chapter 1.

73 Refill the cooling system as described in Chapter 1.

4.66 Secure the driveshaft to the differential using a new double roll pin (arrowed)

2B

74 Where applicable, refill the power steering fluid reservoir, and bleed the system as described in Chapter 10.

75 Check the gearbox oil level, and top up if necessary, as described in Chapter 1.

76 Prime and bleed the fuel system as described in Chapter 4.

77 On Turbo models, before starting the engine, ensure that the oil circuit has been primed as described in Chapter 1, Section 6.

5 Engine overhaul - dismantling sequence

1 It is much easier to disassemble and work on the engine if it is mounted on a portable engine stand. These stands can often be hired from a tool hire shop. Before the engine is mounted on a stand, the flywheel should be removed from the engine, so that the engine stand bolts can be tightened into the end of the cylinder block.

2 If a stand is not available, it is possible to disassemble the engine with it blocked up on a sturdy workbench or on the floor. Be extra-careful not to tip or drop the engine when working without a stand.

3 If you are going to obtain a reconditioned engine, all the external components must come off first, in order to be transferred to the replacement engine (just as they will if you are doing a complete engine overhaul yourself). Check with the engine supplier for details. Normally these components include.

a) *Alternator mounting bracket.*
b) *Fuel injection pump and mounting bracket, and fuel injectors and glow plugs (see Chapter 4).*
c) *Thermostat and cover.*
d) *Turbocharger (where applicable).*
e) *Inlet and exhaust manifolds.*
f) *Oil cooler.*
g) *Engine lifting brackets, hose brackets and wiring brackets.*
h) *Ancillary (power steering pump, air conditioning compressor) brackets.*
i) *Oil pressure warning light switch and oil level sensor (where applicable) (see Chapter 5).*
j) *Coolant temperature sensors (see Chapters 3 and 5).*
k) *Wiring harnesses and brackets.*
l) *Coolant pipes and hoses.*
m) *Oil filler tube and dipstick.*
n) *Clutch (Chapter 6).*

Note: *When removing the external components from the engine, pay close attention to details that may be helpful or important during refitting. Note the fitted position of gaskets, seals, spacers, pins, washers, bolts and other small items.*

4 If you are obtaining a "short" motor (which, when available, consists of the engine cylinder block, crankshaft, pistons and connecting rods all assembled), then the cylinder head, flywheel, sump, oil pump, and

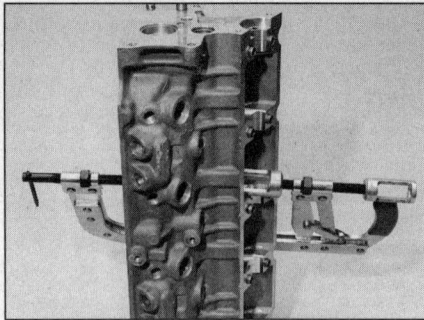
6.3 Using a valve spring compressor tool to remove a valve

timing belt (where applicable) will have to be removed also.

5 If you are planning a complete overhaul, the engine can be disassembled and the internal components removed in the following order:

a) *Inlet and exhaust manifolds (and turbocharger where applicable).*
b) *Timing belt and sprockets.*
c) *Cylinder head.*
d) *Flywheel.*
e) *Sump.*
f) *Oil pump.*
g) *Pistons.*
h) *Crankshaft.*

6 Before beginning the disassembly and overhaul procedures, make sure that you have all of the correct tools necessary. Refer to the introductory pages at the beginning of this manual for further information.

6 Cylinder head - dismantling

Note: *New and reconditioned cylinder heads are available from the manufacturers or from engine overhaul specialists. Due to the fact that some specialist tools are required for the dismantling and inspection procedures, and new components may not be readily available, it may be more practical and economical for the home mechanic to purchase a reconditioned head rather than to dismantle, inspect and recondition the original head. A valve spring compressor tool will be required for this operation.*

1 With the cylinder head removed as described in Chapter 2A, clean away all external dirt, then remove the following components, if not already done.

a) *Manifolds (and turbocharger, where applicable) (Chapter 4).*
b) *Fuel injection pump and mounting bracket (Chapter 4).*
c) *Thermostat - where applicable (Chapter 3).*
d) *Brake vacuum pump (Chapter 9).*
e) *Fuel injectors (Chapter 4).*
f) *Glow plugs (Chapter 5).*
g) *Camshaft (Chapter 2A).*

2 Withdraw the bucket tappets, together with

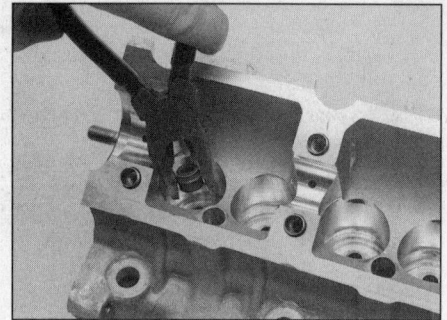
6.7 Removing a valve stem oil seal using pliers

their respective shims, keeping them all identified for location. Place them on a sheet of cardboard numbered 1 to 8, with No 1 at the flywheel end. It is a good idea to write the shim thickness size on the card alongside each bucket, in case the shims are accidentally knocked off their buckets and mixed up. The size is etched on the shim bottom face.

3 To remove a valve, fit a valve spring compressor tool. Ensure that the arms of the compressor tool are securely positioned on the head of the valve and the spring cap. The valves are deeply recessed, so the end of the compressor may need to be extended with a tube or box section with a "window" for access **(see illustration)**.

4 Compress the valve spring to relieve the pressure of the spring cap acting on the split collets.

> **HAYNES HINT** *If the valve spring cap sticks to the valve stem, support the compressor tool and give the end a light tap with a soft-faced mallet to help free the spring cap.*

5 Extract the two split collets, then slowly release the compressor tool.

6 Remove the spring cap, spring, and the spring seat, then withdraw the valve.

7 Remove the valve stem oil seal, using pliers if necessary, as the seals must be renewed on refitting **(see illustration)**.

8 Repeat the procedure for the remaining valves, keeping all components in strict order so that they can be refitted in their original positions, unless all the components are to be renewed. If the components are to be kept and used again, place each valve assembly in a labelled polythene bag or a similar small container **(see illustrations)**. Note that as with cylinder numbering, the valves are normally numbered from the flywheel end of the engine.

9 If desired, any remaining brackets can be unbolted from the cylinder head, noting their locations before removal.

10 Dismantling of the cylinder head is now complete.

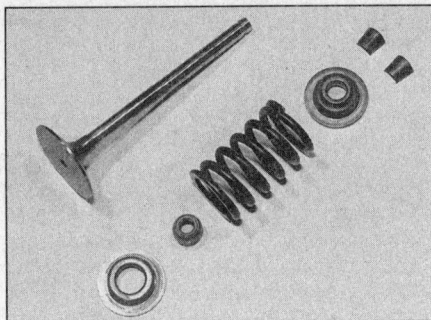
6.8a Valve components

6.8b Store the valve components in a labelled polythene bag

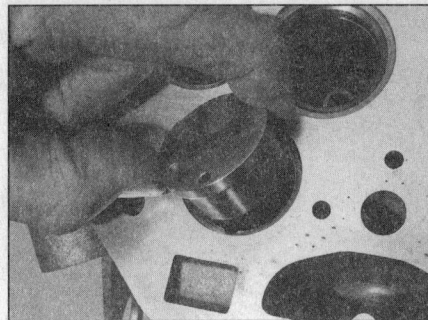
7.5 Removing a swirl chamber

7 Cylinder head and valve components - cleaning, inspection and renovation

1 Thorough cleaning of the cylinder head and valve components, followed by a detailed inspection, will enable a decision to be made on whether further work is necessary before reassembling the components.

Cleaning

2 Scrape away all traces of old gasket material and sealing compound from the cylinder head surfaces. Take care not to damage the cylinder head surfaces.

3 Scrape away the carbon from the surfaces of the cylinder head surrounding the valves, then wash the cylinder head thoroughly with paraffin or a suitable solvent.

4 Scrape off any heavy carbon deposits that may have formed on the valves, then use a power-operated wire brush to remove deposits from the valve heads and stems.

5 Ideally, for complete cleaning, the core plugs should be removed. Drill a small hole in the plugs, then insert a self-tapping screw and pull out the plugs using a pair of grips or a slide hammer. Additionally, the swirl chambers should be removed from their locations if they are loose (if this is done, mark the swirl chambers so that they can be refitted in their original locations) **(see illustration)**.

6 If the head is extremely dirty, it should be steam cleaned.

7 If the head has been steam cleaned, clean all oil holes and oil galleries one more time on

> **⚠ Warning: Wear eye protection when using compressed air!**

completion. Flush all internal passages with warm water until the water runs clear, dry the head thoroughly and wipe all machined surfaces with a light oil. If you have access to compressed air, use it to speed the drying process and to blow out all the oil holes and galleries.

8 If the head is relatively clean, an adequate cleaning job can be achieved with hot soapy water and a stiff brush. Take plenty of time and do a thorough job. Regardless of the cleaning method used, be sure to clean all oil holes and galleries very thoroughly, dry the head completely and coat all machined surfaces with light oil.

9 The threaded holes in the cylinder head must be clean to ensure accurate torque readings when tightening fixings during reassembly. Run the correct size tap (which can be determined from the size of the relevant bolt which fits in the hole) into each of the holes to remove rust, corrosion, thread sealant or other contamination, and to restore damaged threads. If possible, use compressed air to clear the holes of debris produced by this operation. Do not forget to clean the threads of all bolts and nuts as well.

10 After coating the mating surfaces of the new core plugs with suitable sealant, fit them to the cylinder head. Make sure that they are driven in straight and seated correctly, or leakage could result. Special tools are

available for this purpose, but a large socket, with an outside diameter which will just fit into the core plug will work just as well.

Inspection

Note: *Be sure to perform all the following inspection procedures before concluding that the services of a machine shop or engine overhaul specialist are required. Make a list of all items that require attention.*

Cylinder head

Note: *A dial test indicator will be required for this operation.*

11 Inspect the head very carefully for cracks, evidence of coolant leakage and other damage. If cracks are found, a new cylinder head should be obtained.

12 Use a straight-edge and feeler blade to check that the cylinder head gasket surface is not distorted **(see illustration)**. Check the head surface both diagonally, and along its edge. Do not position the straight-edge over the swirl chambers, as these may be proud of the cylinder head face. If the specified distortion limit is exceeded, machining of the gasket face is not recommended by the manufacturers, so the only course of action is to renew the cylinder head.

13 Check that the overall height of the cylinder head is as specified, which will indicate if the head has been machined in a mistaken attempt to compensate for surface distortion **(see illustration)**.

14 Inspect the valve seats and swirl chambers for burning or cracks **(see illustration)**. Both can be renewed but the

2B

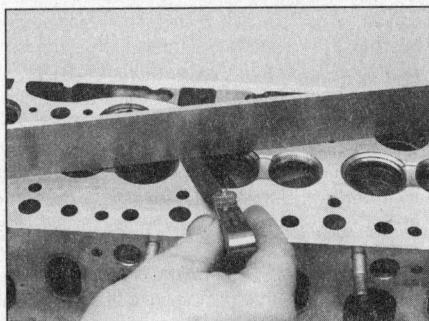
7.12 Checking the cylinder head gasket face for distortion

7.13 Check the overall height of the cylinder head

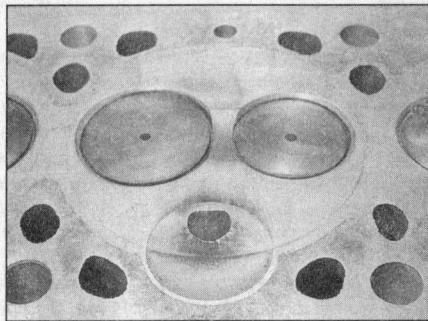
7.14 This swirl chamber shows the initial stages of cracking and burning

7.15 Measuring swirl chamber protrusion using a dial gauge

7.16 Measuring the valve depth

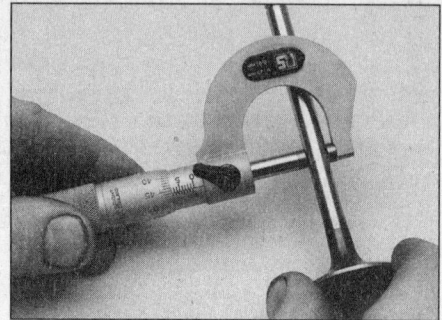

7.21 Measuring a valve stem using a micrometer

work should be entrusted to a specialist.

15 Using a dial test indicator check that the swirl chamber protrusion is within the limits given in the Specifications. Zero the dial test indicator on the gasket surface of the cylinder head, then measure the protrusion of the swirl chamber **(see illustration)**.

16 Examine the valve seats in the cylinder head. If the seats are severely pitted, cracked or burned, then they will need to be recut or renewed by an engine overhaul specialist. If only slight pitting is evident, this can be removed by grinding the valve heads and seats together with coarse, then fine, grinding paste as described later in this Section. Note that the valve seats can only be recut to a limited depth, to avoid decreasing the compression ratio. Using a dial test indicator, check that the valve depth below the cylinder head gasket surface is within the limits given in the Specifications **(see illustration)**.

17 Check for play (side-to-side movement) of the valves in the valve guides. Excessive play in the guide may be caused by wear in either component. Measure the valve stem with a micrometer, or try the fit of a new valve, if available, to establish whether it is the valve or the guide which is worn. If the valve guides are worn, they can be renewed, but this work is best carried out by a Renault dealer or an engine overhaul specialist.

18 Check the tappet bores in the cylinder head for wear. If excessive wear is evident, the cylinder head must be renewed.

19 Examine the camshaft bearing surfaces in the cylinder head and bearing caps. Wear here can only be corrected by renewing the head. Also examine the camshaft as described in Chapter 2A.

20 Inspect the studs for the manifolds and camshaft bearing caps. Renew them if necessary by using a proprietary stud extractor, or lock two nuts together on the exposed threads. Studs which have come out by mistake should be cleaned up and refitted using thread locking fluid.

Valves

Note: *A micrometer will be required for this operation.*

21 Examine the head of each valve for pitting, burning, cracks and general wear, and check the valve stem for scoring and wear

ridges. Rotate the valve and check for any obvious indication that it is bent. Look for pitting and excessive wear on the end of each valve stem. If the valve appears satisfactory at this stage, measure the valve stem diameter at several points using a micrometer **(see illustration)**. Any significant difference in the readings obtained indicates wear of the valve stem. Should any of these conditions be apparent, the valve(s) must be renewed.

22 If the valves are in satisfactory condition, they should be ground (lapped) onto their respective seats to ensure a smooth gas-tight seal.

23 Valve grinding is carried out as follows. Place the cylinder head upside down on a bench, with a block of wood at each end to give clearance for the valve stems.

24 Smear a trace of coarse carborundum paste on the seat face in the cylinder head, and press a suction grinding tool onto the relevant valve head. With a semi-rotary action, grind the valve head to its seat, lifting the valve occasionally to redistribute the grinding paste **(see illustration)**. When a dull, matt, even surface is produced on the faces of both the valve seat and the valve, wipe off the paste and repeat the process with fine carborundum paste. A light spring placed under the valve head will greatly ease this operation. When a smooth unbroken ring of light grey matt finish is produced on both the valve and seat faces, the grinding operation is complete. Carefully clean away every trace of grinding paste, taking great care to leave none in the ports or in the valve guides. Clean the valves and valve seats with a paraffin-soaked

rag, then with a clean rag, and finally, if an air line is available, blow the valves, valve guides and cylinder head ports clean.

Valve springs

25 Check that all the valve springs are intact. If any one is broken, all should be renewed.

⚠ *Warning: Wear eye protection when using compressed air!*

26 Check the free length of the springs against the figure given in the Specifications, then stand each spring on a flat surface and check it for squareness **(see illustration)**. If a spring is found to be too short, or damaged in any way, renew all the springs as a set. Springs suffer from fatigue, and it is a good idea to renew them even if they look serviceable.

Tappets

27 Examine the surfaces of the bucket tappets for wear or scoring. If excessive wear is evident, the tappet should be renewed.

Valve stem oil seals

28 All valve stem oil seals should be renewed as a matter of course.

---

8 Cylinder head - reassembly

Note: *A valve spring compressor will be required for this operation. New valve stem oil seals should be fitted on reassembly.*

7.24 Grinding a valve to its seat - lift the valve to redistribute the paste

7.26 Checking a valve spring free length

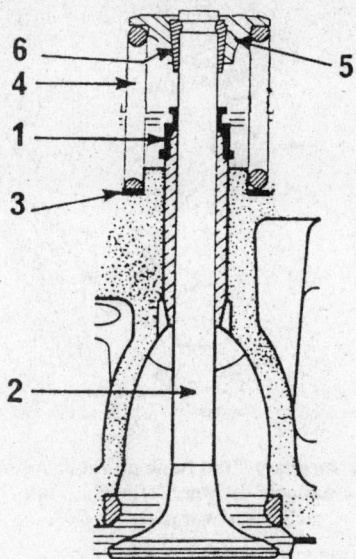

8.1 Fit the valve components in the order shown

1 *Valve stem oil seal*   4 *Spring*
   seal   5 *Spring cap*
2 *Valve*   6 *Split collets*
3 *Spring seat*

1 If the swirl chambers have been removed, refit them to their original locations. With all the components cleaned, starting at one end of the cylinder head, fit the valve components as follows **(see illustration)**. If the original components are being refitted, all components must be refitted in their original positions.

2 Lubricate the valve stem oil seal with clean engine oil, then fit the oil seal by pushing it into position in the cylinder head using a suitable socket **(see illustration)**. Ensure that the seal is fully engaged with the cylinder head.

3 Insert the appropriate valve into its guide (if new valves are being fitted, insert each valve into the location to which it has been ground), ensuring that the valve stem is well lubricated with clean engine oil **(see illustration)**. Take care not to damage the valve stem oil seal as the valve is fitted.

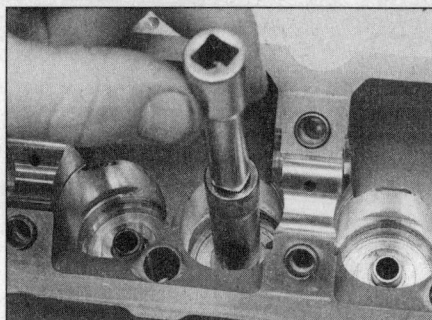

8.2 Fitting a valve stem oil seal

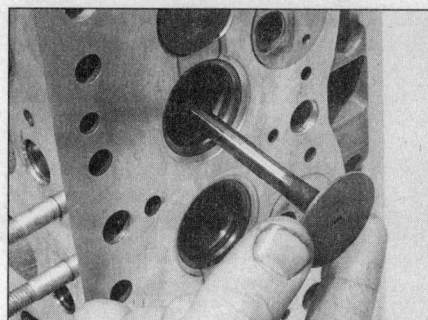

8.3 Inserting a valve into its guide

8.4 Fit the spring seat . . .

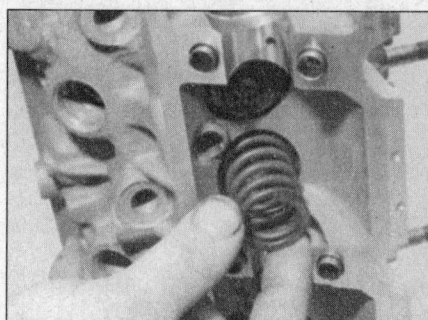

8.5a . . . spring . . .

4 Fit the spring seat **(see illustration)**.
5 Fit the valve spring (either way up) and the spring cap **(see illustrations)**.
6 Fit the spring compressor tool, and compress the valve spring until the spring cap passes beyond the collet groove in the valve stem.
7 Apply a little grease to the collet groove, then fit the split collets into the groove, with the narrow ends nearest the spring. The grease should hold them in the groove **(see illustration)**.
8 Slowly release the compressor tool, ensuring that the collets are not dislodged from the groove. When the compressor is fully released, give the top of the valve assembly a tap with a soft-faced mallet to settle the components.
9 Repeat the procedure for the remaining valves, ensuring that if the original components are being used, they are all refitted in their original positions.
10 Oil and insert the bucket tappets, together

with their respective shims, making sure that they are fitted in the correct locations, and with the size markings downwards (where applicable) **(see illustration)**. Make a note of the shim thickness fitted at each position, if not already done, for reference when checking the valve clearances.

11 Refit the following components, as applicable (if desired, these components can be refitted after refitting the cylinder head).

a) *Camshaft (Chapter 2A).*
b) *Glow plugs (Chapter 5).*
c) *Fuel injectors (Chapter 4).*
d) *Brake vacuum pump (Chapter 9).*
e) *Thermostat - where applicable (Chapter 3).*
f) *Fuel injection pump and mounting bracket (Chapter 4).*
g) *Manifolds (and turbocharger, where applicable) (Chapter 4).*

12 Ensure that any brackets removed during dismantling are refitted in their correct positions.

2B

8.5b . . . and cap

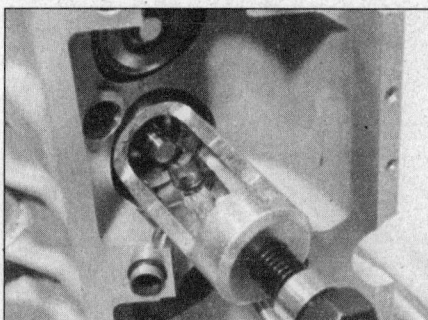

8.7 Fitting a split collet

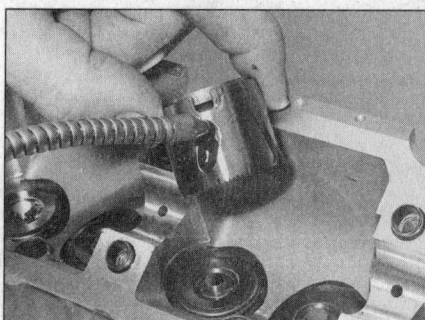

8.10 Oil and insert the bucket tappets

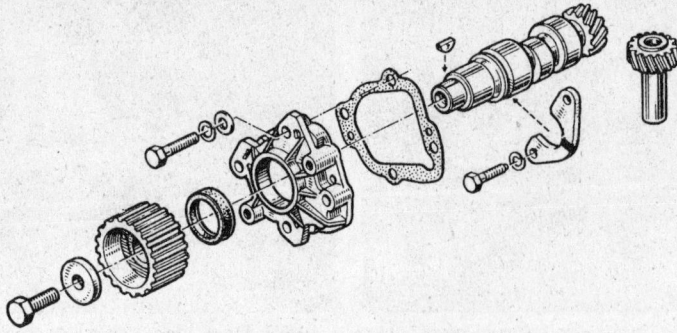

9.5a Auxiliary shaft components

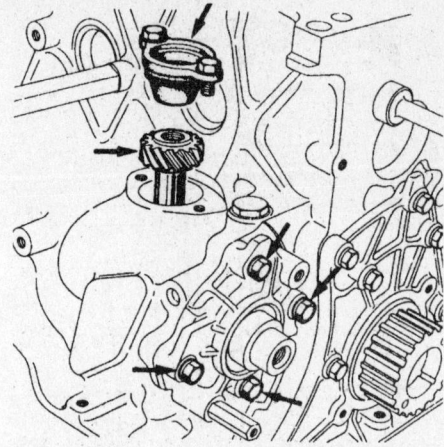

9.5b Auxiliary shaft housing retaining bolt locations, oil pump driveshaft and cover plate

9 Auxiliary shaft - removal and refitting

Note: *A new auxiliary shaft oil seal, housing gasket (or suitable sealant, as applicable), and oil pump drivegear cover plate O-ring will be required on refitting.*

Removal

1 With the engine removed from the vehicle, proceed as follows.

2 Remove the timing belt as described in Chapter 2A.

3 Remove the auxiliary shaft sprocket with reference to Chapter 2A, Section 6.

4 Unbolt the timing belt rear lower cover from the cylinder block, and remove it.

5 Unscrew the four bolts and withdraw the auxiliary shaft housing **(see illustrations)**, then remove the gasket (if fitted). Note that the housing locates on two dowels.

6 Unscrew the two bolts and withdraw the oil pump drivegear cover plate/breather noting the location of the O-ring. Withdraw the drivegear from its location. Use a screwdriver or similar tool to hook the drivegear out if necessary **(see illustrations)**.

7 Unscrew the two bolts and washers, and lift out the auxiliary shaft thrustplate and the auxiliary shaft **(see illustrations)**.

Inspection

8 Examine the auxiliary shaft and oil pump driveshaft for pitting, scoring or wear ridges on the bearing journals, and for chipping or wear of the gear teeth. Renew as necessary. Check the auxiliary shaft bearings in the cylinder block for wear and, if worn, have these renewed by your Renault dealer or suitably-equipped engineering works. Wipe them clean if they are still serviceable.

9 Temporarily fit the thrustplate to its position on the auxiliary shaft, and use a feeler gauge to check that the endfloat is as given in the Specifications **(see illustration)**. If it is greater than the upper tolerance, a new thrustplate should be obtained, but first check the thrust surfaces on the shaft to ascertain if wear has occurred here.

Refitting

10 Clean off all traces of the old gasket or sealant from the auxiliary shaft housing, and prise out the oil seal with a screwdriver. Install the new oil seal using a block of wood, or a

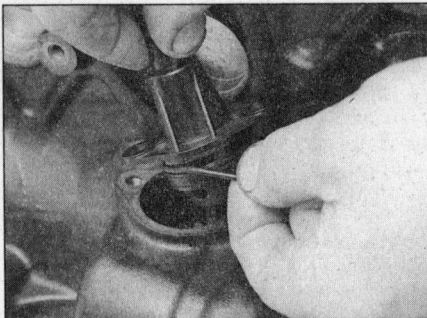

9.6a Removing the oil pump drivegear cover plate/breather and O-ring

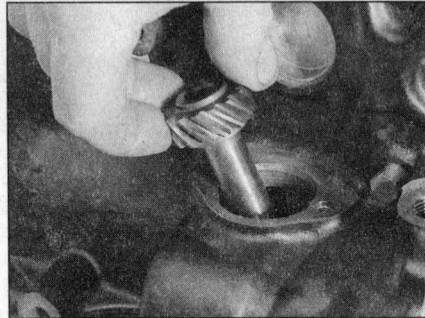

9.6b Removing the oil pump drivegear

9.7a Removing the auxiliary shaft thrust plate . . .

9.7b . . . and the auxiliary shaft

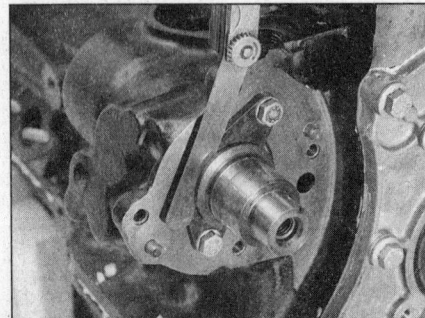

9.9 Measuring the auxiliary shaft endfloat

9.10a Prising the auxiliary shaft oil seal from the housing

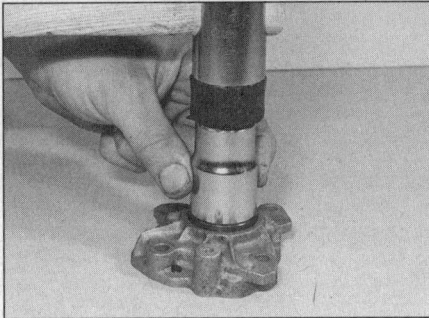

9.10b Fitting a new auxiliary shaft oil seal

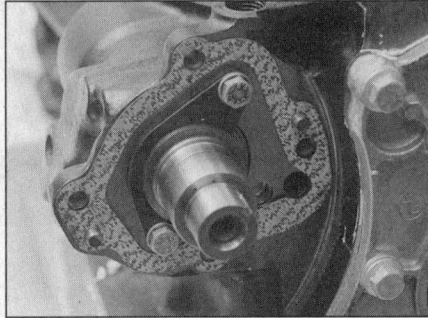

9.13 Auxiliary shaft gasket positioned over the dowels

9.14 Refitting the auxiliary shaft housing. Note tape around front of shaft

suitable socket, and tap it in until it is flush with the outer face of the housing. The open side of the seal must be towards the engine **(see illustrations)**.

11 Liberally lubricate the auxiliary shaft, and slide it into its bearings.

12 Place the thrustplate in position with its curved edge away from the crankshaft, and refit the two retaining bolts, tightening them securely.

13 Place a new housing gasket in position over the dowels of the cylinder block **(see illustration)**. If a gasket was not used previously, apply a bead of CAF 4/60 THIXO sealant (or an alternative) to the housing mating face.

14 Wind a length of tape around the end of the auxiliary shaft to prevent damage to the oil seal as the housing is refitted. Liberally lubricate the oil seal lips, and then locate the housing in place, engaging it with the dowels **(see illustration)**. Refit and tighten the housing retaining bolts progressively in a diagonal sequence. Remove the tape from the end of the shaft.

15 Lubricate the oil pump drivegear, and lower the gear into its location. Ensure that the splines on the drivegear engage with the oil pump.

16 Inspect the O-ring seal on the oil pump drivegear cover plate/breather, and renew it if necessary. Fit the cover plate/breather and secure with the two retaining bolts.

17 Refit the rear lower timing belt cover to the cylinder block, and tighten the bolts.

18 Refit the auxiliary shaft sprocket with

reference to Chapter 2A, Section 6.

19 Refit and tension the timing belt as described in Chapter 2A.

10 Piston/connecting rod assemblies - removal

1 Before proceeding, the following components must be removed as described in Chapter 2A.

a) Cylinder head.
b) Sump.
c) Oil pump.

2 Rotate the crankshaft so that No 1 big-end cap (nearest the flywheel end of the engine) is at the lowest point of its travel. If the big-end cap and rod are not already numbered, mark them with a centre-punch **(see illustration)**. Mark both cap and rod to identify the cylinder they operate in, noting that No 1 is nearest the flywheel end of the engine.

3 Before removing the big-end cap, use a feeler blade to check the amount of side play between the cap and the crankshaft webs **(see illustration)**.

4 Unscrew and remove the big-end bearing cap bolts. Withdraw the cap, complete with bearing shell, from the connecting rod **(see illustration)**. Strike the cap with a wooden or copper mallet if it is stuck. Tape the bearing shell to the cap if it is to be re-used.

5 If only the bearing shells are being attended to, push the connecting rod up and off the

crankpin, and remove the upper bearing shell. Again, tape the bearing shell to the rod if it is to be re-used.

6 If desired, push the connecting rod up, and remove the piston and rod assembly from the bore. Note that if there is a pronounced wear ridge at the top of the bore, there is a risk of damaging the piston as the rings foul the ridge. However, it is reasonable to assume that a rebore and new pistons will be required in any case if the ridge is so pronounced.

7 Repeat the procedure for the remaining piston/connecting rod assemblies. Ensure that the caps and rods are marked before removal, as described previously, and keep all components in order.

11 Crankshaft - removal

1 Before proceeding, the following components must be removed.

a) Timing belt, sprockets and tensioner, and upper rear timing belt cover (Chapter 2A).
b) Flywheel (Chapter 2A).
c) Piston/connecting rod assemblies (Section 10).

2 Unscrew the securing bolts, and remove the lower rear timing belt cover.

3 Unscrew the securing bolts, and remove the crankshaft front oil seal housing, along with the oil seal. Note that the housing is fitted using sealant.

2B

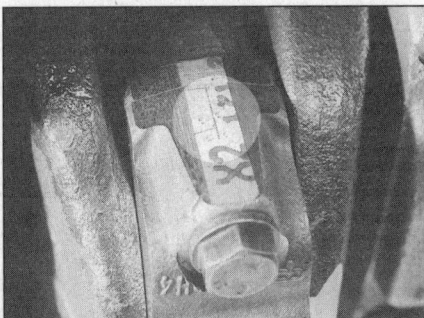

10.2 Identification marks on No 4 big-end cap

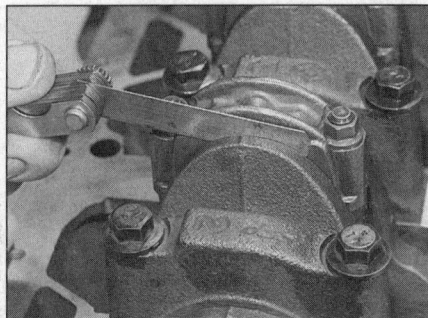

10.3 Checking the side play between a big-end cap and the crankshaft web

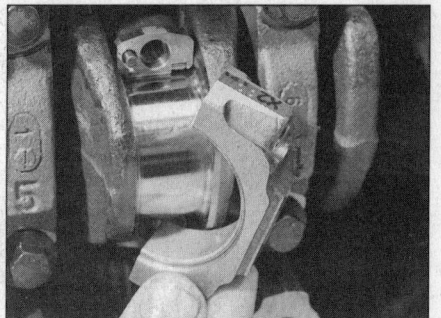

10.4 Removing a big-end bearing cap

11.4 Checking the crankshaft endfloat using a dial gauge

11.6 Identification marking on No 2 main bearing cap

11.9 Lifting the crankshaft from the crankcase

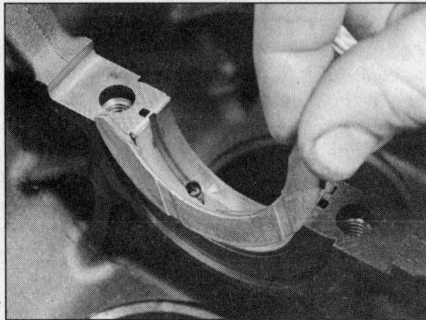
11.10 Remove the thrust washers

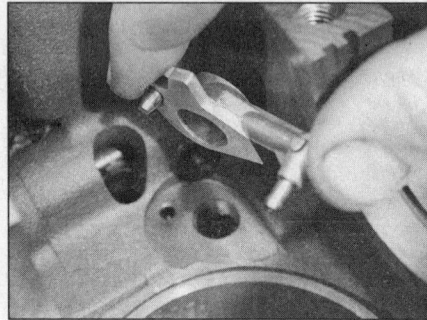
12.1 Removing a piston oil spray jet - Turbo model

4 Before the crankshaft is removed, check the endfloat using a dial gauge in contact with the end of the crankshaft **(see illustration)**. Push the crankshaft fully one way, and then zero the gauge. Push the crankshaft fully the other way, and check the endfloat. The result can be compared with the specified amount, and will give an indication as to whether new thrustwashers are required.

5 If a dial gauge is not available, feeler blades can be used. First push the crankshaft fully towards the flywheel end of the engine, then slip the feeler blade between the web of No 1 crankpin and the thrust washer of No 2 main bearing (located in the crankcase).

6 Identification numbers should already be cast onto the base of each main bearing cap on the auxiliary shaft side of the engine. If not, number the caps and crankcase using a centre-punch, as was done for the connecting rods and caps **(see illustration)**. Again note that No 1 cylinder is at the flywheel end of the engine.

7 Unscrew and remove the main bearing cap securing bolts, noting their locations, as two different types and lengths of bolts are used, and they are not interchangeable. In most cases, hexagonal head bolts are used to secure all except No 1 (flywheel end), which is secured by Allen bolts.

8 Withdraw the caps, complete with the bearing shells. Tap the caps with a wooden or copper mallet if they are stuck. Note that the sides of No 1 bearing cap are sealed to the cylinder block using silicon sealant or butyl seals. Tape the shells to their relevant caps if

they are to be re-used.

9 Carefully lift the crankshaft from the crankcase **(see illustration)**.

10 Remove the thrustwashers at each side of No 2 main bearing, then remove the bearing shell upper halves from the crankcase **(see illustration)**. Place each shell with its respective bearing cap.

11 Remove the oil seal from the rear of the crankshaft.

12 Cylinder block/crankcase - cleaning and inspection

Cleaning

1 For complete cleaning, the core plugs should be removed. Drill a small hole in them, then insert a self-tapping screw and pull out the plugs using a pair of grips or a slide-hammer. Also remove all external components, brackets and senders (if not already done), noting their locations. On Turbo models, remove the securing bolts, and withdraw the piston oil spray jets from the bottom of the cylinder block **(see illustration)**.

2 Scrape all traces of gasket and sealant from the cylinder block, taking care not to damage the head and sump mating faces.

3 If the block is extremely dirty, it should be steam-cleaned.

4 After the block has been steam-cleaned, clean all oil holes and oil galleries one more time. Flush all internal passages with warm

water until the water runs clear, dry the block thoroughly and wipe all machined surfaces with a light rust-preventative oil. If you have access to compressed air, use it to speed up the drying process and to blow out all the oil holes and galleries.

> ⚠ **Warning: Wear eye protection when using compressed air!**

5 If the block is not very dirty, you can do an adequate cleaning job with hot soapy water and a stiff brush. Take plenty of time, and do a thorough job. Regardless of the cleaning method used, be sure to clean all oil holes and galleries very thoroughly, dry the block completely and coat all machined surfaces with light oil.

6 The threaded holes in the block must be clean to ensure accurate torque wrench readings during reassembly. Run the proper-size tap into each of the holes to remove rust, corrosion, thread sealant or sludge, and to restore damaged threads. If possible, use compressed air to clear the holes of debris produced by this operation, noting the warning given in paragraph 4. Now is a good time to clean the threads on the head bolts and the main bearing cap bolts as well.

7 Refit the main bearing caps, and tighten the bolts finger-tight.

8 After coating the mating surfaces of the new core plugs with suitable sealant, refit them in the cylinder block. Make sure that they are driven in straight and seated properly, or leakage could result. Special tools are available for this purpose, but a large socket, with an outside diameter that will just slip into the core plug, will work just as well.

9 On Turbo models, check the gauze filters and the oil holes in the piston oil spray jet securing bolts, and the oil holes in the jets themselves for blockage **(see illustrations)**. Clean if necessary, then refit the jets and tighten the securing bolts. Ensure that the locating pegs on the jets engage with the corresponding holes in the cylinder block.

10 If the engine is not going to be reassembled right away, cover it with a large plastic bag to keep it clean and prevent it rusting.

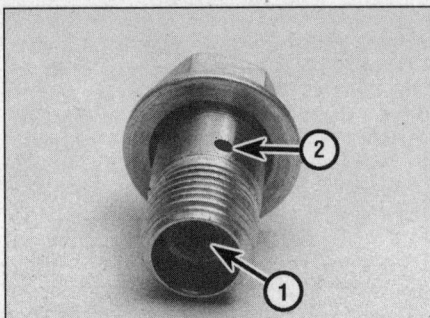

12.9a Check the gauze filters (1) and the oil holes (2) in the oil spray jet securing bolts . . .

12.9b . . . and the oil holes (arrowed) in the jets for blockage

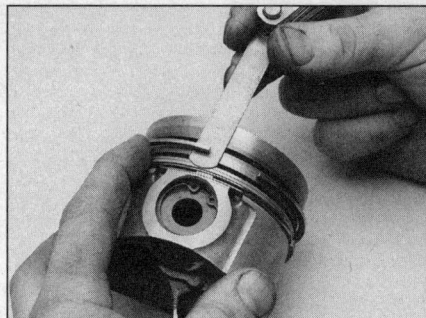

13.2 Removing a piston ring with the aid of a feeler blade

Inspection

11 Visually check the block for cracks, rust and corrosion. Look for stripped threads in the threaded holes. If there has been any history of internal water leakage, it may be worthwhile having an engine overhaul specialist check the block with special equipment. If defects are found, have the block repaired, if possible, or renewed.

12 Check the cylinder bores for scuffing and scoring. Normally, bore wear will be evident in the form of a wear ridge at the top of the bore. This ridge marks the limit of piston travel.

13 Measure the diameter of each cylinder at the top (just under the ridge area), centre and bottom of the cylinder bore, parallel to the crankshaft axis.

14 Next measure each cylinder's diameter at the same three locations across the crankshaft axis. If the difference between any of the measurements is greater than 0.20 mm, indicating that the cylinder is excessively out-of-round or tapered, then remedial action must be considered.

15 Repeat this procedure for the remaining cylinders.

16 If the cylinder walls are badly scuffed or scored, or if they are excessively out-of-round or tapered, have the cylinder block rebored. New pistons (oversize in the case of a rebore) will also be required.

17 If the cylinders are in reasonably good condition, then it may only be necessary to renew the piston rings.

18 If this is the case, the bores should be honed in order to allow the new rings to bed in correctly and provide the best possible seal. The conventional type of hone has spring-loaded stones, and is used with a power drill. You will also need some paraffin or honing oil and rags. The hone should be moved up and down the cylinder to produce a crosshatch pattern, and plenty of honing oil should be used. Ideally, the crosshatch lines should intersect at approximately a 60° angle. Do not take off more material than is necessary to produce the required finish. If new pistons are being fitted, the piston manufacturers may specify a finish with a different angle, so their instructions should be followed. Do not withdraw the hone from the cylinder while it is

still being turned, but stop it first. After honing a cylinder, wipe out all traces of the honing oil. If equipment of this type is not available, or if you are not sure whether you are competent to undertake the task yourself, an engine overhaul specialist will carry out the work at a moderate cost.

19 Where applicable, refit all external components and senders in their correct locations, as noted before removal.

13 Piston/connecting rod assemblies - inspection and reassembly

1 Before the inspection process can begin, the piston/connecting rod assemblies must be cleaned, and the original piston rings removed from the pistons.

2 Carefully expand the old rings over the top of the pistons. The use of two or three old feeler blades will be helpful in preventing the rings dropping into empty grooves **(see illustration)**. Note that the oil control ring has two sections.

3 Scrape away all traces of carbon from the top of the piston. A hand-held wire brush or a piece of fine emery cloth can be used once the majority of the deposits have been scraped away.

4 Remove the carbon from the ring grooves in the piston by cleaning them using an old ring. Break the ring in half to do this. Be very careful to remove only the carbon deposits; do not remove any metal, nor nick or scratch the sides of the ring grooves. Protect your fingers - piston rings are sharp.

5 Once the deposits have been removed, clean the piston/connecting rod assembly with paraffin or a suitable solvent, and dry thoroughly. Make sure the oil return holes in the back sides of the ring grooves are clear.

6 If the pistons and cylinder bores are not damaged or worn excessively, and if the cylinder block does not need to be rebored, the original pistons can be re-used. Normal piston wear appears as even vertical wear on the piston thrust surfaces, and slight looseness of the top ring in its groove. New piston rings, however, should always be used

when the engine is reassembled.

7 Carefully inspect each piston for cracks around the skirt, at the gudgeon pin bosses, and at the piston ring lands (between the piston ring grooves).

8 Look for scoring and scuffing on the sides of the skirt, holes in the piston crown, and burned areas at the edge of the crown. If the skirt is scored or scuffed, the engine may have been suffering from overheating and/or abnormal combustion, which caused excessively-high operating temperatures. The cooling and lubricating systems should be checked thoroughly. Scorch marks on the sides of the pistons show that blow-by has occurred. A hole in the piston crown, or burned areas at the edge of the piston crown indicates that abnormal combustion (pre-ignition, knocking, or detonation) has been occurring. If any of the above problems exist, the causes must be investigated and corrected, or the damage will occur again. The causes may include incorrect injection pump timing, or a faulty injector.

9 Corrosion of the piston, in the form of small pits, indicates that coolant is leaking into the combustion chamber and/or the crankcase. Again, the cause must be corrected, or the problem may persist in the rebuilt engine.

10 If new rings are being fitted to old pistons, measure the piston ring-to-groove clearance by placing a new piston ring in each ring groove and measuring the clearance with a feeler blade. Check the clearance at three or four places around each groove. No values are specified, but if the measured clearance is excessive - say greater than 0.10 mm - new pistons will be required. If the new ring is excessively tight, the most likely cause is dirt remaining in the groove.

11 Check the piston-to-bore clearance by measuring the cylinder bore (see Section 11) and the piston diameter. Measure the piston across the skirt, at a 90° angle to the gudgeon pin, approximately half way down the skirt. Subtract the piston diameter from the bore diameter to obtain the clearance. If this is greater than the figures given in the Specifications, the block will have to be rebored and new pistons and rings fitted. The piston diameter grade, which corresponds to the

2B

13.11a Measuring a piston diameter using a micrometer

13.11b Piston diameter grade marked on piston crown

13.13 Gudgeon pin retaining circlip (arrowed)

cylinder bore grade, is marked on the piston crown **(see illustrations)**.

12 Check the fit of the gudgeon pin by twisting the piston and connecting rod in opposite directions. Any noticeable play indicates excessive wear, which must be corrected.

13 To separate a piston from its connecting rod, prise out the circlips and push out the gudgeon pin **(see illustration)**. Hand pressure is sufficient to remove the pin. Identify the piston and rod to ensure correct reassembly.

14 The connecting rods themselves should not be in need of renewal unless seizure or some other major mechanical failure has occurred. Check the alignment of the connecting rods visually, and if the rods are not straight, take them to an engine overhaul specialist for a more detailed check.

15 Examine the mating faces of the big-end caps and connecting rods to see if they have ever been filed, in a mistaken attempt to take up bearing wear. This is extremely unlikely, but if evident, the offending connecting rods and caps must be renewed.

16 Where applicable, reassemble the pistons and rods. Make sure that the pistons are fitted the right way round - the oil hole in the connecting rod small-end should face away from the combustion chamber in the piston crown **(see illustration)**. Oil the gudgeon pins before fitting them. When assembled, the piston should pivot freely on the rod.

17 Before refitting the rings to the pistons, check their end gaps by inserting each of them in their cylinder bores. Use the piston to make sure that they are square **(see illustrations)**. No values are specified, but typical gaps would be of the order of 0.50 mm for compression rings, perhaps somewhat

greater for the oil control rings. Renault rings are supplied pre-gapped; no attempt should be made to adjust the gaps by filing.

18 Once the ring end gaps have been checked, the rings can be fitted to the pistons.

19 Fit the piston rings using the same technique as for removal. Fit the bottom (oil control) ring first and work up. When fitting the oil control ring, first insert the expander, then fit the ring. Where applicable, ensure that the "TOP" marking on the face of the piston ring faces the piston crown. Arrange the gaps of the middle and upper rings 120° either side of the oil control ring gap **(see illustrations)**. **Note:** *Always follow the instructions supplied with the new piston ring sets - different manufacturers may specify different procedures. Do not mix up the top and middle rings, as they have different cross sections.*

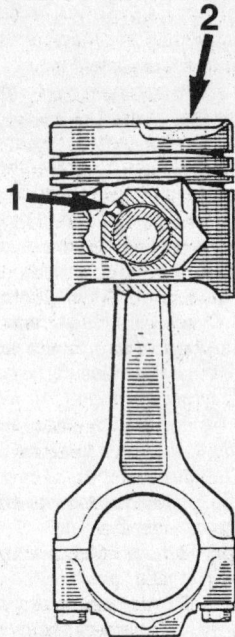

13.16 The oil hole (1) in the connecting rod small-end should face away from the combustion chamber (2) in the piston crown

13.17a Use the piston to push the rings into the cylinder bores . . .

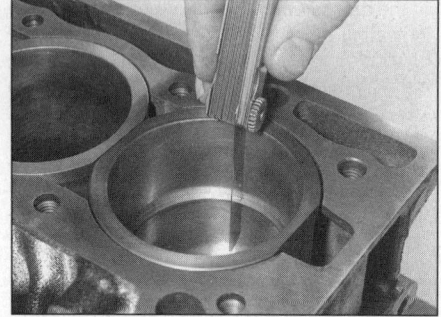

13.17b . . . then measure the ring end gaps

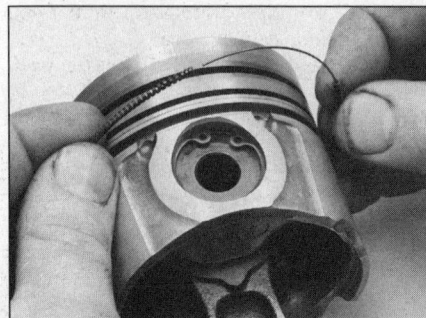

13.19a Fit the oil control ring expander . . .

13.19b . . . followed by the ring

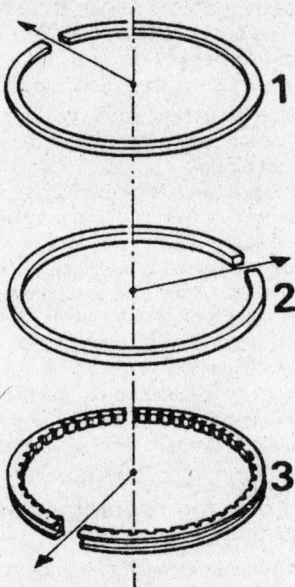

13.19c Position the piston ring end gaps 120° apart as shown
1 Top compression ring
2 Lower compression ring
3 Oil control ring

14 Crankshaft - inspection

Note: *A micrometer will be required for this operation.*

1 Clean the crankshaft using paraffin or a suitable solvent, and dry it, preferably with compressed air if available.

⚠️ *Warning: Wear eye protection when using compressed air! Be sure to clean the oil holes with a pipe cleaner or similar probe, to ensure that they are not obstructed.*

2 Check the main and big-end bearing journals for uneven wear, scoring, pitting and cracking.
3 Big-end bearing wear is accompanied by distinct metallic knocking when the engine is running, particularly noticeable when the engine is pulling from low revs, and some loss of oil pressure.
4 Main bearing wear is accompanied by severe engine vibration and rumble - getting progressively worse as engine revs increase - and again by loss of oil pressure.
5 Check the bearing journal for roughness by running a finger lightly over the bearing surface. Any roughness (which will be accompanied by obvious bearing wear) indicates the that the crankshaft requires regrinding.
6 If the crankshaft has been reground, check for burrs around the crankshaft oil holes (the

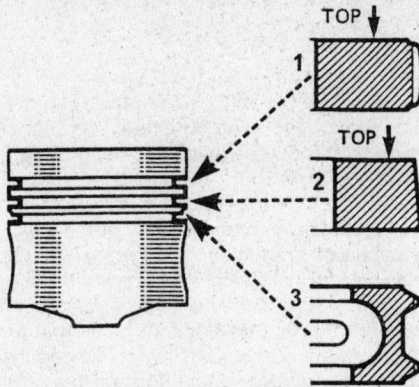

13.19d Piston ring profiles
1 Top compression ring
2 Lower compression ring
3 Oil control ring
Where applicable position the "TOP" markings as shown

14.7 Measuring a main bearing journal diameter using a micrometer

holes are usually chamfered, so burrs should not be a problem unless regrinding has been carried out carelessly). Remove any burrs with a fine file or scraper, and thoroughly clean the oil holes as described previously.
7 Using a micrometer, measure the diameter of the main and big-end bearing journals and compare the results with the Specifications **(see illustration)**. By measuring the diameter at a number of points around each journal's circumference, you will be able to determine

whether or not the journal is out-of-round. Take the measurement at each end of the journal, near the webs, to determine if the journal is tapered. If the crankshaft journals are damaged, tapered, out-of-round or worn beyond the limits given in the Specifications, the crankshaft will have to be reground and undersize bearings fitted.
8 Check the oil seal contact surfaces at each end of the crankshaft for wear and damage. If the seal has worn an excessive groove in the surface of the crankshaft, consult an engine overhaul specialist who will be able to advise whether a repair is possible or if a new crankshaft is necessary.

15 Main and big-end bearings - inspection

1 Even though the main and big-end bearings should be renewed during engine overhaul, the old bearings should be retained for close examination, as they may reveal valuable information about the condition of the engine. The bearing shells carry identification marks to denote their size in the form of a code marked on the back of the shell. If the shells are to be renewed, without carrying out any crankshaft regrinding, the old shells should be taken along when obtaining new shells to ensure that the correct shells are obtained.
2 Bearing failure occurs because of lack of lubrication, the presence of dirt or other foreign particles, overloading the engine, or corrosion. If a bearing fails, the cause must be found and eliminated before the engine is reassembled to prevent the failure from happening again **(see illustration)**.
3 To examine the bearing shells, remove them from the cylinder block, the main bearing caps, the connecting rods and the big-end bearing caps, and lay them out on a clean surface in the same order as they were fitted to the engine. This will enable any bearing problems to be matched with the corresponding crankshaft journal.
4 Dirt and other foreign particles can enter the engine in a variety of ways. Contamination may be left in the engine during assembly, or it may pass through filters or the crankcase

2B

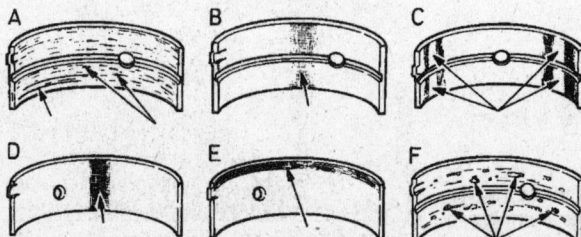

15.2 Typical bearing failures
A Scratched by dirt; dirt embedded into bearing material
B Lack of oil; overlay wiped out
C Improper seating; bright (polished) sections
D Tapered journal; overlay gone from entire surface
E Radius ride
F Fatigue failure; craters or pockets

ventilation system. Normal engine wear produces small particles of metal, which can eventually cause problems. If particles find their way into the lubrication system, it is likely that they will eventually be carried to the bearings. Whatever the source, these foreign particles often end up embedded in the soft bearing material and are easily recognized. Large particles will not embed in the bearing and will score or gouge the bearing and journal. To prevent possible contamination, clean all parts thoroughly and keep everything spotlessly clean during engine assembly. Once the engine has been installed in the vehicle, ensure that regular engine oil and filter changes are carried out at the recommended intervals.

5 Lack of lubrication (or lubrication breakdown) has a number of interrelated causes. Excessive heat (which thins the oil), overloading (which squeezes the oil from the bearing face) and oil leakage (from excessive bearing clearances, worn oil pump or high engine speeds) all contribute to lubrication breakdown. Blocked oil passages, which may be the result of misaligned oil holes in a bearing shell, will also starve a bearing of oil and destroy it. When lack of lubrication is the cause of bearing failure, the bearing material is wiped or extruded from the steel backing of the bearing. Temperatures may increase to the point where the steel backing turns blue from overheating.

6 Driving habits can have a definite effect on bearing life. Full throttle, low speed operation (labouring the engine) puts very high loads on bearings, which tends to squeeze out the oil film. These loads cause the bearings to flex, which produces fine cracks in the bearing face (fatigue failure). Eventually the bearing material will loosen in pieces and tear away from the steel backing. Regular short journeys can lead to corrosion of bearings because insufficient engine heat is produced to drive off the condensed water and corrosive gases which form inside the engine. These products collect in the engine oil, forming acid and sludge. As the oil is carried to the bearings, the acid attacks and corrodes the bearing material.

7 Incorrect bearing installation during engine assembly will also lead to bearing failure. Tight fitting bearings leave insufficient bearing lubrication clearance and will result in oil starvation. Dirt or foreign particles trapped behind a bearing shell results in high spots on the bearing which can lead to failure.

8 If new bearings are to be fitted, the bearing running clearances should be measured before the engine is finally reassembled, to ensure that the correct bearing shells have been obtained (see Sections 17 and 18). If the crankshaft has been reground, the engineering works which carried out the work will advise on the correct size bearing shells to suit the work carried out. If there is any doubt as to which bearing shells should be used, seek advice from a Renault dealer.

16 Engine overhaul - reassembly sequence

1 Before reassembly begins, ensure that all new parts have been obtained, and that all necessary tools are available. Read through the entire procedure to familiarise yourself with the work involved, and to ensure that all items necessary for reassembly of the engine are at hand. In addition to all normal tools and materials, a thread-locking compound will be needed. A tube of RTV sealing compound will also be required for the joint faces that are fitted without gaskets; it is recommended that CAF 4/60 THIXO paste (obtainable from Renault dealers) is used, as it is specially-formulated for this purpose.

2 In order to save time and avoid problems, engine reassembly can be carried out in the following order.

a) Crankshaft.
b) Pistons/connecting rod assemblies.
c) Oil pump.
d) Sump.
e) Flywheel.
f) Cylinder head.
g) Timing belt and sprockets.
h) Engine external components.

17 Crankshaft - refitting and main bearing running clearance check

Note: *Suitable seals and/or a suitable sealant kit will be required when refitting No 1 main bearing cap - see text. New crankshaft oil seals should be used on refitting.*

1 Before fitting the crankshaft and main bearings, a decision has to be made on the method to be used to seal the No 1 main bearing cap. The cap has sealing grooves in the sides of the cap, which can be sealed using

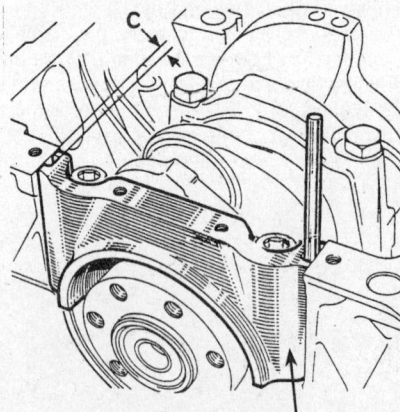

17.1 Measuring No 1 main bearing cap side seal grooves using a dowel rod
Bearing cap (arrowed)
C Seal groove measurement

butyl seals or silicone sealant. If butyl seals are to be used, it is necessary to determine the correct thickness of the seals to obtain from Renault, as follows **(see illustration)**.

a) *Place the bearing cap in position without any seals, and secure it with the two retaining bolts.*
b) *Locate a twist drill, dowel rod or any other suitable implement which will just fit in the side seal groove.*
c) *Now measure the implement - this dimension is the side seal groove size. If the dimension is less than or equal to 5.0 mm, a 5.10 mm thick side seal is needed. If the dimension is more than 5.0 mm, a 6.0 mm thick side seal is required.*
d) *Having determined the side seal size and obtained the necessary seals, proceed as follows.*

Main bearing running clearance check

Note: *Suitable measuring equipment will be required for this check - see text.*

2 Clean the backs of the bearing shells and the bearing recesses in both the cylinder block and main bearing caps. If new shells are being fitted, ensure that all traces of the protective grease are cleaned off using paraffin.

3 Press the bearing shells without oil holes into the caps, ensuring that the tag on the shell engages in the notch in the cap.

4 Press the bearing shells with the oil holes/grooves into the recesses in the cylinder block. Note that if the original main bearing shells are being re-used, these must be refitted to their original locations in the block and caps.

5 Before the crankshaft can be permanently installed, the main bearing running clearance should be checked; this can be done in either of two ways. One method is to fit the main bearing caps to the cylinder block, with the bearing shells in place. With the cap retaining bolts tightened to the specified torque, measure the internal diameter of each assembled pair of bearing shells using a vernier dial indicator or internal micrometer. If the diameter of each corresponding crankshaft journal is measured and then subtracted from the bearing internal diameter, the result will be the main bearing running clearance. The second (and more accurate) method is to use an American product known as "Plastigage". This consists of a fine thread of perfectly-round plastic which is compressed between the bearing cap and the journal. When the cap is removed, the deformation of the plastic thread is measured with a special card gauge supplied with the kit. The running clearance is determined from this gauge. Plastigage is sometimes difficult to obtain in the UK, but enquiries at one of the larger specialist chains of quality motor factors should produce the name of a stockist in your area. The procedure for using Plastigage is as follows.

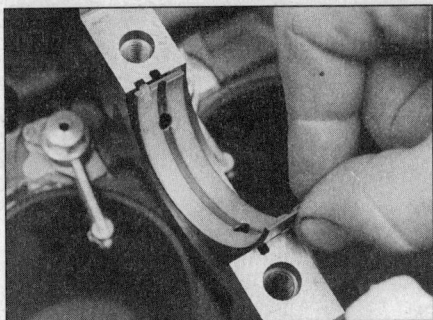

17.6 The upper main bearing shells have oil grooves

17.7 Thread of Plastigage (arrowed) placed on a crankshaft main journal

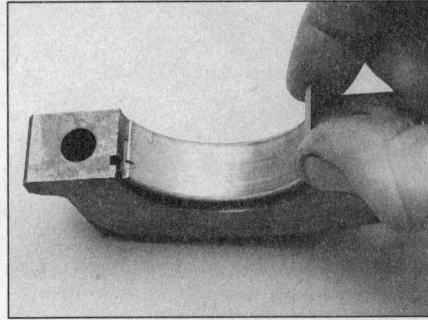

17.8 The lower main bearing shells have no oil grooves

6 With the upper main bearing shells in place (the upper shells have oil grooves), carefully lay the crankshaft in position (see illustration). Do not use any lubricant; the crankshaft journals and bearing shells must be perfectly clean and dry.

7 Cut several pieces of the appropriate-size Plastigage (they should be slightly shorter than the width of the main bearings), and place one piece on each crankshaft journal axis (see illustration).

8 With the bearing shells in position in the caps (the shells have no oil grooves), fit the caps to their numbered or previously-noted locations (see illustration). Take care not to disturb the Plastigage.

9 Starting with the centre main bearing and working outward, tighten the main bearing cap bolts progressively to their specified torque setting (Chapter 2A). Don't rotate the crankshaft at any time during this operation.

10 Remove the bolts and carefully lift off the main bearing caps, keeping them in order. Don't disturb the Plastigage or rotate the crankshaft. If any of the bearing caps are difficult to remove, tap them from side-to-side with a soft-faced mallet.

11 Compare the width of the crushed Plastigage on each journal to the scale printed on the Plastigage envelope to obtain the main bearing running clearance (see illustration).

12 If the clearance is not as specified, the bearing shells may be the wrong size (or excessively-worn if the original shells are being re-used). Before deciding that different size shells are needed, make sure that no dirt or oil was trapped between the bearing shells and the caps or block when the clearance was measured. If the Plastigage was wider at one end than at the other, the journal may be tapered.

13 Carefully scrape away all traces of the Plastigage material from the crankshaft and bearing shells, using a fingernail or something similar which is unlikely to score the shells.

Final refitting

14 Carefully lift the crankshaft out of the cylinder block once more.

15 Using a little grease, stick the thrustwashers to each side of No 2 main bearing location in the crankcase. Ensure that the oilway grooves on each thrustwasher face outwards from the bearing location, towards the crankshaft webs.

16 Liberally lubricate each bearing shell in the cylinder block, and lower the crankshaft into position.

17 Lubricate the bearing shells, then fit the bearing caps in their numbered or previously-noted locations. Note the following points (see illustrations):

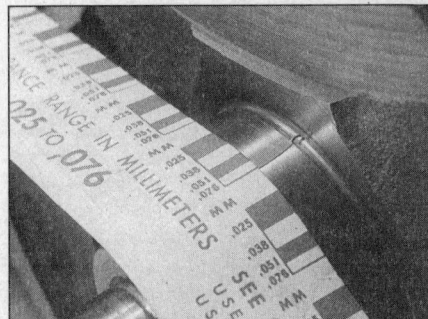

17.11 Measuring the Plastigage width with the special gauge

a) If using butyl seals to seal No 1 main bearing cap (see paragraph 1), fit the seals with their grooves facing outwards. Position the seals so that approximately 0.2 mm of seal protrudes at the lower face of the cap (the side towards the crankcase). Lubricate the seals with a little oil, and apply a little CAF 4/60 THIXO sealant to the bottom corners of the cap prior to fitting it. When the cap is being fitted, use the bolts as a guide by just starting them in their threads, then pressing the cap firmly into position. When the cap is almost fully home, check that the seals still protrude slightly at the cylinder block mating face.

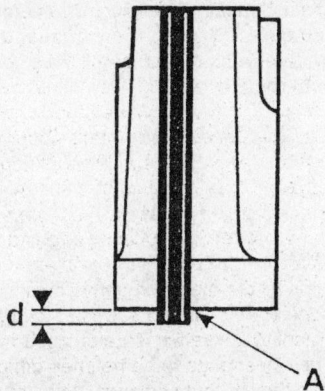

17.17a The butyl seals should protrude (d = 0.2 mm) beyond the lower face (A) of No 1 main bearing cap

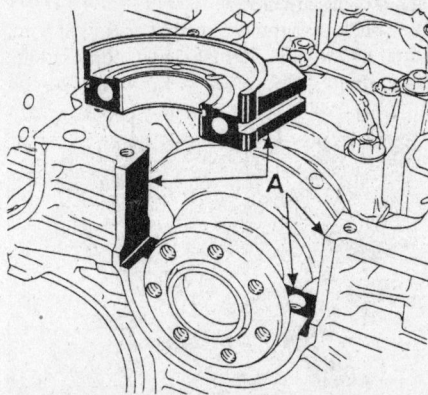

17.17b Clean the cylinder block and bearing cap mating faces (A) when using silicone sealant to seal No 1 main bearing cap . . .

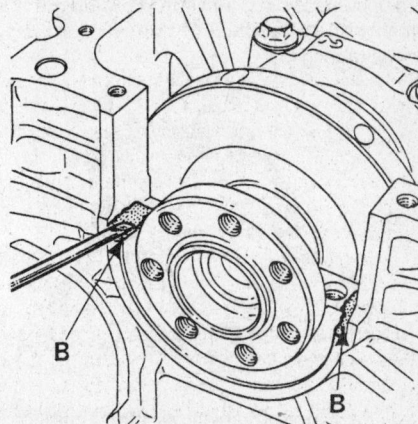

17.17c . . . and coat the lower faces of the cylinder block (B) with sealant

2B

17.18a Fitting No 1 main bearing cap bolts

17.18b Tightening a main bearing cap bolt

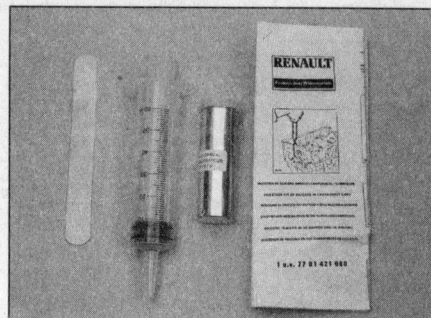

17.20a Renault silicone sealant kit for sealing No 1 main bearing cap

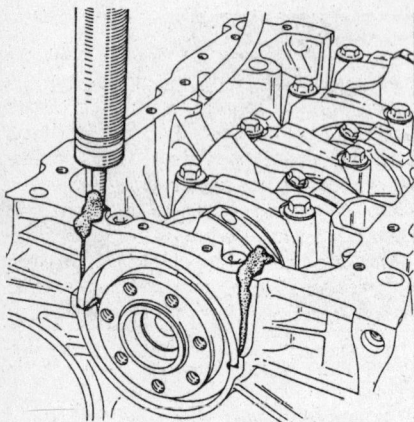

17.20b Injecting sealant into the sealing grooves of No 1 main bearing cap

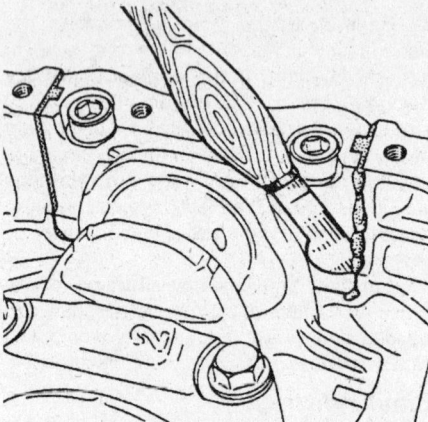

17.20c Cut away the surplus sealant from inside the block . . .

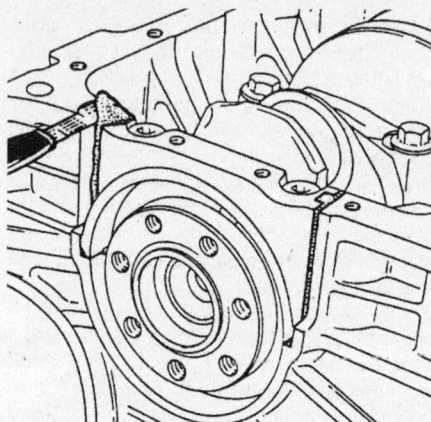

17.20d . . . and from the sump mating face

b) *If silicone sealant is to be used to seal No 1 main bearing cap (see paragraph 1), clean all the mating faces of the cylinder block and bearing cap using a degreasing agent, then allow the cleaned areas to dry. Lightly coat the lower faces of the cylinder block with CAF 4/60 THIXO sealant.*

18 Fit the main bearing cap bolts, and tighten them progressively to the specified torque (Chapter 2A) **(see illustrations)**.

19 Where butyl seals have been fitted to seal No 1 bearing cap, trim the protruding ends flush with the surface of the cylinder block sump mating face.

20 Where silicone sealant is to be used to seal No 1 main bearing cap, mix the sealant and the hardener as described in the instructions supplied with the kit. Inject the mixture into the bearing cap grooves, allowing the mixture to flow out slightly either side of the grooves, and at the cylinder block sump mating face, to ensure that the grooves are completely filled. Allow the sealant to dry for a few minutes, then cut away surplus sealant from the joint face, both inside and outside the cylinder block, and at the sump mating face **(see illustrations)**.

21 Check that the crankshaft is free to turn. Some stiffness is normal if new components have been fitted, but there must be no jamming or tight spots.

22 Check the crankshaft endfloat with reference to Section 11.

23 Fit a new oil seal to the crankshaft front oil seal housing, with reference to Chapter 2A, Section 12.

24 Smear the cylinder block mating face of the oil seal housing liberally with CAF 4/60 THIXO sealant (or an alternative), ensuring that the oilway is not blocked **(see illustration)**.

25 Lubricate the inner lips of the oil seal, then fit the housing over the front of the crankshaft, taking care not to damage the seal. Refit and tighten the housing securing bolts **(see illustrations)**.

26 Fit a new crankshaft rear oil seal, with reference to Chapter 2A.

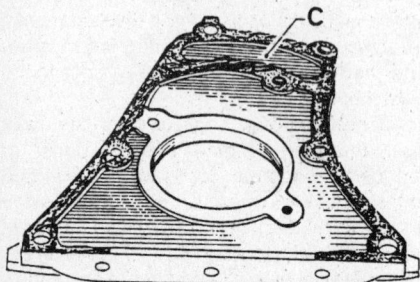

17.24 Smear the cylinder block mating face of the front oil seal housing with sealant, ensuring that the oilway (C) is not blocked

17.25a Fit the crankshaft front oil seal housing . . .

17.25b . . . and tighten the securing bolts

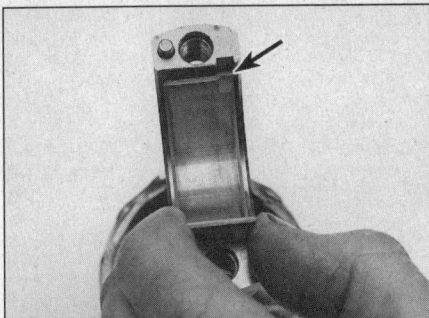

18.2 The locating tabs (arrowed) in the shells engage with the cut-outs in the connecting rods

18.4 Fitting a piston/connecting rod assembly to the cylinder block using a piston ring compressor and a hammer handle

18.8 Tightening a big-end bearing cap bolt

27 Refit the lower rear timing belt cover.

28 On completion, refit the piston/connecting rod assemblies as described in Section 18, and the flywheel, timing belt, sprockets and tensioner, and the upper rear timing belt cover as described in Chapter 2A.

18 Piston/connecting rod assemblies - refitting and big-end bearing clearance check

Note: *A piston ring compressor tool will be required for this operation.*

1 Clean the backs of the big-end bearing shells and the recesses in the connecting rods and big-end caps. If new shells are being fitted, ensure that all traces of the protective grease are cleaned off using paraffin. Wipe the shells and connecting rods dry with a lint-free cloth.

2 Press the big-end bearing shells into the connecting rods and caps, in their correct locations if the original shells are to be re-used. Make sure that the locating tabs are engaged with the cut-outs in the connecting rods (see illustration).

Big-end bearing running clearance check

Note: *Suitable measuring equipment will be required for this check - see text.*

3 Lubricate No 1 piston and piston rings, and check that the ring gaps are spaced at 120° intervals to each other.

4 Fit a ring compressor to No 1 piston, then insert the piston and connecting rod into No 1 cylinder. The combustion chamber in the piston crown should be on the oil filter side of the engine. With No 1 crankpin at its lowest point, drive the piston carefully into the cylinder with the wooden handle of a hammer (see illustration), at the same time guiding the connecting rod onto the crankpin.

5 To measure the big-end bearing running

clearance, refer to the information contained in Section 17; the same general procedures apply. If the Plastigage method is being used, ensure that the crankpin journal and the big-end bearing shells are clean and dry, then engage the connecting rod with the crankpin. Place the Plastigage strip on the crankpin, fit the bearing cap in its previously-noted position (see Section 10), then tighten the bolts to the specified torque. Do not rotate the crankshaft during this operation. Remove the cap and check the running clearance by measuring the Plastigage as previously described.

6 Repeat the above procedures on the remaining piston/connecting rod assemblies.

Final refitting

7 Having checked the running clearance of all the crankpin journals and taken any corrective action necessary, clean off all traces of Plastigage from the bearing shells and crankpin.

8 Liberally lubricate the crankpin journals and big-end bearing shells. Refit the bearing caps once more, ensuring correct positioning as previously described. Tighten the bearing cap bolts to the specified torque (Chapter 2A), and turn the crankshaft each time to make sure that it is free before moving on to the next assembly (see illustration).

9 On completion, refit the oil pump, sump and cylinder head as described in Chapter 2A.

19 Engine - initial start-up after overhaul

1 With the engine refitted to the vehicle, check the engine oil and coolant levels, and check that the battery is well charged.

2 Prime the fuel system as described in Chapter 4.

3 On Turbo models, prime the turbocharger lubrication circuit by disconnecting the stop

solenoid and cranking the engine on the starter motor in several ten-second bursts, pausing for half a minute or so between each burst. Reconnect the solenoid when satisfied that oil pressure has been established (ensure that the oil pressure warning light on the facia extinguishes when the engine is cranked).

4 Fully depress the accelerator pedal, turn the ignition key to position "M" and wait for the preheating warning light to go out.

5 Start the engine. Additional cranking may be necessary to bleed the fuel system before the engine starts.

6 Once started, keep the engine running at fast tickover. Check that the oil pressure light goes out, then check that there are no leaks of oil, fuel and coolant. Where applicable, check the power steering pipe/hose unions for leakage. Do not be alarmed if there are some odd smells and smoke from parts getting hot and burning off oil deposits.

7 Keep the engine idling until hot coolant is felt circulating through the radiator top hose, indicating that the engine is at normal operating temperature, then stop the engine and allow it to cool.

8 Recheck the oil and coolant levels and top up if necessary.

9 Check the fuel injection pump timing and the idle speed as described in Chapters 4 and 1 respectively.

10 On Turbo models, tighten the cylinder head bolts to the final stage (see Chapter 2A) after running the engine until it reaches normal operating temperature (cooling fan cuts in), and then allowing the engine to cool for at least 2 hours.

11 If new pistons, rings or bearings have been fitted, the engine must be run-in at reduced speeds and loads for the first 500 miles (800 km) or so. Do not operate the engine at full throttle, or allow it to labour in any gear during this period. It is beneficial to change the engine oil and filter at the end of this period.

2B

Notes

Chapter 3
Cooling, heating and air conditioning systems

Contents

Degrees of difficulty

Easy, suitable for novice with little experience

Fairly easy, suitable for beginner with some experience

Fairly difficult, suitable for competent DIY mechanic

Difficult, suitable for experienced DIY mechanic

Very difficult, suitable for expert DIY or professional

Specifications

General
Cooling system type .... Pressurised, with belt-driven pump, front-mounted radiator and electric cooling fan
Coolant type .... See Chapter 1 (*"Lubricants, fluids and capacities"*)
Coolant capacity .... See Chapter 1 (*"Lubricants, fluids and capacities"*)
System pressure:
　Brown cap .... 1.2 bars
　Blue cap .... 1.6 bars

Thermostat
Type .... Wax

	Starts to open	Fully open
Opening temperatures	83°C	94°C

Travel (closed to fully open) .... 7.5 mm

Temperature gauge/warning light sender unit
Resistance values (typical):
　20°C .... 3550 ± 500 ohms
　80°C .... 335 ± 35 ohms
　90°C .... 240 ± 30 ohms

1 General information and precautions

General information

The cooling system is of the pressurised type. The main components are a belt-driven pump, an aluminium crossflow radiator, an expansion tank, an electric cooling fan, a thermostat, and the associated hoses **(see illustrations)**.

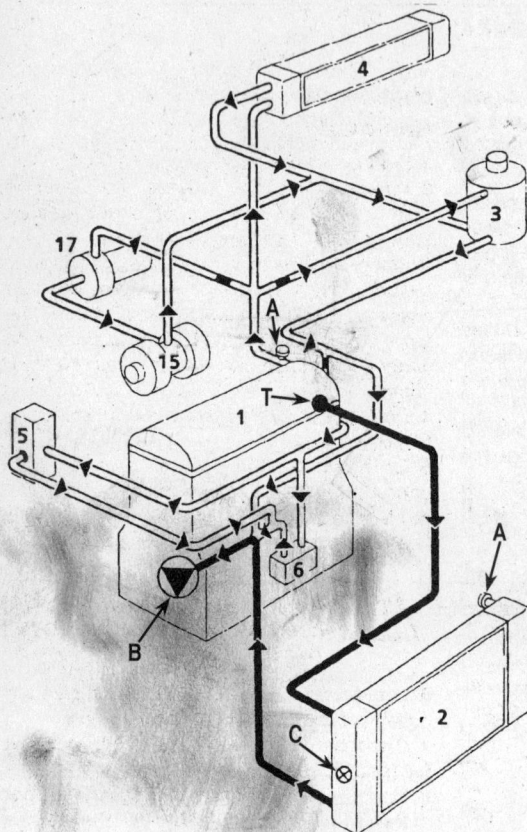

1.1a Cooling system schematic view - non-Turbo engines

1 *Cylinder block*
2 *Radiator*
3 *Expansion tank*
4 *Heater matrix*
5 *Fuel filter/heater*
A *Bleed screw*
B *Water pump*
C *Cooling fan switch*
T *Thermostat*

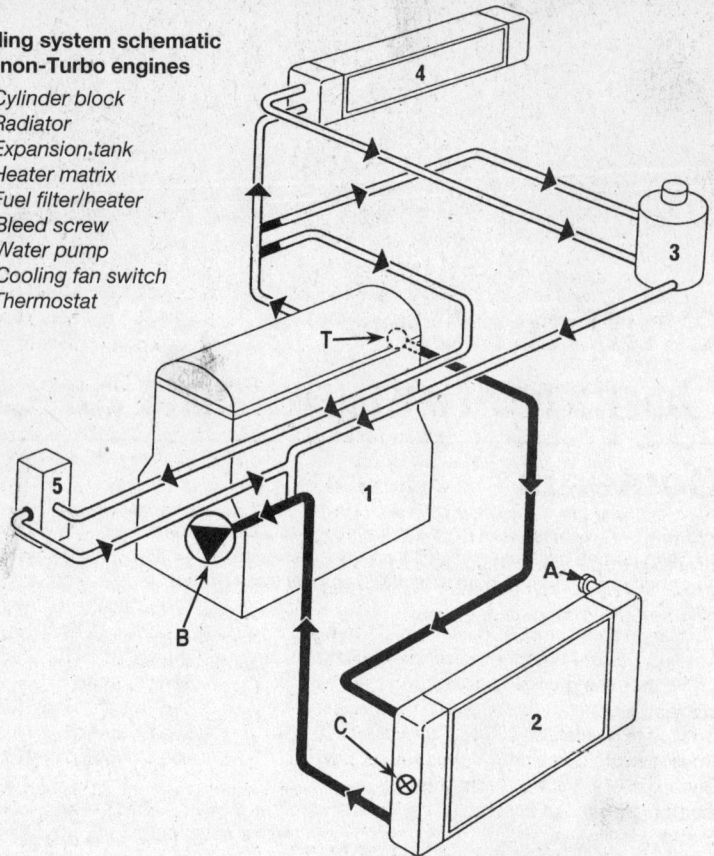

1.1b Cooling system schematic view - Turbo engines

1 *Cylinder block*
2 *Radiator*
3 *Expansion tank*
4 *Heater matrix*
5 *Fuel filter/heater*
6 *Oil cooler*
15 *Turbocharger*
17 *Auxiliary (electric) water pump*
A *Bleed screws*
B *Water pump*
C *Cooling fan switch*
T *Thermostat*

The system functions as follows. When the engine is cold, coolant is pumped around the cylinder block and head passages and the engine oil cooler. After cooling the cylinder bores, combustion surfaces and valve seats, the coolant passes through the heater and fuel heater, and on Turbo models, through the turbocharger, and is returned to the water pump.

When the coolant reaches a predetermined temperature, the thermostat opens, and the hot coolant passes through the top hose to the radiator. As the coolant circulates through the radiator, it is cooled by the inrush of air when the vehicle is in motion. The airflow is supplemented by the action of the electric cooling fan (or twin fans on certain models) when necessary. Upon reaching the bottom of the radiator, the coolant returns to the pump via the radiator bottom hose, and the cycle is repeated.

As the coolant warms up, it expands; the increased volume is accommodated in an expansion tank. The tank is "hot", coolant circulating through the tank all the time that the engine is running.

The electric cooling fan (or twin fans on certain models), mounted behind the radiator, is/are controlled by a thermostatic switch located in the side of the radiator. At a predetermined coolant temperature, the switch contacts close, actuating the fan via a relay.

An engine oil cooler is fitted, mounted between the oil filter and the cylinder block.

The cooling system on Turbo models has an auxiliary electric water pump, which circulates coolant through the turbocharger to cool the bearings after the engine has stopped. This prevents overheating of the bearings and prolongs their life.

For details of the air conditioning system (when fitted) and the precautions associated with it, refer to Section 19.

Precautions

⚠ *Warning: Do not attempt to remove the expansion tank filler cap or disturb any part of the cooling system while the engine is hot, as there is a high risk of scalding. If the expansion tank filler cap must be removed before the engine and radiator have fully cooled (even though this is not recommended) the pressure in the cooling system must first be relieved. Cover the cap with a thick layer of cloth, to avoid scalding, and slowly unscrew the filler cap until a hissing sound can be heard. When the hissing has stopped, indicating that the pressure has reduced, slowly unscrew the filler cap until it can be removed; if more hissing sounds are heard, wait until they have stopped before unscrewing the cap completely. At all times keep well away from the filler cap opening.*

3.2 Removing the plastic radiator shield

3.3 Move the power steering fluid reservoir and bracket clear of the radiator

3.6 Disconnecting the top hose from the radiator

⚠️ *Warning: Do not allow antifreeze to come into contact with skin or painted surfaces of the vehicle. Rinse off spills immediately with plenty of water. Never leave antifreeze lying around in an open container or in a puddle in the driveway or on the garage floor. Children and pets are attracted by its sweet smell. Antifreeze can be fatal if ingested.*

⚠️ *Warning: If the engine is hot, the electric cooling fan may start rotating even if the engine is not running, so be careful to keep hands, hair and loose clothing well clear when working in the engine compartment.*

⚠️ *Warning: Refer to Section 19 for precautions to be observed when working on models equipped with air conditioning.*

2 Cooling system hoses - renewal

Note: *Refer to the warnings given in Section 1 of this Chapter before proceeding. Hoses should only be disconnected once the engine has cooled sufficiently to avoid scalding.*

1 The number, routing and pattern of hoses will vary according to model, but the same basic procedure applies. Before commencing work, make sure that the new hoses are to hand, along with new hose clips if needed. It is good practice to renew the hose clips at the

same time as the hoses.
2 Drain the cooling system, saving the coolant if it is fit for re-use (Chapter 1). Squirt a little penetrating oil onto the hose clips if they are rusty.
3 Release the hose clips from the hose concerned. Three types of clip are used: worm-drive, spring and "sardine-can". The worm-drive clip is released by turning its screw anti-clockwise. The spring clip is released by squeezing its tags together with pliers, at the same time working the clip away from the hose stub. The "sardine-can" clip is not re-usable, and is best cut off with snips or side cutters.
4 Unclip any wires, cables or other hoses which may be attached to the hose being removed. Make notes for reference when reassembling if necessary.
5 Release the hose from its stubs with a twisting motion. Be careful not to damage the stubs on delicate components such as the radiator. If the hose is stuck fast, the best course is often to cut it off using a sharp knife, but again be careful not to damage the stubs.
6 Before fitting the new hose, smear the stubs with washing-up liquid or a suitable rubber lubricant to aid fitting. **Do not** use oil or grease, which may attack the rubber.
7 Fit the hose clips over the ends of the hose, then fit the hose over its stubs. Work the hose into position. When satisfied, locate and tighten the hose clips.
8 Refill the cooling system (Chapter 1). Run the engine, and check that there are no leaks.
9 Recheck the tightness of the hose clips on any new hoses after a few hundred miles.
10 Top up the coolant level if necessary.

3 Radiator - removal, inspection, cleaning and refitting

Note: *Refer to the warnings given in Section 1 of this Chapter before proceeding.*

Removal

1 Disconnect the battery negative lead.
2 Where applicable, release the securing clips, and remove the plastic shield from above the radiator **(see illustration)**.
3 Where applicable, remove the bolts and nut securing the power steering fluid reservoir bracket to the radiator, and move the reservoir and bracket clear of the radiator **(see illustration)**. Take care not to strain the fluid hoses.
4 Drain the cooling system as described in Chapter 1.
5 On models fitted with air conditioning, unbolt the condenser assembly from the radiator, and move it clear of the radiator, leaving the refrigerant lines connected.

⚠️ *Warning: Do not under any circumstances attempt to disconnect the refrigerant lines (see Section 19).*

6 Loosen the clip and disconnect the top hose from the radiator **(see illustration)**.
7 Disconnect the wiring plug from the cooling fan **(see illustration)**.
8 Unscrew the bolts securing the upper radiator mounting brackets to the engine compartment cross panel. Move the radiator to the rear and remove the mounting brackets **(see illustrations)**.

3.7 Disconnecting the wiring plug from the cooling fan

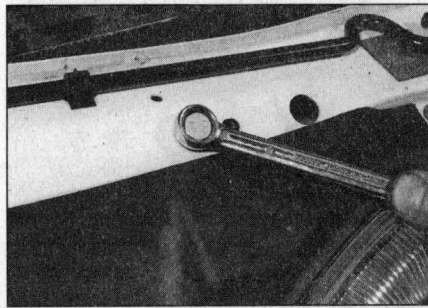

3.8a Unscrew the left-hand . . .

3.8b . . . and right-hand radiator bracket securing bolts

3

3.8c Removing the left-hand radiator mounting bracket

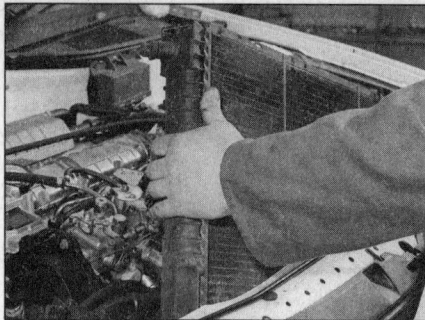
3.9 Lifting out the radiator

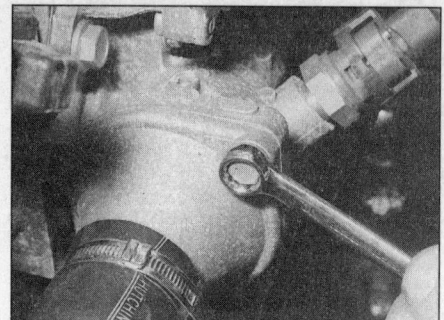
5.5a Remove the securing bolts . . .

5.5b . . . withdraw the cover . . .

5.5c . . . and remove the thermostat and sealing ring - Turbo model

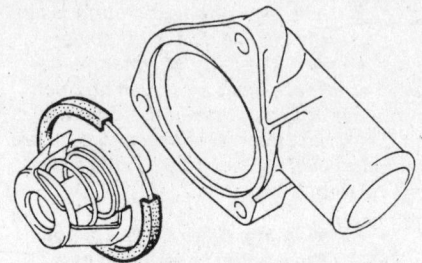
5.5d Thermostat and housing - non-Turbo models

9 Lift the radiator up from the lower locating rubber bushes, until the thermostatic switch wiring plug can be disconnected, then withdraw the radiator from the engine compartment (see illustration).

Inspection and cleaning

10 Radiator repair is best left to a specialist, but minor leaks may be sealed using a radiator sealant. Clear the radiator matrix of flies and small leaves with a soft brush, or by hosing.

11 If the radiator is to be left out of the vehicle for more than 48 hours, special precautions must be taken to prevent the brazing flux used during manufacture from reacting with the chloride elements remaining from the coolant. This reaction could cause the aluminium core to oxidize causing leakage. To prevent this, either flush the radiator thoroughly with clean water, dry with compressed air and seal all outlets, or refill the radiator with coolant and temporarily plug all outlets.

Refitting

12 Refitting is a reversal of removal, but check the condition of the mounting bushes and if necessary renew them. Refill the cooling system with reference to Chapter 1.

4 Expansion tank - removal, inspection and refitting

Note: *Refer to the warnings given in Section 1 of this Chapter before proceeding.*

Removal

1 With the engine cold, drain some coolant from the system until the expansion tank is empty.
2 Release the strap or the clip (as applicable) which secures the tank. Disconnect the hoses and remove the tank.

Inspection

3 Clean the tank and inspect it for cracks and other damage. Renew it if necessary. Also inspect the cap; if there is evidence that coolant has been vented through the cap, renew it.

Refitting

4 Refit by reversing the removal operations. Refill and bleed the cooling system as described in Chapter 1.

5 Thermostat - removal, testing and refitting

Note: *Refer to the warnings given in Section 1 of this Chapter before proceeding. A new sealing ring may be required on refitting.*

1 The thermostat is located in a housing bolted to the left-hand end of the cylinder head.

Removal

2 Where necessary, disconnect the crankcase breather hose and move the hose to one side to improve access to the thermostat housing.

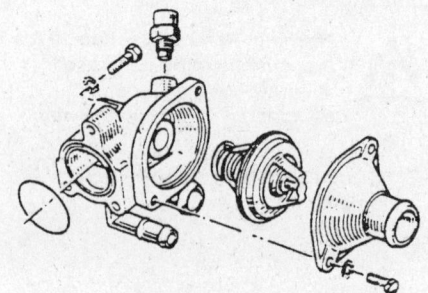
5.5e Thermostat and housing components - Turbo models

3 Partially drain the cooling system, so that the coolant level is below the thermostat location.
4 Where applicable, disconnect the battery negative lead, then disconnect the wiring plug from the coolant temperature sensor located in the thermostat housing.
5 Unbolt the housing (non-Turbo models), or the housing cover (Turbo models), and remove the thermostat, then remove the sealing ring (see illustrations).
6 If the housing or cover (as applicable) is stuck, tap it sharply with a plastic or hide mallet.

Testing

7 To test whether the unit is serviceable, suspend it on a string in a saucepan of cold water, together with a thermometer. Heat the water, and note the temperature at which the thermostat begins to open. Continue heating

5.8 Thermostat opening temperature (83°C)

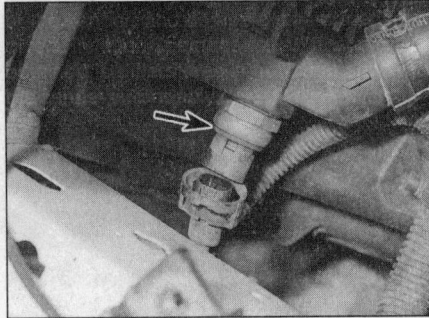

7.1 Cooling fan thermostatic switch (arrowed) in radiator

8.1 Temperature gauge/warning light sender unit (arrowed) - Turbo model

the water until the thermostat is fully open, and then remove it from the water.

8 The temperature at which the thermostat should start to open is stamped on the unit **(see illustration)**. If the thermostat does not start to open at the specified temperature, does not fully open in boiling water, or does not fully close when removed from the water, then it must be discarded and a new one fitted.

Refitting

9 Refitting is a reversal of removal, but where applicable renew the sealing ring. Refill the cooling system as described in Chapter 1.

6 Electric cooling fan assembly - removal and refitting

Removal

1 Where applicable, for improved access, release the securing clips, and remove the plastic shield from above the radiator.
2 Where applicable, remove the nut or bolt securing the power steering fluid reservoir bracket to the side of the cooling fan shroud.
3 Remove the shroud/fan assembly from the radiator by unscrewing the bolts or, where necessary, by drilling the heads off the rivets.
4 Unscrew the nut or extract the retaining clip and slide the fan off the motor shaft.
5 The motor can now be removed by drilling out the retaining rivets, or unscrewing the mounting nuts and bolts, as applicable.

Refitting

6 Refitting is a reversal of removal, but where applicable, use new rivets.

7 Electric cooling fan thermostatic switch - testing, removal and refitting

Testing

1 The thermostatic switch is located in the side of the radiator. The switch may be on the left or the right-hand side of the radiator depending on model **(see illustration)**. If it develops a fault it is most likely to fail

open-circuit. This will result in the fan motor remaining stationary even though the coolant temperature exceeds the switch-on point. The coolant may even reach boiling point.
2 To test for a faulty thermostatic switch, disconnect the wiring from the switch, then bridge the two wires with a suitable length of wire. If the fan now operates with the ignition switched on, the thermostatic switch is proved faulty and must be renewed. If the fan is still inoperative, this proves that there is a fault in the fan motor or associated wiring.

Removal

Note: *Refer to the warnings given in Section 1 of this Chapter before proceeding.*
3 To remove the switch, disconnect the battery negative terminal and drain the cooling system, as described in Chapter 1.
4 Disconnect the wiring plug, then unscrew the switch from the radiator. Remove the sealing washer.

Refitting

5 Refitting is a reversal of removal, but fit a new sealing washer and fully tighten the switch.
6 On completion, refill the cooling system as described in Chapter 1.

8 Temperature gauge/warning light sender unit - testing, removal and refitting

1 The location of the temperature gauge/warning light sender unit varies according to model. On non-Turbo models, the sender is located at the front or rear left-hand end of the cylinder head (depending on model). On Turbo engines, the sender is located in the thermostat housing **(see illustration)**. In all cases, the procedures are the same.

Testing

Note: *An ohmmeter will be required for testing.*
2 Disconnect the wiring plug from the sender. Using an ohmmeter, measure the resistance of the sender, and compare it with the values given in the Specifications. If the value obtained is differs greatly from that specified, the sender is probably defective.

3 For accurate testing across the temperature range, the sender unit will have to be removed.

Removal

Note: *Refer to the warnings given in Section 1 of this Chapter before proceeding. Suitable sealant will be required when refitting.*
4 Drain the cooling system (Chapter 1). Alternatively, remove the expansion tank cap to depressurise the system, and have the new sender or a suitable bung to hand.
5 Disconnect the wiring plug and unscrew the sender.

Refitting

6 Apply a little sealant to the sender threads, and screw it into position. Reconnect the wiring plug.
7 Top-up or refill the cooling system as necessary (see Chapter 1).

9 Water pump - removal and refitting

Note: *Refer to the warnings given in Section 1 of this Chapter before proceeding. A new gasket must be used on refitting.*

Removal

1 Disconnect the battery negative lead, then refer to Chapter 1 and drain the cooling system.
2 Remove the alternator as described in Chapter 5.
3 Unscrew the three bolts and remove the pump pulley **(see illustration)**.

9.3 Removing the water pump pulley

4 Working through the top of the engine compartment, unscrew the bolts securing the water pump to the cylinder block **(see illustration)**. Note that some of the bolts cannot be removed completely due to limited clearance, and must be removed with the pump.

5 Withdraw the pump from its location **(see illustration)**. It may be necessary to lever the engine slightly away from the right-hand body panel, using a suitable lever, to allow sufficient clearance to remove the pump (the engine should move sufficiently without disconnecting the mountings). If this is done, take care not to damage any of the surrounding components. If the pump is stuck, tap it sharply with a plastic or hide mallet. Remove the gasket.

Refitting

6 Clean the mating faces of the water pump and cylinder block.

7 Locate the water pump on the cylinder block together with a new gasket, and with the relevant bolts fitted to the pump flange. If necessary, lever the engine slightly away from the body as during removal.

8 Insert the remaining bolts and tighten them.

9 Refit the pump pulley and tighten the bolts.

10 Refit the alternator as described in Chapter 5, and tension the drivebelt with reference to Chapter 1.

11 Refill the cooling system (Chapter 1), then re-connect the battery leads.

10 Auxiliary water pump (Turbo models) - general

The auxiliary water pump fitted to Turbo models is electrically operated.

The pump is connected in parallel with the heater coolant circuit, and circulates coolant through the turbocharger to cool the bearings. The pump continues to operate for a period after the engine stops, preventing the turbocharger bearings from overheating and prolonging their life.

11 Auxiliary water pump (Turbo models) - removal and refitting

Note: *Refer to the warnings given in Section 1 of this Chapter before proceeding.*

Removal

1 The pump is located in a clamp mounted on the front suspension subframe, behind the gearbox **(see illustration)**.

2 Disconnect the battery negative lead.

3 Drain the cooling system as described in Chapter 1.

4 Apply the handbrake, then jack up the front of the vehicle and support securely on axle stands (see *"Jacking, towing and wheel changing"*). Where applicable, remove the

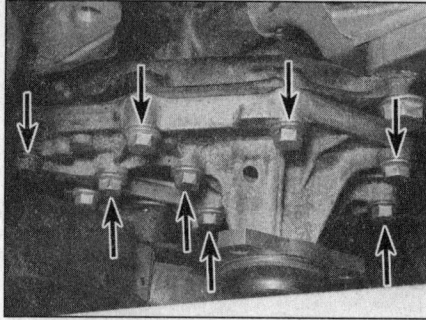

9.4 Water pump securing bolts (arrowed) - not all bolts are visible

engine undershield to improve access.

5 Disconnect the pump wiring plug, and unclip the connector from the pump clamp bracket.

6 Loosen the securing clips, and disconnect the two coolant hoses from the pump, noting their locations to ensure correct refitting **(see illustration)**.

7 Unscrew the pump clamp bolt, and unclip the top half of the clamp **(see illustration)**.

8 Working at the rear of the subframe, lift out the pump complete with its rubber, then remove the rubber from the pump **(see illustration)**.

Refitting

9 Refitting is a reversal of removal, noting that the wider shoulder of the mounting rubber fits towards the front of the vehicle.

10 Refill the cooling system as described in Chapter 1.

12 Heating system - general information and checks

General information

The heater and fresh air ventilation unit works on the principle of mixing hot and cold air in the proportions selected by means of the central (temperature) control knob. Coolant flows through the heater matrix all the time that the engine is running, regardless of the temperature selected.

Air distribution is selected by the left-hand control knob. Additional control is possible by

9.5 Withdrawing the water pump

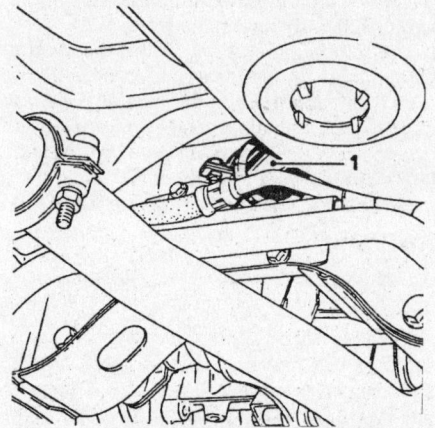

11.1 Auxiliary water pump location (1) - Turbo models

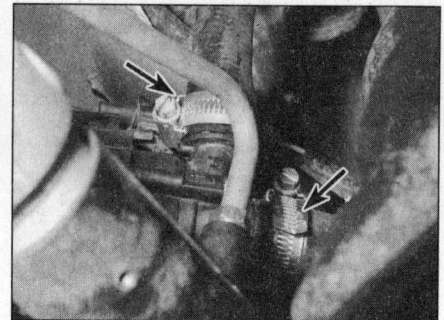

11.6 Auxiliary water pump coolant hose connections (arrowed)

11.7 Unclip the top half of the auxiliary water pump clamp (arrowed)

11.8 Lifting out the auxiliary water pump

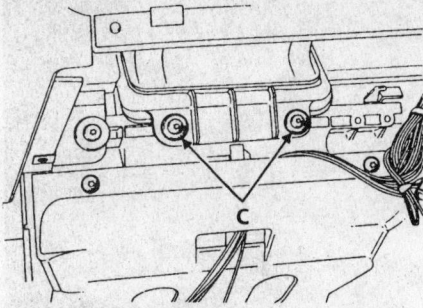

13.8 Heater unit-to-facia bracket securing bolts (C)

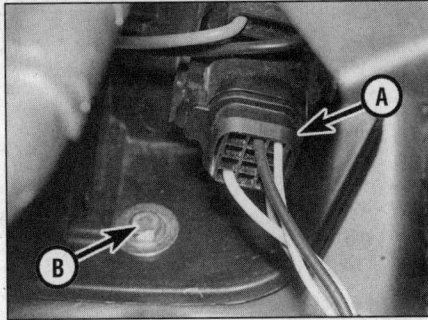

14.2 Heater blower unit wiring (A) and mounting bolt (B)

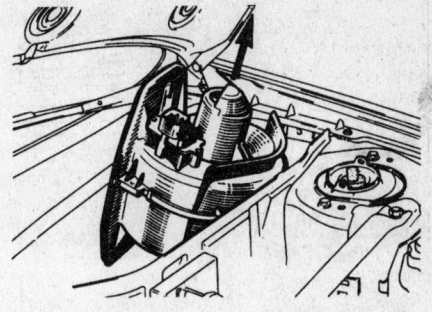

14.3 Removing the heater blower unit

opening, closing or redirecting individual vents in the facia panel.

A three-speed blower is controlled by the right-hand knob.

For details of the air conditioning system fitted to some models, refer to Section 19.

Checks

Periodically check that all the controls operate as intended. Problems related to the temperature and air distribution controls may be due to cables being broken or disconnected (Section 18).

If the blower does not operate at all, check the fuse and the blower multi-plug before condemning the motor. If one or two speeds do not work, the fault is almost certainly in the resistor unit (Section 16).

Check the condition and security of the coolant hoses which feed the heater matrix. The matrix-to-hose joints are at the bulkhead under the bonnet. If water leaks inside the vehicle seem to be coming from the heater, establish whether the leak is of coolant (indicating a leaking heater matrix) or of rainwater (indicating a defective scuttle seal). Cooling system antifreeze has a distinctive sweet smell.

13 Heater unit - removal and refitting

Note: *Refer to the warnings given in Section 1 of this Chapter before proceeding.*

Removal

1 Disconnect the battery negative lead.
2 Remove the complete facia panel with reference to Chapter 11.
3 Remove the upper seal from the scuttle to the rear of the engine compartment. Also remove the external air inlet grilles.
4 Disconnect the wiring from the heater blower motor.
5 Remove the heater blower unit with reference to Section 14.
6 Drain the cooling system with reference to Chapter 1.
7 Loosen the two clips and disconnect the hoses from the heater matrix.

8 Unbolt the heater unit and remove it from inside the vehicle **(see illustration)**.

Refitting

9 Check that the seals are in good condition, then locate the unit on the bulkhead.
10 Position the blower motor over the heater and insert the bolts finger-tight. Also insert the heater mounting bolts.
11 Check and if necessary adjust the heater control cables (Section 18).
12 Connect the hoses to the heater unit and tighten the clips.
13 Tighten the heater and blower motor mounting bolts, then reconnect the wiring to the blower motor.
14 Refit the upper seal to the scuttle and also refit the external air inlet grilles.
15 Refit the facia panel with reference to Chapter 11.
16 Refill the cooling system with reference to Chapter 1.
17 Reconnect the battery leads with reference to Chapter 5.

14 Heater blower unit - removal and refitting

Removal

1 Working under the bonnet, remove the scuttle upper seal and the external air inlet grille.
2 Disconnect the wiring from the blower unit **(see illustration)**.
3 Unscrew the two mounting bolts, then remove the unit from the left-hand side of the bulkhead **(see illustration)**. It is necessary to turn the unit on its side to do this.
4 Release the clips, then separate the two half-casings of the unit and remove the motor assembly **(see illustrations)**. If the unit has not previously been separated from new, the two casings will be hot-crimped together and it will be necessary to split them apart with a knife.

Refitting

5 Locate the motor assembly in the two half-casings making sure that the wiring connector can be fitted without stress.

6 Fit the casings together and secure with clips which are available in a kit from Renault dealers. The kit also contains a new seal for fitting to the unit. Do not refit the original seal, since if it does not seal correctly, there is a risk of water entry into the passenger compartment.
7 Refit the unit and tighten the mounting bolts.
8 Reconnect the wiring to the blower unit.
9 Refit the external air inlet grille and the scuttle upper seal.

15 Heater matrix - removal and refitting

Removal

1 Remove the heater unit with reference to Section 13.
2 Prise out the retaining clips, then pull out the matrix **(see illustration)**. Take care not to damage the air control flaps.

14.4a Release the securing clips . . .

14.4b . . . and separate the two half-casings for access to the motor assembly

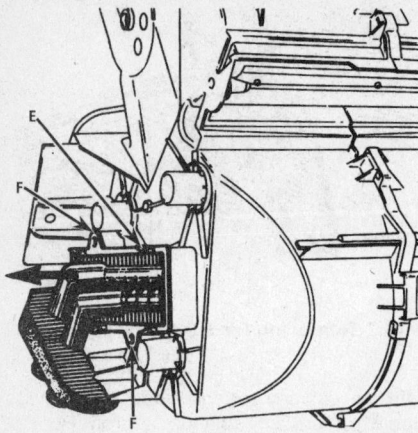

15.2 Removing the heater matrix

E *Retaining clips*
F *Mounting screw locations*

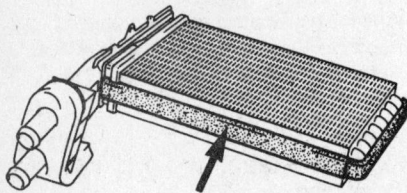

15.3 Heater matrix sealing foam (arrowed)

Refitting

3 Check that the sealing foam is in good condition, then insert the matrix and retain with the clips **(see illustration)**. If the clips have been broken during removal, fit two screws instead (see illustration 15.2).
4 Refit the heater unit with reference to Section 13.

16 Heater resistor unit - removal and refitting

Removal

1 Working under the bonnet, remove the scuttle upper seal and external air inlet grille.
2 Unplug the wiring connector, then unscrew the two mounting screws.
3 Pull the clips apart and remove the resistor unit **(see illustration)**.

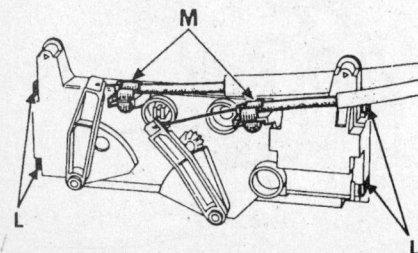

16.3 Heater resistor unit location

A *Wiring connector*   H *Securing clip*
G *Mounting screw*

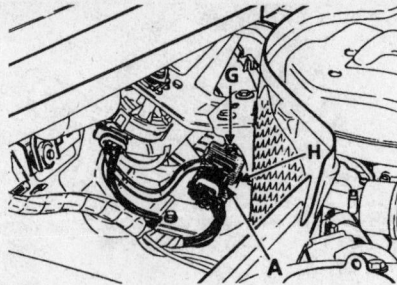

17.2a Heater control panel mounting screw (arrowed)

Refitting

4 If the resistor unit is being removed because it has been damaged, check that the heater fan motor turns freely before refitting it.
5 Refitting is a reversal of removal.

17 Heater control panel - removal and refitting

Removal

1 Unscrew the two screws securing the central lower cover beneath the heater control panel. Remove the cover **(see illustration)**.
2 Unscrew the two mounting screws, then remove the control panel by releasing it at the bottom and removing the four clips **(see illustrations)**.
3 Disconnect the cables by releasing the clips.
4 If desired, the trim panel can be removed

17.1 Removing the lower heater cover

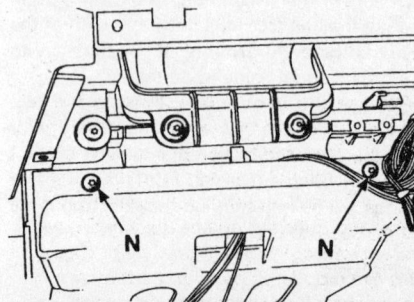

17.2b Removing the heater control panel

from the control panel by releasing the four securing clips **(see illustration)**.

Refitting

5 Refitting is a reversal of removal.

18 Heater control cables - removal and refitting

Removal

1 Remove the control panel as described in Section 17.
2 Remove the air deflector (two screws) **(see illustration)**.
3 Release the relevant cable from the flap control lever by releasing the clip and turning it through a quarter turn.

Refitting

4 Refit the cable so that it is flush with the sheath stop.

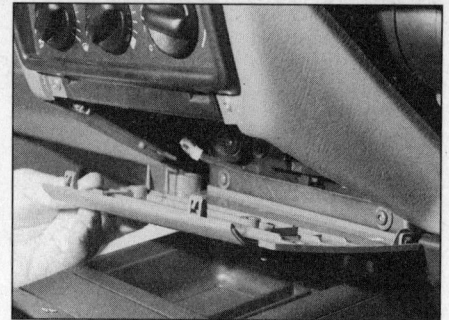

17.4 Heater control panel trim securing clips (L) and control cable clips (M)

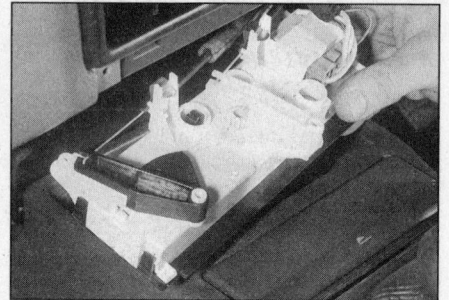

18.2 Air deflector securing screws (N)

18.8 Heater unit mixer flap return spring location (P)

5 Turn the control knobs to the "ventilation" and "cold" positions.
6 Refit the control panel.
7 Place the control flaps in the "ventilation" and "cold" positions, then align the marks on the flap control sections.
8 Refit the mixer flap return spring (air mixer control), then the air deflector and lower cover **(see illustration)**. Note that the control cables are of different lengths - the longer one controls the mixer flap.

19 Air conditioning system - general information and precautions

General information

1 An air conditioning system is available on some models. It enables the temperature of incoming air to be lowered; it also dehumidifies the air, which makes for rapid demisting and increased comfort **(see illustration)**.
2 The cooling side of the system works in the same way as a domestic refrigerator. Refrigerant gas is drawn into a belt-driven compressor, and passes into a condenser in front of the radiator, where it loses heat and becomes liquid. The liquid passes through an expansion valve to an evaporator, where it changes from liquid under high pressure to gas under low pressure. This change is accompanied by a drop in temperature, which cools the evaporator. The refrigerant returns to the compressor and the cycle begins again.
3 Air blown through the evaporator passes to the air distribution unit, where it is mixed with hot air blown through the heater matrix, to achieve the desired temperature in the passenger compartment.
4 The heating side of the system is identical to that for models without air conditioning.

Precautions

⚠️ *Warning: The refrigerant (Freon R12) is potentially dangerous, and should only be handled by qualified persons. If it is splashed onto the skin, it can cause frostbite. It is not itself poisonous, but in the presence of a naked flame (including a cigarette) it forms a poisonous gas.*

⚠️ *Warning: Uncontrolled discharging of the refrigerant is dangerous, and potentially damaging to the environment. It follows that any work on the air conditioning system which involves opening the refrigerant circuit must only be carried out by a Renault dealer or an air conditioning specialist.*

⚠️ *Warning: Do not operate the air conditioning system if it is known to be short of refrigerant; the compressor may be damaged.*

19.1 Air conditioning system components
A *Passenger compartment*
B *Engine compartment*
C *Outside air*
D *To air distribution unit*
E *Bulkhead*
F *Incoming air (fresh or recirculated)*
1 *Compressor*
2 *Condenser*
3 *Reservoir*
4 *Pressure switch*
5 *High pressure bleed*
6 *Pressure relief valve*
7 *Thermostat*
8 *Evaporator*
9 *Low-pressure bleed*
10 *Blower*
11 *Cooling fans*
12 *Cooling system radiator*
13 *Liquid at high pressure*
14 *Gas at low pressure*
15 *Gas at high pressure*

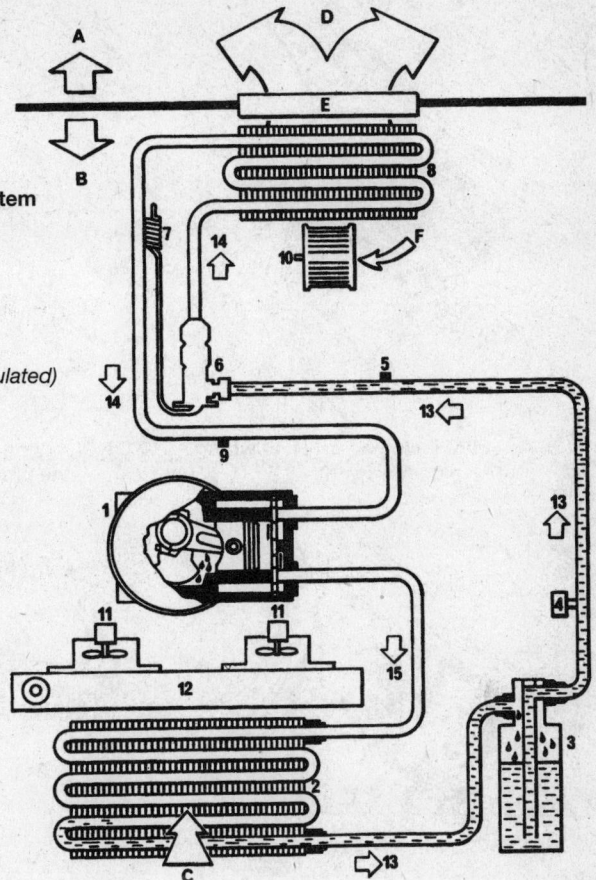

20 Air conditioning system - checking and maintenance

1 Routine maintenance is limited to checking the tension and condition of the compressor drivebelt, and checking the refrigerant sight glass for bubbles. Refer to Chapter 1.
2 Periodic recharging of the system will be required, since there is inevitably a slow loss of refrigerant. It is suggested that the system is inspected by a specialist every 2 years, or at once if a loss of performance is noticed.

21 Air conditioning system components - removal and refitting

⚠️ *Warning: The system should be professionally discharged before carrying out any of the following work. Under no circumstances attempt to open any of the connections or discharge the system without professional help. Cap or plug the pipe lines as soon as they are disconnected to prevent the entry of moisture. Refer to the precautions given in Section 1 before proceeding.*

Blower unit and fan motor
Removal

1 Disconnect the battery leads.
2 Where applicable, unbolt and remove the strengthening bar from between the front suspension turrets.
3 Remove the preheating control unit from the bulkhead.
4 Remove the five securing screws, and withdraw the scuttle bulkhead cover **(see illustration)**.

21.4 Three of the scuttle bulkhead cover securing screws (A)

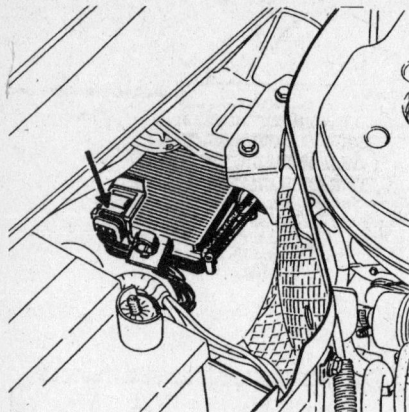

21.5 Air conditioning control unit wiring plug (arrowed)

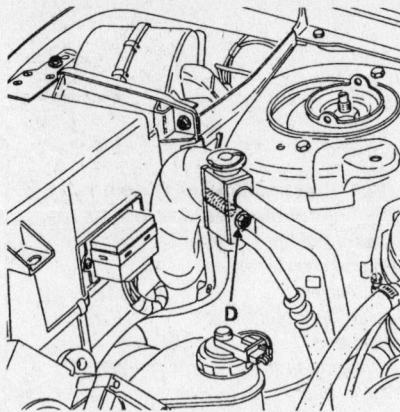

21.6 Disconnect the refrigerant pipes from the pressure relief valve (D)

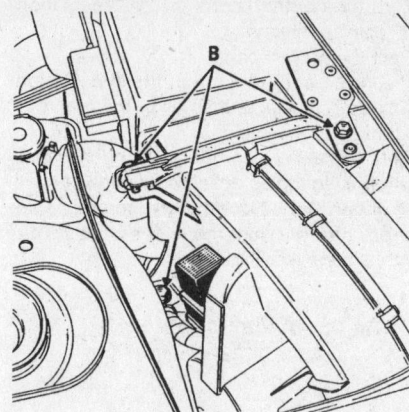

21.7 Three bolts (B) securing the blower unit assembly to the ventilation unit body

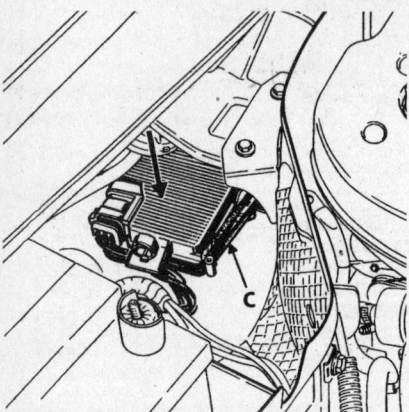

21.8 Remove the control unit assembly (arrowed) for access to the ventilation unit mounting bolt (C)

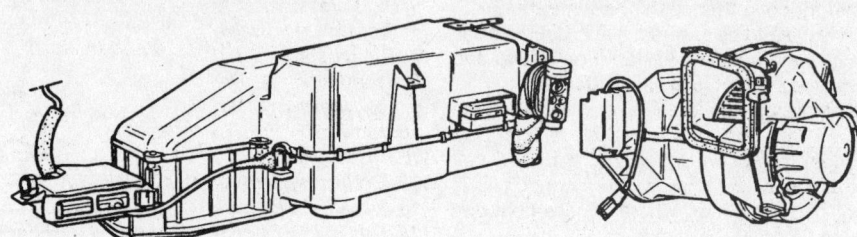

21.9 Blower unit assembly and ventilation unit removed from vehicle

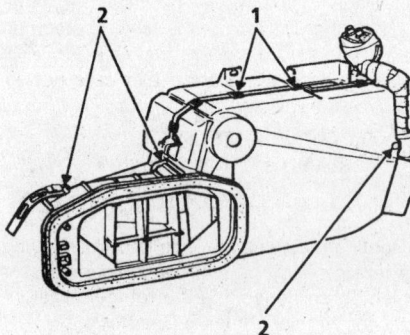

21.16 Clips (1) and screws (2) securing the ventilation unit half-casings together

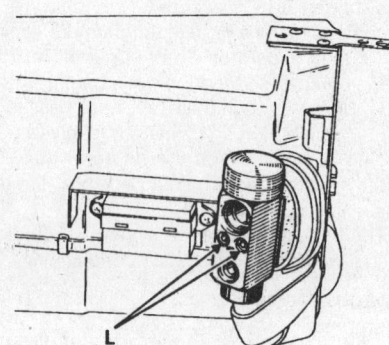

21.17 Pressure relief valve securing bolts (L)

5 Disconnect the wiring plug from the air conditioning control unit assembly (see illustration).

6 Refer to the warning at the beginning of this Section, then disconnect the refrigerant pipes from the pressure relief valve (see illustration). Plug or cover the ends of the pipes to prevent dirt ingress.

7 Unscrew the three bolts, and separate the blower unit assembly from the ventilation unit body (see illustration).

8 Release the retaining strap, and remove the control unit assembly from the scuttle for access to the ventilation unit mounting bolt (see illustration). Remove the mounting bolt.

9 Working inside the vehicle, unscrew the two ventilation unit mounting bolts from under the left-hand side of the facia panel, then withdraw the ventilation unit and the blower unit assembly separately (see illustration).

10 To remove the fan motor, proceed as follows.

11 Pull the rubber cover from the blower unit, then unsolder the wiring.

12 Prise off the clips and separate the two half-casings.

13 Using a screwdriver, push back the rubber beads holding the motor in the casing. Pull the fan motor directly from the casings.

Refitting

14 Refitting is a reversal of removal, but make sure that the foam seals are in good condition and renew them if necessary. Have the system refilled by a refrigeration specialist.

Evaporator

Removal

15 Remove the blower unit as described previously.

16 Remove the clips and the three screws securing the two ventilation unit half-casings together (see illustration).

17 Unscrew the two securing bolts, and remove the pressure relief valve from the ventilation unit (see illustration).

18 Withdraw the evaporator.

Refitting

19 Refitting is a reversal of removal, but make sure that the foam seals are in good condition and renew them if necessary. Have the system recharged by a Renault dealer, or a refrigeration specialist.

Compressor

Note: *Due to changes in production procedures, certain models may be fitted with compressor mounting arrangements which differ in detail from those described in this Section. Where this is the case, make comprehensive notes during removal, to ensure correct refitting.*

Removal

20 Disconnect the battery leads.

21 Remove the alternator as described in Chapter 5.

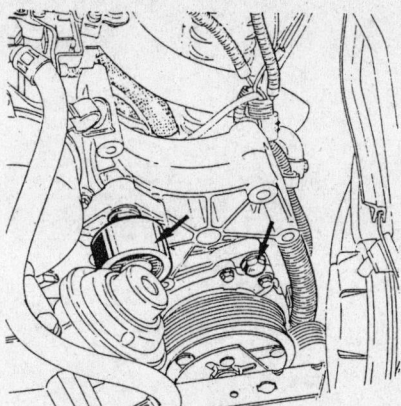

21.23 Auxiliary drivebelt guide roller/bracket assembly, and one of the upper air conditioning compressor-to-alternator mounting bracket securing bolts (arrowed)

22 Unscrew the securing bolts, and remove the power steering pump pulley from the pump drive flange. Note that it will be necessary to counterhold the pulley (eg, using an old drivebelt) in order to loosen the bolts.

23 Remove the securing bolts, and withdraw the auxiliary drivebelt guide roller/bracket assembly **(see illustration)**.

24 Remove the two upper bolts securing the air conditioning compressor to the alternator mounting bracket.

25 Apply the handbrake, then jack up the front of the vehicle and support securely on axle stands (see *"Jacking, towing and wheel changing"*).

26 Remove the engine undershield, where applicable.

27 Remove the right-hand front roadwheel and the wheel arch liner.

28 Loosen the lower air conditioning compressor mounting nuts and bolts, then pivot the compressor downwards to enable the alternator mounting bracket to be removed from above **(see illustration)**.

29 Disconnect the wiring from the compressor.

30 Unscrew the unions, and disconnect the two refrigerant pipes from the compressor.

31 Remove the lower mounting nuts and bolts, and withdraw the compressor.

Refitting

32 Refitting is a reversal of removal, bearing in mind the following points.

a) Before refitting the compressor, the oil level should be checked by a Renault dealer.

b) Check that all seals and pipes are in good condition, and renew any which are not, as necessary.

c) Refit the alternator as described in Chapter 5.

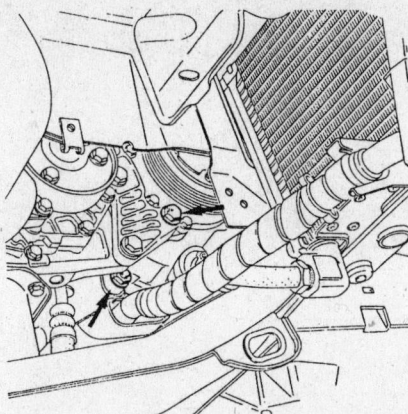

21.28 Air conditioning compressor lower mounting nuts and bolts (arrowed)

d) On completion, have the system recharged by a Renault dealer or air conditioning specialist.

Condenser

Removal

33 Drain the cooling system with reference to Chapter 1.

34 Where applicable, for improved access release the securing clips, and remove the plastic shield from above the radiator.

35 Where applicable, remove the nut securing the power steering fluid reservoir to the mounting bracket on the radiator, and move the reservoir clear. Take care not to strain the fluid hoses.

36 Disconnect the refrigerant lines from the condenser while counterholding the unions with a further spanner.

37 Disconnect the wiring plug from the cooling fan motor.

38 Remove the bolts securing the radiator upper mounting brackets to the engine compartment front panel.

39 Disconnect the top hose from the radiator.

40 Lift the radiator and condenser assembly upwards from the engine compartment.

41 Remove the screws and separate the condenser from the radiator **(see illustration)**.

Refitting

42 Refitting is a reversal of removal, but when reconnecting the lines to the condenser, oil them and hold the unions with a spanner to prevent any damage to the condenser.

43 Refill the cooling system as described in Chapter 1.

Fan control module

Removal

44 Remove the five securing screws, and withdraw the scuttle bulkhead cover.

45 Remove the two bolts securing the module to the control unit assembly, and withdraw the module **(see illustration)**.

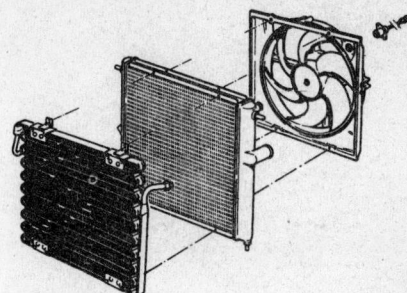

21.41 Air conditioning condenser, radiator and electric cooling fan

Refitting

46 Refitting is a reversal of removal.

Temperature sensor

Removal

47 Remove the five securing screws, and withdraw the scuttle bulkhead cover.

48 The sensor is located in the side of the air conditioning control unit assembly **(see illustration)**.

49 Disconnect the sensor wiring plug.

50 Release the locating tab, and turn the sensor 90° clockwise to remove it from the control unit.

Refitting

51 Refitting is a reversal of removal.

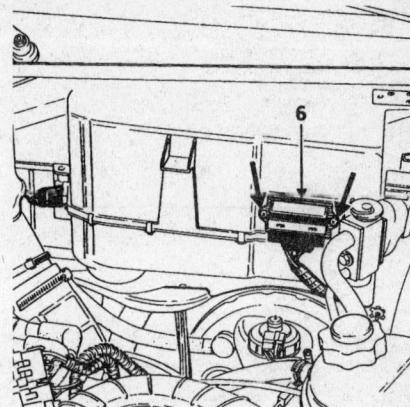

21.45 Fan control module (6) and securing bolts (arrowed)

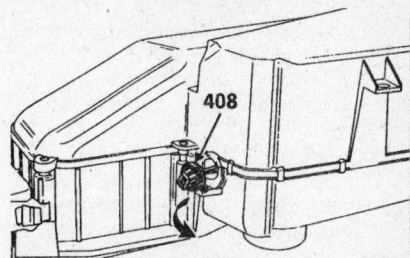

21.48 Air conditioning temperature sensor (408)

Chapter 4
Fuel, exhaust and emission control systems

Contents

Degrees of difficulty

Easy, suitable for novice with little experience	**Fairly easy,** suitable for beginner with some experience	**Fairly difficult,** suitable for competent DIY mechanic	**Difficult,** suitable for experienced DIY mechanic	**Very difficult,** suitable for expert DIY or professional

Specifications

Note: *The engine code appears on a plate attached to the engine. Refer to "Buying spare parts and vehicle identification numbers" for further details.*

General

System type . . . . Rear-mounted fuel tank, distributor fuel injection pump with integral transfer pump, indirect injection. Turbocharger and intercooler on F8Q 740 and F8Q 744 engines

Firing order . . . . 1-3-4-2 (No 1 at flywheel end)

Fuel

Type . . . . Commercial diesel fuel for road vehicles (DERV)
Fuel tank capacity . . . . 55 litres

Maximum speed

Bosch injection pump:
   F8Q 706 engine . . . . 5200 to 5400 rpm
   F8Q 742 engine . . . . 5100 to 5300 rpm
Lucas injection pump:
   F8Q 706 and F8Q 764 engines . . . . 5100 to 5300 rpm
   F8Q 740 and F8Q 744 engines . . . . 4800 to 5000 rpm

Fast idle speed

Bosch injection pump . . . . 1000 ± 50 rpm
Lucas injection pump . . . . Not adjustable (factory set)

4

Injection pump (Bosch)

Direction of rotation	Clockwise viewed from sprocket end
Static timing:	
Engine position	No 1 cylinder at TDC (see Section 16)
Pump position:	
All engines except F8Q 706 from early 1993*	0.70 ± 0.02 mm
F8Q 706 engine from early 1993*	0.82 ± 0.02 mm
Dynamic timing	No information available at time of writing

From early 1993, the pump on F8Q 706 engines was modified to meet revised European exhaust emissions regulations. Applicable pumps can be identified from the timing value marked on the pump accelerator lever.

Injection pump (Lucas CAV/Roto-Diesel)

Direction of rotation	Clockwise viewed from sprocket end
Static timing:	
Engine position	No 1 cylinder at TDC (see Section 15)
Pump position	Value shown on pump (see Section 15)
Dynamic timing	No information available at time of writing

Injectors

Type	Pintle
Opening pressure:	
All except F8Q 706 and F8Q 764 engines with Lucas pump	130 + 8 bars - 5
F8Q 706 and F8Q 764 engines with Lucas injection pump	118 + 7 bars - 5

Turbocharger

Type	Garrett T2	
Boost pressure (full load)	0.8 to 0.9 bar approximately	
Speed of rotation	Approximately 150 000 rpm	
Wastegate pressure settings:	**Control pressure**	**Adjustment pressure**
Actuator rod movement 0.38 mm	1020 to 1080 mbars	1050 to 1080 mbars
Actuator rod movement 4.0 mm	1180 to 1260 mbars	1220 to 1260 mbars

Torque wrench settings

	Nm	**lbf ft**
Fuel injectors to cylinder head	70	52
Fuel pipe union nuts and bolts	25	18
Injection pump timing hole blanking plug:		
Lucas pump	5	4
Bosch pump	10	7
Injection pump mounting nuts and bolts	25	18
Injection pump sprocket securing nut	50	37
Injection pump sprocket adjuster bolts (two-piece adjustable sprocket)	20	15
Fast idle thermostatic actuator-to-cylinder head	35	26
Turbocharger-to-manifold nuts	45	33
Exhaust front section-to-turbocharger nuts	45	33
Wastegate bracket-to-turbocharger bolts*	15	11
Wastegate actuator rod locknut	6 to 8	4 to 6
Coolant pipe-to-turbocharger union nuts	20 to 30	15 to 22
Oil feed pipe-to-turbocharger union nut	15 to 25	11 to 18
Oil return pipe-to-turbocharger union nut	40	30

Coat the bolt threads with thread-locking compound

1 General information and precautions

General information

1 The fuel system consists of a rear-mounted fuel tank, a fuel filter with integral water separator, a fuel injection pump, injectors and associated components (see illustration). As it passes through the filter, the fuel is heated by coolant flowing through the filter bowl. A turbocharger and intercooler are fitted to the F8Q 740 and F8Q 744 engines. The exhaust system is conventional, but on certain models, an exhaust gas recirculation (EGR) system and/or an unregulated catalytic converter may be fitted to reduce exhaust gas emissions (see Section 26 for further details).

2 Fuel is drawn from the fuel tank to the fuel injection pump by a vane-type transfer pump incorporated in the fuel injection pump. Before reaching the pump the fuel passes through a fuel filter where foreign matter and water are removed. Excess fuel lubricates the moving components of the pump and is then returned to the tank.

3 The fuel injection pump is driven at half crankshaft speed by the timing belt. The high pressure required to inject the fuel into the compressed air in the swirl chambers is achieved by a cam plate acting on a single piston on the Bosch pump, or by two opposed pistons forced together by rollers running in a cam ring on the Lucas/CAV pump (see illustration). The fuel passes through a central rotor with a single outlet drilling which aligns with ports leading to the injector pipes.

4 Fuel metering is controlled by a centrifugal governor which reacts to accelerator pedal position and engine speed. The governor is linked to a metering valve which increases or

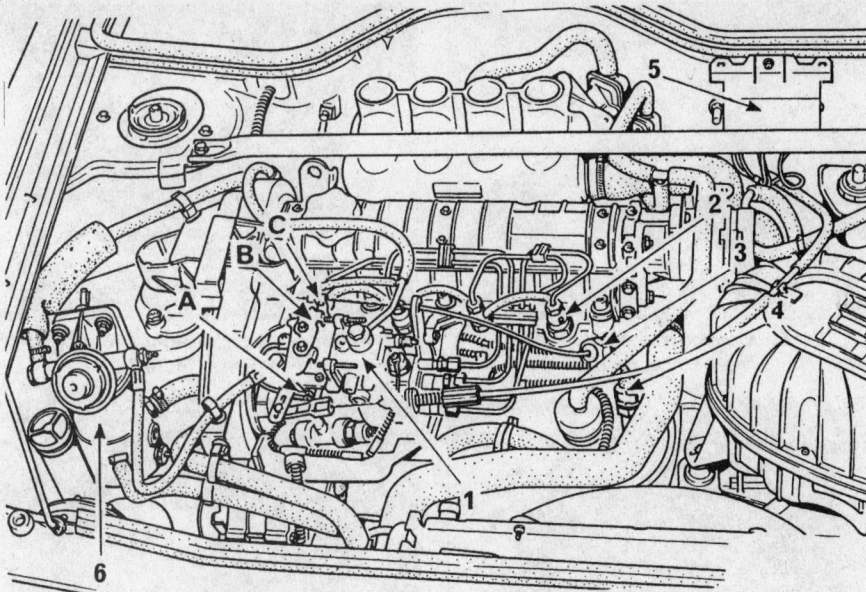

1.1 Typical underbonnet fuel system component locations - non-Turbo models

1 *Injection pump*
2 *Fuel injector*
3 *Fast idle thermostatic actuator*
4 *Coolant temperature switch (post-heating cut-off)*
5 *Preheating control unit*
6 *Fuel filter*
A *No-load switch*
B *Accelerator lever*
C *Idle and fast idle lever*

decreases the amount of fuel delivered at each pumping stroke. On turbocharged models a separate device also increases fuel delivery with increasing boost pressure.

5 Basic injection timing is determined when the pump is fitted. When the engine is running it is varied automatically to suit the prevailing engine speed by a mechanism which turns the cam plate or ring.

6 A solenoid valve in the pump is used to advance the injection timing briefly after a cold start. The system operates by increasing the pump transfer pressure via a restrictor valve.

7 The four fuel injectors produce a homogeneous spray of fuel into the swirl chambers located in the cylinder head. The injectors are calibrated to open and close at critical pressures to provide efficient and even combustion. Each injector needle is lubricated by fuel which accumulates in the spring chamber and is channelled to the injection pump return hose by leak-off pipes.

8 Bosch or Lucas CAV/Roto-Diesel fuel system components may be fitted, depending on model. Components from the latter manufacturer are marked either "CAV", "Roto-Diesel" or "Con-Diesel", depending on their date and place of manufacture. Replacement components must be of the same make as those originally fitted.

9 Cold starting is assisted by preheater or "glow" plugs fitted to each swirl chamber (see Chapter 5 for further details).

10 The fast idle system is operated either by a thermostatic actuator, or a vacuum actuator, depending on model.

11 On models with a thermostatic fast idle actuator, a thermostatic sensor in the cooling system operates a fast idle lever on the injection pump, via a cable, to increase the idling speed when the engine is cold.

12 On models with a vacuum actuator, the fast idle cable is operated by a vacuum-controlled (brake servo vacuum) actuator, via a solenoid valve. The solenoid valve is controlled by the preheating system control unit, and on models with air conditioning, an additional input is provided by the air conditioning compressor clutch relay.

13 A stop solenoid cuts the fuel supply to the injection pump rotor when the ignition is switched off, and there is also a hand-operated stop lever for use in an emergency **(see illustration)**.

14 Provided that the specified maintenance is carried out, the fuel injection equipment will give long and trouble-free service. The injection pump itself may well outlast the engine. The main potential cause of damage to the injection pump and injectors is dirt or water in the fuel.

15 Servicing of the injection pump and injectors is very limited for the home mechanic, and any dismantling or adjustment other than that described in this Chapter must be entrusted to a Renault dealer or fuel injection specialist.

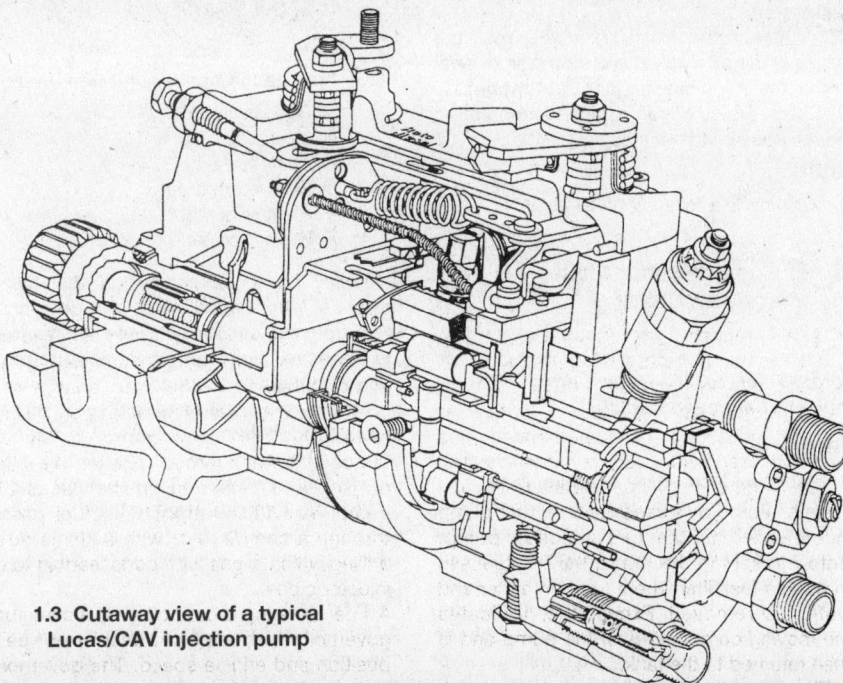

1.3 Cutaway view of a typical Lucas/CAV injection pump

1.13 Hand-operated stop lever (arrowed) - Lucas injection pump

2.3 Air cleaner body mounting nut - non-Turbo model

2.4 Air cleaner rubber mounting - non-Turbo model

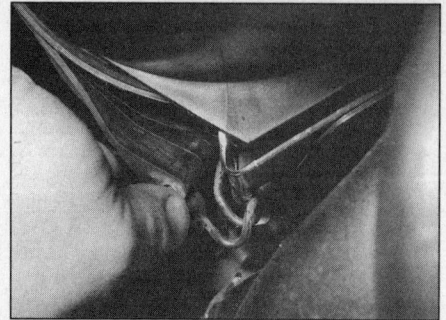
2.7 Release the air cleaner securing strap - Turbo model

2.8 Disconnect the air trunking . . .

2.9 . . . and lift out the air cleaner - Turbo model

3.2 Fuel gauge sender unit and connections

Precautions

⚠️ **Warning: It is necessary to take certain precautions when working on the fuel system components, particularly the fuel injectors. Before carrying out any operations on the fuel system, refer to the precautions given in "Safety first!" at the beginning of this manual, and to any additional warning notes at the start of the relevant Sections.**

2 Air cleaner housing assembly - removal and refitting

Non-Turbo models

Removal

1 Remove the air cleaner filter element as described in Chapter 1.
2 Disconnect the fresh air hose from the bottom of the air cleaner and from the front left-hand corner of the engine compartment.
3 Unscrew the mounting nuts and withdraw the air cleaner body from the engine compartment **(see illustration)**.
4 Check the condition of the rubber mountings where applicable and renew them as necessary **(see illustration)**. Also check the hoses and hose clips for condition.

Refitting

5 Refitting is a reversal of removal.

Turbo models

Removal

6 Remove the air cleaner filter element as described in Chapter 1.
7 Release the strap securing the air cleaner body to the support bracket **(see illustration)**.
8 Disconnect the air trunking connecting the air cleaner casing to the turbocharger **(see illustration)**.
9 Disconnect the fresh air hose from the bottom of the air cleaner, and lift the air cleaner from its mounting bracket **(see illustration)**.
10 Check the condition of the securing strap and the hoses and hose clips.

Refitting

11 Refitting is a reversal of removal.

3 Fuel gauge sender unit - removal and refitting

Note: *Refer to the precautions given in Section 1 before proceeding.*

Removal

1 Disconnect the battery negative lead.
2 Working in the rear luggage compartment, lift the carpet and prise out the rubber cover to gain access to the fuel gauge sender unit **(see illustration)**.
3 Disconnect the wiring connector from the sender unit, and secure it in the luggage compartment to prevent it from falling out of reach beneath the rear floor.

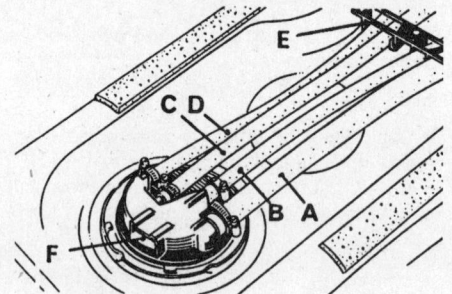
3.4 Fuel gauge sender unit and hoses

A Degassing pipe
B Vent pipe
C Fuel feed pipe
D Fuel return pipe
E Hose retaining clip
F Wiring connector socket

4 Identify the hoses for position, then loosen the clips, where applicable, and disconnect them from the sender unit **(see illustration)**. Tie the hoses and wiring connector together and move them to one side.
5 Unscrew the plastic ring nut. To do this it is recommended that a removal tool is made out of a U-shaped piece of metal which will engage with the lugs on the ring nut.
6 With the ring nut removed, withdraw the sender unit from the fuel tank, followed by the special gasket. Be prepared for fuel spillage.

Refitting

7 Refitting is a reversal of removal, but use a new gasket if the old one is damaged or shows signs of deterioration.

4.5 Fuel tank mounting bolt (arrowed)

4 Fuel tank - removal and refitting

Note: *Refer to the precautions given in Section 1 before proceeding.*

Removal

1 A drain plug is not provided on the fuel tank, and it is therefore preferable to carry out the removal operation when the tank is nearly empty. Before proceeding, disconnect the battery negative lead and then syphon or hand pump the remaining fuel from the tank.
2 Chock the front wheels, then jack up the rear of the vehicle and support it securely on axle stands (see *"Jacking, towing and wheel changing"*).
3 Remove the spare wheel, then unbolt the spare wheel carrier from the underbody.
4 Loosen the clip(s) and disconnect the filler hose from the fuel tank.
5 Take the weight of the fuel tank using a trolley jack together with an interposed block of wood. Unscrew and remove the fuel tank mounting bolts **(see illustration)**.
6 Lower the fuel tank sufficiently to gain access to the hose connections on the fuel gauge sender unit. As the tank is being lowered, release the hose retaining clip on the top of the tank.
7 Disconnect the fuel gauge sender wiring connector.
8 Identify the hoses for position, then loosen the clips and disconnect them from the sender unit.
9 Lower the fuel tank to the ground.

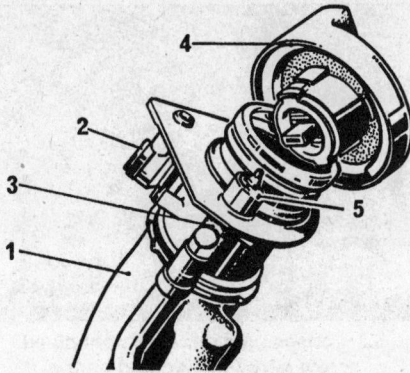

5.3 Fuel tank filler pipe

1 Filler pipe   4 Cap
2 Safety valve 5 Plunger
3 Filling limiter

10 If the tank is contaminated with sediment or water, remove the sender unit as described in Section 3 and swill the tank out with clean fuel. If the tank is damaged, or if leaks are apparent, it should be repaired by a specialist, or alternatively, renewed.

Refitting

11 Refitting is a reversal of removal, but make sure that the hoses are correctly reconnected and that they are not trapped as the tank is lifted into place.

5 Fuel tank filler pipe - removal and refitting

Note: *Refer to the precautions given in Section 1 before proceeding.*

Removal

1 A drain plug is not provided on the fuel tank, and it is therefore preferable to carry out the removal operation when the tank is nearly empty. Before proceeding, disconnect the battery negative lead and then syphon or hand pump the remaining fuel from the tank.
2 Chock the front wheels, then jack up the rear of the vehicle, and support it securely on axle stands (see *"Jacking, towing and wheel changing"*).

6.1 Disconnecting the accelerator cable from the injection pump

3 Loosen the clip and disconnect the filler hose from the filler pipe **(see illustration)**.
4 Identify the pipes for position, then disconnect them from the filler pipe.
5 Open the fuel filler flap and remove the cap.
6 Unscrew the cross-head screws located inside the filler flap recess, and remove the filler pipe assembly.

Refitting

7 Refitting is a reversal of removal.

6 Accelerator cable - removal, refitting and adjustment

Removal

1 Working in the engine compartment, operate the accelerator lever on the fuel injection pump, and release the cable inner from the lever. Alternatively, on models with a press-fit balljoint cable end fitting, pull the cable end from the lever **(see illustration)**.
2 Pull the cable outer ferrule from the grommet in the fuel injection pump bracket. Note that on models with a balljoint end fitting, it will be necessary to prise the balljoint from the rubber cable end fitting to enable the cable to pass through the pump bracket **(see illustrations)**.
3 Working inside the vehicle, release the cable end fitting which is a push fit in the accelerator pedal rod **(see illustration)**.
4 Release the cable from the remaining clips

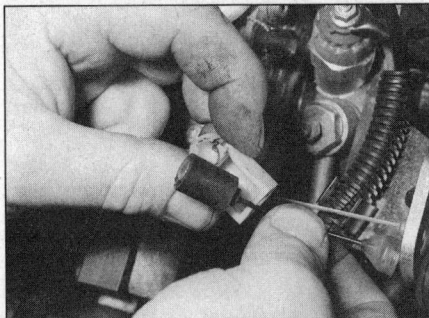

6.2a Remove the balljoint . . .

6.2b . . . to enable the cable to pass through the bracket

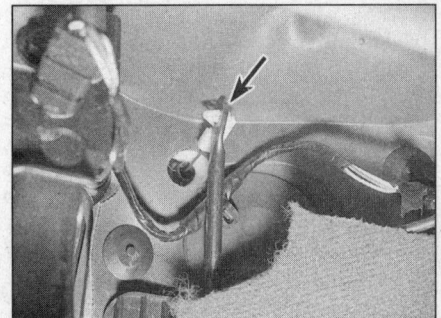

6.3 Accelerator cable end fitting (arrowed) at accelerator pedal

4

and brackets in the engine compartment, noting its routing.

5 Withdraw the cable through the bulkhead into the engine compartment.

Refitting and adjustment

6 Refitting is a reversal of removal, ensuring that the cable is routed as noted before removal, and on completion, check the cable adjustment as follows.

7 Have an assistant fully depress the accelerator pedal, then check that the accelerator lever on the injection pump is touching the maximum speed adjustment screw. If adjustment is required, remove the spring clip from the adjustment ferrule, reposition the ferrule as necessary, then insert the clip in the next free groove on the ferrule.

8 With the accelerator pedal fully released, check that the accelerator lever is touching the anti-stall adjustment screw.

7 Accelerator pedal - removal and refitting

Removal

1 Working inside the vehicle, release the accelerator cable end fitting which is a push fit in the pedal rod.

2 Unscrew the bolt securing the pedal assembly to the bulkhead and withdraw it from inside the vehicle.

Refitting

3 Refitting is a reversal of removal, but check the accelerator cable adjustment as described in Section 6.

8 Fuel system - priming and bleeding

Note: *Refer to the precautions given in Section 1 before proceeding.*

1 After disconnecting part of the fuel supply system or running out of fuel, it is necessary to prime the system and bleed off any air which may have entered the system components.

2 All models are fitted with a hand-operated priming pump, operated by a plunger located on the top of the fuel filter head, on the right-hand side of the engine compartment.

3 To prime the system, loosen the bleed screw, located on the filter head outlet union, or on the fuel pump inlet union **(see illustration)**. If no bleed screw is fitted, loosen the outlet union itself.

4 Pump the priming plunger until fuel free from air bubbles emerges from the outlet union or bleed screw (as applicable) **(see illustration)**. Retighten the bleed screw or outlet union.

5 Switch on the ignition (to activate the stop

8.3 Loosening the fuel system bleed screw (arrowed) located on the fuel pump inlet union

solenoid) and continue pumping the priming plunger until firm resistance is felt, then pump a few more times.

6 If a large amount of air has entered the pump, place a wad of rag around the fuel return union on the pump (to absorb spilt fuel), then slacken the union. Operate the priming plunger (with the ignition switched on to activate the stop solenoid), or crank the engine on the starter motor in 10 second bursts, until fuel free from air bubbles emerges from the fuel union. Tighten the union and mop up split fuel.

⚠️ **Warning: Be prepared to stop the engine if it should fire, to avoid excessive fuel spray and spillage.**

7 If air has entered the injector pipes, place wads of rag around the injector pipe unions at the injectors (to absorb spilt fuel), then slacken the unions. Crank the engine on the starter motor until fuel emerges from the unions, then stop cranking the engine and retighten the unions. Mop up spilt fuel.

⚠️ **Warning: Refer to the warning given in the previous paragraph.**

8 Start the engine with the accelerator pedal fully depressed. Additional cranking may be necessary to finally bleed the system before the engine starts.

9 Maximum speed - checking and adjustment

Caution: The maximum speed adjustment screw is sealed by the manufacturers at the factory using paint or a locking wire and a lead seal. There is no reason why it should require adjustment. Do not disturb the screw if the vehicle is still within the warranty period otherwise the warranty will be invalidated. This adjustment requires the use of a tachometer - refer to Chapter 1, Section 26 for alternative methods.

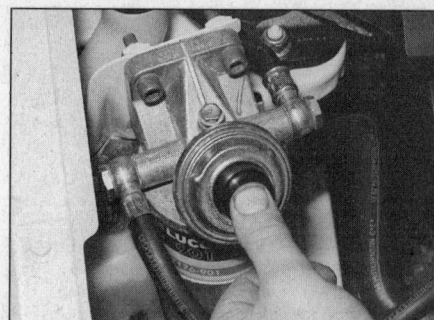

8.4 Pumping the fuel system priming plunger

9.3 Maximum speed adjustment screw (arrowed) - Lucas injection pump

1 Run the engine to normal operating temperature.

2 Have an assistant fully depress the accelerator pedal and check that the maximum engine speed is as given in the Specifications. Do not keep the engine at maximum speed for more than two or three seconds.

3 If adjustment is necessary, stop the engine then loosen the locknut, turn the maximum speed adjustment screw as necessary, and retighten the locknut **(see illustration)**. (Refer to illustration 10.12 for the location of the adjustment screw on the Bosch pump.)

4 Repeat the procedure in paragraph 2 to check the adjustment.

5 Stop the engine and disconnect the tachometer.

10 Fast idle thermostatic actuator and cable - removal, refitting, testing and adjustment

Note: *A new sealing ring will be required on refitting.*

Removal

1 The thermostatic actuator is located at the left-hand end of the cylinder head.

2 Partially drain the cooling system as described in Chapter 1.

3 Loosen the clamp screw or nut (as applicable) and slide the fast idle cable end fitting from the inner cable at the fast idle lever on the injection pump **(see illustration)**.

10.3 Fast idle cable end fitting (arrowed) - Lucas injection pump

10.5a Unscrew the thermostatic actuator . . .

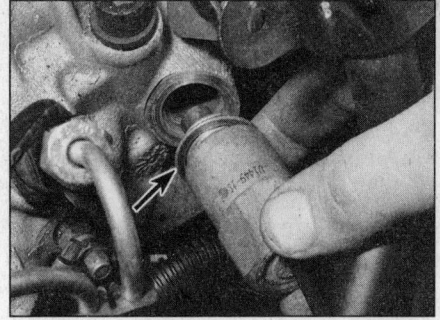
10.5b . . . and withdraw it from the cylinder head. Note the sealing ring (arrowed)

4 Slide the cable outer from the bracket on the fuel injection pump.

5 Using a suitable open-ended spanner, unscrew the thermostatic actuator from the cylinder head, and withdraw the actuator complete with the cable. Recover the sealing ring **(see illustrations)**.

Refitting

6 Fit the actuator, using a new sealing ring, and tighten it.

7 Refill the cooling system as described in Chapter 1.

8 Insert the cable outer through the bracket on the injection pump.

9 Insert the inner cable through the fast idle lever, and position the end fitting on the cable, but do not tighten the clamp screw or nut (as applicable).

10 Adjust the cable as described in the following paragraphs.

Testing and adjustment

Bosch injection pump

Note: *During this procedure, it is necessary to measure the engine speed. The usual type of tachometer (rev counter), which works from ignition system pulses, cannot be used on diesel engines. A diagnostic socket is provided*

for the use of Renault test equipment, but this will not normally be available to the home mechanic. If it is not felt that adjusting the idle speed "by ear" is satisfactory, or that (where fitted) the instrument panel tachometer is not sufficiently reliable, one of the following alternatives may be used.
a) Purchase or hire of an appropriate tachometer.
b) Delegation of the job to a Renault dealer or other specialist.
c) Timing light (strobe) operated by a petrol engine running at the desired speed. If the timing light is pointed at a mark on the camshaft pump pulley, the mark will appear stationary when the two engines are running at the same speed (or multiples of that speed). The pulley will be rotating at half the crankshaft speed but this will not affect the adjustment. (In practice it was found impossible to use this method on the crankshaft pulley due to the acute viewing angle.)

11 With the engine warm (the cooling fan should have cut in and out once) and running at the correct idle speed (see Chapter 1), proceed as follows.

12 Move the fast idle lever on the injection pump towards the flywheel end of the engine so that it contacts the fast idle adjustment screw **(see illustration)**.

13 Check the fast idle speed. If necessary, loosen the locknut and turn the adjustment screw to give the specified fast idle speed. Retighten the locknut on completion.

14 Stop the engine, and disconnect the tachometer where applicable.

15 The fast idle cable should now be adjusted as follows.

16 With the engine still at normal operating temperature, and the fast idle lever in its rest position (resting against the idle speed adjustment screw, **not** the fast idle adjustment screw), gently pull the fast idle cable taught.

17 Position the end fitting on the cable so that the dimension between the end of the fast idle lever and the end fitting is as shown **(see illustration)**.

18 With the end fitting correctly positioned, tighten the clamp screw.

19 When the engine has cooled, check that the cable has pulled the fast idle lever so that it rests against the fast idle adjustment screw. Re-check that with the engine at normal operating temperature the dimension "x" between the end of the fast idle lever and the cable end fitting is as specified. If not, it is likely that the thermostatic actuator is faulty.

Lucas injection pump

20 The fast idle speed is set at the factory on a test bench and cannot be adjusted.

21 With the engine cold, note the length of the exposed inner fast idle cable, measured from the end of the cable to the point where it enters the cable outer.

22 Run the engine until it is at normal operating temperature (the cooling fan should have cut in and out once), then stop the engine.

23 Again measure the length of the exposed inner fast idle cable, which should have increased by 7.0 to 8.5 mm. If the cable travel between cold and normal operating temperature is not as specified, it is likely that the thermostatic actuator is faulty.

24 With the engine still at normal operating temperature, and the fast idle lever in the rest position, gently pull the fast idle cable taught.

25 Position the fast idle cable end fitting on the cable so that the dimension between the

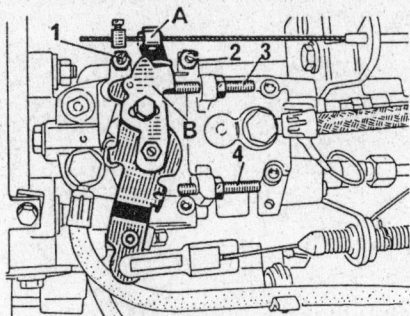
10.12 Bosch injection pump adjustment screws

A Fast idle lever
B Accelerator lever
1 Fast idle adjustment screw
2 Idle adjustment screw
3 Anti-stall adjustment screw
4 Maximum speed adjustment screw

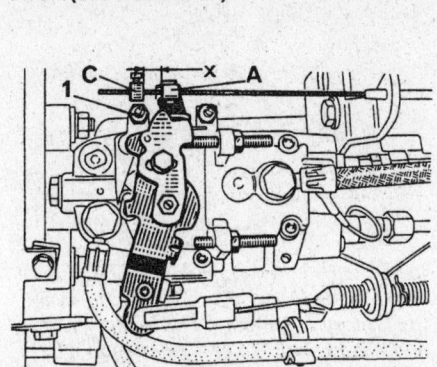
10.17 Bosch injection pump fast idle cable adjustment (thermostatic actuator)

A Fast idle lever
C Cable end fitting
1 Fast idle adjustment screw
x = 6. mm

4

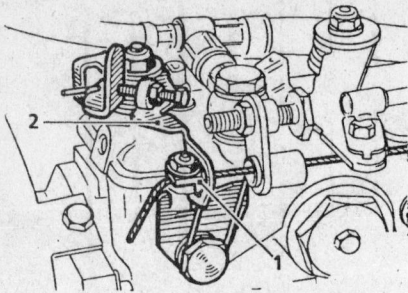

10.25 Lucas injection pump fast idle cable adjustment (thermostatic actuator)

1 Cable end fitting   *2 Fast idle lever*

end of the fast idle lever and the end fitting is 3.0 ± 1.0 mm **(see illustration)**.

26 With the end fitting correctly positioned, tighten the clamp nut.

11 Fast idle actuator, cable and solenoid valve - removal, refitting, testing and adjustment

Vacuum actuator and cable

Removal

1 The vacuum actuator is attached to a bracket located on the end of the injection pump **(see illustration)**.

2 Loosen the clamp screw or nut (as applicable) and slide the fast idle cable end fitting from the inner cable at the fast idle lever on the injection pump.

3 Disconnect the vacuum hose from the actuator.

4 Unscrew the nut securing the actuator to the bracket, and withdraw the actuator, passing the cable through the bracket as it is withdrawn **(see illustrations)**.

Refitting

5 Refit the actuator to the bracket, and tighten the securing nut.

6 Reconnect the vacuum hose.

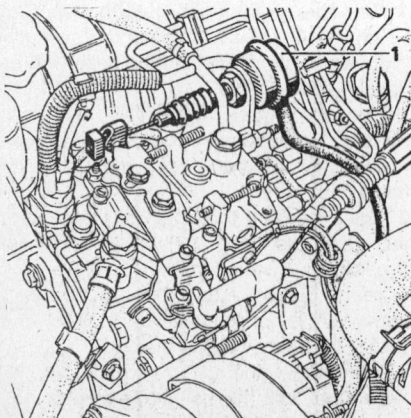

11.1 Fast idle vacuum actuator and solenoid valve components

1 Vacuum actuator
2 Solenoid valve
A Hose from brake vacuum pump to servo

7 Insert the inner cable through the fast idle lever, and position the end fitting on the cable, but do not tighten the clamp screw or nut (as applicable).

8 Adjust the cable as described in the following paragraphs.

Testing and adjustment - Bosch injection pump

9 Proceed as described in Section 10, paragraphs 11 to 18 inclusive, with reference to the note at the beginning of paragraph 11.

10 If a faulty vacuum actuator is suspected, first test the solenoid valve as described later in this Section.

11 The actuator can be tested using a vacuum pump. With the engine stopped, disconnect the vacuum hose from the actuator, and connect the vacuum pump in its place. With a vacuum of 500 mbars applied, the actuator should operate the cable sufficiently to pull the fast idle lever so that it rests against the fast idle adjustment screw. If not, it is likely that the vacuum actuator is faulty.

Testing and adjustment - Lucas injection pump

12 The fast idle speed is set at the factory on a test bench and cannot be adjusted.

13 With the engine stopped, and the fast idle lever in the rest position, gently pull the fast idle cable taught.

14 Position the fast idle cable end fitting on the cable so that the dimension between the end of the fast idle lever and the end fitting is 3.0 ± 1.0 mm (see illustration 10.25).

15 With the end fitting correctly positioned, tighten the clamp nut.

16 The actuator can be tested with reference to paragraphs 10 and 11, but note that the fast idle lever should rest against the lever stop rather than the fast idle adjustment screw.

Solenoid valve

Removal

17 The solenoid valve is located on a bracket attached to the front body panel in the engine compartment **(see illustration)**.

18 Disconnect the wiring plug and the vacuum hoses from the valve.

19 Unscrew the two securing nuts, and withdraw the valve, complete with its bracket.

Refitting

20 Refitting is a reversal of removal, ensuring that the vacuum hoses are securely reconnected.

Testing

21 Remove the solenoid valve as described previously.

22 Attempt to blow gently through one of the vacuum hose connections. No air should pass through the valve.

23 With a 12-volt supply connected across the solenoid terminals, again attempt to blow through the valve. Air should now pass through.

24 If the valve proves to be faulty, it should be renewed.

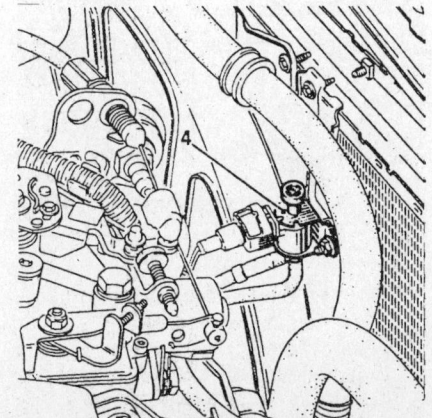

11.4a Fast idle vacuum actuator (1) - Bosch injection pump

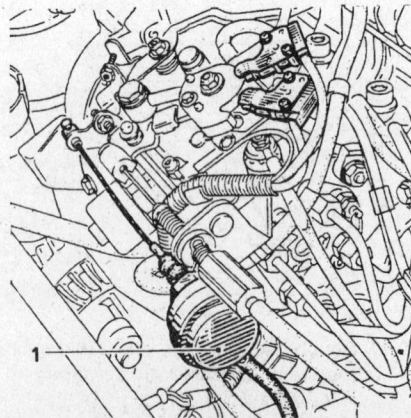

11.4b Fast idle vacuum actuator (1) - Lucas injection pump

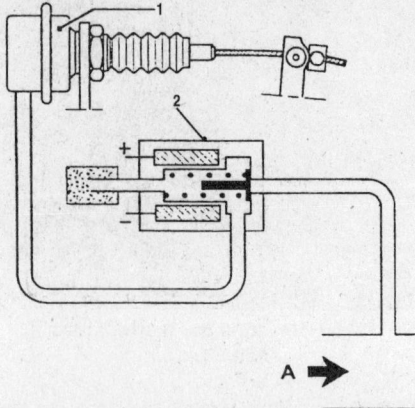

11.17 Fast idle solenoid valve location (4) - vacuum fast idle actuator

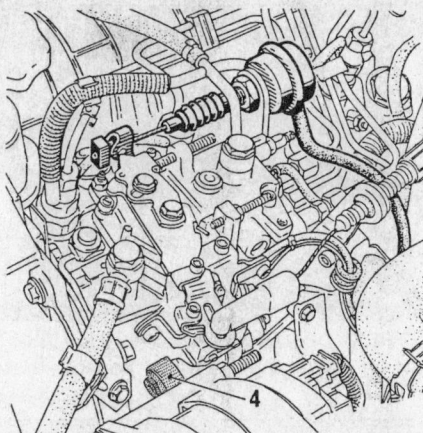

12.4a Cold start timing advance solenoid
location (4) - Bosch injection pump

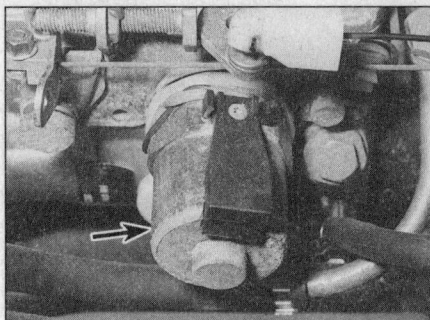

12.4b Cold start timing advance
solenoid location (arrowed) -
Lucas injection pump

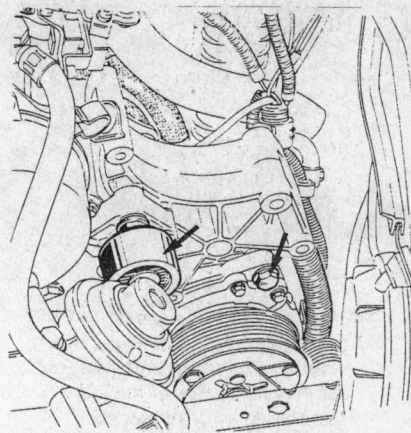

13.5 Auxiliary drivebelt guide
roller/bracket assembly, and one of the
upper air conditioning compressor-to-
alternator mounting bracket
securing bolts (arrowed)

12 Cold - start timing advance solenoid - testing, removal and refitting

Testing

1 To check the operation of the system, start the engine from cold, and listen for a knocking or harshness, disappearing after between 30 seconds and 2 minutes 45 seconds. This shows that the system is working correctly. (If dynamic timing equipment is available, this can be used to check the advance.)

2 If the system does not seem to be working, check for voltage at the solenoid feed wire with the starter motor cranking, and for 5 to 6 seconds after start-up (the feed to the solenoid is controlled by the preheating system control unit).

3 If voltage is present, but the system is still not working, the solenoid valve is probably faulty, and should be renewed.

Removal

Note: *Be careful not to allow dirt into the injection pump during this procedure. A new sealing washer must be used on refitting.*

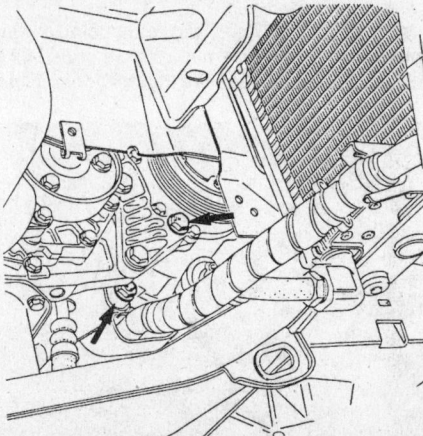

13.10 Air conditioning compressor lower
mounting nuts and bolts (arrowed)

4 Disconnect the battery negative lead, then disconnect the solenoid wiring connector **(see illustrations)**.

5 Unscrew the solenoid valve from the pump and recover the sealing washer. Take great care not to allow dirt to enter the pump.

Refitting

6 Refitting is a reversal of removal, using a new sealing washer.

13 Fuel injection pump - removal and refitting

Note: *Refer to the precautions given in Section 1 of this Chapter before proceeding. Be careful not to allow dirt into the pump or injector pipes during this procedure. New sealing rings should be used on the fuel pipe banjo unions when refitting.*

Removal

Non-turbo models with air conditioning

Note: *At the time of writing, it was not possible to obtain a vehicle on which to carry out detailed work. It is therefore possible that some differences to the sequence of work described in the following paragraphs may be noted. It is*

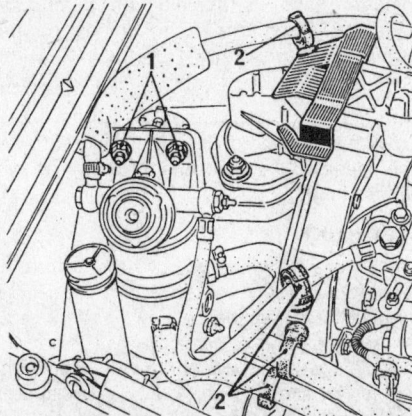

13.13 Fuel filter assembly securing bolts
(1), and fuel and coolant hose
securing clips (2)

recommended that notes and, where necessary, sketches are made during removal, where any differences to procedures are noted.

1 In order to gain access to the injection pump securing bolts, the alternator and its mounting bracket must be removed.

2 Disconnect the battery negative lead.

3 Remove the alternator as described in Chapter 5, then proceed as follows.

4 Unscrew the securing bolts, and remove the power steering pump pulley from the pump drive flange. Note that it will be necessary to counterhold the pulley (eg, using an old drivebelt) in order to loosen the bolts.

5 Remove the securing bolts, and withdraw the auxiliary drivebelt guide roller/bracket assembly **(see Illustration)**.

6 Remove the two upper bolts securing the air conditioning compressor to the alternator mounting bracket.

7 Apply the handbrake, then jack up the front of the car and support securely on axle stands (see *"Jacking, towing and wheel changing"*).

8 Remove the engine undershield, where applicable.

9 Remove the right-hand front roadwheel and the wheel arch liner.

10 Loosen the lower air conditioning compressor mounting nuts and bolts, then pivot the compressor downwards to enable the alternator mounting bracket to be removed from above **(see illustration)**.

11 Proceed as described in the following paragraphs.

All models

12 If not already done, disconnect the battery negative lead.

13 If not already done, remove the two bolts securing the fuel filter assembly to the body panel, unbolt the hose bracket from the fuel injection pump mounting bracket, and move the fuel filter assembly to one side, leaving the hoses connected **(see illustration)**. Take care not to strain the hoses.

4

13.21 Disconnect the hose (arrowed) connecting the boost pressure fuel delivery corrector to the inlet manifold - Turbo models

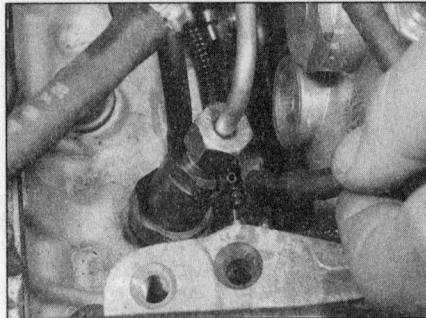

13.23 Disconnect the main fuel leak-off return hose from the relevant fuel injector

13.24 Disconnecting the auxiliary fuel return hose - Turbo model

14 Turn the crankshaft to bring No 1 piston to TDC on the compression stroke, and fit the tool to lock the crankshaft in position, as described in Chapter 2A.

15 Unscrew the securing bolts, and remove the timing belt cover which covers the fuel injection pump sprocket.

16 If an injection pump sprocket locking tool is available (Renault tool Mot.1131 for one-piece sprockets, or Mot.1200 for two-piece adjustable sprockets), remove the crankshaft locking tool, turn the engine back from TDC by one camshaft sprocket tooth, and fit the injection pump sprocket locking tool (turning the engine back by one sprocket tooth will ensure that sufficient adjustment is available to set the pump timing on refitting).

17 If a locking tool is not available, remove the timing belt as described in Chapter 2A.

18 Disconnect the accelerator cable from the injection pump, with reference to Section 6 if necessary.

19 On models with a fast idle thermostatic actuator, disconnect the fast idle cable from the injection pump, with reference to Section 10 if necessary.

20 On models with a fast idle vacuum actuator, disconnect the vacuum hose from the actuator (see Section 11).

21 On Turbo models, disconnect the hose connecting the boost pressure fuel delivery corrector to the inlet manifold **(see illustration)**.

22 Loosen the clip or undo the banjo union, as applicable and disconnect the fuel supply hose from the injection pump. Recover the sealing washers from the banjo union, where applicable. Cover the open end of the hose or pipe, and plug the opening in the injection pump to keep dirt out (on models with a banjo union, the banjo bolt can be refitted to the pump and covered).

23 Disconnect the main fuel leak-off return hose (connected to the main fuel return pipe) from the relevant fuel injector **(see illustration)**.

24 Where applicable, disconnect the auxiliary fuel return hose from the pump. On Turbo models, the auxiliary hose is connected to the boost pressure fuel delivery corrector on the pump (also unclip it from the accelerator cable bracket) **(see illustration)**.

13.25a Disconnecting the main fuel return pipe union - Turbo model

25 Disconnect the main fuel return pipe banjo union from the injection pump. Recover the sealing washers from the banjo union. Again, cover the open end of the hose and the banjo bolt to keep dirt out **(see illustrations)**. Take care not to get the inlet and outlet banjo unions mixed up.

26 Disconnect all relevant wiring from the pump. Note that on certain pumps, this can be achieved by simply disconnecting the wiring connectors at the brackets on the pump **(see illustration)**. On some pumps it will be necessary to disconnect the wiring from the individual components (some connections may be protected by rubber covers).

27 Unscrew the union nuts securing the injector pipes to the injection pump and injectors. Counterhold the unions on the pump, when unscrewing the pipe-to-pump union nuts. Remove the pipes as a set. Cover

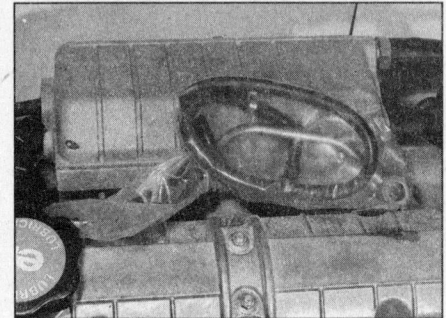

13.25b Cover the open ends of the pipe and hoses to keep dirt out

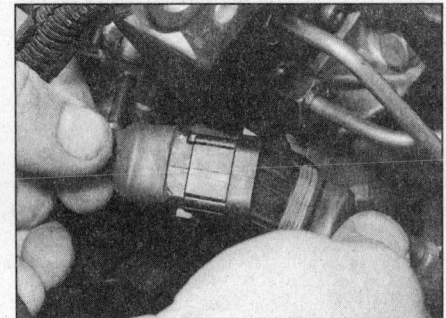

13.26 Disconnecting the main fuel injection pump wiring connector - Turbo model

open unions to keep dirt out, using small plastic bags or fingers cut from discarded (but clean!) rubber gloves **(see illustrations)**. Note

13.27a Unscrewing an injector pipe-to-injection pump union . . .

13.27b . . . and an injector pipe-to-injector union - Turbo model

13.27c Cover the injectors to keep dirt out

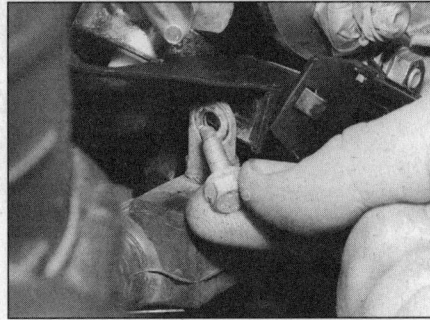

13.28 Removing the alternator plastic shield securing bolt. Note the location of the bracket

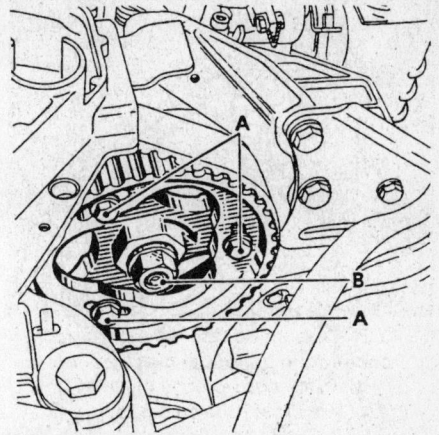

13.30 Two-piece sprocket adjuster bolts (A) and sprocket securing nut (B). Turn sprocket boss in direction arrowed before removing pump

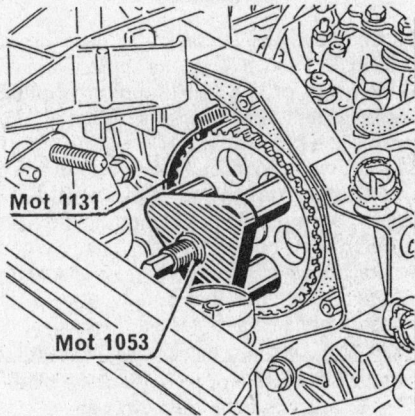

13.31a Renault sprocket locking tool and puller in position - one-piece sprocket

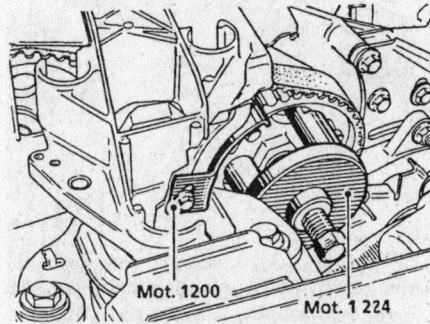

13.31b Renault sprocket locking tool and puller in position - two-piece adjustable sprocket

13.34 Unscrew the bolts securing the rear injection pump mounting bracket to the cylinder head - Turbo model shown

that the leak-off hoses will have to be removed from the fuel injectors to enable the injectors to be covered.

28 Where applicable, remove the alternator plastic shield from below the injection pump. Note the locations of any brackets secured by the shield nut and bolt **(see illustration)**.

29 Loosen the injection pump sprocket securing nut, and unscrew it to the end of the thread on the pump shaft (do not remove the nut at this stage. If a Renault sprocket locking tool is not available (see paragraph 16), counterhold the sprocket using an improvised tool engaged with the holes in the sprocket (**not** the sprocket teeth).

30 On models with a two-piece adjustable pump sprocket, loosen the three sprocket

adjuster bolts **(see illustration)**. Using the centre boss, turn the sprocket rear section clockwise, (viewed from the timing belt end of the engine - effectively turning the pump shaft) so that the adjuster bolts are positioned at the ends of the elongated slots. Retighten the adjuster bolts.

31 Fit a puller to the pump sprocket, acting on the sprocket nut, and free the sprocket from the taper on the pump shaft **(see illustrations)**. **Note:** *The puller must bear on the sprocket holes (between the two sprocket halves on models with two-piece adjustable sprockets)*, **not** *on the teeth.* **Do not** hammer on the end of the pump shaft to free it, as this will damage the internal components of the pump.

32 On models with a one-piece sprocket, mark the sprocket in relation to the end of the pump shaft to ensure correct refitting. This is necessary regardless of whether the timing belt has been removed, because there are two keyways in the sprocket (for use with different injection pump types), and it is possible to refit the sprocket to the pump shaft incorrectly (see Chapter 2A, Section 6).

33 Remove the puller and the sprocket nut. Unless an injection pump sprocket locking tool has been fitted (see paragraph 16), remove the sprocket.

34 Unscrew the bolts securing the rear injection pump mounting bracket to the cylinder head **(see illustration)**.

35 Make a final check to ensure that all relevant pipes, hoses and wires have been disconnected to facilitate pump removal.

36 Make alignment marks between the pump and the mounting bracket. This will aid pump timing on refitting.

37 Unscrew the three pump securing bolts, and withdraw the pump from its mounting bracket, leaving the sprocket engaged with the timing belt, where applicable **(see illustrations)**. Access to the lower pump mounting bolt is most easily obtained from the rear of the pump, using a deep socket and extension.

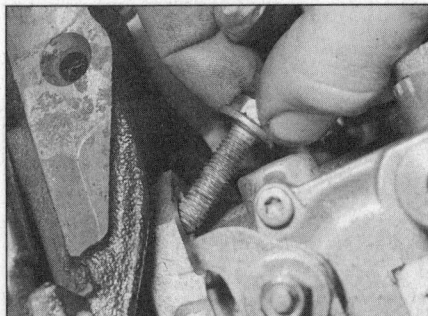

13.37a Remove the securing bolts . . .

13.37b . . . and withdraw the fuel injection pump - Turbo model shown

4

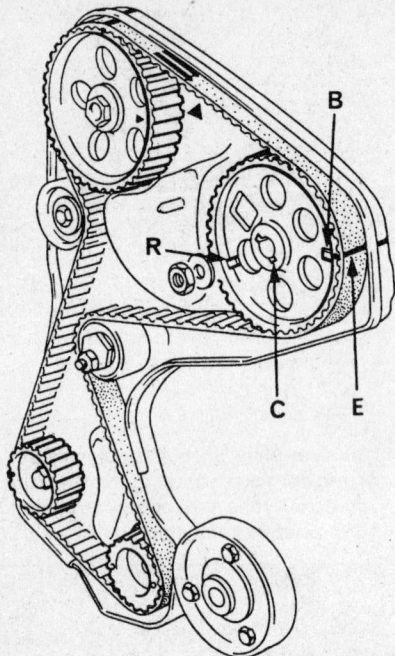

13.42a One-piece injection pump sprocket orientation - Bosch injection pump (engine shown with No 1 piston at TDC)

B Sprocket alignment mark for Bosch injection pump
C Position of injection pump shaft Woodruff key
E Sprocket alignment mark on timing belt
R Sprocket alignment mark for Lucas injection pump

38 Recover the Woodruff key from the end of the pump shaft if it is loose.
39 If desired, the rear pump mounting bracket and the accelerator cable bracket can be unbolted from the rear of the pump.

Refitting

40 Where applicable, refit the rear mounting bracket and the accelerator cable bracket to the rear of the pump.
41 Commence refitting by fitting the Woodruff key to the end of the pump shaft, where applicable.
42 Offer the pump to the mounting bracket. If the sprocket is still engaged with the timing belt, engage the pump shaft with the sprocket. On models with a one-piece sprocket, align the marks made on the sprocket and the pump shaft before removal (this will ensure that the key engages with the correct keyway in the sprocket - see paragraph 32) **(see illustrations)**. Ensure that the Woodruff key does not fall out of the shaft as the sprocket is engaged.
43 Where applicable, align the marks made on the pump and the mounting bracket before removal. If a new pump is being fitted, transfer the mark from the old pump to give an approximate setting.

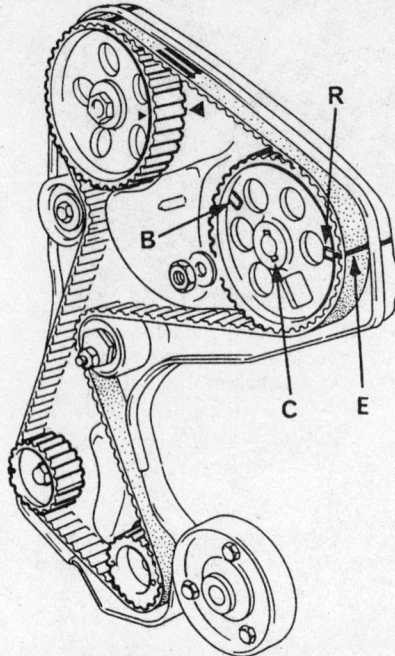

13.42b One-piece injection pump sprocket orientation - Lucas injection pump (engine shown with No 1 cylinder at TDC)

B Sprocket alignment mark for Bosch injection pump
C Position of injection pump shaft Woodruff key
E Sprocket alignment mark on timing belt
R Sprocket alignment mark for Lucas injection pump

44 Refit and lightly tighten the front pump mounting bolts.
45 Refit and tighten the bolts securing the rear pump mounting bracket to the cylinder head.
46 Where applicable, refit the sprocket to the pump shaft, ensuring that the Woodruff key engages correctly. On models with a one-piece sprocket, align the marks made on the sprocket and the pump shaft before removal, to ensure that the key engages with the correct keyway in the sprocket (see paragraph 32).
47 Tighten the pump sprocket securing nut to the specified torque, counterholding the sprocket as during removal **(see illustration)**.
48 If the timing belt has been removed, refit and tension it as described in Chapter 2A.
49 On models with a two-piece adjustable sprocket, loosen the three sprocket adjuster bolts. Using the centre boss, turn the sprocket rear section anti-clockwise (viewed from the timing belt end of the engine - effectively turning the pump shaft) so that the adjuster bolts are positioned at the ends of the elongated slots. Lightly tighten the adjuster bolts.
50 Where applicable, remove the sprocket locking tool, then turn the crankshaft to bring No 1 piston to TDC on the compression stroke, and fit the tool to lock the crankshaft in position, as described in Chapter 2A.

13.47 Tightening the injection pump sprocket bolt

51 Carry out injection timing as described in Sections 14, and 15 or 16, as applicable.
52 Refit the plastic shield under the pump, ensuring that any brackets noted during removal are in place.
53 Refit and reconnect the injector fuel pipes, and tighten the unions. Counterhold the unions on the pump when tightening the pipe-to-pump union nuts.
54 Reconnect all relevant wiring to the pump.
55 Reconnect the fuel supply and return pipes and hoses, and tighten the unions, as applicable. Use new sealing washers on the banjo unions. Also reconnect the leak-off hoses.
56 On Turbo models, reconnect the hose connecting the boost pressure fuel delivery corrector to the inlet manifold.
57 Reconnect the accelerator cable and adjust as described in Section 6.
58 Refit the fuel filter assembly and tighten the securing bolts, and refit the hose bracket.
59 On non-Turbo models with air conditioning, reverse the operations carried out in paragraphs 1 to 10. Refit and tighten the auxiliary drivebelt as described in Chapter 1.
60 On models with a fast idle thermostatic actuator, reconnect and adjust the fast idle cable as described in Section 10, noting that final adjustment must be carried out after the engine has been started and reached normal operating temperature.
61 On models with a fast idle vacuum actuator, reconnect the hose to the actuator, and check the fast idle cable adjustment as described in Section 11.
62 Check the no-load switch adjustment as described in Chapter 5.
63 Reconnect the battery negative lead.
64 Prime and bleed the fuel system as described in Section 8.
65 Start the engine, and check the idle speed and anti-stall speed, as described in Chapter 1.

14 Injection timing - checking methods and adjustment

1 Checking the injection timing is not a routine operation. It is only necessary after the injection pump has been disturbed.

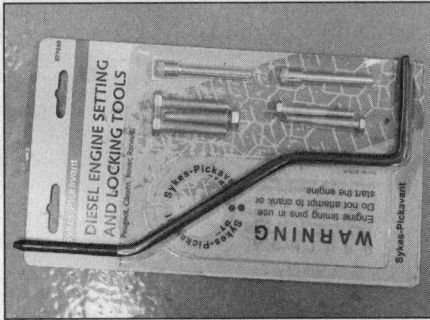

14.3 TDC locking tools for setting injection timing on Renault diesel engines

2 Dynamic timing equipment does exist, but it is unlikely to be available to the home mechanic. The equipment works by converting pressure pulses in an injector pipe into electrical signals. If such equipment is available, use it in accordance with its maker's instructions.

3 Static timing as described in this Chapter gives good results if carried out carefully. A dial test indicator will be needed, with probes and adaptors appropriate to the type of injection pump (see illustration). Read through the procedures before starting work to find out what is involved.

15 Injection timing (Lucas injection pump) - checking and adjustment

Caution: The maximum engine speed and transfer pressure settings, together with timing access plugs, are sealed by the manufacturers at the factory using locking wire and lead seals. Do not disturb the wire if the vehicle is still within the warranty period otherwise the warranty will be invalidated. Also do not attempt the timing procedure unless accurate instrumentation is available. Suitable special tools for carrying out pump timing are available from motor factors, and a dial test indicator will be required regardless of the method used. Refer to the precautions given in Section 1 of this Chapter before proceeding.

1 Disconnect the battery negative lead.

2 Apply the handbrake, then jack up the front right-hand corner of the vehicle until the wheel is just clear of the ground. Support the vehicle on an axle stand and engage 4th or 5th gear. This will enable the crankshaft to be turned easily by turning the right-hand wheel. Alternatively, the engine can be turned using an open-ended spanner on the crankshaft pulley bolt.

3 Turn the crankshaft to bring No 1 piston to TDC on the compression stroke, and fit the tool to lock the crankshaft in position, as described in Chapter 2A.

4 A dial test indicator will now be required, along with a suitable special probe (Renault tool Mot.1079, or an alternative available from

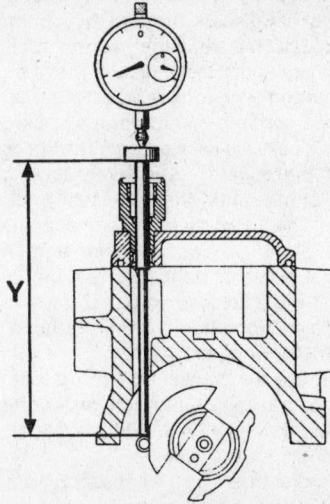

15.4 Timing probe details (Renault tool Mot.1079) - Lucas injection pump

$Y = 95.5 \pm 0.1$ mm

motor factors). Note that the probe must seat on the sealing washer surface in the timing aperture, **not** on the top surface of the timing aperture. The probe is "waisted" to allow it to clear the pump rotor (see illustration).

5 Remove the inspection plug from the top of the pump (see illustration), and recover the sealing washer. Position the timing probe in the aperture so that the tip of the probe rests on the rotor timing piece.

6 Position the dial test indicator securely on the injection pump body, so that it can read the movement of the timing probe. Ensure that the gauge is positioned directly in line with the probe, with the gauge plunger at the mid-point of its travel.

Models with one-piece fixed injection pump sprocket

7 Remove the crankshaft locking tool, then turn the crankshaft approximately a quarter-turn anti-clockwise (viewed from the timing belt end of the engine), and zero the dial test indicator. Check that the timing probe is seated against the sealing washer surface of the timing aperture (see paragraph 4).

8 Turn the crankshaft clockwise slowly until the crankshaft locking tool can be re-inserted (bringing the engine back to TDC).

9 Read the dial test indicator; the reading should correspond to the value marked on the pump. The timing value may be marked on a plastic disc on the front of the pump, or alternatively may appear on a label attached to the top of the pump, or a tag attached to the accelerator pump lever (see illustration).

10 If the reading is not as specified, proceed as follows.

11 Cover the alternator with a plastic bag or rags as a precaution against spillage of fuel.

12 Unscrew the union nuts securing the injector pipes to the fuel injection pump and the fuel injectors. Counterhold the unions on

15.5 Unscrewing the timing inspection plug from the top of a Lucas injection pump

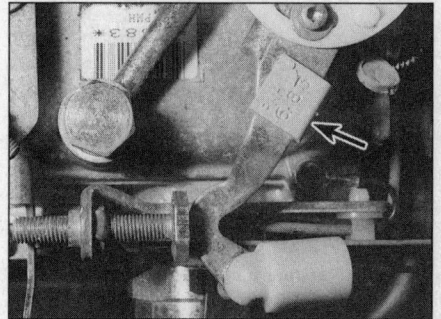

15.9 Injection pump timing value marked on accelerator lever tag (arrowed) - Lucas injection pump

the pump, when unscrewing the nuts. Cover open unions to keep dirt out, using small plastic bags or fingers cut from discarded (but clean!) rubber gloves.

13 Slacken the three front pump mounting bolts, and the two rear pump mounting nuts, and slowly rotate the pump body until the point is found where the specified reading is obtained on the dial gauge. When the pump is correctly positioned, tighten the mounting nuts and bolts, ensuring that the reading on the dial gauge does not change as the fixings are tightened.

14 Withdraw the timing probe slightly, so that it is positioned clear of the pump rotor, and remove the crankshaft locking tool. Rotate the crankshaft through one and three quarter turns clockwise.

15 Slide the timing probe back into position, ensuring that it is correctly seated against the sealing washer surface, as described previously, then zero the dial test indicator.

16 Rotate the crankshaft slowly clockwise until the crankshaft locking tool can be reinserted (bringing No 1 piston back to TDC). Recheck the timing measurement.

17 If adjustment is necessary, slacken the pump mounting nuts and bolts, and repeat the operations described in paragraphs 13 to 16.

18 When the timing is correct, reconnect the fuel injector pipes to the pump and the injectors, and remove the dial test indicator. Remove the probe from the inspection hole, and refit the inspection plug, ensuring that the sealing washer is in place.

4

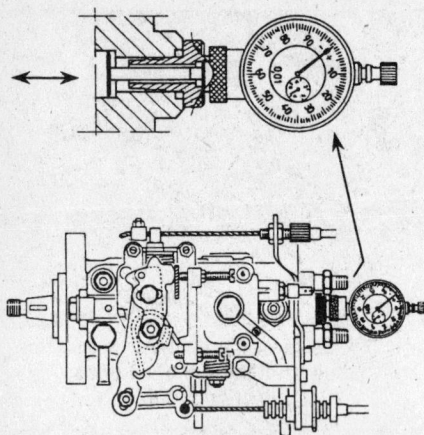

16.5 Dial test indicator and timing probe for use with Bosch injection pump

Note: Pump cable linkages may differ from that shown

19 Where applicable, remove the plastic bag or rags from the alternator.

20 Remove the crankshaft locking tool.

21 Lower the vehicle to the ground and reconnect the battery negative lead.

22 Bleed the fuel system as described in Section 8.

23 Check and if necessary adjust the idle speed and anti-stall speed as described in Chapter 1.

Models with two-piece adjustable injection pump sprocket

24 Remove the crankshaft locking tool, then turn the crankshaft approximately a quarter-turn anti-clockwise (viewed from the timing belt end of the engine), and zero the dial test indicator. Check that the timing probe is seated against the sealing washer surface of the timing aperture (see paragraph 4).

25 Turn the crankshaft clockwise slowly until the crankshaft locking tool can be re-inserted (bringing the engine back to TDC).

26 Read the dial test indicator; the reading should correspond to the value marked on the pump. The timing value may be marked on a plastic disc on the front of the pump, or alternatively may appear on a label attached to the top of the pump, or a tag attached to the accelerator pump lever (see illustration 15.9).

27 If the reading is not as specified, proceed as follows.

28 Loosen the three sprocket adjuster bolts. Using the centre boss, turn the sprocket rear section anti-clockwise (viewed from the timing belt end of the engine - effectively turning the pump shaft) so that the adjuster bolts are positioned at the ends of the elongated slots. Tighten the adjuster bolts.

29 Zero the dial test indicator. Check that the timing probe is seated against the sealing washer surface of the timing aperture (see paragraph 4).

30 Remove the crankshaft locking tool, then turn the crankshaft through two complete turns clockwise, refit the locking tool, and check that the dial test indicator is still zeroed.

31 Loosen the sprocket adjuster bolts, and using the centre boss, turn the sprocket rear section clockwise (viewed from the timing belt end of the engine - effectively turning the pump shaft) until the dial test indicator displays the appropriate timing value marked on the pump. In this position, tighten the sprocket adjuster bolts (the reading on the dial test indicator should not change as the bolts are tightened), then remove the crankshaft locking tool.

32 Remove the crankshaft locking tool, then turn the crankshaft through two complete turns clockwise, refit the locking tool, and recheck the timing value.

33 If adjustment is necessary, slacken the sprocket adjuster bolts, and repeat the operations described in paragraphs 31 and 32.

34 When the timing is correct, remove the dial test indicator. Remove the probe from the inspection hole, and refit the inspection plug, ensuring that the sealing washer is in place.

35 Proceed as described in paragraphs 20 to 23.

16 Injection timing (Bosch injection pump) - checking and adjusting

Caution: Some of the injection pump settings and access plugs may be sealed by the manufacturers at the factory using paint or locking wire and lead seals. Do not disturb the seals if the vehicle is still within the warranty period, otherwise the warranty will be invalidated. Also do not attempt the timing procedure unless accurate instrumentation is available. Refer to the precautions given in Section 1 of this Chapter before proceeding.

1 Disconnect the battery negative lead.

2 Apply the handbrake, then jack up the front right-hand corner of the vehicle until the wheel is just clear of the ground. Support the vehicle on an axle stand and engage 4th or 5th gear. This will enable the engine to be turned easily by turning the right-hand wheel. Alternatively, the engine can be turned using an open ended spanner on the crankshaft pulley bolt.

3 Turn the crankshaft to bring No 1 piston to TDC on the compression stroke, and fit the tool to lock the crankshaft in position, as described in Chapter 2A.

4 Cover the alternator with a plastic bag or rags as a precaution against spillage of fuel.

5 A dial test indicator will now be required, along with a special probe and adaptor to screw into the hole in the rear of the pump (designed specifically for the Bosch pump and available from motor factors) **(see illustration)**.

6 Unscrew the union nuts securing the

injector pipes to the fuel injection pump. Counterhold the unions on the pump, when unscrewing the nuts. Cover open unions to keep dirt out, using small plastic bags or fingers cut from discarded (but clean!) rubber gloves.

7 Unscrew the blanking plug from the end of the injection pump between the injector pipe connections. Be prepared for the loss of some fuel.

8 Insert the probe and connect it to the dial test indicator positioned directly over the inspection hole.

Models with one-piece fixed injection pump sprocket

9 Remove the locking tool from the flywheel, and turn the engine approximately a quarter-turn anti-clockwise (viewed from the timing belt end of the engine), and zero the dial test indicator.

10 Turn the crankshaft clockwise slowly until the crankshaft locking tool can be re-inserted (bringing the engine back to TDC).

11 Read the dial test indicator; the reading should correspond to the value given in the Specifications. Note that on later pumps, the timing value is marked on the pump accelerator lever.

12 If the reading is not as specified, proceed as follows.

13 Slacken the three front pump mounting bolts, and the rear pump mounting nuts, and slowly rotate the pump body until the point is found where the specified reading is obtained on the dial gauge. When the pump is correctly positioned, tighten the mounting nuts and bolts, ensuring that the reading on the dial gauge does not change as the fixings are tightened.

14 Remove the crankshaft locking tool, and rotate the crankshaft through one and three quarter turns clockwise. Check that the dial test indicator is reading zero.

15 Rotate the crankshaft slowly clockwise until the crankshaft locking tool can be reinserted (bringing No 1 piston back to TDC). Recheck the timing measurement.

16 If adjustment is necessary, slacken the pump mounting nuts and bolts, and repeat the operations described in paragraphs 13 to 15.

17 When the timing is correct, remove the dial test indicator, remove the probe from the inspection hole, and refit the blanking plug.

18 Reconnect the fuel injector pipes to the pump.

19 Where applicable, remove the plastic bag or rags from the alternator.

20 Remove the crankshaft locking tool.

21 Lower the vehicle to the ground and reconnect the battery negative lead.

22 Bleed the fuel system as described in Section 8.

23 Check and if necessary adjust the idle speed and anti-stall speed as described in Chapter 1.

17.4 Pull the leak-off pipes from
the fuel injectors

17.6 Disconnect the fuel pipes
from the injectors

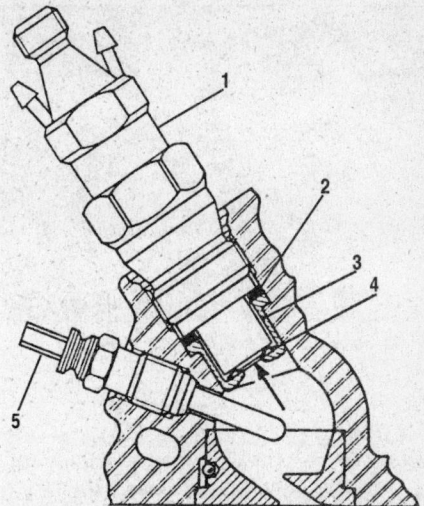

17.7a Cross-section of fuel injector

1 Fuel injector   4 Fire seal washer
2 Copper washer   5 Glow plug
3 Sleeve

Models with two-piece adjustable injection pump sprocket

24 Remove the locking tool from the flywheel, and turn the engine approximately a quarter-turn anti-clockwise (viewed from the timing belt end of the engine), and zero the dial test indicator.

25 Turn the crankshaft clockwise slowly until the crankshaft locking tool can be re-inserted (bringing the engine back to TDC).

26 Read the dial test indicator; the reading should correspond to the value given in the Specifications. Note that on later pumps, the timing value is marked on the pump accelerator lever.

27 If the reading is not as specified, proceed as follows.

28 Loosen the three sprocket adjuster bolts. Using the centre boss, turn the sprocket rear section anti-clockwise (viewed from the timing belt end of the engine - effectively turning the pump shaft) so that the adjuster bolts are positioned at the ends of the elongated slots. Tighten the adjuster bolts.

29 Zero the dial test indicator.

30 Remove the crankshaft locking tool, then turn the crankshaft through two complete turns, refit the locking tool, and check that the dial test indicator is still zeroed.

31 Loosen the sprocket adjuster bolts, and using the centre boss, turn the sprocket rear section clockwise (viewed from the timing belt end of the engine - effectively turning the pump shaft) until the dial test indicator displays the appropriate timing given in the Specifications. In this position, tighten the sprocket adjuster bolts (the reading on the dial test indicator should not change as the bolts are tightened), then remove the crankshaft locking tool.

32 Turn the crankshaft through two complete turns clockwise, refit the locking tool, and recheck the timing value.

33 If adjustment is necessary, slacken the sprocket adjuster bolts, and repeat the operations described in paragraphs 31 and 32.

34 When the timing is correct, proceed as described in paragraphs 17 to 23.

17 Fuel injectors - testing, removal and refitting

Warning: Exercise extreme caution when working on the fuel injectors. Never expose the hands or any part of the body to injector spray, as the high working pressure can cause the fuel to penetrate the skin, with possibly fatal results. You are strongly advised to have any work which involves testing the injectors under pressure carried out by a dealer or fuel injection specialist. Refer to the precautions given in Section 1 of this Chapter before proceeding.

Testing

1 Injectors do deteriorate with prolonged use and it is reasonable to expect them to need reconditioning or renewal after 60 000 miles (100 000 km) or so. Accurate testing, overhaul and calibration of the injectors must be left to a specialist. A defective injector which is causing knocking or smoking can be located without dismantling as follows.

2 Run the engine at a fast idle. Slacken each injector union in turn, placing rag around the union to catch spilt fuel and being careful not to expose the skin to any spray. When the union on the defective injector is slackened, the knocking or smoking will stop.

Removal

Note: *Take great care not to allow dirt into the injectors or fuel pipes during this procedure.*

3 Carefully clean around the injectors and injector pipe union nuts.

4 Pull the leak-off pipes from the injectors (see illustration).

5 Unscrew the union nuts securing the injector pipes to the fuel injection pump. Counterhold the unions on the pump, when unscrewing the nuts. Cover open unions to keep dirt out, using small plastic bags or fingers cut from discarded (but clean!) rubber gloves.

6 Unscrew the union nuts and disconnect the pipes from the injectors (see illustration). If

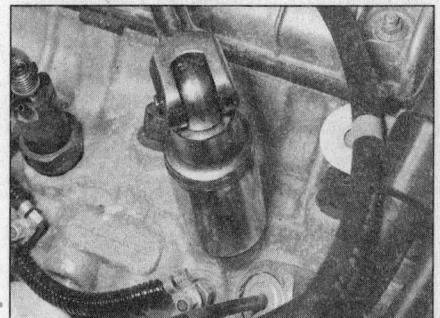

17.7b Unscrew the injectors . . .

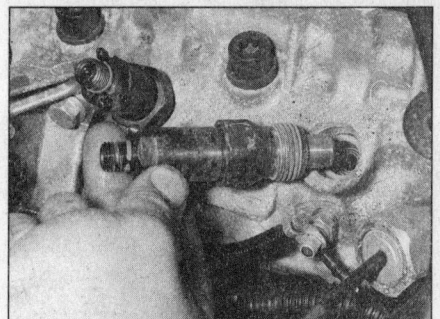

17.7c . . . and withdraw them from
the cylinder head

necessary the injector pipes may be completely removed. Note the locations of any clips attached to the pipes. Cover the ends of the injectors to prevent dirt ingress.

7 Unscrew the injectors using a deep socket or box spanner (27 mm across flats) and remove them from the cylinder head (see illustrations).

8 Recover the copper washers and fire seal washers from the cylinder head. Also recover the sleeves if they are loose (see illustrations).

4

17.8a Recover the copper washers . . .

17.8b . . . and the fire seal washers

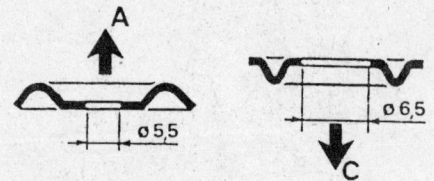

17.12 Fire seal washer fitting details

A Early type washer - fits with convex side upwards

C Later type washer - fits with convex side downwards

Refitting

9 Obtain new copper washers and fire seal washers. Also renew the sleeves if they are damaged.

10 Take care not to drop the injectors or allow the needles at their tips to become damaged. The injectors are precision-made to fine limits and must not be handled roughly. In particular, do not mount them in a bench vice.

11 Commence refitting by inserting the sleeves (if removed) into the cylinder head.

12 Fit the new fire seal washers to the cylinder head. Note that two types of fire seal washers have been fitted to the engines covered by this manual. The earlier type of washer has a hole diameter of 5.5 mm, and should be fitted with the convex side upwards (towards the fuel injector). The later type of washer has a hole diameter of 6.5 mm, and should be fitted with the convex side downwards (towards the cylinder head) **(see illustration)**. It is likely that the new washers supplied by a Renault parts centre will be of the later type. Ensure that the washers are fitted correctly, according to type.

13 Fit the copper washers to the cylinder head.

14 Insert the injectors and tighten them to the specified torque.

15 Refit the injector pipes and tighten the union nuts. Position any clips attached to the pipes as noted before removal.

16 Reconnect the leak-off pipes.

17 Start the engine. If difficulty is experienced, bleed the fuel system as described in Section 8.

18 Manifolds - removal and refitting

Note: *A new gasket must be used on refitting.*

Non-Turbo models

Removal

1 Although the manifolds are separate, they are retained by the same nuts, since the stud holes are split between the manifold flanges.

2 To improve access, unscrew the securing bolts, and remove the strengthening bar from between the front suspension strut turrets.

3 Note the location of any wiring or hose brackets/clips attached to the manifolds, and remove them.

4 Release the securing clip, and disconnect the air inlet hose from the inlet manifold.

5 Where applicable, disconnect the hoses from the oil separator mounted on the inlet manifold. If desired, the oil separator can be unbolted from its bracket.

6 Where applicable, disconnect the breather hose(s) from the inlet manifold.

7 On models fitted with an EGR system, remove the recirculation valve and pipe as described in Section 26.

8 Unscrew and remove the two nuts, then remove the washers, tension springs and sleeves securing the exhaust front section to the manifold. Slide the flange plate off the manifold studs and separate the joint.

9 Progressively unscrew the nuts securing the inlet and exhaust manifolds and withdraw them from the cylinder head. Recover the manifold gasket.

Refitting

10 Refitting is a reversal of removal, bearing in mind the following points.

a) Ensure that the cylinder head and manifold mating surfaces are clean and use a new gasket.

b) Reconnect the exhaust front section to the manifold with reference to Section 24.

c) Where applicable, refit the EGR recirculation valve and pipe (see Section 26).

d) Ensure that any wiring or hose brackets/clips are positioned as noted before removal.

Turbo models

Removal

11 Although the manifolds are separate, they are retained by the same nuts, since the stud holes are split between the manifold flanges.

12 To improve access, unscrew the securing bolts, and remove the strengthening bar from between the front suspension strut turrets.

13 Note the location of any wiring or hose brackets/clips attached to the manifolds, and remove them.

18.18 Manifold securing nuts (arrowed) - Turbo model (viewed with engine removed for clarity)

14 Disconnect the breather hoses from the inlet manifold, noting their locations to aid refitting.

15 Remove the turbocharger as described in Section 20.

16 On models fitted with an EGR system, remove the recirculation valve and pipe as described in Section 26.

17 Unbolt the engine earth strap from the engine lifting bracket at the right-hand end of the inlet manifold, then unbolt the bracket from the manifold.

18 Progressively unscrew the nuts securing the inlet and exhaust manifolds and withdraw them from the cylinder head. Recover the manifold gasket **(see illustration)**.

Refitting

19 Refitting is a reversal of removal, bearing in mind the following points.

a) Ensure that the cylinder head and manifold mating surfaces are clean and use a new gasket.

b) Where applicable, refit the EGR recirculation valve and pipe with reference to Section 26.

c) Refit the turbocharger as described in Section 20.

d) Ensure that the breather hoses are correctly reconnected as noted before removal.

e) Ensure that any wiring or hose brackets/clips are positioned as noted before removal.

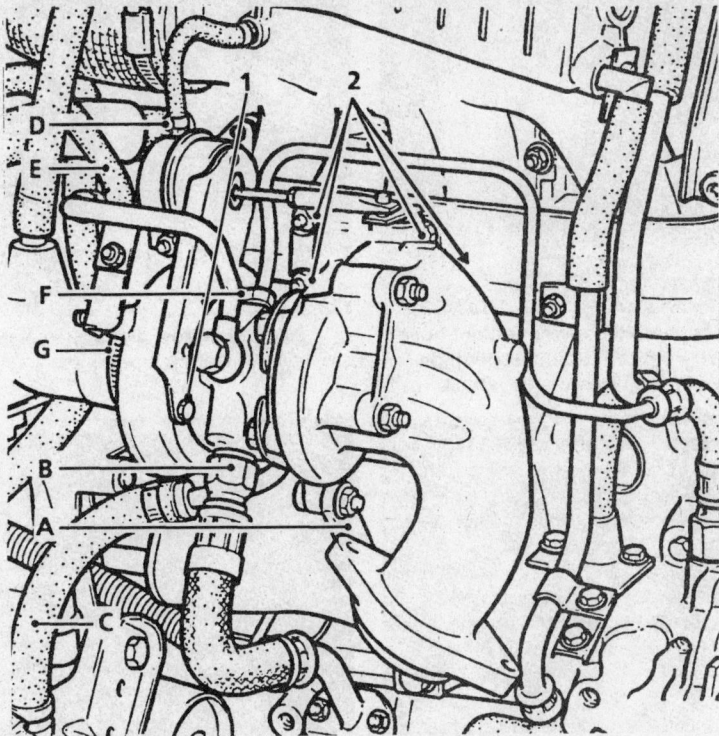

20.6a Turbocharger mountings and hose/pipe connections

1 Wastegate bracket bolts
2 Turbocharger-to-manifold nuts
A Lower support bracket
B Oil return pipe union
C Lower turbocharger coolant hose

D Cylinder head-to-T-piece coolant hose
E Upper turbocharger coolant hose
F Oil feed pipe union
G Air trunking (air cleaner-to-turbocharger)

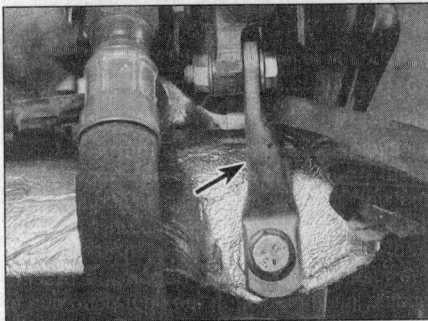

20.6b Turbocharger lower support bracket (arrowed) - viewed with engine removed for clarity

19 Turbocharger - description and precautions

Description

1 A turbocharger is fitted to the F8Q 740 and F8Q 744 engines. It increases engine efficiency by raising the pressure in the inlet manifold above atmospheric pressure. Instead of the air simply being sucked into the cylinders, it is forced in. Additional fuel is supplied by the injection pump in proportion to the increased air intake.

2 Energy for the operation of the turbocharger comes from the exhaust gas. The gas flows through a specially-shaped housing (the turbine housing) and in so doing, spins the turbine wheel. The turbine wheel is attached to a shaft, at the end of which is another vaned wheel known as the compressor wheel. The compressor wheel spins in its own housing and compresses the inducted air on the way to the inlet manifold.

3 Between the turbocharger and the inlet manifold, the compressed air passes through an intercooler. This is an air-to-air heat exchanger, mounted on the left-hand side of the car behind the front bumper, and supplied with cooling air ducted through the front spoiler. The purpose of the intercooler is to remove, from the inducted air, some of the heat gained in being compressed. Because cooler air is denser, removal of this heat further increases engine efficiency.

4 Boost pressure (the pressure in the inlet manifold) is limited by a wastegate, which diverts the exhaust gas away from the turbine wheel in response to a pressure-sensitive actuator.

5 The turbo shaft is pressure-lubricated by an oil feed pipe from the main oil gallery. The shaft "floats" on a cushion of oil. A drain pipe returns the oil to the sump.

6 The turbocharger bearings are cooled by circulating engine coolant. After switching off the ignition, an electric pump continues to circulate coolant for several minutes to prevent overheating of the bearings and to prolong their life.

Precautions

⚠️ *Warning:*
a) The turbocharger operates at extremely high speeds and temperatures. Certain precautions must be observed to avoid premature failure of the turbo or injury to the operator.
b) Do not operate the turbo with any parts exposed. Foreign objects falling onto the rotating vanes could cause excessive damage and (if ejected) personal injury.
c) Do not race the engine immediately after start-up, especially if it is cold. Give the oil a few seconds to circulate.
d) Always allow the engine to return to idle speed before switching it off - do not blip the throttle and switch off, as this will leave the turbo spinning without lubrication.
e) Allow the engine to idle for several minutes before switching off after a high-speed run.
f) Observe the recommended intervals for oil and filter changing, and use a reputable oil of the specified quality. Neglect of oil changing, or use of inferior oil, can cause carbon formation on the turbo shaft and subsequent failure.

20 Turbocharger - removal and refitting

Note: *New turbocharger-to-manifold nuts must be used on refitting. If a new turbocharger is to be fitted, new exhaust elbow-to-turbocharger nuts and new coolant pipe seals will be required.*

Removal

1 Whilst the engine is still warm, spray the turbocharger mounting bolts with a penetrating oil to ease removal.

2 Apply the handbrake, then jack up the front of the vehicle, and support securely on axle stands (see *"Jacking, towing and wheel changing"*).

3 Ensure that the engine has cooled sufficiently to avoid scalding, then drain the cooling system as described in Chapter 1.

4 Where applicable, remove the engine undershield.

5 Remove the exhaust front section with reference to Section 24.

6 Working under the vehicle, unscrew the upper securing nut and bolt, and the lower bolt, and remove the turbocharger lower support bracket **(see illustrations)**.

7 Unscrew the turbocharger oil return pipe

4

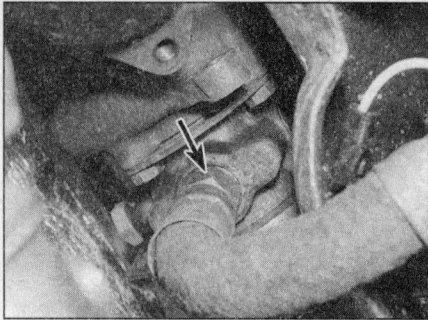

20.7 Turbocharger oil return pipe union (arrowed) - viewed from underneath vehicle

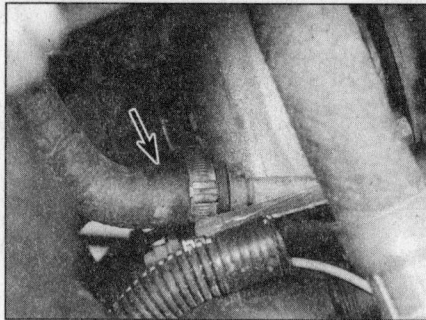

20.8 Disconnect the lower coolant hose (arrowed) from the turbocharger pipe - viewed from underneath vehicle

20.15 Unscrew the brake vacuum pump pipe union

20.16 Disconnect the coolant hose (arrowed) from the rear of the cylinder head

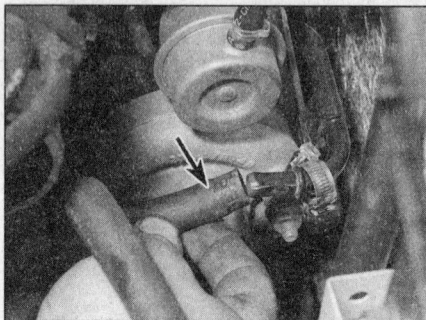

20.17 Disconnecting the upper turbocharger coolant hose (arrowed)

20.18 Unscrewing the turbocharger oil feed pipe union nut (arrowed)

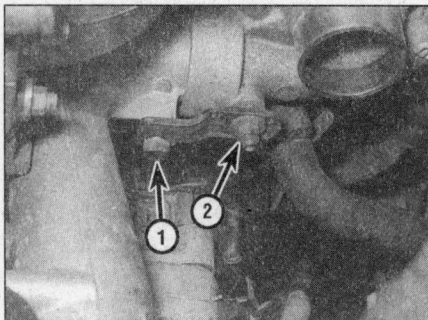

20.19 Turbocharger-to-air elbow bracket bolt (1) and nut (2)

20.20 Disconnecting the boost pressure pipe (arrowed) from the inlet manifold

20.21 Two of the turbocharger-to-manifold nuts (arrowed)

union from the outlet on the underside of the turbocharger **(see illustration)**. Be prepared for oil spillage.

8 Cut the hose clamp, and disconnect the lower coolant hose from the turbocharger pipe **(see illustration)**. Be prepared for coolant spillage.

9 Working in the engine compartment, unscrew the securing bolts, and remove the strengthening bar from between the front suspension strut turrets.

10 Remove the air cleaner assembly as described in Section 2.

11 Loosen the clamps, and remove the air trunking connecting the inlet manifold to the intercooler tube.

12 Loosen the clamps, and remove the air trunking connecting the air cleaner to the turbocharger. Also disconnect the breather

hose connecting the air trunking to the inlet manifold. Note the locations of any clips attached to the air trunking.

13 Loosen the clamp and disconnect the air outlet trunking (running to the intercooler) from the turbocharger.

14 Remove the nut securing the preheating system control unit to the bulkhead, and move the unit to one side, leaving the wiring connected.

15 Unscrew the union nut, and disconnect the vacuum pipe from the brake vacuum pump **(see illustration)**.

16 Disconnect the coolant hose from the rear of the cylinder head, and move the hose to one side, clear of the working area **(see illustration)**. Be prepared for coolant spillage.

17 Similarly, disconnect the upper turbocharger coolant hose **(see illustration)**.

18 Unscrew the union nut, and disconnect the oil feed pipe from the top of the turbocharger **(see illustration)**. It may be necessary to remove the wastegate bracket bolts to enable access to the union nut.

19 Remove the bolt and the nut securing the turbocharger-to-air elbow bracket, and withdraw the bracket **(see illustration)**.

20 Disconnect the boost pressure pipe from the inlet manifold **(see illustration)**.

21 Unscrew the four turbocharger-to-manifold nuts, and slide the turbocharger from the manifold studs **(see illustration)**. Access to the lower right-hand nut is easiest from underneath the vehicle. For improved access to the nuts, unbolt the exhaust elbow from the turbocharger.

22 Withdraw the turbocharger from above the engine compartment, by passing it below

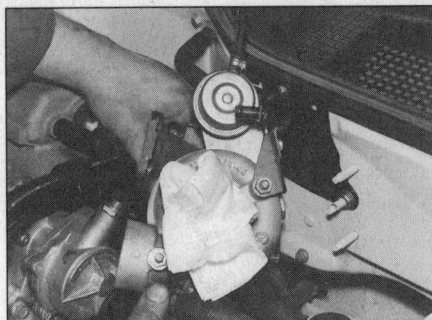

20.22 Withdrawing the turbocharger

the brake vacuum pump, and then manipulating it between the vacuum pump and the coolant reservoir **(see illustration)**.
23 If a new turbocharger is to be fitted, remove the coolant pipes and the exhaust elbow (if not already done) from the old unit, and transfer them to the new unit. Use new nuts when fitting the exhaust elbow, and new seals when fitting the coolant pipes.

Refitting

24 Refitting is a reversal of removal, but renew any damaged hose clamps, and use new turbocharger-to-manifold nuts. Where applicable, the exhaust elbow should be refitted to the turbocharger using new nuts. Note that if the wastegate bracket bolts were removed, they should be refitted using a suitable thread-locking compound. Refill the cooling system as described in Chapter 1.
25 On completion, the following procedure must be observed before starting the engine.
a) *Disconnect the wiring from the stop solenoid on the injection pump, and insulate the connector.*
b) *Crank the engine on the starter motor until the instrument panel oil pressure warning light goes out (this may take several seconds).*
c) *Reconnect the wiring to the stop solenoid, then start the engine using the normal procedure.*
d) *Run the engine at idle speed, and check the turbocharger oil and coolant unions for leakage. Rectify any problems without delay.*
26 After the engine has been run, check the engine oil level, and top up if necessary.

21 Turbocharger - examination and renovation

1 With the turbocharger removed, inspect the housing for cracks or other visible damage.
2 Spin the turbine or the compressor wheel to verify that the shaft is intact and to feel for excessive shake or roughness. Some play is normal since in use the shaft is "floating" on a film of oil. Check that the wheel vanes are undamaged.

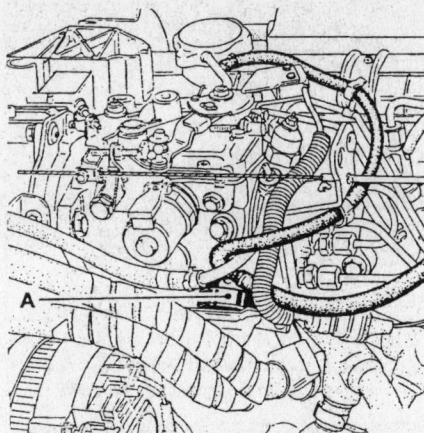

22.1 Boost pressure fuel delivery corrector location (A) - Turbo models

3 The wastegate actuator is a separate unit, and can be renewed independently of the turbocharger. Consult a Renault dealer or other specialist if it is thought that testing or renewal is necessary.
4 If the exhaust or inlet passages are oil-contaminated, the turbo shaft oil seals have probably failed. (On the inlet side, this will also have contaminated the intercooler, which if necessary should be flushed with a suitable solvent.)
5 Check the oil feed and return pipes for contamination or blockage and clean if necessary.
6 No DIY repair of the turbocharger is possible. A new unit may be available on an exchange basis.

22 Boost pressure fuel delivery corrector (Turbo models) - general information

This device is mounted on the side of the injection pump, and its purpose is to adjust the injection pump fuel metering in relation to the turbocharger boost pressure **(see illustration)**. Effectively, the quantity of fuel injected is increased as the boost pressure increases.
An adjustment screw is provided, but this is sealed at factory, and no attempt should be made to carry out adjustments without the use of specialist test equipment.
If a fault with the device is suspected, consult a Renault dealer or a suitably qualified specialist.

23 Intercooler - removal and refitting

Removal

1 The intercooler is located at the front left-hand side of the engine compartment, behind the front bumper.

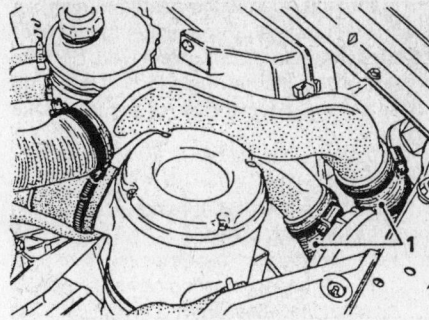

23.3 Disconnect the air trunking (1) from the intercooler

23.4 Intercooler bracket mounting bolts and nut (2)

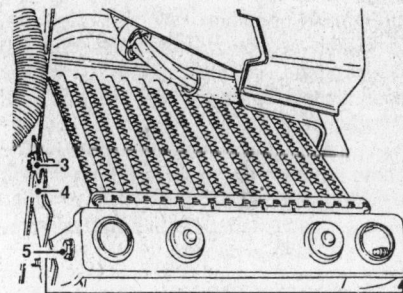

23.5 Intercooler clamp plate securing bolt (3), clamp plate (4) and intercooler-to-bracket bolts (5)

2 Remove the front bumper as described in Chapter 11.
3 Loosen the securing clamps, and disconnect the air trunking from the intercooler **(see illustration)**.
4 Working from outside the wing panel, unscrew the two bolts securing the intercooler mounting bracket to the body panel. Where applicable, also remove the bracket mounting nut **(see illustration)**.
5 Working at the inner edge of the intercooler, remove the bolt securing the clamp plate to the body panel, and withdraw the clamp plate **(see illustration)**.
6 Push the intercooler up to release the upper securing clip from the lip of the body panel (the clip is visible from the engine

4

compartment), then withdraw the intercooler and bracket assembly from under the vehicle.

7 The intercooler can be removed from its bracket after unscrewing the two securing bolts, and removing the lower section of the bracket.

Refitting

8 Refitting is a reversal of removal, bearing in mind the following points.

a) *When positioning the a]ssembly, take care not to damage the wiring harness located beneath the wheel arch.*

b) *Ensure that the upper securing clip is correctly located on the body panel (push the intercooler upwards until the clip engages over the lip of the body panel).*

c) *Ensure that the air trunking securing clamps are securely tightened.*

24 Exhaust system - general information and component renewal

General information

1 The exhaust system consists of three sections, the sections varying in detail depending on model **(see illustrations)**. Note that the intermediate section may contain one or two silencers, depending on model. Both the front pipe and tail pipe can be removed leaving the remaining exhaust system sections in position. To remove the intermediate section, it is recommended that the tail pipe is removed first, before disconnecting the intermediate section from the front pipe.

2 Where applicable, the catalytic converter is located between the exhaust front pipe and the intermediate section. The catalytic converter is attached to the exhaust front pipe and intermediate section by flange joints.

Component renewal

Note: *Where applicable, gaskets should be renewed on refitting.*

3 To remove the system or part of the system, first jack up the front or rear of the vehicle, as applicable, and support it securely on axle stands (see *"Jacking, towing and wheel changing"*). Alternatively, position the vehicle on car ramps.

Front pipe

4 To remove the front pipe, unscrew and remove the two nuts, then remove the washers, tension springs and sleeves securing the exhaust front pipe to the manifold or turbocharger, as applicable. Slide the flange plate off the manifold studs and separate the joint. Recover the sealing ring **(see illustrations)**.

5 Unscrew the nuts and remove the clamp securing the front pipe to the intermediate section. Pull the front pipe from the

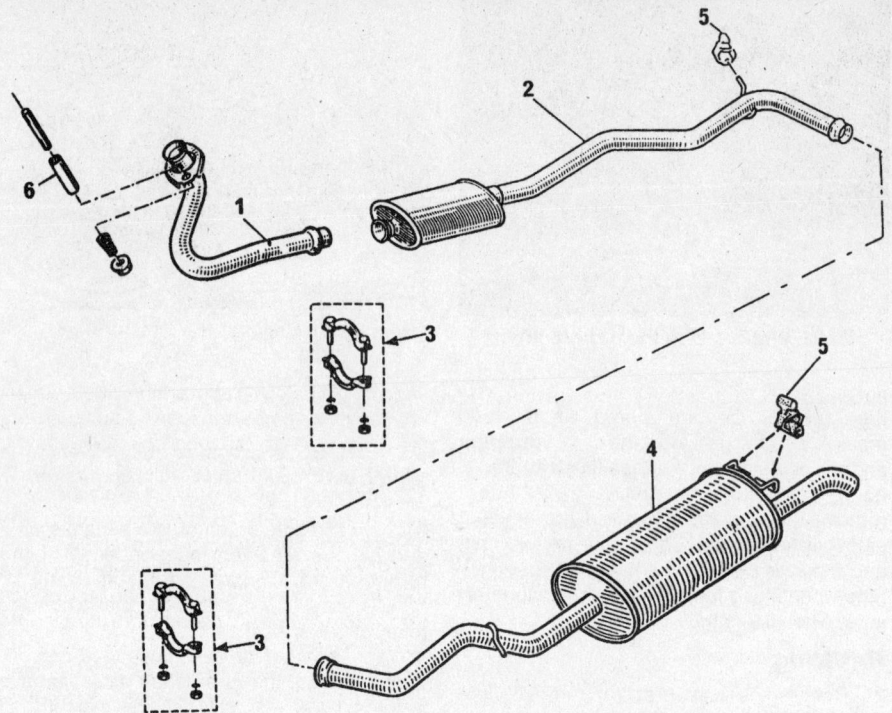

24.1a Typical exhaust system components - models without catalytic converter

1 *Front section*
2 *Intermediate section and resonator*
3 *Connecting clamp*
4 *Rear section and silencer*
5 *Exhaust rubber mounting*
6 *Spacer to limit tightening of front section nut*

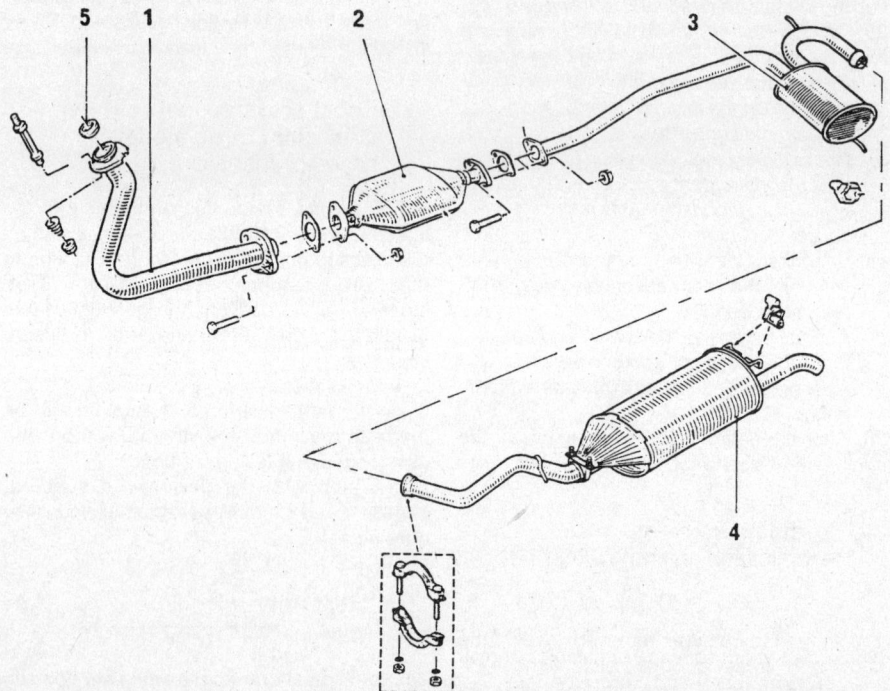

24.1b Typical exhaust system components - models with catalytic converter

1 *Front section*
2 *Catalytic converter*
3 *Intermediate section and resonator*
4 *Rear section*
5 *Front-section-to-manifold gasket*

24.4a Exhaust front pipe-to-turbocharger nuts (arrowed)

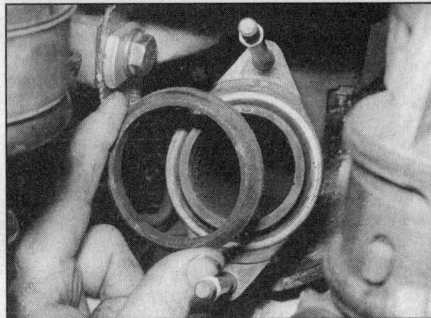

24.4b Recover the sealing ring

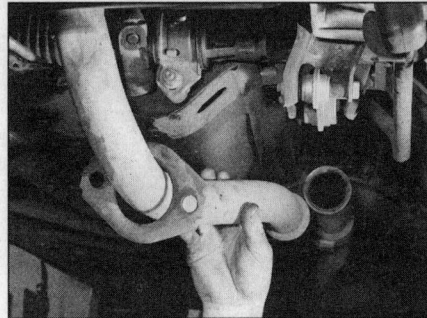

24.5 Removing the exhaust front section

intermediate section (see illustration). If a catalytic converter is fitted, simply unscrew the flange nuts and bolts securing the front pipe to the catalytic converter, and recover the gasket.

6 Refitting is a reversal of removal, but use a new sealing ring between the front pipe and the manifold or turbocharger (as applicable), and on models with a catalytic converter, use a new flange gasket.

Tailpipe

7 To remove the tailpipe, unscrew the nuts and remove the clamp securing the tailpipe to the intermediate section.

8 Slide the rubber mountings off the bars, and if necessary remove them from the underbody by turning them through 90°. Separate the tailpipe from the intermediate section.

9 Refitting is a reversal of removal, but tighten the clamp nuts securely and renew the rubber mountings if necessary.

Intermediate section

10 To remove the intermediate section, first remove the tailpipe as described previously.

11 Unscrew the nuts and remove the clamp securing the front pipe to the intermediate

section. If a catalytic converter is fitted, simply unscrew the flange nuts and bolts securing the intermediate section to the catalytic converter, and recover the gasket.

12 Slide the rubber mountings off the bars, and if necessary remove them from the underbody by turning them through 90°.

13 Separate the intermediate section from the front pipe or catalytic converter (as applicable) and if necessary unbolt the strengthening bracket.

14 Refitting is a reversal of removal, tighten the clamp nuts (and bolts, where applicable) securely and renew the rubber mountings if necessary. On models with a catalytic converter, use a new flange gasket.

Catalytic converter

15 The catalytic converter can be removed without disturbing the surrounding exhaust components after unscrewing the flange nuts and bolts. Recover the joint gaskets.

16 When refitting the catalytic converter, use new gaskets.

25 Emission control systems - general information

1 Certain engines are equipped with systems designed to reduce the emission of harmful by-products of the combustion process into the atmosphere.

2 The following systems may be fitted according to model.

Crankcase emission control system

3 A crankcase ventilation system is fitted to all models. A number of different system configurations may be encountered depending on the engine type (see illustrations).

4 Oil fumes and piston blow-by gases (combustion gases which have passed by the piston rings) are drawn from the crankcase through an auxiliary oil separator (two separators, located at the front and rear of the

4

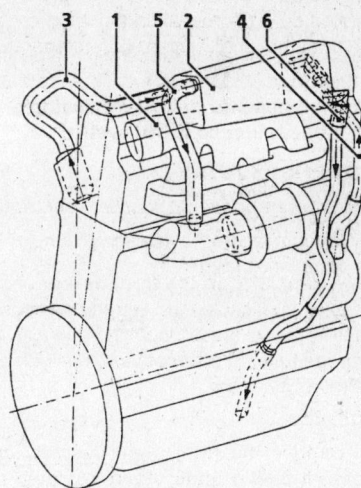

25.3a Typical crankcase emission control system - early non-Turbo models

1 Auxiliary oil separators
2 Main oil separator
3 Inlet manifold
4 Return pipe to sump
5 Calibrated orifice

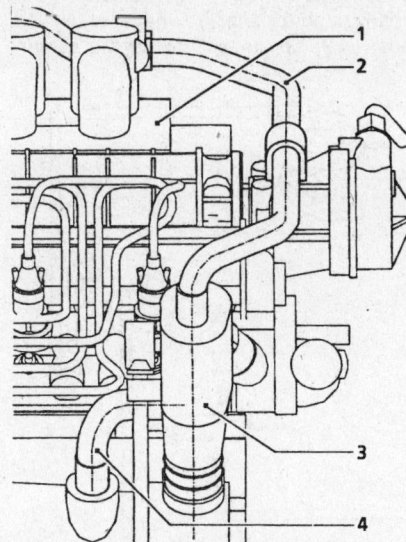

25.3b Typical crankcase emission control system - later non-Turbo models

1 Inlet manifold
2 Hose to inlet manifold
3 Oil separator
4 Return pipe to sump

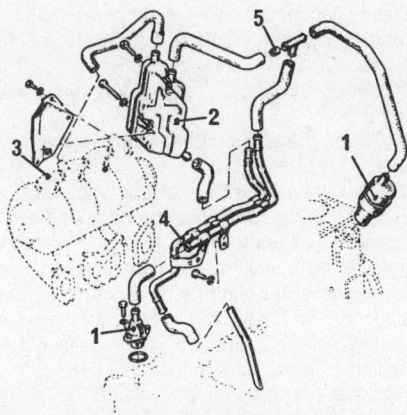

25.3c Typical crankcase emission control system - Turbo models

1 Inlet manifold
2 Vapour separator
3 Breather hose (from crankcase)
4 Breather hose (from crankcase)
5 Breather hose (to turbocharger inlet)
6 Return hose to sump

cylinder block on some engines), through the main oil separator, into the air inlet tract. The gases are then drawn into the engine together with fresh air/fuel mixture. Condensed oil vapour is returned from the main oil separator to the engine sump.

Exhaust emission control system

5 This system is fitted to all models with the F8Q 744 engine, and certain models with the F8Q 742 engine.

6 To minimise the level of exhaust gas pollutants released into the atmosphere, a catalytic converter is fitted, located in the exhaust system.

7 The catalytic converter consists of a canister containing a fine mesh impregnated with a catalyst material, over which the exhaust gases pass. The catalyst speeds up the oxidation of harmful carbon monoxide, unburnt hydrocarbons and soot, effectively reducing the quantity of harmful products reaching the atmosphere.

Exhaust gas recirculation (EGR) system

8 This system is fitted to models with the F8Q 742 and F8Q 744 engines.

9 The system is designed to recirculate small quantities of exhaust gas into the inlet tract, and therefore into the combustion process **(see illustration)**. This process reduces the level of oxides of nitrogen present in the final exhaust gas which is released into the atmosphere, and also lowers the combustion temperature.

10 The volume of exhaust gas recirculated is controlled by vacuum supplied from the brake servo vacuum pump, via a solenoid valve controlled by a micro-switch mounted on the injection pump (see Chapter 4). A temperature

25.9 Schematic view of exhaust gas recirculation (EGR) system

1 *Recirculation valve*
2 *Temperature valve*
3 *Fast idle vacuum actuator*
4 *Vacuum take-off between vacuum pump and servo*
5 *Fast idle solenoid valve*
6 *EGR solenoid valve*

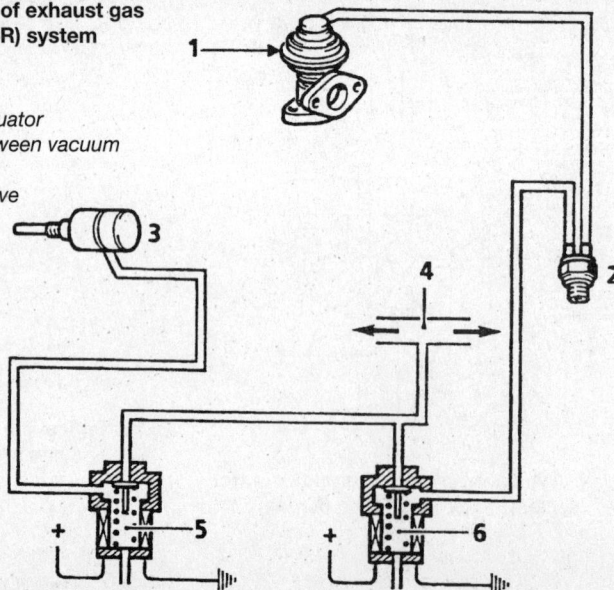

valve fitted in the vacuum supply line cuts off the vacuum supply until the engine reaches normal operating temperature.

11 A vacuum-operated recirculation valve is fitted to the exhaust manifold to regulate the quantity of exhaust gas recirculated. The valve is operated by the vacuum supplied by the brake vacuum pump via the solenoid valve and the temperature valve.

12 Between idling speed and a pre-determined engine load, the micro-switch on the injection pump closes to supply power to the solenoid valve, which allows the recirculation valve to open. Under full-load conditions, the micro-switch opens to cut off exhaust gas recirculation. Additional control is provided by the temperature valve, which cuts off the vacuum supply until the coolant temperature reaches 40°C, preventing the recirculation valve from opening during the engine warm-up phase. An "altimetric" capsule is also fitted, which cuts off the electrical supply to the solenoid valve (overriding the injection pump micro-switch) if atmospheric pressure drops below 900 mbars due to altitude.

26 Emission control systems - testing and component renewal

Crankcase emission control system components

Testing

1 If the system is thought to be faulty, firstly, check that the hoses are unobstructed. On high mileage vehicles, particularly when regularly used for short journeys, a jelly-like deposit may be evident inside the system

hoses and oil separators. If excessive deposits are present, the relevant component(s) should be removed and cleaned.

2 Periodically inspect the system components for security and damage, and renew them as necessary. Note that damaged or loose hoses can cause various engine running problems (erratic idle speed, stalling, etc) which can be difficult to trace.

Component renewal

3 Renewal procedures for the hoses and oil separators are self-evident.

Exhaust emission control system

Testing

4 The system can only be tested accurately using a suitable exhaust gas analyser (suitable for use with diesel engines).

Component renewal

5 The catalytic converter is fitted in the exhaust system between the front and intermediate sections.

6 Removal and refitting are described in Section 24.

Exhaust gas recirculation system

Testing

7 Start the engine, and run it until it reaches normal operating temperature (the cooling fan should have cut in and out at least once).

8 With the engine idling, disconnect the vacuum hose from the recirculation valve. As the hose is disconnected, it should be possible to hear the valve click shut. If no click is heard, proceed as follows.

9 Check that vacuum is present at the recirculation valve end of the vacuum hose. If a vacuum gauge is available, check that the vacuum is at least 500 mbars. If vacuum is present, it is likely that the recirculation valve is faulty (jammed or pierced diaphragm). If no vacuum is present, carry out the following checks.

10 Check the security of all vacuum hose connections.

11 Check the electrical feed to the solenoid valve.

12 Check the operation of the temperature valve. This can be done by checking that vacuum will pass through the valve with the engine at normal operating temperature. Stop the engine and disconnect the temperature valve vacuum hoses at the recirculation valve and the solenoid valve, and check that it is possible to blow through the hoses. If not, it is likely that the temperature valve is faulty, or the hoses are obstructed.

13 Check the operation of the micro-switch on the injection pump, using a continuity tester or an ohmmeter. With the pump accelerator lever in the idle position, the switch should be open (no continuity/infinite resistance). As the accelerator lever is moved from the idle position, the switch should close (continuity/zero resistance), until the lever reaches a predetermined position towards the end of its travel, when the switch should open again. Note that adjustment of the switch should **not** be attempted. If it is suspected that adjustment is required, or if a new switch is fitted, consult a Renault dealer who will have access to the specialist calibration equipment required to carry out accurate adjustment.

Component renewal

Recirculation valve

Note: *Where applicable, new gaskets should be used on refitting.*

14 The valve is located at the rear of the engine, and is bolted to the exhaust manifold on F8Q 742 engines, or the inlet manifold on F8Q 744 engines **(see illustration)**. The valve is connected to the remaining manifold via a metal pipe bolted between the valve and the manifold.

15 Disconnect the vacuum hose from the valve.

16 Remove the securing bolts, and disconnect the valve pipe from the inlet manifold (F8Q 742 engines) or exhaust manifold (F8Q 744 engines). Recover the gasket.

17 Unbolt the valve body from the relevant manifold, and recover the gasket, where applicable. Remove the valve complete with the pipe.

18 If a new valve is to be fitted, unscrew the securing bolts, and transfer the pipe to the new valve, using a new gasket.

19 Refitting is a reversal of removal, using new gaskets where applicable.

Solenoid valve

20 The valve is located on a bracket attached to the engine compartment bulkhead.

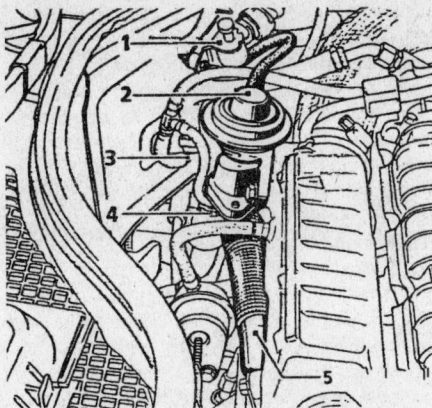

26.14 Exhaust gas recirculation (EGR) system components - F8Q 744 engine

1 *Solenoid valve*
2 *Recirculation valve*
3 *Vacuum take-off*
4 *Temperature valve*
5 *Recirculation pipe*

21 Disconnect the wiring plug and the vacuum hoses from the valve.

22 Unscrew the securing nut(s), and withdraw the valve complete with its bracket.

23 Refitting is a reversal of removal, ensuring that the vacuum hoses are securely reconnected.

Temperature valve

24 The temperature valve is located in the coolant hose at the left-hand front corner of the cylinder block.

25 To remove the valve, simply disconnect the wiring plug and unscrew the valve from the hose. Be prepared for coolant spillage.

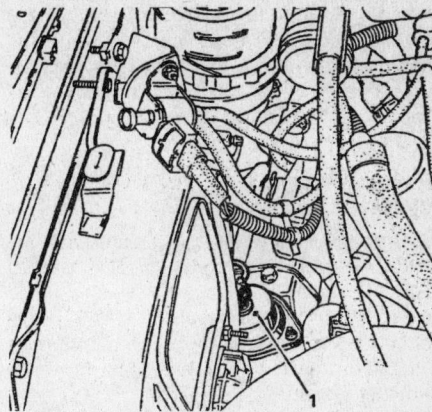

26.27 Exhaust gas recirculation (EGR) system "altimetric" capsule location (1)

26 Refitting is reversal of removal, but check for coolant leaks on completion, and if necessary, top up the coolant level.

"Altimetric" capsule

27 The capsule is located on the crossmember at the front of the engine compartment **(see illustration)**.

28 Disconnect the wiring plug from the capsule, then unscrew the securing nut(s) and withdraw the capsule.

29 Refitting is a reversal of removal.

Injection pump micro-switch (EGR cut-off switch)

30 Removal and refitting of the switch is self-explanatory, but note that on completion the switch must be adjusted by a Renault dealer using specialist calibration equipment. Refer to Chapter 5, Section 18 for details of the switch location.

4

Chapter 5
Engine electrical systems

Contents

Degrees of difficulty

Easy, suitable for novice with little experience	Fairly easy, suitable for beginner with some experience	Fairly difficult, suitable for competent DIY mechanic	Difficult, suitable for experienced DIY mechanic	Very difficult, suitable for expert DIY or professional

5

Specifications

General

Electrical system type .... 12 volt negative earth

Battery

Type .... Lead-acid, low-maintenance or "maintenance-free" (sealed for life)

Alternator

Type .... Paris-Rhone, Valeo or Ducellier
Maximum output (at 13.5 volts and 8000 (alternator) rpm .... 70, 90 or 110 amps, according to model
Regulated voltage .... 13.5 to 14.8 volts

Starter motor

Make and type .... Bosch reduction gear

Glow plugs

Type:
  Non-Turbo models .... Champion CH88 or CH137
  Turbo models .... Champion CH69

Torque wrench settings	**Nm**	**lbf ft**
Glow plugs	20	15
Stop solenoid	20	15

1 General information and precautions

General information

The engine electrical system includes all charging, starting and pre-heating components and engine oil sensors. Because of their engine-related functions, these components are covered separately from the body electrical devices such as the lights, instruments, etc (which are covered in Chapter 12).

The electrical system is of the 12-volt negative earth type.

The battery is of the low maintenance or "maintenance-free" (sealed for life) type and is charged by the alternator, which is belt-driven from a crankshaft-mounted pulley.

The starter motor is of the pre-engaged reduction gear type, incorporating an integral solenoid. On starting, the solenoid moves the drive pinion into engagement with the flywheel ring gear before the starter motor is energised. Once the engine has started, a one-way clutch prevents the motor armature being driven by the engine until the pinion disengages from the flywheel. The motor is fitted with a reduction gear mechanism, in order to achieve the high torque necessary to turn the engine against the high compression pressures encountered in a diesel engine.

Precautions

Further details of the various systems are given in the relevant Sections of this Chapter. While some repair procedures are given, the usual course of action is to renew the component concerned. The owner whose interest extends beyond mere component renewal should obtain a copy of the "Automobile Electrical & Electronic Systems Manual", available from the publishers of this manual.

It is necessary to take extra care when working on the electrical system to avoid damage to semi-conductor devices (diodes and transistors), and to avoid the risk of personal injury. In addition to the precautions given in "Safety first!" at the beginning of this manual, observe the following when working on the system:

Always remove rings, watches, etc before working on the electrical system. Even with the battery disconnected, capacitive discharge could occur if a component's live terminal is earthed through a metal object. This could cause a shock or nasty burn.

Do not reverse the battery connections. Components such as the alternator, pre-heating electronic control unit, or any other components having semi-conductor circuitry could be irreparably damaged.

If the engine is being started using jump leads and a slave battery, connect the batteries positive-to-positive and negative-to-

negative (see "Booster battery (jump) starting"). This also applies when connecting a battery charger.

Never disconnect the battery terminals, the alternator, any electrical wiring or any test instruments when the engine is running.

Do not allow the engine to turn the alternator when the alternator is not connected.

Never "test" for alternator output by "flashing" the output lead to earth.

Never use an ohmmeter of the type incorporating a hand-cranked generator for circuit or continuity testing.

Always ensure that the battery negative lead is disconnected when working on the electrical system.

Before using electric-arc welding equipment on the car, disconnect the battery, alternator and components such as the pre-heating electronic control unit, ABS electronic control unit, etc, to protect them from the risk of damage.

The radio/cassette unit fitted as standard equipment by Renault may be equipped with a built-in security code to deter thieves. If the power source to the unit is cut, the anti-theft system will activate. Even if the power source is immediately reconnected, the radio/cassette unit will not function until the correct security code has been entered. Therefore, if you do not know the correct security code for the radio/cassette unit **do not** disconnect the negative terminal of the battery or remove the radio/cassette unit from the vehicle. Refer to the manufacturer's handbook supplied with the vehicle for details of how to enter the security code.

2 Electrical fault finding - general information

Refer to Chapter 12.

3 Battery - testing and charging

Note: Refer to the precautions given in "Safety first!" and in Section 1 of this Chapter before proceeding.

Testing

1 Most vehicles are fitted with a "maintenance-free" (sealed-for-life) battery, in which case the electrolyte level cannot be checked. In this case, refer to the battery manufacturer's recommendations for maintenance and charging procedures.

2 Where a conventional battery is fitted, the electrolyte level of each cell should be checked, and if necessary topped-up with distilled or de-ionised water, at the intervals given in Chapter 1. On some batteries, the case is translucent, and incorporates

minimum and maximum level marks.

3 If the vehicle covers a very small annual mileage, it is worthwhile checking the specific gravity of the electrolyte every three months, to determine the state of charge of the battery. Use a hydrometer to make the check, and compare the results obtained with the following table.

	Normal climates	Tropics
Discharged	1.080	1.120
Half-charged	1.200	1.160
Fully-charged	1.280	1.230

4 If the battery condition is suspect, where possible, first check the specific gravity of the electrolyte in each cell. A variation of 0.040 or more between cells indicates loss of electrolyte or deterioration of the internal plates.

5 An accurate test of battery condition can be made by a battery specialist, using a heavy-discharge meter. Alternatively, connect a voltmeter across the battery terminals, and disconnect the stop solenoid (see Section 21); operate the starter motor with the headlamps, heated rear window and heater blower switched on. If the voltmeter reading remains above 9.6 volts, the battery condition is satisfactory. If the voltmeter reading drops below 9.6 volts, and the battery has already been charged, it is faulty.

Charging

Note: The following is intended as a guide only. Always refer to the battery manufacturer's recommendations (often printed on a label attached to the battery) before charging.

6 In normal use, the battery should not require charging from an external source, unless it is discharged accidentally (for instance by leaving the lamps on). Charging can also temporarily revive a failing battery, but if frequent recharging is required (and the alternator output is correct), the battery is worn out.

7 Unless the battery manufacturer advises differently, the charging rate in amps should be no more than one-tenth of the battery capacity in amp-hours (for instance, 6.5 amps for a 65 amp-hour battery). Most domestic battery chargers have an output of 5 amps or so, and these can safely be used overnight. Rapid "boost" charging is not recommended; if it is not carefully controlled, it can cause serious damage to the battery plates through overheating.

8 Both battery terminal leads must be disconnected before connecting the charger leads (disconnect the negative lead first). Connect the charger leads **before** switching on at the mains. When charging is complete, switch off at the mains **before** disconnecting the charger. If this procedure is followed, there is no risk of creating a spark at the battery terminals. Continue to charge the battery until no further rise in specific gravity

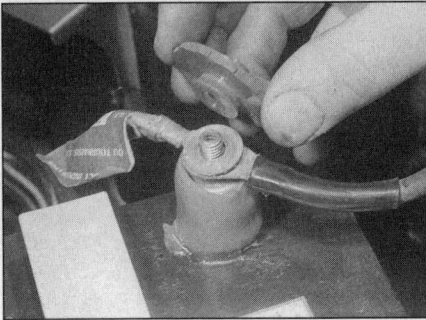

4.4 Disconnecting the positive terminal lead from the battery

4.5 Unscrewing the extended clamp bolt to remove the battery

7.3 Unbolt the hose bracket from the fuel injection pump mounting bracket

is noted over a four-hour period, or until vigorous gassing is observed.

9 On completion of charging, check the electrolyte level (if possible) and top-up if necessary, using distilled or de-ionised water.

4 Battery - removal and refitting

Note: *Refer to the precautions given in "Safety first!" and in Section 1 of this Chapter before proceeding.*

Removal

1 The battery is located beneath a plastic cover on the right-hand side of the bulkhead. First check that all electrical components are switched off in order to avoid a spark occurring as the negative lead is disconnected. Note also that if the radio has a security coding, it will be necessary to insert this code when the battery is re-connected.

2 Remove the plastic cover from over the battery. To do this, first pull up the weatherseal, then remove the screws and lift the cover from the battery. The cover may be stuck to the windscreen, however a sharp pull will release it.

3 Loosen the plastic nut on the negative terminal clamp, then lift the clamp and lead from the terminal and place it on the bulkhead. This is the terminal to disconnect before working on any electrical component on the vehicle. If the terminal is tight, carefully ease it off by moving it from side to side.

4 Loosen the plastic nut on the positive terminal clamp **(see illustration)**, then lift the clamp and lead from the terminal and place it on the bulkhead. If necessary, the nut can be removed completely and the lead disconnected from the clamp.

5 Unscrew the extended clamp bolt and remove the clamp from the front of the battery **(see illustration)**.

6 Lift the battery from the tray, keeping it upright and taking care not to let it touch clothing.

7 If necessary, remove the battery tray from the bulkhead.

8 Clean the battery terminal posts, clamps,

tray and battery casing. If the bulkhead is rusted as a result of battery acid spillage, clean it thoroughly and re-paint with reference to Chapter 11.

Refitting

9 Refitting is a reversal of removal, but always connect the positive terminal clamp first and the negative terminal clamp last.

5 Charging system - testing

Note: *Refer to the warnings given in "Safety first!" and in Section 1 of this Chapter before proceeding.*

1 If the ignition (no-charge) warning light fails to illuminate when the ignition is switched on, first check the security of the alternator wiring connections. If satisfactory, check that the warning light bulb has not blown, and that the bulbholder is secure in its location in the instrument panel. If the light still fails to illuminate, check the continuity of the warning light feed wire from the alternator to the bulbholder. If all is satisfactory, the alternator is at fault, and should be renewed or taken to an auto-electrician for testing and repair.

2 If the ignition warning light illuminates when the engine is running, stop the engine and check that the drivebelt is correctly tensioned (Chapter 1) and that the alternator connections are secure. If all is so far satisfactory, check the alternator brushes and slip rings (see Section 8). If the fault persists, the alternator should be renewed, or taken to an auto-electrician for testing and repair.

3 If the alternator output is suspect even though the warning light functions correctly, the regulated voltage may be checked as follows.

4 Connect a voltmeter across the battery terminals, and start the engine.

5 Increase the engine speed until the voltmeter reading remains steady; the reading should be between 13.5 and 14.8 volts.

6 Switch on as many electrical accessories (headlamps, heated rear window, heater blower etc) as possible, and check that the alternator maintains the regulated voltage

between 13.5 and 14.8 volts. It may be necessary to increase engine speed slightly.

7 If the regulated voltage is not as stated, the fault may be due to worn brushes, weak brush springs, a faulty voltage regulator, a faulty diode, a severed phase winding, or worn or damaged slip rings. The brushes and slip rings may be checked (see Section 8), but if the fault persists, the alternator should be renewed or taken to an auto-electrician for testing and repair.

6 Auxiliary drivebelts - removal, refitting and adjustment

Refer to Chapter 1.

7 Alternator - removal and refitting

Note: *Refer to the warnings given in "Safety first!" and in Section 1 of this Chapter before proceeding. Due to changes in production procedures, certain models may be fitted with alternator mounting arrangements which differ in detail from those described in this Section. Where this is the case, make comprehensive notes during removal, to ensure correct refitting.*

Models without air conditioning

Removal

1 Disconnect the battery leads.

2 Where applicable, to improve access, remove the securing clips, and withdraw the cover panel from the top of the radiator.

3 To allow sufficient clearance to enable the alternator to be removed, remove the two bolts securing the fuel filter assembly to the body panel, unbolt the hose bracket from the fuel injection pump mounting bracket, and move the fuel filter assembly to one side, leaving the hoses connected **(see illustration)**. Take care not to strain the hoses.

4 Where necessary for improved access, remove the plastic shield from above the alternator.

5

7.7 Unscrewing the drivebelt tensioner bolt
1 Alternator pivot bolt
2 Adjustment locknut

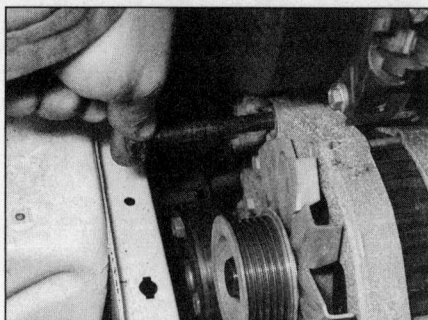

7.8a Remove the alternator pivot bolt . . .

7.8b . . . then withdraw the alternator

8.3 Alternator brush and regulator lead to the B+ terminal (arrowed)

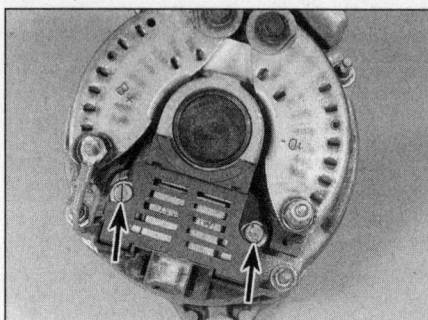

8.4a Unscrew the two small screws (arrowed) . . .

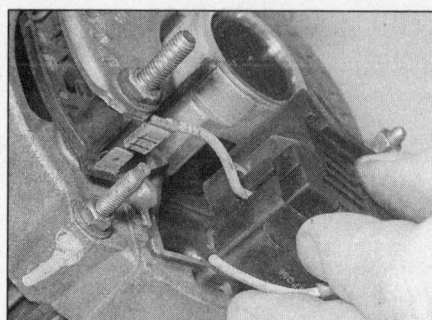

8.4b . . . and remove the regulator and brushbox assembly

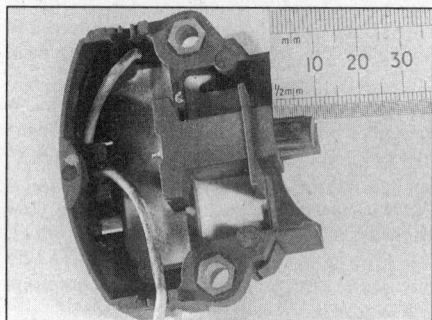

8.5 Measuring the length of the alternator brushes

5 Make a note of the electrical lead locations at the rear of the alternator and disconnect them.

6 Loosen the alternator pivot nut and bolt and, where applicable, the tensioner locknut on the adjustment bracket.

7 Unscrew the tensioner bolt, or release the tensioner, as applicable, so that the drivebelt tension is fully released. Remove the drivebelt from the alternator pulley **(see illustration)**.

8 Remove the alternator pivot bolt and nut, and where applicable, the adjustment locknut and bolt, then withdraw the alternator from the engine **(see illustrations)**.

Refitting

9 Refitting is a reversal of removal. Tension the drivebelt with reference to Chapter 1.

Models with air conditioning

Removal

10 Proceed as described in paragraphs 1 to 5 inclusive.

11 Remove the auxiliary drivebelt with reference to Chapter 1.

12 Remove the cover from the rear of the right-hand headlamp to allow sufficient clearance to withdraw the lower alternator mounting through-bolt. (On certain models, it may be necessary to move the headlamp unit forwards with reference to Chapter 12.)

13 Unscrew the nut and remove the lower alternator mounting through-bolt.

14 Similarly, remove the upper through-bolt, and withdraw the alternator.

Refitting

15 Refitting is a reversal of removal. Tension the drivebelt with reference to Chapter 1.

8 Alternator brushes and regulator - removal, inspection and refitting

Note: *Refer to the warnings given in "Safety first!" and in Section 1 of this Chapter before proceeding.*

Removal

1 Disconnect the battery negative lead. On certain models, it may be necessary to remove the alternator, as described in Section 7, to enable access to the regulator and brushbox assembly.

2 Note the locations of the wiring connectors and leads at the rear of the alternator and disconnect them.

3 Note the location of the lead on the B+ terminal, then unscrew and remove the nuts and lead and remove the plastic rear cover **(see illustration)**.

4 Unscrew the two small screws or nuts securing the regulator and brushbox assembly to the rear of the alternator. Lift off the regulator and brushbox, disconnect the electrical lead(s), noting their locations, then remove the regulator and brushbox assembly from the alternator **(see illustrations)**.

Inspection

5 Measure the length of each brush from the end of the holder to the top of the brush **(see illustration)**. No dimension is given by Renault, but as a rough guide 5 mm should be regarded as a minimum. If either brush is worn below this amount, obtain and fit a new brushbox. If the brushes are still serviceable, clean them with a petrol-moistened cloth. Check that the brush spring pressure is equal for both brushes and gives reasonable tension. If in doubt about the condition of the brushes and springs, compare them with new parts at a Renault parts dealer. The regulator can be separated from the brushbox after removing the cover if necessary.

6 Clean the alternator slip rings with a petrol-moistened cloth, then check for signs

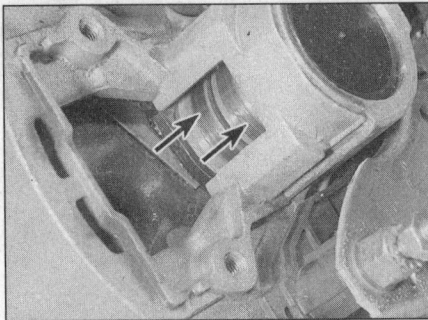

8.6 Alternator slip rings (arrowed)

of scoring, burning or severe pitting **(see illustration)**. If evident, the slip rings should be attended to by an automobile electrician.

Refitting

7 Refitting is a reversal of removal.

9 Starting system - testing

Note: *Refer to the precautions given in "Safety first!" and in Section 1 of this Chapter before proceeding.*

1 If the starter motor fails to operate when the ignition key is turned to the appropriate position, the possible causes are as follows.
 a) *The battery is faulty.*
 b) *The electrical connections between the switch, solenoid, battery and starter motor are somewhere failing to pass the necessary current from the battery through the starter to earth.*
 c) *The solenoid is faulty.*
 d) *The starter motor is mechanically or electrically defective.*

2 To check the battery, switch on the headlamps. If they dim after a few seconds, this indicates that the battery is discharged - recharge (see Section 3) or renew the battery. If the headlamps glow brightly, operate the starter switch and observe the lamps. If they dim, then this indicates that current is reaching the starter motor, therefore the fault must lie in the starter motor. If the lamps continue to glow brightly (and no clicking sound can be heard from the starter motor solenoid), this indicates that there is a fault in the circuit or solenoid - see the following paragraphs. If the starter motor turns slowly when operated, but the battery is in good condition, then this indicates either that the starter motor is faulty, or there is considerable resistance somewhere in the circuit.

3 If a fault in the circuit is suspected, disconnect the battery leads (including the earth connection to the body), the starter/solenoid wiring and the engine/gearbox earth strap. Thoroughly clean the connections, and reconnect the leads and wiring. Use a voltmeter or test lamp to check that full battery voltage is available at the

battery positive lead connection to the solenoid. Smear petroleum jelly around the battery terminals to prevent corrosion - corroded connections are among the most frequent causes of electrical system faults.

4 If the battery and all connections are in good condition, check the circuit by disconnecting the wire from the solenoid blade terminal. Connect a voltmeter or test lamp between the wire end and a good earth (such as the battery negative terminal), and check that the wire is live when the ignition switch is turned to the "start" position. If it is, then the circuit is sound - if not, there is a fault in the ignition/starter switch or wiring.

5 The solenoid contacts can be checked by connecting a voltmeter or test lamp between the battery positive feed connection on the starter side of the solenoid, and earth. When the ignition switch is turned to the "start" position, there should be a reading or lighted bulb, as applicable. If there is no reading or lighted bulb, the solenoid is faulty and should be renewed.

6 If the circuit and solenoid are proved sound, the fault must lie in the starter motor. Begin checking the starter motor by removing it (see Section 10), and checking the brushes (see Section 11). If the fault does not lie in the brushes, the motor windings must be faulty. In this event, the starter motor must be renewed, unless an auto-electrical specialist can be found who will overhaul the unit at a cost significantly less than that of a new or exchange starter motor.

10 Starter motor - removal and refitting

Note: *Refer to the precautions given in "Safety first!" and in Section 1 of this Chapter before proceeding.*

Non-Turbo models

Removal

1 Open the bonnet and disconnect the battery negative lead.

2 Unscrew the three bolts securing the starter motor to the gearbox bellhousing. Where applicable, note the location of any wiring brackets secured by the bolts.

3 Apply the handbrake, then jack up the front of the vehicle and support it securely on axle stands (see *"Jacking, towing and wheel changing"*). For improved access, remove the front right-hand roadwheel. Where applicable, also remove the engine undershield.

4 Unscrew the nuts/bolts securing the exhaust heat shield/rear starter motor mounting bracket assembly to the cylinder block and the starter motor bracket, and withdraw the assembly.

5 Disconnect the wiring from the terminals on the starter motor solenoid.

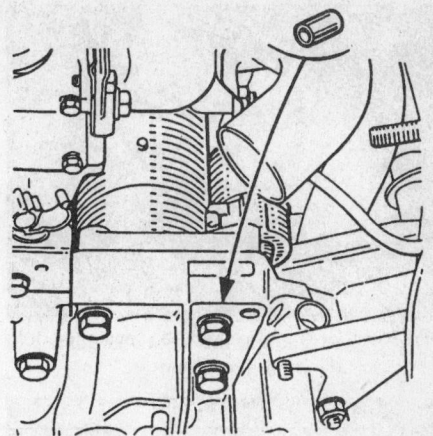

10.7 Starter motor locating dowel location (arrowed) - non-Turbo models

6 Working from in the engine compartment, withdraw the motor from the engine. Note the locating dowel in the bellhousing hole.

Refitting

7 Refitting is a reversal of removal, bearing in mind the following points.
 a) *Ensure that the locating dowel is correctly positioned in the bellhousing bolt hole, as noted during removal (see illustration).*
 b) *When reconnecting the wiring to the motor, make sure that the terminal on the end of the wiring is positioned clear of the starter motor body and surrounding components.*
 c) *Ensure the exhaust heat shield is refitted.*
 d) *Where applicable, refit the any wiring brackets to the starter motor mounting bolts.*

Turbo models

Removal

8 Disconnect the battery negative lead.

9 Apply the handbrake, then jack up the front of the vehicle and support it securely on axle stands (see *"Jacking, towing and wheel changing"*). Remove the right-hand roadwheel. Where applicable, also remove the engine undershield.

10 Loosen the securing clips, and remove the air ducting connecting the inlet manifold to the intercooler **(see illustration)**.

10.10 Remove the air ducting connecting the inlet manifold to the intercooler . . .

5

10.11 . . . and the turbocharger to the intercooler

10.14 Drive the roll pin from the right-hand driveshaft

10.16 Release the driveshaft from the stub shaft

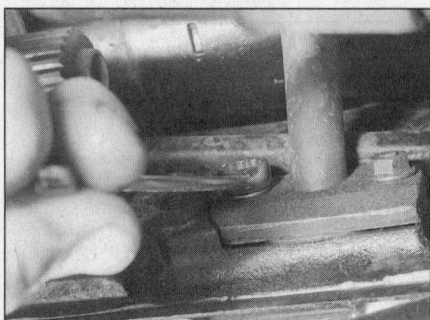

10.18a Unscrew the two securing nuts . . .

10.18b . . . and disconnect the turbocharger oil return pipe

10.19 Remove the nut securing the wiring to the starter motor bracket, then disconnect the wiring (arrowed)

11 Similarly, remove the air ducting connecting the turbocharger to the intercooler **(see illustration)**.

12 Unscrew the three bolts securing the starter motor to the gearbox bellhousing. Where applicable, note the location of any wiring brackets secured by the bolts.

13 Remove the exhaust front section as described in Chapter 4.

14 Working beneath the right-hand side of the vehicle, use a pin punch to drive out the double roll pin securing the right-hand driveshaft to the gearbox differential sun wheel stub shaft **(see illustration)**.

15 Loosen the two nuts and bolts securing the right-hand stub axle carrier to the suspension strut. Remove the upper nut and bolt, but leave the lower nut and bolt in

position. Note that the nuts are on the rear side of the strut.

16 Pull the top of the stub axle carrier outwards until the inner end of the driveshaft is released from the stub shaft **(see illustration)**. Support the driveshaft using string or wire - do not allow it to hang under its own weight.

17 Move the driveshaft as necessary for access to the two nuts securing the turbocharger oil return pipe to the cylinder block.

18 Remove the two securing nuts, and disconnect the turbocharger oil return pipe from the cylinder block. Recover the gasket. Plug the hole in the cylinder block to prevent dirt ingress **(see illustrations)**.

19 Remove the nut securing the wiring bracket to the bottom of the rear starter motor

mounting bracket, then disconnect the wiring from the starter motor **(see illustration)**.

20 Remove the bolt securing the turbocharger support bracket to the rear starter motor support bracket (note that the bolt also secures the heat shield) **(see illustration)**. Loosen the nut and bolt securing the support bracket to the turbocharger, and pivot the support bracket clear of the starter motor.

21 Remove the nuts and bolts securing the rear starter motor mounting bracket to the engine and the starter motor.

22 Remove the remaining bolt securing the heat shield **(see illustration)**.

23 Withdraw the starter motor, rear mounting bracket and heat shield from underneath the vehicle **(see illustration)**. Take care not to drop the starter motor.

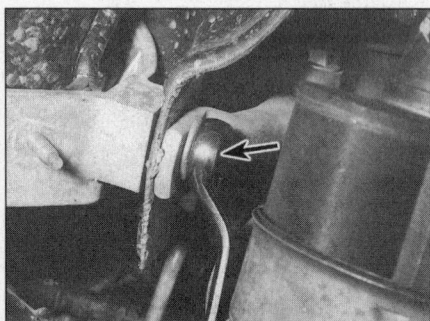

10.20 Remove the bolt (arrowed) securing the turbocharger support bracket

10.22 Upper heat shield securing bolt (arrowed) - viewed from above with engine removed

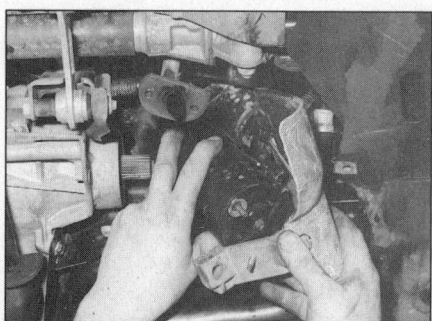

10.23 Removing the starter motor, rear mounting bracket and heat shield

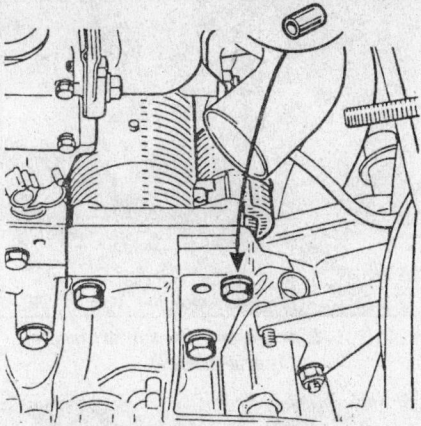

10.24 Starter motor locating dowel location (arrowed) - Turbo models

Refitting

24 Refitting is a reversal of removal, bearing in mind the following points.

a) Ensure that the locating dowel is correctly positioned in the bellhousing bolt hole and that the motor engages correctly with the dowel **(see illustration)**.

b) When reconnecting the wiring to the motor, make sure the terminal on the end of the wiring is positioned clear of the starter motor body and surrounding components.

c) Ensure the exhaust heat shield is refitted.

d) Tighten the stub axle carrier-to-suspension strut nuts and bolts to the specified torque (Chapter 10).

e) Refit the exhaust front section as described in Chapter 4.

f) Where applicable, refit any wiring brackets to the starter motor mounting bolts.

11 Starter motor - brush renewal

1 With the starter motor removed from the vehicle as described in Section 10, proceed as follows **(see illustration)**.

2 Make alignment marks on the armature end cover and the motor body.

3 Where applicable, unscrew the two securing nuts, and remove the mounting

11.1 Exploded view of the Bosch reduction gear type starter motor

1 Bolt	10 Armature shaft end	16 End cap screw
2 Solenoid	circlips and shims	17 Armature shaft end cap
4 Through-bolt	11 Armature end cover	18 Terminal nut and washer
5 Drive end housing	12 Armature	19 Brush spring
6 Armature retaining plate	13 Brush holder	20 Bush
7 Ring gear	14 Brush holder plate	21 Field windings
8 Rubber wiring grommet	15 Motor body	22 Bush
9 Reduction gear assembly		

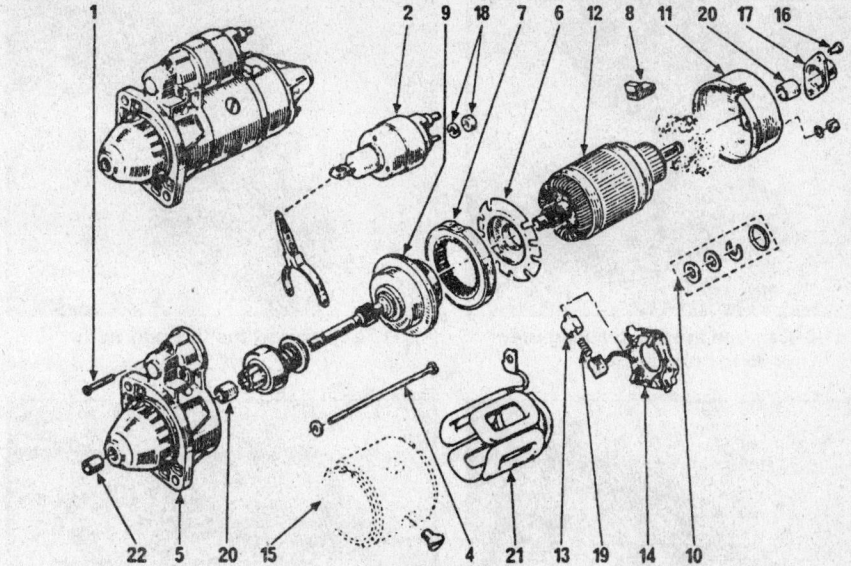

11.3 Removing the mounting bracket from the rear of the starter motor

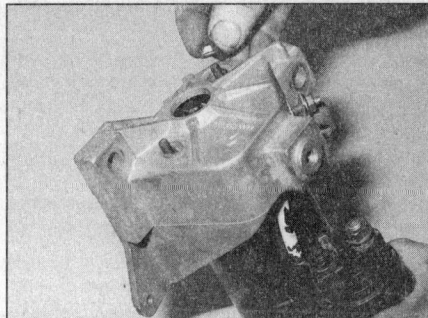

11.4a Unscrew the securing screws . . .

bracket from the rear of the starter motor **(see illustration)**.

4 Unscrew the securing screws, and remove the armature shaft end cap **(see illustrations)**.

5 Remove the circlip from the end of the armature shaft. Recover the washers and spacers, noting their orientation **(see illustrations)**.

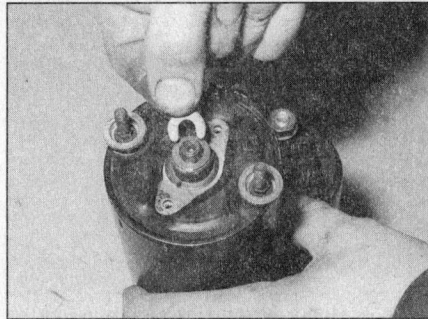

11.4b . . . and remove the armature shaft end cap

11.5a Remove the circlip . . .

11.5b . . . and recover the washers and spacers

5

11.6 Remove the nut securing the field brush wiring

11.7a Unscrew the through-bolts . . .

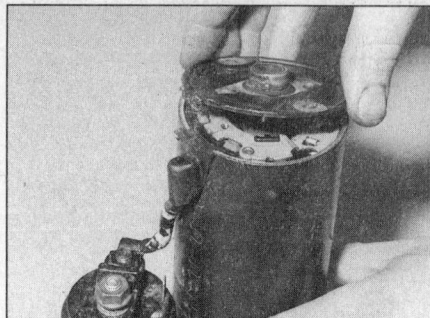

11.7b . . . and withdraw the armature end cover

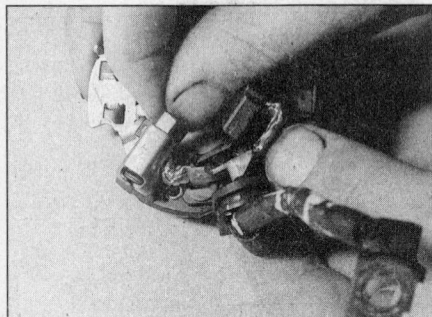

11.9a Withdraw the brushes . . .

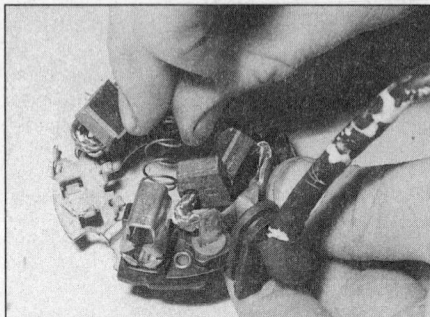

11.9b . . . springs . . .

11.9c . . . and brush holders from the brush plate

6 Remove the nut securing the field brush wiring to the solenoid **(see illustration)**.

7 Unscrew the two through-bolts and withdraw the armature end cover, along with the mounting bracket, when fitted **(see illustrations)**.

8 Withdraw the brush plate assembly from the rear of the starter motor, pulling the rubber wiring grommet from the motor casing as it is withdrawn.

9 Withdraw the brushes and the springs from the brush holders, then unclip the brush holders from the brush plate **(see illustrations)**.

10 Examine the brushes for wear and damage. If they are damaged, or worn to the extent where the springs are unable to exert sufficient pressure to maintain good contact with the commutator, they should be renewed. If renewal is necessary, unsolder the old brushes, and solder new ones into place.

11 Clean the brush holder assemblies, and wipe the commutator with a petrol-moistened cloth. If the commutator is dirty, it may be cleaned with fine glass paper, then wiped with the cloth.

12 Fit the brush holders to the brush plate, then refit the springs and the brushes to the brush holders. Ensure that the brushes move freely in their holders. Ensure that the brush springs provide adequate pressure on the brushes, and renew any worn springs.

13 Push the brushes into the brush holders, and use a suitable socket to hold them in position as shown **(see illustration)**.

14 Position the brush plate over the rear of the armature shaft, then withdraw the socket so that the brushes contact the commutator **(see illustration)**.

15 Further refitting is a reversal of removal, bearing in mind the following points.
a) Align the marks made on the end cover and the motor body before removal.
b) Ensure that the washers and spacers on the end of the armature shaft are fitted as noted before removal.
c) Refit the starter motor (see Section 10).

12 Ignition switch - removal and refitting

Removal

1 Disconnect the battery negative lead.

2 Unscrew the cross-head screws and remove the steering column shrouds. Where applicable, also remove the internal cover **(see illustrations)**.

11.13 Use a suitable socket to hold the brushes in position

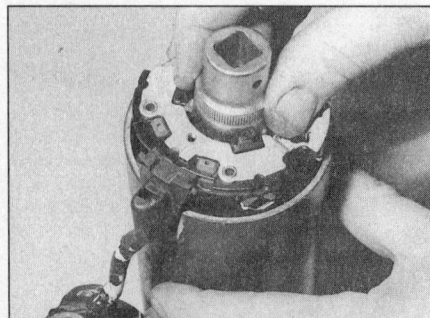

11.14 Fitting the brush plate over the armature shaft

12.2a Remove the screws . . .

12.2b . . . and withdraw the steering column shrouds

12.2c Removing the ignition switch internal cover

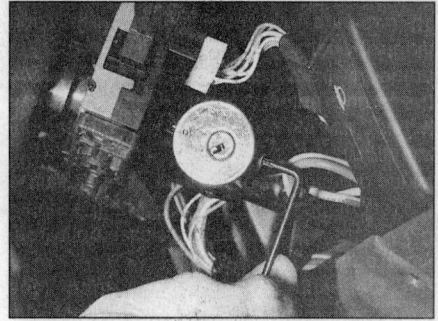

12.4 Unscrewing the ignition switch grub screw

3 Note the routing of the wiring, then disconnect the two ignition switch wiring connectors.

4 Using an angled cross-head screwdriver (or a similar tool to enable access), remove the small grub screw located at the rear, or on the top of the ignition switch **(see illustration)**.

5 Insert the ignition key and turn it to the position between "A" and "M".

6 Depress the retaining lug (located under the switch), using a pin punch, and withdraw the switch assembly using the key **(see illustration)**. Feed the wiring through the housing in the steering column.

Refitting

7 Refitting is a reversal of removal, ensuring that the wiring is correctly routed as noted during removal.

13 Oil pressure warning light switch - removal and refitting

Removal

1 The oil pressure warning light switch is located at the lower front right-hand side of the cylinder block **(see illustration)**.

2 Disconnect the battery negative lead, then release the wiring connector from the switch.

3 Carefully unscrew the switch and withdraw it from the cylinder block. Be prepared for some oil spillage.

4 Recover the sealing ring, where applicable.

Refitting

5 Refitting is a reversal of removal, but clean the threads of the switch before screwing it into the cylinder block, and where applicable, use a new sealing ring.

14 Oil level sensor - removal and refitting

Where fitted, the oil level sensor is located in the front lower face of the cylinder block or in the side of the sump **(see illustration)**. Removal and refitting details are as described for the oil pressure warning light switch in Section 13.

15 Preheating system - description and testing

Description

1 Each swirl chamber has a heater plug (commonly called a glow plug) screwed into it. The plugs are electrically operated before, during, and a short time after start-up when the engine is cold. Electrical feed to the glow plugs is controlled by the preheating control unit.

2 The glow plugs also provide a "post-heating" function, whereby the glow plugs remain switched on for a period after the engine has started. Once the starter has been switched off, the glow plugs are supplied with full current for 10 seconds, then the plugs are supplied with half the "preheating" current, alternately, in pairs, for up to 3 minutes. The exact "post-heating" time is controlled by the preheating control unit, and is dependant on the prevailing engine operating conditions. The supply to the plugs will be interrupted by:

a) *Opening of the "no-load" switch. The supply is cut off 3 seconds after the switch opens (ie 3 seconds after the accelerator pedal is depressed). The current supply is restored as soon as the switch closes.*

b) *A coolant temperature of more than 60°C.*

3 A warning light in the instrument panel tells the driver that preheating is taking place. When the light goes out, the engine is ready to be started. The voltage supply to the glow plugs continues for several seconds after the light goes out. If no attempt is made to start, the timer then cuts off the supply in order to avoid draining the battery and overheating of the glow plugs.

Testing

4 If the system malfunctions, testing is ultimately by substitution of known good units, but some preliminary checks may be made as follows.

5 Connect a voltmeter or 12 volt test lamp between the glow plug supply cable and earth (engine or vehicle metal). Make sure that the live connection is kept clear of the engine and bodywork.

5

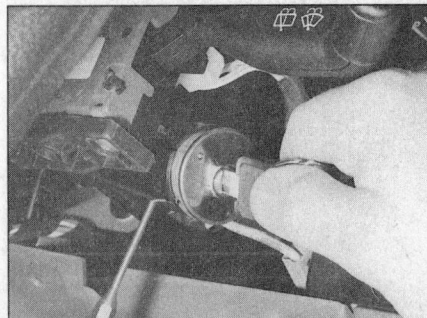

12.6 Depress the retaining lug and withdraw the switch assembly

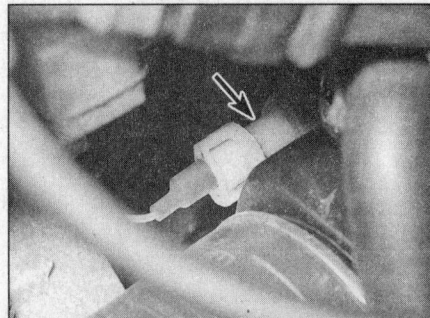

13.1 Oil pressure warning light switch (arrowed)

14.1 Oil level sensor (arrowed)

6 Have an assistant switch on the ignition and check that voltage is applied to the glow plugs. Note the time for which the warning light is lit and the total time for which voltage is applied before the system cuts out. Switch off the ignition.

7 At an under-bonnet temperature of 20°C typical times noted should be 5 or 6 seconds for warning light operation, followed by a further 4 to 5 seconds supply after the light goes out (provided the starter motor is not operated). Warning light time will increase with lower temperatures and decrease with higher temperatures.

8 If there is no supply at all, the relay or associated wiring is at fault.

9 To locate a defective glow plug, disconnect the main supply cable and the interconnecting wire or strap from the top of the glow plugs. Be careful not to drop the nuts and washers.

10 Use a continuity tester, or a 12 volt test lamp connected to the battery positive terminal, to check for continuity between each glow plug terminal and earth. The resistance of a glow plug in good condition is very low (less than 1 ohm), so if the test lamp does not light or the continuity tester shows a high resistance the glow plug is certainly defective.

11 If an ammeter is available, the current draw of each glow plug can be checked. After an initial surge of around 15 to 20 amps, each plug should draw around 10 amps. Any plug which draws much more or less than this is probably defective.

12 As a final check the glow plugs can be removed and inspected as described in Section 17.

16 Preheating system control unit - removal and refitting

Removal

1 The unit Is located on the engine compartment bulkhead. Disconnect the battery negative lead.

2 Unscrew the securing nut, and withdraw the unit from the bracket on the bulkhead **(see illustration)**.

16.2 Unscrew the securing nut . . .

3 Disconnect the wiring from the base of the unit, noting the connector locations **(see illustration)**.

Refitting

4 Refitting is a reversal of removal, ensuring that the wiring connectors are correctly connected.

17 Glow plugs - removal, inspection and refitting

Removal

Caution: If the preheating system has just been energised, or if the engine has been running, the glow plugs may be very hot.

1 Disconnect the battery negative lead.

2 Unscrew the nuts from the glow plug terminals, and recover the washers. Disconnect the wiring **(see illustration)**. Note that the main electrical feed wiring is connected to two of the plugs.

3 Where applicable, carefully move any obstructing pipes or wires to one side to enable access to the glow plugs.

4 Unscrew the glow plugs and remove them from the cylinder head **(see illustrations)**.

Inspection

5 Inspect the glow plugs for physical damage. Burnt or eroded glow plug tips can be caused by a bad injector spray pattern.

16.3 . . . then withdraw the preheating system control unit and disconnect the wiring

Have the injectors checked if this sort of damage is found.

6 If the glow plugs are in good physical condition, check them electrically using a 12 volt test lamp or continuity tester as described in the previous Section.

7 The glow plugs can be energised by applying 12 volts to them to verify that they heat up evenly and in the required time. Observe the following precautions:

a) Support the glow plug by clamping it carefully in a vice or self-locking pliers. Remember it will become red-hot.

b) Make sure that the power supply or test lead incorporates a fuse or overload trip to protect against damage from a short-circuit.

c) After testing, allow the glow plug to cool for several minutes before attempting to handle it.

8 A glow plug in good condition will start to glow red at the tip after drawing current for 5 seconds or so. Any plug which takes much longer to start glowing, or which starts glowing in the middle instead of at the tip, is defective.

Refitting

9 Refit by reversing the removal operations. Apply a smear of copper-based anti-seize compound to the plug threads and tighten the glow plugs to the specified torque. Do not overtighten, as this can damage the glow plug element.

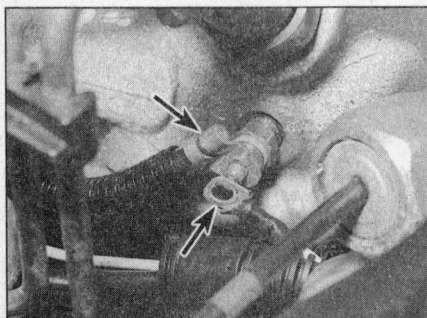

17.2 Disconnect the wiring (arrowed) from the glow plug terminal

17.4a Unscrew the glow plug . . .

17.4b . . . and remove it from the cylinder head

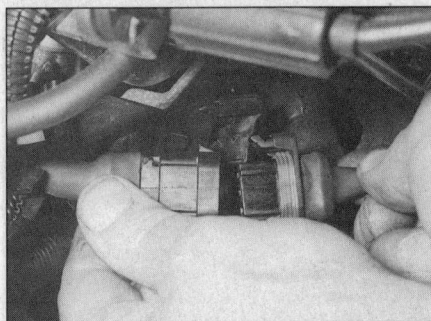

18.1 Disconnecting the no-load switch wiring connector - Lucas injection pump

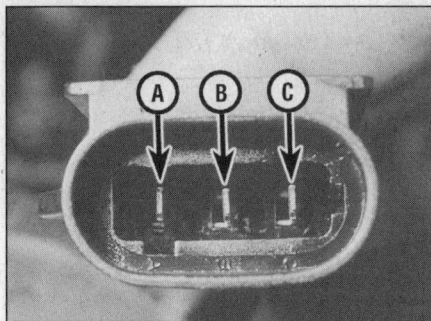

18.2 No-load switch wiring connector terminal identification - Lucas injection pump

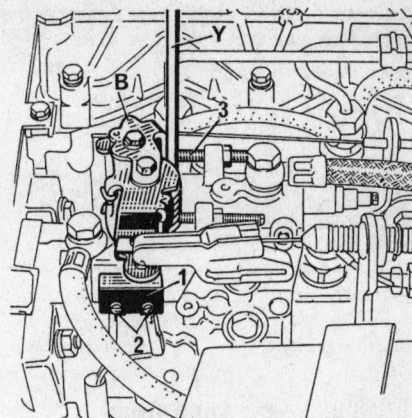

18 No-load switch - testing, adjustment, removal and refitting

Testing and adjustment

Note: *A continuity tester or an ohmmeter will be required for testing.*

1 To test and adjust the switch, first disconnect the switch wiring connector **(see illustration)**.

2 Connect a continuity tester or an ohmmeter across wiring connector terminals "B" and "C" **(see illustration)**.

3 Insert feeler gauges of different thicknesses between the injection pump accelerator lever and the anti-stall adjustment screw, and note the readings on the continuity tester or ohmmeter, as applicable **(see illustrations)**.

18.3b Adjusting the no-load switch - Lucas injection pump (model without air conditioning)

B *Accelerator lever*
Y *Feeler gauges*
1 *No-load switch*
2 *Switch wiring connector*
3 *Anti-stall adjustment screw*
4 *Bolt*
5 *Cam*

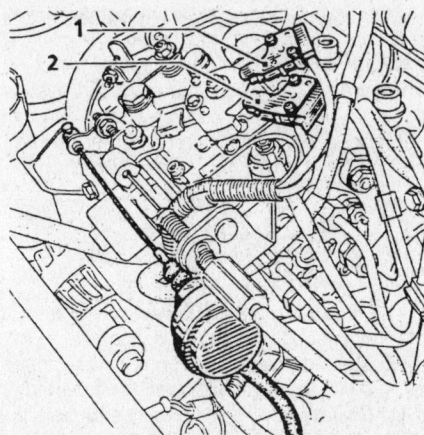

The readings obtained should be as follows.
Note: *Refer to Section 19 for details of the switch locations on models with air conditioning.*

Bosch injection pump

Spacer thickness	Test reading
Up to 7.0 mm (0.28 in)	Continuity/zero resistance
More than 8.0 mm (0.32 in)	No continuity/infinite resistance

Lucas injection pump

Spacer thickness	Test reading
Up to 9.0 mm (0.35 in)	Continuity/zero resistance
More than 11.0 mm (0.43 in)	No continuity/infinite resistance

4 If the switch does not behave as described, slacken its mounting screws and reposition it as necessary. Note that on certain Lucas fuel injection pumps, the adjustment is made by loosening the screw and adjusting the position of the cam in relation to the accelerator lever.

5 If the switch is permanently open or closed, renew it.

18.3c No-load switch location on Turbo models fitted with EGR (see Chapter 4)
1 *No-load switch*
2 *EGR cut-off switch*

18.3a Adjusting the no-load switch - Bosch injection pump (model without air conditioning)

B *Accelerator lever*
Y *Feeler gauge*
1 *No-load switch*
2 *Mounting screws*
3 *Anti-stall adjustment screw*

Removal

6 Disconnect the switch wiring connector, then remove the two securing screws, and withdraw the switch from its bracket on the injection pump.

Refitting

7 Refitting is a reversal of removal, but where applicable, before tightening the securing screws, adjust the switch as described previously.

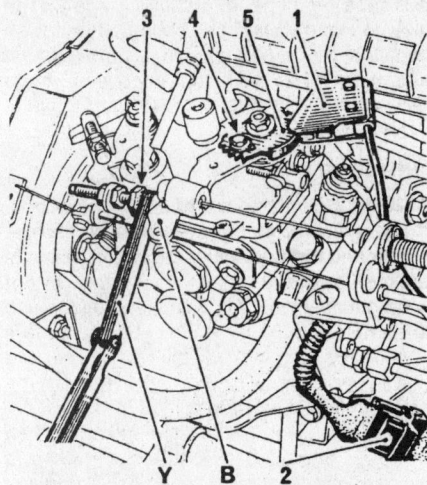

19 Air conditioning cut-off switches - testing, adjustment, removal and refitting

1 The cut-off switches are fitted in order to switch off the air conditioning compressor during starting and warm-up. Two switches are fitted, one to the clutch pedal, and one on the injection pump.

2 In order for the system to operate, the clutch pedal must be depressed, and the accelerator pedal must be depressed to provide an engine load above a preset level. When both these conditions are met, power is supplied to the compressor via a timer relay, which prevents the compressor from operating for four seconds.

Testing and adjustment

Note: *A continuity tester or an ohmmeter will be required for testing.*

Injection pump-mounted switch

3 The procedure is as described in Section 18 for the no-load switch, but the readings obtained should be as follows **(see illustration)**. Note that on models fitted with a Lucas injection pump, the location of the air

5

conditioning cut-off switch is as shown for the EGR cut-off switch in illustration 18.3c.

Bosch injection pump

Spacer thickness	Test reading
Up to 17.5 mm	Continuity/zero resistance
More than 18.5 mm	No continuity/infinite resistance

Lucas injection pump

Spacer thickness	Test reading
Up to 27.0 mm	Continuity/zero resistance
More than 29.0 mm	No continuity/infinite resistance

Clutch pedal-mounted switch

4 There is no requirement to adjust the switch, but when the clutch pedal is released (in the rest position), the switch plunger must be fully depressed.

5 To test the switch, disconnect the wiring connector, and connect a continuity tester or an ohmmeter across the switch contacts. With the pedal released (in the rest position), there should be continuity/zero resistance between the switch contacts. With the pedal depressed, there should be no continuity/infinite resistance between the switch contacts.

Removal

6 Disconnect the wiring connector, then remove the securing screw(s), and withdraw the switch from its bracket.

Refitting

7 Refitting is a reversal of removal, but when refitting the injection pump-mounted switch, carry out the adjustment described previously before tightening the securing screws.

20 Coolant temperature switch (post-heating cut-off) - testing, removal and refitting

Testing

Note: *A continuity tester or an ohmmeter will be required for testing.*

1 Remove the switch as described in paragraphs 7 to 9.

2 Connect a continuity tester or an ohmmeter across the switch terminals. There should be continuity/zero resistance between the terminals.

3 Now suspend the switch in a container of water (using wire or string), along with a thermometer.

4 Gently heat the water, keeping note of the rise in temperature.

5 Periodically remove the switch from the water, ensure that the terminals are dry, and again check for continuity/resistance. The

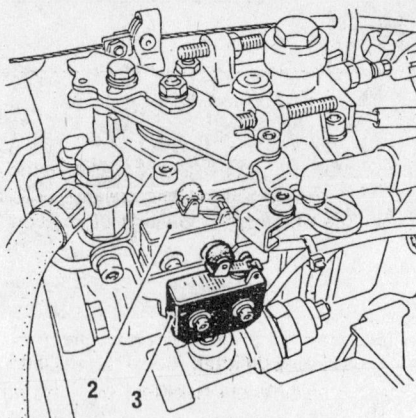

19.3 Injection pump-mounted air conditioning cut-off switch (3) and no-load switch (2) - Bosch injection pump

results obtained should be as follows.
Water temperature below 55°C ± 2°C - Continuity/zero resistance
Water temperature above 65°C ± 2°C - No continuity/infinite resistance

6 If the results obtained are not as specified, the switch is proved faulty and should be renewed.

Removal

7 The switch is located in a housing in the coolant hose at the left-hand front corner of the engine.

8 Drain the cooling system as described in Chapter 1. Alternatively have the new switch or a suitable bung to hand.

9 Disconnect the switch wiring plug, then unscrew and remove the switch **(see illustration)**. Recover the sealing ring, where applicable.

Refitting

10 Refitting is a reversal of removal, using a new sealing ring, where applicable.

11 On completion, check the coolant level, and top up or refill and bleed the cooling system, as necessary, as described in Chapter 1.

21 Stop solenoid - description, removal and refitting

Description

1 The stop solenoid is located on the end of the fuel injection pump. Its purpose is to cut the fuel supply when the ignition is switched off. If an open circuit occurs in the solenoid or supply wiring it will be impossible to start the engine, as the fuel will not reach the injectors. The same applies if the solenoid plunger jams in the "stop" position. If the solenoid jams in

20.9 Disconnecting the coolant temperature switch wiring plug

21.4 Disconnecting the stop solenoid wiring - Lucas injection pump

the "run" position, the engine will not stop when the ignition is switched off.

2 If the solenoid has failed and the engine will not run, a temporary repair may be made by removing the solenoid as described in the following paragraphs. Refit the solenoid body without the plunger and spring. Tape up the wire so that it cannot touch earth. The engine can now be started as usual, but it will be necessary to use the manual stop lever on the fuel injection pump (or to stall the engine in gear) to stop it.

Removal

Caution: Be careful not to allow dirt into the injection pump during this procedure. A new sealing washer or O-ring must be used on refitting.

3 Disconnect the battery negative lead.

4 Withdraw the rubber boot (where applicable), then unscrew the terminal nut and disconnect the wire from the top of the solenoid **(see illustration)**.

5 Carefully clean around the solenoid, then unscrew and withdraw the solenoid, and recover the sealing washer or O-ring (as applicable). Recover the solenoid plunger and spring if they remain in the pump. Operate the hand priming pump as the solenoid is removed to flush away any dirt.

Refitting

6 Refitting is a reversal of removal, using a new sealing washer or O-ring.

Chapter 6 Clutch

Contents

Degrees of difficulty

Easy, suitable for novice with little experience	**Fairly easy,** suitable for beginner with some experience	**Fairly difficult,** suitable for competent DIY mechanic	**Difficult,** suitable for experienced DIY mechanic	**Very difficult,** suitable for expert DIY or professional

Specifications

General
Clutch type . . . .   Single dry plate, diaphragm spring, cable-operated
Adjustment . . . .   Automatic

Clutch disc
Diameter . . . .   200.0 mm
Lining thickness (new, and in compressed position) . . . .   7.7 mm

Torque wrench settings

	Nm	lbf ft
Clutch cover bolts	25	19

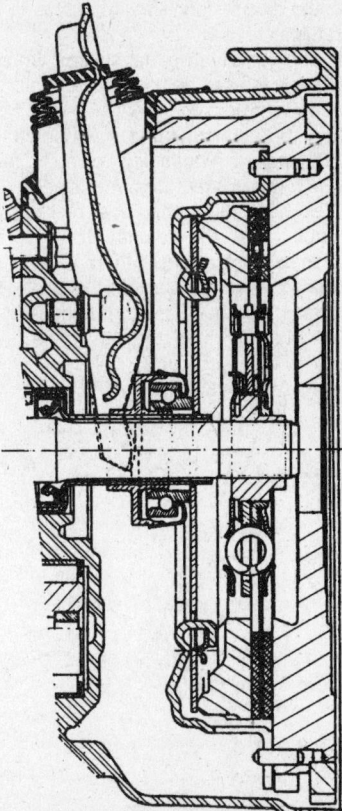

1.1 Cross-section of the clutch components

1 General information

All models are equipped with a cable-operated clutch. The unit consists of a steel cover which is dowelled and bolted to the rear face of the flywheel, and contains the pressure plate and diaphragm spring **(see illustration)**.

The clutch disc is free to slide along the gearbox splined input shaft. The disc is held in position between the flywheel and the pressure plate by the pressure of the diaphragm spring. Friction lining material is riveted to the clutch disc, which has a spring-cushioned hub to absorb transmission shocks and to help ensure a smooth take-up of the drive.

The clutch is actuated by a cable, controlled by the clutch pedal. The clutch release mechanism consists of a release arm and bearing which are in permanent contact with the fingers of the diaphragm spring **(see illustration)**.

Depressing the clutch pedal actuates the release arm by means of the cable. The arm pushes the release bearing against the diaphragm fingers, so moving the centre of

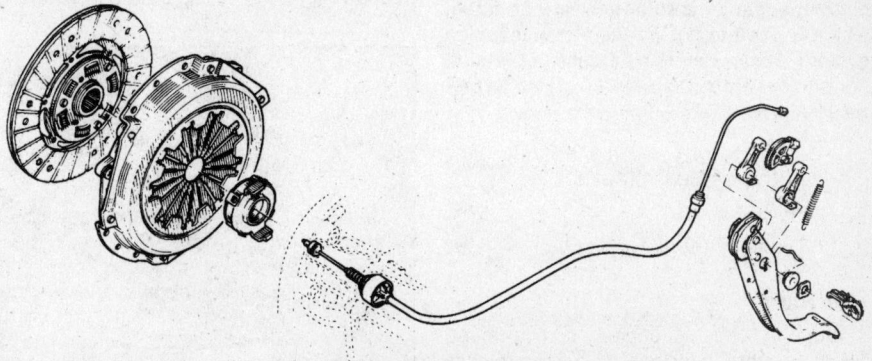

1.3 Clutch cable and pedal components

6

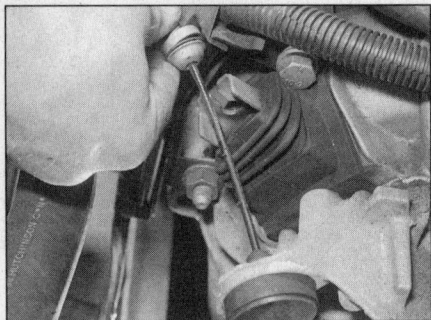

2.1 Withdrawing the outer cable from the bellhousing bracket

2.3 Clutch cable end retainer (arrowed) in the quadrant on the self-adjusting mechanism

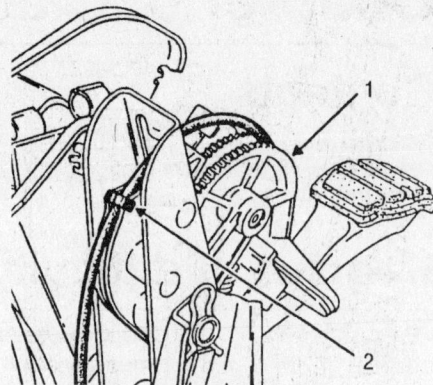

2.4 Clutch cable self-adjusting quadrant (1) and guide (2)

the diaphragm spring inwards. As the centre of the spring is pushed in, the outside of the spring pivots out, so moving the pressure plate backwards and disengaging its grip on the clutch disc.

When the pedal is released, the diaphragm spring forces the pressure plate into contact with the friction linings on the clutch disc. The disc is now firmly sandwiched between the pressure plate and the flywheel, thus transmitting engine power to the gearbox.

Wear of the friction material on the clutch disc is automatically compensated for by a self-adjusting mechanism attached to the clutch pedal. The mechanism consists of a serrated quadrant, a notched cam and a tension spring. One end of the clutch cable is attached to the quadrant, which is free to pivot on the pedal, but is kept in tension by a spring. When the pedal is depressed, the notched cam contacts the quadrant, thus locking it and allowing the pedal to pull the cable and operate the clutch. When the pedal is released, the tension spring causes the notched cam to move free of the quadrant; at the same time tension is maintained on the cable, keeping the release bearing in contact with the diaphragm spring. As the friction material on the disc wears, the self-adjusting quadrant will rotate when the pedal is released, and the pedal free play will be maintained between the notched cam and the quadrant.

On certain models with air conditioning, a clutch pedal-operated switch may be fitted, which is used to cut off the air conditioning system under certain engine operating conditions. Refer to Chapter 5 for further details.

2 Clutch cable - removal and refitting

Removal

1 Working in the engine compartment, disengage the inner cable from the release fork located on the clutch bellhousing, then withdraw the outer cable from the bracket on

the bellhousing **(see illustration)**.
2 On certain models, it may be necessary to unclip the trim panel from under the facia to improve access to the pedal assembly.
3 Press the clutch pedal to the floor, and then release it and pull the cable end retainer from the quadrant on the pedal assembly **(see illustration)**.
4 Pull the end of the cable down, and release it from the quadrant, then manipulate the cable out through the guide at the rear of the pedal **(see illustration)**.
5 Using a screwdriver, release the retaining tangs, and push the cable outer retaining bush from the bulkhead **(see illustration)**.
6 To aid refitting, tie a suitable length of string to the pedal end of the cable.
7 Pull the cable through into the engine compartment, and detach it from the support clips.
8 Untie the string from the end of the cable, and leave it in position to aid refitting. Remove the cable from the car.

Refitting

9 To refit the cable, tie the end of the string left in the engine compartment to the pedal end of the cable, then use the string to draw the cable through into the inside of the car.
10 From inside the vehicle (the aid of an assistant will ease the job), align the cable outer retaining bush with the appropriate locating hole in the bulkhead.
11 Working in the engine compartment, push the retaining bush through the bulkhead until

it locks in position.
12 Untie the string from the end of the cable.
13 Ensure that the cable passes through the guide on the rear of the pedal, then lay the cable over the quadrant.
14 Position the cable end in the end of the quadrant, then refit the cable end retainer. Make sure that the self-adjusting cam support arms return to their rest position freely under the tension of the return spring.
15 Working in the engine compartment, slip the other end of the cable through the bellhousing bracket, and connect the inner cable to the release fork. Refit the cable to the support clips.
16 Depress the clutch pedal several times in order to allow the self-adjusting mechanism to set the correct free play.
17 When the self-adjusting mechanism on the clutch pedal is functioning correctly, there should be a minimum of 20.0 mm slack in the cable. To check this dimension, pull out the inner cable near the release fork on the gearbox **(see illustration)**. If there is less than the specified minimum slack in the cable, the self-adjusting quadrant should be checked for seizure or possible restricted movement.
18 Depress the clutch pedal fully, and check that the total movement at the top of the

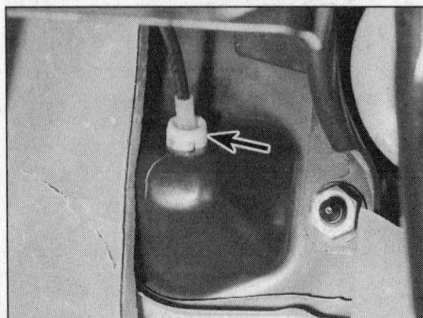

2.5 Clutch cable retaining bush (arrowed) at bulkhead

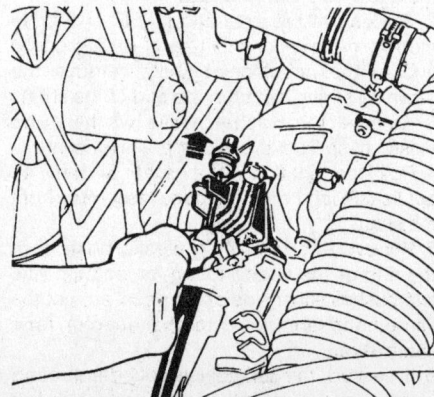

2.17 Checking the clutch inner cable slack at the release fork end

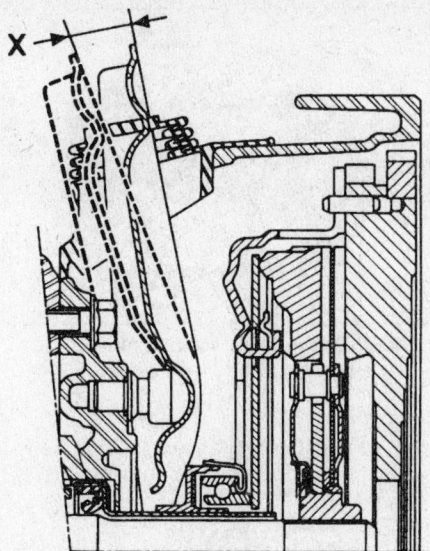

2.18 Checking the clutch release fork movement (X)
For dimension X, see text

release fork is between 17.0 and 18.0 mm **(see illustration)**. This movement ensures that the clutch pedal stroke is correct. If the movement is not as specified, make sure that the quadrant and support arms are free to turn on their respective pivots, and that the spring has not lost its tension. If necessary check the free length of the spring against a new one. Also check that the inner cable is not seizing in the outer cable.

19 Where applicable, refit the trim panel under the facia.

3 Clutch pedal - removal and refitting

Removal

1 Disconnect the cable end from the clutch pedal assembly as described in the previous Section. Note that there is no need to remove the cable from the bulkhead.

2 Working at the left-hand (right-hand-drive models) or right-hand (left-hand-drive models) end of the pedal pivot shaft, remove the retaining spring clip from the end of the shaft.

3 Remove the washer, wave washer, and plastic bush from the end of the pivot shaft.

4 Pull the shaft to the right or left, as applicable, and slide the pedal assembly from the shaft.

5 Recover the remaining plastic bush from the end of the shaft, noting its location (the two bushes either side of the pedal are not the same, and are not interchangeable) **(see illustration)**.

6 If desired, the self-adjuster quadrant return spring can be unhooked and removed, but note the position of all the components to

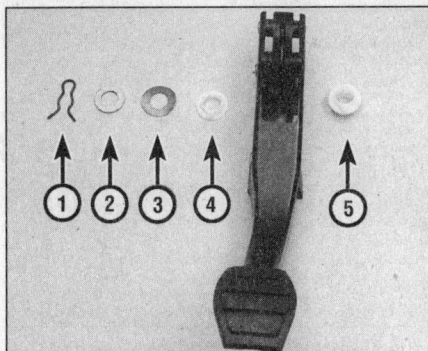

3.5 Clutch pedal components

1 Spring clip
2 Washer
3 Wave washer
4 Plastic bush
5 Plastic bush

ensure correct refitting.

7 Similarly, remove the bushes and withdraw the self-adjuster support arms and quadrant. Inspect these components and renew them if worn.

Refitting

8 Apply some multi-purpose grease to the bushes, and to the bearing surfaces or the support arms, quadrant and pivot shaft.

9 Locate the plastic bushes on the pedal, making sure that the thick bush is on the brake pedal side, and ensuring that the lugs on the bushes locate in the cut-outs in the pedal and the self-adjuster support arms. Reconnect the self-adjuster quadrant return spring.

10 To facilitate the refitting procedure, and to hold the bushes and support arms together, it is helpful to assemble the pedal on a dummy shaft. If a suitable shaft is not available, the pedal can still be refitted, but it will be necessary to hold the bushes together until the retaining spring clip is refitted to the end of the pivot shaft.

11 Locate the pedal assembly in the bracket, and push the pedal shaft through the pedal.

12 Refit the wave washer, washer and spring clip to the end of the shaft. Where applicable, make sure that the ends of the clip engage correctly with the cut-out in the pedal bracket,

4.2 Unscrewing the clutch cover retaining bolts, showing a screwdriver engaged with the starter ring gear to hold the flywheel stationary

and ensure that the clip engages with the groove in the pivot shaft.

13 Reconnect the clutch cable to the pedal assembly, and check the operation of the self-adjusting mechanism as described in the previous Section. Where applicable, check the operation of the air conditioning cut-off switch, with reference to Chapter 5.

4 Clutch assembly - removal, inspection and refitting

Warning: Dust created by clutch wear and deposited on the clutch components may contain asbestos which is a health hazard. DO NOT blow it out with compressed air or inhale any of it. DO NOT use petrol or petroleum-based solvents to clean off the dust. Brake system cleaner or methylated spirit should be used to flush the dust into a suitable receptacle. After the clutch components are wiped clean with rags, dispose of the contaminated rags and cleaner in a sealed, marked container.

Removal

1 On non-Turbo models, access to the clutch may be gained in one of two ways; either the gearbox may be removed independently, as described in Chapter 7, or the engine/gearbox unit may be removed as described in Chapter 2B, and the gearbox separated from the engine on the bench. On Turbo models, the gearbox cannot be removed independently from the engine, therefore the engine/gearbox unit must be removed as described in Chapter 2B.

2 Having separated the gearbox from the engine, unscrew and remove the clutch cover retaining bolts. Work in a diagonal sequence and slacken the bolts only a few turns at a time. Hold the flywheel stationary by positioning a screwdriver over the gearbox location dowel on the cylinder block and engaging it with the starter ring gear **(see illustration)**.

3 Ease the clutch cover off its locating dowels. Be prepared to catch the clutch disc,

4.3a Ease the clutch cover off its locating dowels

6

4.3b Be prepared to catch the clutch disc

4.5 Inspect the clutch disc lining (A), springs (B) and splines (C)

4.6a Check the machined face of the pressure plate (arrowed) . . .

4.6b . . . and the diaphragm springs, paying particular attention to the tips (arrowed)

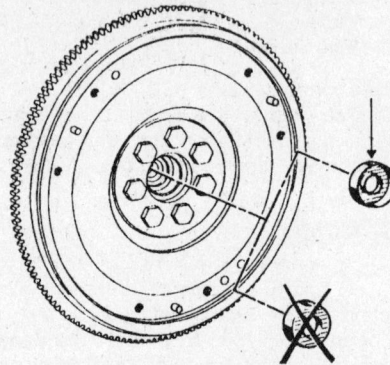
4.9 Fit the dummy bush in the crankshaft bore with the open end facing outwards

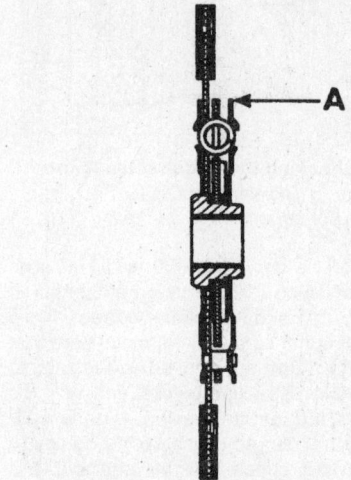
4.12 Clutch disc offset (A) faces away from flywheel

which will drop out as the cover is removed. Note which way round the disc is fitted **(see illustrations)**.

Inspection

4 With the clutch assembly removed, clean off all traces of asbestos dust using a dry cloth. This is best done outside or in a well-ventilated area; refer to the warning at the beginning of this Section.

5 Examine the linings of the clutch disc for wear or loose rivets, and the disc rim for distortion, cracks, broken torsion springs and worn splines **(see illustration)**. The surface of the friction linings may be highly glazed, but as long as the friction material pattern can be clearly seen, this is satisfactory. If there is any sign of oil contamination, indicated by shiny black discoloration, the disc must be renewed and the source of the contamination traced and rectified. This will be a leaking crankshaft oil seal, gearbox input shaft oil seal, or both. The renewal procedure for the former is given in Chapter 2A. Renewal of the gearbox input shaft oil seal should be entrusted to a Renault garage, as it involves dismantling the gearbox (JB3-type) and the renewal of the clutch release bearing guide tube using special tools. The disc must also be renewed if the linings have worn down to, or just above, the level of the rivet heads.

6 Check the machined faces of the flywheel and pressure plate. If either is grooved, or heavily scored, renewal is necessary. The pressure plate must also be renewed if any

cracks are apparent, or if the diaphragm spring is damaged or its pressure suspect **(see illustrations)**.

7 Take the opportunity to check the condition of the release bearing, as described in Section 5.

8 It is good practice to renew the clutch disc, pressure plate and release bearing as an assembly. Renewing the disc alone is not always satisfactory. A clutch repair kit can be obtained containing the new components.

9 Renault clutch kits contain a special dummy bush which may be fitted in the crankshaft bore to enable the use of the clutch centring tool also supplied in the kit. To fit this bush, first clean the bore in the end of the crankshaft and apply locking fluid to the outer surface of the bush. Press the bush fully into the crankshaft using a length of tubing of 38 mm outside diameter, making sure that the open end of the bush faces outwards **(see illustration)**.

Refitting

10 Before commencing the refitting procedure, apply a little high-melting-point grease to the splines of the gearbox input shaft. (A sachet of suitable grease may be supplied with the clutch kit.) Distribute the grease by sliding the clutch disc on and off the splines a few times. Remove the disc and wipe away any excess grease.

11 It is important that no oil or grease is

allowed to come into contact with the friction material of the clutch disc, or the pressure plate and flywheel faces. It is advisable to refit the clutch assembly with clean hands, and to wipe the pressure plate and flywheel faces with a clean dry rag before assembly begins.

12 Begin reassembly by placing the clutch disc against the flywheel, with the larger offset of the disc facing away from the flywheel **(see illustration)**.

13 Place the clutch cover over the dowels. Refit the retaining bolts and tighten them finger-tight so that the clutch disc is gripped, but can still be moved.

14 The clutch disc must now be centralised so that, when the engine and gearbox are mated, the splines of the gearbox input shaft will pass through the splines in the centre of the clutch disc hub. If this is not done accurately, it will be impossible to refit the gearbox.

15 Centralisation can be carried out quite easily by inserting a round bar through the hole in the centre of the clutch disc, so that the end of the bar rests in the hole in the end of the crankshaft. Note that a plastic centralising tube is supplied with Renault clutch kits, making the use of a bar

4.15a Centralising the clutch disc using a socket and extension bar

4.15b Centralising the clutch disc using the special tube supplied with Renault clutch kits

4.17 Using a clutch alignment tool to centralise the clutch disc

unnecessary **(see illustrations)**.

16 If a bar is being used, move it sideways or up and down until the clutch disc is centralised. Centralisation can be judged by removing the bar and viewing the clutch disc hub in relation to the bore in the end of the crankshaft. When the bore appears exactly in the centre of the clutch disc hub, all is correct.

17 If a non-Renault clutch is being fitted, an alternative and more accurate method of centralisation is to use a commercially-available clutch aligning tool obtainable from most accessory shops **(see illustration)**.

18 Once the clutch is centralised, progressively tighten the cover bolts in a diagonal sequence to the torque setting given in the Specifications **(see illustration)**. Remove the centralising device.

19 The gearbox can now be refitted to the engine, referring to the appropriate Chapter of this manual.

20 On completion, check the functioning of the clutch pedal as described in Section 2.

5 Clutch release bearing - removal, inspection and refitting

Removal

1 To gain access to the release bearing, it is necessary to separate the engine and gearbox as described at the beginning of the previous Section.

4.18 Tightening the clutch cover bolts

2 With the gearbox removed from the engine, tilt the release fork and slide the bearing assembly off the gearbox input shaft guide tube.

3 To remove the release fork, disengage the rubber cover and then pull the fork off its pivot ball stud.

Inspection

4 Check the bearing for smoothness of operation. Renew it if there is any roughness or harshness as the bearing is spun. It is good practice to renew the bearing as a matter of course during clutch overhaul, regardless of its apparent condition.

Refitting

5 Refitting the release fork and release bearing is the reverse sequence to removal,

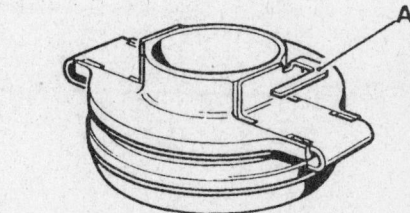

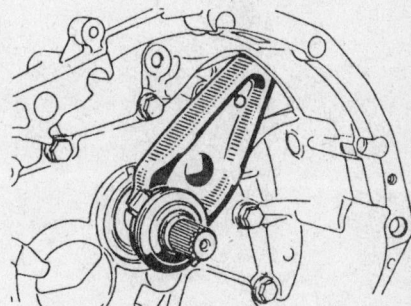

5.5 Clutch release components. Clip (A) on bearing carrier must engage with release fork

but note the following points.

a) Lubricate the release fork pivot ball stud and the release bearing-to-diaphragm spring contact areas sparingly with molybdenum disulphide grease.

b) Ensure that the clip on the bearing carrier engages with the release fork **(see illustration)**.

6

Chapter 7
Manual gearbox

Contents

Degrees of difficulty

Easy, suitable for novice with little experience	**Fairly easy,** suitable for beginner with some experience	**Fairly difficult,** suitable for competent DIY mechanic	**Difficult,** suitable for experienced DIY mechanic	**Very difficult,** suitable for expert DIY or professional

Specifications

General

Type . . . . Five forward speeds (all synchromesh) and reverse. Final drive differential integral with main gearbox

Designation:
   Non-Turbo models JB3
   Turbo models JC5

Gear ratios (typical)

1st 3.7:1
2nd 2.0:1
3rd 1.3:1
4th 1.0:1
5th 0.8:1
Reverse 3.6:1

Final drive ratio

JB3-type gearbox 3.6:1
JC5-type gearbox 3.3:1

Torque wrench settings

	Nm	lbf ft
Gearchange casing nuts	15	11
Gearchange link rod clamp nuts and bolts	30	22

7

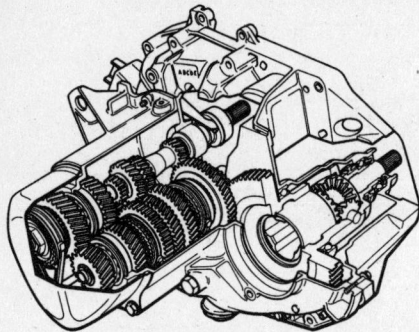

1.1a Cutaway view of the JB3-type gearbox

1 General information

The manual gearbox is of five-speed (JB3 or JC5) type, with one reverse gear **(see illustrations)**. Baulk ring synchromesh gear engagement is used on all the forward gears. The final drive (differential) unit is integral with the main gearbox, and is located between the main gearbox casing and the clutch bellhousing. The gearbox and differential both share the same lubricating oil.

The JC5-type gearbox is basically a

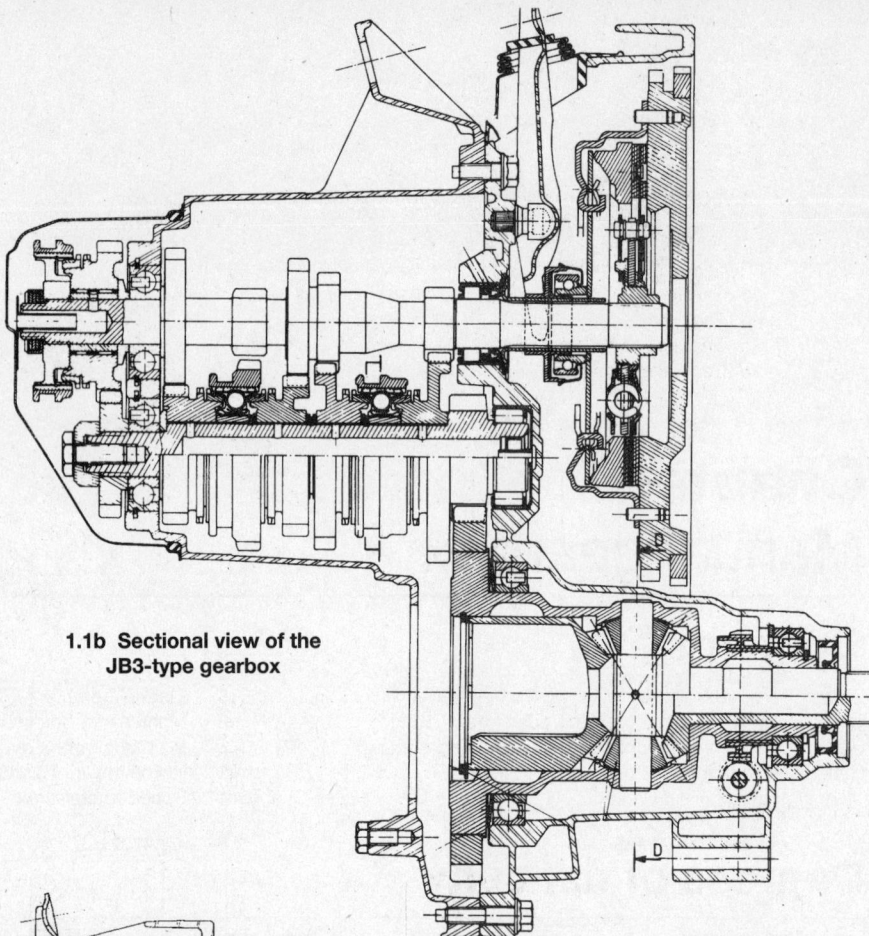

1.1b Sectional view of the JB3-type gearbox

strengthened version of the JB3-type gearbox, with uprated bearings and gears, and a strengthened casing, to cope with the additional power and torque produced by the Turbo engines.

Gearshift is by means of a floor-mounted lever, connected by a remote control linkage to the gearbox selector mechanism **(see illustration)**.

2 Gearchange linkage/mechanism - adjustment

Note: *The following details refer to the JB3-type gearbox. At the time of writing, no information was available for gearchange linkage adjustment on models equipped with the JC5-type gearbox.*

1 Apply the handbrake, then jack up the front of the vehicle and support it securely on axle stands (see *"Jacking, towing and wheel changing"*). Where necessary, remove the engine/gearbox undershield.

2 If desired, to improve access, lower or remove the exhaust system and if necessary the heat shield, with reference to Chapter 4.

3 Select 1st gear on the gearbox by moving the lever to the appropriate position. Renault

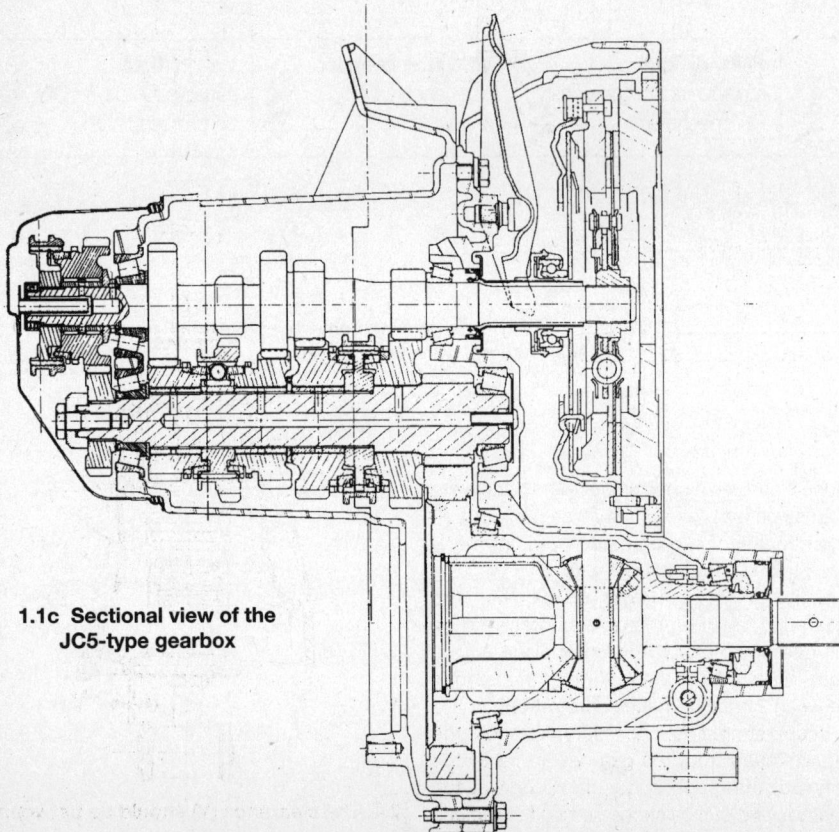

1.1c Sectional view of the JC5-type gearbox

1.3 Gearchange linkage/mechanism components

1 Link rod
2 Spring
3 Casing
4 Pad
5 Gear lever assembly
6 Gear lever boot

7 Knob
8 Circlip
9 Bush
10 Sleeve
11 Cover
12 Clevis

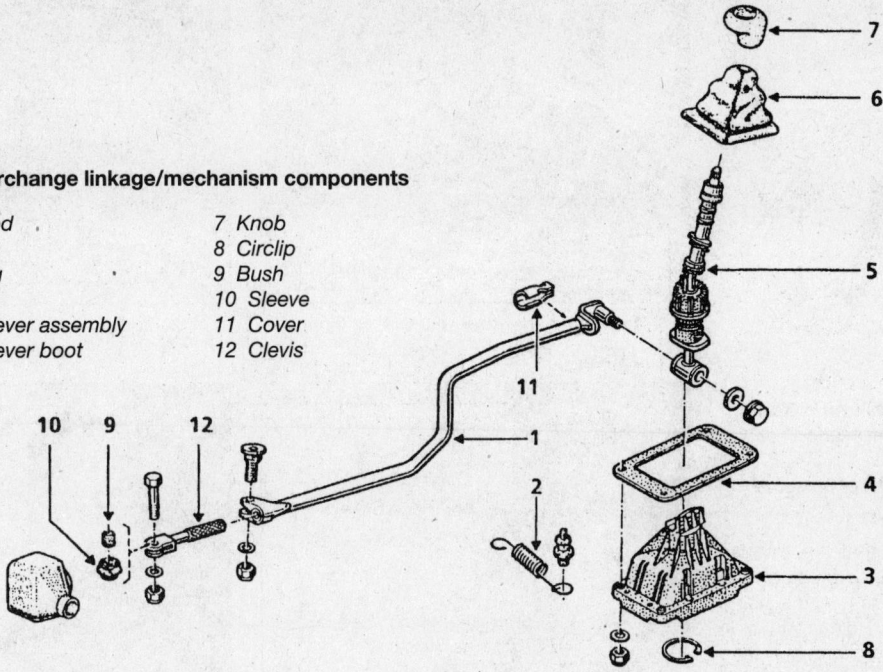

2.3a Gear positions for the gearbox lever

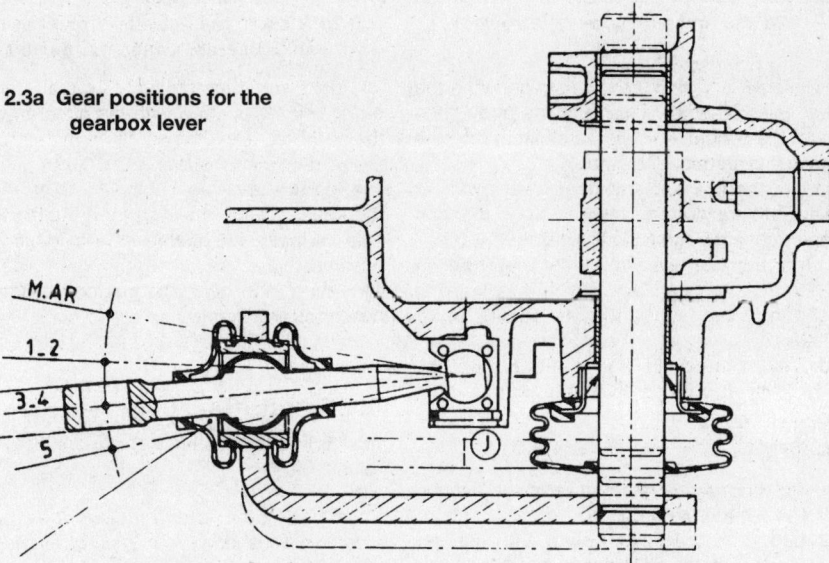

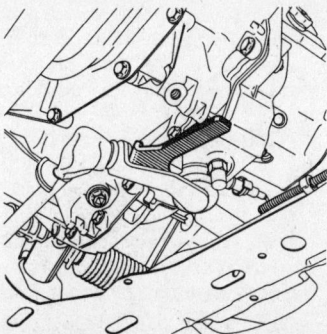

2.3b Using the special Renault tool to hold the gearbox lever in 1st gear position

technicians use a special tool to hold the lever in position and take up any free play, but an alternative tool can be made from flat metal bar or wood **(see illustrations)**.

4 Using a feeler blade, check that the clearance between the reverse stop-ring on the gear lever and the inclined plane on the right-hand side of the gear lever housing is between 2 and 5 mm **(see illustration)**.

5 If adjustment is necessary, unhook the return spring from the gear lever end of the link rod, then loosen the clamp bolt at the gearbox end of the link rod so that the rod can be moved on the clevis.

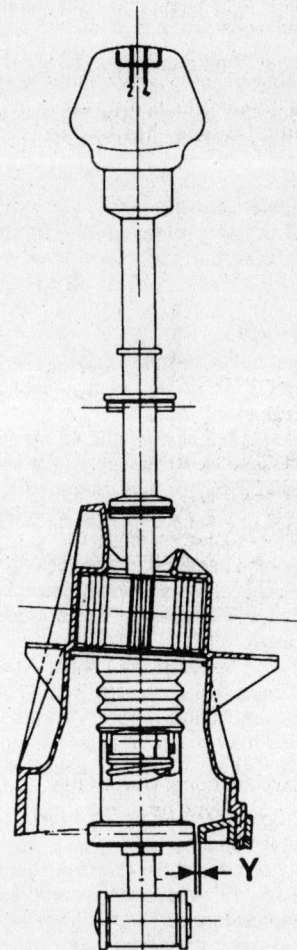

2.4 The clearance (Y) should be between 2 and 5 mm

7

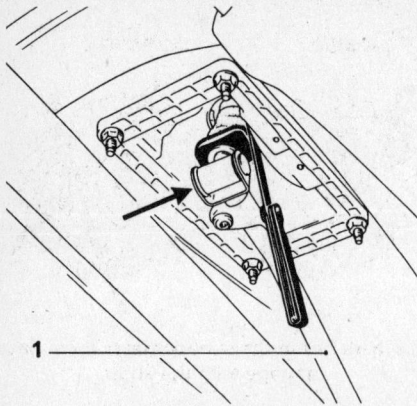

2.6 Adjusting the gearchange linkage using a 2 mm feeler blade
1 Link rod
Arrow indicates direction of pressure

6 Move the gear lever so that the reverse stop-ring is against the inclined plane on the housing, then insert a 2 mm feeler blade between the ring and plane. Hold the lever in this position, then tighten the clamp bolt **(see illustration)**.
7 Remove the holding tool and refit the return spring.
8 Recheck the clearance shown in illustration 2.4.
9 Check that all gears can be selected, then lower the vehicle to the ground.

---

3 Gearchange linkage/mechanism - removal and refitting

Removal

1 Working inside the vehicle, prise the gear lever boot from the centre console **(see illustration)**.
2 Unscrew the screws and lift off the centre console **(see illustrations)**. Where applicable, disconnect the battery negative lead, and disconnect the wiring plugs from the centre console-mounted switches.
3 Apply the handbrake, then jack up the front of the vehicle and support it securely on axle stands (see *"Jacking, towing and wheel changing"*).
4 Working beneath the vehicle, disconnect the flexible exhaust pipe mountings, and where applicable, remove the screws securing the exhaust heat shield. Ensure that the exhaust system is adequately supported to prevent damage to the system.
5 Unhook the return spring from the link rod **(see illustration)**.
6 Pull back the rubber boot from the front end of the link rod, then unscrew and remove the bolt and disconnect the rod from the gearbox lever. Recover the bush and sleeve. Note that the clevis at the front end of the rod is offset, and must be refitted correctly.

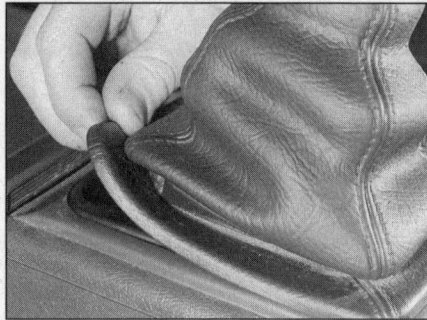

3.1 Removing the gear lever boot from the centre console

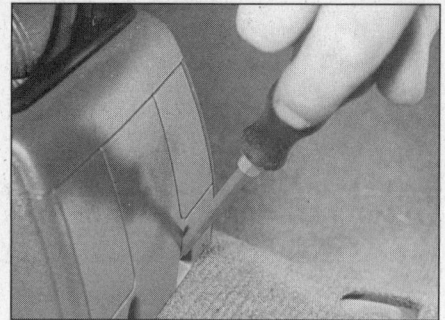

3.2b . . . and side screws (arrowed)

7 Unscrew and remove the nuts securing the gear lever assembly casing to the body, then lower the assembly while carefully pulling the exhaust system to one side.
8 Mark the link rod and gear lever clevis in relation to each other. Unscrew the clamp bolt and remove the rod from the clevis.
9 Grip the gear lever in a vice, then remove the knob and gear lever boot. The knob is bonded to the lever and may be difficult to remove.
10 Extract the circlip from the bottom of the gear lever and withdraw the lever and latch from the casing.

Refitting

11 Refitting is a reversal of removal, bearing in mind the following points.
12 Lubricate the pivot points with grease, and use a suitable adhesive to bond the knob to the lever.

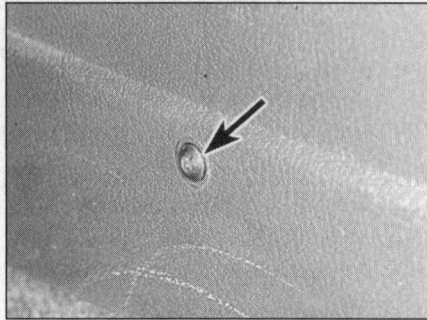

3.5 Unhook the link rod return spring (arrowed)

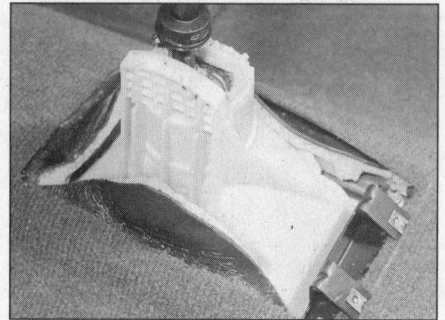

3.2a Remove the centre console rear screws . . .

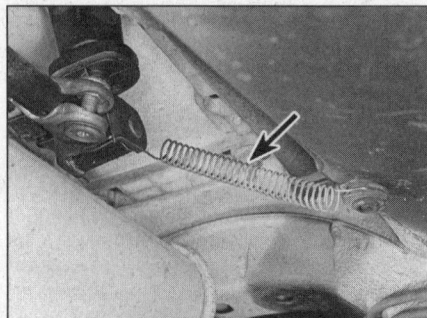

3.2c View of the gear lever and casing with the centre console removed

13 Make sure that the clevis on the front end of the link rod is fitted with the offset towards the gearbox. If the clevis has been removed, or if a new clevis is being fitted, connect the link rod to the clevis leaving 10 to 12 mm of the knurled area showing **(see illustration)**. This will locate the gear lever in its longitudinal position.
14 Adjust the gearchange mechanism as described in Section 2.

---

4 Speedometer drive - removal and refitting

Note: *On some later models, the speedometer drive is taken from the right-hand side of the gearbox, just above the driveshaft. It is not possible to remove the drive on this type.*

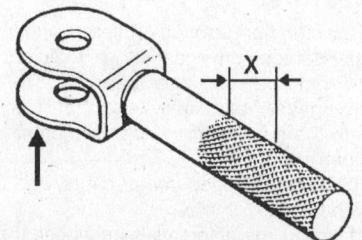

3.13 Link rod offset (arrowed) must face towards gearbox
Knurled area showing (X) = 10 to 12 mm

4.0 **Speedometer drive plastic cable connection (arrowed) on later models**

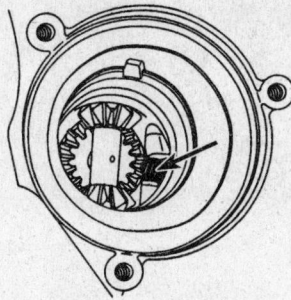

4.3 **View of the speedometer drivegear (arrowed) with the differential sun wheel removed**

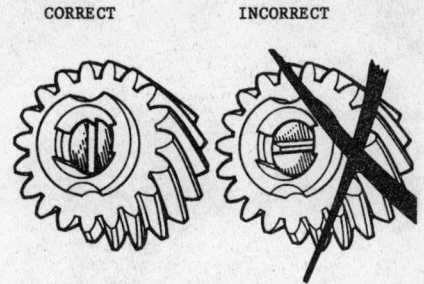

4.9 **Notches in the speedometer drive gear engage with the shaft**

The later type can be identified by the plastic cable connection to the gearbox instead of the clip type connection on earlier models (see illustration).

Removal

1 Disconnect the left-hand driveshaft at the gearbox end - refer to Chapter 8. There is no need to disturb the hub end of the driveshaft; the driveshaft/stub axle carrier assembly can be withdrawn together, as described for engine removal (Chapter 2B).
2 Extract the circlip and thrustwasher, then withdraw the left-hand sun wheel from the differential. The sun wheel also acts as the driveshaft spider housing.
3 Turn the differential until the planet wheels are in a vertical plane so that the speedometer drivegear is visible (see illustration).
4 Pull out the clip and disconnect the speedometer cable from the outside of the gearbox.
5 Using long-nosed pliers, extract the speedometer drivegear shaft vertically from the outside of the gearbox.
6 Using the same pliers, extract the speedometer drivegear from inside the differential housing, being very careful not to drop it.
7 Examine the drivegear teeth for wear and damage. Renew it if necessary. Note that if the drivegear teeth on the differential are worn or damaged, it will be necessary to dismantle the gearbox - this work should be entrusted to a Renault dealer.

Refitting

8 Using long-nosed pliers, insert the speedometer drivegear into its location.
9 From outside the gearbox, refit the drivegear shaft. Make sure that it engages with the gear location notches correctly (see illustration).
10 Refit the speedometer cable, and secure with the clip.
11 Insert the differential sun wheel, then refit the thrustwasher and circlip.
12 Reconnect the left-hand driveshaft with reference to Chapter 8.

5 Differential output oil seal (right-hand side) - renewal

Note: *New driveshaft-to-differential side gear roll pins will be required on refitting.*

1 Apply the handbrake, then jack up the front of the car and support it on axle stands. Remove the right-hand wheel.
2 Position a suitable container beneath the gearbox, then unscrew the drain plug and allow the oil to drain. (On some models, it may be necessary to remove a splash guard from the bottom of the gearbox first). When most of the oil has drained, clean and refit the drain plug, tightening it securely.
3 Using a pin punch (5 mm diameter), drive out the double roll pins securing the inner end of the right-hand driveshaft to the differential side gear. New pins will be required when reassembling.
4 Unscrew the nut securing the steering track rod end to the steering arm. Use a balljoint separator tool to separate the balljoint taper.
5 Refer to Chapter 9 and unbolt the brake caliper from the stub axle carrier. Do not disconnect the hydraulic hose from the caliper. Tie the caliper to the suspension coil spring without straining the hydraulic hose.
6 Loosen (but do not remove) the lower bolt securing the stub axle carrier to the bottom of the suspension strut. Unscrew and remove the upper bolt, then tilt the stub axle carrier

and disconnect the driveshaft. Take care not to damage the driveshaft rubber bellows.
7 Recover the O-ring from the side gear shaft.
8 Wipe clean the old oil seal, and measure its fitted depth below the casing edge. This is necessary to determine the correct fitted position of the new oil seal if the special Renault fitting tool is not being used.
9 Free the old oil seal, using a small drift to tap the outer edge of the seal inwards so that the opposite edge of the seal tilts out of the casing (see illustration). A pair of pliers or grips can then be used to pull out the oil seal. Take care not to damage the splines of the differential side gear.
10 Wipe clean the oil seal seating in the casing.
11 Before fitting the new oil seal, it is necessary to cover the splines on the side gear to prevent damage to the oil seal lips. Ideally, a close-fitting plastic cap should be located on the splines. If this is not available, wrap some adhesive tape over the splines.
12 Smear a little grease on the lips of the new oil seal and on the protective cap or tape.
13 Carefully locate the new oil seal over the splines of the side gear, and enter it squarely into the casing. Using a piece of metal tube or a socket, tap the oil seal into position to its correct depth, as noted previously (see illustrations). Renault use a special tool to ensure that the oil seal is fitted to the correct depth; it may be possible to hire this tool from a Renault garage or tool hire shop.

7

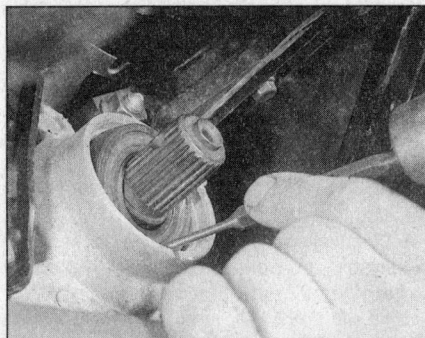

5.9 **Tap the old differential output oil seal with a small drift to remove it**

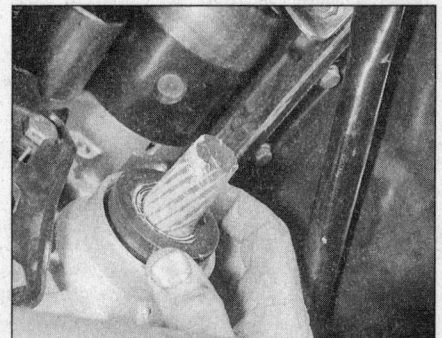

5.13a **Locate the new differential output oil seal over the side gear splines . . .**

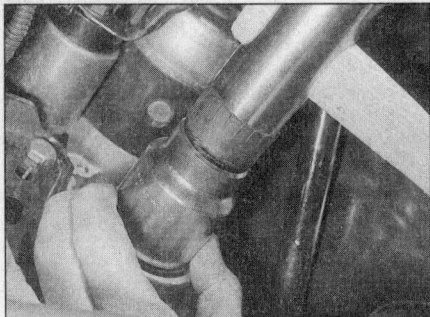

5.13b . . . and tap it into position with a socket or metal tube

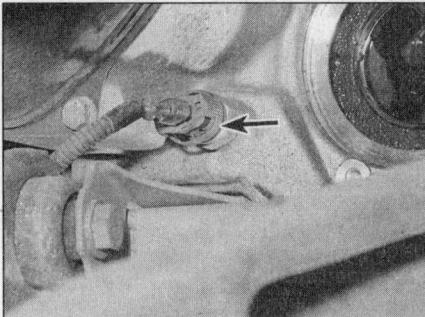

6.4 Reversing light switch (arrowed) viewed with driveshaft removed

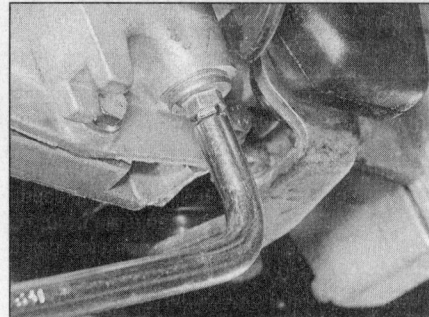

7.4 Unscrewing the gearbox oil drain plug

14 Remove the plastic cap or adhesive tape, and apply a little grease to the splines of the side gear. Fit a new O-ring to the side gear shaft.

15 Engage the driveshaft with the splines on the side gear so that the roll pin holes are correctly aligned. Tilt the stub axle carrier and slide the driveshaft onto the side gear, making sure that it enters the oil seal centrally.

16 With the holes aligned, tap the new roll pins into position. Seal the ends of the roll pins with a suitable sealant.

17 Refit the upper bolt securing the stub axle carrier to the bottom of the suspension strut, then tighten both upper and lower bolts to the specified torque (see Chapter 10).

18 Refit the brake caliper to the stub axle carrier, and tighten the bolts to the specified torque with reference to Chapter 9.

19 Clean the track rod end balljoint taper and the steering arm, then refit the balljoint to the arm and tighten the nut to the specified torque (see Chapter 10).

20 Refill the gearbox with the correct quantity and grade of oil, with reference to Chapter 1. Refit the splash guard where necessary.

21 Refit the roadwheel and lower the car to the ground.

6 Reversing light switch - removal and refitting

Removal

1 Apply the handbrake, then jack up the front of the car and support it on axle stands.

2 Where applicable, unbolt and remove the splash guard from the bottom of the gearbox.

3 Position a suitable container beneath the gearbox, then unscrew the drain plug and allow the oil to drain. When all of the oil has drained, clean and refit the drain plug, tightening it securely.

4 The switch is located on the left-hand side of the gearbox, next to the driveshaft (see illustration). Disconnect the wiring from the switch.

5 Unscrew the switch from the gearbox, and remove the washer.

Refitting

6 Clean the location in the gearbox and the threads of the switch.

7 Insert the switch together with a new washer, and tighten it securely.

8 Reconnect the wiring.

9 Refill the gearbox with the correct quantity and grade of oil, with reference to Chapter 1.

10 Refit the gearbox splash guard, where applicable.

11 Lower the car to the ground.

7 Manual gearbox (JB3-type) - removal and refitting

Note: *This Section describes the removal of the gearbox leaving the engine in position in the car, however if an adequate lifting hoist is available it may be easier to remove both the engine and the gearbox together as described in Chapter 2B and then to separate the gearbox from the engine on the bench. Suitable means of supporting both the engine and gearbox will be required during this procedure. A balljoint separator will be required.*

Removal

1 The manual gearbox is removed upwards from the engine compartment after disconnecting it from the engine. Due to the weight of the unit, it will be necessary to have some form of lifting equipment available, such as an engine crane or suitable hoist to enable the unit to be removed in this way.

2 Apply the handbrake, then jack up the front of the vehicle, and support it securely on axle stands (see *"Jacking, towing and wheel changing"*). Remove both the front roadwheels.

3 Where applicable, remove the engine splash guard.

4 Position a suitable container beneath the gearbox, then unscrew the drain plug and allow the oil to drain (see illustration). When all of the oil has drained, clean and refit the drain plug, tightening it securely.

5 Disconnect the battery negative lead.

6 Unscrew the nut securing the left-hand

steering track rod end to the steering arm, then use a balljoint separator tool to separate the balljoint taper.

7 Working in the engine compartment, where applicable, remove the air cleaner assembly and mounting bracket from its location above the gearbox bellhousing. Refer to Chapter 4 for further details.

8 Working in the engine compartment, unscrew the three bolts securing the left-hand driveshaft rubber gaiter retaining plate to the gearbox.

9 Refer to Chapter 9 and unbolt the left-hand brake caliper from the stub axle carrier. Do not disconnect the hydraulic hose from the caliper. Tie the caliper to the suspension coil spring without straining the hydraulic hose.

10 Unbolt the front left-hand inner wing protective cover. The cover is secured by two Torx screws and one self-tapping screw (see illustration).

11 Unscrew and remove the pinch-bolt securing the front suspension lower arm balljoint to the bottom of the stub axle carrier.

12 Support the weight of the stub axle carrier and driveshaft on a trolley jack or an axle stand, then slacken and remove the two nuts and washers from the bolts securing the stub axle carrier to the suspension strut, noting that the nuts are positioned on the rear side of the strut. Withdraw the bolts and separate the stub axle carrier from the bottom of the suspension strut.

13 Withdraw the left-hand driveshaft and stub axle carrier assembly from the gearbox. Be prepared for some oil spillage as the

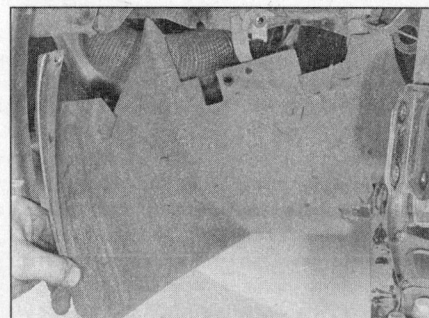

7.10 Removing the left-hand inner wing protective cover

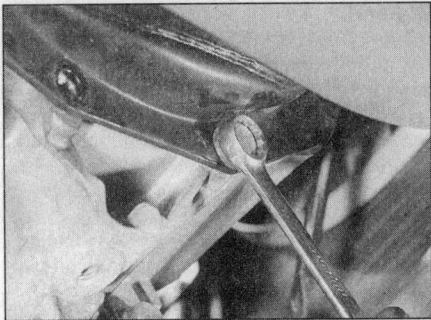

7.18a Remove the bolts securing the tie-rod bracket to the gearbox . . .

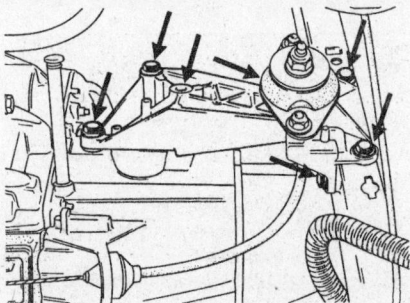

7.18b . . . and the engine

7.20a Pull back the rubber boot . . .

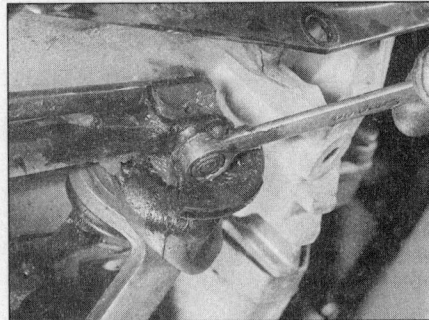

7.20b . . . then disconnect the gear lever rod from the lever on the gearbox

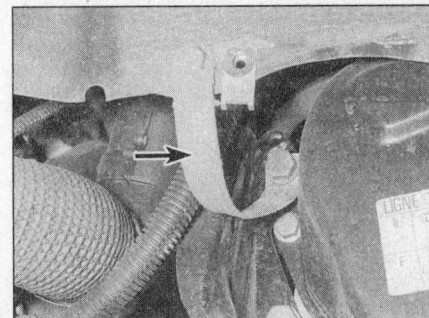

7.26 Unscrewing an engine-to-gearbox nut

driveshaft is withdrawn. Make sure that the rollers on the end of the driveshaft tripod remain in position, otherwise they may fall into the gearbox.

14 Working on the right-hand driveshaft, rotate the driveshaft until the double roll pin, securing the inner constant velocity joint to the sun wheel shaft, is visible. Using a hammer and a 5 mm diameter pin punch, drive out the double roll pin. New roll pins must be used on refitting.

15 Slacken and remove the two nuts and washers from the bolts securing the stub axle carrier to the suspension strut, again noting that the nuts are positioned on the rear side of the strut. Withdraw the upper bolt, but leave the lower bolt in position.

16 Pull the top of the stub axle carrier outwards until the driveshaft inner constant velocity joint splines are released from the sun wheel shaft in the differential. Remove the O-ring from the sun wheel shaft splines.

17 Support the driveshaft to one side using wire or string attached to a suitable point on the vehicle body - do not allow the driveshaft to hang under its own weight, as this may damage the joints.

18 Where applicable, unscrew and remove the bolts securing the engine-to-gearbox tie-rod bracket to the gearbox (note that the tie-rod bracket is fixed to the gearbox bellhousing cover plate). Loosen the tie-rod mounting bolts on the engine, or alternatively remove them and remove the tie-rod completely **(see illustrations)**.

19 Where applicable, if not already done, unbolt the gearbox bellhousing cover plate.

20 Working under the gearbox, cut the plastic tie and pull back the rubber boot from the gear linkage. Disconnect the gear lever rod from the lever on the gearbox by unscrewing the nut and removing the bolt **(see illustrations)**. Recover the bush from inside the lever.

21 Disconnect the wiring from the starter motor.

22 Disconnect the wiring from the reversing light switch.

23 Disengage the clutch inner cable from the release fork located on the clutch bellhousing

24 Withdraw the outer cable from the bracket on the bellhousing. Position the cable to one side, clear of the gearbox.

25 Pull out the clip and disconnect the speedometer cable from the outside of the gearbox.

26 Unscrew and remove the engine-to-gearbox nuts and bolts from around the

gearbox and from the starter motor **(see illustration)**. There is no need to remove the starter motor.

27 Connect a suitable hoist to the engine and lift it slightly. Alternatively the engine may be supported using a trolley jack and interposed block of wood positioned under the sump, so that the hoist can be used to remove the gearbox.

28 Remove the left-hand engine/gearbox mounting with reference to Chapter 2A. Note that the complete mounting assembly must be removed to provide sufficient clearance to remove the gearbox **(see illustration)**.

29 Unbolt the earth strap from the body, beneath the left-hand front wing, or from the end of the gearbox (in which case note the location to ensure correct refitting) **(see illustration)**.

30 Remove the lower engine steady bracket with reference to Chapter 2A **(see illustration)**.

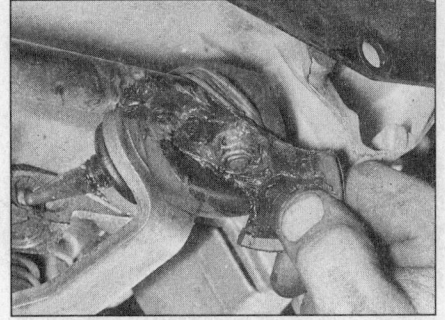

7.28 Left-hand front engine mounting assembly securing bolts (arrowed)

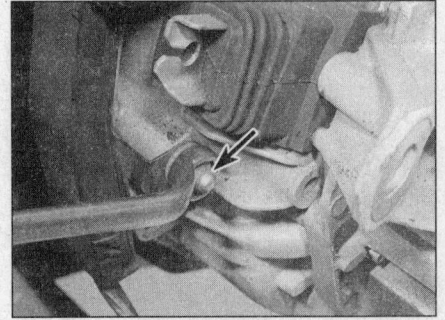

7.29 Earth strap (arrowed) beneath the left-hand front wing

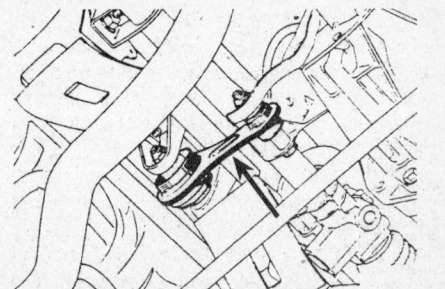

7.30 Lower engine steady bracket (arrowed)

7

7.32 Using two nuts locked together to unscrew a gearbox locating stud

7.37 Lifting the gearbox from the engine compartment

31 Remove the radiator as described in Chapter 3.

32 Remove the gearbox locating studs by using two nuts locked together to unscrew each of them from their locations on the front and rear of the bellhousing **(see illustration)**. The front stud protrudes to the left-hand side and the rear stud protrudes to the right-hand side at the rear of the engine.

33 On models with power-assisted steering, remove the two clips securing the fluid hose to the body panel and subframe.

34 Attach a hoist and lifting tackle to the gearbox. Connect one end of the lifting tackle to the clutch cable mounting lug, and connect

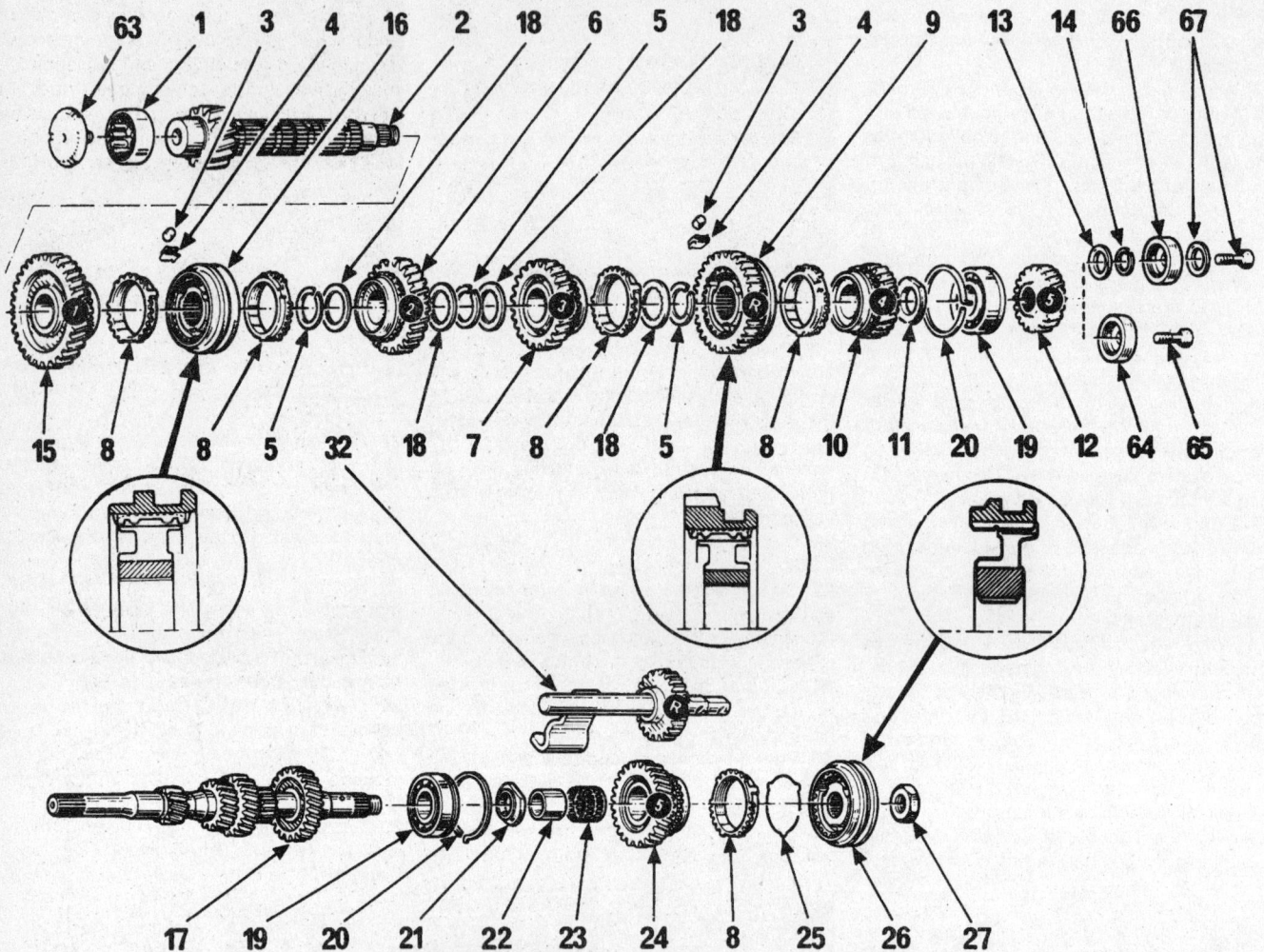

9.4a Gearbox internal components - JB3-type gearbox

1 Roller race	10 4th speed gear	19 Ball race	32 Reverse shaft and gear
2 Output shaft	11 Washer	20 Circlip	63 Oil baffle
3 Roller	12 5th speed gear	21 Washer	64 Thrustwasher
4 Spring	13 Washer	22 5th speed ring	65 5th speed end bolt on
5 Circlip	14 5th speed circlip	23 Needle race	output shaft
6 2nd speed gear	15 1st speed gear	24 5th speed gear (primary)	66 Shouldered washer
7 3rd speed gear	16 1st/2nd gear hub	25 5th speed spring	67 Retaining bolt and washer
8 Synchro-ring	17 Input shaft	26 5th speed gear hub	
9 3rd/4th gear hub	18 Splined ring	27 5th speed nut	

the other end to a bolt temporarily fitted to the gearbox.

35 Ensure that the weight of the gearbox is supported by the hoist and lifting tackle. Separate the gearbox from the engine while sliding the 5th speed housing between the subframe and the side panel beneath the left-hand front wing. Careful use of a wide-blade screwdriver may be necessary to free the bellhousing from the locating dowels.

36 Raise the engine slightly and move it to the rear, then turn the gearbox to the front and release it from the engine.

37 Lift the gearbox from the engine compartment **(see illustration)**.

Refitting

38 Refitting is a reversal of removal, noting the following points:

a) *Make sure that the locating studs are correctly positioned in the gearbox.*

b) *Apply a little high melting-point grease to the splines of the gearbox input shaft. Do*

not apply too much, otherwise there is the possibility of the grease contaminating the clutch friction disc. Make sure that the clutch release bearing is correctly located on the release arm.

c) *Refit the lower engine steady bracket and the left-hand engine/gearbox mounting, and adjust the position of the engine/gearbox assembly with reference to Chapter 2A.*

d) *Fit new roll pins to the right-hand driveshaft and seal the ends using a suitable sealant.*

e) *Refit and tighten the brake caliper mounting bolts with reference to Chapter 9.*

f) *Refill the gearbox with oil and check the level with reference to Chapter 1.*

g) *Refill and bleed the cooling system as described in Chapter 1.*

h) *Tighten all nuts and bolts to the specified torque.*

8 Manual gearbox (JC5-type) - removal and refitting

On models fitted with the JC5-type gearbox, the gearbox cannot be removed independently from the engine. The engine and gearbox must be removed as an assembly and then separated as described in Chapter 2B.

9 Manual gearbox overhaul - general information

Overhauling a manual gearbox is a difficult and involved job for the DIY home mechanic. In addition to dismantling and reassembling many small parts, clearances must be precisely measured and, if necessary, changed by selecting shims and spacers. Gearbox internal components are also often

7

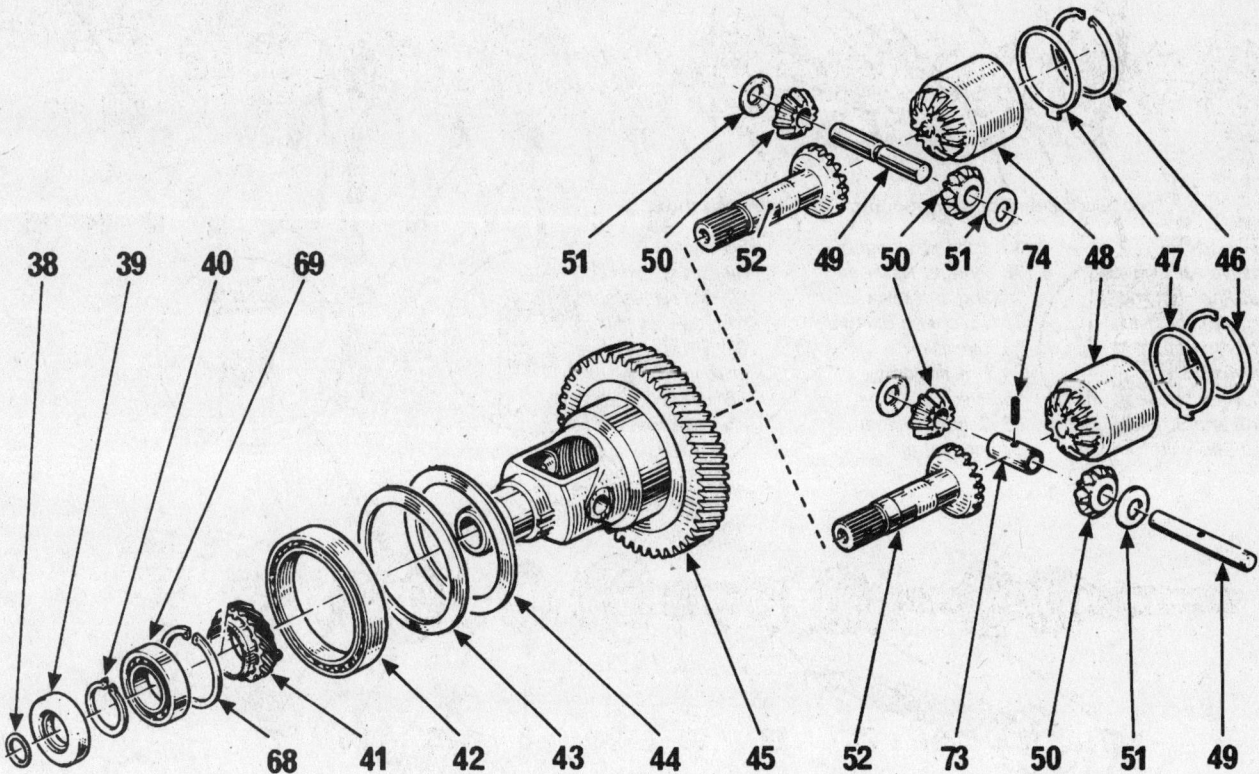

9.4b Differential components - JB3-type gearbox

38 O-ring	43 Spacer washer	48 Spider-type sun wheel	68 Circlip
39 Oil seal	44 Spring washer	49 Planet wheel shaft	69 Ball race
40 Circlip	45 Differential housing	50 Planet wheels	73 Sleeve
41 Speedometer drivegear	46 Circlip	51 Planet wheel washer	74 Pin
42 Ball race	47 Shim	52 Sun wheel with splined shaft	

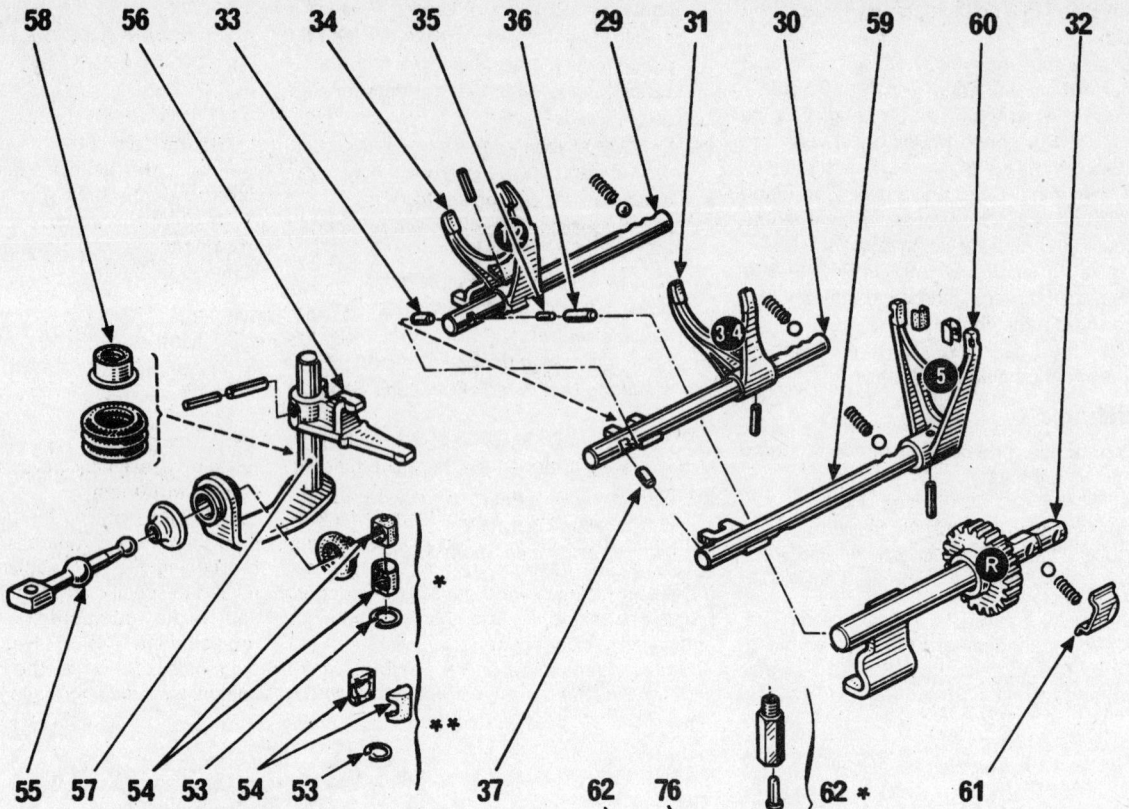

9.4c Gear selector components - JB3-type gearbox

Note: * and ** = alternative assemblies

29 1st/2nd shift rod
30 3rd/4th shift rod
31 3rd/4th gear fork
32 Reverse shaft
33 Plunger between 1st/2nd and 3rd/4th
34 1st/2nd shift fork

35 1st/2nd plunger
36 Plunger between 1st/2nd and reverse
37 5th speed plunger
53 Circlip
54 Link support
55 Link
56 Selector finger
57 Input shaft

58 Bush
59 5th speed rod
60 5th speed shift fork
61 Reverse stirrup
62 5th speed detent assembly
76 5th speed detent shim washer

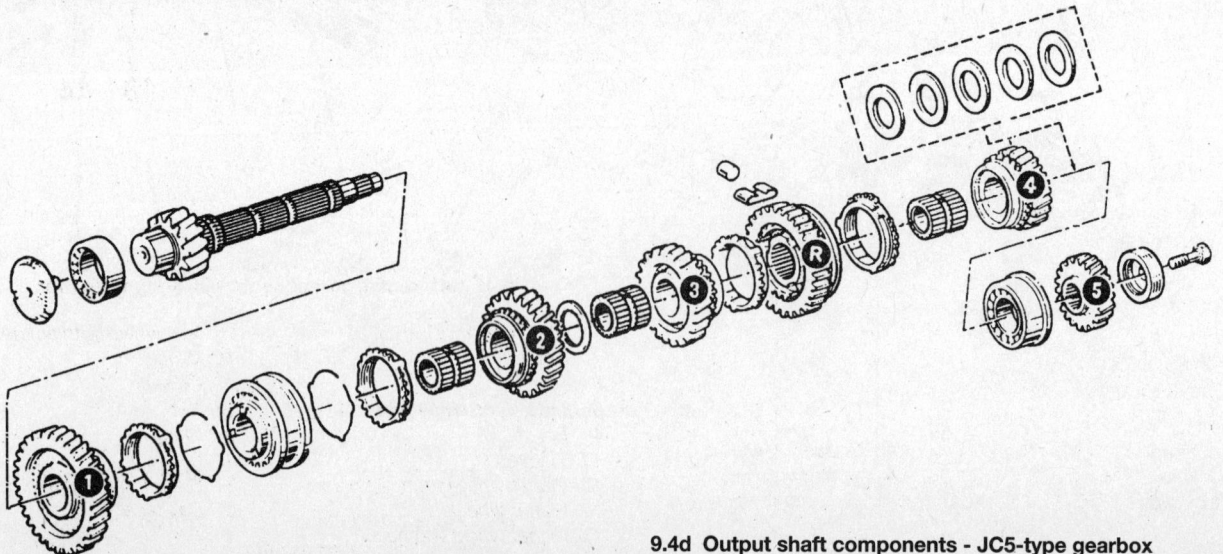

9.4d Output shaft components - JC5-type gearbox

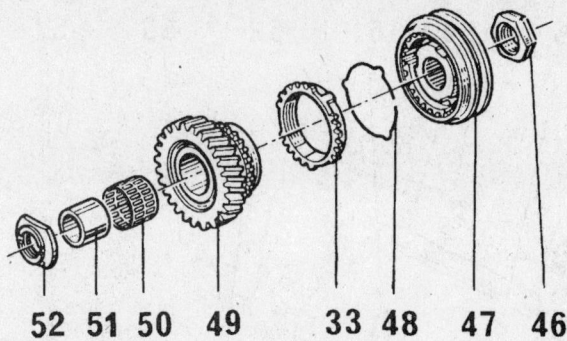

9.4e 5th gear components - JC5-type gearbox

33 Synchro-ring
46 5th speed nut
47 5th speed gear hub
48 5th speed spring
49 5th speed gear (primary)
50 Needle race
51 5th speed ring
52 Washer

difficult to obtain, and in many instances, extremely expensive. Because of this, if the gearbox develops a fault or becomes noisy, the best course of action is to have the unit overhauled by a specialist repairer, or to obtain an exchange reconditioned unit.

Nevertheless, it is not impossible for the more experienced mechanic to overhaul a gearbox, provided the special tools are available and the job is done in a deliberate step-by-step manner so that nothing is overlooked.

The tools necessary for an overhaul include internal and external circlip pliers, bearing pullers, a slide-hammer, a set of pin punches, a dial test indicator, and possibly a hydraulic press. In addition, a large, sturdy workbench and a vice will be required.

During dismantling of the gearbox, make careful notes of how each component is fitted, to make reassembly easier and more accurate **(see illustrations)**.

Before dismantling the gearbox, it will help if you have some idea of which area is mal-functioning. Certain problems can be closely related to specific areas in the gearbox, which can make component examination and replacement easier. Refer to the *Fault diagnosis* Section at the beginning of this manual for more information.

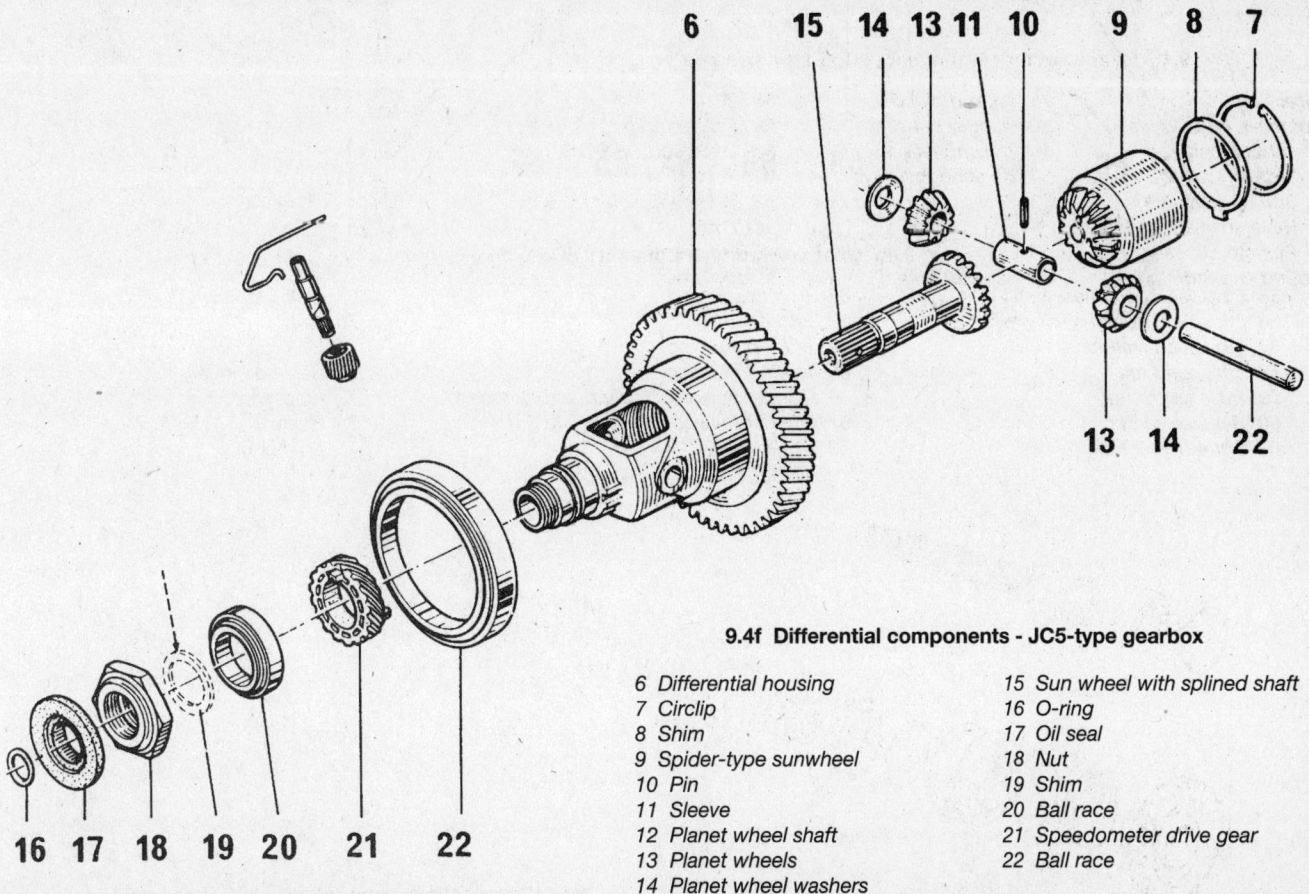

9.4f Differential components - JC5-type gearbox

6 Differential housing
7 Circlip
8 Shim
9 Spider-type sunwheel
10 Pin
11 Sleeve
12 Planet wheel shaft
13 Planet wheels
14 Planet wheel washers
15 Sun wheel with splined shaft
16 O-ring
17 Oil seal
18 Nut
19 Shim
20 Ball race
21 Speedometer drive gear
22 Ball race

7

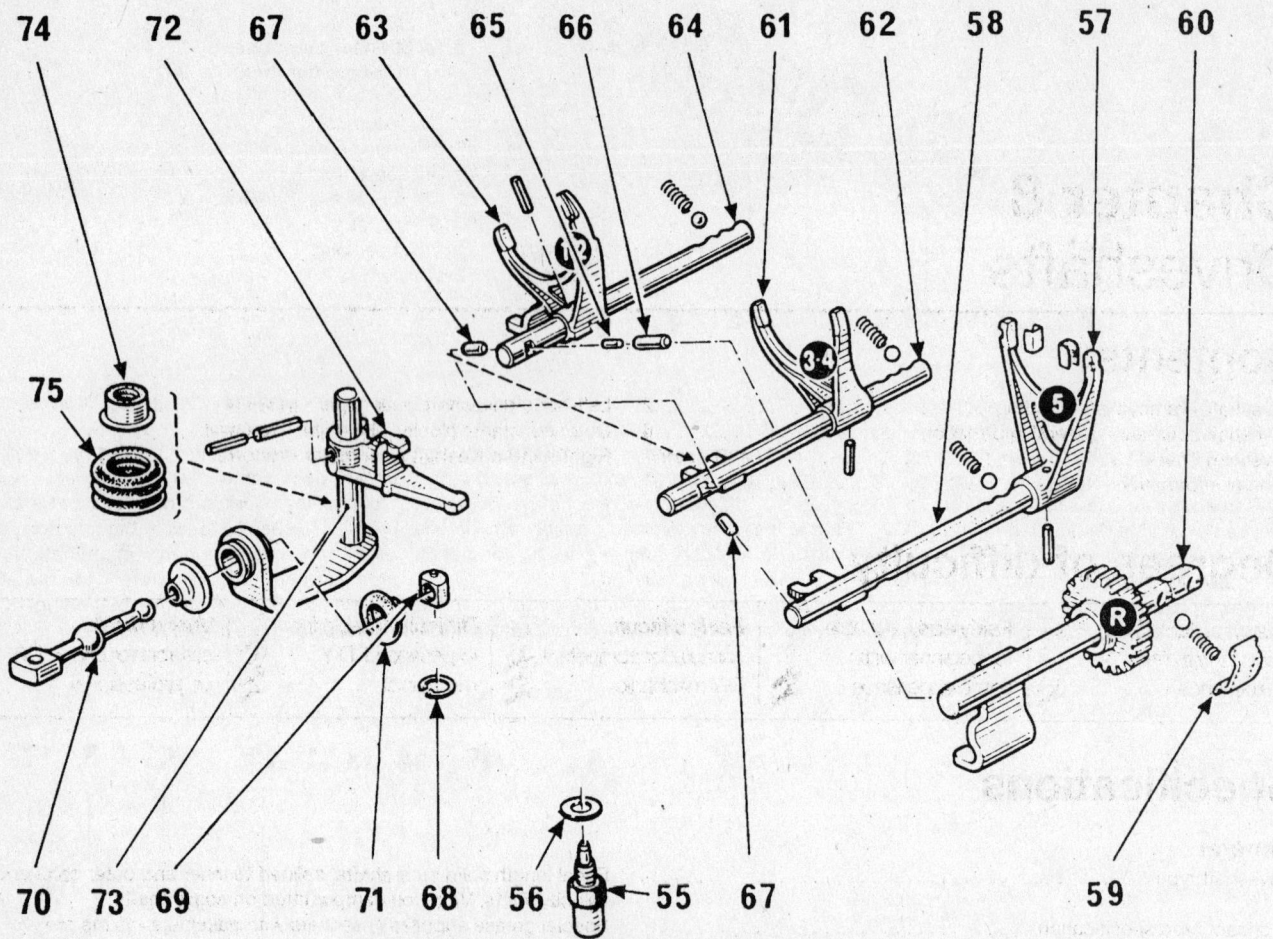

9.4g Gear selector components - JC5-type gearbox

55 5th speed detent assembly	62 3rd/4th shift rod	69 Link support
56 5th speed detent shim washer	63 1st/2nd shift fork	70 Link
57 5th speed shift fork	64 1st/2nd shift rod	71 Link cup
58 5th speed rod	65 1st/2nd plunger	72 Selector finger
59 Reverse stirrup	66 Plunger between 1st/2nd and reverse	73 Input shaft
60 Reverse shaft	67 Plunger between 1st/2nd and 3rd/4th	74 Bush
61 3rd/4th gear fork	68 Circlip	75 Dust boot

Chapter 8
Driveshafts

Contents

Degrees of difficulty

| **Easy,** suitable for novice with little experience | ⤜ | **Fairly easy,** suitable for beginner with some experience | ⤜ | **Fairly difficult,** suitable for competent DIY mechanic | ⤜ | **Difficult,** suitable for experienced DIY mechanic | ⤜ | **Very difficult,** suitable for expert DIY or professional | ⤜ |

Specifications

General

Driveshaft type	Equal length solid steel shafts, splined to inner and outer constant velocity joints. Vibration damper fitted on some shafts
Lubricant type/specification	Special grease supplied in sachets with gaiter kits - joints are otherwise pre-packed with grease and sealed

Torque wrench settings

	Nm	lbf ft
Driveshaft nut*	250	185
Left-hand driveshaft gaiter retaining plate bolts	25	19

Use a new nut

1 General information

Drive is transmitted from the differential to the front wheels by means of two, equal-length, open driveshafts.

Both driveshafts are fitted with a constant velocity (CV) joint at their outer ends, which may be of the spider-and-yoke type or of the ball-and-cage type. Each joint has an outer member, which is splined at its outer end to accept the wheel hub and is threaded so that it can be fastened to the hub by a large nut. The joint contains either a spring-loaded plunger or six balls within a cage, which engage with the inner member. The complete assembly is protected by a flexible gaiter secured to the driveshaft and joint outer member **(see illustrations)**.

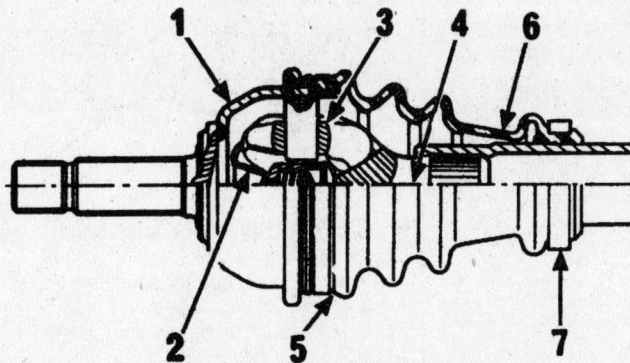

1.2a Sectional view of the spider-and-yoke type outer constant velocity joint

1 Outer member
2 Thrust plunger
3 Driveshaft spider
4 Driveshaft
5 Outer retaining clip
6 Gaiter
7 Inner retaining clip

8

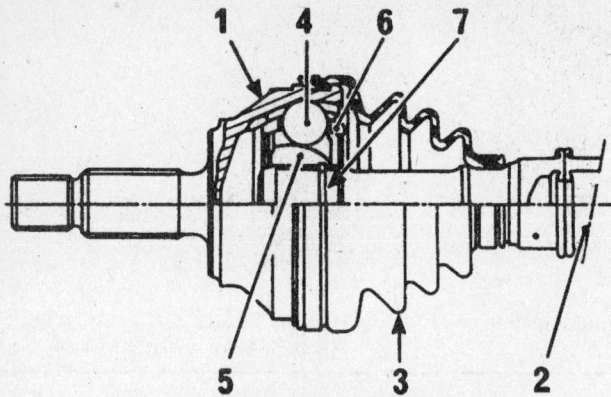

1.2b Sectional view of the ball-and-cage type outer constant velocity joint

1 Outer member
2 Driveshaft
3 Gaiter
4 Ball
5 Inner member
6 Ball cage
7 Circlip

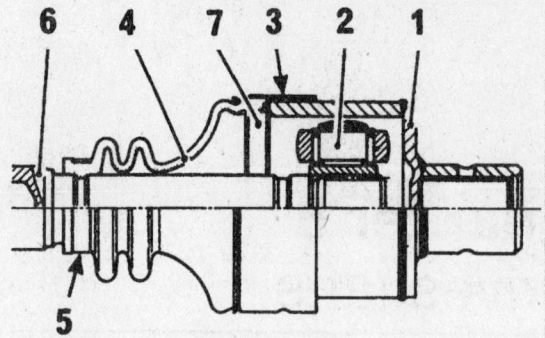

1.3 Sectional view of a right-hand inner constant velocity joint - RC490 type

1 Outer member
2 Tripod joint
3 Metal cover
4 Gaiter
5 Inner retaining clip
6 Driveshaft
7 Metal insert

A different inner constant velocity joint arrangement is fitted to each driveshaft. On the right-hand side, the driveshaft is splined to engage with a tripod joint, containing needle roller bearings and cups. The tripod joint is free to slide within the yoke of the joint outer member, which is splined and retained by a roll pin to the differential sun wheel stub shaft. As on the outer joints, a flexible gaiter secured to the driveshaft and outer member protects the complete assembly **(see illustration)**. On the left-hand side, the driveshaft also engages with a tripod joint, but the yoke in which the tripod joint is free to slide is an integral part of the differential sun wheel. On this side, the gaiter is secured to the gearbox casing with a retaining plate, and to a ball-bearing on the driveshaft with a retaining clip. The bearing allows the driveshaft to turn within the gaiter, which does not revolve.

2 Driveshaft - removal and refitting

Note: *A new driveshaft nut must be used on refitting. If a new driveshaft is fitted on models*

with ABS, the ABS wheel sensor reluctor ring must be removed from the old driveshaft, and fitted to the new driveshaft (see Chapter 9).

Removal

1 Apply the handbrake, then jack up the front of the vehicle and support it on axle stands. Remove the appropriate front roadwheel.
2 Refit at least two roadwheel bolts to the front hub, and tighten them securely. Have an assistant firmly depress the brake pedal to prevent the front hub from rotating. Using a socket and a long extension bar, slacken and remove the driveshaft retaining nut and washer. This nut is extremely tight. Discard the driveshaft nut; a new one should be used on refitting **(see illustration)**
3 Unscrew the two bolts securing the brake

TOOL TiP

A tool to hold the front hub stationary can be fabricated from two lengths of steel strip (one long, one short) and a nut and bolt; the nut and bolt form the pivot of a forked tool. Bolt the tool to the hub using two wheel bolts, and hold the tool to prevent the hub from rotating as the driveshaft retaining nut is undone.

caliper assembly to the stub axle carrier, and slide the caliper assembly off the disc. Using a piece of wire or string, tie the caliper to the front suspension coil spring, to avoid placing any strain on the hydraulic brake hose.
4 Slacken and remove the nut securing the steering gear track rod end balljoint to the stub axle carrier. Release the balljoint tapered shank using a universal balljoint separator.
5 Slacken and remove the two nuts and washers from the bolts securing the stub axle carrier to the suspension strut, noting that the nuts are positioned on the rear side of the strut **(see illustration)**. Withdraw the upper bolt, but leave the lower bolt in position at this stage. Now proceed as described under the relevant sub-heading.

Left-hand driveshaft

6 Position a suitable container beneath the gearbox drain plug, then remove the drain plug and allow the oil to drain from the gearbox. Once the oil has drained, wipe the threads of the drain plug clean, refit it to the gearbox and tighten it securely.
7 Slacken and remove the three bolts securing the rubber gaiter retaining plate to the side of the gearbox **(see illustration)**.

2.2 Removing the driveshaft retaining nut and washer

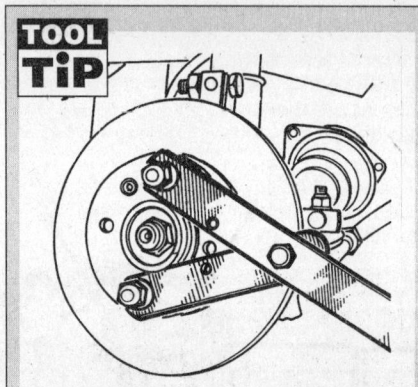

2.5 Unscrewing a stub axle carrier-to-suspension strut nut

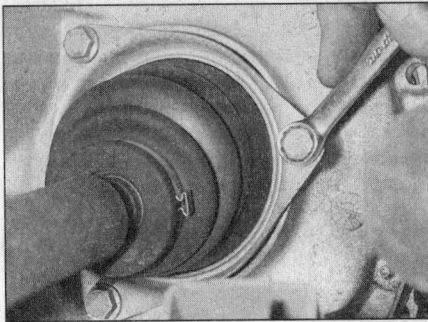
2.7 Remove the left-hand gaiter retaining plate bolts. . .

2.8 . . . and release the tripod joint from the gearbox

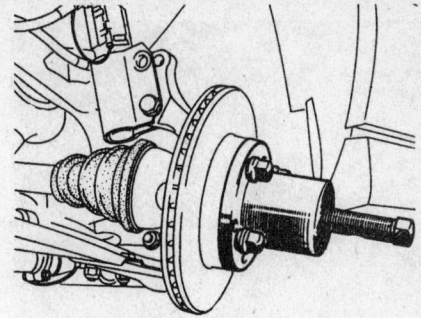
2.9 Using an extractor to press the driveshaft out of the front hub

8 Pull the top of the stub axle carrier outwards until the driveshaft tripod joint is released from its yoke; be prepared for some oil spillage as the joint is withdrawn **(see illustration)**. Be careful that the rollers on the end of the tripod do not fall off.

9 Remove the lower bolt securing the stub axle carrier to the suspension strut. Taking care not to damage the driveshaft gaiters, release the outer constant velocity joint from the hub and remove the driveshaft. Note that locking fluid is applied to the outer constant velocity joint splines during assembly, so it is likely that they will be a tight fit in the hub splines. Use a hammer and a soft metal drift to tap the joint out of the hub, or use an extractor to push the driveshaft out of the hub **(see illustration)**.

Right-hand driveshaft

Note: *New roll pins must be used on refitting.*

10 Rotate the driveshaft until the double roll pin, securing the inner constant velocity joint to the sun wheel shaft, is visible. Using a hammer and a 5 mm diameter pin punch, drive out the double roll pin **(see illustration)**. New roll pins must be used on refitting.

11 Pull the top of the stub axle carrier outwards until the inner constant velocity joint splines are released from the sun wheel shaft **(see illustration)**. Remove the O-ring from the sun wheel shaft splines.

12 Remove the driveshaft as described in paragraph 9.

Refitting

13 All new driveshafts supplied by Renault are equipped with cardboard or plastic protectors to prevent damage to the gaiters. Even the slightest knock to the gaiter can puncture it, allowing the entry of water or dirt at a later date, which may lead to the premature failure of the joint. The protectors should be left on the driveshafts until the end of the refitting procedure.

> **HAYNES HiNT** *If the original driveshaft is being refitted, it is worthwhile making up some cardboard protectors as a precaution to prevent damage to the gaiters. They can be held in position with elastic bands.*

Left-hand driveshaft

14 Wipe clean the side of the gearbox. Insert the tripod joint into the sun wheel yoke, keeping the driveshaft horizontal as far as possible.

15 Align the gaiter retaining plate with its bolt holes. Refit the retaining bolts, and tighten them to the specified torque. Ensure that the gaiter is not twisted.

16 Check that the splines on the driveshaft outer constant velocity joint and hub are clean and dry. Apply a coat of locking fluid to the splines.

17 Move the top of the stub axle carrier inwards, at the same time engaging the driveshaft with the hub.

18 Slide the hub fully onto the driveshaft splines, then insert the two suspension strut mounting bolts from the front side of the strut. Refit the washers and nuts to the rear of the bolts, and tighten them to the specified torque (Chapter 10).

19 Slide on the washer, then fit the new driveshaft retaining nut, tightening it by hand only at this stage.

20 Reconnect the steering track rod balljoint to the stub axle carrier, and tighten its retaining nut to the specified torque (see Chapter 10).

21 Slide the brake caliper assembly into position over the brake disc. Refit the caliper mounting bolts, having first applied a few drops of locking fluid to their threads, and tighten them to the specified torque (see Chapter 9).

22 Using the method employed during removal to prevent the hub from rotating, tighten a new driveshaft retaining nut to the specified torque **(see illustration)**. Check that the hub rotates freely, then remove the protectors from the driveshaft, taking great care not to damage the flexible gaiters.

23 Refit the roadwheel. Lower the car to the ground and tighten the roadwheel bolts to the specified torque (Chapter 10).

24 Refill the gearbox with oil; refer to Chapter 1 for details.

Right-hand driveshaft

25 Ensure that the inner constant velocity joint and sun wheel shaft splines are clean and dry. Apply a smear of molybdenum

8

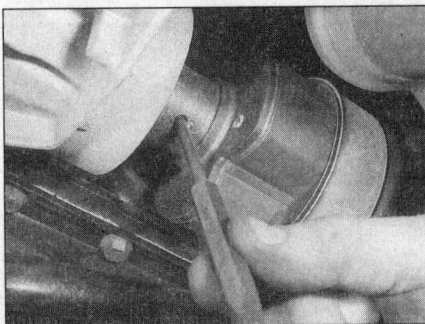
2.10 Drive out the roll pins with a suitable pin punch

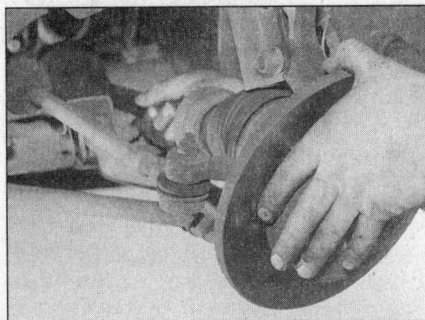
2.11 Pulling out the right-hand driveshaft

2.22 Tighten the driveshaft retaining nut to the specified torque

2.25 Fit the new O-ring onto the sun wheel shaft . . .

2.26 . . . and engage the driveshaft, ensuring that the roll pin holes (arrowed) are correctly aligned

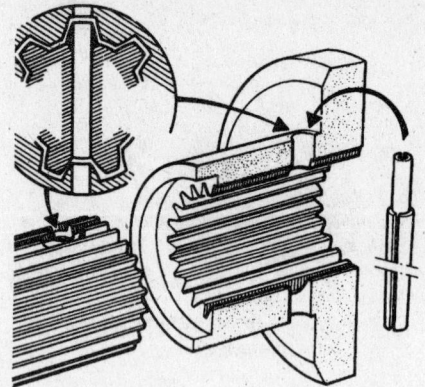

2.27a Right-hand driveshaft inner constant velocity joint roll pin arrangement

disulphide grease to the splines. Fit a new O-ring over the end of the sun wheel shaft, and slide the O-ring along the shaft until it abuts the gearbox oil seal **(see illustration)**.

26 Engage the driveshaft splines with those of the sun wheel shaft, making sure that the roll pin holes are in alignment **(see illustration)**. Slide the driveshaft onto the sun wheel shaft until the roll pin holes are aligned.

27 Drive in new roll pins with their slots 90° apart, then seal the ends of the pins with sealing compound (Renault CAF 4/60 THIXO paste or equivalent) **(see illustrations)**.

28 Carry out the procedures described in paragraphs 16 to 23.

3 Outer constant velocity joint gaiter - renewal

1 Remove the driveshaft (see Section 2).

2 Cut through the gaiter retaining clip(s) or release the retaining spring and inner collar (as applicable), then slide the gaiter down the shaft to expose the outer constant velocity joint.

3 Scoop out as much grease as possible from the joint, and determine which type of constant velocity joint is fitted. Proceed as described under the relevant sub-heading.

Ball-and-cage type joint

4 Using circlip pliers, expand the joint internal circlip. At the same time, tap the exposed

face of the ball hub with a mallet to separate the joint from the driveshaft. Slide off the gaiter and rubber collar.

5 With the constant velocity joint removed from the driveshaft, clean the joint using paraffin, or a suitable solvent, and dry it thoroughly. Carry out a visual inspection of the joint.

6 Move the inner splined driving member from side to side, to expose each ball in turn at the top of its track. Examine the balls for cracks, flat spots or signs of surface pitting.

7 Inspect the ball tracks on the inner and outer members. If the tracks have widened, the balls will no longer be a tight fit. At the same time, check the ball cage windows for wear or cracking between the windows.

8 If on inspection any of the constant velocity joint components are found to be worn or damaged, it will be necessary to renew the complete driveshaft assembly, since no components are available separately. If the joint is in satisfactory condition, obtain a repair kit from your Renault dealer consisting of a new gaiter, rubber collar, retaining spring, and the correct type and quantity of grease.

9 Tape over the splines on the end of the driveshaft, then slide the rubber collar and gaiter onto the shaft. Locate the inner end of the gaiter on the driveshaft, and secure it in position with the rubber collar.

10 Remove the tape, then slide the constant velocity joint coupling onto the driveshaft until the internal circlip locates in the driveshaft groove.

11 Check that the circlip holds the joint securely on the driveshaft, then pack the joint with the grease supplied. Work the grease well into the ball tracks, and fill the gaiter with any excess.

12 Locate the outer lip of the gaiter in the groove on the joint outer member. With the coupling aligned with the driveshaft, lift the lip of the gaiter to equalise the air pressure. Secure the gaiter in position with the large retaining spring, using two lengths of hollow metal tubing to ease the spring into position **(see illustration)**.

13 Check that the constant velocity joint moves freely in all directions, then refit the driveshaft to the vehicle as described in Section 2.

Spider-and-yoke type joint

14 Remove the inner constant velocity joint, bearing and gaiter (as applicable), as described in Section 4 or 5 of this Chapter.

15 Where a vibration damper is fitted, clearly mark the position of the damper on the driveshaft, then use a puller or press to remove it from the inner end of the driveshaft, noting which way around it is fitted **(see illustration)**. Ensure that the legs of the puller or support plate rest only on the damper inner

2.27b Seal the ends of the roll pins with a suitable sealing compound

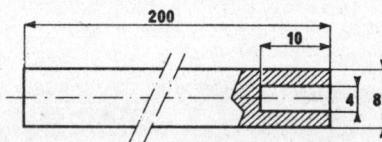

3.12 Using two lengths of hollow metal tubing to install the gaiter retaining spring. Tube dimensions in mm

3.15 Removing the vibration damper from the driveshaft

3.19 Renault driveshaft gaiter repair kit

3.21 Pack the joint with the grease supplied in the repair kit . . .

3.22 . . . then slide the gaiter into position over the joint

rubber bush, otherwise the damper will distort and break away from the outer metal housing as it is removed.

16 Slide the outer constant velocity joint gaiter off the inner end of the driveshaft.

17 Clean the outer constant velocity joint using paraffin or a suitable solvent, and dry it thoroughly. Carry out a visual inspection of the joint.

18 Check the driveshaft spider and outer member yoke for signs of wear, pitting or scuffing on their bearing surfaces. Also check that the outer member pivots smoothly and easily, with no traces of roughness.

19 If inspection reveals signs of wear or damage, it will be necessary to renew the driveshaft complete, since no components are available separately. If the joint components are in satisfactory condition, obtain a repair kit consisting of a new gaiter, retaining clips, and the correct type and quantity of grease **(see illustration)**.

20 Tape over the splines on the inner end of the driveshaft, then carefully slide the outer gaiter onto the shaft.

21 Pack the joint with the grease supplied in the repair kit. Work the grease well into the joint, and fill the gaiter with any excess **(see illustration)**.

22 Ease the gaiter over the joint, and ensure that the gaiter lips are correctly located in the grooves on the driveshaft and on the joint **(see illustration)**. With the coupling aligned with the driveshaft, lift the lip of the gaiter to equalise the air pressure.

23 Fit the large metal retaining clip to the gaiter. Remove any slack in the gaiter retaining clip by carefully compressing the raised section of the clip. In the absence of the special tool, a pair of pincers may be used. Secure the small retaining clip using the same procedure **(see illustrations)**. Check that the constant velocity joint moves freely in all directions before proceeding further.

24 To refit the vibration damper (when applicable), lubricate the driveshaft with a solution of soapy water. Press or drive the vibration damper along the shaft, using a tubular spacer which bears only on the damper inner bush, until it is aligned with the mark made prior to removal.

25 Refit the inner constant velocity joint

3.23a Fit the large retaining clip . . .

3.23b . . . and the small retaining clip. Note use of pincers to secure the clip

components as described in Section 4 or 5 (as applicable), then refit the driveshaft to the vehicle as described in Section 2.

4 Right-hand driveshaft inner gaiter - renewal

1 Remove the driveshaft (see Section 2).
2 On these models, two different types of inner constant velocity joint are used on the right-hand driveshaft: type GI62 and type RC490. The joints can be identified by the shape of their outer members. The GI62 joint has a smooth, circular outer member; the RC490 joint has a recessed outer member which appears clover-shaped when viewed end-on. Identify the type of joint fitted, then proceed as described under the relevant sub-heading.

GI62-type joint

3 Release the large retaining spring and the inner retaining collar, then slide the gaiter down the shaft to expose the joint.
4 Using pliers, carefully bend up the anti-separation plate tangs at their corners **(see illustration)**. Slide the outer member off the tripod joint. Be prepared to hold the rollers in place, otherwise they may fall off the tripod ends as the outer member is withdrawn. If necessary, secure the rollers in place using tape after removal of the outer member. The rollers are matched to the tripod joint stems, and it is important that they are not interchanged.

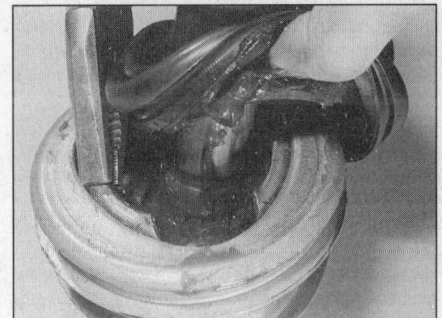
4.4 Bend up the anti-separation tangs with pliers to release the joint outer member - GI62-type

4.5 Remove the circlip . . .

5 Using circlip pliers, extract the circlip securing the tripod joint to the driveshaft **(see illustration)**. Note that on some models, the joint may be staked in position; if so, relieve the staking using a file. Mark the position of

8

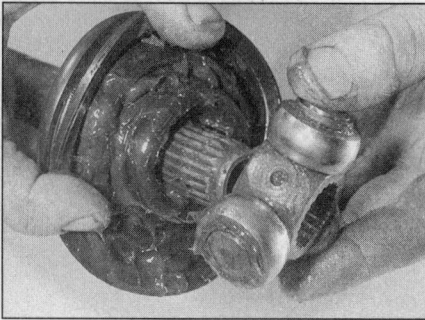

4.6 . . . and withdraw the tripod joint from the driveshaft end

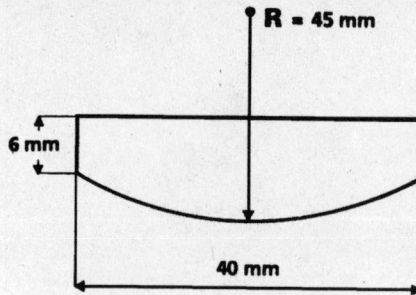

4.15 Support plate dimensions for re-forming the anti-separation plate tangs - GI62-type joint

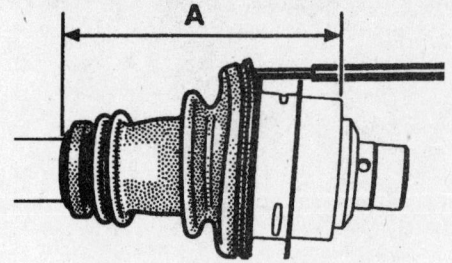

4.19 Fitting dimension for the right-hand driveshaft inner constant velocity joint gaiter - GI62-type joint
A = 153 ± 1 mm

the tripod in relation to the driveshaft, using a dab of paint or a punch.

6 The tripod joint can now be removed **(see illustration)**. If it is tight, draw the joint off the driveshaft end using a puller. Ensure that the legs of the puller are located behind the joint inner member and do not contact the joint rollers. Alternatively, support the inner member of the tripod joint, and press the shaft out using a hydraulic press, again ensuring that no load is applied to the joint rollers.

7 With the tripod joint removed, slide the gaiter and inner retaining collar off the end of the driveshaft.

8 Wipe clean the joint components, taking care not to remove the alignment marks made on dismantling. **Do not** use paraffin or other solvents to clean this type of joint.

9 Examine the tripod joint, rollers and outer member for any signs of scoring or wear. Check that the rollers move smoothly on the tripod stems. If wear is evident, the tripod joint and roller assembly can be renewed, but it is not possible to obtain a replacement outer member. Obtain a new gaiter, retaining spring/collar and a quantity of the special lubricating grease. These parts are available in the form of a repair kit from your Renault dealer.

10 Tape over the splines on the end of the driveshaft, then carefully slide the inner retaining collar and gaiter onto the shaft.

11 Remove the tape, then, aligning the marks made on dismantling, engage the tripod joint with the driveshaft splines. Use a hammer and soft metal drift to tap the joint onto the shaft, taking great care not to damage the driveshaft splines or joint rollers. Alternatively, support the driveshaft, and press the joint into position using a hydraulic press and suitable tubular spacer which bears only on the joint inner member.

12 Secure the tripod joint in position with the circlip, ensuring that it is correctly located in the driveshaft groove. Where no circlip is fitted, secure the joint in position by staking the end of the driveshaft in three places, at intervals of 120°, using a hammer and punch.

13 Evenly distribute the grease contained in the repair kit around the tripod joint and inside

the outer member. Pack the gaiter with the remainder of the grease.

14 Slide the outer member into position over the tripod joint.

15 Using a piece of 2.5mm thick steel or similar material, make up a support plate to the dimensions shown **(see illustration)**.

16 Position the support plate under each anti-separation plate tang in the outer member in turn, and tap the tang down onto the support plate. Remove the plate when all the tangs have been returned to their original shape.

17 Slide the gaiter up the driveshaft. Locate the gaiter in the grooves on the driveshaft and outer member.

18 Slide the inner retaining collar into place over the inner end of the gaiter.

19 Using a blunt rod, carefully lift the outer lip of the gaiter to equalise the air pressure. With the rod in position, compress the joint until the dimension from the inner end of the gaiter to the flat end face of the outer member is as shown **(see illustration)**. Hold the outer member in this position and withdraw the rod.

20 Slip the new retaining spring into place to secure the outer lip of the gaiter to the outer member. Take care to ensure that the retaining spring is not overstretched during the fitting process.

21 Check that the constant velocity joint moves freely in all directions, then refit the driveshaft as described in Section 2.

RC490-type joint

22 Using a pair of grips, bend up the metal joint cover at the points where it has been staked into the outer member recesses.

23 Using a pair of snips, cut the gaiter inner retaining clip.

24 Using a soft metal drift, tap the metal joint cover off the outer member **(see illustration)**. Slide the outer member off the end of the tripod joint. Be prepared to hold the rollers in place, otherwise they may fall off the tripod ends as the outer member is withdrawn. If necessary, secure the rollers in place using tape after removal of the outer member. The rollers are matched to the tripod joint stems, and it is important that they are not interchanged.

25 Remove the tripod joint and gaiter assembly, and examine the joint components for wear, using the information given in paragraphs 6 to 9 of this Section. Make alignment marks between the spider and the shaft for use when refitting. Obtain a repair kit consisting of a gaiter, retaining clip, metal insert and joint cover, and the correct type and amount of grease.

26 Fit the metal insert into the inside of the gaiter, then locate the gaiter assembly inside the metal joint cover.

27 Tape over the driveshaft splines, and slide the gaiter and joint cover assembly onto the driveshaft.

28 Refit the tripod joint as described in paragraphs 11 and 12.

29 Evenly distribute the grease contained in the repair kit around the tripod joint and inside the outer member. Pack the gaiter with the remainder of the grease.

30 Slide the outer member into position over the tripod joint.

31 Slide the metal joint cover onto the outer member until it is flush with the outer member guide panel. Secure the joint cover in position by staking it into the recesses in the outer member, using a hammer and a round-ended punch.

32 Using a blunt rod, carefully lift the inner lip of the gaiter to equalise the air pressure. With the rod in position, compress the joint until the dimension from the inner end of the gaiter to

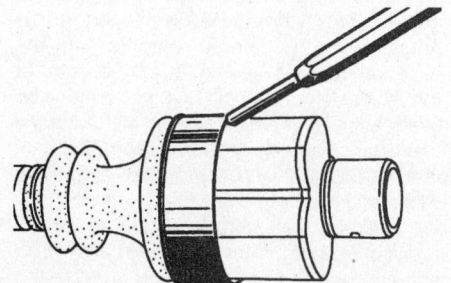

4.24 Removing the metal cover from the right-hand driveshaft inner constant velocity joint - RC490-type

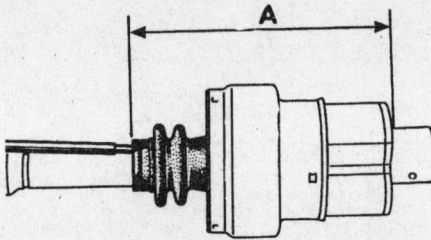

4.32 Fitting dimension for the right-hand driveshaft inner constant velocity joint gaiter - RC490-type joint
A = 156 ± 1 mm

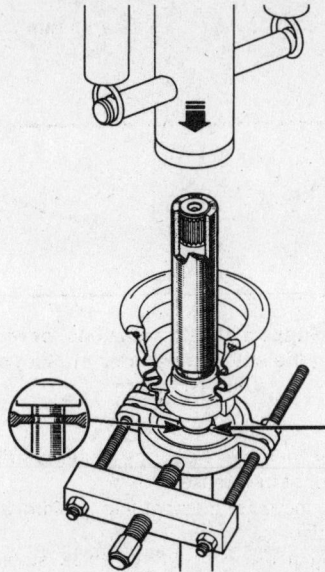

5.8a Pressing the inner bearing/gaiter onto the end of the left-hand driveshaft

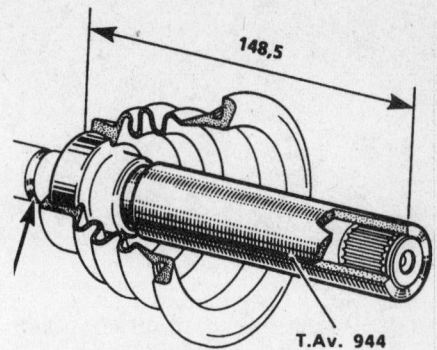

5.8b Fitting dimension (in mm) for the left-hand driveshaft inner bearing/gaiter
T.Av.944 = Renault special tool

the flat end face of the outer member is as shown **(see illustration)**. Hold the outer member in this position and withdraw the rod.
33 Fit the small retaining clip to the inner end of the gaiter. Remove any slack in the gaiter retaining clip by carefully compressing the raised section of the clip. In the absence of the special tool, a pair of pincers may be used.
34 Check that the constant velocity joint moves freely in all directions, then refit the driveshaft as described in Section 2.

5 Left-hand driveshaft inner gaiter - renewal

1 Remove the driveshaft as described in Section 2.
2 Using circlip pliers, extract the circlip securing the tripod joint to the driveshaft. Note that on some models, the joint may be staked in position; if so, relieve the stakings using a file. Using a dab of paint or a hammer and punch, mark the position of the tripod joint in relation to the driveshaft, to use as a guide to refitting.
3 The tripod joint can now be removed. If it is tight, draw the joint off the driveshaft end using a puller. Ensure that the legs of the puller are located behind the joint inner member and do not contact the joint rollers. Alternatively, support the inner member of the tripod joint and press the shaft out of the joint, again ensuring that no load is applied to the joint rollers.
4 The gaiter and bearing assembly is removed in the same way, either by drawing the bearing off the driveshaft, or by pressing the driveshaft out of the bearing. Remove the retaining plate, noting which way round it is fitted.

5 Obtain a new gaiter, which is supplied complete with the small bearing.
6 Owing to the lip-type seal used in the bearing, the bearing and gaiter must be pressed into position. If a hammer and tubular drift are used to drive the assembly onto the driveshaft, there is a risk of distorting the seal.
7 Refit the retaining plate to the driveshaft, ensuring that it is fitted the correct way around.
8 Support the driveshaft, and press the gaiter bearing onto the shaft, using a tubular spacer which bears only on the bearing inner race. Position the bearing so that the distance from the end of the driveshaft to the inner face of the bearing is as shown **(see illustrations)**.
9 Align the marks made on dismantling, and engage the tripod joint with the driveshaft splines. Use a hammer and soft metal drift to tap the joint onto the shaft, taking care not to damage the driveshaft splines or joint rollers. Alternatively, support the driveshaft, and press the joint into position using a tubular spacer which bears only on the joint inner member.
10 Secure the tripod joint in position with the circlip, ensuring that it is correctly located in the driveshaft groove. Where no circlip is fitted, secure the joint in position by staking the end of the driveshaft in three places, at intervals of 120°, using a hammer and punch.
11 Refit the driveshaft to the vehicle as described in Section 2.

6 Driveshaft overhaul - general information

1 If any of the checks described in Chapter 1 reveal wear in a driveshaft joint, first remove the roadwheel trim or centre cap (as appropriate) and check that the driveshaft retaining nut is still correctly tightened; if in doubt, use a torque wrench to check it. Refit the centre cap or trim, and repeat the check on the other driveshaft.
2 Road test the vehicle, and listen for a metallic clicking from the front as the vehicle is driven slowly in a circle with the steering on full-lock. If a clicking noise is heard, this indicates wear in the outer constant velocity joint.
3 If vibration, consistent with road speed, is felt through the vehicle when accelerating, there is a possibility of wear in the inner constant velocity joints.
4 Constant velocity joints can be dismantled and inspected for wear as described in Sections 3, 4 and 5.
5 Wear in the outer constant velocity joint can only be rectified by renewing the driveshaft. This is necessary since no outer joint components are available separately. For the inner joint, the tripod joint and roller assembly is available separately, but wear in any of the other components will also necessitate driveshaft renewal.
6 On models with ABS, the reluctor ring should be removed from the old driveshaft and fitted to the new one. See Chapter 9.

8

Chapter 9
Braking system

Contents

Degrees of difficulty

Easy, suitable for novice with little experience	**Fairly easy,** suitable for beginner with some experience	**Fairly difficult,** suitable for competent DIY mechanic	**Difficult,** suitable for experienced DIY mechanic	**Very difficult,** suitable for expert DIY or professional

Specifications

General

System type:
Conventional system .... Dual hydraulic circuit, split diagonally, with servo assistance
Bendix ABS .... Dual hydraulic circuit, split diagonally, with electric high-pressurepump
Bosch ABS .... Dual hydraulic circuit, split diagonally, with servo assistance
Front brakes .... Disc, with single-piston sliding caliper
Rear brakes .... Self-adjusting drum or disc, according to model
Handbrake .... Cable-operated, to rear wheels

Front brakes

	New	Minimum
Disc diameter .... 238.0 mm		
Disc thickness:	**New**	**Minimum**
Non-Turbo models (except models with ABS)	12.0 mm	10.5 mm
Turbo models and all models with ABS	20.0 mm	18.0 mm
Maximum disc run-out	0.07 mm	
Brake pad thickness (friction material and backing plate)	18.0 mm	6.0 mm

Rear drum brakes

	New	Minimum
Drum diameter:		
New	180.25 mm	
Maximum diameter after machining	181.25 mm	
	New	**Minimum**
Brake shoe thickness (friction material and shoe)	6.5 mm	2.5 mm

Rear disc brakes

Disc diameter . . . . 238.0 mm

	New	Minimum
Disc thickness	12.0 mm	10.5 mm
Maximum disc run-out	0.07 mm	
Brake pad minimum thickness (friction material and backing plate) . . .	11.0 mm	5.0 mm

Anti-lock braking system (ABS)

	Front	Rear
Wheel sensor-to-reluctor ring clearance:		
Bendix ABS system	0.15 to 1.15 mm	0.20 to 0.81 mm
Bosch ABS system	0.21 to 1.03 mm	0.40 to 1.50 mm
Wheel sensor electrical resistance:		
Bendix ABS system	No information available at time of writing	
Bosch ABS system	1130 ohms (approximately)	

Torque wrench settings

	Nm	lbf ft
Vacuum servo-to-bulkhead nuts	20	15
Brake fluid pipe and hose unions	13	10
Master cylinder-to-servo nuts	13	10
Bendix front brake caliper mounting bolts	100	74
Girling front brake caliper:		
Guide pin bolts*	35	26
Mounting bracket-to-stub axle carrier bolts	100	74
Front brake disc securing screws	25	19
Rear hub nut*	160	118
Rear drum brake backplate	45	33
Fluid bleed screw	7	5
ABS wheel sensor bolts	9	7

*Note: Use a new nut/bolts.

1 General information

The braking system is of the servo-assisted, dual circuit hydraulic type. The arrangement of the hydraulic system is such that each circuit operates one front and one rear brake from a tandem master cylinder. Under normal circumstances, both circuits operate in unison. However, in the event of hydraulic failure in one circuit, full braking force will still be available at two wheels **(see illustration)**.

Certain Turbo models, and all models fitted with an anti-lock braking system (ABS) are equipped with disc brakes all round as standard, whereas all other models without ABS are fitted with front disc brakes and rear drum brakes. ABS is offered as an option on certain models (refer to Section 22 for further information on ABS operation).

The front disc brakes are actuated by single-piston sliding type calipers, which ensure that equal pressure is applied to each disc pad.

On models with rear drum brakes, the rear brakes incorporate leading and trailing shoes, which are actuated by twin-piston wheel cylinders (one cylinder per drum). The wheel cylinders incorporate integral pressure-regulating valves, which control the hydraulic pressure applied to the rear brakes. The regulating valves help to prevent rear wheel lock-up during emergency braking. As the brake shoe linings wear, footbrake operation automatically operates a self-adjuster mechanism, which effectively lengthens the strut between the shoes and reduces the lining-to-drum clearance.

On models with rear disc brakes, the brakes are actuated by single-piston sliding calipers which incorporate mechanical handbrake mechanisms. A load-sensitive pressure-regulating valve is connected into the brake lines to the rear calipers. The regulating valve is similar to that fitted to the rear wheel cylinders (on rear drum brake models), and helps to prevent rear wheel lock-up during emergency braking. It does this by varying the hydraulic pressure applied to the rear calipers in proportion to the load being carried by the vehicle.

On all models, the handbrake provides an independent mechanical means of rear brake application.

On all models except those fitted with the Bendix ABS system, a vacuum servo is fitted to reduce the pedal effort required to operate the braking system.

As with all diesel engines, since there is insufficient vacuum in the inlet manifold to operate the vacuum servo, a vacuum pump is fitted to the engine to provide the required vacuum. The pump is mounted on the left-hand end of the cylinder head, and is driven directly from the end of the camshaft.

Note: *When servicing any part of the system, work carefully and methodically; also observe scrupulous cleanliness when overhauling any part of the hydraulic system.*

Always renew components (in axle sets, where applicable) if in doubt about their condition, and use only genuine Renault replacement parts, or at least those of known good quality. Note the warnings given in "Safety first!" and at relevant points in this Chapter, concerning the dangers of asbestos dust and hydraulic fluid.

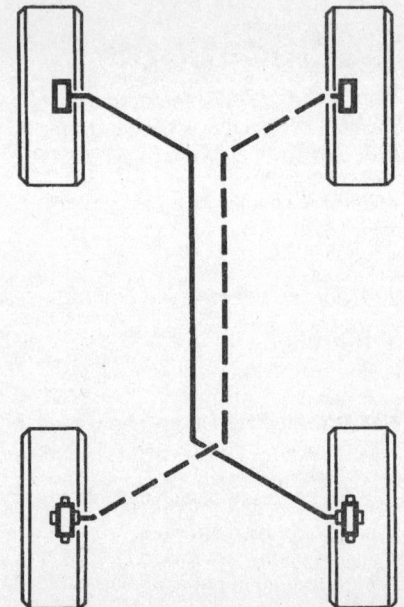

1.1 Diagonally split brake hydraulic system (rear drum brake model shown)

2.1 Removing the lower facia panel

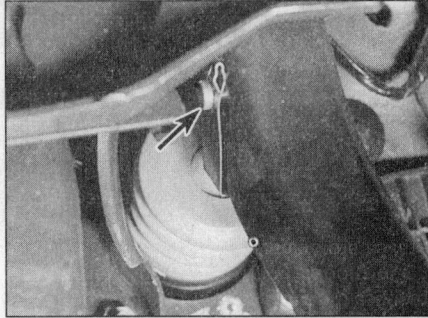
2.2a Clevis pin (arrowed) securing the vacuum servo unit pushrod to the brake pedal

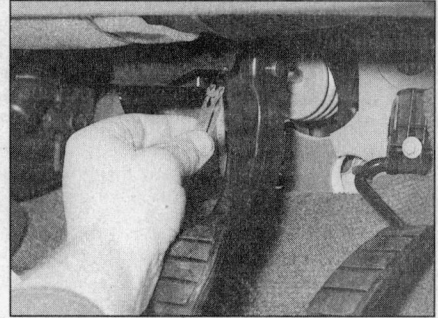
2.2b Removing the spring clip from the clevis pin

2 Brake pedal - removal and refitting

Removal

1 Working inside the vehicle, remove the lower facia panel from beneath the steering column for access to the pedal bracket (see illustration).
2 Extract the spring clip, washer and clevis pin securing the vacuum servo unit pushrod to the brake pedal (see illustrations). Note the location of the plastic spacer on the right-hand end of the clevis pin.
3 Remove the clutch pedal, as described in Chapter 6.
4 Slide the remaining spacer from the clutch pedal end of the pedal pivot shaft.
5 Slide out the pivot shaft to the right, until the brake pedal can be withdrawn (see illustration).
6 Examine the pivot bushes for wear and renew them if necessary.

Refitting

7 Refitting is a reversal of removal, but lubricate the bushes, pivot shaft and pushrod clevis pin with molybdenum disulphide grease.
8 Refit the clutch pedal as described in Chapter 6.

3 Vacuum servo unit - testing, removal and refitting

Testing

1 To test the operation of the servo unit, depress the footbrake four or five times to exhaust the vacuum, then start the engine while keeping the footbrake depressed. As the engine starts there should be a noticeable "give" in the brake pedal as vacuum builds up. Allow the engine to run for at least two minutes and then switch it off. If the brake pedal is now depressed again, it should be possible to detect a hiss from the servo when the pedal is depressed. After about four or five

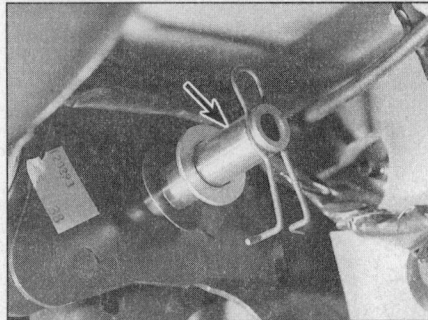
2.5 Slide out the pedal pivot shaft (arrowed)

applications no further hissing will be heard and the pedal will feel considerably firmer.

Removal

2 The servo must be removed upwards from the engine compartment. On certain right-hand-drive models, it will be necessary to remove the inlet and/or exhaust manifold assemblies (see Chapter 4) to enable sufficient access and clearance for the servo to be removed.
3 Where applicable, unbolt the brackets or release the clips and move any heat shields, hoses, pipes or wiring obscuring the servo to one side.
4 Disconnect the battery negative lead.
5 Refer to Section 8 and remove the master cylinder.
6 Disconnect the vacuum hose at the servo non-return valve.
7 Working inside the vehicle, remove the lower facia panel from beneath the steering column.
8 Extract the spring clip, washer and clevis pin securing the servo unit pushrod to the brake pedal.
9 Unscrew the four nuts and remove the washers securing the servo to the bulkhead, then withdraw the unit into the engine compartment.
10 Note that the servo unit cannot be dismantled for repair or overhaul and, if faulty, must be renewed.

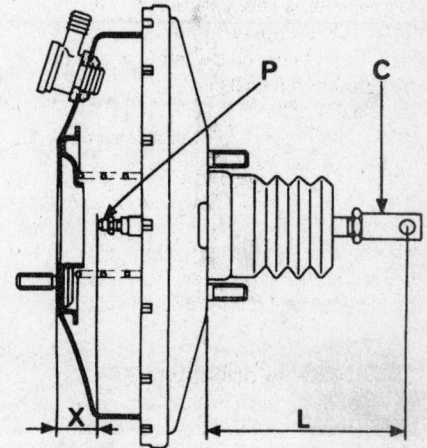
3.11 Vacuum servo unit adjustment dimensions

C Pushrod clevis   L = 117.5 mm
P Pushrod nut   X = 22.3 mm

Refitting

11 Before refitting the servo unit, check the pushrod and clevis dimensions as shown, and if necessary adjust them (see illustration). Make sure that the locknuts are tight after making an adjustment.
12 Refitting is a reversal of removal, but refit the master cylinder with reference to Section 8, and where applicable, refit the manifold(s) with reference to Chapter 4.

4 Vacuum servo unit non-return valve - removal, testing and refitting

Removal

1 Slacken the clip (where applicable) and disconnect the vacuum pipe from the non-return valve on the front face of the servo unit.
2 Withdraw the valve from its rubber sealing grommet by pulling and twisting. Remove the sealing grommet from the servo unit.

9

Testing

3 Examine the non-return valve and sealing grommet for damage and signs of deterioration and renew if necessary. The valve may be tested by blowing through it in both directions - it should only be possible to blow from the servo end to the manifold end.

Refitting

4 Refitting is a reversal of removal.

5 Vacuum servo unit air filter - renewal

1 Working inside the vehicle, remove the lower facia panel from beneath the steering column.
2 Ease the convoluted rubber cover off the rear of the servo unit and move it up the pushrod.
3 Using a screwdriver or scriber, hook out the old air filter and remove it from the servo.
4 Make a cut in the new filter as shown, and place it over the pushrod and into position in the servo end **(see illustration)**.
5 Refit the rubber cover, then refit the lower facia panel beneath the steering column.

6 Hydraulic system - bleeding

⚠️ **Warning: Hydraulic fluid is poisonous; wash off immediately and thoroughly in the case of skin contact, and seek immediate medical advice if any fluid is swallowed or gets into the eyes. Certain types of hydraulic fluid are inflammable, and may ignite when allowed into contact with hot components; when servicing any hydraulic system, it is safest to assume that the fluid is inflammable, and to take precautions against the risk of fire as though it is petrol that is being handled. Finally, it is hygroscopic (it absorbs moisture from the air) - old fluid may be contaminated and unfit for further use. When topping-up or renewing the fluid, always use the recommended type (see Chapter 1), and ensure that it comes from a freshly-opened, previously-sealed container**

HAYNES HINT *Hydraulic fluid is an effective paint stripper, and will attack plastics; if any is spilt, it should be washed off immediately using copious quantities of fresh water.*

Note: *On models with ABS, before disconnecting any part of the hydraulic system, the system must be depressurised as*

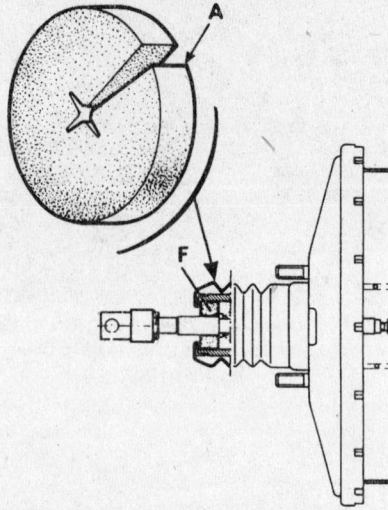

5.4 Vacuum servo unit air filter renewal
A Cut the new filter as shown
F Correct fitted position of filter in servo unit

described later in this Section. Failure to do so could result in personal injury.

Non-ABS models

1 The correct operation of any hydraulic system is only possible after removing all air from the components and circuit; this is achieved by bleeding the system.
2 During the bleeding procedure, add only clean, unused hydraulic fluid of the recommended type; never re-use fluid that has already been bled from the system. Ensure that sufficient fluid is available before starting work.
3 If there is any possibility of incorrect fluid being already in the system, the system must be flushed completely with uncontaminated, correct fluid, and new seals should be fitted to the various components.
4 If air has entered the hydraulic system because of a leak, ensure that the fault is cured before proceeding further.
5 Park the vehicle on level ground, switch off the engine and select first or reverse gear. Chock the wheels and release the handbrake.
6 Check that all pipes and hoses are secure, unions tight and bleed screws closed. Clean any dirt from around the bleed screws.
7 Unscrew the fluid reservoir cap and top the reservoir up to the "MAX" level line; refit the cap loosely. Remember to maintain the fluid level at least above the "MIN" level line throughout the procedure, or there is a risk of further air entering the system.
8 There are a number of one-man, do-it-yourself brake bleeding kits currently available from motor accessory shops. It is recommended that one of these kits is used whenever possible, as they greatly simplify the bleeding operation, and also reduce the risk of expelled air and fluid being drawn back into the system. If such a kit is not available, the basic (two-man) method must be used,

which is described in detail below.
9 If a kit is to be used, prepare the vehicle as described previously, and follow the kit manufacturer's instructions. The procedure may vary slightly according to the type of kit being used; general procedures are as outlined below in the relevant sub-section.
10 Whichever method is used, the correct bleeding sequence must be followed to ensure the removal of all air from the system.

Bleeding sequence

11 If the system has been only partially disconnected, and suitable precautions were taken to minimise fluid loss, it should be necessary only to bleed that part of the system (ie the primary or secondary circuit).
12 If the complete system is to be bled, then it should be done working in the following sequence:
a) *Left-hand rear brake.*
b) *Right-hand front brake.*
c) *Right-hand rear brake.*
d) *Left-hand front brake.*

Bleeding - basic (two-man) method

13 Collect a clean glass jar, a suitable length of plastic or rubber tubing which is a tight fit over the bleed screw, and a ring spanner to fit the screw. The help of an assistant will also be required.
14 Remove the dust cap from the first bleed screw in the sequence. Fit the spanner and tube to the screw, place the other end of the tube in the jar, and pour in sufficient fluid to cover the end of the tube.
15 Ensure that the fluid reservoir fluid level is maintained at least above the "MIN" level line throughout the procedure.
16 Have the assistant fully depress the brake pedal several times to build up pressure, then maintain it on the final stroke.
17 While pedal pressure is maintained, unscrew the bleed screw (approximately one turn) and allow the compressed fluid and air to flow into the jar. The assistant should maintain pedal pressure, following it down to the floor if necessary, and should not release it until instructed to do so. When the flow stops, tighten the bleed screw again. Have the assistant release the pedal slowly.
18 Repeat the steps given in paragraphs 16 and 17 until the fluid emerging from the bleed screw is free from air bubbles. Remember to recheck the fluid level in the reservoir every five strokes or so. If the master cylinder has been drained and refilled, and air is being bled from the first screw in the sequence, allow approximately five seconds between strokes for the master cylinder passages to refill.
19 When no more air bubbles appear, tighten the bleed screw securely, remove the tube and spanner, and refit the dust cap. Do not overtighten the bleed screw.
20 Repeat the procedure on the remaining screws in the sequence until all air is removed from the system and the brake pedal feels firm.
21 Proceed to paragraph 30.

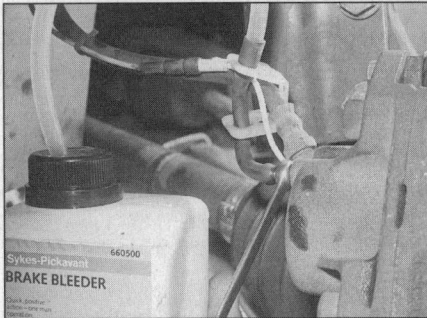

6.22 Bleeding a front brake caliper

Bleeding - using a one-way valve kit

22 As their name implies, these kits consist of a length of tubing with a one-way valve fitted, to prevent expelled air and fluid being drawn back into the system; some kits include a translucent container, which can be positioned so that the air bubbles can be more easily seen flowing from the end of the tube **(see illustration)**.

23 The kit is connected to the bleed screw, which is then opened. The user returns to the driver's seat and depresses the brake pedal with a smooth, steady stroke and slowly releases it; this is repeated until the expelled fluid is clear of air bubbles.

24 Note that these kits simplify work so much that it is easy to forget the reservoir fluid level; ensure that this is maintained at least above the "MIN" level line at all times.

25 Proceed to paragraph 30.

Bleeding - using a pressure-bleeding kit

26 These kits are usually operated by the reservoir of pressurised air contained in the spare tyre, although it may be necessary to reduce the pressure to lower than normal; refer to the instructions supplied with the kit.

27 By connecting a pressurised, fluid-filled container to the fluid reservoir, bleeding can be carried out simply by opening each screw in turn (in the specified sequence) and allowing the fluid to flow out until no more air bubbles can be seen in the expelled fluid.

28 This method has the advantage that the large reservoir of fluid provides an additional safeguard against air being drawn into the system during bleeding.

29 Pressure-bleeding is particularly effective when bleeding "difficult" systems, or when bleeding the complete system at the time of routine fluid renewal.

All methods

30 When bleeding is complete and firm pedal feel is restored, wash off any spilt fluid, tighten the bleed screws securely and refit their dust caps.

31 Check the hydraulic fluid level, and top-up if necessary (Chapter 1).

32 Discard any hydraulic fluid that has been bled from the system; it will not be fit for re-use.

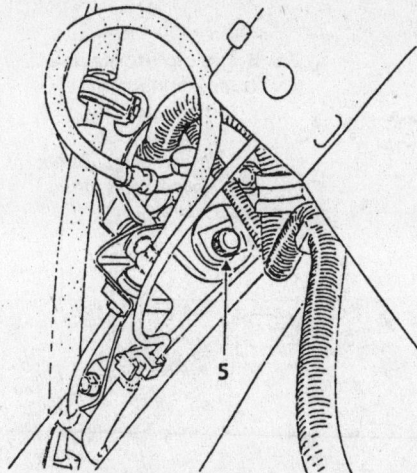

6.34 Slacken the bolt (5) to depressurise the ABS hydraulic system

33 Check the feel of the brake pedal. If it feels at all spongy, air must still be present in the system, and further bleeding is required. Failure to bleed satisfactorily after several repetitions of the bleeding procedure may be due to worn master cylinder seals.

Bendix ABS system

⚠️ *Warning: Before carrying out any work involving disconnection of fluid lines, or loosening of bleed screws, it is essential to depressurise the system as described in the following paragraphs. Failure to observe this could result in personal injury. Due to the complex nature of the ABS, it is recommended that this work is carried out by a Renault dealer.*

Note: *Due to the requirement for special test equipment, and the associated risk of personal injury if the equipment is not available, no procedure is given here for bleeding of the braking system on models with Bendix ABS. It is strongly recommended that bleeding of the system is entrusted to a Renault dealer, who will have the required specialist knowledge and equipment.*

Depressurising the system

34 Working under the front of the vehicle, slacken the bolt on the underside of the pump unit by one turn. **Note:** *Do not slacken the bolt by more than two turns, otherwise the O-ring seal will be damaged.* Check that the accumulator has emptied by checking the fluid level in the reservoir which should be level with the upper mark **(see illustration)**.

35 Retighten the bolt on the underside of the pump.

Bleeding the system

36 Bleeding of the system should be entrusted to a Renault dealer, due to the requirement for specialist knowledge and test equipment.

Bosch ABS system

37 At the time of writing, no information was available regarding the Bosch ABS system fitted to certain later models (from 1994 model year). Before attempting to carry out any work on a vehicle fitted with this system, consult a Renault dealer for advice.

7 Hydraulic pipes and hoses - inspection, removal and refitting

⚠️ *Warning: Before attempting to disconnect any fluid pipes or hoses on models with ABS, refer to the information given for depressurising and bleeding the ABS system in Section 6.*

Note: *Before starting work, refer to the warning at the beginning of Section 6 concerning the dangers of hydraulic fluid.*

Inspection

1 The hydraulic pipes, hoses, hose connections and pipe unions should be regularly examined.

2 First check for signs of leakage at the pipe unions, then examine the flexible hoses for signs of cracking, chafing and fraying **(see illustration)**.

3 The brake pipes should be examined carefully for signs of dents, corrosion or other damage. Corrosion should be scraped off, and if the depth of pitting is significant, the pipes renewed. This is particularly likely in those areas underneath the vehicle body where the pipes are exposed and unprotected.

Removal

4 If any pipe or hose is to be renewed, minimise fluid loss by removing the fluid reservoir cap and then tightening it down onto a piece of polythene (taking care not to damage the level sender unit) to obtain an airtight seal. Alternatively, flexible hoses can

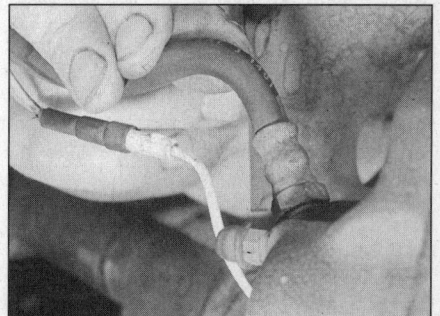

7.2 Checking a brake flexible hose for cracking

9

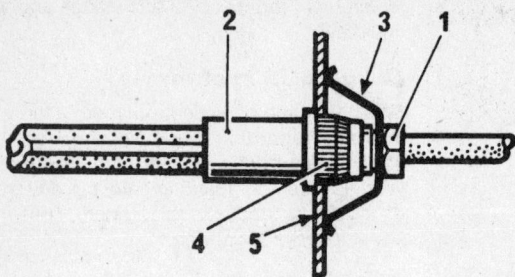

7.5 Brake pipe-to-flexible hose connection
1 Union nut
2 Flexible hose
3 Spring clip support
4 Splined end fitting
5 Bodywork

be sealed, if required, using a proprietary brake hose clamp; metal brake pipe unions can be plugged (if care is taken not to allow dirt into the system) or capped immediately they are disconnected. Place a wad of rag under any union that is to be disconnected, to catch any spilt fluid. If a section of pipe is to be removed from the master cylinder, the reservoir should be emptied by syphoning out the fluid or drawing out the fluid with a pipette.

5 If a flexible hose is to be disconnected, unscrew the brake pipe union nut before removing the spring clip which secures the hose to its mounting bracket **(see illustration)**.

6 To unscrew the union nuts, it is preferable to obtain a brake pipe spanner of the correct size (11 mm/13 mm split ring); these are available from motor accessory shops **(see illustration)**. Failing this, a close-fitting open-ended spanner will be required, though if the nuts are tight or corroded, their flats may be rounded off if the spanner slips. In such a case, a self-locking wrench is often the only way to unscrew a stubborn union, but it follows that the pipe and the damaged nuts must be renewed on reassembly. Always clean a union and surrounding area before disconnecting it.

> **HAYNES HINT** *If disconnecting a component with more than one union, make a careful note of the connections before disturbing any of them.*

7 If a brake pipe is to be renewed, it can be obtained, cut to length and with the union nuts and end flares in place, from Renault dealers. All that is then necessary is to bend it to shape, following the line of the original, before fitting it to the vehicle. Alternatively, most motor accessory shops can make up brake pipes from kits, but this requires very careful measurement of the original to ensure that the replacement is of the correct length. The safest answer is usually to take the original to the shop as a pattern.

Refitting

8 On refitting, do not overtighten the union nuts. The specified torque wrench settings (where given) are not high, and it is not necessary to exercise brute force to obtain a sound joint.

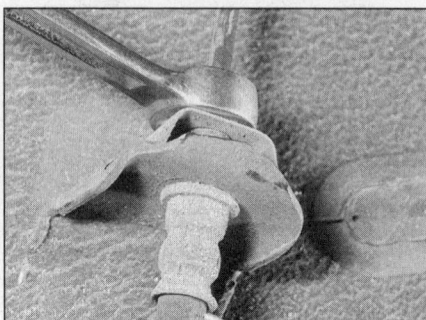

7.6 Using a brake pipe spanner to unscrew a hydraulic union nut

9 Ensure that the pipes and hoses are correctly routed with no kinks, and that they are secured in the clips or brackets provided. In the case of flexible hoses, make sure that they cannot contact other components during movement of the steering and/or suspension assemblies.

10 After fitting, remove the polythene from the reservoir (or remove the plugs or clamps, as applicable), and bleed the hydraulic system as described in Section 6. Wash off any spilt fluid, and check carefully for fluid leaks.

8 Master cylinder (non-ABS models) - removal and refitting

> ⚠ **Warning: Before attempting to disconnect any fluid pipes or hoses on models with ABS, refer to the information given for depressurising and bleeding the ABS system in Section 6.**

Note: *A new master cylinder-to-servo seal will be required on refitting.*

Removal

1 Where applicable, unbolt and remove the strengthening bar from between the front suspension turrets.

2 On certain models, it may be necessary to remove the inlet and/or exhaust manifolds, as described in Chapter 4.

3 Where applicable, unbolt the brackets or release the clips and move any heat shields, hoses, pipes or wiring obscuring the master

cylinder to one side.

4 Syphon the brake fluid from the reservoir (not by mouth - use an old poultry baster or a pipette), or alternatively place a container beneath the master cylinder and cover the surrounding components with rags.

5 On models with a remotely-mounted fluid reservoir, disconnect the hoses leading from the reservoir to the master cylinder, at the master cylinder. Wipe up any fluid spillage immediately.

6 On models where the fluid reservoir is mounted directly on the master cylinder, pull the reservoir from the top of the master cylinder.

7 Identify the brake pipes for position, then unscrew the union nuts and disconnect them. Tape over the pipe ends to prevent the entry of dust and dirt.

8 Unscrew the mounting nuts and withdraw the master cylinder from the servo unit. Where applicable, note the position of the vacuum hose support bracket **(see illustration)**.

9 It is not possible to obtain seals or internal components for the master cylinder, therefore if it is faulty it should be renewed complete. Where applicable, the reservoir locating seals may be renewed if necessary. The seal between the master cylinder and the vacuum servo should be renewed as a matter of course whenever the unit is removed, as a leak at this point will allow atmospheric pressure into the servo unit.

Refitting

10 Before refitting the master cylinder, clean the mounting faces and check that the distance between the tip of the master cylinder end of the pushrod and the front of the servo unit (dimension "X") is as shown in illustration 3.11. If required, adjust by repositioning the pushrod nut "P".

11 Refitting is a reversal of removal, but tighten the securing nuts to the specified torque. Fit a new seal between the master cylinder and the servo, and when offering the master cylinder to the servo, make sure that it is correctly aligned so that the pushrod enters the piston centrally.

12 On completion, bleed the hydraulic system as described in Section 6.

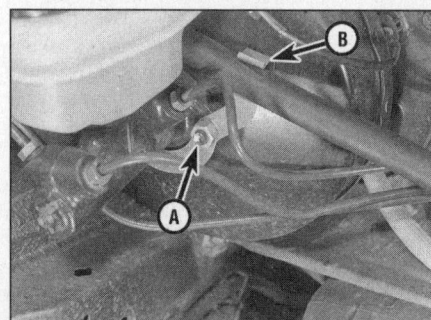

8.8 Master cylinder mounting nut (A) and vacuum hose support bracket (B)

9.4a Extract the small spring . . .

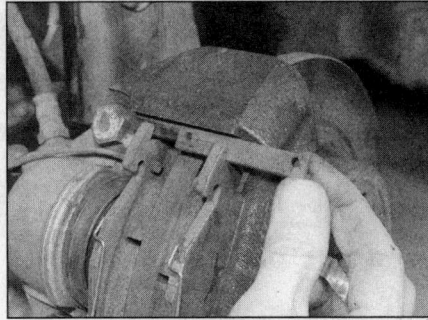

9.4b . . . and withdraw the pad retaining key (Bendix caliper)

9.5a Removing the outer brake pad . . .

9.5b . . . and the inner brake pad (Bendix caliper)

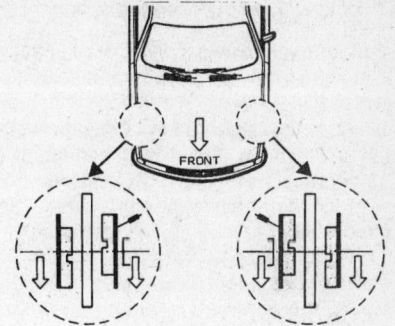

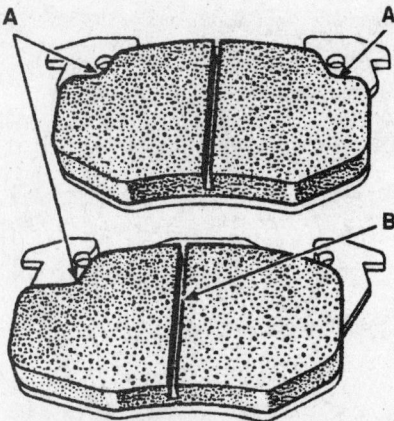

9 Front brake pads - renewal

Warning: Disc brake pads must be renewed on both front wheels at the same time - never renew the pads on only one wheel, as uneven braking may result. Also, the dust created by wear of the pads may contain asbestos, which is a health hazard. Never blow it out with compressed air and don't inhale any of it. An approved filtering mask should be worn when working on the brakes. DO NOT use petroleum based solvents to clean brake parts. Use brake cleaner or methylated spirit only.

1 Apply the handbrake then jack up the front of the vehicle and support it securely on axle stands (see "*Jacking, towing and wheel changing*"). Remove the front roadwheels.

Bendix calipers

2 Disconnect the brake pad wear warning sensor wire at the connector.

3 Push the piston into its bore by pulling the caliper outwards.
4 Extract the small spring clip and then withdraw the pad retaining key **(see illustrations)**.
5 Using pliers if necessary, withdraw the pads from the caliper, and remove the anti-rattle spring from each pad **(see illustrations)**. If required, the thickness of the pad linings can be checked at this stage using a steel rule.
6 With the pads removed, check that the caliper is free to slide on the guide sleeves and that the rubber dust excluders around the piston and guide sleeves are undamaged. If attention to these components is necessary refer to Section 10.
7 To refit the pads, move the caliper sideways as far as possible towards the centre of the car. Fit the anti-rattle spring to the innermost pad making sure that this pad is the one with the wear warning sensor wire, then locate the pad in position, with the backing plate against the piston.
8 Note that the pads are of the offset type, having only one cutaway on their outer edge, compared with the two cutaways on the symmetrical type. Looking at the pads from the front of the car, the innermost pad groove must be higher than the outer pad groove. Make sure that the pads are fitted correctly **(see illustrations)**.

9.8a Bendix caliper symmetrical-lining pad (top) and offset-lining pad (bottom). Offset lining has only a single cut-out (A) and the groove in the friction material (B) is not central

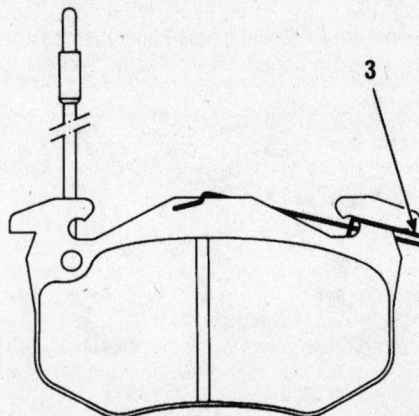

9.8b Anti-rattle spring (3) correctly fitted to Bendix inner brake pad

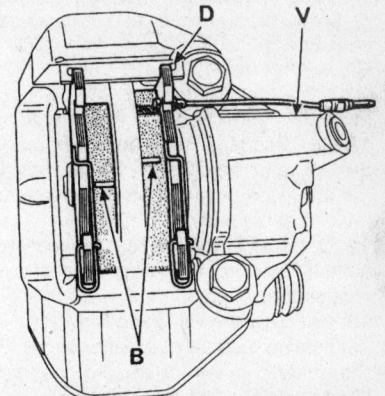

9.8c Correct fitting of Bendix offset lining brake pads

B Grooves
D Pad retaining plate spring clip location
V Bleed screw

9

9.8d Correct fitted positions of the Bendix offset lining brake pads

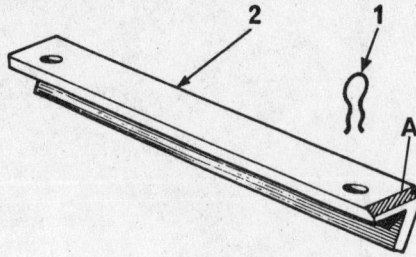

9.10 Bendix disc pad retaining plate (2) and spring clip (1) showing filed chamfer (A)

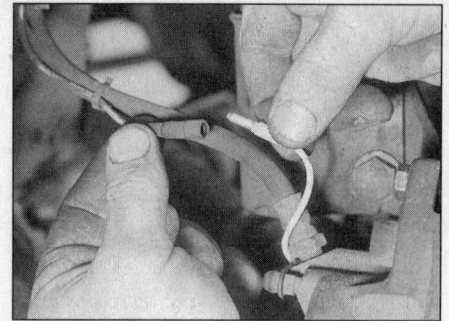

9.14 Disconnecting the brake pad wear warning sensor wiring (Girling caliper)

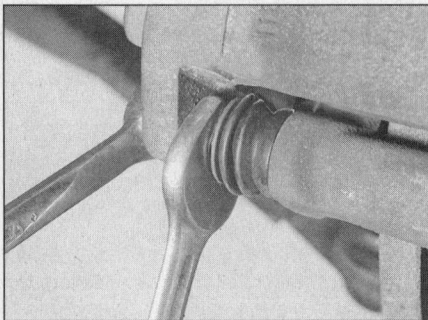

9.15a On Girling calipers, slacken the guide pin bolts whilst holding the guide pins with an open-ended spanner . . .

9.15b . . . then withdraw the bolts and lift off the brake caliper

9 Move the caliper outwards, then fit the anti-rattle spring to the outer pad and locate the pad in the caliper.

10 Slide the retaining key into place and refit the small spring clip at the inner end. It may be necessary to file an entry chamfer on the edge of the retaining key to enable it to be fitted without difficulty **(see illustration)**.

11 Reconnect the brake pad wear warning sensor wire, then refit the roadwheel and repeat the renewal procedure on the other front brake.

12 On completion, check the hydraulic fluid level in the reservoir, then depress the brake pedal two or three times to bring the pads into contact with the disc. Lower the vehicle to the ground.

Girling calipers

13 Pull the caliper body outwards, away from the centre of the car. This will push the piston back into its bore to facilitate removal and refitting of the pads.

14 Disconnect the brake pad wear warning sensor wiring at the connector **(see illustration)**.

15 Unscrew the upper and lower guide pin bolts using a suitable spanner, while holding the guide pins with a second spanner **(see illustrations)**. Note that new guide pin bolts will be required on reassembly.

16 With the guide pins removed, lift the caliper off the brake pads and carrier bracket, and tie it up in a convenient place under the wheelarch. Do not allow the caliper to hang

unsupported on the flexible brake hose.

17 Withdraw the two brake pads from the carrier bracket **(see illustration)**. If required, the thickness of the pads can be checked at this stage using a steel rule.

18 Before refitting the pads, check that the guide pins are free to slide in the carrier bracket and check that the rubber dust excluders around the guide pins are undamaged. Brush the dust and dirt from the caliper and piston but do not inhale it as it is injurious to health. Inspect the dust excluder around the piston for damage and inspect the piston for evidence of fluid leaks, corrosion or damage. If attention to any of these components is necessary, refer to Section 10.

19 To refit the pads, place them in position on the carrier bracket, noting that the pad with the warning sensor wire must be nearest to

the centre of the car. The anti-rattle springs must be located as shown **(see illustration)**.

20 Make sure that the caliper piston is fully retracted in its bore. If not, carefully push it in, preferably using a G-clamp or, alternatively, using a flat bar or screwdriver as a lever.

21 Position the caliper over the pads, then fit the new lower guide pin bolt, having first coated its threads with locking fluid. Apply locking fluid to the new upper guide pin bolt, press the caliper into position, then fit the bolt. Tighten the bolts to the specified torque, starting with the lower bolt.

22 Reconnect the brake pad wear warning sensor wiring, then refit the roadwheel and repeat the renewal procedure on the other front brake.

23 On completion, check the hydraulic fluid level in the reservoir, then depress the brake pedal two or three times to bring the pads into contact with the disc. Lower the vehicle to the ground.

9.17 Removing the outer brake pad from the carrier bracket (Girling caliper)

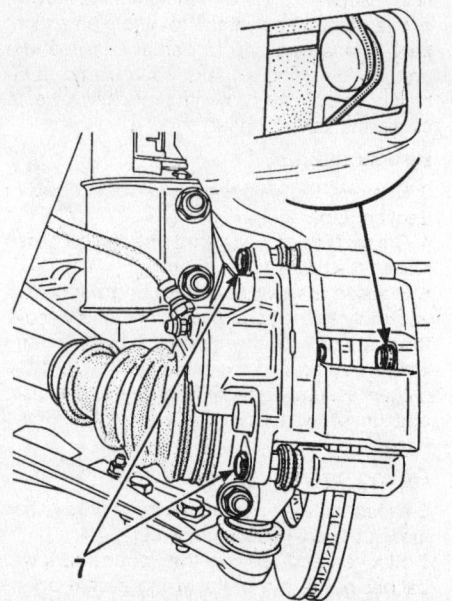

9.19 Girling caliper showing guide pin bolts (7) and correct fitted position of anti-rattle spring

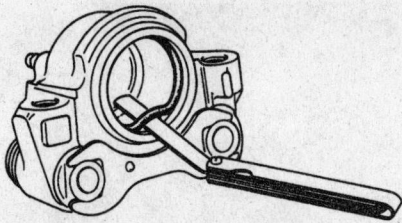

10.11 Using a feeler gauge to remove the piston seal from a Bendix type caliper

10.14 Bendix type brake caliper components

1 Mounting plate
2 Guide sleeve inner rubber gaiters
3 Guide sleeves
4 Guide sleeve seals
5 Caliper body
6 Guide sleeve outer rubber gaiters
7 Mounting bracket retaining bolts
8 Mounting bracket
9 Piston
10 Piston seal
11 Piston dust seal

10 Front brake caliper - removal, overhaul and refitting.

Warning: Before attempting to disconnect any fluid pipes or hoses on models with ABS, refer to the information given for depressurising and bleeding the ABS system in Section 6.

Note: *Before starting work, refer to the warnings at the beginning of Sections 6 and 9 concerning the dangers of hydraulic fluid and asbestos dust.*

Removal

1 Apply the handbrake, then jack up the front of the vehicle and support it securely on axle stands (see *"Jacking, towing and wheel changing"*). Remove the appropriate roadwheel.
2 Minimise fluid loss, either by removing the fluid reservoir cap and then tightening it down onto a piece of polythene to obtain an airtight seal (taking care not to damage the sender unit), or by using a brake hose clamp, a G-clamp, or a similar tool with protected jaws, to clamp the flexible hose.

Bendix caliper

3 Remove the brake pads as described in Section 9, paragraphs 2 to 5.
4 Clean the area around the union, then loosen the brake hose union nut.
5 Slacken the two bolts securing the caliper assembly to the stub axle carrier, and remove them along with the mounting plate, noting which way around the plate is fitted. Lift the caliper assembly away from the brake disc, and unscrew it from the end of the brake hose.

Girling caliper

6 Clean the area around the hose union, then loosen the brake hose union nut.
7 Slacken and remove the upper and lower caliper guide pin bolts, using a slim open-ended spanner to prevent the guide pin itself from rotating. Discard the guide pin bolts; new bolts must be used on refitting. With the guide pin bolts removed, lift the caliper away from the brake disc, then unscrew the caliper from

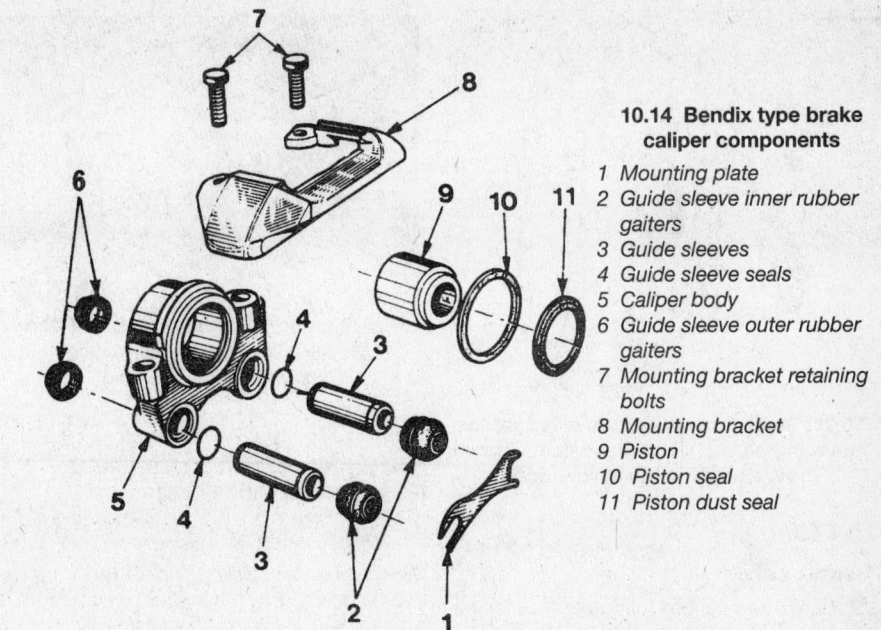

the end of the brake hose. Note that the brake pads need not be disturbed, and can be left in position in the caliper mounting bracket.

Overhaul

Note: *Ensure that an appropriate overhaul kit can be obtained before dismantling the caliper.*
8 With the caliper on the bench, wipe away all traces of dust and dirt, but *avoid inhaling the dust, as it is injurious to health.*
9 On the Girling caliper, using a small flat-bladed screwdriver, carefully prise the dust seal retaining clip out of the caliper bore.
10 On all calipers, withdraw the partially-ejected piston from the caliper body and remove the dust seal. The piston can be withdrawn by hand, or if necessary forced out by applying compressed air to the union bolt hole. *Caution: The piston may be ejected with some force.* Only low pressure should be required, such as is generated by a foot pump.
11 Extract the piston hydraulic seal using a blunt instrument such as a knitting needle or a feeler gauge, taking care not to damage the caliper bore **(see illustration)**.
12 Withdraw the guide sleeves or pins from the caliper body or mounting bracket (as applicable) and remove the rubber gaiters.
13 Thoroughly clean all components using only methylated spirit, isopropyl alcohol or clean hydraulic fluid as a cleaning medium. Never use mineral-based solvents, such as petrol or paraffin, which will attack the hydraulic system rubber components. Dry the components immediately, using compressed air or a clean, lint-free cloth. Use compressed air to blow clear the fluid passages.
14 Check all components and renew any that are worn or damaged **(see illustration)**. Check particularly the cylinder bore and

piston; if they are scratched, worn or corroded in any way, they must be renewed (note that this means the renewal of the complete body assembly). Similarly, check the condition of the guide sleeves or pins and their bores; they should be undamaged and (when cleaned) a reasonably tight sliding fit in the body or mounting bracket bores. If there is any doubt about the condition of a component, renew it.
15 If the assembly is fit for further use, obtain the appropriate repair kit; the components are available from Renault dealers, in various combinations.
16 Renew all rubber seals, dust covers and caps disturbed on dismantling as a matter of course; these should never be re-used.
17 Before commencing reassembly, ensure that all components are absolutely clean and dry.
18 Dip the piston and the new piston (fluid) seal in clean hydraulic fluid. Smear clean fluid on the cylinder bore surface.
19 Fit the new piston (fluid) seal, using only the fingers to manipulate it into the cylinder bore groove. Fit the new dust seal to the piston. Refit the piston to the cylinder bore using a twisting motion, ensuring that the piston enters squarely into the bore. Press the piston fully into the bore, then press the dust seal into the caliper body.
20 On the Girling caliper, install the dust seal retaining clip, ensuring that it is correctly seated in the caliper groove.
21 On all calipers, apply the grease supplied in the repair kit, or a good quality high-temperature brake grease or anti-seize compound to the guide sleeves or pins. Fit the sleeves or pins to the caliper body or mounting bracket. Fit the new rubber gaiters, ensuring that they are correctly located in the grooves on both the sleeve or pin, and body or mounting bracket (as applicable).

9

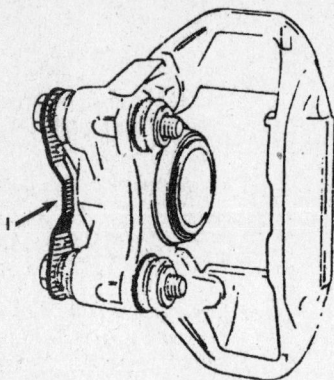

10.22 On Bendix calipers, ensure that the mounting plate (1) is fitted so that its bend curves towards the caliper body

Refitting

Bendix caliper

22 Screw the caliper fully onto the flexible hose union nut. Position the caliper over the brake disc, then refit the two caliper mounting bolts and the mounting plate. Note that the mounting plate must be fitted so that its bend curves towards the caliper body **(see illustration)**; this is necessary to prevent the plate contacting the driveshaft gaiter when the steering is on full-lock. With the plate correctly positioned, tighten the caliper bolts to the specified torque setting.

23 Tighten the brake hose union nut to the specified torque, then refit the brake pads as described in Section 9.

24 Proceed to paragraph 28.

Girling caliper

25 Screw the caliper body fully onto the flexible hose union nut. Check that the brake pads are still correctly fitted in the caliper mounting bracket.

26 Position the caliper over the pads. Coat the threads of the new lower guide pin bolt with locking fluid, and fit the bolt. Apply locking fluid to the new upper guide pin bolt, press the caliper into position, and fit the bolt. Check that the anti-rattle springs are correctly located (see illustration 9.19), then tighten the guide pin bolts to the specified torque, starting with the lower bolt.

27 Tighten the brake hose union nut to the specified torque.

All calipers

28 Remove the brake hose clamp or polythene, where fitted, and bleed the hydraulic system as described in Section 6. Providing the precautions described were taken to minimise brake fluid loss, it should only be necessary to bleed the relevant front brake.

29 Refit the roadwheel, then lower the vehicle to the ground and tighten the roadwheel bolts to the specified torque (Chapter 10).

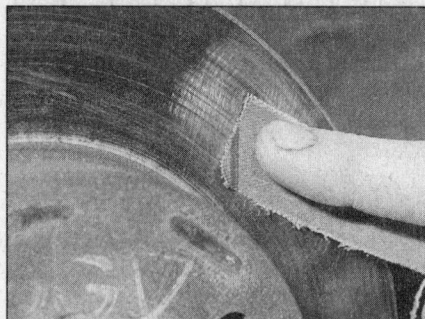

11.2 Using emery tape to remove light scoring from the disc

11 Front brake disc - inspection, removal and refitting

Note: *Before starting work, refer to the warning at the beginning of Section 9 concerning the dangers of asbestos dust. If either disc requires renewal, both should be renewed at the same time, to ensure even and consistent braking. In principle, new pads should be fitted also.*

Inspection

1 Apply the handbrake, then jack up the front of the vehicle and support it securely on axle stands (see *"Jacking, towing and wheel changing"*). Remove the appropriate front roadwheel.

2 Slowly rotate the brake disc so that the full area of both sides can be checked; remove the brake pads, as described in Section 9, if better access is required to the inboard surface. Light scoring is normal in the area swept by the brake pads, and can be removed using emery tape **(see illustration)**. If heavy scoring is found, the disc must be renewed.

3 It is normal to find a lip of rust and brake dust around the disc's perimeter; this can be scraped off if required. If, however, a lip has formed due to wear of the brake pad swept area, the disc thickness must be measured using a micrometer **(see illustration)**. Take measurements at several places around the

11.4 Checking brake disc run-out with a dial gauge

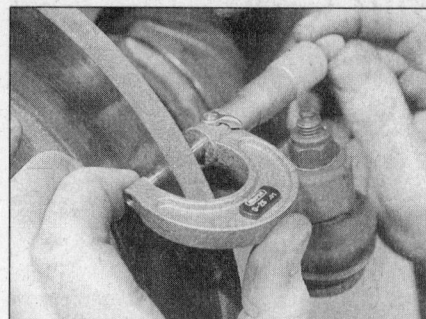

11.3 Measuring brake disc thickness with a micrometer

disc at the inside and outside of the pad swept area; if the disc has worn at any point to the specified minimum thickness or less, it must be renewed.

4 If the disc is thought to be warped, it can be checked for run-out, ideally by using a dial gauge mounted on any convenient fixed point, while the disc is slowly rotated **(see illustration)**. In the absence of a dial gauge, use feeler blades to measure (at several points all around the disc) the clearance between the disc and a fixed point such as the caliper mounting bracket. If the measurements obtained are at the specified maximum or beyond, the disc is excessively warped, and must be renewed; however, it is worth checking first that the hub bearing is in good condition (Chapters 1 and 10). Also try the effect of removing the disc and turning it through 180° to reposition it on the hub; if run-out is still excessive, the disc must be renewed.

5 Check the disc for cracks (especially around the wheel bolt holes), and for any other wear or damage. Renew the disc if necessary.

Removal

6 Unscrew the two bolts securing the brake caliper assembly to the stub axle carrier, and slide the caliper assembly, complete with pads, off the disc. Using a piece of wire or string, tie the caliper to the front suspension coil spring, to avoid placing any strain on the hydraulic brake hose **(see illustration)**.

11.6 Girling brake caliper assembly suspended from the front suspension coil spring (pads removed)

12.2 Prise the cap from the centre of the brake drum . . .

12.3 . . . then remove the rear hub nut and thrustwasher

7 If the same disc is to be refitted, use chalk or paint to mark the relationship of the disc to the hub. Remove the two screws securing the brake disc to the hub, and remove the disc. If it is tight, lightly tap its rear face with a hide or plastic mallet.

Refitting

8 Refitting is the reverse of the removal procedure, noting the following points:

a) Ensure that the mating surfaces of the disc and hub are clean and flat.

b) If applicable, align the marks made on removal.

c) Securely tighten the disc retaining screws.

d) If a new disc has been fitted, use a suitable solvent to wipe any preservative coating from the disc before refitting the caliper.

e) Apply locking fluid to the threads of the brake caliper mounting bolts, and tighten them to the specified torque.

f) Refit the roadwheel, then lower the vehicle to the ground and tighten the roadwheel bolts to the specified torque.

g) On completion, depress the brake pedal several times to bring the brake pads into contact with the disc.

---

12 Rear brake drum - removal, inspection and refitting

Note: *Before starting work, refer to the warning at the beginning of Section 9 concerning the dangers of asbestos dust. If either drum requires renewal or refinishing, both should be dealt with at the same time, to ensure even and consistent braking. In principle, new shoes should be fitted also. A new rear hub nut will be required on refitting.*

Removal

1 Chock the front wheels, engage reverse gear and release the handbrake. Jack up the rear of the vehicle and support it securely on axle stands (see *"Jacking, towing and wheel changing"*). Remove the appropriate rear wheel.

2 Using a hammer and suitable large flat-bladed screwdriver, carefully tap and prise the cap out of the centre of the brake drum **(see illustration)**.

3 Using a socket and long bar, slacken and remove the rear hub nut, and withdraw the thrustwasher **(see illustration)**. Discard the hub nut; a new nut must used on refitting.

4 It should now be possible to withdraw the brake drum and hub bearing assembly from the stub axle by hand. It may be difficult to remove the drum due to the tightness of the hub bearing on the stub axle, or due to the brake shoes binding on the inner circumference of the drum. If the bearing is tight, tap the periphery of the drum using a hide or plastic mallet, or use a universal puller, secured to the drum with the wheel bolts, to pull it off. If the brake shoes are binding, proceed as follows.

5 First ensure that the handbrake is fully off. From underneath the vehicle, slacken the handbrake cable adjuster locknut, then back off the adjuster nut on the handbrake lever rod. Note that on some models, it will first be necessary to remove the mounting nut(s) and lower the exhaust heat shield to gain access to the adjuster nut.

6 Insert a screwdriver through one of the wheel bolt holes in the brake drum, so that it contacts the handbrake operating lever on the trailing brake shoe **(see illustrations)**. Push the lever until the stop-peg slips behind the brake shoe web, allowing the brake shoes to retract fully. Withdraw the brake drum, and slide the spacer off the stub axle.

Inspection

7 Working carefully, remove all traces of brake dust from the drum, but *avoid inhaling the dust, as it is injurious to health.*

8 Scrub clean the outside of the drum, and check it for obvious signs of wear or damage such as cracks around the roadwheel bolt holes; renew the drum if necessary.

9 Carefully examine the inside of the drum. Light scoring of the friction surface is normal, but if heavy scoring is found, the drum must be renewed. It is usual to find a lip on the drum's inboard edge which consists of a mixture of rust and brake dust; this should be scraped away to leave a smooth surface which can be polished with fine (120 to 150

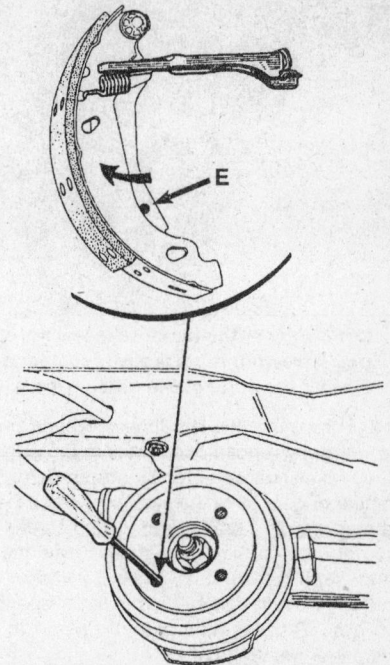

12.6a Using a screwdriver inserted through the brake drum to release the handbrake operating lever
E Handbrake operating lever stop-peg location

12.6b Releasing the handbrake operating lever using a screwdriver

grade) emery paper. If the lip is due to the friction surface being recessed by wear, then the drum must be refinished (within the specified limits) or renewed.

10 If the drum is thought to be excessively worn or oval, its internal diameter must be measured at several points using an internal micrometer. Take measurements in pairs, the second at right-angles to the first, and compare the two to check for signs of ovality. Minor ovality can be corrected by machining; otherwise, renew the drum.

Refitting

11 If a new brake drum is to be installed, use a suitable solvent to remove any preservative coating that may have been applied to its interior.

9

12.12 Ensure the handbrake lever stop-peg (arrowed) is correctly repositioned against the edge of the brake shoe web

12 Ensure that the handbrake lever stop-peg is correctly repositioned against the edge of the brake shoe web **(see illustration)**. Apply a smear of gear oil to the stub axle, and slide on the spacer and brake drum, being careful not to get oil onto the brake shoes or the friction surface of the drum. Fit the thrustwasher and a new hub nut; tighten the nut to the specified torque. Tap the hub cap into place in the centre of the brake drum.

13 Depress the footbrake several times to operate the self-adjusting mechanism.

14 Repeat the above procedure on the other rear brake assembly (where necessary), then adjust the handbrake as described in Chapter 1.

15 On completion, refit the roadwheel(s), lower the vehicle to the ground and tighten the wheel bolts to the specified torque (Chapter 10).

13 Rear brake shoes - inspection and renewal

⚠️ **Warning: Brake shoes must be renewed on both rear wheels at the same time - never renew the shoes on only one wheel, as uneven braking may result. Also, the dust created by wear of the shoes may contain asbestos, which is a health hazard. Never blow it out with compressed air, and don't inhale any of it. An approved filtering mask should be worn when working on the brakes. DO NOT use petroleum-based solvents to clean brake parts - use brake cleaner or methylated spirit only.**

Inspection

1 Remove the brake drum as described in Section 12.

2 Working carefully, remove all traces of brake dust from the brake drum, backplate and shoes.

3 Measure the thickness of each brake shoe (friction material and shoe) at several points; if either shoe is worn at any point to the specified minimum thickness or less, all four shoes must be renewed as a set. Also, the

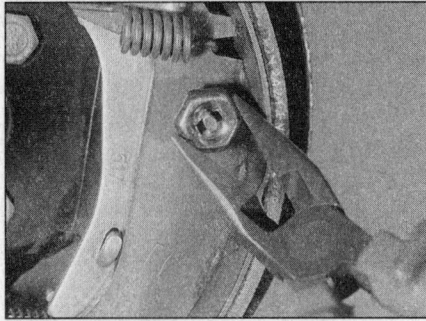

13.6 Removing a rear brake shoe retainer spring cup - Bendix brakes

13.8a Easing the upper ends of the brake shoes from the wheel cylinder - Bendix brakes

shoes should be renewed if any are fouled with oil or grease; there is no satisfactory way of degreasing friction material once contaminated.

4 If any of the brake shoes are worn unevenly, or fouled with oil or grease, trace and rectify the cause before reassembly.

Renewal

5 The procedure now varies according to which make of brake is fitted.

Bendix brake shoes

6 Using a pair of pliers, remove the shoe retainer spring cups by depressing and turning them through 90° **(see illustration)**. With the cups removed, lift off the springs and withdraw the retainer pins.

13.8c Removing the leading shoe and adjuster bolt from the adjuster strut - Bendix rear brakes

13.7 Ease the shoes out of the lower pivot point and disconnect the lower return spring - Bendix brakes

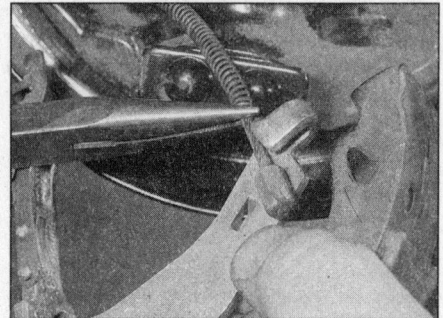

13.8b Disconnecting the handbrake cable from the trailing shoe - Bendix brakes

7 Ease the shoes out one at a time from the lower pivot point, to release the tension of the return spring, then disconnect the lower return spring from both shoes **(see illustration)**.

8 Ease the upper ends of both shoes out from their wheel cylinder locations, taking care not to damage the wheel cylinder seals, and disconnect the handbrake cable from the trailing shoe. The brake shoe and adjuster strut assembly can then be manoeuvred out of position and away from the backplate **(see illustrations)**. Do not depress the brake pedal until the brakes are reassembled; wrap a strong elastic band around the wheel cylinder pistons to retain them.

9 With the shoe and adjuster strut assembly on the bench, make a note of the correct fitted positions of the springs and adjuster strut, to

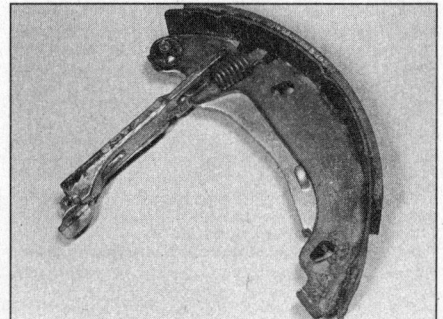

13.9a Rear brake trailing shoe and adjuster strut - Bendix rear brakes

13.9b Rear brake leading shoe and adjuster bolt - Bendix rear brakes

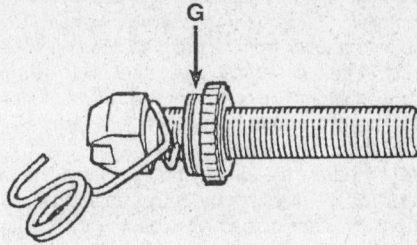

13.11 Bendix rear drum brake left-hand adjuster strut bolt can be identified by groove (G) on adjuster wheel collar

13.12 Correct fitted position of Bendix adjuster spring components

use as a guide on reassembly **(see illustrations)**. Release the handbrake lever stop-peg (if not already done), then detach the adjuster strut bolt retaining spring from the leading shoe. Disconnect the upper return spring, then detach the leading shoe and return spring from the trailing shoe and strut assembly. Unhook the spring securing the adjuster strut to the trailing shoe, and separate the two.

10 If genuine Renault brake shoes are being installed, it will be necessary to remove the handbrake lever from the original trailing shoe and fit it to the new shoe. Secure the lever in position with the new retaining clip which is supplied with the brake shoes. All return springs should be renewed, regardless of their apparent condition; spring kits are also available from Renault dealers.

11 Withdraw the adjuster bolt from the strut, and carefully examine the assembly for signs of wear or damage, paying particular attention to the threads of the adjuster bolt and the knurled adjuster wheel, and renew if necessary. Note that left-hand and right-hand struts are not interchangeable - they are marked "G" (gauche/left) and "D" (droit/right) respectively. Also note that the strut adjuster bolts are not interchangeable; the left-hand strut bolt has a left-hand thread, and the right-hand bolt a right-hand thread. The left-hand bolt can be identified by the groove on its adjuster wheel collar **(see illustration)**. The right-hand bolt does not have a groove on the adjuster wheel collar, but the bolt itself is painted.

12 Ensure the components on the end of the strut are correctly positioned **(see illustration)**, then apply a little high melting-point grease to the threads of the adjuster bolt. Screw the adjuster wheel onto the bolt until only a small gap exists between the wheel and the head of the bolt, then install the bolt in the strut.

13 Fit the adjuster strut retaining spring to the trailing shoe, ensuring that the shorter hook of the spring is engaged with the shoe. Attach the adjuster strut to the spring end, then ease the strut into position in its slot in the trailing shoe.

14 Engage the upper return spring with the

trailing shoe. Hook the leading shoe onto the other end of the spring, and lever the leading shoe down until the adjuster bolt head is correctly located in its groove. Once the bolt is correctly located, hook its retaining spring into the slot on the leading shoe.

15 Remove the elastic band fitted to the wheel cylinder. Peel back the rubber protective caps, and check the wheel cylinder for fluid leaks or other damage. Also check that both cylinder pistons are free to move easily. Refer to Section 14, if necessary, for information on wheel cylinder renewal.

16 Prior to installation, clean the backplate and apply a thin smear of high-temperature brake grease or anti-seize compound to all those surfaces of the backplate which bear on the shoes, particularly the wheel cylinder pistons and lower pivot point **(see illustration)**. Do not use too much, and don't allow the lubricant to contaminate the friction material.

17 Ensure that the handbrake lever stop-peg is correctly located against the edge of the trailing shoe.

18 Manoeuvre the shoe and strut assembly into position on the vehicle. Engage the upper ends of both shoes with the wheel cylinder pistons. Attach the handbrake cable to the trailing shoe lever. Fit the lower return spring to both shoes, and ease the shoes into position on the lower pivot point.

19 Centralise the shoes relative to the backplate by tapping them. Refit the shoe

retainer pins and springs, and secure them in position with the spring cups **(see illustration)**.

20 Using a screwdriver, turn the strut adjuster wheel until the diameter of the shoes is between 178.7 and 179.2 mm. This should allow the brake drum to just pass over the shoes.

21 Slide the drum into position over the linings, but do not refit the hub nut yet.

22 Repeat the above procedure on the remaining rear brake.

23 Once both sets of rear shoes have been renewed, adjust the lining-to-drum clearance by repeatedly depressing the brake pedal. Whilst depressing the pedal, have an assistant listen to the rear drums, to check that the adjuster strut is functioning correctly; if this is so, a clicking sound will be emitted by the strut as the pedal is depressed.

13.16 Apply a little high-melting point grease to the shoe contact points on the backplate - Bendix brakes

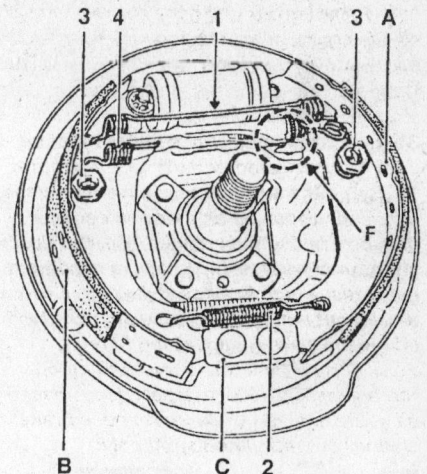

13.19 Correct fitted position of Bendix rear brake components

A Leading shoe
B Trailing shoe
C Lower pivot point
F Adjuster strut mechanism
1 Upper return spring
2 Lower return spring
3 Retaining pin, spring and spring cup
4 Adjuster strut-to-trailing shoe spring

9

24 Remove both the rear drums, and check that the handbrake lever stop-pegs are still correctly located against the edges of the trailing shoes, and that each lever operates smoothly. If all is well, with the aid of an assistant, adjust the handbrake cable so that the handbrake lever on each rear brake assembly starts to move as the handbrake is moved between the first and second notch (click) of its ratchet mechanism, ie so that the stop-pegs are still in contact with the shoes when the handbrake is on the first notch of the ratchet, but no longer contact the shoes when the handbrake is on the second notch. Once the handbrake adjustment is correct, hold the adjuster nut and securely tighten the locknut. Where necessary, refit the exhaust system heat shield to the vehicle underbody.

25 Refit the brake drums as described in Section 12.

26 On completion, check the hydraulic fluid level as described in Chapter 1.

27 If new shoes have been fitted, full braking efficiency will not be obtained until the linings have bedded-in. Be prepared for longer stopping distances, and avoid harsh braking as far as possible for the first hundred miles or so after fitting new shoes.

Girling brake shoes

28 Make a note of the correct fitted positions of the springs and adjuster strut, to use as a guide on reassembly.

29 Carefully unhook both the upper and lower return springs, and remove them from the brake shoes.

30 Using a pair of pliers, remove the leading shoe retainer spring cup by depressing it and turning through 90°. With the cup removed, lift off the spring, then withdraw the retainer pin and remove the shoe from the backplate. Unhook the adjusting lever spring, and remove it from the leading shoe.

31 Detach the adjuster strut and remove it from the trailing shoe.

32 Remove the trailing shoe retainer spring cup, spring and pin as described previously, then detach the handbrake cable and remove the shoe from the vehicle. Do not depress the brake pedal until the brakes are reassembled; wrap a strong elastic band around the wheel cylinder pistons to retain them.

33 If genuine Renault brake shoes are being installed, it will be necessary to remove the adjusting lever from the original leading shoe and install it on the new shoe. All return springs should be renewed, regardless of their apparent condition; spring kits are also available from Renault dealers.

34 Withdraw the forked end from the adjuster strut. Carefully examine the assembly for signs of wear or damage, paying particular attention to the threads and the knurled adjuster wheel, and renew if necessary. Note that left-hand and right-hand struts are not interchangeable; the left-hand fork has a right-hand thread, and the right-hand fork a left-hand thread. The forks can also be identified by their colour: the left-hand fork is silver, and the right-hand fork is gold.

35 Remove the elastic band fitted to the wheel cylinder. Peel back the rubber protective caps, and check the wheel cylinder for fluid leaks or other damage. Check that both cylinder pistons are free to move easily. Refer to Section 14, if necessary, for information on wheel cylinder renewal.

36 Prior to installation, clean the backplate and apply a thin smear of high-temperature brake grease or anti-seize compound to all those surfaces of the backplate which bear on the shoes, particularly the wheel cylinder pistons and lower pivot point. Do not allow the lubricant to contaminate the friction material.

37 Ensure that the handbrake lever stop-peg is correctly located against the edge of the trailing shoe.

38 Locate the upper end of the trailing shoe in the wheel cylinder piston, then refit the retainer pin and spring, and secure it in position with the spring cup. Connect the handbrake cable to the lever.

39 Screw in the adjuster wheel until the minimum strut length is obtained, then hook the strut into position on the trailing shoe. Rotate the adjuster strut forked end so that the cut-out of the fork will engage with the leading shoe adjusting lever **(see illustration)**.

40 Fit the spring to the leading shoe adjusting lever, so that the shorter hook of the spring engages with the lever.

41 Slide the leading shoe assembly into position, ensuring that it is correctly engaged

with the adjuster strut fork, and that the fork cut-out is engaged with the adjusting lever. Engage the upper end of the shoe in the wheel cylinder piston, then secure the shoe in position with the retainer pin, spring and spring cup.

42 Install the upper and lower return springs, then tap the shoes to centralise them on the backplate.

43 Using a screwdriver, turn the strut adjuster wheel until the diameter of the shoes is between 178.7 and 179.2 mm. This should just allow the brake drum to pass over the shoes.

44 Slide the drum into position over the linings, but do not refit the hub nut yet.

45 Repeat the above procedure on the remaining rear brake.

46 Carry out the procedures described previously in paragraphs 23 to 27.

14 Rear wheel cylinder - removal and refitting

Note: *Before starting work, refer to the warnings at the beginning of Section 6 concerning the dangers of hydraulic fluid, and at the beginning of Section 9 concerning the dangers of asbestos dust.*

Removal

1 Remove the brake drum (see Section 12).

2 Using pliers, carefully unhook the brake shoe upper return spring and remove it from the brake shoes. Pull the upper ends of the shoes away from the wheel cylinder to disengage them from the pistons.

3 Minimise fluid loss, either by removing the fluid reservoir cap and then tightening it down onto a piece of polythene to obtain an airtight seal (taking care not to damage the fluid level sender unit), or by using a brake hose clamp, a G-clamp or a similar tool with protected jaws to clamp the flexible hose at the nearest convenient point to the wheel cylinder **(see illustration)**.

4 Wipe away all traces of dirt around the brake pipe union at the rear of the wheel cylinder, and unscrew the union nut **(see illustration)**. Carefully ease the pipe out of the

13.39 On Girling rear brakes, adjuster strut fork cut-out (A) must engage with leading shoe adjusting lever on refitting

14.3 Brake hose clamp fitted to the rear brake flexible hose

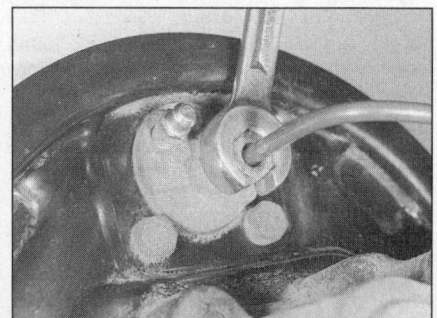

14.4 Unscrewing the union nut from the rear of the wheel cylinder

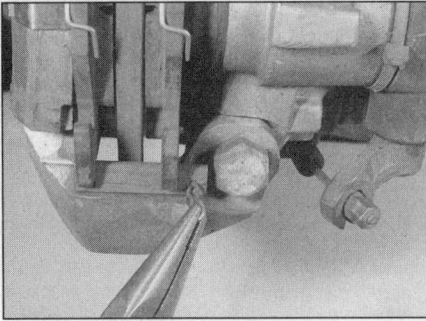

15.2a To remove the rear brake pads, remove the spring clip . . .

15.2b . . . then withdraw the retaining plate from the caliper

15.3a Slide out the inner brake pad . . .

wheel cylinder, and plug or tape over its end to prevent dirt entry. Wipe off any spilt fluid immediately.

5 Unscrew the two wheel cylinder retaining bolts from the rear of the backplate. Remove the cylinder, taking care not to allow hydraulic fluid to contaminate the brake shoe linings.

6 It is not possible to overhaul the cylinder, since no components are available separately. If faulty, the complete wheel cylinder assembly must be renewed.

Refitting

7 Ensure the backplate and wheel cylinder mating surfaces are clean, then spread the brake shoes and manoeuvre the wheel cylinder into position.

8 Engage the brake pipe, and screw in the union nut two or three turns to ensure that the thread has started.

9 Insert the two wheel cylinder retaining bolts, and tighten them securely. Now fully tighten the brake pipe union nut.

10 Remove the clamp from the brake hose, or the polythene from the fluid reservoir (as applicable).

11 Ensure that the brake shoes are correctly located in the cylinder pistons. Carefully refit the brake shoe upper return spring, using a screwdriver to stretch the spring into position.

12 Refit the brake drum as described in Section 12.

13 Bleed the brake hydraulic system as described in Section 6. Providing suitable precautions were taken to minimise loss of fluid, it should only be necessary to bleed the relevant rear brake.

15 Rear brake pads - inspection and renewal

⚠️ **Warning: Renew both sets of rear brake pads at the same time - never renew the pads on only one wheel, as uneven braking may result. Note that the dust created by wear of the pads may contain asbestos, which is a health hazard. Never blow it out with compressed air, and don't inhale any of it. An approved filtering mask should be worn when working on the brakes. DO NOT use petroleum-based solvents to clean brake parts - use brake cleaner or methylated spirit only.**

Inspection

1 Chock the front wheels, then engage reverse gear and release the handbrake. Jack up the rear of the vehicle and support it on axle stands (see *"Jacking, towing and wheel changing"*). Remove the rear wheels.

2 Extract the small spring clip from the pad retaining plate. Slide the plate out of the caliper **(see illustrations)**.

3 Withdraw the inner pad from the caliper, using pliers if necessary. Where applicable, slacken and remove the two outer pad retaining screws, then withdraw the outer pad from the caliper **(see illustrations)**. Make a note of the correct fitted position of the anti-rattle springs, and remove the springs from each pad.

4 First measure the thickness of each brake pad (friction material and backing plate). If either pad is worn at any point to the specified minimum thickness or less, all four pads must be renewed. Also, the pads should be renewed if any are contaminated with oil or grease; there is no satisfactory way of degreasing friction material once contaminated. If any of the brake pads are worn unevenly, or fouled with oil or grease, trace and rectify the cause before reassembly. New brake pads and spring kits are available from Renault dealers.

5 If the brake pads are still serviceable, carefully clean them using a clean, fine wire brush or similar, paying particular attention to the sides and back of the metal backing. Clean out the grooves in the friction material, and pick out any large embedded particles of dirt or debris. Clean the pad locations in the caliper body/mounting bracket.

6 Prior to fitting the pads, check that the guide sleeves are free to slide easily in the caliper body, and that the guide sleeve rubber gaiters are undamaged. Brush the dust and dirt from the caliper and piston, but *do not inhale it, as it is injurious to health.* Inspect the dust seal around the piston for damage, and the piston for evidence of fluid leaks, corrosion or damage. If attention to any of these components is necessary, refer to Section 16.

Renewal

7 If new brake pads are to be fitted, it will be necessary to retract the piston fully into the caliper bore by rotating it in a clockwise

15.3b . . . undo the two retaining screws . . .

15.3c . . . and withdraw the outer brake pad

15.7 Retract the piston using a square-section bar

9

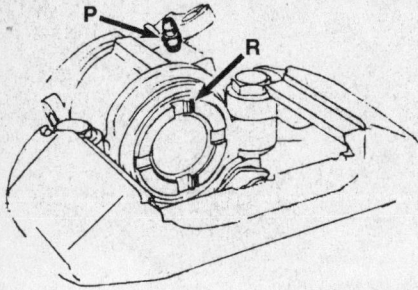

15.8 Prior to installing rear brake pads, align groove on caliper piston (R) with bleed screw (P)

15.9 Inner brake pad can be identified by its locating lug (arrowed). Note correct fitted positions of anti-rattle springs

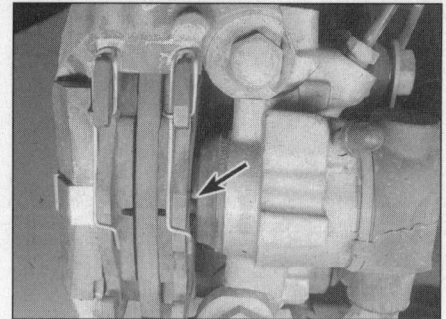

15.13 Ensure inner pad locating lug is correctly located in piston slot (arrowed)

direction. This can be achieved using a suitable square-section bar, such as the shaft of a suitable screwdriver, which locates snugly in the caliper piston slots **(see illustration)**. Provided that the fluid reservoir has not been overfilled with hydraulic fluid, there should be no spillage, but keep a careful watch on the fluid level while retracting the piston. If the fluid level rises above the "MAX" level, the surplus should be syphoned off (not by mouth - use an old poultry baster or a pipette), or ejected via a plastic tube connected to the bleed screw (see Section 16).

8 Position the caliper piston so that the small groove scribed across the piston points in the direction of the caliper bleed screw. This is necessary to ensure that the lug on the inner pad will locate with the caliper piston slot on installation **(see illustration)**.

9 Refit the anti-rattle springs to the pads, so that when the pads are installed in the caliper, the spring end will be located at the opposite end of the pad in relation to the pad retaining plate **(see illustration)**. The brake pad with the lug on its backing plate is the inner pad.

10 Locate the outer brake pad in the caliper body, ensuring that its friction material is against the brake disc. Where applicable, insert the retaining screws and tighten them securely.

11 Slide the inner pad into position in the caliper, ensuring that the lug on the pad backing plate is aligned with the slot in the caliper piston. Recheck that the anti-rattle spring ends on both pads are at the opposite end of the pad to which the retaining plate is to be inserted.

12 Slide the retaining plate into place, and install the small spring clip at its inner end. It may be necessary to file an entry chamfer on the edge of the retaining key, to enable it to be fitted without difficulty.

13 Depress the brake pedal repeatedly until the pads are pressed into firm contact with the brake disc. Check that the inner pad lug is correctly engaged with one of the caliper piston slots **(see illustration)**.

14 Repeat the procedure on the remaining rear brake caliper.

15 Check the handbrake cable adjustment as

described in Chapter 1, then refit the roadwheels and lower the vehicle to the ground. Tighten the roadwheel bolts to the specified torque (Chapter 10).

16 Check the hydraulic fluid level as described in Chapter 1.

17 If new pads have been fitted, full braking efficiency will not be obtained until the linings have bedded-in. Be prepared for longer stopping distances, and avoid harsh braking as far as possible for the first hundred miles or so after fitting new pads.

16 Rear brake caliper - removal, overhaul and refitting

⚠️ **Warning: Before attempting to disconnect any fluid pipes or hoses on models with ABS, refer to the information given for depressurising and bleeding the ABS system in Section 6.**

Note: *Before starting work, refer to the warnings at the beginning of Section 6 concerning the dangers of hydraulic fluid, and at the beginning of Section 9 concerning the dangers of asbestos dust.*

Removal

1 Chock the front wheels, engage reverse gear and release the handbrake. Jack up the rear of the vehicle and support it securely on axle stands (see *"Jacking, towing and wheel changing"*). Remove the relevant rear wheel.

2 Remove the brake pads as described in paragraphs 2 and 3 of Section 15.

3 Free the handbrake inner cable from the caliper handbrake operating lever, then tap the outer cable out of its bracket on the caliper body.

4 Minimise fluid loss, either by removing the fluid reservoir cap and then tightening it down onto a piece of polythene to obtain an airtight seal (taking care not to damage the fluid level sender unit), or by using a brake hose clamp, a G-clamp or a similar tool with protected jaws to clamp the flexible hose at the nearest convenient point to the brake caliper.

5 Wipe away all traces of dirt around the brake pipe union on the caliper, and unscrew the union nut. Carefully ease the pipe out of position, and plug or tape over its end to prevent dirt entry. Wipe off any spilt fluid immediately.

6 Slacken the two bolts securing the caliper assembly to the trailing arm, and remove them along with the mounting plate, noting which way around the plate is fitted **(see illustration)**. Lift the caliper assembly away from the brake disc.

Overhaul

Note: *Ensure that an appropriate overhaul kit can be obtained before dismantling the caliper.*

7 With the caliper on the bench, wipe away all traces of dust and dirt, but *avoid inhaling the dust, as it is injurious to health.*

8 Using a small screwdriver, carefully prise out the dust seal from the caliper bore, taking care not to damage the piston.

9 Remove the piston from the caliper bore by rotating it in an anti-clockwise direction. This can be achieved using a suitable square-section bar, such as the shaft of a suitable screwdriver, which locates snugly in the caliper piston slots. Once the piston turns freely but does not come out any further, the piston can be withdrawn by hand, or if necessary forced out by applying compressed air to the union bolt hole. *Caution: The piston may be ejected with some force - only low*

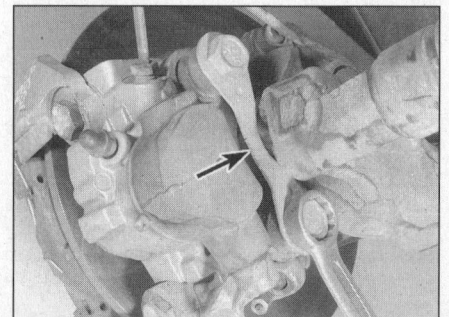

16.6 Remove the caliper mounting bolts, noting which way around the mounting plate is fitted (arrowed)

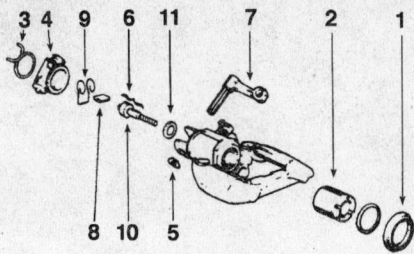

16.12 Exploded view of the rear brake caliper

1 Dust seal
2 Piston
3 Retaining clip
4 Handbrake mechanism dust cover
5 Circlip
6 Spring washers
7 Handbrake operating lever
8 Plunger cam
9 Return spring
10 Adjusting screw
11 Thrustwasher

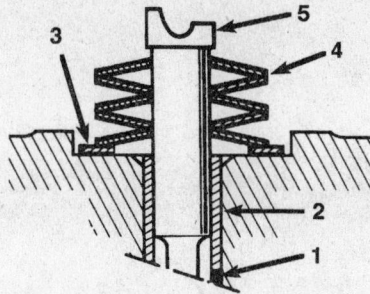

16.15 Correct fitted positions of rear brake caliper handbrake mechanism adjuster screw and associated components

1 O-ring
2 Adjusting screw bush
3 Thrustwasher
4 Correct arrangement of spring washers
5 Adjustng screw

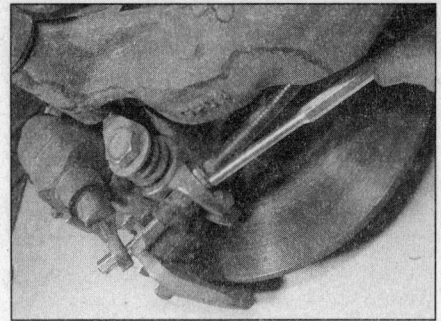

16.23 Tap the handbrake outer cable into position using a hammer and punch

pressure should be required, such as is generated by a foot pump.

10 Using a blunt instrument such as a knitting needle or feeler gauge, extract the piston hydraulic seal, taking care not to damage the caliper bore.

11 Withdraw the guide sleeves from the caliper body, and remove the guide sleeve gaiters.

12 Inspect the caliper components as described in Section 10, paragraphs 13 to 17 **(see illustration)**. Renew the components as necessary, noting that the inside of the caliper piston must **not** be dismantled. If necessary, the handbrake mechanism can be overhauled as described in the following paragraphs. If it is not wished to overhaul the handbrake mechanism, proceed to paragraph 16.

13 Release the handbrake mechanism dust cover retaining clip, and peel the cover away from the rear of the caliper. Make a note of the correct fitted positions of the relative components to use as a guide on reassembly. Remove the circlip from the base of the operating lever shaft, then compress the adjusting screw spring washers, and withdraw the operating lever and dust cover from the caliper body. With the lever withdrawn, remove the return spring, plunger cam, adjusting screw, spring washers and thrustwasher from the rear of the caliper body. Using a suitable pin punch, carefully tap the adjusting screw bush out of the caliper body and remove the O-ring.

14 Clean all the handbrake mechanism components in methylated spirit, and examine them for wear. If there is any sign of wear or damage, the complete handbrake mechanism assembly should be renewed; a kit is available from your Renault dealer.

15 Ensure that all components are clean and dry. Install the O-ring, then press the adjusting screw bush into position until its outer edge is flush with the rear of the caliper body; if

necessary, tap the bush into position using a suitable tubular drift. Fit the thrustwasher, then install the adjusting screw and spring washers, ensuring that the washers are positioned as shown **(see illustration)**. Locate the plunger cam in the end of the adjusting screw, and position the return spring in the caliper housing. Fit the new dust cover to the operating lever, then compress the adjusting screw spring washers and insert the lever shaft through the caliper body, ensuring that it is correctly engaged with the return spring and plunger cam. Secure the operating lever in position with the circlip, then release the spring washers and check the operation of the handbrake mechanism. Apply a smear of high-melting point grease to the operating lever shaft and adjusting screw. Slide the dust cover over the caliper body, and secure it in position with a cable tie.

16 Soak the piston and the new piston (fluid) seal in clean hydraulic fluid. Smear clean fluid on the cylinder bore surface.

17 Fit the new piston (fluid) seal, using only the fingers to manipulate it into the cylinder bore groove, and refit the piston assembly. Turn the piston in a clockwise direction, using the method employed on dismantling, until it is fully retracted into the caliper bore.

18 Fit the dust seal to the caliper, ensuring that it is correctly located in the caliper and also the groove on the piston.

19 Apply the grease supplied in the repair kit, or a good-quality high-temperature brake grease or anti-seize compound to the guide sleeves. Fit the guide sleeves to the caliper body, and fit the new gaiters, ensuring that the gaiters are correctly located in the grooves on both the guide sleeve and caliper body.

Refitting

20 Position the caliper over the brake disc. Refit the two caliper mounting bolts and the mounting plate, noting that the mounting plate must be fitted so that its bend curves towards

the caliper body. With the plate correctly positioned, tighten the caliper bolts to the specified torque.

21 Wipe clean the brake pipe union. Refit the pipe to the caliper, and tighten its union nut securely.

22 Remove the clamp from the brake hose, or the polythene from the fluid reservoir (as applicable).

23 Insert the handbrake cable through its bracket on the caliper, and tap the outer cable into position using a hammer and a pin punch **(see illustration)**. Reconnect the inner cable to the caliper operating lever.

24 Refit the brake pads as described in Section 15.

25 Bleed the hydraulic system as described in Section 6. Note that, providing the precautions described were taken to minimise brake fluid loss, it should only be necessary to bleed the relevant rear brake.

26 Repeatedly apply the brake pedal to bring the pads into contact with the disc. Check and if necessary adjust the handbrake cable as described in Chapter 1.

27 Refit the roadwheel, lower the vehicle to the ground and tighten the wheel bolts to the specified torque (Chapter 10).

28 On completion, check the hydraulic fluid level as described in Chapter 1.

17 Rear brake disc - inspection, removal and refitting

Note: *Before starting work, refer to the warning at the beginning of Section 16 concerning the dangers of asbestos dust. If either disc requires renewal, both should be renewed at the same time, to ensure even and consistent braking. A new rear hub nut will be required on refitting.*

Inspection

1 Chock the front wheels, engage reverse gear and release the handbrake. Jack up the rear of the vehicle and support it securely on axle stands (see *"Jacking, towing and wheel changing"*). Remove the appropriate rear roadwheel.

9

17.5 Prising out the rear disc hub cap

17.9a Refit the spacer to the rear of the brake disc . . .

17.9b . . . and slide the disc onto the stub axle

17.10 Tighten the rear hub nut to the specified torque

17.11a Apply locking fluid to the retaining bolts, then refit the caliper bracket . . .

17.11b . . . and tighten the bolts

2 Inspect the disc as described in Section 11, paragraphs 2 to 5.

Removal

3 Remove the brake pads as described in paragraphs 2 and 3 of Section 15.

4 Remove the two caliper frame retaining bolts. Remove the frame from the caliper body.

5 Using a hammer and a large flat-bladed screwdriver, carefully tap and prise the cap out of the centre of the brake disc (see illustration).

6 Using a socket and long bar, slacken and remove the rear hub nut and withdraw the thrustwasher. Discard the hub nut; a new nut must be used on refitting.

7 It should now be possible to withdraw the brake disc and hub bearing assembly from the stub axle by hand. It may be difficult to remove the disc, due to the tightness of the hub bearing on the stub axle. If the bearing is tight, tap the periphery of the disc using a hide or plastic mallet, or use a universal puller, secured to the disc with the wheel bolts, to pull it off. Remove the spacer from the rear of the disc, noting which way round it is fitted.

Refitting

8 Prior to refitting the disc, smear the stub axle shaft with gear oil. Be careful not to contaminate the friction surfaces with oil. If a new disc is to be fitted, use a suitable solvent to wipe any preservative coating from its surface.

9 Refit the spacer to the rear of the disc, noting that its slightly bigger protrusion

should face the hub bearing. Slide the disc onto the stub axle, and tap it into position using a soft-faced mallet (see illustrations).

10 Slide on the thrustwasher, then fit the new rear hub nut and tighten it to the specified torque (see illustration). Tap the cap back into position in the centre of the disc.

11 Apply a few drops of locking fluid to the threads of the caliper frame retaining bolts. Offer up the frame and refit the bolts. Tighten both bolts to the specified torque (see illustrations).

12 Refit the brake pads as described in Section 15.

13 Check the handbrake cable adjustment as described in Chapter 1.

14 Refit the roadwheels and lower the vehicle to the ground. Tighten the roadwheel bolts to the specified torque (Chapter 10).

18 Load-sensitive pressure-regulating valve (models with rear disc brakes) - general

1 On models with rear disc brakes, a load-sensitive pressure-regulating valve is incorporated in the hydraulic circuit. The valve regulates the pressure applied to the rear brakes, and reduces the risk of the rear wheels locking under heavy braking. It is mounted underneath the rear of the vehicle, above the rear axle assembly (see illustration).

2 Removal and refitting of the valve is a straightforward process, but on completion, specialist equipment is required to check and

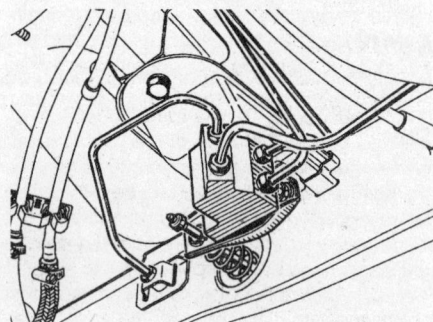

18.1 Load-sensitive pressure-regulating valve - models with rear disc brakes

adjust the operation of the valve. Therefore, if the valve is to be removed or if it is thought to be faulty, the work should be entrusted to a Renault dealer, who will have the necessary test equipment.

19 Handbrake lever - removal and refitting

Removal

1 Chock the front wheels, then jack up the rear of the vehicle and support it securely on axle stands (see "Jacking, towing and wheel changing"). Fully release the handbrake.

2 Working under the vehicle, unscrew the handbrake cable adjuster locknut and the adjuster nut from the end of the handbrake

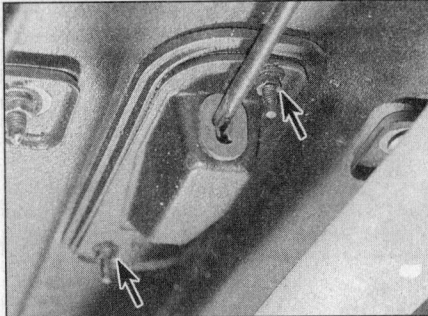

19.7 View of handbrake lever mounting bolts (arrowed) from under the vehicle

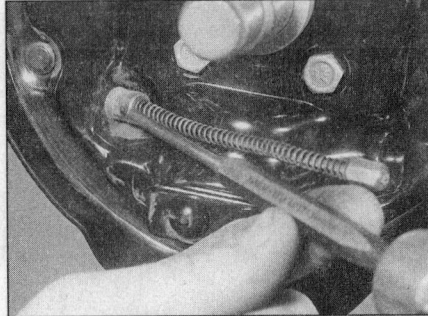

20.5 Tapping the handbrake outer cable from the brake backplate

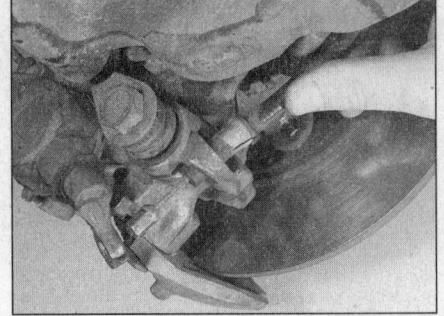

20.6 On rear disc brake models, disconnect the handbrake cable from the brake caliper

lever rod. Remove the cable compensator from the handbrake lever rod.

3 Release the handbrake lever rod from the support/guide block.

4 Working inside the vehicle, remove the covers (two screws in each case), then unbolt the two seat belt flexible stalk anchorages.

5 Make a slit in the carpet, just to the rear of the lever assembly to provide access to the lever mountings.

6 Spread the carpet and disconnect the "handbrake on" warning light switch wiring.

7 Unscrew the two bolts securing the lever assembly to the floor and remove the assembly from inside the vehicle (see illustration).

Refitting

8 Refitting is a reversal of removal but, on completion, adjust the handbrake as described in Chapter 1.

20 Handbrake cables - removal and refitting

Removal

1 The handbrake cable consists of two sections, a right- and left-hand section, which are linked to the lever assembly by an equalizer plate. Each section can be removed individually as follows.

2 Chock the front wheels, engage reverse gear and release the handbrake. Jack up the rear of the vehicle and support it securely on axle stands (see *"Jacking, towing and wheel changing"*).

3 Where applicable, working from underneath the vehicle, undo the nut(s) securing the exhaust system heat shield to the vehicle underbody. Lower the rear of the heat shield to gain access to the handbrake cable adjuster nuts. If necessary, disconnect the exhaust system from its rubber mountings to give additional clearance (make sure that the system is not strained).

4 Slacken the cable locknut and adjuster nut until there is sufficient slack in the inner cable to allow it to be disconnected from the equalizer plate.

5 On models with rear drum brakes, remove the rear brake shoes from the appropriate side as described in Section 13. Using a hammer and pin punch, carefully tap the outer cable from the brake backplate (see illustration).

6 On models with rear disc brakes, disengage the inner cable from the caliper handbrake lever. Using a hammer and pin punch, tap the outer cable out of its mounting bracket on the caliper (see illustration).

7 Working along the length of the cable, remove any retaining bolts and screws, and free the cable from any retaining clips and ties (see illustration). Remove the cable from under the vehicle.

Refitting

8 Refitting is a reversal of removal, but adjust the handbrake as described in Chapter 1. Note that on models with rear drum brakes, the cable is adjusted before the brake drum is refitted.

21 Stop light switch - removal, refitting and adjustment

Removal

1 The stop light switch is located on the pedal bracket, beneath the facia (see illustration).

2 To remove the switch, reach up behind the facia, pull off the wiring plug, and unscrew the switch from the bracket.

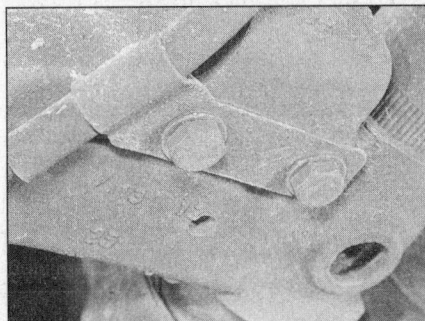

20.7 Handbrake cable support clip

Refitting and adjustment

3 Screw the switch back into position in the pedal bracket.

4 Connect a continuity tester (ohmmeter or self-powered test lamp) across the switch terminals. Screw the switch in until an open-circuit is present between the switch terminals (infinite resistance, or lamp goes out). Gently depress the pedal and check the continuity exists between the switch terminals (zero resistance, or lamp comes on) after the pedal has travelled approximately 6.0 mm. If necessary, reposition the switch until it operates as specified.

5 In the absence of a continuity tester, the same adjustment can be made by reconnecting the wiring to the switch, and having an assistant observe the stop lights (ignition on).

6 Once the switch is correctly adjusted, reconnect the wiring, if not already done, and recheck the operation of the stop lights.

22 Anti-lock braking system (ABS) - general information

⚠️ *Warning: Before attempting to disconnecting any fluid pipes or hoses on models with ABS, refer to the information given for depressurising and bleeding the ABS system in Section 6.*

21.1 Stop light switch and wiring (arrowed)

9

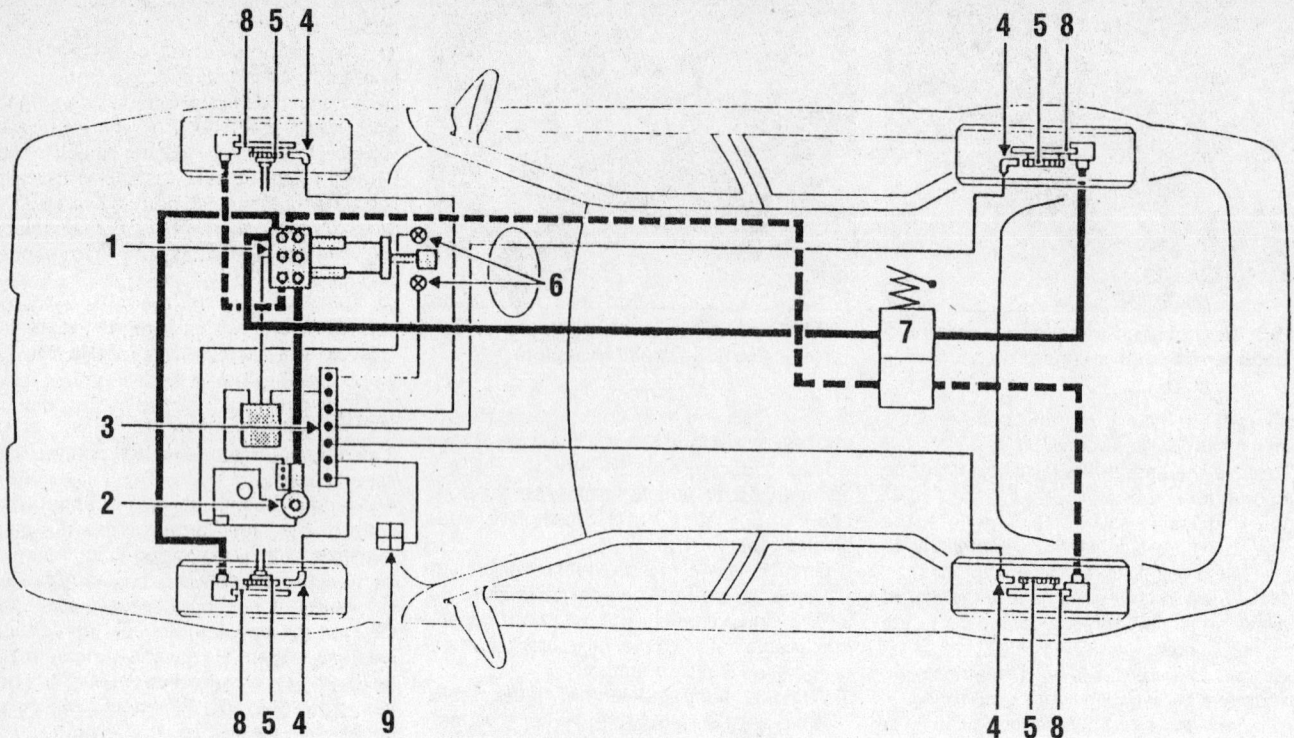

22.2a Bendix ABS components

1 Hydraulic modulator/master cylinder unit
2 Electric pump assembly
3 Computer

4 Wheel sensors
5 Sensor reluctor rings
6 Instrument panel warning lights

7 Pressure regulating valve
8 Disc brakes
9 Diagnostic socket

Bendix ABS

1 ABS is available as an option on certain models. The purpose of the system is to prevent wheel(s) locking during heavy braking. This is achieved by automatic release of the brake on the relevant wheel, followed by reapplication of the brake.

2 The main components of the system are four wheel sensors (one per wheel), a master cylinder/regulator assembly, an electric pump unit (used to return fluid to the reservoir), and the ABS computer **(see illustrations)**.

3 The solenoids are controlled by the computer, which receives signals from the wheel sensors. The sensors detect the speed of rotation of a toothed ring, known as a reluctor ring, attached to the wheel hub. By comparing the speed signals from the four wheels, the computer can determine when a wheel is decelerating at an abnormal rate, and can therefore predict when a wheel is about to lock. During normal operation, the system functions in the same way as a non-ABS braking system.

4 If the computer senses that a front wheel is about to lock, the ABS system regulates the fluid pressure supplied to the relevant caliper(s) as follows. The computer operates the relevant solenoid valve(s) in the regulator block. If the computer determines that a rapid pressure release is required, the high

pressure input to the relevant caliper(s) is shut off, and the return to the reservoir is opened. If a slow pressure release is required, the direct return to the reservoir is closed off, so that the fluid has to pass through calibrated holes on its way back to the reservoir. If a wheel picks up speed, the relevant solenoid valve(s) are opened to reapply fluid pressure as required.

5 If the computer senses that a rear wheel is about to lock, the high pressure input to the calipers is shut off, and the return to the reservoir is opened. At the same time, the pressure differential between the high pressure side and the return side causes a mechanical valve to close. The fluid pressure to both rear wheels is regulated similarly, and the computer establishes the degree of control to be applied using information from the rear wheel with the lowest level of grip.

6 If a rear wheel picks up speed, the high pressure circuit is opened, and the return to the reservoir is closed. The fluid flows through a circuit which is parallel with the mechanical valve (which is still closed), passing through calibrated holes until the pressure differential between the high pressure and return sides falls to zero.

7 The cycling of applying and releasing the brakes can be carried out at up to 10 times a second.

8 The action of the solenoid valves and the

electric pump creates pulses in the hydraulic circuit. When the ABS is functioning, these pulses can be felt through the brake pedal.

9 The operation of the ABS system is entirely dependent on electrical signals. To prevent the system responding to any inaccurate signals, a built-in safety circuit monitors all signals received by the computer. If an inaccurate signal or low battery voltage is detected, the ABS system is automatically shut down, and the warning light on the instrument panel is illuminated to inform the driver that the ABS system is not operational. Normal braking is unaffected, although in some instances, greater pedal pressure may be required to operate the brakes due to the lack of servo assistance.

10 If a fault does develop in the ABS system, the vehicle must be taken to a Renault dealer for fault diagnosis and repair. Check first, however, that the problem is not due to loose or damaged wiring connections, or badly-routed wiring picking up spurious signals from the ignition system.

Bosch ABS

11 The purpose of the system is to prevent wheel(s) locking during heavy braking. This is achieved by automatic release of the brake on the relevant wheel, followed by reapplication of the brake.

12 The main components of the system are

these pulses can be felt through the brake pedal.

17 The solenoid valves connected to the front calipers operate independently, but the valve connected to the rear calipers, together with the load-sensitive pressure-regulating valve, operates both calipers simultaneously. Since the braking circuit is split diagonally, a separate mechanical plunger valve in the modulator block divides the rear solenoid valve hydraulic outlet into two separate circuits.

18 The operation of the ABS system is entirely dependent on electrical signals. To prevent the system responding to any inaccurate signals, a built-in safety circuit monitors all signals received by the computer. If an inaccurate signal or low battery voltage is detected, the ABS system is automatically shut down, and the warning light on the instrument panel is illuminated to inform the driver that the ABS system is not operational. Normal braking is unaffected.

19 If a fault does develop in the ABS system, the vehicle must be taken to a Renault dealer for fault diagnosis and repair. Check first, however, that the problem is not due to loose or damaged wiring connections, or badly-routed wiring picking up spurious signals from the ignition system.

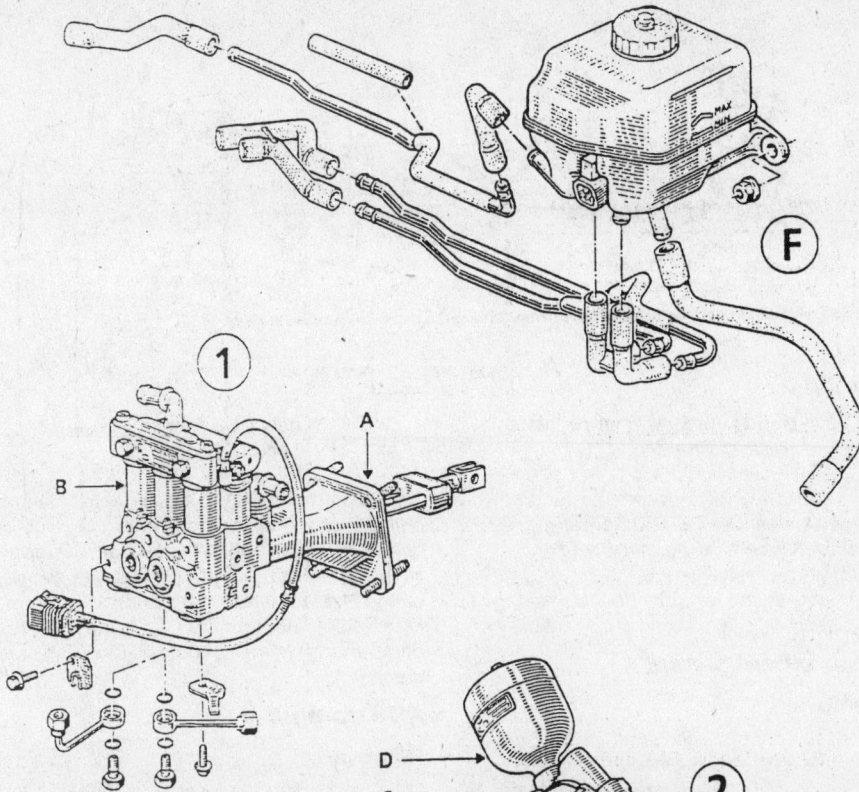

22.2b Bendix ABS hydraulic components

1 *Hydraulic modulator/master cylinder unit*
2 *Electric pump assembly*
A *Master cylinders*
B *Modulator unit*
C *Electric pump*
D *Pressure accumulator*
E *Pressure switches*
F *Fluid reservoir assembly*

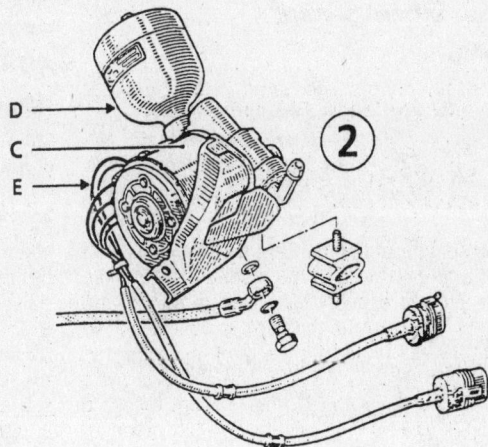

22.12 Bosch ABS components

1 *Modulator assembly*
2 *Master cylinder and servo unit*
3 *Wheel sensor*
4 *Sensor reluctor ring*
5 *Pressure regulating valve*

four wheel sensors (one per wheel), and a modulator block which contains the ABS computer, the hydraulic solenoid valves and accumulators, and an electrically-driven return pump **(see illustration)**.

13 The solenoids are controlled by the computer, which receives signals from the wheel sensors. The sensors detect the speed of rotation of a toothed ring, known as a reluctor ring, attached to the wheel hub. By comparing the speed signals from the four wheels, the computer can determine when a wheel is decelerating at an abnormal rate, and can therefore predict when a wheel is about to lock. During normal operation, the system functions in the same way as a non-ABS braking system does.

14 If the computer senses that a wheel is about to lock, the ABS system enters the "pressure-maintain" phase. The computer

operates the relevant solenoid valve in the modulator block; this isolates the brake caliper on the wheel in question from the master cylinder, effectively sealing-in the hydraulic pressure.

15 If the speed of rotation of the wheel continues to decrease at an abnormal rate, the ABS system then enters the "pressure-decrease" phase. The return pump operates and pumps the hydraulic fluid back into the master cylinder, releasing pressure on the brake caliper. When the speed of rotation of the wheel returns to an acceptable rate, the pump stops and the solenoid valve opens, allowing hydraulic pressure to return to the caliper and reapply the brake. This cycle can be carried out at up to 10 times a second.

16 The action of the solenoid valves and return pump creates pulses in the hydraulic circuit. When the ABS system is functioning,

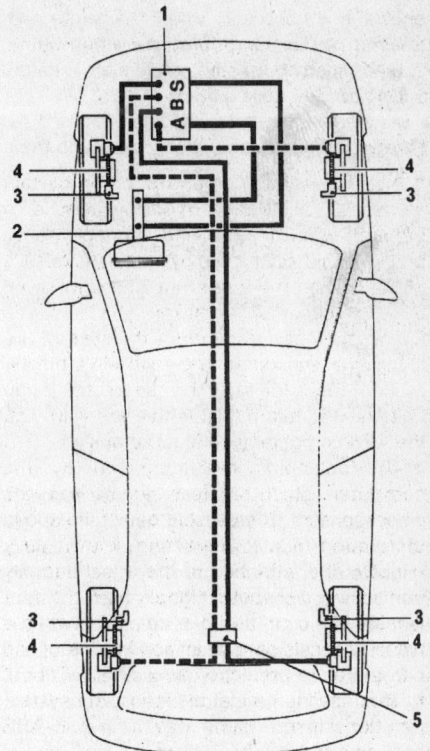

9

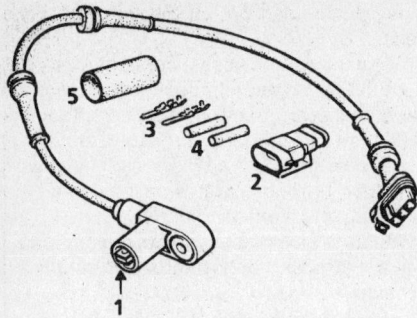

23.1 Bendix ABS front wheel sensor fitting kit

1 Sensor
2 Tab connector
3 Tabs
4 Sleeves containing sealing mastic
5 Heat shrinking cover

23 Anti-lock braking system components (Bendix ABS) - removal and refitting

Front wheel sensor

Removal

1 The front wheel sensors are originally supplied complete with the computer, and for renewal it is necessary to cut the wiring and obtain a new sensor, complete with a fitting kit (see illustration). The sensors are located in the front stub axle carriers.
2 Disconnect the battery negative lead.
3 Apply the handbrake, then jack up the front of the vehicle, and support securely on axle stands (see *"Jacking, towing and wheel changing"*). Remove the relevant roadwheel.
4 Remove the sensor securing screw (see illustration).
5 Release the sensor wiring from any clips and brackets, and peel back the plastic sleeving.
6 Cut the wiring at the point where the connector is to be fitted, then remove the sensor.

Refitting

7 Fit the female half of the connector supplied in the fitting kit to the wiring running from the computer. Place the sleeves full of sealing mastic over the wiring approximately 5.0 mm from the wire apertures in the connector. Fit the heat shrink cover, taking great care to ensure that the connection is absolutely leak-proof.
8 Coat the sensor with light grease, then fit it to the stub axle carrier and tighten the securing screw.
9 Connect the two halves of the wiring connector, and clip the wiring into position.
10 For reference, it is possible to check the air gap between the sensor and the reluctor ring, as follows. Note that the gap cannot be adjusted; the check will merely give an indication as to whether the components (sensor and reluctor ring) are damaged.

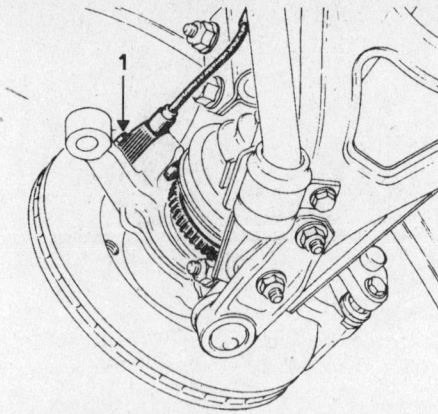

23.4 Bendix ABS front wheel sensor securing screw (1)

11 Turn the wheel hub/brake disc until the crest of one of the reluctor ring teeth is directly opposite the tip of the sensor.
12 Using a feeler gauge, check that the air gap between the reluctor ring tooth and the tip of the sensor is as given in the Specifications.

Rear wheel sensor

Removal

13 The sensors are located in brackets attached to the trailing arms.
14 Disconnect the battery negative lead.
15 Chock the front wheels, engage reverse gear and release the handbrake. Jack up the rear of the vehicle and support it securely on axle stands (see *"Jacking, towing and wheel changing"*). Remove the relevant rear wheel.
16 Remove the sensor securing screw, and withdraw the sensor from its bracket (see illustration).
17 Unclip the wiring from any support clips and brackets, then separate the two halves of the wiring connector (located near the rear suspension assembly left-hand mounting point) (see illustration).

Refitting

18 Coat the sensor with light grease, then refit it using a reversal of the removal procedure. Ensure that the wiring connector halves are securely reconnected.

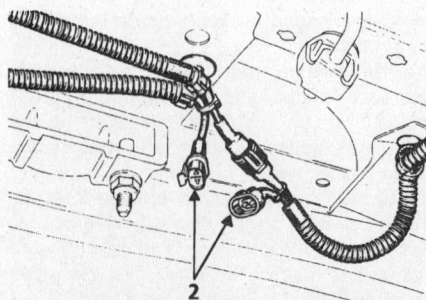

23.16 Bendix ABS rear wheel sensor securing screw (1)

19 On completion, using a feeler gauge, check that the air gap between the reluctor ring tooth and the tip of the sensor is as given in the Specifications. Note that the air gap cannot be adjusted; the check will merely give an indication as to whether the components (sensor and reluctor ring) are damaged.

ABS computer

Removal

20 The computer is located in the left-hand corner of the scuttle, in front of the windscreen (see illustration).
21 Disconnect the battery negative lead.
22 Remove the securing screws, and withdraw the plastic cover from in front of the windscreen.
23 Release the securing clip, and disconnect the wiring plug from the computer.
24 Unscrew the three bolts securing the computer mounting plate to the bodyshell, then lift the assembly clear of the scuttle.
25 Remove the three bolts securing the computer to the mounting plate, and withdraw the computer.

Refitting

26 Refitting is a reversal of removal, ensuring that the wiring connector is securely reconnected.

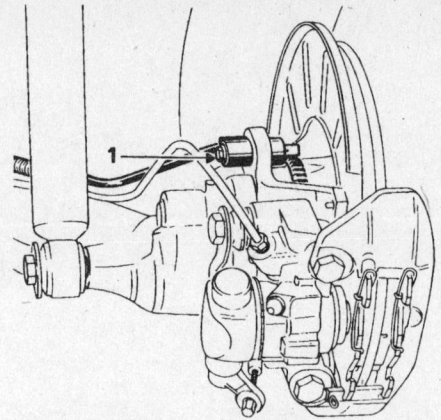

23.17 Bendix ABS rear wheel sensor wiring connector (2)

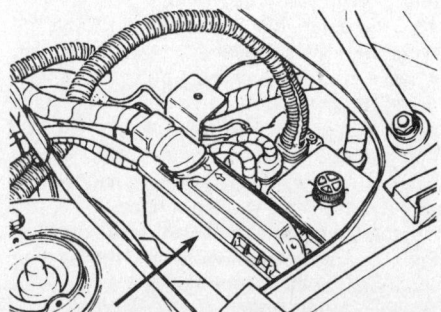

23.20 Bendix ABS computer location (arrowed)

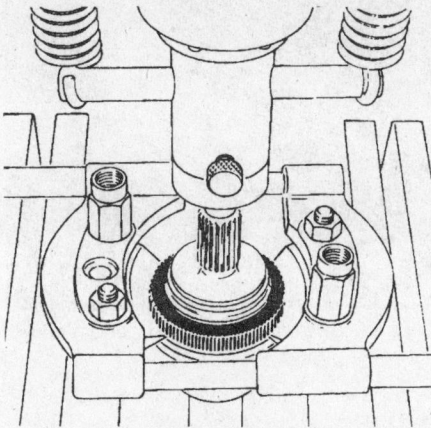

23.29 Pressing the ABS reluctor ring from a driveshaft

Front wheel sensor reluctor ring

Removal

27 The reluctor ring is attached to the driveshaft.
28 Remove the driveshaft as described in Chapter 8.
29 Support the reluctor ring in a suitable press, then press the driveshaft from the ring **(see illustration)**. Alternatively, use a suitable three-legged puller to pull the ring from the end of the driveshaft.

Refitting

30 Ensure that the mating faces of the driveshaft and the reluctor ring are absolutely clean.
31 Coat the inner mating face of the reluctor ring with locking compound, then fit it over the end of the driveshaft.
32 Carefully tap the reluctor ring into position on the driveshaft using a soft-faced mallet. Tap evenly around the outside of the ring, making sure that it does not tilt, and ensuring that it seats firmly against the driveshaft shoulder.
33 On completion, check the air gap between the wheel sensor and the reluctor ring, as described in paragraphs 10 to 12 of this Section.

Rear wheel sensor reluctor ring

34 The reluctor ring is an integral part of the brake disc/hub assembly, and cannot be removed.
35 Refer to Section 17 of this Chapter for details of brake disc/hub removal and refitting.

Hydraulic system components

⚠ *Warning: Before attempting to disconnect any fluid pipes or hoses on models with ABS, refer to the information given for depressurising and bleeding the ABS system in Section 6.*

24.1a Loosening a front wheel sensor securing screw - Bosch ABS

24.1c Checking a front wheel sensor-to-reluctor ring clearance - Bosch ABS

36 After removal and refitting of any of the hydraulic system components, it is necessary to bleed the complete hydraulic system, and test the operation of the system. Due to the requirement for specialist knowledge and equipment to carry out these operations, it is recommended that any tasks involving the removal and refitting of hydraulic system components are entrusted to a Renault dealer.

24 Anti-lock braking system components (Bosch ABS) - removal and refitting

Wheel sensors

1 Refer to the procedure given in the previous Section for models with the Bendix ABS

24.5 Disconnect the three wiring connectors (arrowed) . . .

24.1b Removing a front wheel sensor - Bosch ABS

24.4 Slackening the relay cover retaining screw - Bosch ABS

system. The front wheel sensor is connected to the ABS wiring harness using a conventional connector, therefore the references to cutting the wiring and the use of a fitting kit can be ignored **(see illustrations)**.

ABS computer

Removal

2 The computer is located on the ABS modulator unit in the engine compartment.
3 Disconnect the battery negative lead.
4 Slacken the retaining screw, and remove the relay cover from the modulator assembly **(see illustration)**.
5 Disconnect the three wiring connectors from the computer unit **(see illustration)**.
6 Remove the six Torx retaining screws, and lift the computer away from the modulator assembly **(see illustrations)**.

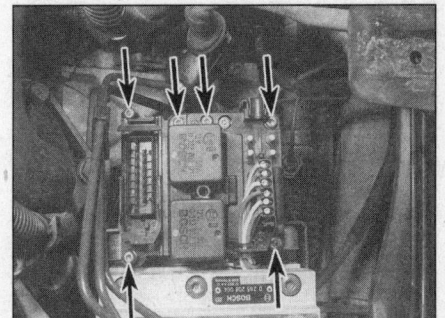

24.6a . . . remove the six retaining screws . . .

9

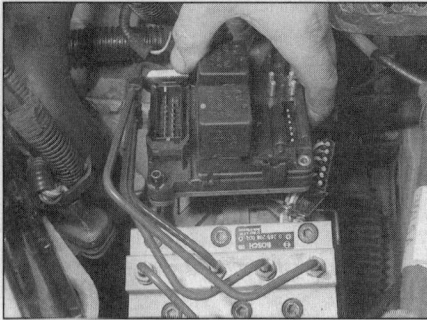
24.6b . . . and remove the ABS computer from the modulator

25.2 Unscrew the vacuum pipe union nut

25.3 Withdrawing the brake vacuum pump

Refitting

7 Refitting is a reversal of removal.

Wheel sensor reluctor rings

8 The procedures are as described for the Bendix ABS in the previous Section.

Hydraulic system components

9 At the time of writing, no information was available for removal and refitting of the Bosch ABS hydraulic system components.

25 Vacuum pump - removal and refitting

All except non-Turbo models without power steering or air conditioning

Note: *A new gasket will be required on refitting.*

Removal

1 The vacuum pump is driven directly from the camshaft at the flywheel end of the engine.

2 Unscrew the union nut, and disconnect the vacuum pipe from the pump **(see illustration)**.

3 Unscrew the nuts and bolts, and withdraw the pump unit from the cylinder head **(see illustration)**. Note the location of any brackets secured by the nuts and bolts. If the pump is stuck, tap it gently with a soft-faced mallet. Recover the gasket.

Refitting

4 Refitting is a reversal of removal, but ensure that the drive lugs on the pump shaft engage correctly with the slots in the camshaft, and use a new gasket **(see illustration)**.

25.4 Ensure that the pump drive lugs engage with the slots (arrowed) in the camshaft

Non-Turbo models without power steering or air conditioning

Note: *A new O-ring will be required on refitting.*

Removal

5 Proceed as described in paragraphs 1 and 2.

6 Unscrew the two securing bolts, and

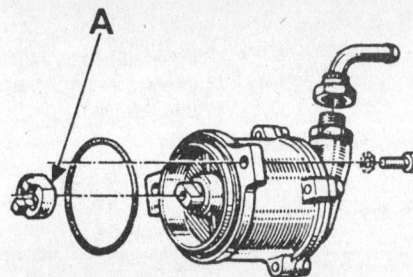
25.7 Brake vacuum pump and drive dog (A) - non-Turbo models without power steering or air conditioning

withdraw the pump unit from the cylinder head. Recover the O-ring.

Refitting

7 Refitting is a reversal of removal, but ensure that the drive dog on the pump shaft engages correctly with the slot in the camshaft, and use a new O-ring. Note that if a new pump is fitted, Renault recommend that a new drive dog is also fitted **(see illustration)**.

26 Vacuum pump - testing and overhaul

Testing

1 The operation of the braking system vacuum pump can be checked using a vacuum gauge.

2 Disconnect the vacuum pipe from the pump and connect the gauge to the pump union using a suitable length of hose.

3 Start the engine and allow it to idle until it reaches normal operating temperature.

4 When warm, accelerate the engine to 4000 rpm, and note the reading on the vacuum gauge. Do not allow the engine to run at this speed for more than a few seconds. The minimum vacuum obtained within 3 seconds should be about 525 mm Hg (700 mbar).

5 If the vacuum registered is significantly less than specified, it is likely that the pump is faulty. However, seek the advice of a Renault dealer before condemning the pump.

Overhaul

6 Overhaul of the pump is not possible since no components are available separately for it. If faulty the complete pump unit must be renewed.

Chapter 10
Suspension and steering

Contents

Degrees of difficulty

Easy, suitable for novice with little experience	**Fairly easy,** suitable for beginner with some experience	**Fairly difficult,** suitable for competent DIY mechanic	**Difficult,** suitable for experienced DIY mechanic	**Very difficult,** suitable for expert DIY or professional

Specifications

Front suspension

Type .... Independent by MacPherson struts, with inclined coil springs and integral shock absorbers. Anti-roll bar on all models

Hub bearing endfloat .... 0 to 0.05 mm
Front underbody height (H1 minus H2 - see text):
  Enclosed-bar type rear suspension .... 37.0 ± 7.5 mm
  Open-bar type rear suspension .... 93.0 ± 7.5 mm
Maximum difference in underbody height between sides (driver's
  side must always be higher) .... 5.0 mm

Rear suspension

Type .... Trailing arms, with transverse torsion bars (enclosed or open type, according to model) and telescopic shock absorbers. Rear anti-roll bar(s) on all models

Hub bearing endfloat .... 0 to 0.03 mm
Rear underbody height checking dimension (H4 minus H5 - see text):
  Enclosed-bar type rear suspension .... 10.0 ± 7.5 mm
  Open-bar type rear suspension .... 25.0 ± 7.5 mm
Dimension "X" (see Section 12):
  Enclosed-bar type rear suspension .... 590 mm
  Open-bar type rear suspension .... 645 mm

Steering

Type .... Rack-and-pinion, power-assisted on certain models

Wheel alignment and steering angles

Front wheel camber angle at underbody height (H1 minus H2) stated:
22.0 mm	+1°35' ± 30'
59.0 mm	+0°30' ± 30'
86.0 mm	-0°05' ± 30'
115.0 mm	-0°30' ± 30'
149.0 mm	-0°45' ± 30'

Maximum front camber angle variation between left- and right-hand sides .... 1°

Front wheel castor angle at underbody height (H5 minus H2) stated:

	Manual steering	Power-assisted steering
21.0 mm	2°55'	5°0'
40.0 mm	2°25'	4°30'
59.0 mm	1°55'	4°0'
78.0 mm	1°25'	3°30'
97.0 mm	0°55'	3°0'

Steering axis inclination/kingpin inclination at underbody height (H1 minus H2) stated:
22.0 mm	10°45' ± 30'
59.0 mm	12°05' ± 30'
86.0 mm	12°55' ± 30'
115.0 mm	13°40' ± 30'
149.0 mm	14°15' ± 30'

Maximum steering axis/kingpin inclination difference between left- and right-hand sides .... 1°
Front wheel toe-setting (all models - vehicle unladen) .... 1.0 ± 1.0 mm (0°10' ± 10') toe-out
Rear wheel camber angle .... -0°50' ± 30'
Rear wheel toe-setting:
Open-bar type rear suspension .... 0.5 to 2.5 mm (0°05' to 0°25') toe-in
Enclosed-bar type rear suspension .... 1.0 to 3.0 mm (0°10' to 0°30') toe-in

Roadwheels

Type .... Pressed steel or alloy (according to model)
Size .... 5Bx13, 5Jx13, 5-1/2Bx13, or 5-1/2Jx14 (depending on model)
Maximum run-out at rim .... 1.2 mm

Tyres

Size .... 165/70 R 13T, 175/70 R 13T, 175/70 R 13T, or 175/65 R 14T (depending on model)
Pressures .... See Chapter 1 Specifications

Torque wrench settings

	Nm	lbf ft
Front suspension		
Lower balljoint-to-stub axle carrier clamp bolt	55	41
Stub axle carrier-to-strut bolts	110	81
Suspension strut upper mounting bolts	25	19
Suspension strut upper mounting nut	60	44
Anti-roll bar mountings	35	26
Lower arm inner pivot bolts	75	55
Balljoint-to-lower arm bolts	75	55
Driveshaft nut	250	185
Rear suspension		
Shock absorber lower mounting bolts	60	44
Shock absorber upper mounting nuts	20	15
Anti-roll bar-to-trailing arm bolts (enclosed bar rear suspension)	45	33
Trailing arm (rear axle) bearing bracket mounting bolts	80	59
Rear hub nut	160	118
Brake backplate-to-trailing arm bolts	45	33
Steering		
Track rod end-to-stub axle carrier nut	35	26
Track rod end locknut	35	26
Steering wheel mounting nut	40	30
Steering gear mounting nuts	50	37
Intermediate shaft-to-pinion shaft clamp bolt	30	22
Roadwheels		
Wheel bolts	80	59

1.1a Front suspension layout

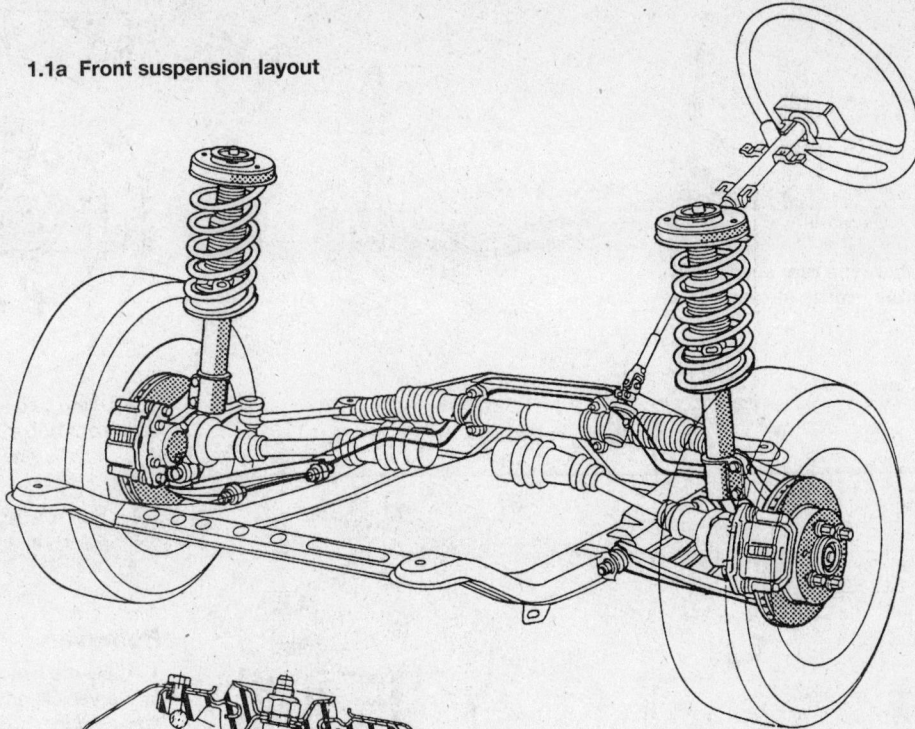

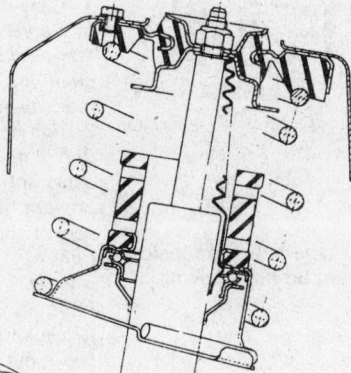

1.1b Cross-section of the front suspension

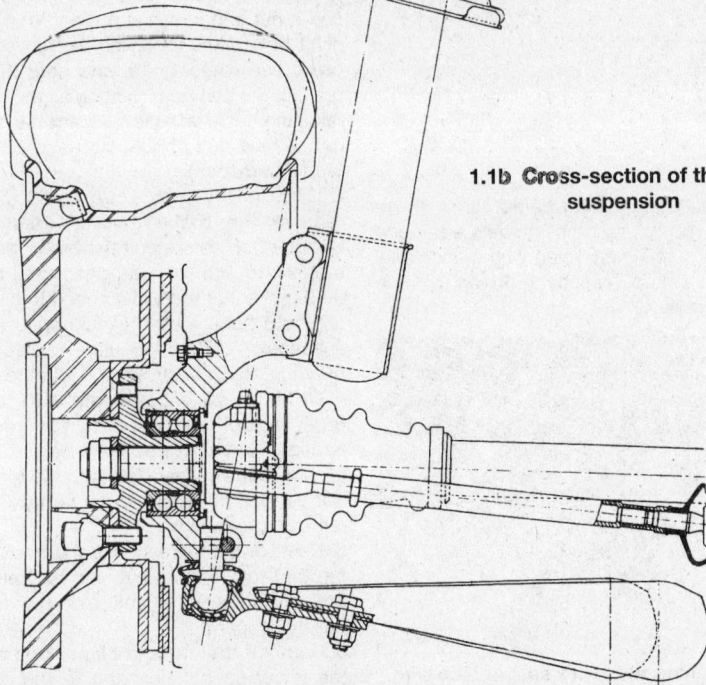

1 General information

The independent front suspension is of the MacPherson strut type, incorporating coil springs and integral telescopic shock absorbers. The MacPherson struts are located by transverse lower suspension arms, which utilize rubber inner mounting bushes and incorporate a balljoint at the outer ends. The front stub axle carriers, which carry the wheel bearings, brake calipers and the hub/disc assemblies, are bolted to the MacPherson struts and connected to the lower arms via the balljoints. A front anti-roll bar is fitted to all models. The anti-roll bar is rubber-mounted onto the subframe, and connects both the lower suspension arms (**see illustrations**).

The rear suspension differs according to model. Non-turbo models without ABS have an enclosed-bar type rear axle, which consists of two torsion bars within a tubular crossmember which connects both the rear trailing arms. An anti-roll bar is situated just to the rear of the crossmember, and is also connected to both trailing arms (**see illustrations**).

Turbo models and models with ABS are fitted with an open-bar rear axle which consists of two torsion bars, two anti-roll bars and an L-section metal crossmember which is connected to both the trailing arms. The two torsion bars and two anti-roll bars are connected at the centre with a link, and at

10

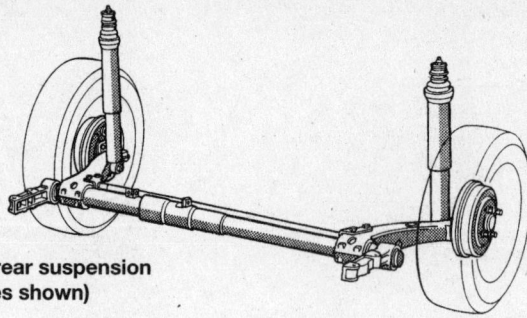

1.2a Enclosed-bar type rear suspension layout (drum brakes shown)

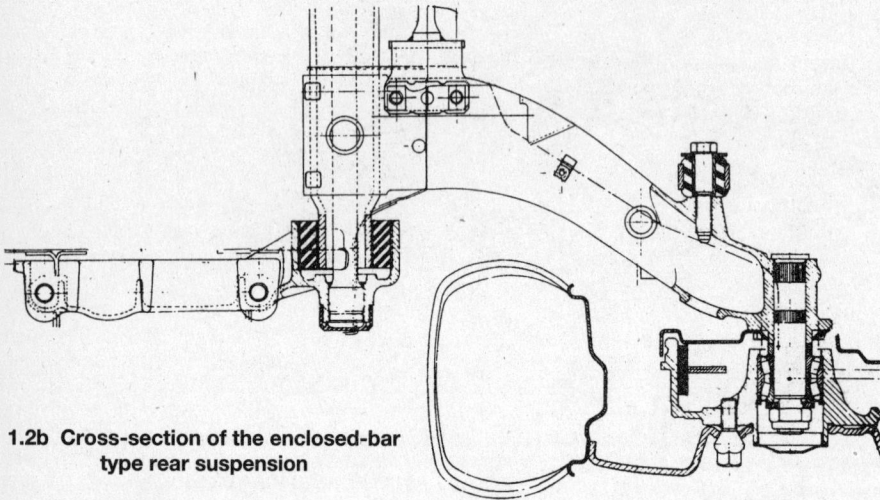

1.2b Cross-section of the enclosed-bar type rear suspension

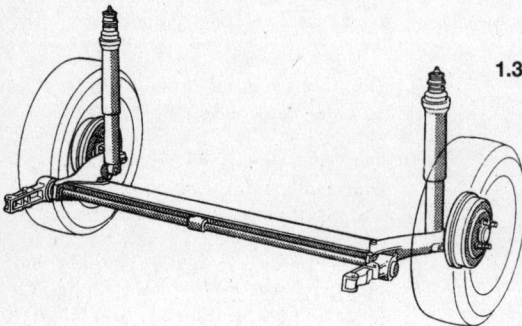

1.3 Open-bar type rear suspension layout (drum brakes shown)

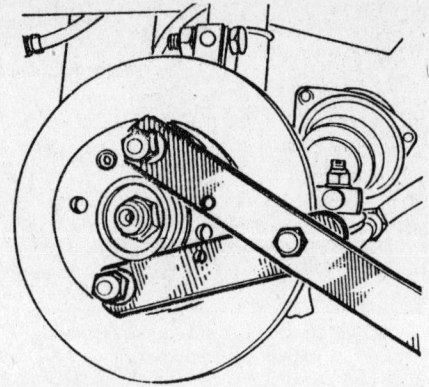

2.2 Using two lengths of metal bar to hold the front hub stationary when unscrewing the driveshaft nut

2 Front stub axle carrier - removal and refitting

Removal

1 Apply the handbrake, then jack up the front of the vehicle and support it securely on axle stands (see *"Jacking, towing and wheel changing"*). Remove the appropriate front roadwheel.

2 Refit at least two roadwheel bolts to the front hub, and tighten them securely. Have an assistant firmly depress the brake pedal to prevent the front hub from rotating. Using a socket and a long extension bar, slacken and remove the driveshaft retaining nut and washer. This nut is extremely tight. Alternatively, a tool can be fabricated from two lengths of steel strip (one long, one short) and a nut and bolt; the nut and bolt form the pivot of a forked tool. Bolt the tool to the hub using two wheel bolts, and hold the tool to prevent the hub from rotating as the driveshaft retaining nut is undone. Discard the driveshaft nut; a new one should be used on refitting **(see illustration)**.

3 If the hub bearings are to be disturbed, remove the brake disc as described in Chapter 9. If not, unbolt the brake caliper and move it to one side, as described in Chapter 9. Note that there is no need to disconnect the fluid hose - tie the caliper to the front suspension coil spring, using a piece of wire or string, to avoid straining the brake hose.

4 On models equipped with ABS, undo the retaining bolt and withdraw the front wheel sensor from the stub axle carrier. Tie the sensor to the suspension strut, so that it does not get damaged during the remainder of the removal procedure.

5 Remove the nut securing the track rod end balljoint to the stub axle carrier. Release the balljoint tapered shank using a universal balljoint separator.

6 Remove the nut and clamp bolt securing the lower suspension arm to the stub axle carrier **(see illustration)**. Carefully lever the

their outer ends to the trailing arms **(see illustration)**.

The steering column is connected by a universal joint to an intermediate shaft, which has a second universal joint at its lower end. The lower universal joint is attached to the steering gear pinion by means of a clamp bolt.

The steering gear is mounted onto the front subframe. It is connected by two track rods and balljoints to steering arms projecting rearwards from the stub axle carriers. The track rod ends are threaded to enable wheel alignment adjustment.

Power-assisted steering is fitted as standard on some models and is available as an option on others. On Turbo models equipped with air conditioning and power steering, an electric power steering pump is used to power the steering hydraulic system; this is due to lack of space in the engine compartment to house

both the air conditioning compressor and a belt-driven pump. All other models equipped with power steering are fitted with a traditional belt-driven pump, which is driven off the crankshaft pulley.

2.6 Loosening the lower suspension arm-to-stub axle carrier clamp bolt and nut

2.7 Stub axle carrier-to-suspension strut nuts (arrowed)

balljoint out of the stub axle carrier, taking care not to damage the balljoint or driveshaft gaiters. Note the plastic protector plate which is fitted to the balljoint shank.

7 Remove the two nuts and washers from the bolts securing the stub axle carrier to the suspension strut, noting that the nuts are positioned on the rear side of the strut **(see illustration)**. Withdraw the bolts and support the stub axle carrier assembly.

8 Release the driveshaft joint from the hub, and remove the stub axle carrier assembly from the vehicle. Note that locking fluid is applied to the joint splines during assembly, so it is likely that they will be a tight fit in the hub. Use a hammer and soft metal drift to tap the joint out of the hub, or use a puller to draw the swivel hub assembly off the joint splines.

Refitting

9 Ensure that the driveshaft joint and hub splines are clean and dry, then apply a coat of locking fluid to the joint splines.

10 Engage the joint splines with the hub, and slide the hub fully onto the driveshaft. Insert the two stub axle carrier-to-suspension strut mounting bolts from the front side of the strut, then refit the washers and nuts to the rear of the bolts and tighten them to the specified torque.

11 Slide on the washer and fit the new driveshaft nut, tightening it by hand only at this stage.

12 Ensure that the plastic protector is still fitted to the lower arm balljoint, then locate the balljoint shank in the stub axle carrier. Refit the balljoint clamp bolt, and tighten its retaining nut to the specified torque.

13 Reconnect the track rod end balljoint to the stub axle carrier, and tighten its retaining nut to the specified torque.

14 On models equipped with ABS, refit the sensor to the stub axle carrier, and tighten its retaining bolt to the specified torque (see Chapter 9).

15 Refit the brake disc (if removed), aligning the marks made on removal, and securely tighten its retaining screw(s). Refit the brake caliper assembly as described in Chapter 9.

16 Insert and tighten two wheel bolts. Tighten the driveshaft nut to the specified torque, using the method employed during removal to prevent the hub from rotating.

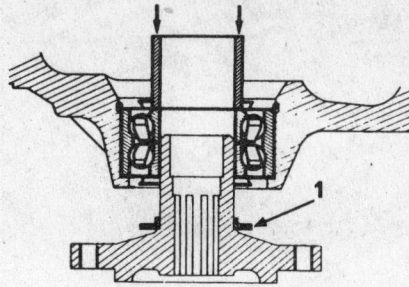

3.12 Refitting the hub flange
1 Thrustwasher

17 Check that the hub rotates freely, then refit the roadwheel and lower the vehicle to the ground. Tighten the roadwheel bolts to the specified torque.

3 Front hub bearings - checking, removal and refitting

Note: *The bearing is a sealed, pre-adjusted and pre-lubricated, double-row roller type, and is intended to last the car's entire service life without maintenance or attention. Do not attempt to remove the bearing unless absolutely necessary, as it will be damaged during the removal operation. Never overtighten the driveshaft nut in an attempt to "adjust" the bearing.*

A press will be required to dismantle and rebuild the assembly; if such a tool is not available, a large bench vice and suitable spacers (such as large sockets) will serve as an adequate substitute. The bearing's inner races are an interference fit on the hub; if the inner race remains on the hub when it is pressed out of the hub carrier, a suitable knife-edged bearing puller will be required to remove it.

Checking

1 Wear in the front hub bearings can be checked by measuring the amount of side play present. To do this, a dial gauge should be fixed so that its probe is in contact with the disc face of the hub. The play should be between 0 and 0.05 mm. If it is greater than this, the bearings are worn excessively, and should be renewed.

Removal

2 Remove the stub axle carrier as described in Section 2. Where applicable, undo the brake disc shield retaining screws and remove the shield from the stub axle carrier.

3 Support the stub axle carrier securely on blocks or in a vice. Using a tubular spacer which bears only on the inner end of the hub flange, press the hub flange out of the bearing. If the bearing outboard inner race remains on the hub, remove it using a bearing puller (see note above), then slide the thrustwasher off the hub flange, noting which way round it is fitted.

4 Extract the bearing retaining circlip from the inner end of the stub axle carrier.

5 Where necessary, refit the inner race in position over the ball cage, and securely support the inner face of the stub axle carrier. Using a tubular spacer which bears only on the inner race, press the complete bearing assembly out of the housing in the stub axle carrier.

6 Thoroughly clean the hub and stub axle carrier, removing all traces of dirt and grease. Polish away any burrs or raised edges which might hinder reassembly. Check for cracks or any other signs of wear or damage, and renew the components if necessary. As noted above, the bearing and its circlip must be renewed whenever they are disturbed. A replacement bearing kit, which consists of the bearing, circlip and thrustwasher, is available from Renault dealers.

Refitting

7 On reassembly, check (if possible) that the new bearing is packed with grease. Apply a light film of oil to the bearing outer race and to the hub flange shaft.

8 Before fitting the new bearing, remove the plastic covers protecting the seals at each end, but leave the inner plastic sleeve in position to hold the inner races together.

9 Securely support the stub axle carrier, and locate the bearing in its housing. Press the bearing into position, ensuring that it enters the housing squarely, using a tubular spacer which bears only on the outer race.

10 Once the bearing is correctly seated, secure it with the new circlip and remove the plastic sleeve. Apply a smear of grease to the oil seal lips.

11 Slide the thrustwasher onto the hub flange, ensuring that its flat surface is facing the flange. Securely support the outer face of the hub flange.

12 Locate the stub axle carrier and the bearing inner race over the end of the hub flange. Press the bearing onto the hub flange, using a tubular spacer which bears only on the inner race, until it seats against the thrustwasher **(see illustration)**. Check that the hub flange rotates freely. Wipe off any excess oil or grease.

13 Where applicable, refit the brake disc shield to the stub axle carrier, and tighten its retaining screws.

14 Refit the stub axle carrier as described in Section 2.

4 Front suspension strut - removal and refitting

10

Removal

1 Apply the handbrake, then jack up the front of the vehicle and support it securely on axle stands (see *"Jacking, towing and wheel changing"*). Remove the appropriate roadwheel.

2 Remove the two nuts and washers from the bolts securing the stub axle carrier to the suspension strut, noting that the nuts are positioned on the rear side of the strut. Withdraw the bolts, and support the stub axle carrier.

3 From within the engine compartment, unscrew the two bolts securing the strut upper mounting to the turret **(see illustration)**. Note that there are two sets of holes - one for models with manual steering, and the other for models with power-assisted steering.

4 Release the strut from the stub axle carrier, and withdraw it from under the wheel arch, while pressing on the lower suspension arm to prevent damage to the driveshaft gaiter.

Refitting

5 Manoeuvre the strut assembly into position, taking care not damage the driveshaft gaiter.

6 Insert the two stub axle carrier-to-suspension strut mounting bolts from the front side of the strut. Refit the washers and nuts to the rear of the bolts, and tighten them to the specified torque.

7 Refit the two bolts securing the upper strut mounting to the turret, ensuring that they are fitted to the correct holes in the turret **(see illustration)**. Tighten the bolts to the specified torque.

8 Refit the roadwheel, lower the vehicle to the ground and tighten the roadwheel bolts to the specified torque.

5.0 Renault spring compressor tool

A Thrust cup   *B Retaining shell*

5.2 Using a spring compressor tool to compress the strut coil spring

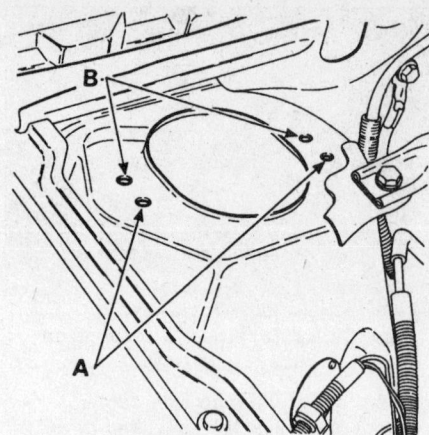

4.3 Front suspension strut upper mounting bolts (arrowed)

| 5 | **Front suspension strut -** dismantling, inspection and reassembly |

Note: Before attempting to dismantle the front suspension strut, a tool to hold the coil spring in compression must be obtained. A Renault special tool is used at Renault dealers (see illustration), however careful use of conventional coil spring compressors will prove satisfactory. Any attempt to dismantle the strut without such a tool is likely to result in damage or personal injury.

Dismantling

1 With the strut removed from the car as described in Section 4, clean away all external dirt then mount the strut upright in a vice.

2 Fit the spring compressor tool and compress the coil spring until all tension is relieved from the upper mounting **(see illustration)**.

3 Withdraw the plastic cap over the strut upper mounting nut, hold the strut piston with an Allen key or a hexagon bit, and unscrew the nut with a ring spanner **(see illustration)**.

4 Lift off the washer, upper mounting, and spring seat assembly.

5 Lift off the spring and compressor tool. Do not remove the tool from the spring unless the spring is to be renewed.

6 Remove the bump stop, convoluted dust cover, and the lower spring seat and bearing components.

5.3 Unscrewing the strut upper mounting nut while holding the strut piston

---

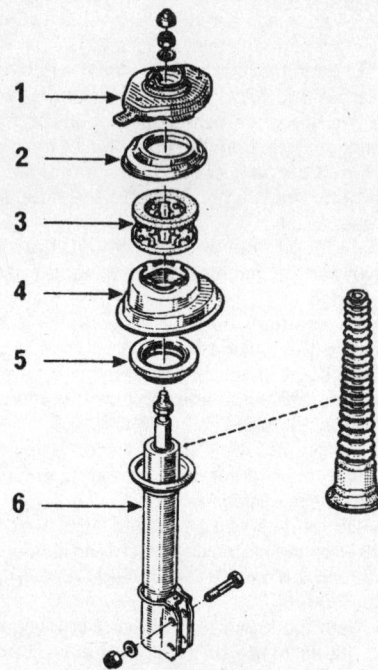

4.7 Front suspension strut upper mounting bolt holes

A Manual steering models
B Power-assisted steering models

Inspection

7 With the strut assembly now completely dismantled, examine all the components for wear, damage or deformation and check the bearing for smoothness of operation. Renew any of the components as necessary **(see illustration)**.

8 Examine the strut for signs of fluid leakage. Check the strut piston for signs of pitting along its entire length and check the strut body for signs of damage or elongation of the mounting bolt holes. Test the operation of the strut, while

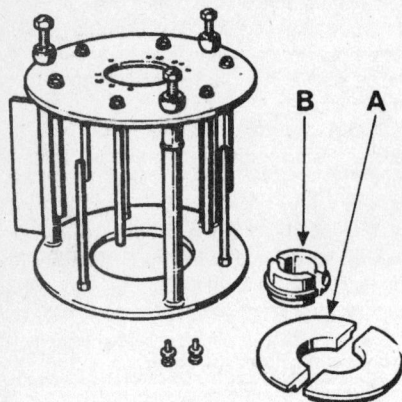

5.7 Exploded view of a front suspension strut

1 Upper mounting   4 Lower spring seat
2 Upper spring seat   5 Bearing
3 Bump stop   6 Strut

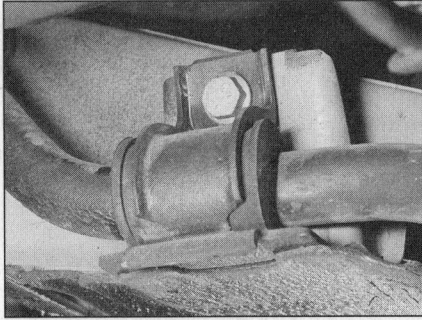

6.5 Front suspension anti-roll bar mounting clamp on the subframe

7.4 Removing the plastic protector plate from the lower arm balljoint shank

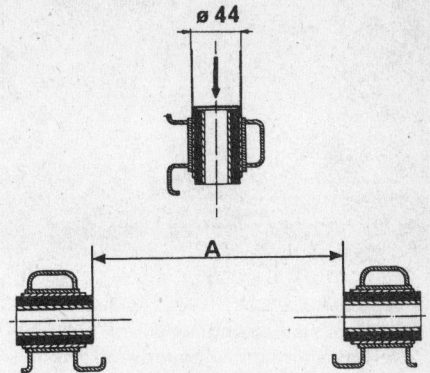

7.7 Front suspension lower arm pivot bush fitting dimension

A = 147.0 ± 0.5 mm

holding it in an upright position, by moving the piston through a full stroke and then through short strokes of 50 to 100 mm. In both cases the resistance felt should be smooth and continuous. If the resistance is jerky, or uneven, or if there is any visible sign of wear or damage to the strut, renewal is necessary.

9 If any doubt exists about the condition of the coil spring, gradually release the spring compressor, and check the spring for distortion and signs of cracking. Since no minimum free length is specified by Renault, the only way to check it is to compare it to a new component. Renew the spring if it is damaged or distorted, or if there is any doubt as to its condition.

10 Inspect all other components for signs of damage or deterioration, and renew any that are suspect.

Reassembly

11 Reassembly is a reversal of dismantling, however make sure that the spring ends are correctly located in the upper and lower seats and tighten the upper nut to the specified torque.

6 Front suspension anti-roll bar - removal and refitting

Removal

1 Apply the handbrake, then jack up the front of the vehicle and support it securely on axle stands (see *"Jacking, towing and wheel changing"*). Remove both front roadwheels.
2 Remove the exhaust downpipe as described in Chapter 4.
3 Disconnect the gearchange mechanism from the gearbox with reference to Chapter 7.
4 Unscrew the nuts and remove the clamp bolts securing the ends of the anti-roll bar to the lower suspension arms. Remove the clamps.
5 Unscrew the nuts and remove the clamp bolts from the clamps on the subframe (**see illustration**). Remove the clamps.
6 Lower the anti-roll bar from the rear of the subframe.
7 Check the bar for damage and the rubber

bushes for wear and deterioration. If the bushes are in need of renewal, slide them off the bar and fit new ones after lubricating them with rubber grease.

Refitting

8 Refitting is a reversal of removal, bearing in mind the following points.
a) *Do not fully tighten the anti-roll bar mountings until the unladen weight of the vehicle is on the suspension (ie, the vehicle is resting on its wheels).*
b) *Reconnect the gearchange mechanism as described in Chapter 7.*
c) *Refit the exhaust downpipe as described in Chapter 4.*

7 Front suspension lower arm - removal, overhaul and refitting

Removal

1 Apply the handbrake, then jack up the front of the vehicle and support it securely on axle stands (see *"Jacking, towing and wheel changing"*). Remove the appropriate front roadwheel.
2 Unscrew the nuts and remove the clamp bolts holding the ends of the anti-roll bar to the lower arms. Remove the clamps, then loosen the mounting clamp bolts and pull the anti-roll bar downwards.
3 Remove the nut and clamp bolt securing the lower arm balljoint to the stub axle carrier. Note which way round the bolt is fitted.
4 Loosen the lower arm inner pivot bolts, then carefully lever the arm down to release the balljoint from the stub axle carrier. Take care not to damage the balljoint or driveshaft gaiters. Remove the plastic protector plate which is fitted to the balljoint shank (**see illustration**).
5 Unscrew the nuts and remove the spacers and pivot bolts from the inner end of the lower arm, then withdraw the arm from the subframe.

Overhaul

6 Clean the lower arm and the area around the arm mountings, then check for cracks, distortion or any other signs of damage. Check that the lower arm balljoint moves

freely, without any sign of roughness, and that the balljoint gaiter is free from cracks and splits. Examine the shanks of the pivot bolts for signs of wear or scoring. Renew worn components as necessary.

7 Inspect the lower arm pivot bushes. If they are worn, cracked, split or perished, they must be renewed. To renew the bushes, support the lower arm, and press the first bush out using a tubular spacer, such as a socket, which bears only on the hard, outer edge of the bush. **Note:** *Remove only one bush at a time from the arm, to ensure that each new bush is correctly positioned on installation.* Thoroughly clean the lower arm bore, removing all traces of dirt and grease, and polish away any burrs or raised edges which might hinder reassembly. Apply a smear of a suitable grease to the outer edge of the new bush. Press the bush into position until the distance "A" between the inner edges of the lower arm bushes is as shown (**see illustration**). Wipe away surplus grease and repeat the procedure on the remaining bush.

Refitting

8 Refitting is a reversal of removal, bearing in mind the following points.
a) *Make sure that the plastic protector plate is positioned over the balljoint gaiter.*
b) *Ensure that the balljoint clamp bolt is orientated as noted before removal.*
c) *Do not fully tighten the lower arm pivot bolts or the anti-roll bar fixings until the unladen weight of the vehicle is on the suspension (ie, the vehicle is resting on its wheels).*
d) *Tighten all fixings to the specified torques, where applicable.*

8 Front suspension lower arm balljoint - removal, inspection and refitting

Removal

1 Apply the handbrake, then jack up the front of the vehicle and support it securely on axle stands (see *"Jacking, towing and wheel*

10

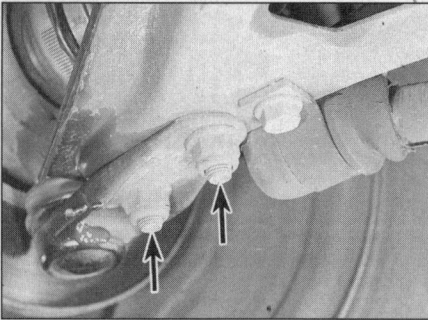

8.4 Front suspension lower arm balljoint-to-lower arm securing nuts (arrowed)

9.3 Exploded view of the rear hub bearing assembly - drum brake model shown

9.5 Extract the circlip . . .

changing"). Remove the appropriate front roadwheel.

2 Unscrew the nut and remove the clamp bolt securing the lower suspension balljoint to the stub axle carrier.

3 Loosen the lower arm inner pivot bolts, then carefully lever the arm down to release the balljoint from the stub axle carrier. Take care not to damage the balljoint or driveshaft gaiters. Remove the plastic protector plate which is fitted to the balljoint shank.

4 Remove the two nuts and bolts securing the balljoint to the lower arm **(see illustration)**. Remove the balljoint.

Inspection

5 Check that the balljoint moves freely, without any sign of roughness or free play. Examine the balljoint gaiter for signs of damage and deterioration such as cracks or splits. Renew the complete balljoint assembly if damaged; it is not possible to renew the balljoint gaiter separately. The balljoint renewal kit obtainable from Renault dealers contains the balljoint, the plastic protector plate and all fixings.

Refitting

6 Refitting is a reversal of removal, bearing in mind the following points.
a) *Do not fully tighten the lower arm inner pivot bolts until the unladen weight of the vehicle is on the suspension (ie, the vehicle is resting on its wheels).*
b) *Tighten all fixings to the specified torques.*

9 Rear hub bearings - checking, removal and refitting

Note: *The bearing is a sealed, pre-adjusted and pre-lubricated, double-row tapered-roller type, and is intended to last the car's entire service life without maintenance or attention. Never overtighten the hub nut in an attempt to "adjust" the bearings.*

Checking

1 Chock the front wheels and engage reverse gear. Jack up the rear of the vehicle and support it securely on axle stands (see *"Jacking, towing and wheel changing"*).

Remove the appropriate rear roadwheel, and fully release the handbrake.

2 Wear in the rear hub bearings can be checked by measuring the amount of side play present. To do this, a dial test indicator should be fixed so that its probe is in contact with the hub outer face. The play should be between 0 and 0.03 mm. If it is greater than this, the bearings are worn excessively and should be renewed.

Removal

3 The rear hub bearing is integral with the brake drum/disc (as applicable) **(see illustration)**.

4 Remove the rear brake disc or drum (as applicable), as described in Chapter 9.

5 Using circlip pliers, extract the bearing retaining circlip from the centre of the brake disc or drum **(see illustration)**.

6 Securely support the disc or drum hub. Press or drive the bearing out of the hub, using a tubular drift of suitable diameter inserted through the inside of the hub and in contact with the bearing outer race **(see illustration)**.

7 Thoroughly clean the hub, removing all traces of dirt and grease. Polish away any burrs or raised edges which might hinder reassembly. Check the hub/drum/disc assembly for cracks or any other signs of damage, and renew if necessary. The bearing and its circlip must be renewed whenever they are disturbed. A replacement bearing kit is available from Renault dealers, consisting of the bearing, circlip, spacer, thrustwasher, hub nut and grease cap.

9.6 . . . then drive out the rear hub bearing using a tubular drift

Refitting

8 On reassembly, check (if possible) that the new bearing is packed with grease. Apply a light film of gear oil to the bearing outer race and to the stub axle.

9 Securely support the hub, then press the bearing into position, using a suitable tube in contact with the bearing outer race. Ensure that the bearing enters the hub squarely.

10 Ensure that the bearing is correctly seated against the hub shoulder, and secure it in position with the new circlip. Ensure that the circlip is correctly seated in its groove.

11 Refit the brake disc or drum (as applicable) as described in Chapter 9.

10 Rear shock absorber - removal, inspection and refitting

Removal

1 Chock the front wheels and engage reverse gear. Jack up the rear of the vehicle and support it securely on axle stands (see *"Jacking, towing and wheel changing"*). Remove the appropriate rear roadwheel.

2 Using a jack, raise the trailing arm slightly until the shock absorber is slightly compressed. Remove the lower mounting bolt and recover the washer **(see illustration)**.

3 Working inside the luggage compartment, pull off the rubber cover, then unscrew the shock absorber upper mounting nut **(see illustrations)**. If necessary, hold the piston

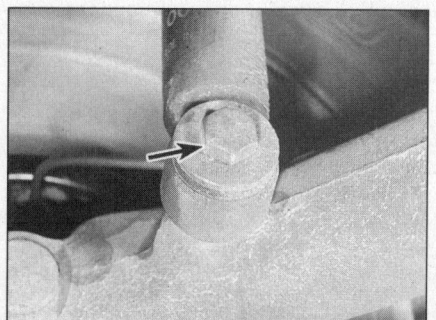

10.2 Rear shock absorber lower mounting bolt (arrowed)

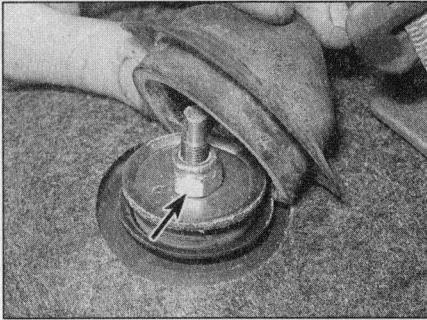

10.3a Rear shock absorber upper mounting nut (arrowed) in the luggage compartment

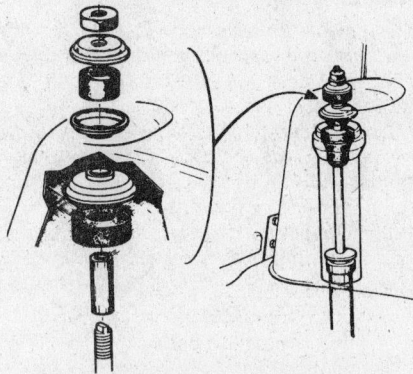

10.3b Exploded view of the rear shock absorber upper mounting

rod stationary using a further spanner.

4 Withdraw the shock absorber from under the vehicle. Recover the mounting rubbers and their seats if they are loose.

Inspection

5 Examine the shock absorber for signs of fluid leakage. Check the piston for signs of pitting along its visible length, and check the shock absorber body for signs of damage. Test the operation of the shock absorber (mounting it in a vice if necessary), while holding it in an upright position, by moving the piston through a full stroke and then through short strokes of 59 to 100 mm. In both cases the resistance felt should be smooth and continuous. If the resistance is jerky, or

uneven, or if there is any visible sign of wear or damage to the shock absorber, renewal is necessary. Note that the mounting bushes are not available separately. Inspect the mounting bolt and nut for signs of wear or damage, and renew as necessary.

Refitting

6 Prior to refitting the shock absorber, mount it upright in a vice, and operate it fully through several strokes in order to prime it. (This is necessary even if a new unit is being fitted, as it may have been stored horizontally, and so need priming). Apply a smear of multi-purpose grease to the shock absorber mounting bolt and nut.

7 Refitting is a reversal of removal, but delay tightening the mounting bolt and nut until the unladen weight of the vehicle is on the suspension (ie, the vehicle is resting on its wheels).

11 Rear suspension anti-roll bar (enclosed-bar rear axle) - removal and refitting

Removal

1 Chock the front wheels and engage reverse gear. Jack up the rear of the vehicle and support it securely on axle stands (see *"Jacking, towing and wheel changing"*).

2 Remove the bolts securing the ends of the anti-roll bar to the rear suspension trailing arms, noting the fitted positions of the handbrake cable retaining clips. Recover the anti-roll bar retaining nut plates from the top of the trailing arms.

3 Withdraw the anti-roll bar from under the vehicle.

Refitting

4 Refit the anti-roll bar to the vehicle, noting that the cutaway ends of the anti-roll bar retaining bolt brackets must face towards the front of the vehicle (see illustration).

5 Position the retaining nut plates on the top of the trailing arms. Refit the retaining bolts, ensuring that the handbrake cable retaining

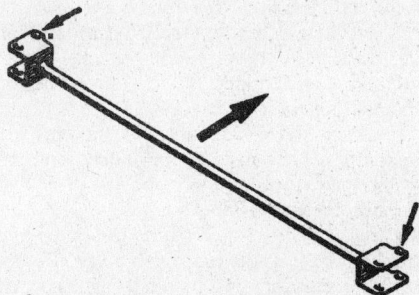

11.4 Cutaway ends of the rear anti-roll bar brackets (small arrows) must face the front of the vehicle

clips are correctly positioned. Tighten the anti-roll bar retaining bolts to the specified torque.

6 Lower the vehicle to the ground.

12 Rear torsion bar - removal and refitting

Removal

1 Chock the front wheels and engage reverse gear. Jack up the rear of the vehicle and support it securely on axle stands (see *"Jacking, towing and wheel changing"*). Remove the appropriate roadwheel.

2 Remove the relevant rear shock absorber, as described in Section 10.

3 On models with an open-bar rear axle, undo the retaining screws and remove the clamp securing the handbrake cable to the torsion bar.

4 Prise off the cap from the trailing arm bearing bracket, to gain access to the torsion bar end.

5 Mark the position of the torsion bar in relation to the bearing bracket. On the open-bar rear axle, also mark the bar in relation to the centre link block. With the trailing arm unsupported, measure the distance between the centres of the shock absorber upper mounting hole in the luggage compartment floor pan, and the lower mounting bolt hole in the trailing arm. Note the distance; if the original bar is to be refitted, this will be required on refitting.

6 The torsion bar can now be withdrawn outwards, using a slide hammer such as Renault tool Emb.880 or a suitable alternative (see illustration). It is possible to improvise by screwing a long bolt with a flat washer into the torsion bar, and placing the jaws of a spanner against the washer. Striking the spanner sharply with a hammer should free the torsion bar.

7 Once the splines of the torsion bar are free, the bar can be withdrawn completely from its location. Note that the left-hand and right-hand bars are not interchangeable; they can be identified by the markings on their ends (see illustration).

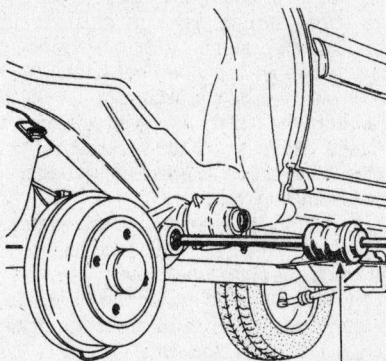

12.6 Using a slide hammer (Renault tool Emb.880 shown)

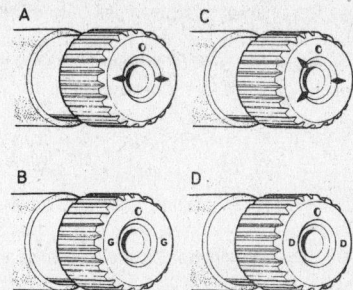

12.7 Rear suspension torsion bar identification markings
A and B Left-hand torsion bar
C and D Right-hand torsion bar

10

Refitting

8 Ensure that the bearing bracket and torsion bar splines are clean and dry. Lubricate the splines with molybdenum disulphide grease, and insert the bar into the bracket.

9 If the original bar is being refitted, position the trailing arm so that the distance between the centres of the shock absorber upper mounting hole in the luggage compartment floor pan, and the lower mounting bolt hole in the trailing arm is as noted prior to removal.

10 If a new torsion bar is being fitted, the trailing arm must be raised until the distance between the centres of the shock absorber upper mounting hole in the luggage compartment floor pan, and the lower mounting bolt hole in the trailing arm is dimension "X" as given in the Specifications. With dimension "X" correctly set, all the torsional forces will be removed from the bar.

11 Raise the trailing arm to the required position using a jack. Alternatively, a tool similar to that shown can be fabricated from a length of threaded bar, and used to position the trailing arm **(see illustration)**.

Original bar (all types)

12 Rotate the torsion bar to align the marks made on removal, then engage the bar with the bearing bracket and bearing/centre link splines. Tap the bar fully into position using a hammer and a soft metal drift.

New bar (enclosed-bar rear axle)

13 Rotate the torsion bar until the position is found where the bar can be freely engaged with the splines on the bearing bracket and bearing. Having found this, tap the bar fully home using a hammer and a soft metal drift.

New bar (open-bar rear axle)

14 Remove the cap from the opposite bearing bracket, and check the position of the drill mark on the end of the torsion bar. Rotate the new bar so that its drill mark is in exactly the same position, then locate its splines with those of the bearing bracket and centre link, and insert the bar. To do this, it may be necessary to rotate the bar slightly, noting that the drill marks on both bars must be no more than two splines away from each other once the splines are engaged. If this proves difficult to achieve, it is permissible to **slightly** lower or raise the trailing arm. If excessive movement of the arm is required to allow the splines to align, it is recommended that the opposite torsion bar is also renewed.

15 Once it is correctly positioned, tap the torsion bar fully into position using a hammer and a soft metal drift.

All types

16 Refit the torsion bar cap(s) to the bearing bracket(s).

17 On models with an open-bar rear axle, refit the handbrake cable clamp to the torsion bar, and securely tighten the screws.

18 Refit the rear shock absorber, as described in Section 10.

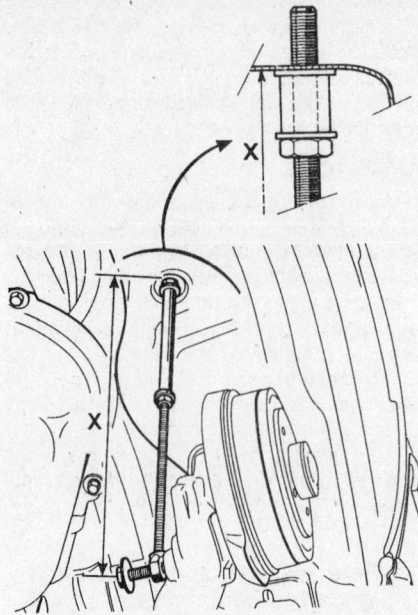

12.11 A tool made from a length of threaded bar can be fitted to the shock absorber mounting holes, and used to set dimension "X" - see text

19 Check the rear underbody height, as described in Section 17.

13 Rear suspension trailing arm (enclosed-bar rear axle) - removal and refitting

Removal

1 Chock the front wheels and engage reverse gear. Jack up the rear of the vehicle and support it securely on axle stands (see *"Jacking, towing and wheel changing"*). Remove the appropriate rear roadwheel.

2 Remove the rear anti-roll bar, as described in Section 11.

3 Remove the appropriate torsion bar, as described in Section 12.

4 Remove the brake drum/hub assembly and brake shoes (drum brake models), or the brake disc/hub assembly (disc brake models), as applicable, as described in Chapter 9. On models with rear disc brakes, also unbolt the caliper from the trailing arm, with reference to Chapter 9 - there is no need to disconnect the fluid line if the caliper is adequately supported to avoid straining the line.

5 On models with rear drum brakes, use a hammer and pin punch to tap the handbrake outer cable out of the backplate.

6 Work along the length of the handbrake cable, and release it from any clips or ties securing it to the trailing arm.

7 On models with rear drum brakes, the brake pipe union must now be unscrewed from the wheel cylinder as follows. Minimise brake fluid loss by removing the master

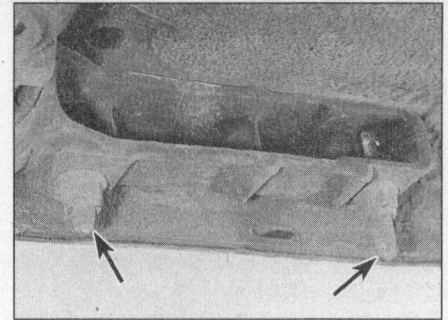

13.10 Trailing arm bearing bracket mounting nuts (arrowed)

13.12 Rear brake backplate retaining bolts (A)

cylinder reservoir cap, and then tightening it down onto a piece of polythene to obtain an airtight seal (taking care not to damage the sender unit). Alternatively, use a brake hose clamp, a G-clamp or a similar tool with protected jaws, to clamp the flexible hose at the nearest convenient point to the wheel cylinder. Wipe away all traces of dirt around the brake pipe union at the rear of the wheel cylinder, and unscrew the union nut. Carefully ease the pipe out of the wheel cylinder, and plug or tape over its end to prevent dirt entry. Wash off any spilt fluid immediately.

8 Support the weight of the trailing arm on a jack.

9 Working inside the luggage compartment, lift the carpet and remove the trim to gain access to the trailing arm bearing bracket mounting bolt heads.

10 Working underneath the vehicle, on the side from which the trailing arm is to be removed, unscrew the trailing arm bearing bracket mounting nuts **(see illustration)**. Tap the bolts through the bearing bracket with a suitable drift. Loosen the mounting nuts on the opposite bearing bracket.

11 Lower the jack until the trailing arm assembly is clear of the sill, then pull the trailing arm out of the opposite arm, and remove it from the vehicle.

12 Inspect the trailing arm bearings and tracks for signs of wear or damage. Renew them if necessary as described in Section 14. On models with rear drum brakes, if a new trailing arm is being fitted, undo the four retaining bolts and remove the brake backplate. Fit the backplate to the new trailing

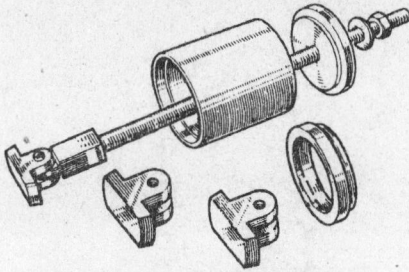

14.3 Renault tool for removing the rear suspension trailing arm bearings - enclosed-bar type rear suspension

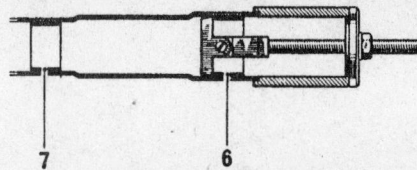

14.4 Using the Renault tool to remove the trailing arm bearings - enclosed-bar type rear suspension

6 Outer bearing *7 Inner bearing*

22 Check the rear underbody height as described in Section 17.

14.7 Removing a trailing arm bearing inner track using a grinder

arm, apply thread-locking compound to the retaining bolts, and tighten them securely **(see illustration)**.

Refitting

13 Ensure that the trailing arm bearings are sufficiently greased, then engage the removed trailing arm with the opposite arm. Temporarily position the anti-roll bar over its mounting bolt holes, ensuring that the cutaway ends of the retaining bolt brackets face towards the front of the vehicle. Push the trailing arm into position until the anti-roll bar bracket holes are correctly aligned with the bolt holes in the trailing arms.

14 Once the trailing arms are correctly interlocked, remove the anti-roll bar. Raise the trolley jack, and insert the bearing bracket mounting bolts from inside the luggage compartment, ensuring that the bolt retaining plate is correctly fitted. Refit the mounting nuts and tighten them to the specified torque. Refit the trim and the carpet in the luggage compartment.

15 On models with rear drum brakes, refit the brake pipe to the wheel cylinder, and securely tighten its union nut. Remove the clamp from the brake hose or the polythene from the master cylinder reservoir (as applicable).

16 Where applicable, tap the handbrake cable back into position in the brake backplate, and secure it in position with the ties or clips.

17 Refit the brake drum/hub assembly and brake shoes (drum brake models), or the brake disc/hub assembly (disc brake models), as applicable, as described in Chapter 9. Where applicable, refit the caliper to the trailing arm and tighten the securing bolts to the specified torque (Chapter 9).

18 Refit the torsion bar as described in Section 12.

19 Refit the anti-roll bar as described in Section 11.

20 Bleed the brake hydraulic system as described in Chapter 9. Providing the precautions described were taken to minimise brake fluid loss, it should only be necessary to bleed the relevant rear brake.

21 Refit the roadwheel, lower the vehicle to the ground and tighten the wheel bolts to the specified torque.

14 Rear suspension trailing arm bearings (enclosed-bar rear axle) - renewal

1 Remove both trailing arms with reference to Section 13.

2 Mount the left-hand trailing arm in a vice.

3 To remove the bearings, it will be necessary to obtain the Renault tool shown **(see illustration)**, or to fabricate a similar tool as follows. First note the exact position of the bearings.

4 Obtain a threaded rod long enough to reach the inner bearing, a tube of suitable diameter, two thick washers of diameter equal to each bearing, a washer of diameter greater than the tube, and two nuts. Cut two sides off the smaller washer so that just a flat strip with a hole in the centre remains. This will form the swivelling end part shown on the Renault tool. Pass the threaded rod through the hole in the strip, and screw on a nut. Feed the strip and rod through the bearing so that the strip locates behind the bearing. Place the tube over the rod and in contact with the edge of the arm. Place the large washer over the end of the tube, and then screw on the remaining nut. Hold the rod with grips, and tighten the nut to draw out the bearing, then repeat this operation to remove the remaining bearing **(see illustration)**.

5 Thoroughly clean the bore, removing all traces of dirt and grease. Polish away any burrs or raised edges which might hinder reassembly. Apply a smear of multi-purpose grease to the outer edge of the new bearings, then carefully press them squarely into position, using a tubular spacer which presses only on the hard outer edge of the bearing.

6 Mount the right-hand trailing arm in the vice.

7 Mark the exact position of the bearing inner tracks on the trailing arm. Cut or grind almost through both bearing inner tracks, taking care not to damage the tube **(see illustration)**. Using a cold chisel, split the tracks and remove them from the tube. Also cut and remove the seal from the tube.

8 Clean the arm and fit the new seal.

9 Press on the new inner tracks, making sure that the lead chamfer goes on first. When doing this, if the load is being taken on the axle support assemblies, make sure that the torsion bars are correctly located in the anchor points.

10 It is not necessary to grease the bearing needle races, as they are supplied already greased.

11 Reassemble and refit the trailing arms with reference to Section 13.

15 Rear suspension bearing bracket bushes (enclosed-bar rear axle) - renewal

Note: *If either bearing bracket bush requires renewal, it will be necessary to renew the complete bearing bracket assembly, since it is not possible to obtain the bush separately.*

1 Remove the trailing arm as described in Section 13.

2 Soak the bearing bracket bush in brake fluid for some time, to soften the bush rubber.

3 Wipe off all traces of brake fluid, then mark the position of the bush inner edge on the trailing arm shaft.

4 Using a two- or three-legged puller, draw the bearing bracket off the trailing arm; the rubber of the bush will tear during this process, leaving the inner part of the bush on the arm **(see illustration)**.

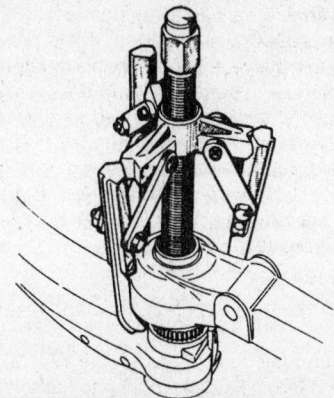

15.4 Using a puller to remove the rear suspension bearing bracket from the trailing arm

10

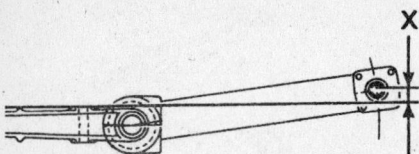

15.7 Correct position of trailing arm bearing bracket in relation to trailing arm

X = 15.0 mm

5 Remove the remaining inner part of the bush by cutting with a hacksaw, taking care not to damage the trailing arm shaft.

6 Thoroughly clean the trailing arm shaft, removing all traces of rubber and grease. Polish away any burrs or raised edges which might hinder reassembly. Apply a smear of suitable grease to the inner edges of the new bush to aid installation.

7 Securely support the trailing arm, then position the new bearing bracket in relation to the trailing arm as shown **(see illustration)**. Press the bracket onto the trailing arm shaft until the bush reaches the alignment mark made prior to removal. Ensure that the bracket is not pushed beyond the mark, as if the bracket is incorrectly positioned, the bush may be damaged when the position of the bracket is adjusted to give the dimension specified in paragraph 8.

8 Temporarily refit the trailing arm into position as described in Section 13, paragraph 13. Check that the dimension between the bolt hole centres of the left and right-hand bearing brackets is as shown **(see illustration)**. If this is not the case, remove the arm and adjust the position of the bearing bracket as necessary, taking care not to damage the bush.

9 With the bearing bracket correctly positioned, refit the trailing arm as described in Section 13.

16 Rear axle (open-bar type) - removal, overhaul and refitting

Removal

1 Chock the front wheels and engage reverse gear. Jack up the rear of the vehicle and support it securely on axle stands (see *"Jacking, towing and wheel changing"*). Remove both rear roadwheels.

2 Support both trailing arms so that the shock absorbers are compressed slightly, then unscrew and remove both shock absorber lower mounting bolts.

3 On models with rear drum brakes, remove the brake drum/hub assemblies and brake shoes as described in Chapter 9. Using a hammer and pin punch, tap the handbrake outer cable out of the backplate.

4 On models with rear disc brakes, remove the brake calipers as described in Chapter 9. If desired, also remove the brake discs.

5 Work back along the length of the handbrake cables, and release them from any clips or ties securing them to the trailing arms.

6 On models equipped with ABS, remove the rear wheel sensors as described in Chapter 9.

7 On models with rear disc brakes, unhook the brake pressure-regulating valve spring from the top of the axle crossmember, using a pair of pliers.

8 Remove the screws securing the handbrake cable retaining clamps to the torsion bars **(see illustration)**.

9 Support the weight of the rear axle on a trolley jack.

10 Working in the luggage compartment, lift the carpet, and remove the trim for access to the trailing arm (rear axle) bearing bracket mounting bolt heads.

11 From underneath the vehicle, unscrew the four trailing arm (rear axle) bearing bracket mounting nuts **(see illustration)**. Tap the bolts up through the bearing bracket with a drift.

12 Lower the jack, and pull the rear axle assembly out from underneath the vehicle.

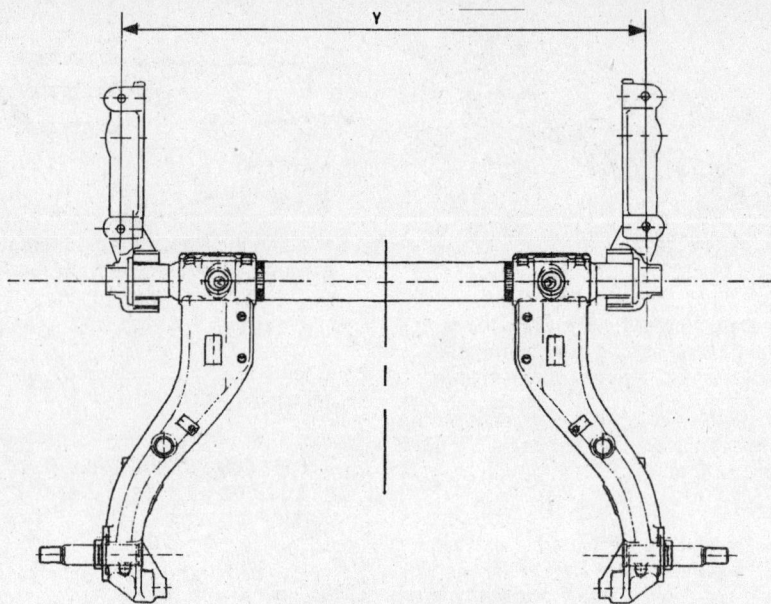

16.8 Handbrake cable retaining clamps (arrowed) on torsion bars - open-bar type rear suspension

15.8 Trailing arm bearing bracket positioning - enclosed-bar type rear suspension shown, open-bar type similar

Distance between left- and right-hand bearing bracket bolt hole centres (Y) = 1268 ± 1.0 mm

Overhaul

13 Remove the two torsion bars with reference to Section 12.

14 Mark the anti-roll bars in relation to the trailing arms and centre link block. Extract them using the same method as that employed when removing the torsion bars.

15 Examine all the components for wear and damage. Check the splines on the torsion bars, anti-roll bars, centre link block and trailing arms **(see illustration)**. If a trailing arm or the L-shaped crossmember is damaged, it will be necessary to obtain a new rear axle (supplied with the bearing brackets already fitted, but requiring the original torsion bars and anti-roll bars to be fitted). If the bearing bracket bushes require renewal, proceed as described below, noting that it is not possible to obtain either bush separately. If worn, the complete bearing bracket and bush assembly must be renewed. If it is not wished to renew the bushes, proceed to paragraph 18.

16.11 Trailing arm (rear axle) bearing bracket mounting nut (arrowed) - open-bar type rear suspension

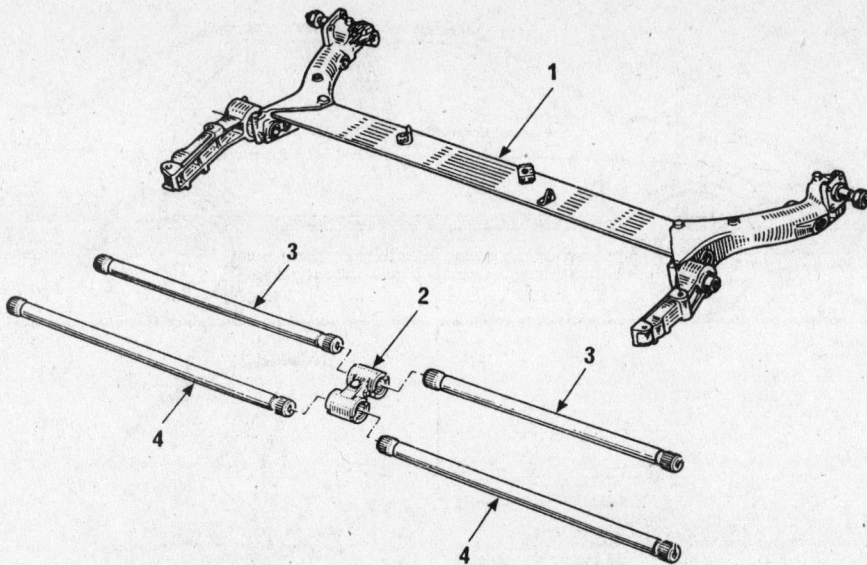

16.15 Open-bar type rear suspension components

1 *Trailing arms and L-shaped*
crossmember assembly
2 *Centre link block*

3 *Anti-roll bars*
4 *Torsion bars*

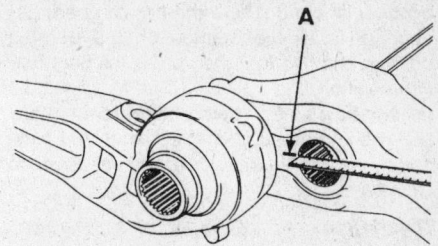

16.20a Mark the trailing arms (A) as described in text before refitting the anti-roll bars - open-bar type rear suspension

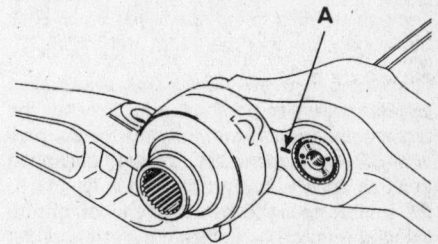

16.20b Fit the anti-roll bars so that their drill marks align with the previously made marks (A) on the trailing arms - open-bar type rear suspension

16 Obtain a nut of suitable diameter which just fits inside the bearing bracket pivot shaft, and weld it securely to the shaft inner surface. Support the outer surface of the trailing arm. Press out the bearing bracket shaft, using a spacer which bears on the top of the welded nut.

17 Thoroughly clean the trailing arm bore. Polish away any burrs or raised edges which might hinder reassembly. Apply a smear of multi-purpose grease to the outer diameter of the new bracket pivot shaft, to aid installation.

18 Support the inner edge of the trailing arm. Position the new bearing bracket in relation to the trailing arm as shown in illustration 15.7. Press the bracket onto the trailing arm shaft until the distance between inner bolt hole centres of the left and right-hand bearing brackets is as shown in illustration 15.8. Wipe away any excess grease.

19 Commence reassembly of the rear axle by placing it upside-down on blocks of wood positioned under the L-shaped crossmember so that the bearing brackets are free.

20 Use a ruler as shown, and mark each trailing arm on the axis between the centres of the torsion bar and anti-roll bar holes. Clean the anti-roll bar splines, and grease them well with molybdenum disulphide grease. Insert one anti-roll bar so that its drill mark is aligned with the mark made on the trailing arm **(see illustrations)**. Fit the centre link block to the anti-roll bar so that it is parallel with the upper section of the crossmember. Insert the remaining anti-roll bar from the opposite side, also aligning its circular drill mark with the mark made on the trailing arm.

21 It is now necessary to adjust the centre link position, in order to avoid any contact with the crossmember during movement of the rear

suspension. First measure the movement possible between the centre link and the crossmember. Note this measurement, then refer to the table below to obtain the amount of adjustment, in terms of splines, necessary.

Movement (mm)	Number of splines to compensate
2 to 4	1
5 to 6	2
7 to 8	3
9 to 10	4
11 to 12	5
13 to 14	6
15 to 16	7
17 to 18	8
19 to 20	9

22 To correct the position of the centre link, withdraw one of the anti-roll bars from the trailing arm. Slide the centre link off the end of the other anti-roll bar, rotate the link away from the crossmember by the specified number of splines, then refit it to the anti-roll bar end **(see illustration)**. Disengage the anti-roll bar and centre link assembly from the trailing arm splines. Rotate the bar by the specified number of splines, so that the centre link is parallel to the crossmember again, then relocate the anti-roll bar in the trailing arm splines. Rotate the second anti-roll bar by the same number of splines in the *opposite* direction, so that its drill mark is at the same position as the one on the opposite bar, then engage its splines with those of the trailing arm and centre link, and slide the bar into position.

23 With the anti-roll bars correctly positioned, use a G-clamp to press the centre link down until it is parallel with the crossmember **(see illustration)**. Temporarily refit the torsion bars. Rotate each bar until the

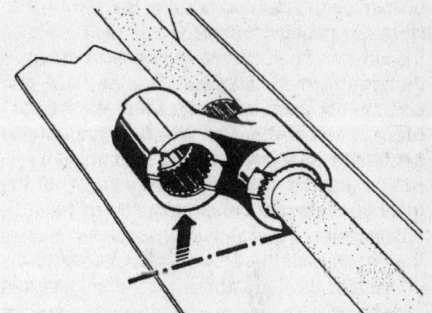

16.22 Calculate the amount of adjustment required, then move the centre link away from the crossmember by the specified number of splines - open-bar type rear suspension

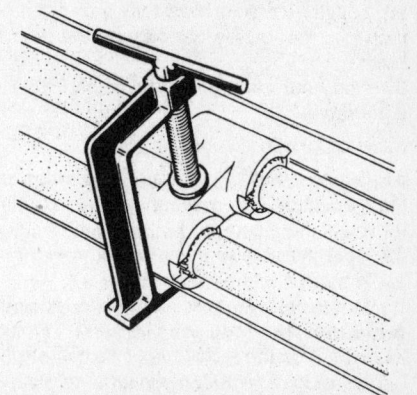

16.23 Using a G-clamp to press the centre link down until parallel with the crossmember

10

position is found where the bar can be freely engaged with the splines on the bearing bracket and bearing, then press the bars fully into position.

24 If a new axle is being fitted, remove any brake components still attached to the axle, and fit them to the new axle, with reference to Chapter 9.

Refitting

25 Place the rear axle assembly on a trolley jack, and lift it into position underneath the vehicle. Insert the bearing bracket mounting bolts from inside the vehicle, ensuring that the retaining plate is correctly fitted. Refit the nuts and tighten them to the specified torque. Refit the luggage compartment trim and carpet.

New axle only

26 Remove the G-clamp from the crossmember, then withdraw the torsion bars again. Position the trailing arms as described in paragraphs 10 and 11 of Section 12.

27 Ensure that the bearing bracket, centre link and torsion bar splines are clean and dry. Lubricate the splines with molybdenum disulphide grease, and insert the bars into the bracket.

28 Rotate the left-hand bar until the position is found where it can be freely engaged with splines on the bearing bracket and centre link. Note the position of the circular drill mark on the left-hand bar. Rotate the right-hand bar so that its drill mark is in the same position, and engage its splines with those of the bearing bracket and centre link; the bar should slide freely into position. If not, it is permissible to rotate the bar slightly, noting that the drill marks on both bars must be no more than two splines away from each other once the splines are engaged. If this proves difficult to achieve, withdraw the left-hand bar and rotate it slightly until it freely engages with the splines (there will be several positions where this will be the case) before trying to install the right-hand bar. Repeat the procedure until a position is found where both torsion bars slide freely into position and the drill marks are satisfactorily positioned.

29 Tap the torsion bars fully into position, then refit the torsion bar caps to the bearing brackets.

30 Carry out the procedures in the following paragraphs.

New or original axle

31 Support the trailing arms, then reconnect the rear shock absorbers and refit and tighten the lower mounting bolts.

32 Refit the screws securing the handbrake cable clamps to the torsion bars.

33 On models with rear disc brakes, hook the brake pressure-regulating valve spring onto its bracket on the top of the crossmember.

34 On models with ABS, refit the rear wheel sensors as described in Chapter 9.

35 Where applicable, reconnect the handbrake cables to the clips or ties securing them to the trailing arms.

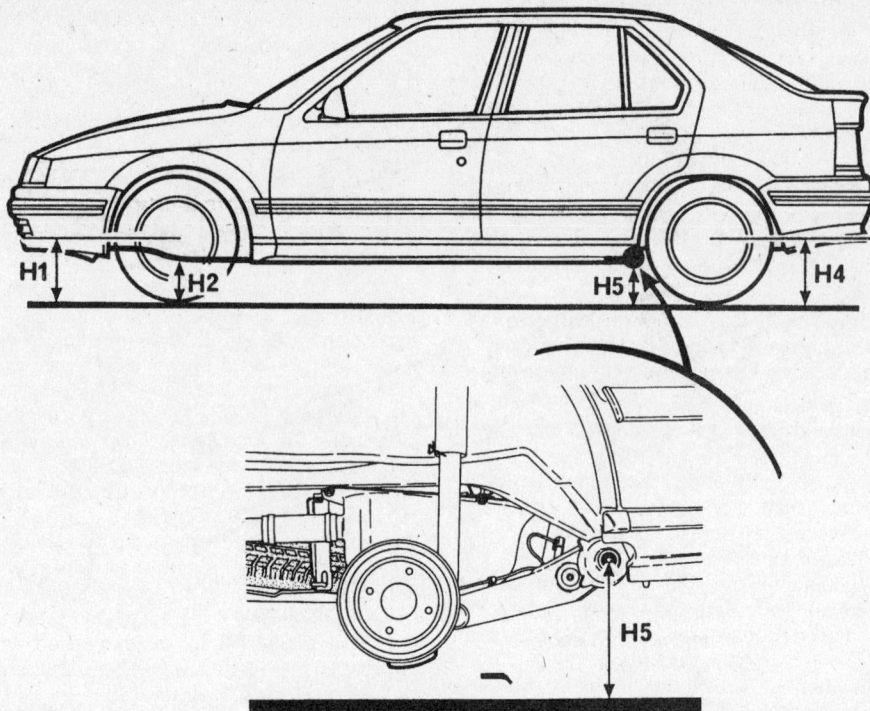

17.2 Underbody height measuring points. Note that H5 is measured from the centre of the torsion bar to the ground

For values refer to Specifications

36 On models with rear disc brakes, refit the discs (where applicable), and the calipers, as described in Chapter 9.

37 On models with rear drum brakes, refit the drum/hub assemblies and brake shoes, and reconnect the handbrake cables as described in Chapter 9.

38 Bleed the brake hydraulic system as described in Chapter 9.

39 Refit the roadwheels, lower the vehicle to the ground and tighten the wheel bolts to the specified torque.

40 Check the rear underbody height as described in Section 17.

17 Underbody height - checking and adjustment

1 Position the unladen vehicle on a level surface, with the tyres correctly inflated and the fuel tank full.

Enclosed-bar rear suspension

2 It is only possible to adjust the rear suspension height in steps of 3 mm. First measure and record the dimensions H4 and H5 on both sides of the vehicle as shown, noting that dimension H5 is measured from the centre of the torsion bar to the ground **(see illustration)**. Subtract H5 from H4 to find the underbody height checking dimension. Check that this dimension is within the range given in the Specifications at the start of this Chapter. If adjustment is necessary, proceed as follows.

3 Determine by how many splines the torsion bar must be moved, noting that one spline is equal to a 3 mm change of height. For example, if the height needs adjusting by 10 mm, the torsion bar should be moved by three splines.

4 Chock the front wheels and engage reverse gear. Jack up the rear of the vehicle and support it securely on axle stands (see *"Jacking, towing and wheel changing"*). Remove the appropriate rear roadwheel.

5 Position a trolley jack beneath the end of the trailing arm, then remove the torsion bar with reference to Section 12. With the bar removed, raise or lower the trailing arm by the required amount, so that it rotates by the required number of splines in relation to the bearing bracket. Once correctly positioned, adjust the trailing arm position slightly until the torsion bar can be slid freely back into position. Use a hammer and a soft metal drift to tap the bar fully home.

6 Refit the roadwheel, lower the vehicle to the ground and tighten the wheel bolts to the specified torque.

7 Recheck that the underbody height is within the specified range. If not, repeat the adjustment procedure. Note that after making the adjustment, it may be necessary to adjust the headlamp beam alignment with reference to Chapter 1.

Open-bar rear suspension

8 Measure and record the dimensions H4 and H5 on both sides of the vehicle as shown, noting that dimension H5 is measured from the centre of the torsion bar to the ground (see illustration 17.2). Subtract H5 from H4 to obtain the underbody height checking dimension. Check that this dimension is within the range given in the Specifications at the start of this Chapter. If necessary, adjust the height(s) using the procedure given under the relevant sub-heading.

Underbody height correct on one side, but difference between sides excessive - new rear axle assembly

9 The difference between the right-hand and left-hand sides is always corrected by altering the position of the anti-roll bar on the lower side, so that the lower side is raised to the same height as the higher side. Calculate the difference in heights between the two sides, then adjust as follows.
10 Mark the relative positions of the two torsion bars and the anti-roll bar to be removed, both on the centre link and on the bearing bracket/trailing arm.
11 Remove both the torsion bars as described in Section 12, then remove the marked anti-roll bar using the same method.
12 Ensure that dimension "X" is correctly set on both sides, as described in paragraphs 10 and 11 of Section 12. Measure the distance from the centre of the stub axle to the ground, on the side on which the anti-roll bar has been removed. Subtract the side-to-side difference from this height to obtain the correct height at which the stub axle should be, then lower the trailing arm until the stub axle is at the correct height.
13 Refit the anti-roll bar, rotating it until the position is found where it can be freely slid back into position, and tap it fully into position. Using the marks made prior to removal, check that the offset of the anti-roll bar splines in relation to the distance the trailing arm was moved is as shown in the following table.

Trailing arm movement (mm)	Number of splines to compensate
5	2
10	4
15	6
20	8
25	10
30	12
35	14
40	16
45	18
50	20

14 Align the marks made prior to removal, then refit both the torsion bars.
15 Refit the shock absorbers as described in Section 10.
16 Refit the roadwheels, lower the vehicle to the ground and tighten the wheel bolts to the specified torque.
17 Recheck the underbody height. If

necessary, repeat the adjustment procedure. Note that after making the adjustment, it will be necessary to adjust the headlamp beam alignment with reference to Chapter 1. It is also recommended that on models with rear disc brakes, the operation of the brake pressure-regulating valve is checked by a Renault dealer at the earliest opportunity.

Underbody heights incorrect on both sides, and difference between sides excessive - new rear axle assembly

18 The difference between the right-hand and left-hand sides is always corrected by altering the position of the anti-roll bar on the lower side, so that the lower side is raised to the same height as the higher side. Calculate the difference in heights between the two sides, and the amount by which the higher side deviates from the specified height.
19 Carry out the procedures described in paragraphs 10 to 13 inclusive.
20 With both trailing arms at the same height, measure the distance from the centre of the stub axle to the ground on each side. Raise or lower both trailing arms equally so that the distance is increased or decreased (as applicable) by the calculated height deviation of the higher side (paragraph 18).
21 Refit the torsion bars, rotating each one until the position is found where it can be freely slid back into place, then tap them fully into position. Using the marks made prior to removal, check that the offset of the bar splines in relation to the distance the trailing arm was moved is as shown in the table in paragraph 13.
22 Carry out the procedures described in paragraphs 15 to 17.

Underbody heights incorrect on both sides, but difference between sides within tolerance - new rear axle assembly

23 In this case, the underbody height is adjusted by repositioning the torsion bars. First calculate the amount by which the actual underbody height dimension deviates from the specified height.
24 Mark the relative positions of the torsion bars in the centre link and bearing bracket, then remove both bars as described in Section 12.
25 Ensure that dimension "X" is correctly set on both sides, as described in paragraphs 10 and 11 of Section 12. Measure the distance from the centre of the stub axles to the ground. Raise or lower both the trailing arms equally so that the distance is increased or decreased (as applicable) by the calculated deviation (paragraph 23).
26 Refit the torsion bars, rotating each one until the position is found where it can be freely slid back into place, then tap them fully into position. Using the marks made prior to removal, check that the offset of the bar splines in relation to the distance the trailing arm was moved is as shown in the table in paragraph 13.

27 Carry out the procedures described in paragraphs 15 to 17.

Underbody height correct on one side, but difference between sides excessive - used rear axle assembly

28 The difference between the right-hand and left-hand sides is always corrected by altering the position of the anti-roll bar on the lower side, so that the lower side is raised to the same height as the higher side. Calculate the difference in heights between the two sides, then proceed as follows.
29 Remove the rear shock absorbers as described in Section 10. Mark the relative positions of the two torsion bars and the anti-roll bar to be removed, both on the centre link and on the bearing bracket/trailing arm.
30 Place a trolley jack under the trailing arm on the side from which the anti-roll bar is to be removed, and raise it until the jack is just supporting the weight. Remove the two torsion bars as described in Section 12. Remove the marked anti-roll bar using the same method.
31 With the bars removed, ensure that the splines are clean and dry. Apply a smear of molybdenum disulphide grease to them.
32 Align the marks made prior to removal, and refit the removed anti-roll bar. If necessary, slightly raise or lower the trailing arm until the position is found where the bar slides freely into position.
33 Once the trailing arm is correctly positioned, so that the bar can freely be removed and refitted without resistance, measure the distance between the centres of the shock absorber upper mounting hole in the luggage compartment floor pan, and the lower mounting bolt hole in the trailing arm. Call this dimension "Y". Remove the anti-roll bar again.
34 Ensuring that dimension "Y" is still correctly set, measure the distance from the centre of the stub axle to the ground, on the side on which the anti-roll bar has been removed. Subtract the side-to-side height difference from this height, then lower the trailing arm until the stub axle is at the height thus calculated.
35 Refit the anti-roll bar, rotating it until the position is found where it can be freely slid back into position, then tap it fully into position. Using the marks made prior to removal, check that the offset of the anti-roll bar splines in relation to the distance the trailing arm was moved is as shown in the table in paragraph 13.
36 Carry out the procedures described in paragraphs 14 to 17.

Underbody heights incorrect on both sides, and difference between sides excessive - used rear axle assembly

37 Calculate the difference in heights between the two sides, and the amount by which the higher side deviates from the specified height.
38 Carry out the operations described in paragraphs 29 to 35.
39 With both trailing arms at the same height, measure the distance from the centre of the

10

stub axles to the ground. Raise or lower both trailing arms equally, so that the distance between the stub axles and the ground is increased or decreased (as applicable) by the calculated height deviation of the higher side (paragraph 37).

40 Refit the torsion bars, rotating each one until the position is found where it can be freely slid back into position, then tap them fully into position. Using the marks made prior to removal, check that the offset of the bar splines in relation to the distance the trailing arm was moved is as shown in the table in paragraph 13.

41 Carry out the procedures described in paragraphs 15 to 17.

Underbody heights incorrect on both sides, but difference between sides within tolerance - used rear axle assembly

42 In this case, the underbody height is adjusted by repositioning the torsion bars. First calculate the amount by which the actual underbody height deviates from the specified height.

43 Remove the rear shock absorbers as described in Section 10. Mark the relative positions of the torsion bars in the centre link and bearing bracket.

44 Place a trolley jack under each trailing arm, and raise it until the jack is just supporting the weight. Remove the two torsion bars as described in Section 12.

45 With the bars removed, ensure the splines are clean and dry. Apply a smear of molybdenum disulphide grease to them.

46 Align the marks made prior to removal, and refit both torsion bars. If necessary, slightly raise or lower the trailing arms by equal amounts until the position is found where both bars slide freely into position.

47 Once the trailing arms are correctly positioned, so that each bar can freely be removed and refitted without resistance, measure the distance between the centres of the shock absorber upper mounting hole in the luggage compartment floor pan, and the lower mounting bolt hole in the trailing arm. Call this dimension "Z".

48 Ensure that dimension "Z" is correctly set on both sides, then measure the distance from the centre of the stub axles to the ground. Raise or lower both trailing arms equally, so that the distance between the stub axles and the ground is increased or decreased (as applicable) by the calculated height deviation (paragraph 42).

49 Refit the torsion bars, rotating each one until the position is found where it can be freely slid back into position, and tap them into position. Using the marks made prior to removal, check that the offset of the bar splines in relation to the distance the trailing arm was moved is as shown in the table in paragraph 13.

50 Carry out the procedures described in paragraphs 15 to 17.

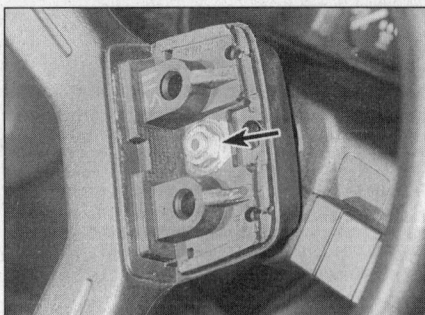

18.2 Steering wheel retaining nut (arrowed)

18 Steering wheel - removal and refitting

Warning: At the time of writing, no information was available regarding the removal and refitting of the steering wheel on models fitted with an air bag. To avoid any possibility of injury or damage, it is therefore strongly recommended that on models fitted with an air bag, any procedures involving the steering wheel are entrusted to a Renault dealer.

Removal

1 Set the front wheels in the straight-ahead position, and release the steering lock by inserting the ignition key.

2 Ease off the steering wheel pad to provide access to the retaining nut **(see illustration)**.

3 Using a socket, unscrew and remove the retaining nut.

4 Mark the steering wheel and steering column shaft in relation to each other and withdraw the wheel from the shaft splines. If it is tight, tap it upwards near the centre, using the palm of your hand, or twist the steering wheel from side-to-side to release it from the splines.

Refitting

5 Refitting is a reversal of removal, but align the previously made marks, and tighten the retaining nut to the specified torque.

19 Steering column - removal, checking and refitting

Removal

1 Disconnect the battery leads.

2 Remove the steering wheel as described in Section 18.

3 Remove the two securing screws, and withdraw the lower facia panel from under the steering wheel.

4 Remove the screws and withdraw the steering column upper and lower shrouds. Note that on models with a radio/cassette player remote control switch, it will be

19.11 Steering column-to-bulkhead securing nuts and bolts (arrowed)

necessary to loosen the switch clamp screw before the shrouds can be removed (see Chapter 12).

5 Remove the steering column combination switch assembly from the column with reference to Chapter 12.

6 Disconnect the wiring from the ignition switch.

7 Remove the two screws which secure the facia panel to the steering column.

8 Apply the handbrake, then jack up the front of the vehicle and support it securely on axle stands (see *"Jacking, towing and wheel changing"*).

9 On manual steering models, cut the retaining clip and release the universal joint rubber boot from the steering gear.

10 Mark the relationship between the intermediate shaft universal joint and the steering gear drive pinion, using a hammer and punch, white paint or similar. Remove the nut and clamp bolt securing the joint to the pinion.

11 Unscrew the two bolts and two nuts securing the steering column to the bulkhead **(see illustration)**.

12 Remove the lower facia fastening, the lower heater control cover, and the facia mounting nuts and bolts with reference to Chapter 11.

13 Slightly lift the facia in order to release it from the clip on the steering column **(see illustration)**.

14 Withdraw the steering column from inside the vehicle. On power-assisted steering models it will be necessary to release the rubber boot from the scuttle when withdrawing the steering column.

Checking

15 The intermediate shaft attached to the bottom of the steering column incorporates a telescopic safety feature. In the event of a front end crash, the shaft collapses and prevents the steering wheel injuring the driver. Before refitting the steering column, the length of the intermediate shaft must be checked. Make sure that the applicable length is as given **(see illustration)**. If the length is shorter than specified, the complete steering column must be renewed. Damage to the intermediate shaft is also implied if it is found that the clamp bolt at its base cannot be

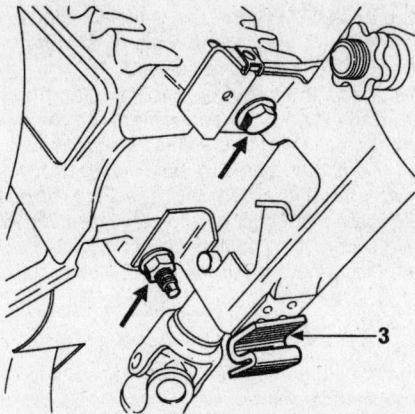

19.13 Steering column-to-bulkhead securing nut and bolt (arrowed) and facia-to-steering column clip (3)

inserted freely when refitting the column.

16 Check the steering shaft for signs of free play in the column bushes, and check the universal joints for signs of damage or roughness in the joint bearings. If damage or wear is found on the steering shaft universal joints or shaft bushes, the column must be renewed as an assembly.

Refitting

17 Refitting is a reversal of removal, bearing in mind the following points.

a) Align the marks made on the intermediate shaft and the steering gear pinion shaft before removal.

b) Before tightening the steering column mounting bolts, check that there is a clearance between the direction indicator return finger, and the lighting multi-function switch mounting.

c) On manual steering models, use a new cable tie to secure the universal joint rubber boot to the steering gear.

d) On models with a height-adjustable steering column, check that the locking

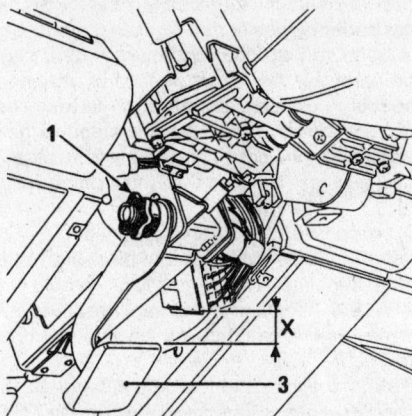

19.17 Checking the position of the height-adjustable steering column lever

1 Lever clamp nut   X = 30.0 mm
3 Locking lever

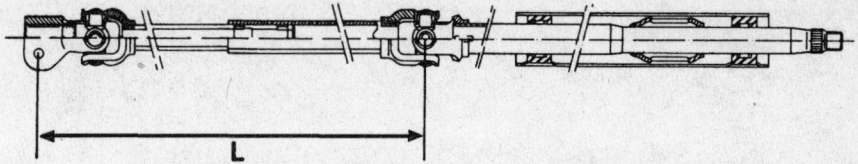

19.15 Steering column intermediate shaft checking dimension (L)

Right-hand- drive models with manual steering - 406.0 ± 1.0 mm
Right-hand-drive models with power steering - 354.5 ± 1.0 mm
Left-hand- drive models with manual steering - 408.0 ± 1.0 mm
Left-hand-drive models with power steering - 355.5 ± 1.0 mm

lever operates freely, and is easily accessible. If the lever is partially concealed and/or difficult to operate, it can be adjusted by removing the lever clamp nut and fully lowering the column. Lock the column by tightening the adjuster nut using the locking lever. Position the locking lever a distance of 30 mm from the steering column support bracket, then refit the lever clamp nut (see illustration). Refit the steering column shrouds, and check that the lever is accessible - if not increase or reduce (as necessary) the dimension between the locking lever and the steering column support bracket by 10 mm.

e) *Tighten all fixings to the specified torque.*

20 Steering gear rubber gaiter - renewal

1 Remove the track rod end balljoint as described in Section 26.
2 Mark the fitted position of the gaiter on the track rod. Release the retaining clips, and slide the gaiter off the steering gear housing and track rod end.
3 Thoroughly clean the track rod and the steering gear housing, using fine abrasive paper to polish off any corrosion, burrs or sharp edges which might damage the sealing lips of the new gaiter on installation.
4 Recover the grease from inside the old

gaiter. If it is uncontaminated with dirt or grit, apply it to the track rod inner balljoint. If the old grease is contaminated, or it is suspected that some has been lost, apply some new molybdenum disulphide grease.
5 Grease the inside of the new gaiter. Carefully slide the gaiter onto the track rod, and locate it on the steering gear housing. Align the outer edge of the gaiter with the mark made on the track rod prior to removal, then secure it in position with new retaining clips.
6 Refit the track rod balljoint as described in Section 26.

21 Steering gear (manual steering) - removal, overhaul and refitting

Removal

1 Apply the handbrake, then jack up the front of the vehicle and support it securely on axle stands (see "Jacking, towing and wheel changing"). Remove both front roadwheels.
2 Working on both sides of the vehicle, remove the nuts securing the track rod end balljoints to the stub axle carriers. Release the balljoint tapered shanks using a universal balljoint separator.
3 Working from underneath the vehicle, cut the retaining clip, then fold the rubber boot back from the steering gear to gain access to the intermediate shaft universal joint clamp bolt (see illustrations).

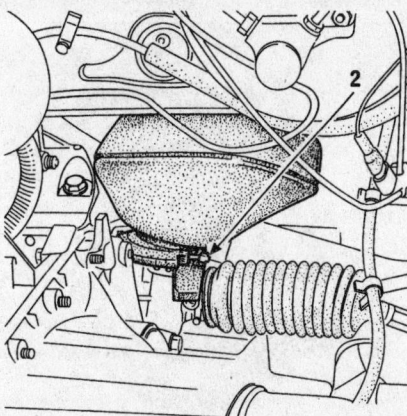

21.3a Cut the retaining clip (2), and fold back the rubber boot . . .

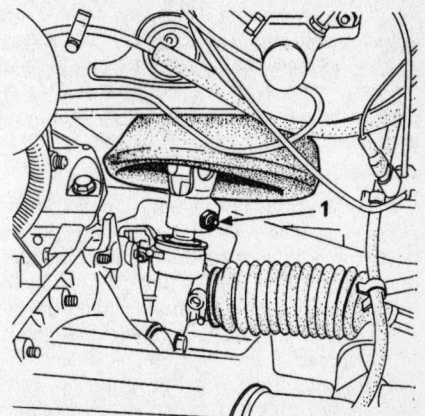

21.3b . . . for access to the universal joint clamp bolt (1) - manual steering gear

10

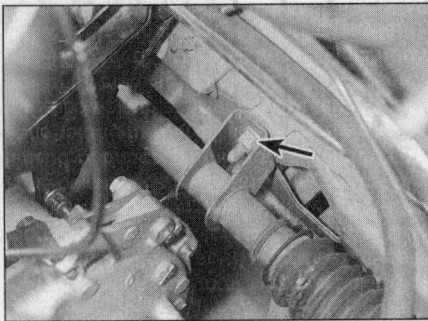

21.5 Manual steering gear mounting nut (arrowed)

4 Mark the relationship between the intermediate shaft universal joint and the steering gear drive pinion, using a hammer and punch, white paint or similar. Remove the nut and clamp bolt securing the joint to the pinion.

5 Remove the two nuts and bolts securing the steering gear assembly to the rear of the subframe. Release the steering gear pinion from the universal joint, and manoeuvre the assembly sideways out of position **(see illustration)**.

Overhaul

General

6 Renewal procedures for the gaiters, the track rod end balljoints and the track rods (complete with inner balljoints) are given in Sections 20, 26 and 27 respectively.

7 Examine the steering gear assembly for signs of wear or damage. Check that the rack moves freely over the full length of its travel, with no signs of roughness or excessive free play between the steering gear pinion and rack. Internal wear or damage can only be cured by renewing the steering gear assembly, but note the points in the following paragraphs.

Thrust plunger adjustment

8 If there is excessive free play of the rack in the steering gear housing, accompanied by a knocking noise, it may be possible to correct this by adjusting the rack thrust plunger. Relieve the staking on the plunger adjusting nut. Using a 10 mm Allen key, tighten the adjusting nut until the free play disappears (but by no more than three flats). Check that the rack still moves freely over its full travel, then secure the adjusting nut by staking it **(see illustration)**.

Anti-noise bush

9 If a grating noise has been noticed from the steering assembly whilst the steering wheel is being turned, this is probably due to the anti-noise bush being dry. To lubricate this bush, first obtain a sachet of the specified grease (Molykote BR2) and a steering gear gaiter retaining clip, from your Renault dealer. Cut the clip securing the gaiter to the opposite end of the steering gear from the pinion housing (ie the left-hand end on right-hand drive models, right-hand end on left-hand drive models). Peel the gaiter back from the

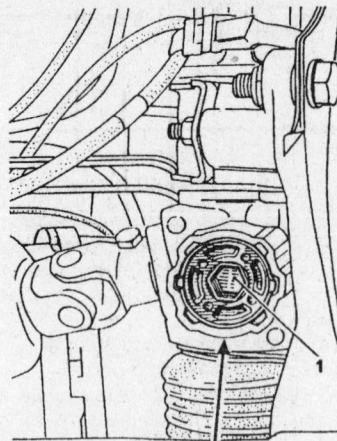

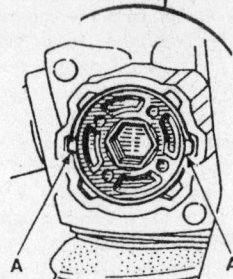

21.8 Manual steering rack thrust plunger adjustment

1 Adjusting nut   A Staking points

housing. Move the steering rack so that its exposed end is fully extended, then smear the grease over the steering rack surface. Refit the gaiter to the housing, and secure it in position with the new retaining clip.

10 The anti-noise bush can be renewed if necessary. After removing the track rod on the side concerned, prise the old bush out using a screwdriver. Fit the new bush, making sure that its lugs engage in the slots in the rack housing **(see illustration)**. Lubricate the bush as described previously.

Refitting

11 Manoeuvre the steering gear assembly

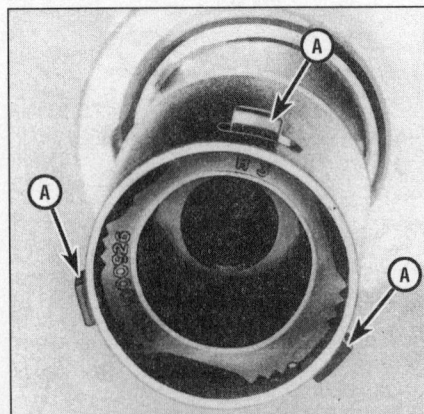

21.10 Manual steering rack anti-noise bush. Lugs (A) must engage in slots

into position. Engage the universal joint with the steering gear pinion splines, aligning the marks made prior to removal.

12 Insert the steering gear mounting bolts from the rear of the subframe. Refit the nuts and tighten them to the specified torque.

13 Refit the universal joint clamp bolt and nut, and tighten to the specified torque. Relocate the rubber boot on the steering gear, and secure it in position with a new cable tie.

14 Reconnect the track rod balljoints to the stub axle carriers, and tighten their retaining nuts to the specified torque.

15 Refit the roadwheels, lower the vehicle to the ground and tighten the wheel bolts to the specified torque.

16 Check the front wheel toe setting as described in Section 28.

22 Steering gear (power-assisted steering) - removal, overhaul and refitting

Removal

1 Apply the handbrake, then jack up the front of the vehicle and support it securely on axle stands (see *"Jacking, towing and wheel changing"*). Remove both front roadwheels.

2 Working on both sides of the vehicle, remove the nuts securing the track rod end balljoints to the stub axle carriers. Release the balljoint tapered shanks using a universal balljoint separator.

3 Mark the relationship between the intermediate shaft universal joint and the steering gear drive pinion, using a hammer and punch, white paint or similar. Remove the nut and clamp bolt securing the joint to the pinion.

4 Using brake hose clamps, clamp both the supply and return hoses near the fluid reservoir. This will prevent unnecessary loss of fluid during subsequent operations.

5 Unscrew the union nuts for the hydraulic fluid supply and return lines at the steering gear. Mark the pipe unions to ensure that they are correctly positioned on reassembly. Also unbolt the fluid line mounting brackets. Be prepared for some loss of fluid by placing a suitable container beneath the line unions. Plug the pipe ends and the steering gear orifices, to prevent dirt ingress and excessive fluid leakage. The spilt fluid must be disposed of.

6 Loosen the clips, then disconnect the short length of hose from the low pressure return line. Completely remove the low pressure line.

7 Where necessary, for improved access, remove the exhaust downpipe with reference to Chapter 4.

8 With the container in place beneath the steering gear, unscrew the union nuts connecting the secondary pipes to the rack and pinion housing. To prevent dirt and dust entering the hydraulic circuit, fit plugs to the apertures in the steering gear and in the ends of the pipes.

22.10 Power-assisted steering gear components

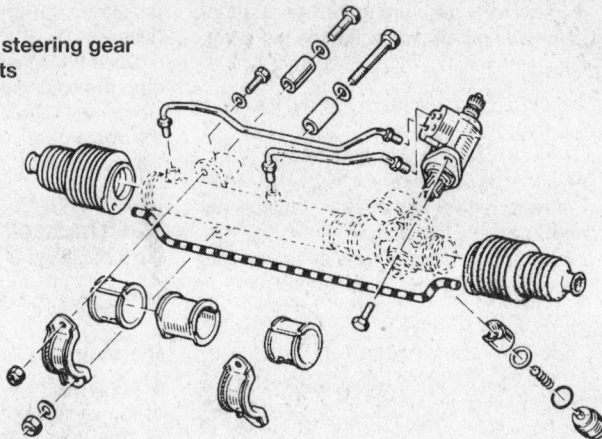

23.3 Clamp the power steering fluid supply and return hoses

9 Unscrew and remove the mounting bolts then release the steering gear pinion from the universal joint, and manoeuvre the steering gear sideways out of position.

Overhaul

10 Examine the steering gear for signs of wear or damage **(see illustration)**. Check that the rack moves freely over the full length of its travel, with no signs of roughness or excessive free play between the pinion and rack. The steering gear must be renewed as an assembly if internal wear or damage is present. Track rod, track rod balljoint and steering gear gaiter renewal procedures are given in Sections 27, 26 and 20 respectively. Note that it is also possible to renew the pinion housing assembly, but it is recommended that this task be entrusted to a Renault dealer.

11 Inspect the steering gear fluid unions for signs of leakage.

12 Examine the steering gear mounting rubbers for signs of damage and deterioration; renew as necessary.

Refitting

13 Manoeuvre the steering gear assembly into position. Aligning the marks made prior to removal, engage the universal joint with the

23.8a Power steering pump bracket securing bolts (B) - models without air conditioning

steering gear pinion splines.

14 Locate the mounting brackets and clamps on the steering gear mounting rubbers, then insert the four steering gear mounting bolts from the rear of the subframe. Refit the nuts and tighten them to the specified torque.

15 Refit the universal joint clamp bolt and nut, and tighten to the specified torque.

16 Remove the plugs from the secondary hydraulic fluid pipes and the rack and pinion housing and wipe the unions clean. Reconnect the pipes to the steering gear, and tighten the union nuts.

17 Where applicable, refit the exhaust downpipe as described in Chapter 4.

18 Reconnect the low pressure fluid return line, and secure with the clips.

19 Wipe clean the fluid supply and return pipe unions, then reconnect them to their respective positions on the steering gear.

23.8b Remove the securing bolts . . .

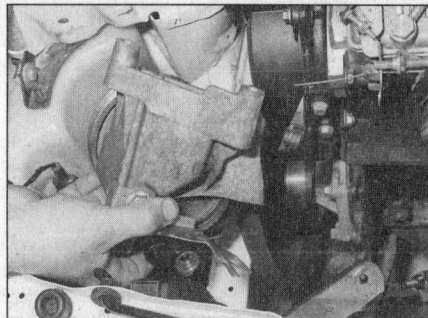

23.8c . . . and remove the bracket and pump assembly

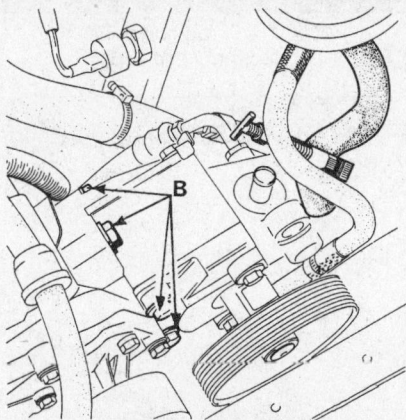

Tighten the union nuts. Refit the fluid line mounting brackets.

20 Reconnect the track rod balljoints to the stub axle carriers. Tighten their retaining nuts to the specified torque.

21 Refit the roadwheels, lower the vehicle to the ground and tighten the wheel bolts to the specified torque.

22 Remove the hose clamps from the reservoir hoses. Top-up the reservoir and bleed the power steering hydraulic system as described in Section 25.

23 On completion, check the front wheel toe setting as described in Section 28.

23 Mechanical power steering pump - removal and refitting

Note: *Due to changes in production procedures, certain models may be fitted with pump mounting arrangements which differ in detail from those described in this Section. Where this is the case, make comprehensive notes during removal, to ensure correct refitting.*

Models without air conditioning

Removal

1 Remove the auxiliary drivebelt, as described in Chapter 1.

2 Remove the alternator, as described in Chapter 5.

3 Using brake hose clamps, clamp both the supply and return hoses leading from the fluid reservoir **(see illustration)**. This will prevent unnecessary loss of fluid during subsequent operations. Also position a suitable container beneath the pump to catch spilled fluid.

4 Where applicable, remove the drivebelt tensioner support bracket.

5 Where applicable, disconnect the wiring plug from the fluid pressure switch, then unbolt the high pressure line support bracket.

6 Disconnect the supply hose from the pump. Be prepared for fluid spillage.

7 Unscrew the union nut and disconnect the high pressure line from the pump. Recover the sealing washer.

8 Unscrew the four bolts securing the pump bracket to the engine, then remove the bracket and pump assembly **(see illustrations)**.

10

9 To remove the pulley, or separate the pump from the bracket, proceed as follows.
10 Measure the dimension from the end of the shaft to the pulley to ensure correct refitting, then use a puller or press to remove the pulley from the shaft.
11 Unbolt the bracket from the pump.

Refitting

12 Refitting is a reversal of removal, bearing in mind the following points.
a) *Ensure that the pump bracket has been refitted before refitting the pulley. Fit the pulley in the position noted before removal.*
b) *Use a new sealing O-ring when reconnecting the high pressure fluid line.*
c) *Refit and tension the auxiliary drivebelt as described in Chapter 1.*
d) *On completion, top up and bleed the fluid circuit, as described in Section 25.*

Models with air conditioning

Note: *Refer to the illustrations provided in Chapter 3, Section 21 for clarification.*

Removal

13 Remove the auxiliary drivebelt, as described in Chapter 1.
14 Remove the alternator, as described in Chapter 5.
15 Unscrew the securing bolts, and remove the power steering pump pulley from the pump drive flange. Note that it will be necessary to counterhold the pulley (eg, using an old drivebelt) in order to loosen the bolts.
16 Remove the securing bolts, and withdraw the auxiliary drivebelt guide roller/bracket assembly.
17 Remove the two upper bolts securing the air conditioning compressor to the alternator mounting bracket.
18 Apply the handbrake, then jack up the front of the vehicle and support securely on axle stands (see *"Jacking, towing and wheel changing"*).
19 Remove the engine undershield, where applicable.
20 Remove the right-hand front roadwheel and the and the wheel arch liner.
21 Loosen the lower air conditioning compressor mounting nuts and bolts, then pivot the compressor downwards to enable the alternator mounting bracket to be removed from above.
22 Using brake hose clamps, clamp both the supply and return hoses leading from the fluid reservoir. This will prevent unnecessary loss of fluid during subsequent operations. Also position a suitable container beneath the pump to catch spilled fluid.
23 Unbolt the fluid pipe securing bracket.
24 Unbolt and remove the rear power steering pump mounting bracket.
25 Disconnect the supply hose from the pump. Be prepared for fluid spillage.
26 Unscrew the union nut and disconnect the high pressure line from the pump. Recover the sealing washer.

27 Remove the remaining power steering pump mounting bolt, and withdraw the pump.

Refitting

28 Refitting is a reversal of removal, bearing in mind the following points.
a) *Use a new sealing washer when reconnecting the high pressure fluid line.*
b) *Refit and tension the auxiliary drivebelt as described in Chapter 1.*
c) *On completion, top up and bleed the fluid circuit, as described in Section 25.*

24 Electric power steering pump - general information, removal and refitting

General information

1 On Turbo models equipped with air conditioning, an electric power steering pump is used. This is because there is not sufficient space in the engine compartment to mount a conventional belt-driven pump; the air conditioning compressor is situated where the power steering pump would normally be.
2 Operation of the system is complex. If any fault develops, the vehicle should be taken to a Renault dealer for the fault to be diagnosed.

Removal and refitting

3 At the time of writing, no information was available for the removal and refitting of the electric power steering pump.

25 Power steering system - bleeding

1 This procedure will only be necessary when any part of the hydraulic system has been disconnected, or if air has entered because of leakage.
2 Remove the fluid reservoir filler cap, and top-up the fluid level to the maximum mark, using only the specified fluid. Refer to Chapter 1 *"Lubricants, fluids and capacities"* for fluid specifications and for details of the different types of fluid reservoir markings.
3 With the engine stopped, slowly move the steering from lock-to-lock several times to expel trapped air, then top-up the level in the fluid reservoir. Repeat this procedure until the fluid level in the reservoir does not drop any further.
4 Start the engine. Slowly move the steering from lock-to-lock several times to expel any air remaining in the system. Repeat this procedure until bubbles cease to appear in the fluid reservoir.
5 If, when turning the steering, an abnormal noise is heard from the fluid pipes, it indicates that there is still air in the system. Check this by turning the wheels to the straight-ahead position and switching off the engine. If the fluid level in the reservoir rises, air is still

present in the system, and further bleeding is necessary.
6 Once all traces of air have been removed, stop the engine and allow the system to cool. Once cool, check that the fluid level is up to the maximum mark on the power steering fluid reservoir; top-up if necessary.

26 Track rod end balljoint - removal and refitting

Removal

1 Apply the handbrake, then jack up the front of the vehicle and support it securely on axle stands (see *"Jacking, towing and wheel changing"*). Remove the appropriate front roadwheel.
2 If the balljoint is to be re-used, use a straight-edge and a scriber, or similar, to mark its relationship to the track rod.
3 Holding the balljoint, unscrew its locknut by one quarter of a turn **(see illustration)**. Do not move the locknut from this position, as it will serve as a reference mark on refitting.
4 Remove the nut securing the track rod balljoint to the stub axle carrier. Release the balljoint tapered shank using a universal balljoint separator. If the balljoint is to be re-used, protect the threaded end of the shank by screwing the nut back on a few turns before using the separator **(see illustration)**.
5 Counting the **exact** number of turns

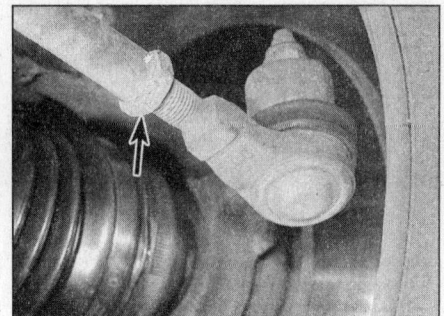

26.3 Track rod end balljoint locknut (arrowed)

26.4 Releasing the track rod end balljoint tapered shank from the stub axle carrier using a balljoint separator tool

necessary to do so, unscrew the balljoint from the track rod end.

6 Count the number of exposed threads between the end of the balljoint and the locknut, and record this figure. If a new balljoint is to be fitted, unscrew the locknut from the old balljoint.

7 Carefully clean the balljoint and the threads. Renew the balljoint if its movement is sloppy or if it is too stiff, if it is excessively worn, or if it is damaged in any way. Carefully check the shank taper and threads. If the balljoint gaiter is damaged, the complete balljoint must be renewed; it is not possible to obtain the gaiter separately.

Refitting

8 If applicable, screw the locknut onto the new balljoint, and position it so that the same number of exposed threads are visible as were noted prior to removal.

9 Screw the balljoint into the track rod by the number of turns noted on removal. This should bring the balljoint locknut to within a quarter of a turn of the end of the track rod, with the alignment marks that were made on removal (if applicable) lined up.

10 Refit the balljoint shank to the stub axle carrier, and tighten the retaining nut to the specified torque. If difficulty is experienced due to the balljoint shank rotating, jam it by exerting pressure on the underside of the balljoint, using a tyre lever or a jack.

11 Refit the roadwheel, lower the vehicle to the ground and tighten the roadwheel bolts to the specified torque.

12 Check the front wheel toe setting as described in Section 28, then tighten the balljoint locknut.

27 Track rod and inner balljoint - removal and refitting

Removal

1 Remove the track rod end balljoint as described in Section 26.

2 Cut the retaining clips, and slide the steering gear gaiter off the track rod.

3 Using a suitable pair of grips, unscrew the track rod inner balljoint from the steering rack end. Prevent the steering rack from turning by holding the balljoint lockwasher with a second pair of grips. Take care not to mark the surfaces of the rack and balljoint.

4 Remove the track rod/inner balljoint assembly and discard the lockwasher; a new one must be used on refitting.

5 Examine the inner balljoint for signs of slackness or tight spots. Check that the track rod itself is straight and free from damage. If necessary, renew the track rod/inner balljoint; the new one will be supplied complete with a new lockwasher and a new end balljoint. It is also recommended that the steering gear gaiter is renewed.

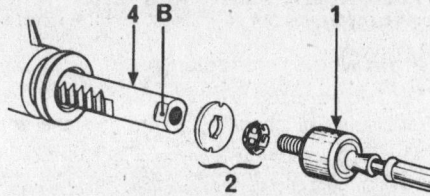

27.7 Track rod inner balljoint components
1 Inner balljoint
2 Lockwasher assembly
4 Steering rack
B Lockwasher locating flats

Refitting

6 If a new track rod is being installed, remove the outer balljoint from the track rod end.

7 Locate the new lockwasher assembly on the end of the steering rack, ensuring that its locating tabs are correctly located with the flats on the rack end **(see illustration)**.

8 Apply a few drops of locking fluid to the inner balljoint threads. Screw the balljoint into the steering rack and tighten it securely. Again, take care not to damage or mark the balljoint or steering rack.

9 Slide the new gaiter onto the track rod end, and locate it on the steering gear housing. Turn the steering from lock-to-lock to check that the gaiter is correctly positioned, then secure it with new retaining clips.

10 Refit the track rod end balljoint as described in Section 26.

28 Wheel alignment and steering angles

General information

1 A vehicle's steering and suspension geometry is defined in four basic settings **(see illustration)**. For this purpose, all angles are expressed in degrees (toe settings are also expressed as a measurement of length). The steering axis is defined as an imaginary line drawn through the axis of the suspension strut, extended where necessary to contact the ground.

2 Camber is the angle between each roadwheel and a vertical line drawn through its centre and tyre contact patch, when viewed from the front or rear of the car. Positive camber is when the roadwheels are tilted outwards from the vertical at the top; negative camber is when they are tilted inwards.

3 Camber is not adjustable. Values are given for reference only. Checking is possible using a camber checking gauge, but if the figure obtained is significantly different from that specified, the vehicle must be taken for careful checking by a professional. Wrong camber settings can only be caused by wear or damage to the body or suspension components.

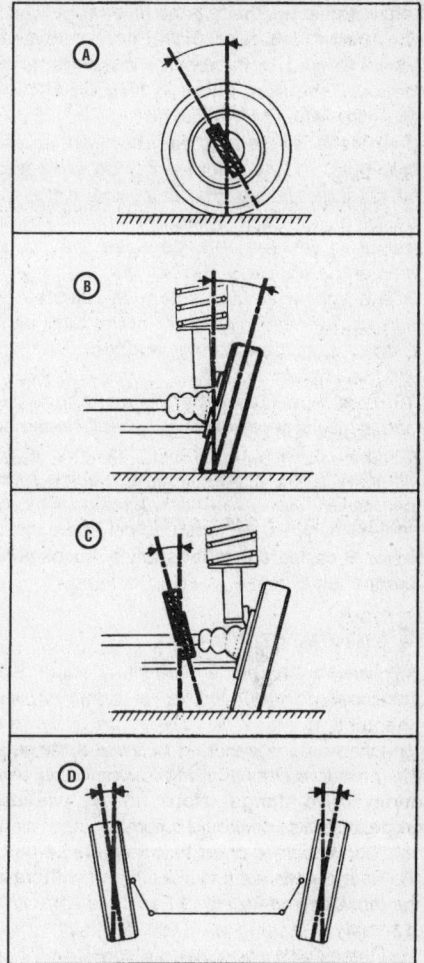

28.1 Wheel alignment and steering angles
A Castor
B Camber
C Steering axis inclination
D Toe

4 Castor is the angle between the steering axis and a vertical line drawn through each roadwheel's centre and tyre contact patch, when viewed from the side of the car. Positive castor is when the steering axis is tilted so that it contacts the ground ahead of the vertical; negative castor is when it contacts the ground behind the vertical.

5 Castor is not adjustable. As with camber, values are given for reference only; deviation can only be due to wear or damage.

6 Steering axis inclination/SAI - also known as **kingpin inclination/KPI** - is the angle between the steering axis and a vertical line drawn through each roadwheel's centre and tyre contact patch, when viewed from the front or rear of the car.

7 SAI/KPI is not adjustable, and is given for reference only.

8 Toe is a measurement of the amount by which the distance between the front inside edges of the roadwheels differs from that

10

between the rear inside edges, when measured at hub height (the amount by which the roadwheels point inwards or outwards when viewed from above). If the distance between the front edges is less than at the rear, the wheels are said to "toe-in". If it is greater than at the rear, the wheels are said to "toe-out". The value for toe can be expressed as an angle (taking the centre-line of the car as zero), or as a measurement of length (taking measurements between the inside rims of the wheels at hub height).

9 The front wheel toe setting is adjusted by screwing the balljoints in or out of their track rods to alter the effective length of the track rod assemblies.

10 Rear wheel toe setting is not adjustable, and is given for reference only. While it can be checked, if the figure obtained is significantly different from that specified, the vehicle must be taken for careful checking by a professional, as the fault can only be caused by wear or damage to the body or suspension components.

Checking - general

11 Due to the special measuring equipment necessary to check the wheel alignment, and the skill required to use it properly, the checking and adjustment of these settings is best left to a Renault dealer or similar expert. Most tyre-fitting shops now possess sophisticated checking equipment.

12 For accurate checking, the vehicle must be at the kerb weight specified in *"General dimensions and weights"*.

13 Before starting work, check first that the tyre sizes and types are as specified, then check tyre pressures and tread wear. Also check roadwheel run-out, the condition of the hub bearings, the steering wheel free play and the condition of the front suspension components (Chapter 1). Correct any faults found.

14 Park the vehicle on level ground, with the front roadwheels in the straight-ahead position. Rock the rear and front ends to settle the suspension. Release the handbrake and roll the vehicle backwards approximately 1 metre (3 feet), then forwards again, to relieve any stresses in the steering and suspension components.

Toe setting - checking and adjusting

Front wheels - checking

15 Two methods are available to the home mechanic for checking the front wheel toe setting. One method is to use a gauge to measure the distance between the front and rear inside edges of the roadwheels. The other method is to use a scuff plate, in which each front wheel is rolled across a movable plate which records any deviation, or scuff, of the tyre from the straight-ahead position as it moves across the plate. Such gauges are available in relatively inexpensive form from accessory outlets. It is up to the owner to decide whether the expense is justified, in view of the small amount of use such equipment would normally receive.

16 Prepare the vehicle as described in paragraphs 12 to 14 above.

17 If the measurement procedure is being used, carefully measure the distance between the front edges of the roadwheel rims and the rear edges of the rims. Subtract the rear measurement from the front measurement, and check that the result is within the specified range. If not, adjust the toe setting as described in paragraph 19.

18 If scuff plates are to be used, roll the vehicle backwards, check that the roadwheels are in the straight-ahead position, then roll it across the scuff plates so that each front roadwheel passes squarely over the centre of its respective plate. Note the angle recorded by the scuff plates. To ensure accuracy, repeat the check three times, and take the average of the three readings. If the roadwheels are running parallel, there will of course be no angle recorded; if a deviation value is shown on the scuff plates, compare the reading obtained for each wheel with that specified. If the value recorded is outside the specified tolerance, the toe setting is incorrect, and must be adjusted as follows.

Front wheels - adjusting

19 Apply the handbrake, then jack up the front of the vehicle and support it securely on axle stands (see *"Jacking, towing and wheel changing"*). Turn the steering wheel onto full-left lock, and record the number of exposed threads on the right-hand track rod end. Now turn the steering onto full-right lock, and record the number of threads on the left-hand side. If there are the same number of threads visible on both sides, then subsequent adjustment should be made equally on both sides. If there are more threads visible on one side than the other, it will be necessary to compensate for this during adjustment. **Note:** *It is important to ensure that, after adjustment, the same number of threads are visible on each track rod end.*

20 First clean the track rod threads; if they are corroded, apply penetrating fluid before starting adjustment. Release the rubber gaiter outboard clips, then peel back the gaiters and apply a smear of grease, so that both gaiters are free and will not be twisted or strained as their respective track rods are rotated.

21 Use a straight-edge and a scriber or similar to mark the relationship of each track rod to its balljoint. Holding each track rod in turn, unscrew its locknut fully.

22 Alter the length of the track rods, bearing in mind the note in paragraph 19, by screwing them into or out of the balljoints. Rotate the track rod using an open-ended spanner fitted to the flats provided. Shortening the track rods (screwing them onto their balljoints) will reduce toe-in and increase toe-out.

23 When the setting is correct, hold the track rods and securely tighten the balljoint locknuts. Check that the balljoints are seated correctly in their sockets, and count the exposed threads. If the number of threads exposed is not the same on both sides, then the adjustment has not been made equally, and problems will be encountered with tyre scrubbing in turns; also, the steering wheel spokes will no longer be horizontal when the wheels are in the straight-ahead position.

24 When the track rod lengths are the same, lower the vehicle to the ground and re-check the toe setting; readjust if necessary. When the setting is correct, tighten the track rod balljoint locknuts. Ensure that the rubber gaiters are seated correctly and are not twisted or strained, then secure them in position with new retaining clips.

Rear wheel toe setting

25 The procedure for checking the rear toe setting is same as described for the front in paragraph 17. However, no adjustment is possible.

Chapter 11
Bodywork and fittings

Contents

Degrees of difficulty

Easy, suitable for novice with little experience	**Fairly easy,** suitable for beginner with some experience	**Fairly difficult,** suitable for competent DIY mechanic	**Difficult,** suitable for experienced DIY mechanic	**Very difficult,** suitable for expert DIY or professional

Specifications

Torque wrench setting	Nm	lbf ft
Seat belt anchorages	20	15

1 General information

The bodyshell and underframe are of all-steel welded construction, incorporating progressive crumple zones at the front and rear and a rigid centre safety cell. The assembly and welding of the main body unit is completed by computer-controlled robots, and is checked for dimensional accuracy using computer and laser technology. All major body panels are protected with an electrolytic zinc coating and are given a zinc phosphate bath.

The front and rear bumpers are of collapsible cellular construction to minimise minor accident damage, and the front wings are bolted in position to facilitate accident damage repair. The plastic side panels are also designed to absorb light impact without damage.

4-door Saloon, 3- and 5-door Hatchback, and 3-door Van body styles are available.

In the Spring of 1992, the "Phase 2" models were introduced, incorporating subtle styling changes to the front grille and the light clusters.

2 Maintenance - bodywork and underframe

The general condition of a vehicle's bodywork is the one thing that significantly affects its value. Maintenance is easy, but needs to be regular. Neglect, particularly after minor damage, can lead quickly to further deterioration and costly repair bills. It is important also to keep watch on those parts of the vehicle not immediately visible, for instance the underside, inside all the wheel arches, and the lower part of the engine compartment.

The basic maintenance routine for the bodywork is washing - preferably with a lot of water, from a hose. This will remove all the loose solids which may have stuck to the vehicle. It is important to flush these off in such a way as to prevent grit from scratching the finish. The wheel arches and underframe need washing in the same way, to remove any accumulated mud, which will retain moisture and tend to encourage rust. Paradoxically enough, the best time to clean the underframe and wheel arches is in wet weather, when the mud is thoroughly wet and soft. In very wet weather, the underframe is usually cleaned of large accumulations automatically, and this is a good time for inspection.

Periodically, except on vehicles with a wax-based underbody protective coating, it is a good idea to have the whole of the underframe of the vehicle steam-cleaned, engine compartment included, so that a thorough inspection can be carried out to see what minor repairs and renovations are necessary. Steam-cleaning is available at

11

many garages, and is necessary for the removal of the accumulation of oily grime, which sometimes is allowed to become thick in certain areas. If steam-cleaning facilities are not available, there are some excellent grease solvents available which can be brush-applied; the dirt can then be simply hosed off. Note that these methods should not be used on vehicles with wax-based underbody protective coating, or the coating will be removed. Such vehicles should be inspected annually, preferably just prior to Winter, when the underbody should be washed down, and any damage to the wax coating repaired. Ideally, a completely fresh coat should be applied. It would also be worth considering the use of such wax-based protection for injection into door panels, sills, box sections, etc, as an additional safeguard against rust damage, where such protection is not provided by the vehicle manufacturer.

After washing paintwork, wipe off with a chamois leather to give an unspotted clear finish. A coat of clear protective wax polish will give added protection against chemical pollutants in the air. If the paintwork sheen has dulled or oxidised, use a cleaner/polisher combination to restore the brilliance of the shine. This requires a little effort, but such dulling is usually caused because regular washing has been neglected. Care needs to be taken with metallic paintwork, as special non-abrasive cleaner/polisher is required to avoid damage to the finish. Always check that the door and ventilator opening drain holes and pipes are completely clear, so that water can be drained out. Brightwork should be treated in the same way as paintwork. Windscreens and windows can be kept clear of the smeary film which often appears, by the use of proprietary glass cleaner. Never use any form of wax or other body or chromium polish on glass.

3 Maintenance - upholstery and carpets

Mats and carpets should be brushed or vacuum-cleaned regularly, to keep them free of grit. If they are badly stained, remove them from the vehicle for scrubbing or sponging, and make quite sure they are dry before refitting. Seats and interior trim panels can be kept clean by wiping with a damp cloth. If they do become stained (which can be more apparent on light-coloured upholstery), use a little liquid detergent and a soft nail brush to scour the grime out of the grain of the material. Do not forget to keep the headlining clean in the same way as the upholstery. When using liquid cleaners inside the vehicle, do not over-wet the surfaces being cleaned. Excessive damp could get into the seams and padded interior, causing stains, offensive odours or even rot.

HAYNES HINT *If the inside of the vehicle gets wet accidentally, it is worthwhile taking some trouble to dry it out properly, particularly where carpets are involved. Do not leave oil or electric heaters inside the vehicle for this purpose.*

4 Minor body damage - repair

Note: *For more detailed information about bodywork repair, Haynes Publishing produce a book by Lindsay Porter called "The Car Bodywork Repair Manual". This incorporates information on such aspects as rust treatment, painting and glass-fibre repairs, as well as details on more ambitious repairs involving welding and panel beating.*

Repairs of minor scratches in bodywork

If the scratch is very superficial, and does not penetrate to the metal of the bodywork, repair is very simple. Lightly rub the area of the scratch with a paintwork renovator, or a very fine cutting paste, to remove loose paint from the scratch, and to clear the surrounding bodywork of wax polish. Rinse the area with clean water.

Apply touch-up paint to the scratch using a fine paint brush; continue to apply fine layers of paint until the surface of the paint in the scratch is level with the surrounding paintwork. Allow the new paint at least two weeks to harden, then blend it into the surrounding paintwork by rubbing the scratch area with a paintwork renovator or a very fine cutting paste. Finally, apply wax polish.

Where the scratch has penetrated right through to the metal of the bodywork, causing the metal to rust, a different repair technique is required. Remove any loose rust from the bottom of the scratch with a penknife, then apply rust-inhibiting paint to prevent the formation of rust in the future. Using a rubber or nylon applicator, fill the scratch with bodystopper paste. If required, this paste can be mixed with cellulose thinners to provide a very thin paste which is ideal for filling narrow scratches. Before the stopper-paste in the scratch hardens, wrap a piece of smooth cotton rag around the top of a finger. Dip the finger in cellulose thinners, and quickly sweep it across the surface of the stopper-paste in the scratch; this will ensure that the surface of the stopper-paste is slightly hollowed. The scratch can now be painted over as described earlier in this Section.

Repairs of dents in bodywork

When deep denting of the vehicle's bodywork has taken place, the first task is to pull the dent out, until the affected bodywork almost attains its original shape. There is little point in trying to restore the original shape completely, as the metal in the damaged area will have stretched on impact, and cannot be reshaped fully to its original contour. It is better to bring the level of the dent up to a point which is about 3 mm below the level of the surrounding bodywork. In cases where the dent is very shallow anyway, it is not worth trying to pull it out at all. If the underside of the dent is accessible, it can be hammered out gently from behind, using a mallet with a wooden or plastic head. Whilst doing this, hold a suitable block of wood firmly against the outside of the panel, to absorb the impact from the hammer blows and thus prevent a large area of the bodywork from being "belled-out".

Should the dent be in a section of the bodywork which has a double skin, or some other factor making it inaccessible from behind, a different technique is called for. Drill several small holes through the metal inside the area - particularly in the deeper section. Then screw long self-tapping screws into the holes, just sufficiently for them to gain a good purchase in the metal. Now the dent can be pulled out by pulling on the protruding heads of the screws with a pair of pliers.

The next stage of the repair is the removal of the paint from the damaged area, and from an inch or so of the surrounding "sound" bodywork. This is accomplished most easily by using a wire brush or abrasive pad on a power drill, although it can be done just as effectively by hand, using sheets of abrasive paper. To complete the preparation for filling, score the surface of the bare metal with a screwdriver or the tang of a file, or alternatively, drill small holes in the affected area. This will provide a really good "key" for the filler paste.

To complete the repair, see the Section on filling and respraying.

Repairs of rust holes or gashes in bodywork

Remove all paint from the affected area, and from an inch or so of the surrounding "sound" bodywork, using an abrasive pad or a wire brush on a power drill. If these are not available, a few sheets of abrasive paper will do the job most effectively. With the paint removed, you will be able to judge the severity of the corrosion, and therefore decide whether to renew the whole panel (if this is possible) or to repair the affected area. New body panels are not as expensive as most people think, and it is often quicker and more satisfactory to fit a new panel than to attempt to repair large areas of corrosion.

Remove all fittings from the affected area, except those which will act as a guide to the original shape of the damaged bodywork (eg headlight shells etc). Then, using tin snips or a hacksaw blade, remove all loose metal and any other metal badly affected by corrosion. Hammer the edges of the hole inwards, in order to create a slight depression for the filler paste.

Wire-brush the affected area to remove the powdery rust from the
surface of the remaining metal. Paint the affected area with rust-inhibiting paint, if the back of the rusted area is accessible, treat this also.

Before filling can take place, it will be necessary to block the hole in some way. This can be achieved by the use of aluminium or plastic mesh, or aluminium tape.

Aluminium or plastic mesh, or glass-fibre matting, is probably the best material to use for a large hole. Cut a piece to the approximate size and shape of the hole to be filled, then position it in the hole so that its edges are below the level of the surrounding bodywork. It can be retained in position by several blobs of filler paste around its periphery.

Aluminium tape should be used for small or very narrow holes. Pull a piece off the roll, trim it to the approximate size and shape required, then pull off the backing paper (if used) and stick the tape over the hole; it can be overlapped if the thickness of one piece is insufficient. Burnish down the edges of the tape with the handle of a screwdriver or similar, to ensure that the tape is securely attached to the metal underneath.

Bodywork repairs - filling and respraying

Before using this Section, see the Sections on dent, deep scratch, rust holes and gash repairs.

Many types of bodyfiller are available, but generally speaking, those proprietary kits which contain a tin of filler paste and a tube of resin hardener are best for this type of repair. A wide, flexible plastic or nylon applicator will be found invaluable for imparting a smooth and well-contoured finish to the surface of the filler.

Mix up a little filler on a clean piece of card or board - measure the hardener carefully (follow the maker's instructions on the pack), otherwise the filler will set too rapidly or too slowly. Using the applicator, apply the filler paste to the prepared area; draw the applicator across the surface of the filler to achieve the correct contour and to level the surface. As soon as a contour that approximates to the correct one is achieved, stop working the paste - if you carry on too long, the paste will become sticky and begin to "pick-up" on the applicator. Continue to add thin layers of filler paste at 20-minute intervals, until the level of the filler is just proud of the surrounding bodywork.

Once the filler has hardened, the excess can be removed using a metal plane or file. From then on, progressively-finer grades of abrasive paper should be used, starting with a 40-grade production paper, and finishing with a 400-grade wet-and-dry paper. Always wrap the abrasive paper around a flat rubber, cork, or wooden block - otherwise the surface of the filler will not be completely flat. During the smoothing of the filler surface, the wet-and-dry paper should be periodically rinsed in water. This will ensure that a very smooth finish is imparted to the filler at the final stage.

At this stage, the "dent" should be surrounded by a ring of bare metal, which in turn should be encircled by the finely "feathered" edge of the good paintwork. Rinse the repair area with clean water, until all of the dust produced by the rubbing-down operation has gone.

Spray the whole area with a light coat of primer - this will show up any imperfections in the surface of the filler. Repair these imperfections with fresh filler paste or bodystopper, and once more smooth the surface with abrasive paper. Repeat this spray-and-repair procedure until you are satisfied that the surface of the filler, and the feathered edge of the paintwork, are perfect. Clean the repair area with clean water, and allow to dry fully.

> **HAYNES HiNT** *If bodystopper is used, it can be mixed with cellulose thinners, to form a really thin paste which is ideal for filling small holes*

The repair area is now ready for final spraying. Paint spraying must be carried out in a warm, dry, windless and dust-free atmosphere. This condition can be created artificially if you have access to a large indoor working area, but if you are forced to work in the open, you will have to pick your day very carefully. If you are working indoors, dousing the floor in the work area with water will help to settle the dust which would otherwise be in the atmosphere. If the repair area is confined to one body panel, mask off the surrounding panels; this will help to minimise the effects of a slight mis-match in paint colours. Bodywork fittings (eg chrome strips, door handles etc) will also need to be masked off. Use genuine masking tape, and several thicknesses of newspaper, for the masking operations.

Before commencing to spray, agitate the aerosol can thoroughly, then spray a test area (an old tin, or similar) until the technique is mastered. Cover the repair area with a thick coat of primer; the thickness should be built up using several thin layers of paint, rather than one thick one. Using 400-grade wet-and-dry paper, rub down the surface of the primer until it is really smooth. While doing this, the work area should be thoroughly doused with water, and the wet-and-dry paper periodically rinsed in water. Allow to dry before spraying on more paint.

Spray on the top coat, again building up the thickness by using several thin layers of paint. Start spraying at one edge of the repair area, and then, using a side-to-side motion, work until the whole repair area and about 2 inches of the surrounding original paintwork is covered. Remove all masking material 10 to 15 minutes after spraying on the final coat of paint.

Allow the new paint at least two weeks to harden, then, using a paintwork renovator, or a very fine cutting paste, blend the edges of the paint into the existing paintwork. Finally, apply wax polish.

Plastic components

With the use of more and more plastic body components by the vehicle manufacturers (eg bumpers. spoilers, and in some cases major body panels), rectification of more serious damage to such items has become a matter of either entrusting repair work to a specialist in this field, or renewing complete components. Repair of such damage by the DIY owner is not really feasible, owing to the cost of the equipment and materials required for effecting such repairs. The basic technique involves making a groove along the line of the crack in the plastic, using a rotary burr in a power drill. The damaged part is then welded back together, using a hot-air gun to heat up and fuse a plastic filler rod into the groove. Any excess plastic is then removed, and the area rubbed down to a smooth finish. It is important that a filler rod of the correct plastic is used, as body components can be made of a variety of different types (eg polycarbonate, ABS, polypropylene).

Damage of a less serious nature (abrasions, minor cracks etc) can be repaired by the DIY owner using a two-part epoxy filler repair material. Once mixed in equal proportions, this is used in similar fashion to the bodywork filler used on metal panels. The filler is usually cured in twenty to thirty minutes, ready for sanding and painting.

If the owner is renewing a complete component himself, or if he has repaired it with epoxy filler, he will be left with the problem of finding a suitable paint for finishing which is compatible with the type of plastic used. At one time, the use of a universal paint was not possible, owing to the complex range of plastics encountered in body component applications. Standard paints, generally speaking, will not bond to plastic or rubber satisfactorily. However, it is now possible to obtain a plastic body parts finishing kit which consists of a pre-primer treatment, a primer and coloured top coat. Full instructions are normally supplied with a kit, but basically, the method of use is to first apply the pre-primer to the component concerned, and allow it to dry for up to 30 minutes. Then the primer is applied, and left to dry for about an hour before finally applying the special-coloured top coat. The result is a correctly-coloured component, where the paint will flex with the plastic or rubber, a property that standard paint does not normally posses.

11

6.2 Foglight wiring plug (5) and front bumper front mounting bolt (6) (arrowed) - "Phase 1" models

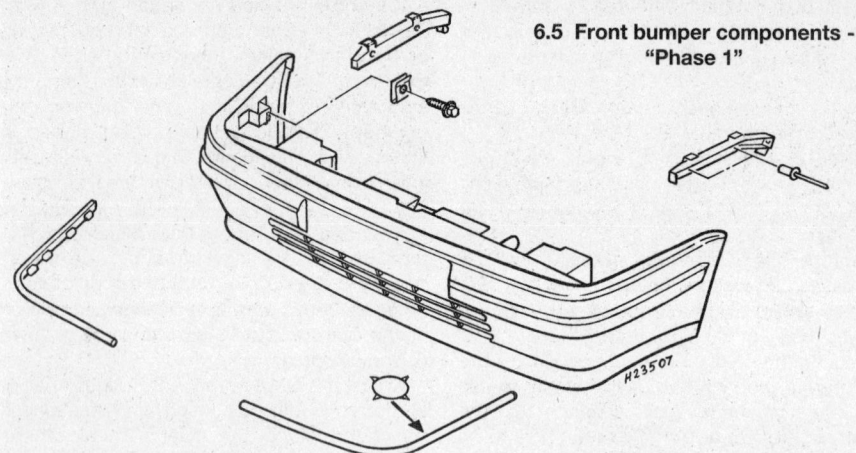

6.5 Front bumper components - "Phase 1"

5 Major body damage - repair

Where serious damage has occurred, or large areas need renewal due to neglect, it means that complete new panels will need welding-in; this is best left to professionals. If the damage is due to impact, it will also be necessary to check the alignment of the bodyshell; this can only be carried out accurately by a Renault dealer using special jigs. If the body is misaligned, it is dangerous, as the vehicle will not handle properly. In addition, uneven stresses will be imposed on the steering, suspension and possibly transmission, causing abnormal wear or complete failure, particularly of items such as the tyres.

6 Front and rear bumpers - removal and refitting

Front bumper - "Phase 1" models

Removal

1 Apply the handbrake, then jack up the front of the vehicle and support it securely on axle stands (see "Jacking, towing and wheel changing").
2 With the bonnet open, unscrew the two front mounting bolts located near the inner side of the headlights (see illustration).
3 Remove the screws (two on each side) securing the sides of the bumper to the wheelarch shields.
4 Unscrew the two bolts securing the bumper to the front subframe.
5 Unscrew the two side mounting bolts (see illustration).
6 Where applicable, disconnect the foglight wiring plug (after disconnecting the battery

negative lead), which is located in front of the radiator (see illustration 6.2).
7 Carefully release the wheel arch shields from the edges of the bumper, and withdraw the bumper from the vehicle.
8 If necessary, unbolt and remove the mounting brackets, and where applicable unbolt the spoiler extension from the bottom of the bumper.

Refitting

9 Refitting is a reversal of removal.

Front bumper - "Phase 2" models

Removal

10 Remove the front grille panels, with reference to Section 24.
11 Where applicable, disconnect the foglight wiring connector(s) (after disconnecting the battery negative lead).
12 Remove the relevant securing screws and clips, and detach the front edges of the wheel arch shields from the bumper.
13 Working in the grille panel aperture, remove the two upper bumper mounting bolts (see illustration).
14 Working in the engine compartment, remove the two side bumper securing screws (one each side), securing the bumper to the wings (see illustration).
15 Working under the front of the vehicle,

6.13 Unscrewing a front bumper upper securing bolt - "Phase 2" model

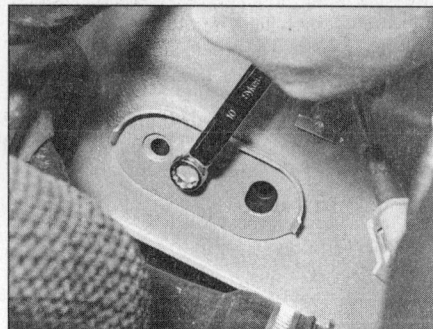

6.14 Unscrewing the front bumper left-hand side securing screw - "Phase 2" model

6.15a Front bumper lower securing bolt (arrowed) - "Phase 2" model

6.15b Front bumper securing rivet (arrowed) - "Phase 2" model

6.18a Withdraw the container carrier . . .

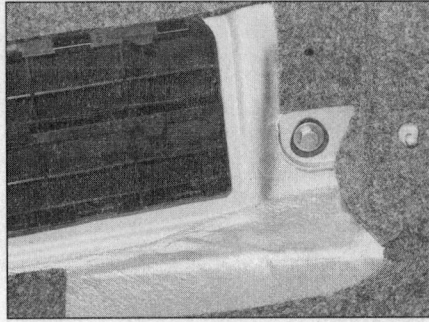
6.18b . . . for access to the rear bumper left-hand side mounting bolt

6.19 Rear bumper centre retaining nut (arrowed)

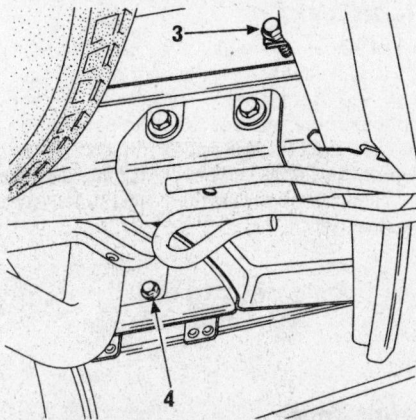
6.22 Rear bumper-to-crossmember bolt (3) and right-hand mounting bolt (4)

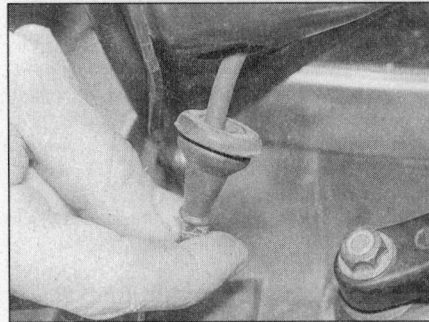
7.2a Prise out the windscreen washer rubber grommet . . .

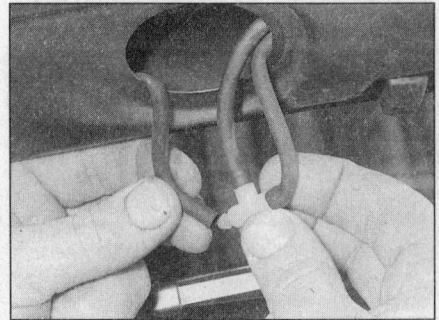
7.2b . . . and disconnect the hose

Refitting

24 Refitting is a reversal of removal.

support the bumper, then remove the two lower bumper mounting bolts, and drill out the centre rivet **(see illustrations)**.
16 Withdraw the bumper from the vehicle.

Refitting

17 Refitting is a reversal of removal, but use a new rivet to secure the lower edge of the bumper to the body.

Rear bumper

Removal

18 Working inside the rear luggage compartment, remove the securing screws, and withdraw the container carrier on the left-hand side for access to the bumper side mounting bolt. Unscrew and remove the bolt **(see illustrations)**.

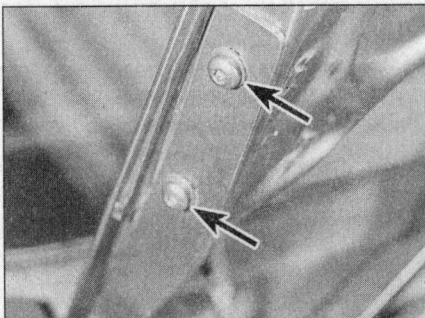
7.3 Bonnet mounting screws (arrowed)

19 For access to the centre bumper retaining nut, prise out the grommet from the centre of the rear luggage compartment panel, or remove the screw and withdraw the lock trim panel, as applicable. Unscrew and remove the centre retaining nut **(see illustration)**.
20 On models with the number plate lights mounted in the bumper, disconnect the battery negative lead, then prise the number plate lights from the bumper, and disconnect the wiring plugs.
21 Chock the front wheels, then jack up the rear of the vehicle and support it securely on axle stands (see *"Jacking, towing and wheel changing"*).
22 Working beneath the vehicle, unscrew the two bolts securing the bumper to the crossmember. Also unscrew the right-hand mounting bolt **(see illustration)**.
23 Remove the screws and/or clips securing the rear wheel arch liners to the bumper, then withdraw the bumper from the vehicle.

7.4 Removing the bonnet

7 Bonnet - removal, refitting and adjustment

Removal

1 Open the bonnet and support it in the open position using the stay.
2 Disconnect the windscreen washer hose by prising out the rubber grommet on the right-hand corner, then pulling the T-connector from the access hole, and disconnecting the right-hand hose **(see illustrations)**.
3 Mark the outline of the hinges with a soft pencil, then loosen the four mounting screws using a Torx key **(see illustration)**.
4 With the help of an assistant, remove the stay, unscrew the four screws and lift the bonnet from the car **(see illustration)**.

Refitting

5 Refitting is a reversal of removal, bearing in mind the following points.
a) *Position the bonnet hinges within the outline marks made during removal, but alter its position as necessary to provide a uniform gap all round.*
b) *Adjust the rear height of the bonnet as necessary by repositioning it on the hinges.*
c) *Adjust the front height if necessary by repositioning the lock with reference to Section 9, then turn the rubber buffers on the engine compartment front cross panel up or down to support the bonnet (see illustration).*

11

7.5 Bonnet front support rubber buffer

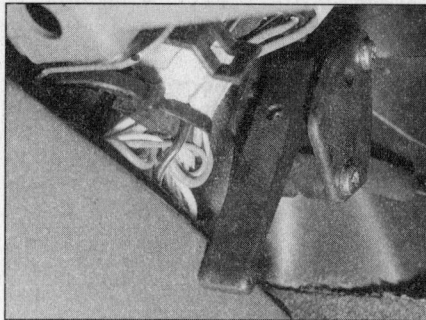

8.6a Bonnet release lever assembly securing bolts - early model

8.6b Removing the bonnet release lever assembly - later model

8 Bonnet release cable - removal and refitting

Removal

1 The bonnet release lever may be located on the driver's or the passenger's side of the vehicle, depending on model.
2 Open the bonnet.
3 On "Phase 2" models, remove the front grille panels, as described in Section 24.
4 Unclip the cable outer from the lock assembly, then manipulate the end of the cable from the lock lever.
5 Working under the facia, if necessary for access, remove the glovebox with reference to Section 31.
6 Remove the bolt(s) securing the release lever assembly to the side of the facia (see illustrations).
7 Note the routing of the cable within the engine compartment, then withdraw the cable through the bulkhead into the vehicle interior.

To aid refitting, a length of string can be tied to the end of the cable before removal. Untie the string from the end of the cable and leave it in position when the cable is removed, then tie the end of the string to the new cable, and use it to pull the cable into position.

Refitting

8 Refitting is a reversal of removal. Ensure the cable is routed as noted during removal.

9 Bonnet lock - removal and refitting

Removal

1 Open the bonnet.
2 On "Phase 2" models, remove the front grille panels, as described in Section 24.
3 Unclip the cable outer from the lock assembly, then manipulate the end of the cable from the lock lever (see illustration).
4 Unscrew the two retaining bolts and remove the lock from the vehicle.

Refitting

5 Refitting is a reversal of removal, but adjust the lock height so that the bonnet line is flush with the front wings and shuts securely without force. If necessary adjust the lock laterally so that the striker enters the lock recess correctly, however it may also be necessary to reposition the striker itself (see illustration).

10 Door inner trim panel - removal and refitting

Front door

Removal

1 Using a screwdriver, prise the plastic insert from the door grip. Unscrew the screws and remove the grip from the inner trim panel (see illustration).

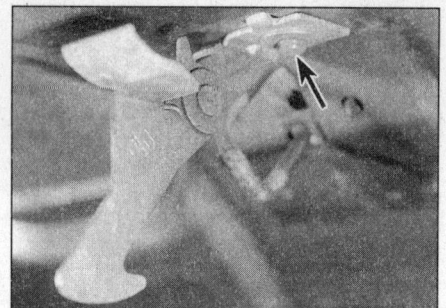

9.5 Bonnet lock striker securing bolt (arrowed)

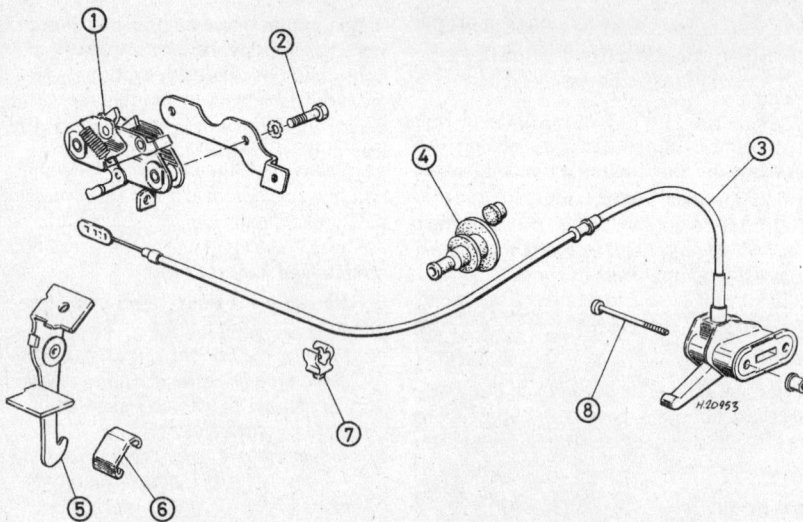

9.3 Bonnet lock and release cable components

1 Lock
2 Lock mounting bolt
3 Cable and handle assembly
4 Grommet
5 Safety catch and striker
6 Guide
7 Clip
8 Handle mounting bolt

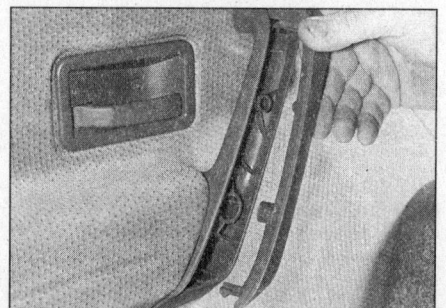

10.1 Removing the plastic insert from the door grip

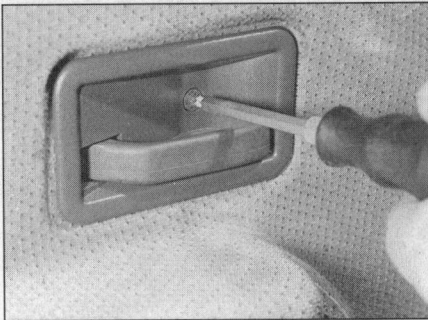

10.2a Remove the screw . . .

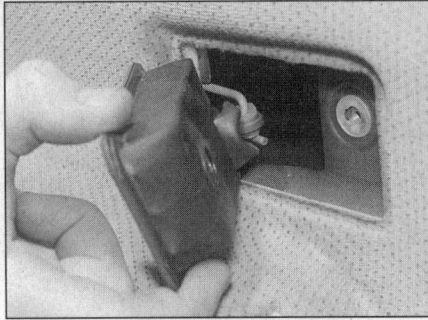

10.2b . . . and remove the interior door handle finger plate

10.3a Removing the loudspeaker cover . . .

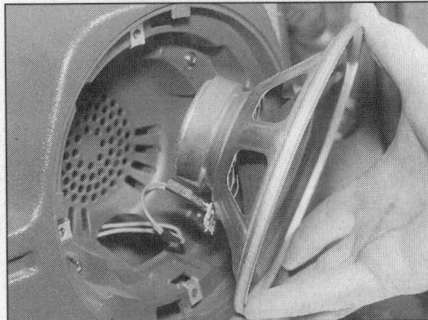

10.3b . . . and loudspeaker

10.4a Remove the front mounting screws (arrowed) . . .

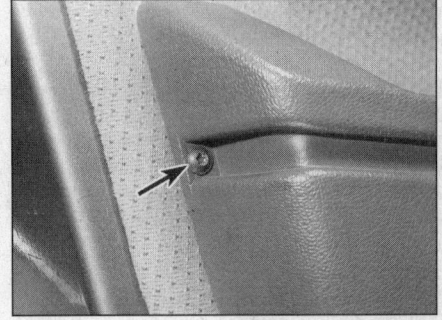

10.4b . . . and rear mounting screws . . .

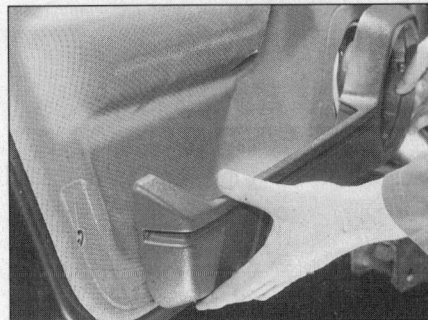

10.4c . . . and remove the loudspeaker holder and side pocket

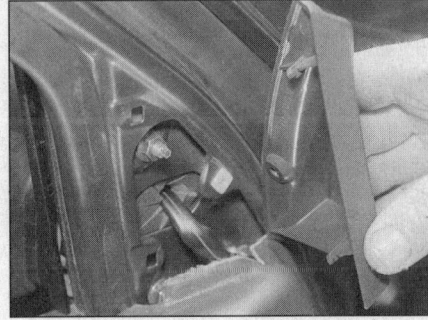

10.5 Removing the exterior mirror inner plastic cover

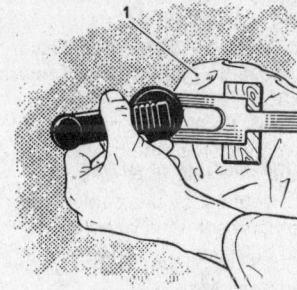

10.6 Using a special tool to remove the window regulator handle
1 Protective cloth

2 Remove the screw from the interior door handle finger plate. Pull the plate out and disconnect it from the pull rod **(see illustrations)**.

3 Turn the loudspeaker cover anti-clockwise and remove it. Remove the screws and withdraw the loudspeaker, then disconnect the wiring **(see illustrations)**.

4 Remove the screws and withdraw the loudspeaker holder and side pocket from the trim panel **(see illustrations)**.

5 Remove the screw, then remove the exterior mirror inner plastic cover taking care not to damage the plastic retaining posts **(see illustration)**.

6 Where applicable, remove the window regulator handle, but first note its position with the window fully shut. If necessary, use a tool similar to that shown together with a piece of cloth **(see illustration)**.

7 The trim panel is clipped in place and sealed with mastic. If the mastic has

hardened, it may be necessary to cut it free using a knife or small saw. Try prising the panel from the door carefully with a wide-bladed screwdriver before cutting the mastic. Prise the panel by inserting the screwdriver under the retaining clips to avoid tearing the inner surface of the panel.

8 Where applicable, disconnect the wiring from the power window switch.

Refitting

9 Refitting is a reversal of removal, but apply suitable mastic to the inner door panel before fitting the trim panel. Check the retaining clips for breakage and renew them if necessary.

Rear door

Removal

10 Using a screwdriver, prise the plastic insert from the door grip. Unscrew the screws and remove the grip from the inner trim panel.

11 Remove the screw from the interior door

handle finger plate. Pull the plate out and disconnect it from the pull rod.

12 Check that the window is fully shut, then note the position of the regulator handle. Pull the handle direct from the splines and remove the bezel - the handle is only a press fit on the splines **(see illustration)**.

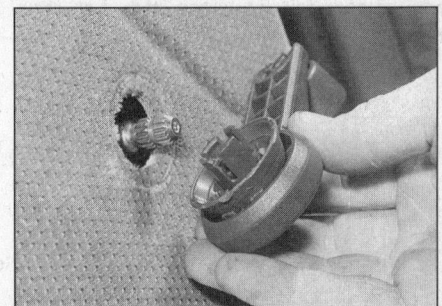

10.12 Removing the rear window regulator handle

11

10.13 Removing the ashtray holder

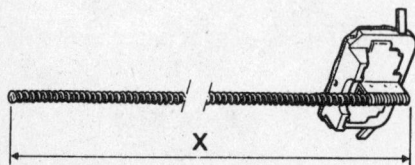

10.15 Applying mastic to the rear inner door panel

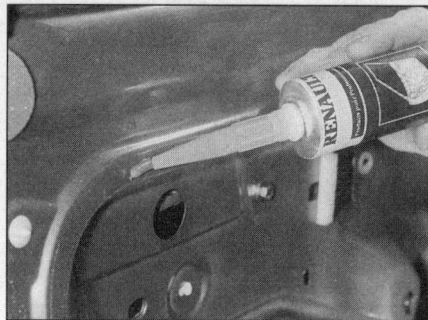

11.3 Front door window lifter (arrowed)

13 Remove the ashtray, then remove the screws and withdraw the ashtray holder from the trim panel **(see illustration)**.

14 The trim panel is clipped in place and sealed with mastic. If the mastic has hardened, it may be necessary to cut it free using a knife or small saw. Try prising the panel from the door carefully with a wide-bladed screwdriver before cutting the mastic. Prise the panel by inserting the screwdriver under the retaining clips to avoid tearing the inner surface of the panel.

Refitting

15 Refer to paragraph 9 **(see illustration)**.

11 Door window glass and regulator - removal and refitting

Front door window glass and regulator

Removal

1 Remove the door inner trim panel as described in Section 10.
2 Remove the lower rubbing strip.
3 Disconnect the lifter from the bottom of the window glass by pulling the fastener sharply from the plate pin **(see illustration)**. With the window free from the pin, lower the plate into the bottom of the door.
4 Release the pad on the rear edge of the window glass from its slide channel, then push the window forwards and lift it out from the outside.
5 Where applicable, reach inside the door and disconnect the wiring plug from the winder motor.

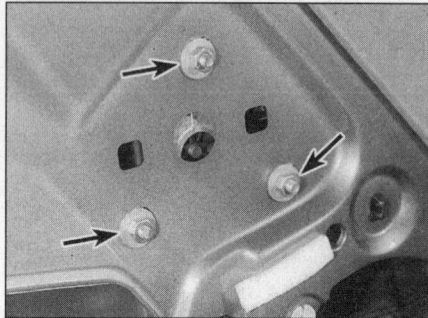

11.8 Front door electric window control cable length for four-door models
X = 1013 ± 5 mm

11.6 Front door window regulator mounting nuts (arrowed)

6 Unscrew the bolts and nuts securing the regulator assembly to the inner door panel **(see illustration)**.
7 Tilt the assembly so that the motor/regulator is at the bottom, then withdraw the assembly through the aperture **(see illustration)**.
8 The electric window control cable may be renewed if necessary, however on four and five-door models, cut the cable to the required length before fitting it **(see illustration)**.

Refitting

9 Refitting is a reversal of removal.

Rear door window regulator

Removal

10 Remove the door inner trim panel as described in Section 10.
11 Lower the window glass so that the lifter is visible, then unscrew the two bolts securing the lifter to the bottom of the window **(see**

11.11 Rear door window regulator-to-glass securing bolts (arrowed)

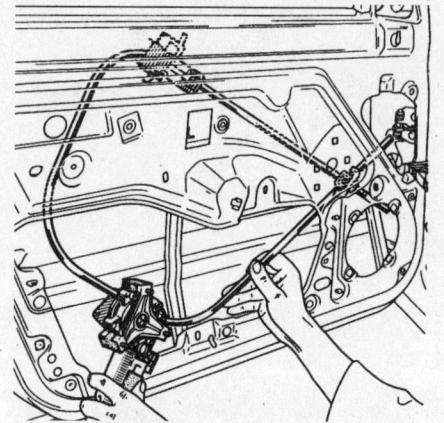

11.7 Removing the front door window regulator and electric motor

illustration). Fully raise the window and hold it in this position using a block of wood or alternatively by using wide adhesive tape.
12 Unscrew the bolts securing the regulator assembly to the inner door panel **(see illustrations)**.
13 Tilt the assembly, taking care not to catch it in the internal locking rod, then withdraw it through the aperture.

Refitting

14 Refitting is a reversal of removal.

Rear door window glass

Removal

15 Remove the door inner trim panel as described in Section 10.

11.12a Rear door window regulator front mounting bolts (arrowed) . . .

11.12b . . . rear upper mounting bolt (arrowed) . . .

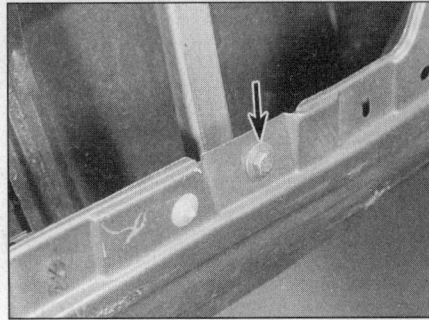

11.12c . . . and rear lower mounting bolt (arrowed)

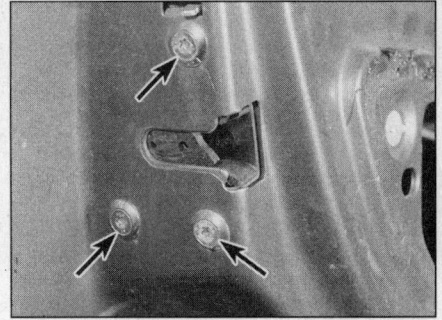

12.3 Door lock mounting screws (arrowed)

16 Remove the inner and outer rubbing strips.

17 Lower the window so that the lifter is visible, unscrew the lifter screws, then lower the window to the bottom of the door.

18 Unscrew the rear guide mounting bolts located at the top and bottom of the guide, then remove the guide.

19 Raise the window and remove it from the inside of the door.

Refitting

20 Refitting is a reversal of removal, but before tightening the lifter screws, have the window 25 to 50 mm open and press it firmly into the rear guide. This will align the window correctly. The lifter screws are accessed through the small hole in the inner door panel with the window in this position.

Rear door fixed window

Removal

21 Remove the main window glass as described previously.

22 Pull the fixed window forwards and withdraw it from the door.

23 Remove the lower stop inside the door.

Refitting

24 Refitting is a reversal of removal.

---

12 Door lock, lock cylinder and handles - removal and refitting

Door lock

Removal

1 Remove the door inner trim panel as described in Section 10.

2 Reach inside the door and disconnect the exterior handle control rod and the locking rod from the lock.

3 Unscrew the lock mounting screws from the rear edge of the door **(see illustration)**.

4 Where applicable, disconnect the wiring from the central locking motor **(see illustration)**.

5 Disconnect the interior handle operating rod, then withdraw the lock through the aperture in the door inner panel.

6 Where applicable, the motor may be removed from the lock by unscrewing the single retaining screw.

Refitting

7 Refitting is a reversal of removal.

Lock cylinder

Removal

8 Remove the door inner trim panel as described in Section 10.

9 Reach inside the door and disconnect the operating rod.

10 Pull out the retaining clip, then withdraw the lock cylinder from the outside of the car.

Refitting

11 Refitting is a reversal of removal.

Interior handle

Removal

12 Remove the door inner trim panel as described in Section 10.

13 Remove the screw from inside the handle finger plate, withdraw the handle, and disconnect it from the operating rod.

Refitting

14 Refitting is a reversal of removal.

Exterior handle

Removal

15 Remove the door inner trim panel as described in Section 10.

16 Disconnect the operating rods from the lock.

17 Insert a screwdriver through the hole in the inner door panel, unscrew the mounting screw, then withdraw the handle from inside the door.

13.2a Front door check link-to-door pillar securing screw (arrowed)

12.4 Disconnect the wiring (arrowed) from the central locking motor

Refitting

18 Refitting is a reversal of removal.

---

13 Door - removal, refitting and adjustment

Removal

1 Where applicable, disconnect the battery negative lead, then remove the door trim panel as described in Section 10, and disconnect the wiring plugs from any electrical components mounted in the door. Note the routing of the wiring to aid refitting, then pass the wiring harness through the front edge of the door.

2 Disconnect the door check link by unscrewing the Torx screw on the door pillar. If necessary, the link may be unbolted from the door **(see illustrations)**.

13.2b Front door check link (arrowed) viewed from inside door

13.7 Door striker

14.2a Pushing the tab (3) outwards to remove the wire spring type exterior mirror

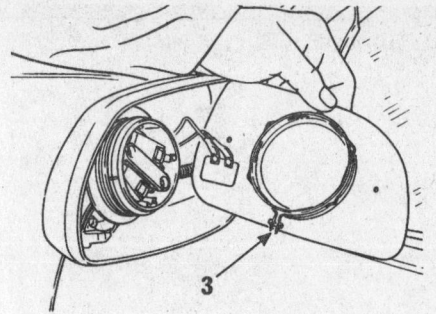

14.2b Inside view of the tab (3) on the wire spring type exterior mirror

3 Support the door on blocks of wood.
4 Prise off the caps covering each hinge pin.
5 Using a cranked metal rod of suitable diameter as a drift, drive out the upper and lower hinge pins.
6 Lift the door from the hinges.

Refitting and adjustment

7 Refitting is a reversal of removal, but check that the door is correctly aligned with the surrounding bodywork with an equal clearance around its edge. Adjustment is made by loosening the Torx screws and moving the door within the elongated mounting holes. A shim is fitted between the hinge plates and door for vertical alignment with the rear pillar. Check that the striker enters the lock centrally when the door is closed, and if necessary loosen it with a Torx key, re-position and re-tighten it **(see illustration)**.

14 Exterior mirror and glass - removal and refitting

Mirror glass

Removal

1 There are two types of mirror glass fitted - one is retained with a wire spring, and the other by plastic clips. The former type is identified by having a small tab located under the bottom edge of the mirror.
2 To remove the wire spring type, use a small

screwdriver to push the tab outwards, then withdraw the mirror and disconnect the heater wiring from the rear of the mirror (where applicable) **(see illustrations)**.
3 To remove the plastic clip type, it is recommended that a suction pad is used to pull it out, together with a small screwdriver to release the clips **(see illustration)**.

Refitting

4 Before refitting the wire spring type, refit the clip then press the mirror into position. To refit the plastic clip type, press the mirror inwards until the clips snap into place.

Mirror assembly

Removal

5 Remove the mirror trim panel, or the door inner trim panel (Section 10), as applicable.
6 Where applicable, disconnect the wiring plug.
7 Unscrew the three nuts and withdraw the mirror assembly from the door while feeding the wiring harness through the rubber grommet where applicable **(see illustration)**.

Refitting

8 Refitting is a reversal of removal.

15 Boot lid - removal, refitting and adjustment

Removal

1 Open the boot lid and mark the position of

the bolts on the hinges with a pencil **(see illustration)**. Where applicable, disconnect the wiring for the central locking.
2 Place cloth rags beneath each corner of the boot lid to prevent damage to the paintwork.
3 Disconnect the strut(s) by prising out the retainer with a small screwdriver and pulling the strut from the boot lid ball.
4 With the help of an assistant, unscrew the bolts and lift the boot lid from the car.
5 If necessary, the boot lid hinges may be unbolted from the body.

Refitting and adjustment

6 Refitting is a reversal of removal, but check that the boot lid is correctly aligned with the surrounding bodywork with an equal clearance around its edge. Adjustment is made by loosening the mounting bolts and moving the boot lid within the elongated mounting holes. Check that the lock enters the striker centrally when the boot lid is closed, and if necessary adjust the positions within the elongated holes.

16 Boot lid support strut - removal and refitting

Removal

1 Support the boot lid in its open position.
2 Disconnect each end of the support strut by prising out the retainers with a small screwdriver and pulling the strut from the ball mountings **(see illustration)**.

14.3 Removing the plastic clip type exterior mirror glass

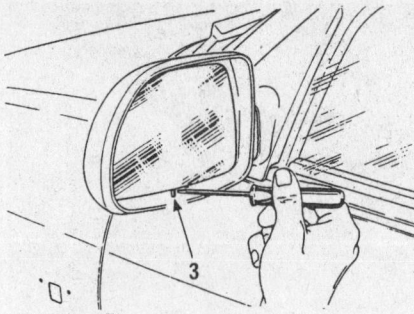

14.7 Removing the exterior mirror

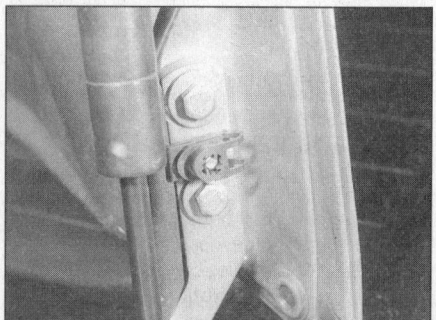

15.1 Hinge mounting on the boot lid

16.2 Prising the retainer from the boot lid upper strut mounting

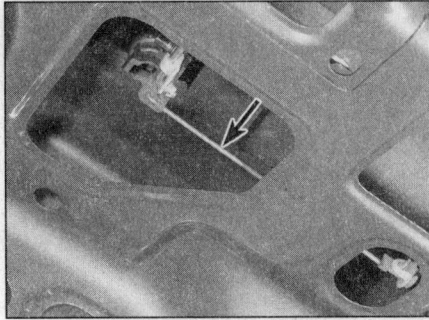

17.4 Boot lid lock operating rod (arrowed)

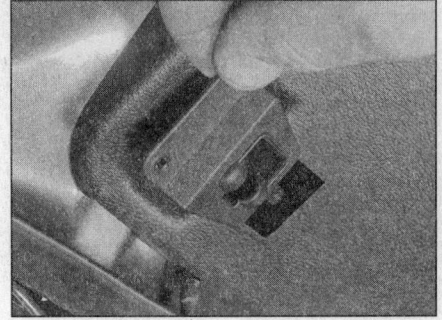

18.2a Remove the screws and hooks . . .

18.2b . . . and unclip the trim panel from the tailgate

18.4 Disconnecting the strut from the tailgate

Check that the striker enters the lock centrally when the tailgate is closed, and if necessary adjust the position of the striker within the elongated holes. The striker position also determines the rear height of the tailgate.

19 Tailgate support strut - removal and refitting

Refitting

3 Refitting is a reversal of removal, but note that the piston end of the strut faces downwards.

Refitting

6 Refitting is a reversal of removal.

18 Tailgate - removal, refitting and adjustment

Removal

1 Open the tailgate and support it in the open position.
2 Remove the screws and hooks, and unclip the trim panel from the tailgate, then disconnect the rear window washer tube (see illustrations). Where applicable also disconnect the wiring for the tailgate wiper motor and the central locking.
3 Unclip and remove the headlining rear cover strip.
4 Support the tailgate in the open position, then disconnect the struts by prising out the spring clip retainers (see illustration).
5 With the help of an assistant, unscrew the mounting nuts and lift the tailgate from the rear of the vehicle.
6 If necessary, the hinge can be removed from the tailgate by driving out the pin with a suitable drift.

Refitting and adjustment

7 Refitting is a reversal of removal, but check that the tailgate is correctly aligned with the surrounding bodywork with an equal clearance around its edge. Adjustment is made by loosening the mounting bolts and moving the tailgate within the elongated mounting holes.

Removal

1 Support the tailgate in its open position.
2 Disconnect each end of the support strut by prising out the spring clip retainers with a small screwdriver and pulling the strut from the ball mountings.

Refitting

3 Refitting is a reversal of removal, but note that the piston end of the strut faces downwards.

20 Tailgate lock and lock cylinder - removal and refitting

Lock

Removal

1 Open the tailgate, then remove the screws and hooks and unclip the inner trim panel.
2 Using a Torx key, unscrew and remove the lock mounting bolts.
3 Pull out the lock and at the same time turn it to release the operating rod from the cylinder assembly. If necessary, also remove the central locking unit (see illustrations).

20.3a Removing the tailgate lock . . .

17 Boot lid lock and cylinder - removal and refitting

Lock

Removal

1 Open the boot lid, then disconnect the operating rod from the lock by reaching through the aperture.
2 Using a Torx key, unscrew the lock mounting bolts and withdraw the lock from the boot lid.

Refitting

3 Refitting is a reversal of removal, but check that the striker enters the lock centrally when the boot lid is closed, and if necessary reposition the striker by loosening the mounting screws.

Lock cylinder

Removal

4 Open the boot lid, then disconnect the operating rods for the lock and central locking unit (where applicable) by reaching through the aperture (see illustration).
5 Using a pair of pliers, pull out the retaining clip, then withdraw the lock cylinder from the boot lid.

11

20.3b ... and central locking unit

20.4 Tailgate lock striker mounting screws (arrowed)

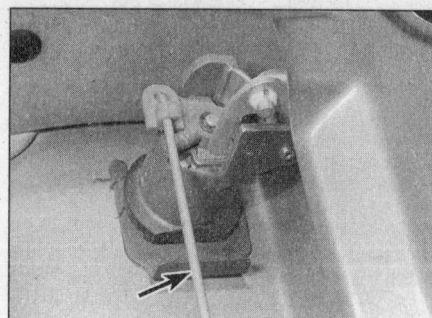

20.5a Central locking unit operating rod (arrowed) on the tailgate lock cylinder

Refitting

4 Refitting is a reversal of removal but, when refitting the lock, check that the striker enters the lock centrally when the tailgate is closed, and if necessary re-position the striker by loosening the mounting screws **(see illustration)**.

Lock cylinder

Removal

5 Open the tailgate, then disconnect the operating rods for the lock and central locking unit (where applicable) by reaching through the aperture **(see illustrations)**.
6 Using a pair of pliers, pull out the retaining clip, then withdraw the lock cylinder from the tailgate **(see illustration)**.

Refitting

7 Refitting is a reversal of removal.

---

21 Rear side window (three-door Hatchback) - removal and refitting

Removal

1 Working inside the vehicle, on the appropriate side, remove the rear side shelf, side panel trim, pillar upper trim and rear quarter panel trim.

21.5 Cross-section of the rear side window (three-door Hatchback) with cord inserted for refitting

A Weatherseal
B Window glass
C Refitting cord
D Groove

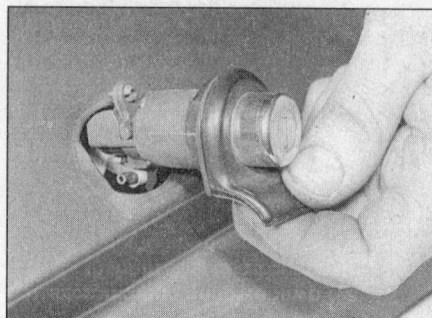

20.5b Disconnecting the lock operating rod from the tailgate lock cylinder

2 Using a blunt ended instrument, push the inner lip of the weatherseal beneath the window frame starting at the top. Support the window on the outside during this operation.
3 With the weatherseal free, withdraw the window from the body.

Refitting

4 Clean the window and aperture in the body.
5 Fit the weatherseal on the window, then insert a cord in the weatherseal groove so that the ends project from the bottom of the window and are overlapped by approximately 200 mm **(see illustration)**.
6 Locate the window on the aperture in the body and pass the ends of the cord inside the car. Have an assistant hold the window.

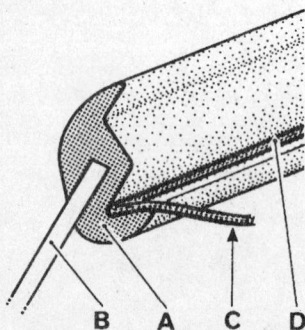

21.7 Pull the cord to locate the lip of the weatherseal over the aperture

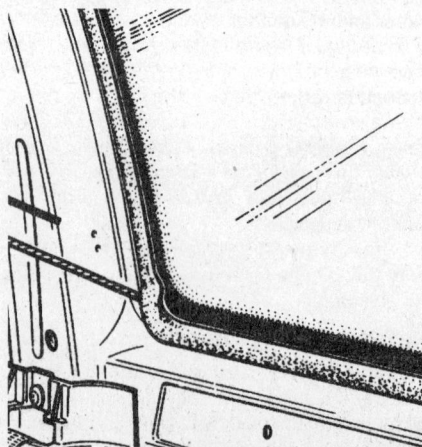

20.6 Removing the lock cylinder from the tailgate

7 Slowly pull one end of the cord so that the lip of the weatherseal goes over the aperture, and at the same time have the assistant press firmly on the outside of the window **(see illustration)**. When the cord reaches the middle top of the window, pull the remaining length of cord to position the other half of the weatherseal.
8 Refit the trim panels in reverse order of removal.

---

22 Windscreen and rear window/tailgate glass - general information

The windscreen and rear window/tailgate glass are bonded in place with special mastic, and special tools are required to cut free the old units and fit replacements, together with cleaning solutions and primers. It is therefore recommended that this work is entrusted to a Renault dealer or windscreen replacement specialist.

---

23 Body exterior fittings/exterior trim panels - general information

The front wing side protection strip can be removed by partially removing the plastic wheelarch, then removing the clip or metal nut from inside the wing. Using a screwdriver, lift the front of the strip to free the pin from the hole, then push the strip to the rear. The strip is refitted by pressing it until the clip engages.

24.2a Remove the securing screw . . .

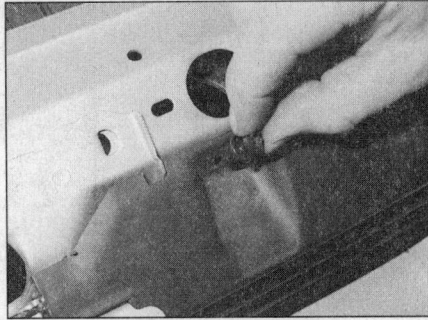

24.2b . . . and the plastic clip . . .

24.2c . . . to release the radiator shield panel

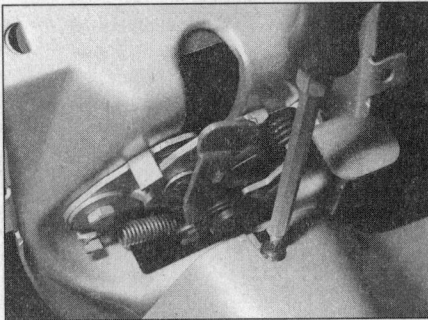

24.3 Slackening the upper grille panel securing screw

24.4 Removing a lower grille panel securing screw

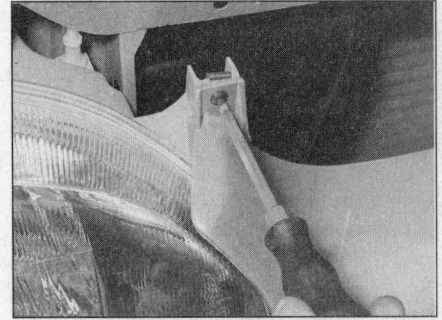

24.5 Removing an inner grille panel-to-headlight securing screw

The door protection strips can be removed by removing the mounting screws from inside the door then pushing the strip forwards. Align the clips when refitting the strips.

The sill protection strips can be removed by prising up their end covers and unscrewing the retaining screws, then pulling the strip forwards. The clips may be removed from the sill by turning them through 90° with a pair of pliers.

24 Front grille panels ("Phase 2" models) - removal and refitting

Removal

1 Open the bonnet. Where applicable, release the two securing clips, and remove the plastic shield panel from the top of the radiator.

2 Remove the securing screws and clips, and withdraw the two radiator shield panels. Each panel is secured by one screw and a plastic clip, which must be turned to release it **(see illustrations)**.

3 Slacken the upper grille panel securing screw (there is no need to remove it) **(see illustration)**.

4 Remove the two lower grille panel securing screws **(see illustration)**.

5 Working in the grille panel aperture, remove the two screws securing the grille panel to the inside of the headlights **(see illustration)**.

6 Remove the front indicator lights as described in Chapter 12.

7 Remove the single screw on each side securing the grille panel to the body bracket **(see illustration)**.

8 Withdraw the grille panel from the vehicle **(see illustration)**.

Refitting

9 Refitting is a reversal of removal.

25 Seats - removal and refitting

Front seat

Removal

1 Working under the vehicle, unscrew the four nuts securing the seat runners to the floor. Lift the seat out from inside the vehicle. Note the location of the spacers between the runners and the floor **(see illustrations)**.

24.7 Removing a grille panel-to-body bracket securing screw

24.8 Removing the front grille panel

25.1a Seat runner mounting nut viewed from under the vehicle

11

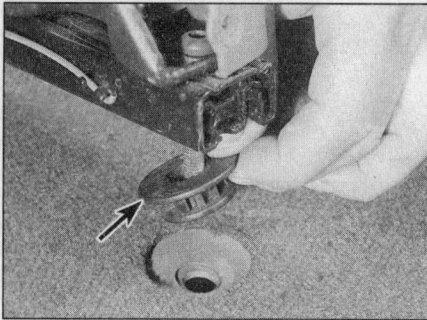

25.1b Removing a seat. Note the spacer (arrowed)

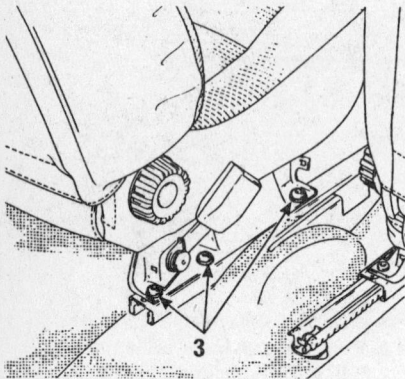

25.2 Seat-to-runner securing bolts (3) on inner side of seat

2 If desired, the seat can be separated from the runners after removing the seat side trim panels (where applicable) and unscrewing the seat-to-runner bolts **(see illustration)**.

Refitting

3 Refitting is a reversal of removal.

Rear seat

Removal

4 Fold the rear seat backrest forwards, then raise the two levers on the hinges and remove the backrest from the vehicle **(see illustration)**.

5 To remove the seat cushion, tilt the cushion forwards then release the two brackets from the location holes and remove the cushion from the vehicle.

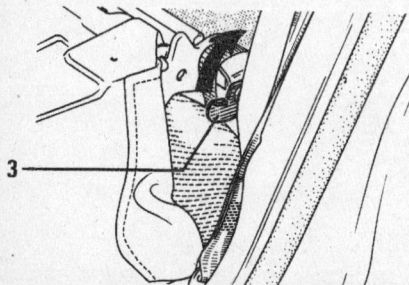

25.4 Rear seat backrest securing lever (3)

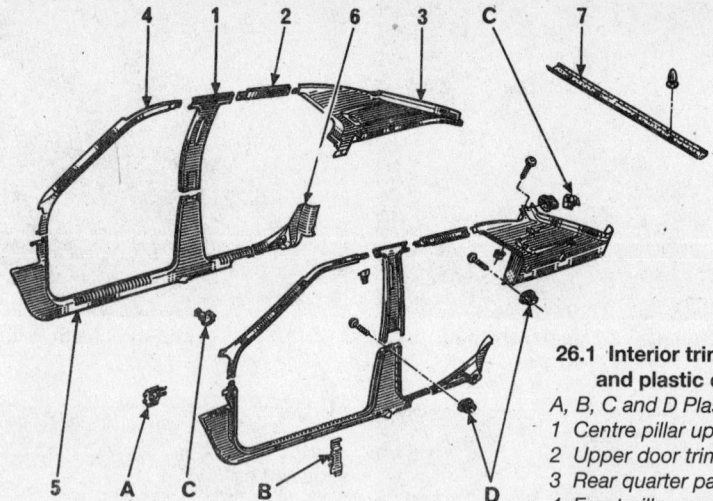

26.1 Interior trim panels and plastic clips

A, B, C and D Plastic clips
1 *Centre pillar upper trim*
2 *Upper door trim*
3 *Rear quarter panel trim*
4 *Front pillar upper trim*
5 *Side lower trim*
6 *Rear lower trim*
7 *Headlining rear panel*

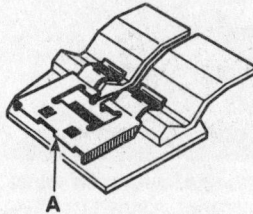

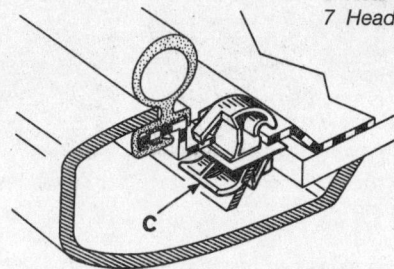

Refitting

6 Refitting is a reversal of removal.

26 Interior trim panels - general information

1 The interior trim panels shown are retained with plastic clips which may easily break on removal **(see illustration)**. It is recommended that the clips are renewed after removal to ensure secure fitting.

2 To remove the centre pillar upper trim, first remove the coat hanger, seat belt mounting and height adjustment pushrod, then release the trim and seals and remove the sliding cover **(see illustration)**.

3 To remove the side lower trim, first remove

the centre pillar upper trim, then remove the screws and the lower belt mounting. Release the rear and front ends then remove the trim from the rear of the vehicle **(see illustration)**.

4 To remove the front pillar upper trim, first remove the centre pillar upper trim, then remove the screws and withdraw the trim downwards and rearwards.

5 To remove the rear quarter panel trim, first remove the centre pillar upper trim, rear door upper and lower trim, and the headlining rear trim. Remove the seal from the luggage compartment aperture frame, the side shelf, and the two upper screws. Release the trim starting at the door seal end **(see illustration)**.

6 To remove the rear side shelf, first remove the centre shelf, then disconnect the wiring from the loudspeaker and remove the five mounting screws.

26.2 Removing the coat hanger

26.3 Side lower trim top screw (arrowed)

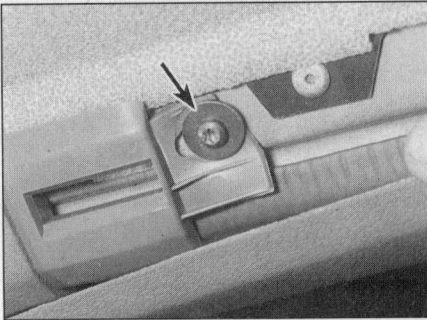

26.5 Rear quarter panel trim front securing screw (arrowed)

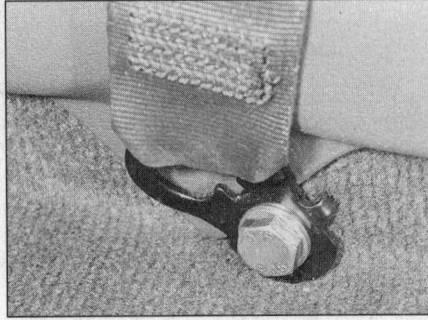

27.2 Front seat belt bottom anchor bolt

27.4 Rear seat belt inertia reel viewed with trim panel removed

27 Seat belts - removal and refitting

Warning: Certain later models may be fitted with a seat belt pretensioning system, which pretensions the front seat belts in the event of a severe frontal impact. Where this system is fitted do not attempt to carry out any work involving the front seat belt stalks. If the system is activated unintentionally, personal injury could result. If the vehicle is involved in an accident, have the system checked by a Renault dealer.

Front seat belt

Removal

1 To remove a front seat belt stalk, move the seat to the rear and, where applicable, remove the trim panel covering the stalk mounting Unscrew the mounting bolt and remove the stalk from the seat.

2 To remove a front seat belt inertia reel and belt, unbolt the bottom anchor bolt from the inner sill, then remove the trim panels and unbolt the inertia reel and upper sliding mounting from the centre pillar **(see illustration)**. On three-door models, unbolt the rail from the inner sill.

Refitting

3 Refitting is a reversal of removal, but tighten the anchorages to the specified torque.

Rear seat belt

Removal

4 To remove the rear seat belts, first remove the rear seat backrest and cushion then prise

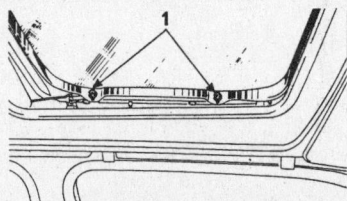

28.2 Two of the sunroof glass panel securing screws (1)

off the plastic caps and unbolt the seat belts from the body. To remove the inertia reel it will first be necessary to remove the trim panels **(see illustration)**.

Refitting

5 Refitting is a reversal of removal, but tighten the anchorages to the specified torque.

28 Sunroof components - removal and refitting

Note: *The sunroof is a complex piece of equipment, consisting of a large number of components. It is strongly recommended that the sunroof mechanism is not disturbed unless absolutely necessary. If the sunroof mechanism is faulty, or requires overhaul, consult a Renault dealer for advice.*

Glass panel

Removal

1 Raise the glass to the tilted position.
2 Remove the four Torx-type glass panel securing screws (two on each side) **(see illustration)**.
3 Tilt the glass slightly rearwards and withdraw it forwards from outside the vehicle.

Refitting and adjustment

4 Lower the glass panel into position, and refit the four securing screws - do not fully tighten them at this stage.
5 Close the sunroof, and adjust the position of the glass panel to bring it flush with the roof.
6 Tighten the securing screws.
7 Open and close the sunroof several times to ensure that it remains flush with the roof,

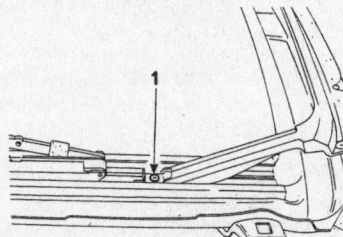

28.9 Sunroof air deflector securing rivet (1)

and if necessary re-adjust as described previously.

Air deflector

Removal

8 Open the sunroof.
9 Carefully drill out the two pop rivets securing the deflector mountings **(see illustration)**.
10 Remove the deflector by pulling it forwards.

Refitting

11 Refitting is a reversal of removal, using new pop rivets.

Crank mechanism and motor

12 For access to these components, it is necessary to remove the headlining, which is clipped and glued to the roof. To remove the headlining, it is necessary to remove the surrounding trim panels. Due to the complicated nature of this procedure, and the risk of damage, it is recommended that any work on the sunroof crank mechanism and motor is entrusted to a Renault dealer.

29 Centre console - removal and refitting

Removal

1 Working inside the vehicle, prise the gear lever boot from the centre console.
2 Remove the mounting screws and lift the centre console from the car. Where applicable, disconnect the wiring from the switches **(see illustrations)**.

Refitting

3 Refitting is a reversal of removal.

30 Facia - removal and refitting

Removal

1 Disconnect the battery negative lead.
2 Remove the centre console with reference to Section 29.

11

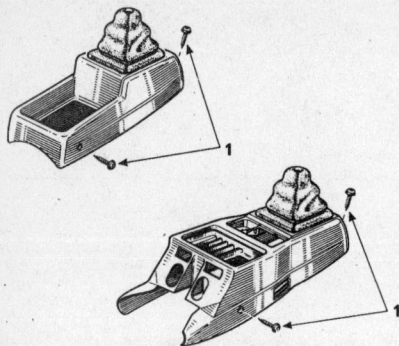

29.2a Alternative types of centre console and securing screws (1)

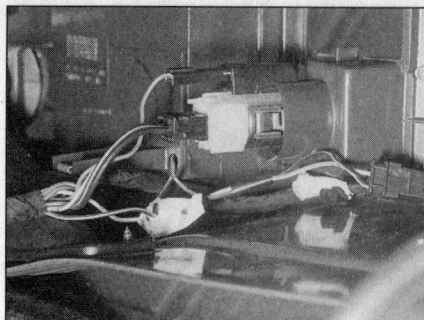

29.2b Switch and cigarette lighter wiring at rear of centre console

30.7 Facia-to-steering column securing screw (arrowed)

30.11a Remove the screws . . .

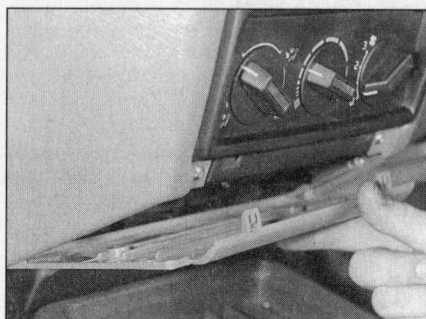

30.11b . . . and remove the heater panel lower cover

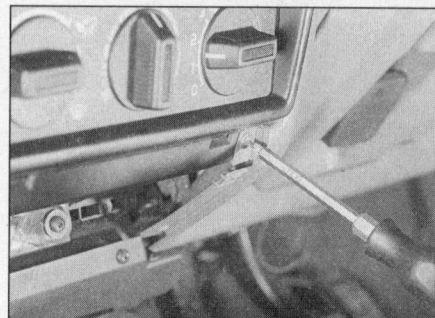

30.11c Removing the heater control panel

30.20 Removing a lower facia mounting nut cover

3 Remove the front left-hand and right-hand pillar upper and lower trim (see Section 26).

4 Remove the steering wheel with reference to Chapter 10, noting the warning given for models fitted with air bags.

5 Remove the steering column upper and lower shrouds. Note that on models with a radio/cassette player remote control switch, it will be necessary to loosen the switch clamp screw before the shrouds can be removed (see Chapter 12).

6 Remove the combination switch from the steering column with reference to Chapter 12.

7 Unscrew and remove the two screws securing the facia to the top of the steering column, then remove the moulding and disconnect the ignition switch **(see illustration)**.

8 On models with a non-adjustable steering column, unscrew and remove the steering column mounting nuts and bolts (Chapter 10), and lower the column away from the facia.

9 On models with an adjustable steering column, set the steering wheel in its lowest position, then remove the adjusting locknut and control lever. The steering column mountings do not have to be removed.

10 Disconnect the speedometer cable.

11 Remove the screws from the heater control panel and lower cover, disconnect the wiring and push the panel inside the facia **(see illustrations)**.

12 Remove the screws securing the heater unit to the facia, and the screws securing the moulding on the heater unit. Release the wiring harness for the centre console.

13 Disconnect the wiring connectors on the left and right-hand A-pillars.

14 Unscrew the earth cable mounting bolts.

15 Remove the courtesy light switches from the A-pillars. Disconnect the wiring plugs located in the pillars.

16 On the left-hand side of the engine compartment, remove the cover and disconnect the engine wiring harness.

17 Remove the plastic shield from the left-hand wheelarch, then unclip the engine wiring harness. Pass the harness inside the car.

18 Remove the scuttle grille from the right-hand side.

19 Disconnect the wiring harness from the windscreen wiper, the battery positive terminal and the heater matrix motor.

20 Using a screwdriver prise off the facia mounting nut covers from the left and right-hand lower corners **(see illustration)**. Unscrew and remove the two nuts.

21 Prise the two upper covers from the left and right-hand speaker locations on the facia, then remove the two nuts from the facia upper mountings.

22 With the help of an assistant, release the facia from the bulkhead and withdraw it from one side of the vehicle, noting the routing of the wiring harness.

Refitting

23 Refitting is a reversal of removal but note the following points:

a) *Check that the plastic centring lug is in position on the top of the bulkhead.*

b) *Ensure that the wiring harness is routed as noted before removal.*

c) *Tighten all nuts and bolts securely.*

d) *Before re-connecting the battery leads, switch off the ignition and all electrical switches. After re-connecting the leads check that all electrical components are operating correctly.*

31 Glovebox - removal and refitting

Removal

1 With the glovebox open, pull out the hinge pins and withdraw the glovebox from the facia.

2 If necessary the lock may be removed from the glovebox lid and the facia.

Refitting

3 Refitting is a reversal of removal.

Chapter 12
Body electrical systems

Contents

Degrees of difficulty

Easy, suitable for novice with little experience | **Fairly easy,** suitable for beginner with some experience | **Fairly difficult,** suitable for competent DIY mechanic | **Difficult,** suitable for experienced DIY mechanic | **Very difficult,** suitable for expert DIY or professional

Specifications

Fuses (main fusebox)

Fuse	Rating (amps)	Circuit(s) protected
1	30	Left-hand window winder
2	30	Right hand window winder
3	10	Left-hand side and rear lights
4	10	Right-hand side and rear lights, lights-on buzzer, switch lighting
5	10	Flasher
7	30	Air conditioning
8	20	Engine electric cooling fan
9	30	Air conditioning
10	5	Seat belt pre-tensioning system
11	20	Protected engine functions
12	5	Automatic transmission
13	15	Anti-lock brakes
14	20	Sunroof, trip computer, heated rear screen, defrosting rear view mirrors, anti-theft switch
15	5	Alarm
16	-	Not used
17	10	Clock, radio, trip computer, alarm
18	20	Heater blower
19	30	Headlight washers
20	10	Windscreen wiper timer
21	30	Central door locking, anti-theft switch
22	20	Heated rear screen
23	15	Radio, interior lights, luggage compartment light
24	30	Accessories cut-off (cuts off power to interior lights, clock, etc, when cranking)
25	15	Clock, trip computer, alarm, rear view mirrors
26	15	Windscreen wiper, windscreen washers
27	10	Heated seats
28	15	Rear screen wiper, cigarette lighter, reversing lights
29	10	Stop lights

12

Fuses (auxiliary fusebox) - "Phase 2" models

Fuse	Rating (amps)		Circuit(s) protected
1	70	Pre-heating circuit	
2	40	Cooling fan	
3	2	Fuel injection computer (petrol engines)	
4	30	Fuel pump (petrol engines)	
5	15	Engine functions (petrol engines)	
6	25	Cooling fan	

Bulbs

	Wattage
Headlight	60/55
Front sidelight:	
Single headlights	5
Dual headlights	3
Front foglight	21
Front direction indicator	21
Front repeater	5
Tail light	5
Rear direction indicator	21
Reversing light	21
Stop light	21
Rear foglight	21
Number plate light	5
Interior lights	10
Instrument panel lights	1.2 or 2

1 General information and precautions

General information

The body electrical system consists of all lights, wash/wipe equipment, interior electrical equipment, and associated switches and wiring.

The electrical system is of the 12-volt negative earth type. Power to the body electrical system is provided by a 12-volt battery which is charged by the alternator (see Chapter 5).

The engine electrical system (battery, alternator, starter motor, pre-heating system, etc) is covered separately in Chapter 5

Precautions

Refer to the precautions given in Chapter 5, Section 1 before carrying out any work on the body electrical system. In particular take note of the precautions to be observed before disconnecting the battery on a vehicle equipped with a security-coded radio/cassette unit.

2 Electrical fault finding - general information

Note: *Refer to the precautions given in "Safety first!" and in Chapter 5, Section 1 before starting work. The following tests relate to testing of the main electrical circuits, and should not be used to test delicate electronic circuits (such as anti-lock braking systems, etc), particularly where an electronic control module is used.*

General

1 A typical electrical circuit consists of an electrical component, any switches, relays, motors, fuses, fusible links or circuit breakers related to that component, and the wiring and connectors which link the component to both the battery and the chassis. To help to pinpoint a problem in an electrical circuit, wiring diagrams are included at the end of this manual.

2 Before attempting to diagnose an electrical fault, first study the appropriate wiring diagram to obtain a complete understanding of the components included in the particular circuit concerned. The possible sources of a fault can be narrowed down by noting if other components related to the circuit are operating properly. If several components or circuits fail at one time, the problem is likely to be related to a shared fuse or earth connection.

3 Electrical problems usually stem from simple causes, such as loose or corroded connections, a faulty earth connection, a blown fuse, a melted fusible link, or a faulty relay (refer to Section 3 for details of testing relays). Visually inspect the condition of all fuses, wires and connections in a problem circuit before testing the components. Use the wiring diagrams to determine which terminal connections will need to be checked in order to pinpoint the trouble spot.

4 The basic tools required for electrical fault-finding include a circuit tester or voltmeter (a 12-volt bulb with a set of test leads can also be used for certain tests); a self-powered test lamp (sometimes known as a continuity tester); an ohmmeter (to measure resistance); a battery and set of test leads; and a jumper wire, preferably with a circuit breaker or fuse incorporated, which can be used to bypass suspect wires or electrical components. Before attempting to locate a problem with test instruments, use the wiring diagram to determine where to make the connections.

5 To find the source of an intermittent wiring fault (usually due to a poor or dirty connection, or damaged wiring insulation), a "wiggle" test can be performed on the wiring. This involves wiggling the wiring by hand to see if the fault occurs as the wiring is moved. It should be possible to narrow down the source of the fault to a particular section of wiring. This method of testing can be used in conjunction with any of the tests described in the following sub-Sections.

6 Apart from problems due to poor connections, two basic types of fault can occur in an electrical circuit - open circuit, or short circuit.

7 Open circuit faults are caused by a break somewhere in the circuit, which prevents current from flowing. An open circuit fault will prevent a component from working, but will not cause the relevant circuit fuse to blow.

8 Short circuit faults are caused by a "short" somewhere in the circuit, which allows the current flowing in the circuit to "escape" along an alternative route, usually to earth. Short circuit faults are normally caused by a breakdown in wiring insulation, which allows a feed wire to touch either another wire, or an earthed component such as the bodyshell. A short circuit fault will normally cause the relevant circuit fuse to blow.

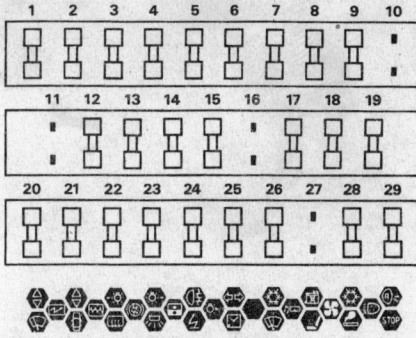

3.2a Fuse location chart (main fusebox) - "Phase 1" models (for fuse identification see Specifications)

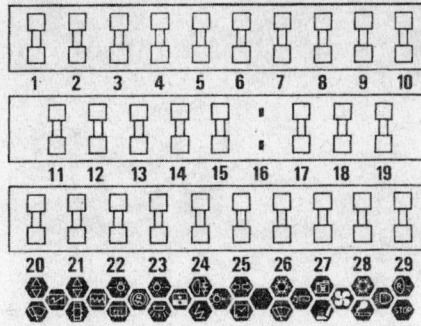

3.2b Fuse location chart (main fusebox) - "Phase 2" models (for fuse identification see Specifications)

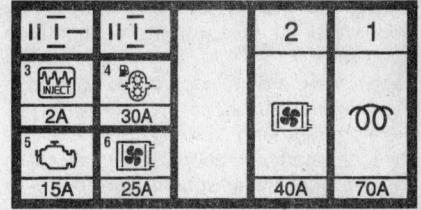

3.4a Fuse location chart (auxiliary fusebox) - "Phase 2" models (for fuse identification see Specifications)

3.4b Auxiliary fusebox with cover removed

Finding an open circuit

9 To check for an open circuit, connect one lead of a circuit tester or voltmeter to either the negative battery terminal or a known good earth.

10 Connect the other lead to a connector in the circuit being tested, preferably nearest to the battery or fuse.

11 Switch on the circuit, bearing in mind that some circuits are live only when the ignition switch is moved to a particular position.

12 If voltage is present (indicated either by the tester bulb lighting or a voltmeter reading, as applicable), this means that the section of the circuit between the relevant connector and the battery is problem-free.

13 Continue to check the remainder of the circuit in the same fashion.

14 When a point is reached at which no voltage is present, the problem must lie between that point and the previous test point with voltage. Most problems can be traced to a broken, corroded or loose connection.

Finding a short circuit

15 To check for a short circuit, first disconnect the load(s) from the circuit (loads are the components which draw current from a circuit, such as bulbs, motors, heating elements, etc).

16 Remove the relevant fuse from the circuit, and connect a circuit tester or voltmeter to the fuse connections.

17 Switch on the circuit, bearing in mind that some circuits are live only when the ignition switch is moved to a particular position.

18 If voltage is present (indicated either by the tester bulb lighting or a voltmeter reading, as applicable), this means that there is a short circuit.

19 If no voltage is present, but the fuse still blows with the load(s) connected, this indicates an internal fault in the load(s).

Finding an earth fault

20 The battery negative terminal is connected to "earth" - the metal of the engine/gearbox unit and the car body - and most systems are wired so that they only receive a positive feed, the current returning via the metal of the car body. This means that the component mounting and the body form part of that circuit. Loose or corroded mountings can therefore cause a range of electrical faults, ranging from total failure of a circuit, to a puzzling partial fault. In particular, lights may shine dimly (especially when another circuit sharing the same earth point is in operation), motors (eg wiper motors or the radiator cooling fan motor) may run slowly, and the operation of one circuit may have an apparently unrelated effect on another. Note that on many vehicles, earth straps are used between certain components, such as the engine/gearbox and the body, usually where there is no metal-to-metal contact between components due to flexible rubber mountings, etc.

21 To check whether a component is properly earthed, disconnect the battery and connect one lead of an ohmmeter to a known good earth point. Connect the other lead to the wire or earth connection being tested. The resistance reading should be zero; if not, check the connection as follows.

22 If an earth connection is thought to be faulty, dismantle the connection and clean back to bare metal both the bodyshell and the wire terminal or the component earth connection mating surface. Be careful to remove all traces of dirt and corrosion, then use a knife to trim away any paint, so that a clean metal-to-metal joint is made. On reassembly, tighten the joint fasteners securely; if a wire terminal is being refitted, use serrated washers between the terminal and the bodyshell to ensure a clean and secure connection. When the connection is remade, prevent the onset of corrosion in the future by applying a coat of petroleum jelly or silicone-based grease or by spraying on (at regular intervals) a proprietary ignition sealer or a water dispersant lubricant.

3 Fuses and relays - general information

Fuses

1 Fuses are designed to break a circuit when a predetermined current is reached, in order to protect components and wiring which could be damaged by excessive current flow. Excessive current flow will be due to a fault in the circuit, usually a short-circuit (see Section 2).

2 The main fuses are located in the fusebox, under the facia/glovebox on the passenger's side (see illustrations).

3 For access to the fuses, turn the two fasteners through a quarter turn, then lower the fusebox panel from the facia. The circuits protected by the fuses are marked on a sticker at the bottom of the fusebox panel.

4 On "Phase 2" models, additional fuses may be located in an auxiliary fusebox under the bonnet, on the left-hand side of the engine compartment. For access to these fuses, unclip the auxiliary fusebox lid. The circuits protected by the fuses are marked on a sticker under the fusebox lid (see illustrations).

5 The fuse for the radio/cassette player is mounted on the rear of the unit.

6 A blown fuse can be recognised from its melted or broken wire (see illustration).

7 To remove a fuse, first ensure that the relevant circuit is switched off.

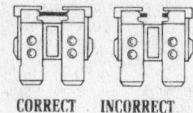

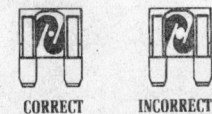

CORRECT   INCORRECT

CORRECT   INCORRECT

3.6 Identifying a blown fuse
Left OK   *Right Blown*

12

8 Using the plastic tool provided in the fusebox, pull the fuse from its location **(see illustration)**.

9 Spare fuses are provided at the right-hand side of the main fusebox.

10 Before renewing a blown fuse, trace and rectify the cause, and always use a fuse of the correct rating. Never substitute a fuse of a higher rating, or make temporary repairs using wire or metal foil; more serious damage, or even fire, could result.

11 Note that the fuses are colour-coded as follows. Refer to the Specifications for details of the fuse ratings and the circuits protected.

Colour	Rating
Orange	5A
Red	10A
Blue	15A
Yellow	20A
Clear or white	25A
Green	30A

Relays

12 A relay is an electrically-operated switch, which is used for the following reasons.

a) *A relay can switch a heavy current remotely from the circuit in which the current is flowing, therefore allowing the use of lighter gauge wiring and switch contacts.*

b) *A relay can receive more than one control input, unlike a mechanical switch.*

c) *A relay can have a "timer" function - for example, the intermittent wiper relay.*

13 Most of the relays are located in the main and auxiliary fuseboxes (see previous sub-Section) **(see illustrations)**.

14 If a circuit controlled by a relay develops a fault, and the relay is suspect, operate the circuit. If the relay is functioning, it should be possible to hear the relay click as it is energised. If this is the case, the fault lies with the components or wiring in the system. If the relay is not being energised, then either the relay is not receiving a switching voltage, or the relay itself is faulty (do not overlook the relay socket terminals when tracing faults). Testing is by the substitution of a known good unit, but be careful; while some relays are identical in appearance and in operation, others look similar, but perform different functions.

3.8 Removing a fuse using the tool provided

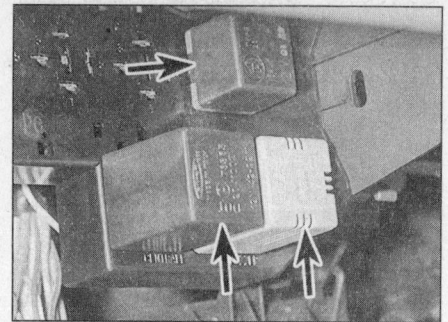

3.13a Relays (arrowed) located in the main fusebox - "Phase 1" models

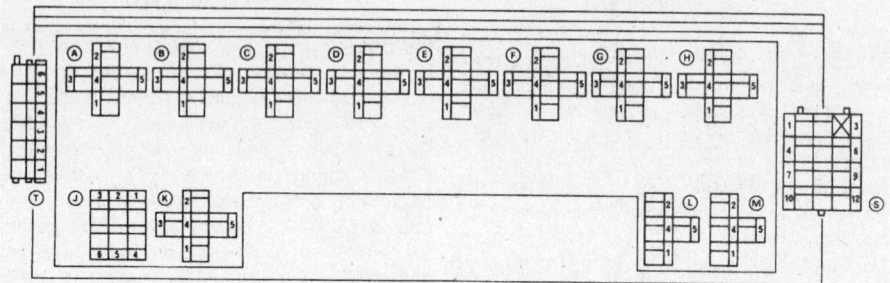

3.13b Relay location chart (main fusebox)

A *Front foglight shunt*
B *Front foglight shunt*
C *Front foglight relay*
D *Not used*
E *Not used*

F *Trip computer lighting rheostat relay*
G *Not used*
H *Heated rear window relay*
J *Door locking timer*
K *Not used*

L *Flasher unit*
M *Lights "on" warning buzzer*
S *Diagnostic plug*
T *Windscreen wiper timer*

---

4 Switches - removal and refitting

Ignition switch

1 Refer to Chapter 5.

Steering column multi-function switches

Removal

2 Disconnect the battery negative lead.

3 Remove the securing screws and withdraw the steering column shrouds. Note that it may be necessary to loosen the radio/cassette player remote control switch clamp screw (see later in this Section), before the shrouds can be removed. Where applicable, also remove the internal cover.

4 Unscrew the mounting screws, withdraw the switch from the steering column, and disconnect the wiring plug **(see illustrations)**.

Refitting

5 Refitting is a reversal of removal.

Facia switches (except for headlight aim adjustment switch)

Removal

6 Disconnect the battery negative lead.

7 Prise the switch from the facia using a small

4.4a Removing a steering column multi-function switch securing screw

4.4b Removing the wash/wipe switch . . .

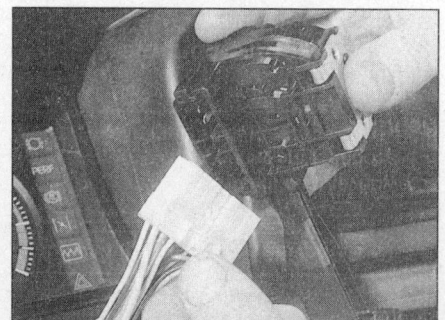

4.4c . . . and disconnecting the wiring plug

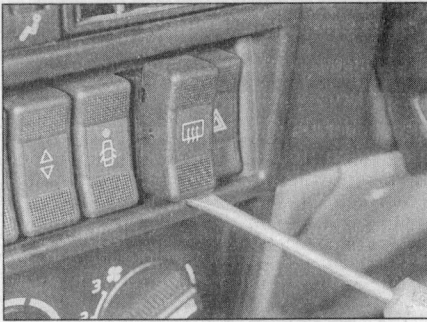

4.7 Prising out a facia switch

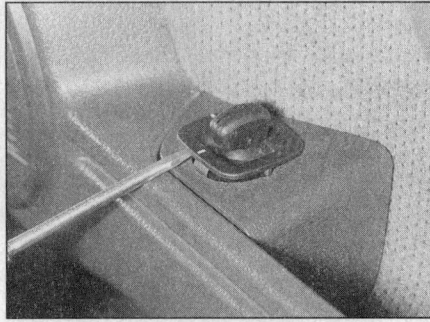

4.10a Prising out a door switch . . .

4.10b . . . for access to the wiring plug

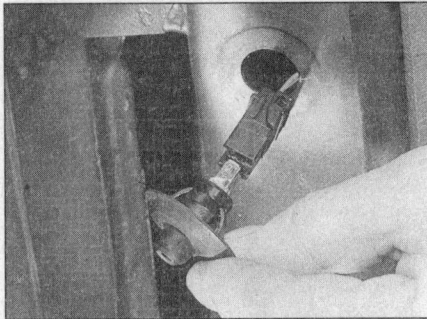

4.12 Removing a courtesy light switch

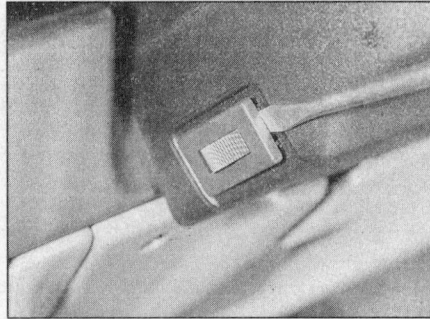

4.16 Prise out the instrument panel rheostat . . .

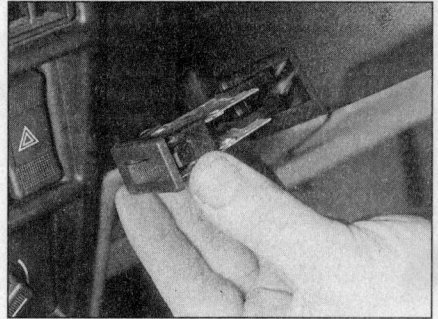

4.17 . . . and disconnect the wiring plug

screwdriver (see illustration).
8 Disconnect the wiring plug.

Refitting

9 Refitting is a reversal of removal.

Door and centre console switches

10 Proceed as described previously for the facia switches (see illustrations).

Courtesy light switches

Removal

11 Disconnect the battery negative lead.
12 With the door open, prise the switch from the door pillar using a small screwdriver (see illustration). Pull out the wiring slightly and tie a piece of string to it to prevent it dropping into the door pillar.
13 Disconnect the wiring from the switch.

Refitting

14 Refitting is a reversal of removal.

Instrument panel rheostat

Removal

15 Disconnect the battery negative lead.
16 Prise the rheostat from the steering column shroud using a small screwdriver (see illustration).
17 Disconnect the wiring plug (see illustration).

Refitting

18 Refitting is a reversal of removal.

Handbrake warning light switch

Removal

19 Disconnect the battery negative lead.
20 Make a slit in the carpet just to the rear of the handbrake lever (see illustration).
21 Disconnect the wiring from the switch (see illustration).
22 Unscrew the mounting bolt and remove the switch.

Refitting

23 Refitting is a reversal of removal.

Map reading and front courtesy light switch

Removal

24 Using a small screwdriver prise off the lens and cover panel.
25 Release the switch assembly from the headlining by depressing the plastic tabs at each end of the switch (see illustration).
26 Disconnect the wiring and remove the switch (see illustration).

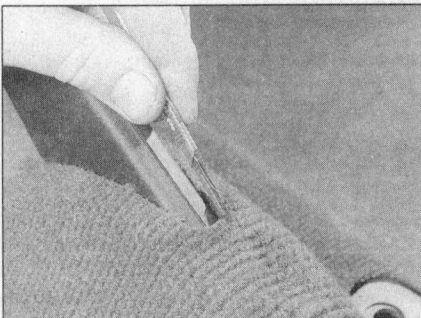

4.20 Make a slit in the carpet with a knife . . .

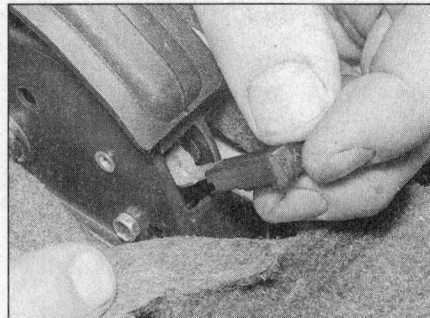

4.21 . . . and disconnect the wiring plug

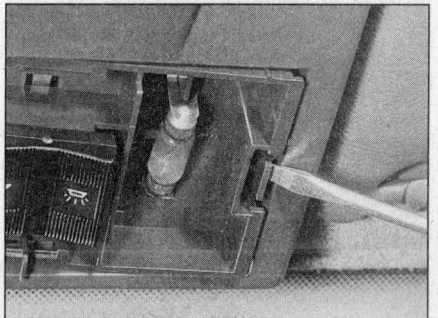

4.25 Depress the plastic tabs to release the switch

12

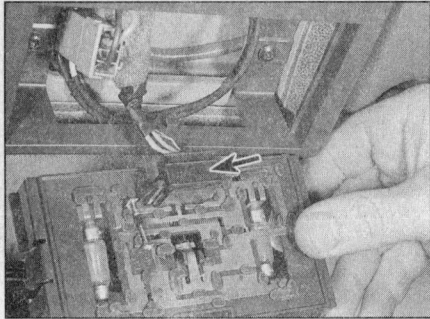

4.26 Wiring plug (arrowed) on the rear of the map reading and front courtesy light switch

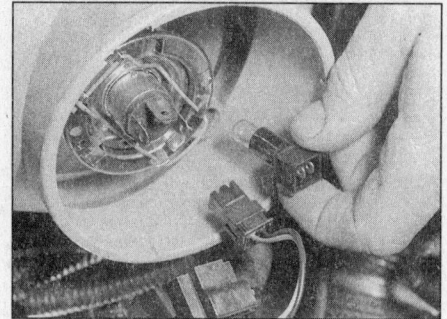

5.5 Removing a headlight bulb - "Phase 1" model

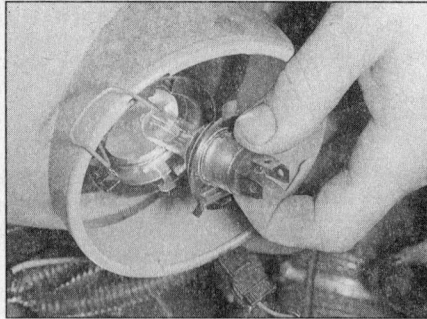

5.8 Removing a front sidelight bulb - "Phase 1" model

Refitting

27 Refitting is a reversal of removal.

Radio/cassette player remote control switch

Removal

28 Disconnect the battery negative lead.
29 Remove the radio/cassette player, as described in Section 18.
30 Disconnect the remote control switch wiring from the rear of the radio/cassette unit.
31 Slide the cover from the switch to reveal the switch clamp screw. Loosen, but do not remove the screw.
32 Remove the steering column shrouds.
33 Slide the switch from its bracket, then feed the wiring through from behind the facia, noting its routing.

Refitting

34 Refitting is a reversal of removal, noting the following points.
a) Refit the radio/cassette player as described in Section 18.
b) Ensure that the wiring is routed as noted before removal.
c) Do not fully tighten the switch clamp screw until the steering column shrouds have been refitted.

Headlight aim adjustment switch

Removal

35 The switch is secured by upper and lower metal clips.

5.12 Removing a front direction indicator bulb

36 Disconnect the battery negative lead.
37 Remove the trim panel from below the switch.
38 Reach up behind the switch (through the aperture provided by removal of the trim panel), and carefully push the switch assembly out from the facia. The clips are tight fit in the facia, so take care not to break the switch surround.
39 Disconnect the wiring plug and withdraw the switch.

Refitting

40 Refitting is a reversal of removal.

5 Bulbs (exterior lights) - renewal

Headlight

1 Disconnect the battery negative lead.
2 On "Phase 1" models, turn the headlight plastic rear cover through 90∞ to remove it. On "Phase 2" models, release the retaining tabs and pull the cover from the rear of the headlight.
3 Pull the wiring connector from the rear of the headlight bulb.
4 Release the spring clip and pivot the clip clear.
5 Withdraw the bulb from its location in the headlight **(see illustration)**. Take care not to touch the bulb glass with your fingers - if touched, clean the bulb with methylated spirit.
6 Fit the new bulb using a reversal of the

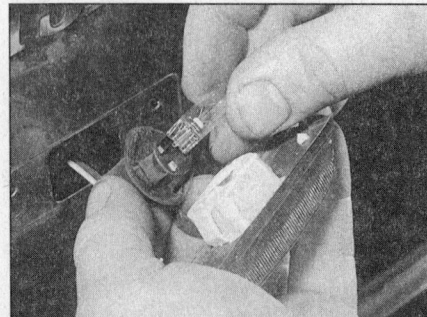

5.24 Removing a front direction indicator repeater bulb - "Phase 1" model

removal procedure, but make sure that the tabs on the bulb support are correctly located in cut-outs in the lens assembly.

Front sidelight

7 Proceed as described in paragraphs 1 to 3 inclusive.
8 On "Phase 1" models, pull the bulbholder from the light unit **(see illustration)**. On "Phase 2" models, twist the bulbholder anti-clockwise to remove it.
9 The bulb is a push-fit in the bulbholder.
10 Fit the new bulb using a reversal of the removal procedure.

Front direction indicator

Front wing-mounted assembly

11 Disconnect the battery negative lead.
12 Twist the bulbholder anti-clockwise to remove it from the rear of the light unit **(see illustration)**.
13 The bulb is a bayonet fit in the bulbholder.
14 Fit the new bulb using a reversal of the removal procedure.

Bumper-mounted assembly

15 Disconnect the battery negative lead.
16 Push one side of the light unit inwards, then insert a screwdriver behind the light unit and lever it out.
17 Release the retaining clips, and remove the lens from the light unit.
18 The bulb is a bayonet fit in the light unit.
19 Fit the new bulb using a reversal of the removal procedure.

Front direction indicator repeater

20 Disconnect the battery negative lead.
21 Carefully prise the light from the front wing, taking care not to damage the paintwork.
22 On "Phase 1" models, pull out the bulbholder and wiring.
23 On "Phase 2" models, twist the bulbholder anti-clockwise and withdraw it from the rear of the light unit.
24 The bulb is a push-fit in the bulbholder **(see illustration)**.
25 Fit the new bulb using a reversal of the removal procedure.

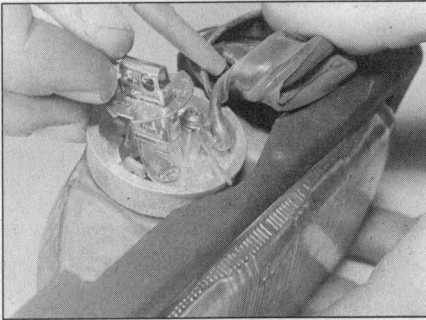
5.30 Removing a front foglight bulb -
"Phase 1" model

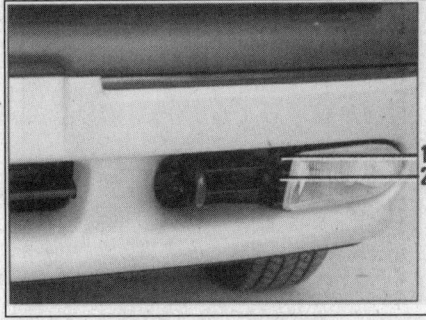
5.34 Front foglight trim plate (2) and beam
adjustment screw (1) - "Phase 2" models

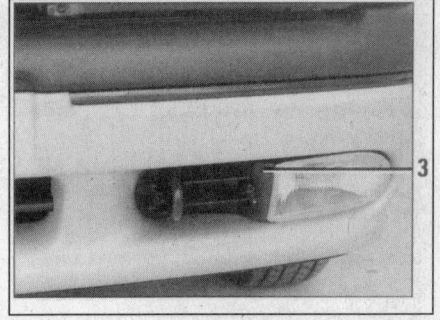
5.35 Front foglight securing screw (3) -
"Phase 2" models

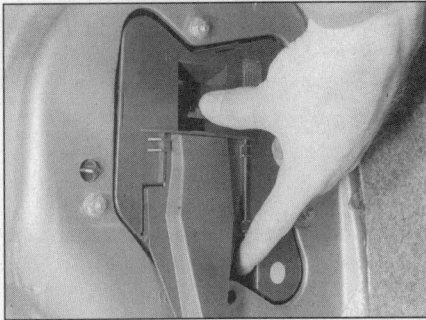
5.42 Releasing the rear light cluster
bulbholder assembly - Saloon model

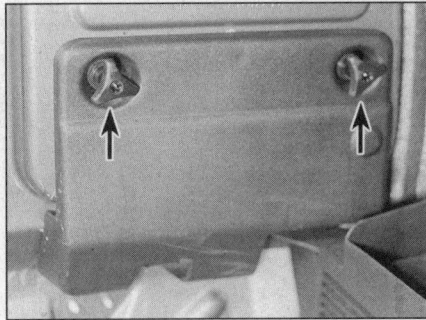
5.46 Rear light cluster cover securing nuts
(arrowed) - Hatchback model

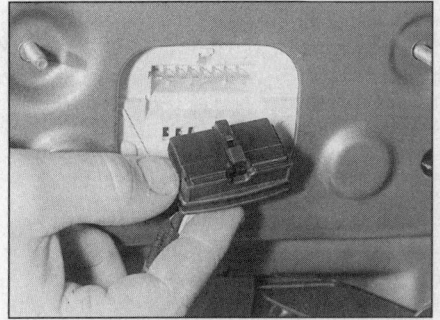
5.47 Disconnecting the rear light cluster
wiring plug - Hatchback model

Front foglight

"Phase 1" models

26 Disconnect the battery negative lead.
27 Unscrew the two screws and pull the lens unit forward.
28 Disconnect the two halves of the wiring connector and remove the lens unit.
29 Pull off the rubber cover, or twist the bulbholder and remove it from the lens unit, as applicable.
30 Depress and twist the bulb to remove it, or release the spring clip and lift out the bulb, as applicable (see illustration).
31 Hold the new bulb in a piece of paper or cloth then fit it in the bulbholder.
32 Refit the bulbholder/cover using a reversal of the removal procedure. On completion, if necessary adjust the light beam alignment using the adjusting screw at the top corner of the light.

"Phase 2" models

33 Disconnect the battery negative lead.
34 Unclip the trim plate from the inside edge of the light unit to reveal the light unit securing screw (see illustration).
35 Remove the securing screw, and withdraw the light unit from the front of the bumper (see illustration).
36 Disconnect the two wires.
37 Twist the rear cover to remove it from the rear of the light unit.
38 Release the spring clip and pivot the clip clear.
39 Withdraw the bulb.
40 Hold the new bulb in a piece of paper or

cloth then fit it using a reversal of the removal procedure.

Rear light cluster

Saloon models

41 Disconnect the battery negative lead.
42 Working in the rear luggage compartment, release the securing clips and release the bulbholder assembly from the rear of the light unit (see illustration).
43 The bulbs are a bayonet fit in the bulbholder.
44 Fit the new bulb using a reversal of the removal procedure.

Hatchback models

45 Disconnect the battery negative lead.
46 Working in the rear luggage compartment, unscrew the two plastic nuts and, where applicable release the securing clip, and withdraw the cover from the rear of the light

5.49 Removing a rear light cluster
bulbholder - Hatchback model

unit (see illustration).
47 Disconnect the wiring plug, and where applicable remove the inner cover (see illustration).
48 Withdraw the light cluster from outside the vehicle.
49 Squeeze together the two tabs and withdraw the bulbholder from the rear of the light cluster (see illustration).
50 The bulbs are a bayonet fit in the bulbholder (see illustration).
51 Fit the new bulb using a reversal of the removal procedure.

Tailgate/boot lid-mounted rear foglights - "Phase 2" models

52 Disconnect the battery negative lead.
53 Open the tailgate, and unclip the cover from the rear of the light unit.
54 Twist the bulbholder anti-clockwise to release it from the rear of the light unit.

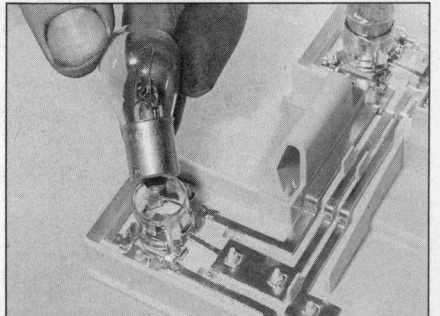
5.50 Removing a bulb from a rear light
cluster bulbholder

12

5.58 Prising out a number plate light - "Phase 1" model

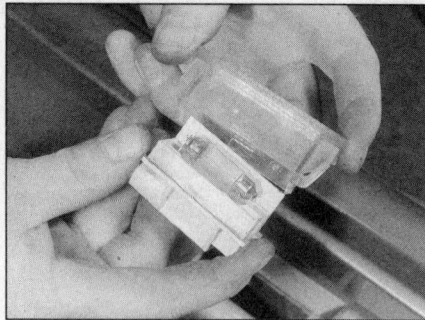

5.60 Removing a number plate light lens cover

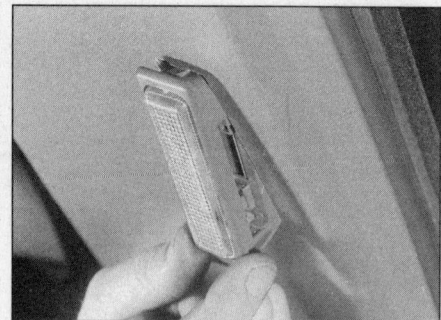

6.2a Removing the courtesy light

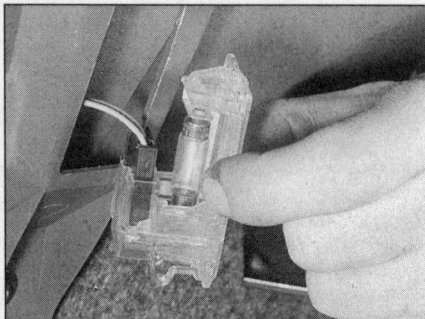

6.2b Removing the luggage compartment light - Hatchback model

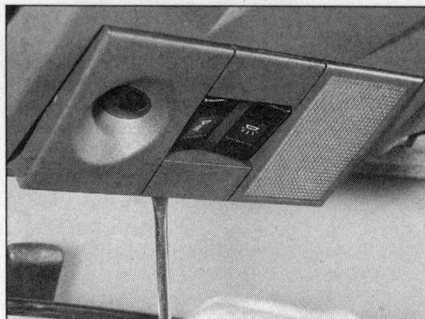

6.6 Prising the lens and cover panel from a map reading and front courtesy light

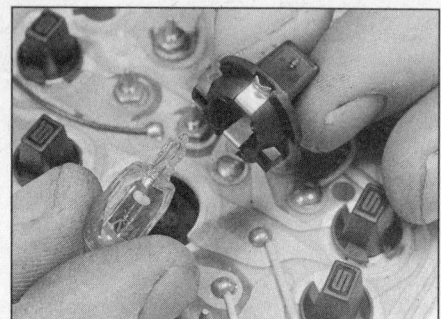

6.10 Removing an instrument panel bulb

55 The bulb is a bayonet fit in the bulbholder.
56 Fit the new bulb using a reversal of the removal procedure.

Number plate lights

57 Disconnect the battery negative lead.
58 Prise the number plate light from the rear bumper using a small screwdriver **(see illustration)**.
59 Disconnect the wiring plug from the light.
60 Remove the lens cover, then release the festoon type bulb from the spring contacts **(see illustration)**.
61 Fit the new bulb using a reversal of the removal procedure, but check the tension of the spring contacts and if necessary bend them so that they firmly contact the bulb end caps.

| 6 | Bulbs (interior lights) - renewal |

Courtesy lights and luggage compartment light

1 Disconnect the battery negative lead.
2 Prise out the light using a small screwdriver **(see illustrations)**.
3 Release the festoon type bulb from the spring contacts.
4 Fit the new bulb using a reversal of the removal procedure, but check the tension of the spring contacts and if necessary bend them so that they firmly contact the bulb end caps.

Map reading and front courtesy light

5 Disconnect the battery negative lead.
6 Using a small screwdriver prise off the lens and cover panel **(see illustration)**.
7 The remainder of the procedure is as described previously for the courtesy lights.

Instrument panel lights

8 Remove the instrument panel (Section 8).
9 Turn the bulbholder a quarter turn to align the shoulders with the slots, then remove
10 The bulbs are a push-fit in the bulbholders **(see illustration)**.
11 Fit the new bulb in reverse order.

Glovebox light

12 Open the glovebox, then proceed as described previously for the courtesy lights **(see illustration)**.

| 7 | Exterior light units - removal and refitting |

Headlight unit
"Phase 1" models

1 Disconnect the battery negative lead.
2 Turn the headlight plastic rear cover through 90° to remove it.
3 Pull off the wiring connectors.
4 Remove the direction indicator assembly as described later in this Section.
5 Unscrew the four mounting nuts from the rear of the headlight.

6.12 Removing a glovebox light

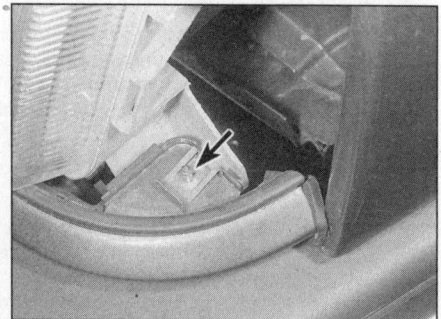

7.7 Headlight retaining screw location (arrowed) - "Phase 1" model

6 Unscrew the screws located on the inner side of the headlight.
7 Withdraw the headlight forwards and at the same time release the lug so that the hidden mounting screw can be removed **(see illustration)**.

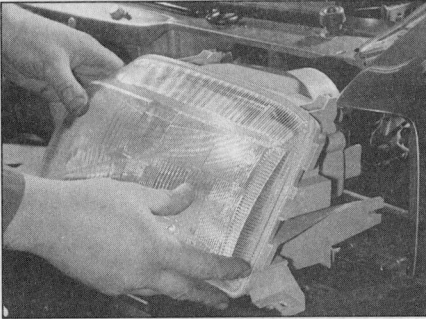

**7.8 Removing the headlight -
"Phase 1" model**

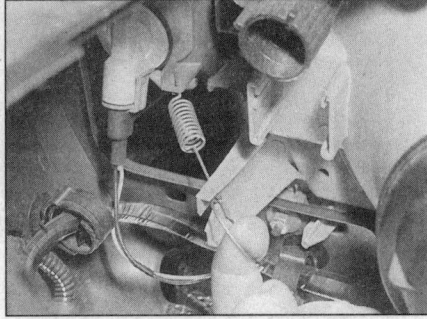

**7.22 Unhooking the front direction
indicator retaining spring -
"Phase 1" model**

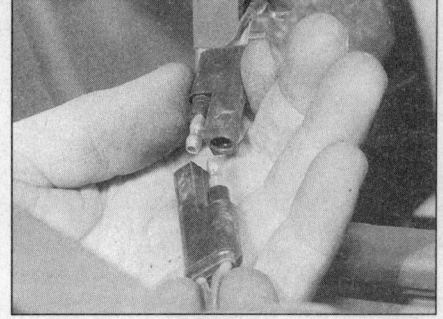

**7.36 Disconnecting the front foglight
wiring connector**

8 Remove the headlight from its location **(see
illustration)**.
9 Refitting is a reversal of removal, but before
tightening the front inner screw, align the
outer edge of the direction indicator in relation
to the front wing.
10 On completion, check the headlight aim
as described in Chapter 1.

"Phase 2" models

11 Disconnect the battery negative lead.
12 Remove the front grille panels as
described in Chapter 11.
13 Remove the direction indicator assembly
as described later in this Section.
14 Unclip the cover from the rear of the
headlight, and disconnect the wiring plugs.
15 Where applicable, disconnect the wiring
plug from the headlight aim adjuster motor.
16 Unscrew the two upper headlight
securing bolts.
17 Remove the lower securing bolt, located
at the inside edge of the headlight, and the
securing nut, located at the outside edge.
18 Withdraw the headlight unit.
19 Refitting is a reversal of removal.
20 On completion, check the headlight beam
alignment as described in Chapter 1.

Front direction indicator

Front wing-mounted assembly

21 Disconnect the battery negative lead.
22 Unhook the retaining spring from the rear
of the headlight unit **(see illustration)**.
23 Move the direction indicator unit forwards
in order to release it.

24 Turn the bulbholder and release it from
the rear of the direction indicator unit.
25 Remove the direction indicator unit from
the vehicle.
26 Refitting is a reversal of removal.

Bumper-mounted assembly

27 Disconnect the battery negative lead.
28 Push one side of the light unit inwards,
then insert a screwdriver behind the light unit
and lever it out.
29 Disconnect the wiring plug and withdraw
the light unit.
30 Refitting is a reversal of removal.

*Front direction indicator
repeater*

31 Disconnect the battery negative lead.
32 Carefully prise the light from the front
wing taking care not to damage the
paintwork.
33 Pull out the bulbholder and wiring, then
remove the light.
34 Refitting is a reversal of removal.

Front foglights

"Phase 1" models

35 Disconnect the battery negative lead.
36 Unscrew the two securing screws,
withdraw the foglight unit from the bumper,
and disconnect the two halves of the wiring
connector **(see illustration)**.
37 Refitting is a reversal of removal, but if
necessary adjust the foglight by turning the
adjustment screw located on the upper corner
of the foglight.

"Phase 2" models

38 Disconnect the battery negative lead.
39 Unclip the trim plate from the inside edge
of the light unit to reveal the light unit screw.
40 Remove the securing screw, and
withdraw the light unit from the front of the
bumper.
41 Disconnect the two wires.
42 Refitting is a reversal of removal, but if
necessary adjust the foglight by turning the
adjustment screw located on the upper corner
of the foglight.

Rear light cluster

Saloon models

43 Disconnect the battery negative lead.
44 Working in the rear luggage compartment,
release the securing clips, and withdraw the
bulbholder assembly from the rear of the light
unit.
45 Unscrew the securing nuts from inside the
luggage compartment, then withdraw the light
unit from outside the vehicle **(see illustration)**.
46 Refitting is a reversal of removal.

Hatchback models

47 Disconnect the battery negative lead.
48 Working in the rear luggage compartment,
unscrew the two plastic nuts and unclip the
cover from the rear of the light cluster.
49 Disconnect the wiring plug and, where
applicable, remove the inner cover.
50 Withdraw the light unit from outside the
vehicle.
51 Refitting is a reversal of removal.

Number plate lights

52 Prise the number plate light from the rear
bumper using a small screwdriver, then
disconnect the wiring plug **(see illustration)**.
53 Refitting is a reversal of removal.

---

8   Instrument panel - removal
and refitting

"Phase 1" models

Removal

1 Disconnect the battery negative lead.

12

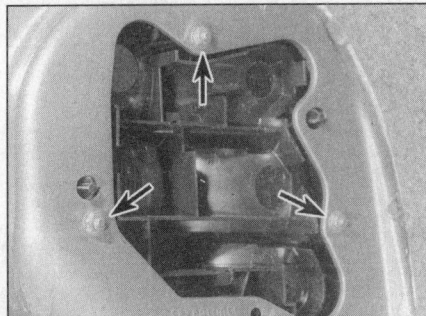

**7.45 Rear light cluster securing nuts
(arrowed) - Saloon model**

**7.52 Disconnecting the number plate light
wiring plug - "Phase 1" model**

8.4 Unscrewing one of the top instrument panel visor securing screws - "Phase 1" model

8.5a Unscrewing a lower instrument panel visor securing screw (arrowed) - "Phase 1" model

8.5b Removing the instrument panel visor - "Phase 1" model

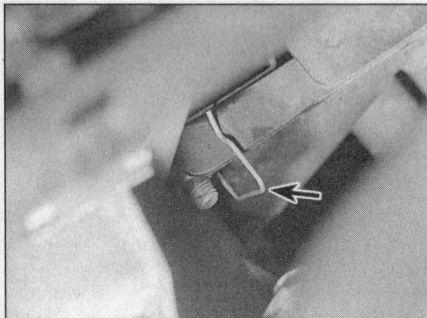

8.6 Speedometer cable retaining spring (arrowed) at the gearbox end

8.7a Remove the securing screws . . .

8.7b . . . and pull out the instrument panel - "Phase 1" models

2 Remove the steering wheel as described in Chapter 10.

3 Remove the securing screws, and remove the steering column shrouds. Note that it may be necessary to loosen the radio/cassette player remote control switch clamp screw (see Section 4) before the shrouds can be removed. Where applicable, also remove the internal cover.

4 Unscrew and remove the screws securing the top of the instrument panel visor to the facia **(see illustration)**.

5 Unscrew and remove the screws securing the bottom of the instrument panel visor to the facia and remove the visor. The screws are located on each side of the steering column **(see illustrations)**.

6 Working in the engine compartment, pull out the spring clip and disconnect the speedometer cable from the gearbox **(see illustration)**. Release the cable from the support clips in the engine compartment.

7 Unscrew the screws securing the top of the instrument panel to the facia, then pull out the panel until there is sufficient room to reach behind it and disconnect the speedometer cable **(see illustrations)**.

8 Note the location of all the wiring connectors then disconnect them from the rear of the instrument panel. Withdraw the instrument panel from the facia.

Refitting

9 Refitting is a reversal of removal. On completion check the function of all electrical components.

"Phase 2" models

Removal

10 Proceed as described in paragraphs 1 to 3 inclusive.

11 Remove the two securing screws, and withdraw the instrument panel visor **(see illustration)**.

12 Unscrew the securing screws, and remove the facia panel from below the steering column.

13 Remove the two upper instrument panel securing screws **(see illustration)**.

14 For access to the lower right-hand instrument panel securing bolt, it is necessary to move the ignition switch wiring connector mounting. Remove the mounting by pulling it towards the steering column before sliding it along its retaining runner.

15 Remove the two lower instrument panel securing screws.

16 Working in the engine compartment, release the securing clip(s) and disconnect the speedometer cable from the gearbox.

17 Tilt the instrument panel for access to the speedometer cable and wiring connections.

18 Disconnect the wiring connectors and the

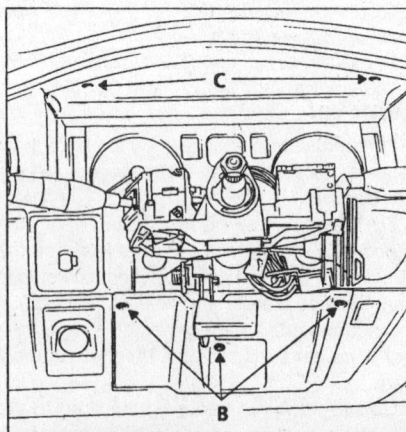

8.11 Facia panel securing screws (B) and instrument panel visor securing screws (C) - "Phase 2" models

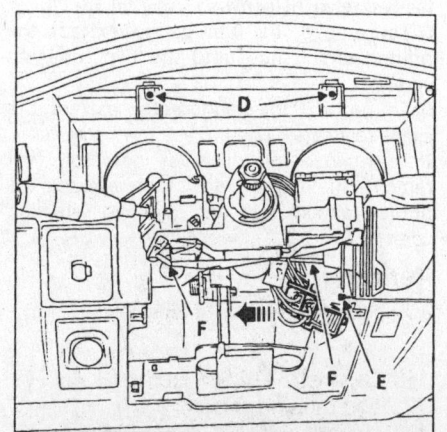

8.13 Upper instrument panel securing screws (D), lower securing bolts (F), and wiring connector mounting (E) - "Phase 2" models

11.2 Prising the clock from the facia

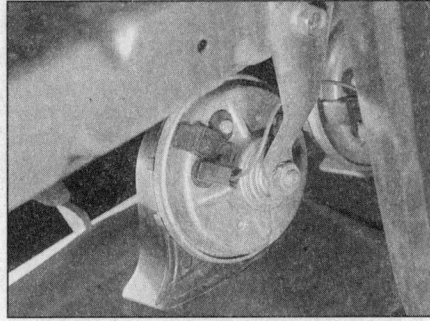

12.1 Typical horn location (viewed from front of vehicle)

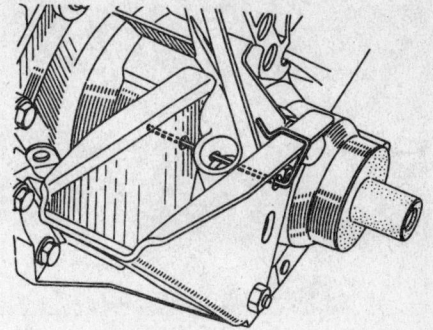

13.5 Correct position of the speedometer cable retaining clip in the rear engine mounting bracket

speedometer cable from the rear of the instrument panel, then withdraw the panel from the facia.

Refitting

19 Refitting is a reversal of removal, but ensure that all wiring connectors and the speedometer cable are securely reconnected.

9 Instrument panel components - removal and refitting

Note: *Various different instrument panel layouts may be encountered depending on model. Although the details may differ from those described, the following paragraphs can be used as a guide for all models.*

Removal

1 Remove the instrument panel as described in Section 8.
2 Prise the plastic hooks outwards and remove the front cover.
3 To remove the speedometer extract the two screws from the front and rear of the unit.
4 To remove the coolant temperature indicator extract the printed circuit nuts and the two retaining screws.
5 To remove the fuel gauge extract the printed circuit nuts and the two retaining screws.
6 To remove the tachometer extract the single rear screw and the two front screws.
7 To remove the oil level indicator, first remove the tachometer, then extract the printed circuit nuts and the two retaining screws.

Refitting

8 Refitting is a reversal of removal.

10 Cigarette lighter - removal and refitting

Removal

1 Disconnect the battery negative lead.

2 Pull out the ashtray.
3 Push the cigar lighter out of its location and disconnect the wiring.
4 To remove the fixed metal section of the cigar lighter, push from behind the main body while releasing the two tabs. Also remove the plastic cover.

Refitting

5 Refitting is a reversal of removal.

11 Clock - removal and refitting

Removal

1 Disconnect the battery negative lead.
2 Carefully prise the clock from the facia and disconnect the wiring plug **(see illustration)**. The clock is retained by plastic clips which are pushed aside as the clock is removed.

Refitting

3 Refitting is a reversal of removal.

12 Horn - removal and refitting

Removal

1 The horn(s) is/are located on the body front valance behind the front bumper **(see illustration)**.
2 To remove a horn, first apply the handbrake, then jack up the front of the vehicle and support it securely on axle stands (see *"Jacking, towing and wheel changing"*).
3 Disconnect the battery negative lead, then reach up and disconnect the horn supply lead.
4 Unscrew the nut securing the horn to the mounting bracket and remove the horn from the vehicle.

Refitting

5 Refitting is a reversal of removal.

13 Speedometer drive cable - removal and refitting

Removal

1 Refer to Section 8 and remove the instrument panel sufficiently to allow the speedometer cable to be disconnected.
2 Where a trip computer is fitted, disconnect the sender unit from the upper and lower cable sections.
3 Working in the engine compartment, unclip or unscrew the end of the speedometer cable from the gearbox. Where applicable, note how the securing clip locates on the gearbox, as several types of clip are used.
4 Withdraw the speedometer drive cable into the passenger compartment through the bulkhead, noting its routing.

Refitting

5 Refitting is a reversal of removal, bearing in mind the following points.
a) On models where the speedometer cable is secured to the gearbox by a wire clip, ensure that the clip is located as shown **(see illustration)**.
b) Make sure that the cable is routed as noted before removal, and be careful not to kink or twist the cable between the bulkhead and the rear of the instrument panel.

14 Windscreen wiper motor and linkage - removal and refitting

Removal

1 Operate the wiper motor then switch it off so that it returns to its rest position.
2 Disconnect the battery negative lead.
3 Remove the windscreen wiper arms with reference to Chapter 1.
4 Remove the battery as described in Chapter 5.
5 Unbolt and remove the plastic cover from

12

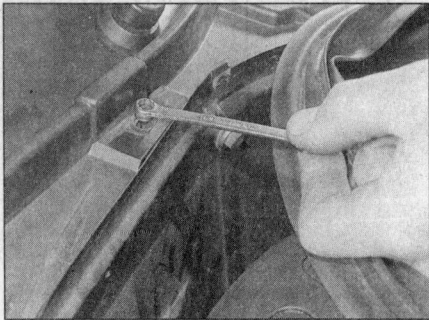

14.5 Unbolting the plastic cover from the plenum chamber

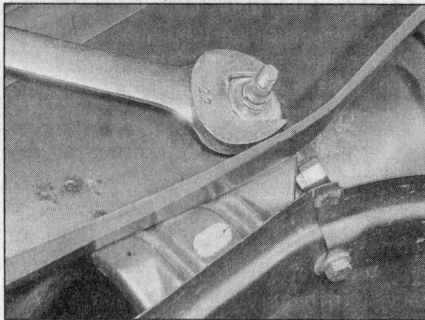

14.6 Unscrewing a wiper spindle nut

14.7 Windscreen wiper motor mounting bolts (arrowed)

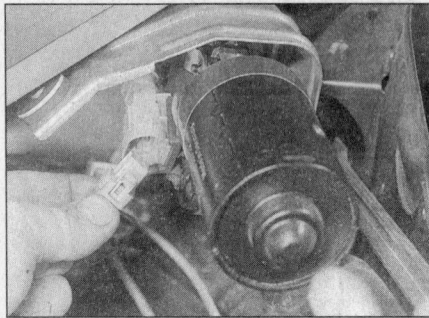

14.8 Disconnecting the wiper motor wiring plug

15.6a Disconnect the wiring plug . . .

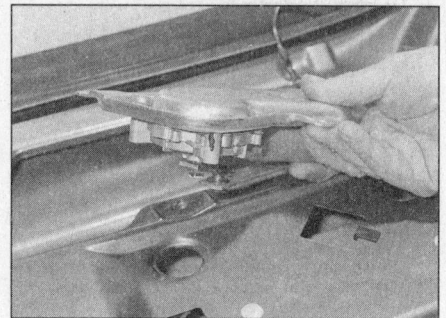

15.6b . . . then unbolt and remove the wiper motor/linkage assembly

the plenum chamber just in front of the windscreen **(see illustration)**.

6 Unscrew the nuts from the wiper spindles protruding through the windscreen valance **(see illustration)**.

7 Unscrew and remove the mounting bolts **(see illustration)**.

8 Disconnect the wiring plug **(see illustration)**.

9 Withdraw the wiper motor and linkage assembly from the bulkhead.

10 If necessary the linkage may be separated from the motor by removing the cranked arm and unbolting the linkage.

Refitting

11 Refitting is a reversal of removal.

15 Tailgate wiper motor and linkage - removal and refitting

Removal

1 Operate the wiper, then switch it off so that it returns to its rest position. Note that the wiper motor will only operate with the tailgate shut as the spring tensioned connector pins must be in contact with the contact plates.

2 Disconnect the battery negative lead.

3 Remove the wiper arm with reference to Chapter 1.

4 Unscrew the nut from the spindle housing protruding through the tailgate.

5 Remove the trim panel from inside the tailgate.

6 Disconnect the wiring plug, then unbolt and

remove the wiper motor/linkage assembly from inside the tailgate **(see illustrations)**.

7 If necessary, the connector pin assembly and connector plate assembly may be removed and the wiring disconnected **(see illustrations)**.

Refitting

8 Refitting is a reversal of removal.

16 Rear window wiper motor and linkage (Saloon models) - removal and refitting

Removal

1 Disconnect the battery negative lead.

2 Remove the wiper arm with reference to Chapter 1.

3 Remove the cover from the spindle nut, then unscrew the nut.

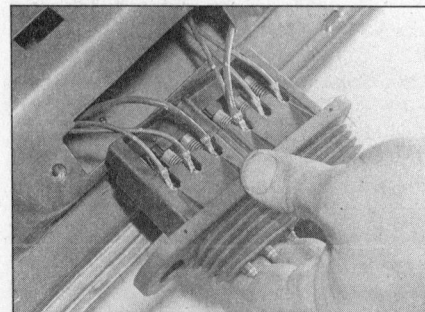

15.7a Removing the tailgate connector pin assembly . . .

4 Remove the plastic washer and the metal cup from the spindle.

5 Pull the rubber grommet from the window, taking care not to damage the glass.

6 Gently pull the washer jet free.

7 Working inside the vehicle, remove the two securing screws and withdraw the cover from the motor.

8 Disconnect the wiring plug.

9 Remove the two screws securing the motor mounting bracket, taking care not to damage the heated rear window with the screwdriver.

10 Lift the motor and its mounting bracket, free the left-hand side of the bracket, and pass it over the wiring harness. Take care not to break the washer jet positioning lug **(see illustration)**.

11 Free the spindle from the hole in the rear window, pivot the assembly, and withdraw it to the right. Remove the assembly carefully, as the washer tube is connected to the motor spacer.

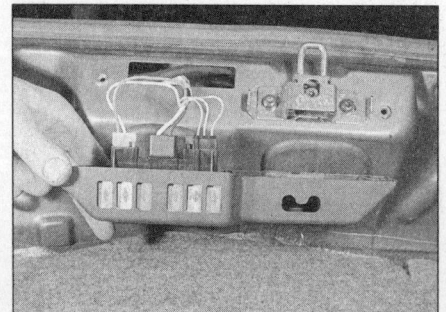

15.7b . . . and tailgate connector plate assembly

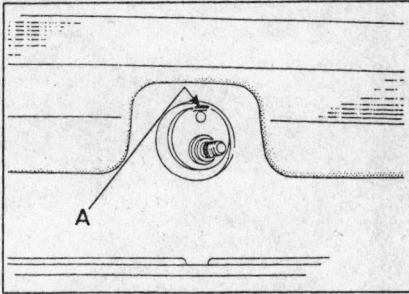

16.10 Rear washer jet positioning lug (A) - Saloon models

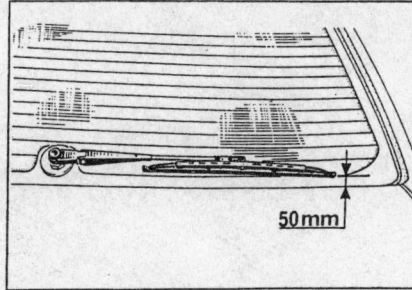

16.19 Rear wiper blade positioning - Saloon models

18.2 Using the U-shaped rods to remove the radio/cassette player

Refitting

12 Manipulate the motor back into position, ensuring that the wiring harness and washer tube are not trapped by the motor bracket.

13 Refit, but do not fully tighten the motor bracket securing screws.

14 Clean the area around the motor spindle on the window glass, then refit the following components in the order given.
 a) A new rubber grommet.
 b) Washer jet.
 c) Metal cup.
 d) Plastic washer.

15 Tighten the motor spindle nut. Note that the motor spindle does not locate in the centre of the hole in the rear window.

16 Working inside the vehicle, tighten the two motor bracket securing screws, again taking care not to damage the heated rear window.

17 Refit the motor cover.

18 Refit the cover to the spindle nut.

19 Ensure that the motor is in the park position, then refit the wiper arm, positioning the end of the wiper arm 50 mm away from the edge of the rear window seal **(see illustration)**.

20 Check that the wiper operates correctly, and if necessary adjust the washer jet.

17 Windscreen/headlight washer system components - removal and refitting

Removal

1 Disconnect the battery negative lead.

2 The reservoir is located at the front right-hand corner of the engine compartment.

3 To enable access, the fuel filter assembly must be unbolted from the front wing. Unclip the fuel and coolant hoses from the clips on the engine, then remove the two securing bolts, and move the assembly clear of the fluid reservoir, taking care not to strain the hoses.

4 Unscrew the mounting screw(s) and lift the reservoir from the front right-hand corner of the engine compartment. Where applicable, the front washer reservoir also supplies the rear window wash by means of a tube running along the right-hand lower edge of the floor area and up the right-hand rear corner pillar.

5 Disconnect the wiring from the pump, then disconnect the tubing from the reservoir.

6 Empty the reservoir of any remaining fluid then pull the pump from the rubber grommet.

7 Disconnect the tubing from the pump and remove the grommet from the reservoir.

Refitting

8 Refitting is a reversal of removal.

18 Radio/cassette player - removal and refitting

Removal

1 Disconnect the battery negative lead. If the radio/cassette has a security code, make sure this is known before disconnecting the battery.

2 In order to release the retaining clips, two U-shaped rods must be inserted into the special holes on each side of the unit **(see illustration)**. If possible, it is preferable to obtain purpose made rods from an audio specialist, as these have cut-outs which snap firmly into the clips so that the radio can be pulled out.

3 Withdraw the unit enough to disconnect the wiring plugs and aerial lead **(see illustration)**.

Refitting

4 Refitting is a reversal of removal.

19 Speakers - removal and refitting

Removal

1 To remove a front speaker located on the top of the facia panel, where applicable, remove the securing screws, then prise out the speaker grille panel. Remove the speaker securing screws, then lift out the speaker and disconnect the wiring.

2 Access to the rear speakers is gained by opening the rear tailgate/boot lid. Disconnect the wiring then remove the screws and withdraw the speaker.

3 To remove a door speaker, first remove the speaker cover. On "Phase 1" models, turn the speaker cover anti-clockwise and remove it. On "Phase 2" models, remove the screws,

then pull the speaker cover from the door. Remove the screws and withdraw the speaker, then disconnect the wiring.

Refitting

4 Refitting is a reversal of removal.

20 Radio aerial - removal and refitting

Removal

1 Remove the map reading and front courtesy light switch assembly with reference to Section 4.

2 Unscrew the nut from the bottom of the aerial, disconnect the lead, then remove the aerial from the outside of the vehicle **(see illustration)**.

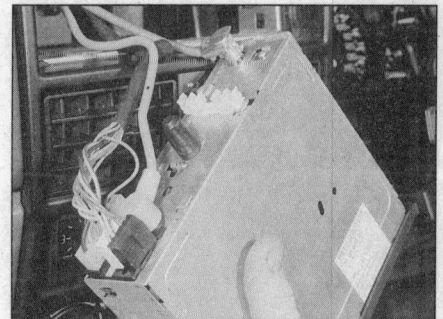

18.3 Aerial lead and wiring plugs on rear of radio/cassette player

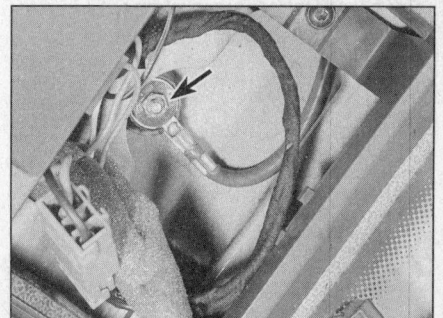

20.2 Radio aerial lead connection to the aerial (arrowed)

12

21.2a Remove the screw from the remote control door locking transmitter . . .

21.2b . . . and separate the covers

22.4 Removing a headlight aim adjustment motor

Refitting

3 Refitting is a reversal of removal.

21 Remote control door locking system - general

1 The ignition key incorporates an infra-red remote control door locking transmitter. The transmitter signal is decoded by a receiver mounted on the roof console and this activates the electro-mechanical system to lock or unlock the doors.
2 The transmitter is powered by two 1.5 volt alkaline type batteries which have a life of approximately 12 months. The batteries can be renewed after unscrewing the transmitter case screw and opening the case to gain access **(see illustrations)**.
3 In the event of a fault occurring in the system it is recommended that you seek the advice of a Renault dealer as specialist knowledge and equipment are necessary for accurate fault diagnosis.

22 Headlight aim adjustment motor - removal and refitting

Removal

1 Disconnect the battery negative lead.
2 Working at the rear of the headlight, disconnect the motor wiring plug.
3 Pull the motor securing clip down to release it, then twist the motor clockwise.

4 Pull the motor sharply from the rear of the light to release the adjuster balljoint **(see illustration)**. Take care, as it is easy to break the balljoint.

Refitting

5 Refitting is a reversal of removal, but hold the rear of the headlight reflector when pushing the motor balljoint into position.

23 Anti-theft alarm system - general

Certain models are fitted with an anti-theft alarm and/or engine immobiliser system as standard or optional equipment.

Various systems may be fitted, some operating in conjunction with the remote control central door locking system.

Some systems have a self-diagnosis function, which can be used to detect faults in conjunction with Renault dedicated test equipment.

No specific details were available for the anti-theft systems at the time of writing. Consult a Renault dealer for further information.

24 Air bag - general information and precautions

General information

Certain models are fitted with a driver's side air bag, located in the steering wheel boss.

The system consists of the air bag unit, a gas cartridge, an electronic unit, two batteries, and a warning light, all incorporated in the steering wheel.

In the event of a severe frontal impact, the air bag inflates (in about 30 milliseconds), softening the impact of the driver's head with the steering wheel. The air bag then deflates.

The warning light, incorporated in the steering wheel illuminates to indicate that the air bag battery charge is low, or there is a fault with the system.

Precautions

The following precautions **must** be observed when working on models equipped with an air bag.

Do not, under any circumstances, attempt to carry out any work on the steering wheel or the air bag system itself. Consult a Renault dealer if any work involving the steering wheel is to be carried out.

Do not cover the steering wheel hub.

If the air bag warning light illuminates, take the vehicle to a Renault dealer as soon as possible to have the system checked.

If the vehicle is involved in an accident, have the air bag system checked by a Renault dealer as soon as possible.

In the event of the vehicle being scrapped, contact a Renault dealer first to have the gas cartridge removed from the steering wheel.

If the vehicle has been stolen, or an attempt has been made to steal the vehicle, have the air bag system checked by a Renault dealer as a precaution.

If you sell the vehicle, inform the new owner that an air bag system is fitted.

NOTES

1. All diagrams are divided into numbered circuits depending on function e.g. Diagram 2 : Exterior lighting.
2. Items are arranged in relation to a plan view of the vehicle.
3. Wires may interconnect between diagrams and are located by using a grid reference e.g. 2/A1 denotes a position on diagram 2 grid location A1.
4. All earth wires are coloured black.
5. Complex items appear on the diagrams as blocks and are expanded on the internal connections page.
6. Brackets show how the circuit may be connected in more than one way.
7. Not all items are fitted to all models.

INTERNAL CONNECTION DETAILS

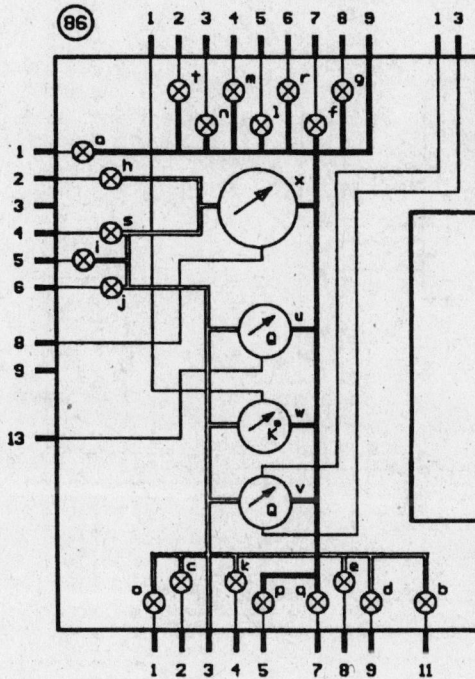

FUSE	RATING	CIRCUIT
1	30A	LH electric window
2	30A	RH electric window
3	10A	LH side lights
4	10A	RH side lights, lights on buzzer and switch lighting
5	10A	Rear foglight
6	10A	Direction indicator flasher unit
7	30A	Air conditioning
8	20A	Cooling fan
9	30A	Air conditioning
10	10A	Automatic transmission
12	5A	Automatic transmission
13	15A	Anti-lock brakes
14	20A	Sunroof, heated rear window and heated door mirrors
15	5A	Alarm
17	10A	Clock, radio and alarm
18	20A	Heater blower
19	30A	Headlight washer
20	10A	Windscreen wiper timer
21	30A	Central door locking
22	20A	Heated rear window
23	15A	Radio, interior light and luggage compartment light
24	30A	Accessories cut-off (cuts off power to interior lights, clock etc. before the ignition)
25	15A	Clock, alarm and electric door mirrors
26	15A	Front wash/wipe
27	10A	Heated seats
28	15A	Rear wash/wipe, cigar lighter and reversing lights
29	10A	Stop lights

KEY TO INSTRUMENT CLUSTER (ITEM 86)

a	=	Hazard warning light
b	=	No charge warning light
c	=	Oil pressure warning light
d	=	Brake system warning light
e	=	High temperature warning light
f	=	Rear foglight warning light
g	=	Heated rear window warning light
h	=	Brake pad wear warning light
i	=	Choke warning light
j	=	Injection warning light
k	=	Preheater warning light
l	=	Sidelight warning light
m	=	Dipped beam warning light
n	=	Main beam warning light
o	=	Low fuel warning light
p	=	Direction indicator LH
q	=	Direction indicator RH
r	=	Front foglight warning light
s	=	ABS warning light
t	=	Instrument illumination
u	=	Fuel gauge
v	=	Oil level gauge
w	=	Coolant temperature gauge
x	=	Tachometer

KEY TO SYMBOLS

PLUG-IN CONNECTOR	
PLUG	
SOCKET	
EARTH	
BULB	
DIODE	
VARIABLE RESISTOR	
MOTOR/PUMP	
PRESSURE ACTUATED	
TEMPERATURE ACTUATED	
LEVEL ACTUATED	
LINE CONNECTORS	
FUSE/ FUSIBLE LINK	

Notes, internal connection details and key to symbols

H24954

WIRE COLOURS

Ba White
Be Blue
Bj Beige
Cy Clear
Gr Grey
Ja Yellow
Ma Brown
No Black
Or Orange
Rg Red
Sa Pink
Ve Green
Vi Mauve

KEY TO ITEMS

7 Alternator
11 Battery
12 Brake pad wear sensor
21 Choke switch
29 Coolant temp. gauge sender unit
31 Cooling fan motor
32 Cooling fan switch
57 Fuel gauge sender unit
65 Handbrake warning switch
79 Ignition switch
82 Glow plug control unit
83 Pre heating thermal switch
84 Glow plugs
86 Instrument cluster
101 Low brake fluid sender unit
104 Oil level sender unit
105 Oil pressure switch
120 Starter motor
138 Throttle position switch
139 Pump advance solenoid
140 Fuel shut off solenoid
141 Cooling fan relay

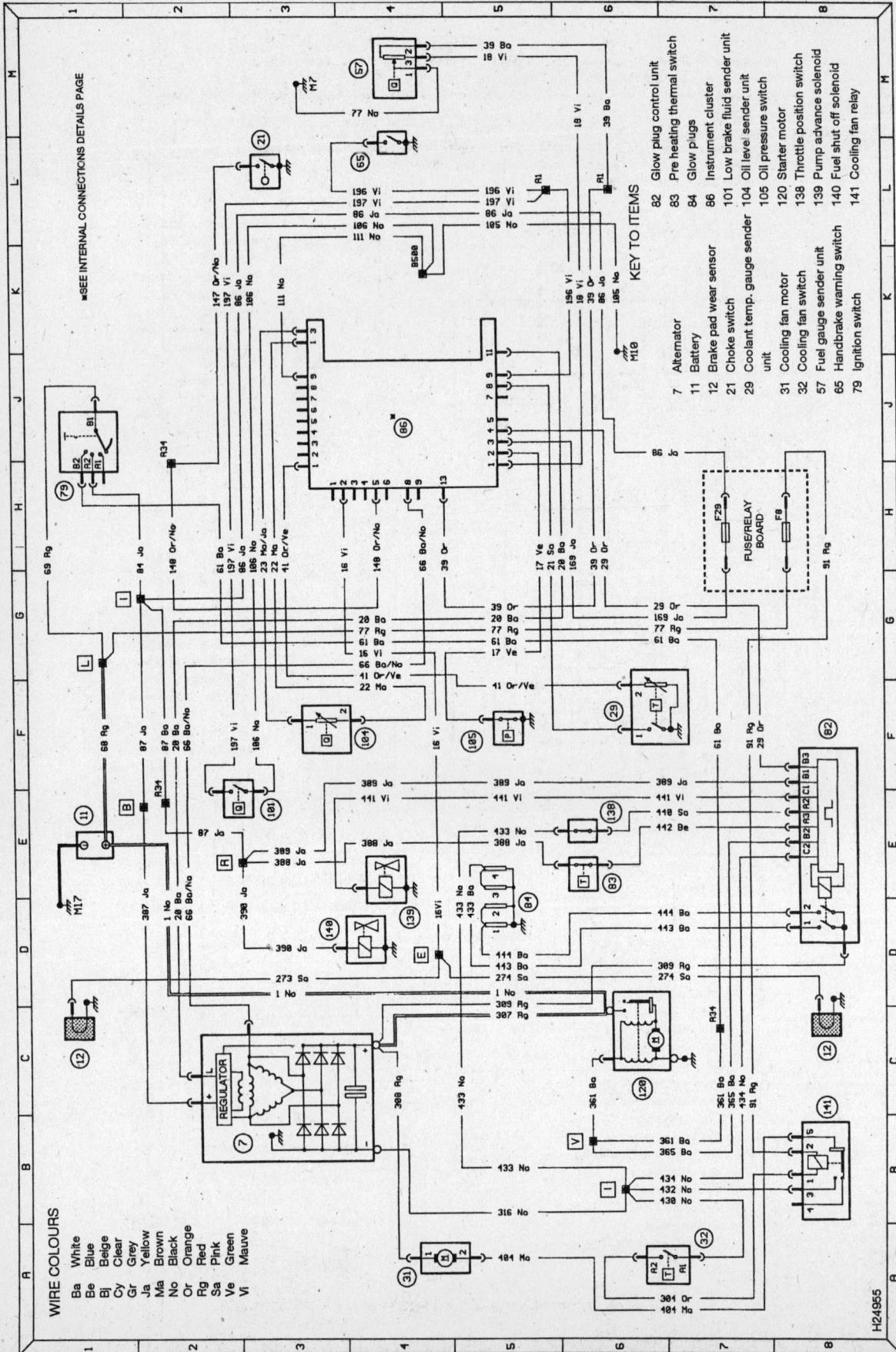

Diagram 1: Starting, charging, glow plugs, cooling fan, warning lights and instruments

H24955

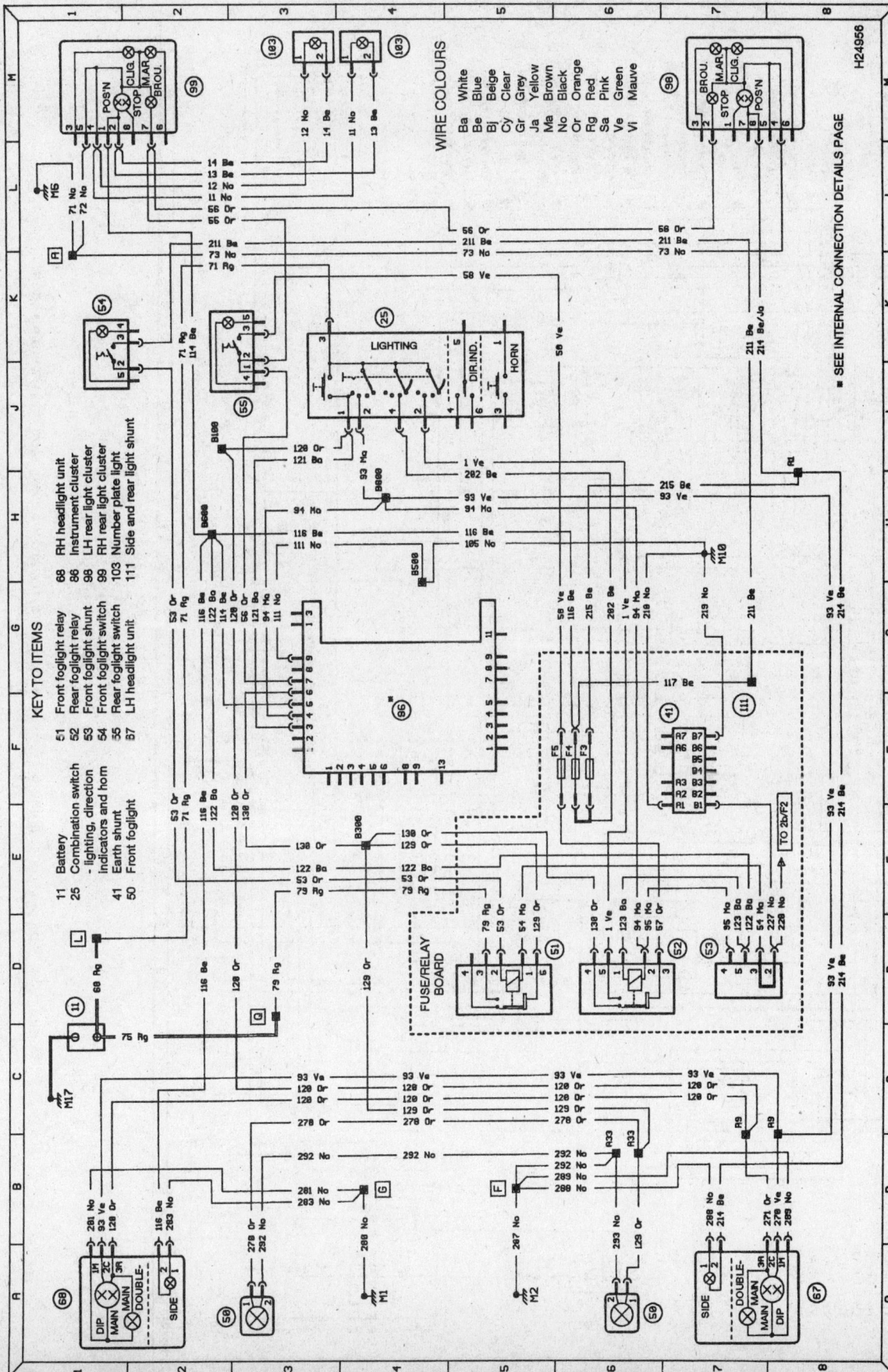

H24956

WIRE COLOURS

Ba	White
Be	Blue
Bj	Beige
Cy	Clear
Gr	Grey
Ja	Yellow
Ma	Brown
No	Black
Or	Orange
Rg	Red
Sa	Pink
Ve	Green
Vi	Mauve

* SEE INTERNAL CONNECTION DETAILS PAGE

KEY TO ITEMS

11	Battery	68	RH headlight unit
25	Combination switch	86	Instrument cluster
	– lighting, direction	98	LH rear light cluster
	indicators and horn	99	RH rear light cluster
41	Earth shunt	103	Number plate light
50	Front foglight	111	Side and rear light shunt
51	Front foglight relay		
52	Rear foglight relay		
53	Front foglight shunt		
54	Front foglight switch		
55	Rear foglight switch		
57	LH headlight unit		

Diagram 2: Typical exterior lighting - fog, side and headlights. All models

12

KEY TO ITEMS

11 Battery
25 Combination switch - lighting, direction indicators and horn
35 Direction indicator flasher relay
36 LH front direction indicator
37 LH direction indicator side repeater
38 RH front direction indicator
39 RH direction indicator side repeater
66 Hazard warning light switch
70 Heated rear window relay
79 Ignition switch
86 Instrument cluster
98 LH rear light cluster
99 RH rear light cluster
109 Reversing light switch
121 Stop light switch

* SEE INTERNAL CONNECTIONS DETAILS PAGE

WIRE COLOURS

Ba White
Be Blue
Bj Beige
Cy Clear
Gr Grey
Ja Yellow
Ma Brown
No Black
Or Orange
Rg Red
Sa Pink
Ve Green
Vi Mauve

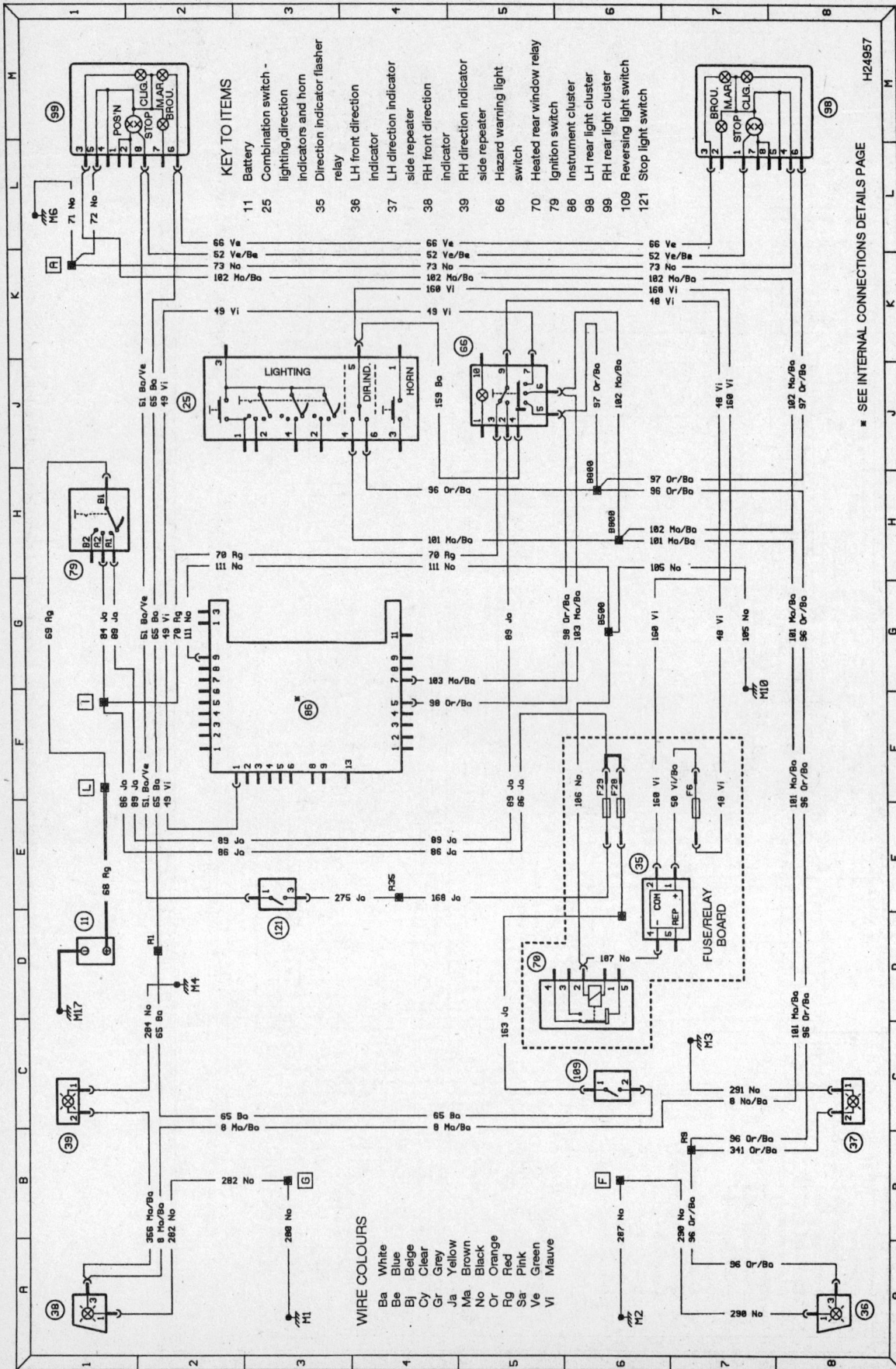

Diagram 2a: Typical exterior lighting - direction indicators, hazard warning, stop and reversing lights

H24957

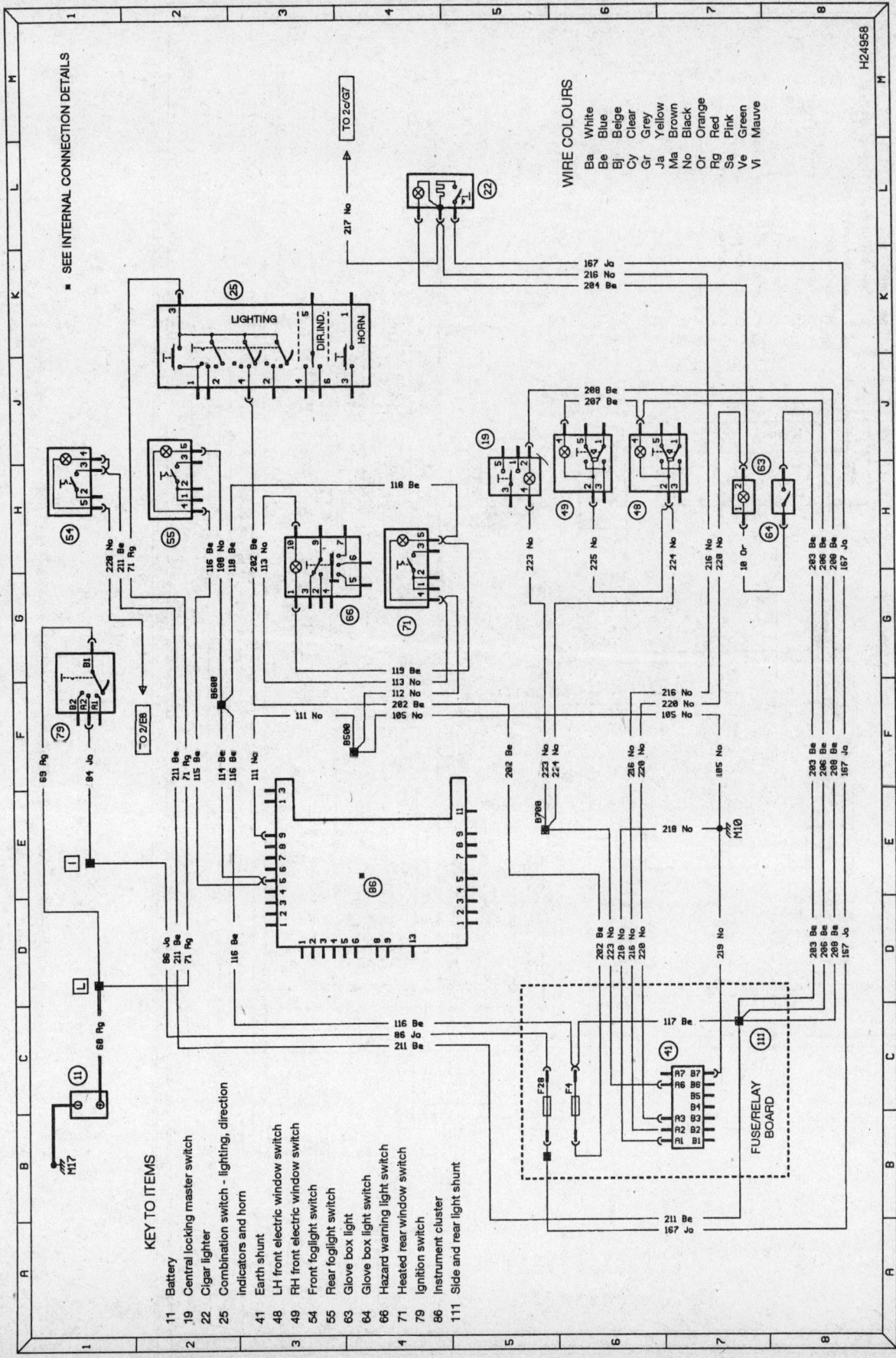

H24958

SEE INTERNAL CONNECTION DETAILS

TO 2c/G7

WIRE COLOURS

Ba	White
Be	Blue
Bj	Beige
Cy	Clear
Gr	Grey
Ja	Yellow
Ma	Brown
No	Black
Or	Orange
Rg	Red
Sa	Pink
Ve	Green
Vi	Mauve

LIGHTING

DIR.IND.

HORN

KEY TO ITEMS

11	Battery
19	Central locking master switch
22	Cigar lighter
25	Combination switch - lighting, direction indicators and horn
41	Earth shunt
48	LH front electric window switch
49	RH front electric window switch
54	Front foglight switch
55	Rear foglight switch
63	Glove box light
64	Glove box light switch
66	Hazard warning light switch
71	Heated rear window switch
79	Ignition switch
86	Instrument cluster
111	Side and rear light shunt

FUSE/RELAY BOARD

Diagram 2b: Typical interior lighting - switch and cigarette lighter illumination, and glovebox light

12

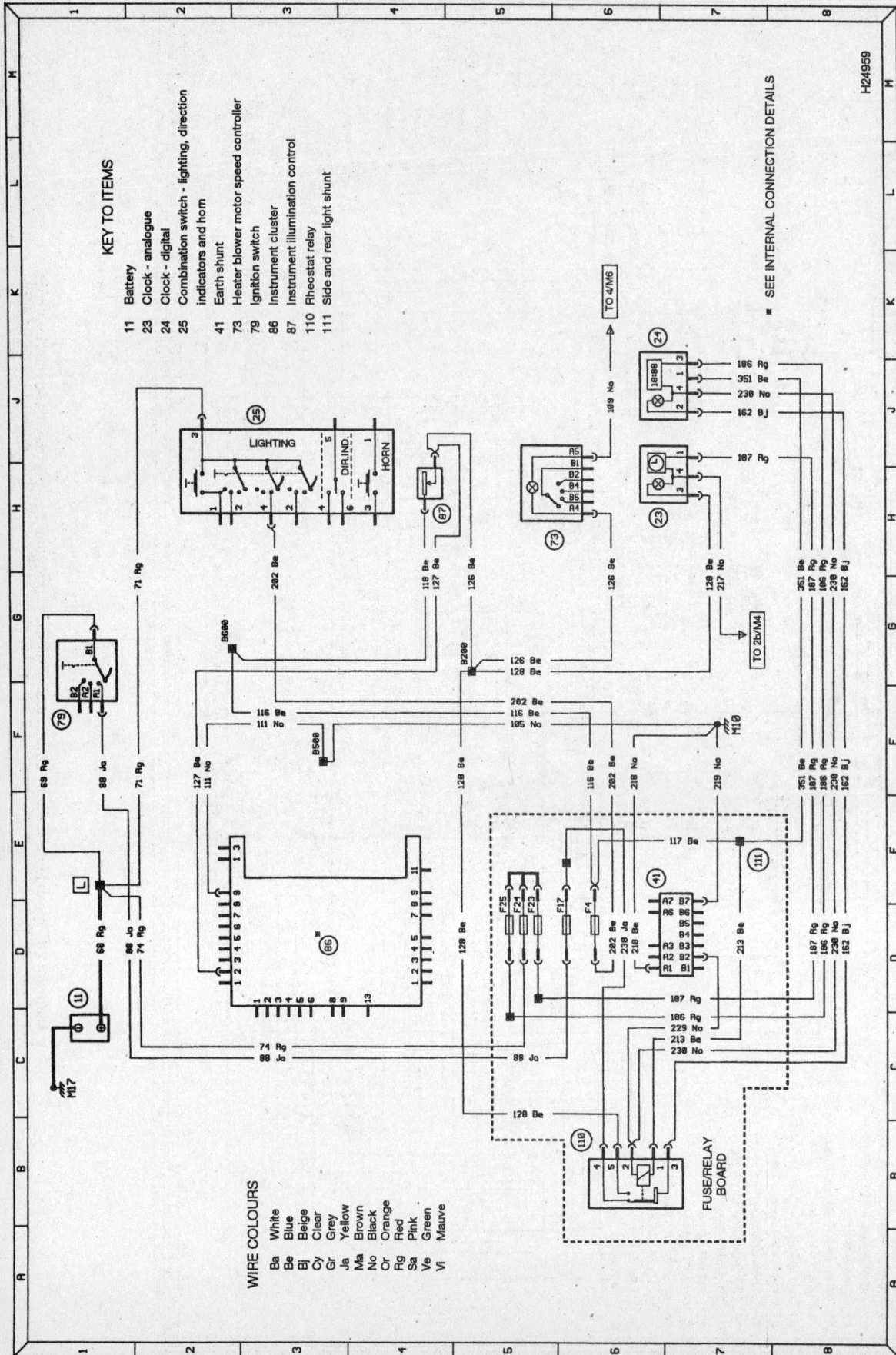

Diagram 2c: Typical interior lighting - clock and switch illumination (dimmer circuit)

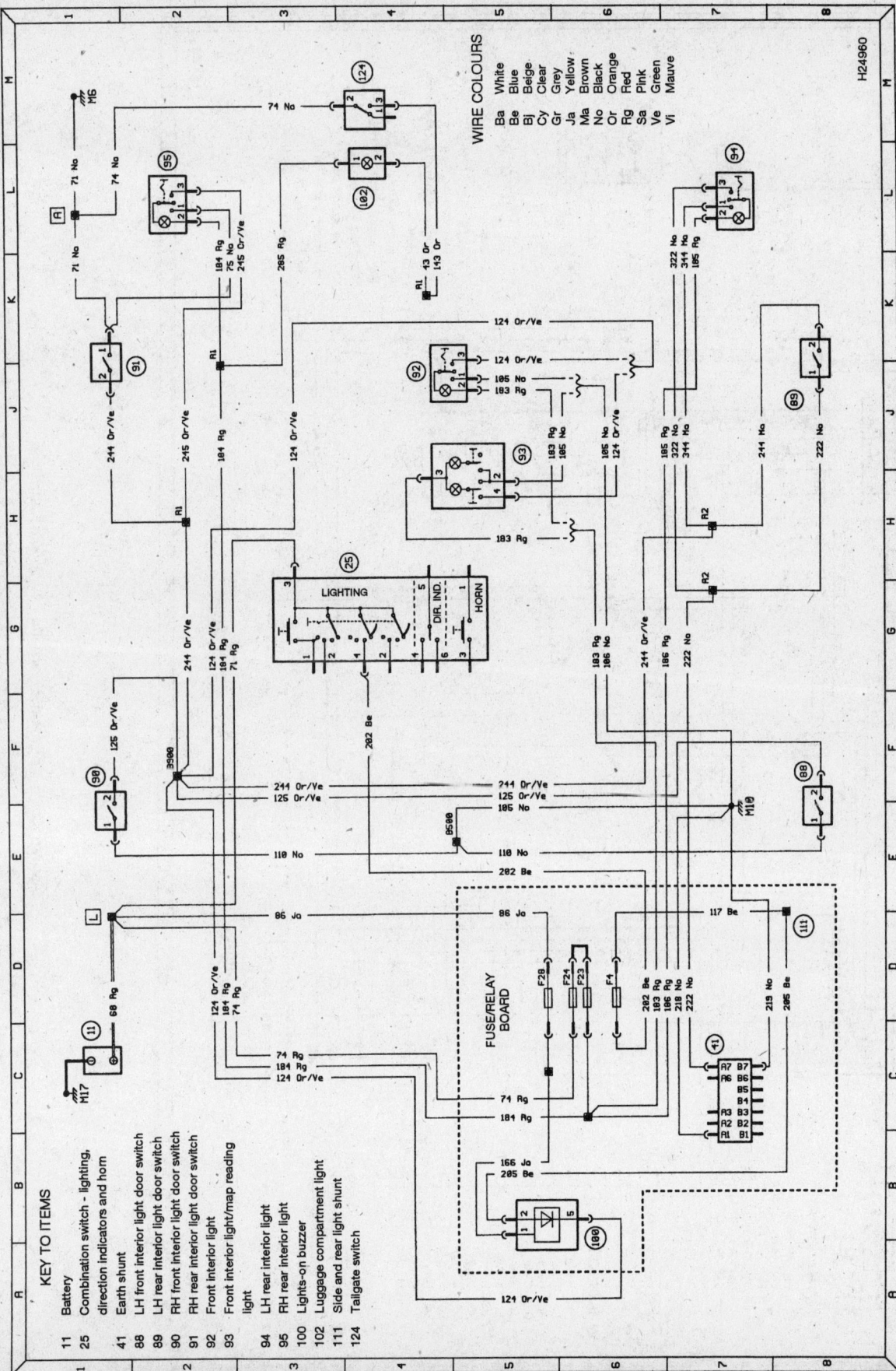

WIRE COLOURS

Ba	White
Be	Blue
Bj	Beige
Cy	Clear
Gr	Grey
Ja	Yellow
Ma	Brown
No	Black
Or	Orange
Rg	Red
Sa	Pink
Ve	Green
Vi	Mauve

Diagram 2d: Typical interior lighting – "lights on" buzzer, luggage compartment and interior lights

KEY TO ITEMS

11	Battery
25	Combination switch – lighting, direction indicators and horn
41	Earth shunt
88	LH front interior light door switch
89	LH rear interior light door switch
90	RH front interior light door switch
91	RH rear interior light door switch
92	Front interior light
93	Front interior light/map reading light
94	LH rear interior light
95	RH rear interior light
100	Lights-on buzzer
102	Luggage compartment light
111	Side and rear light shunt
124	Tailgate switch

H24960

12

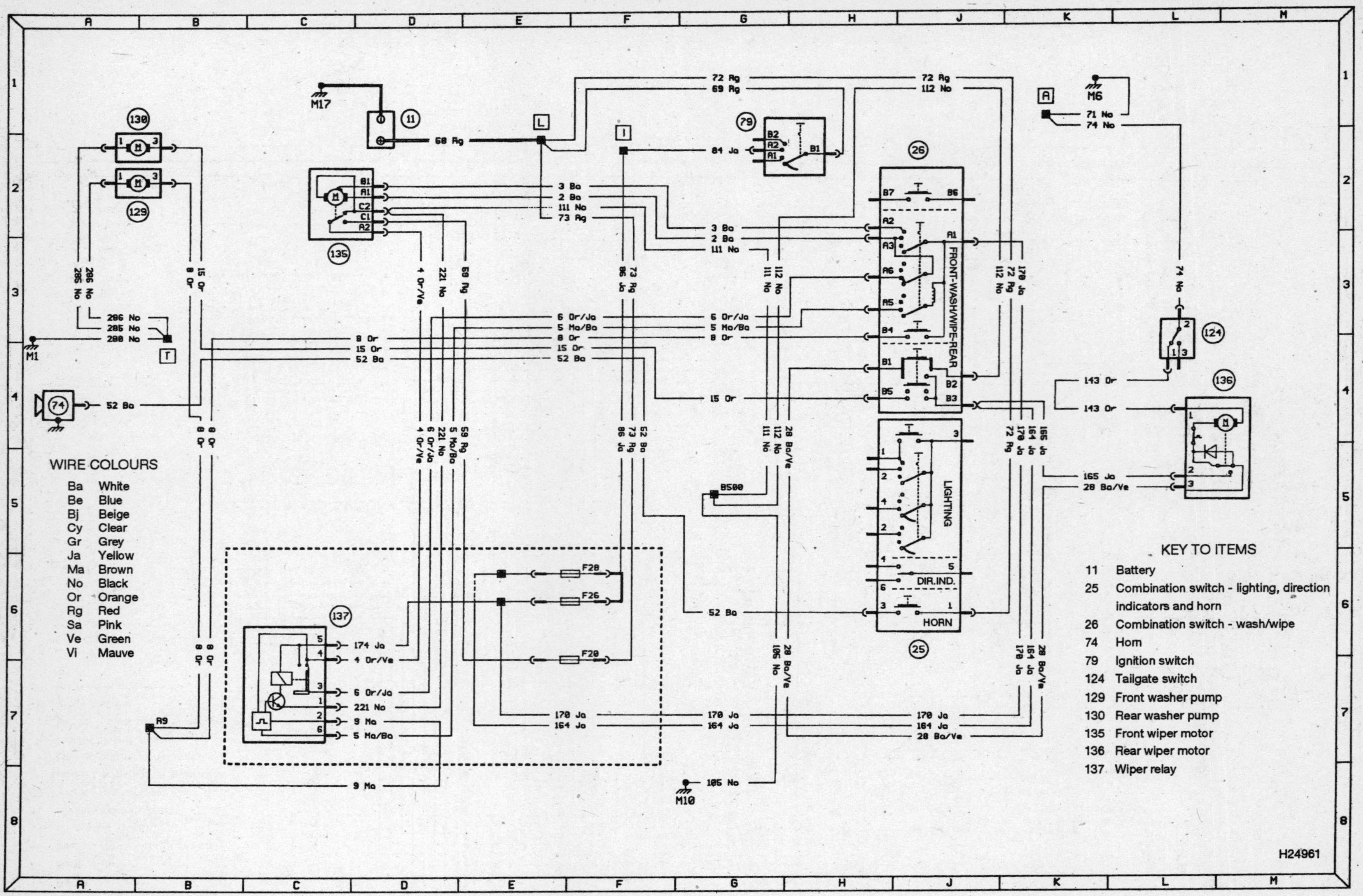

H24961

KEY TO ITEMS

11 Battery
25 Combination switch - lighting, direction indicators and horn
26 Combination switch - wash/wipe
74 Horn
79 Ignition switch
124 Tailgate switch
129 Rear washer pump
130 Rear washer pump
135 Front wiper motor
136 Rear wiper motor
137 Wiper relay

FRONT-WASH/WIPE-REAR

LIGHTING

DIR.IND.

HORN

WIRE COLOURS

Ba White
Be Blue
Bj Beige
Cy Clear
Gr Grey
Ja Yellow
Ma Brown
No Black
Or Orange
Rg Red
Sa Pink
Ve Green
Vi Mauve

Diagram 3: Typical ancillary circuits - wash/wipe and horn

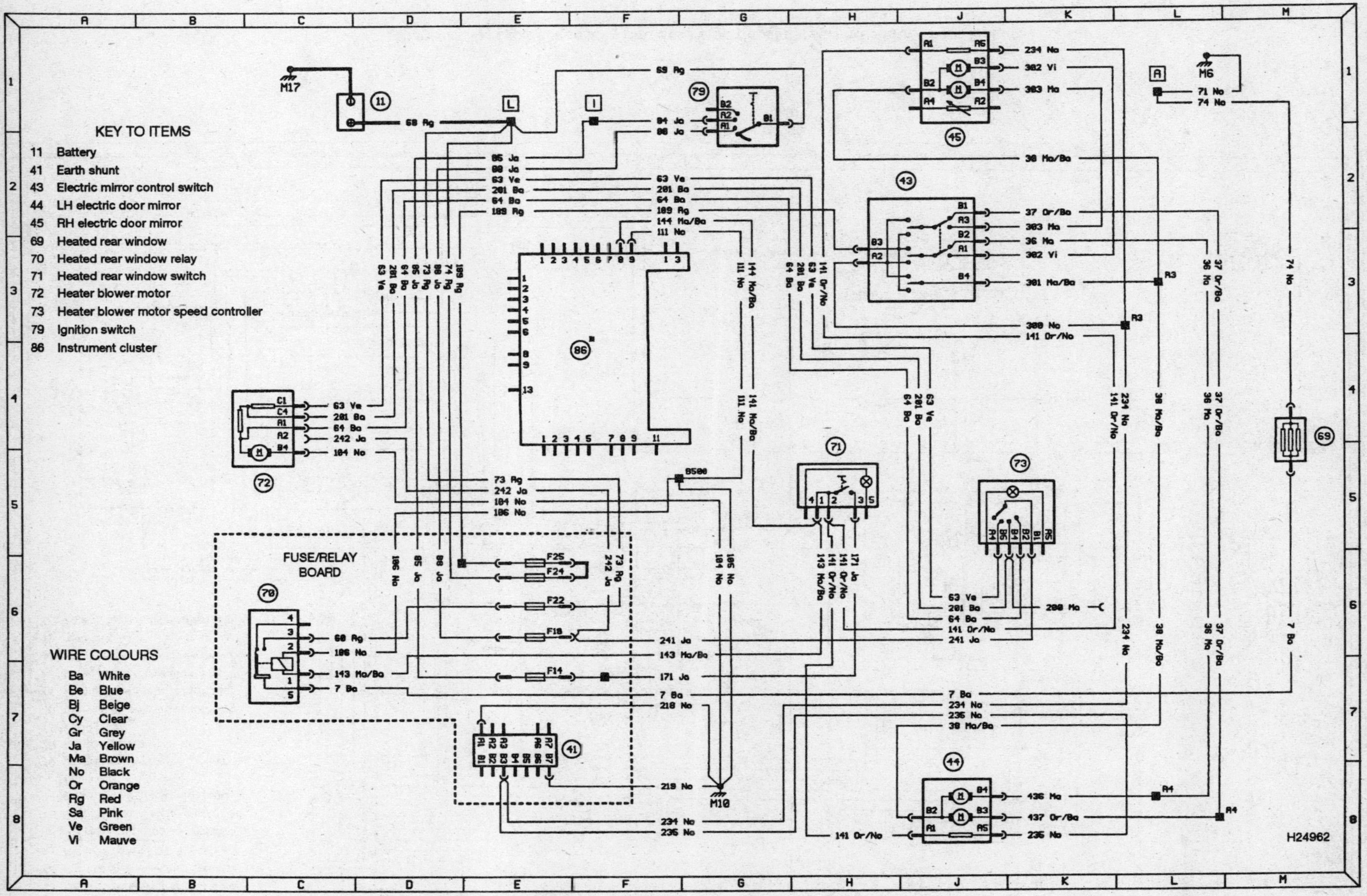

Diagram 3a: Typical ancillary circuits – heated rear window, heater blower and electric door mirrors

KEY TO ITEMS

11 Battery
41 Earth shunt
43 Electric mirror control switch
44 LH electric door mirror
45 RH electric door mirror
69 Heated rear window
70 Heated rear window relay
71 Heated rear window switch
72 Heater blower motor
73 Heater blower motor speed controller
79 Ignition switch
86 Instrument cluster

WIRE COLOURS

Ba White
Be Blue
Bj Beige
Cy Clear
Gr Grey
Ja Yellow
Ma Brown
No Black
Or Orange
Rg Red
Sa Pink
Ve Green
Vi Mauve

12

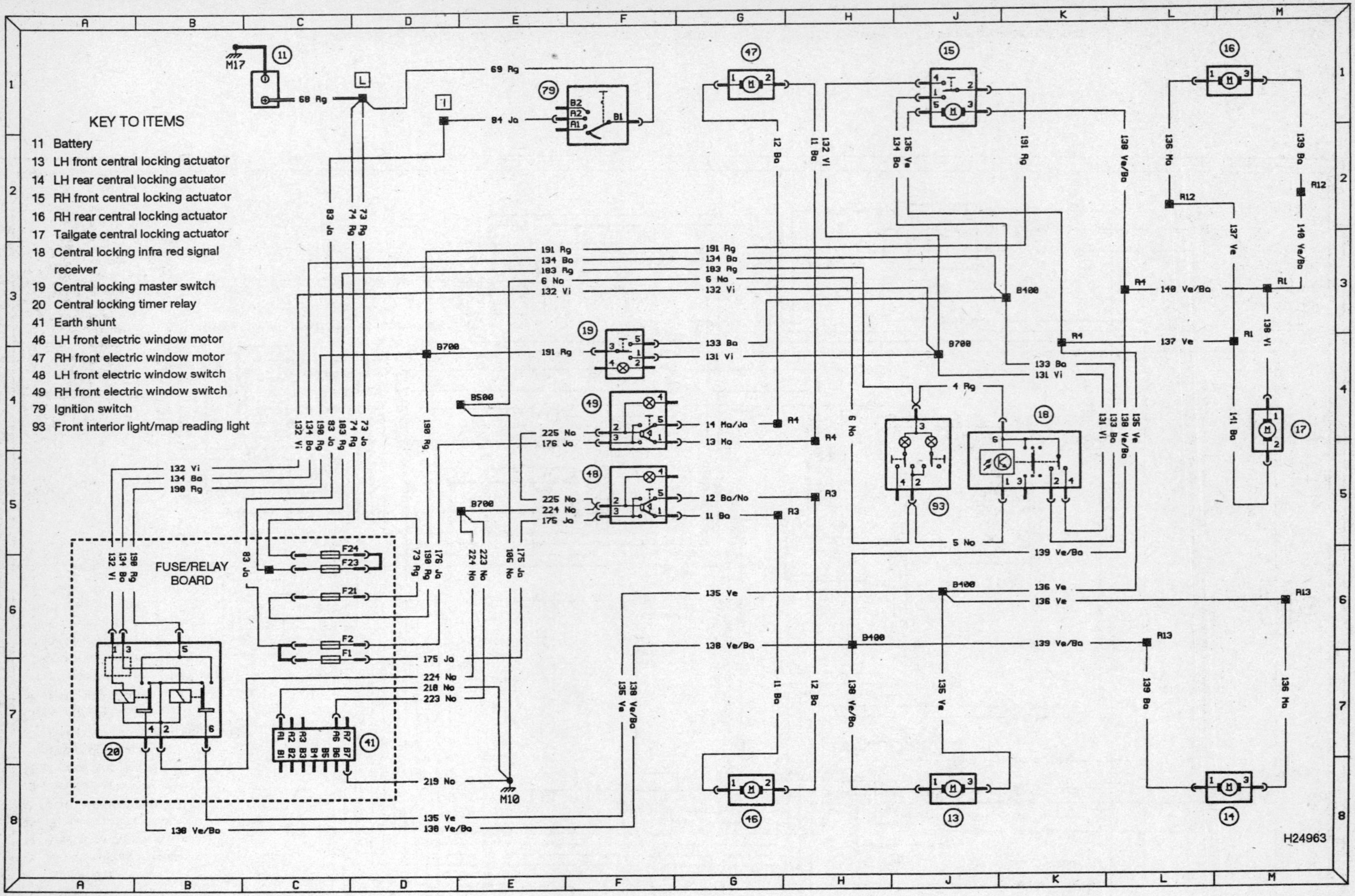

H24963

Diagram 3b: Typical ancillary circuits - electric windows and central door locking

KEY TO ITEMS

11 Battery
13 LH front central locking actuator
14 LH rear central locking actuator
15 RH front central locking actuator
16 RH rear central locking actuator
17 Tailgate central locking actuator
18 Central locking infra red signal receiver
19 Central locking master switch
20 Central locking timer relay
41 Earth shunt
46 LH front electric window motor
47 RH front electric window motor
48 LH front electric window switch
49 RH front electric window switch
79 Ignition switch
93 Front interior light/map reading light

FUSE/RELAY BOARD

H24964

WIRE COLOURS

Ba	White
Be	Blue
Bj	Beige
Cy	Clear
Gr	Grey
Ja	Yellow
Ma	Brown
No	Black
Or	Orange
Rg	Red
Sa	Pink
Ve	Green
Vi	Mauve

TO 2c/K6

ANTENNA

FUSE/RELAY BOARD

KEY TO ITEMS

11	Battery
79	Ignition switch
107	Radio/cassette unit
113	LH front speaker (dashboard)
114	LH front speaker (door)
115	LH rear speaker
116	RH front speaker (dashboard)
117	RH front speaker (door)
118	RH rear speaker
122	Sunroof motor
123	Sunroof switch

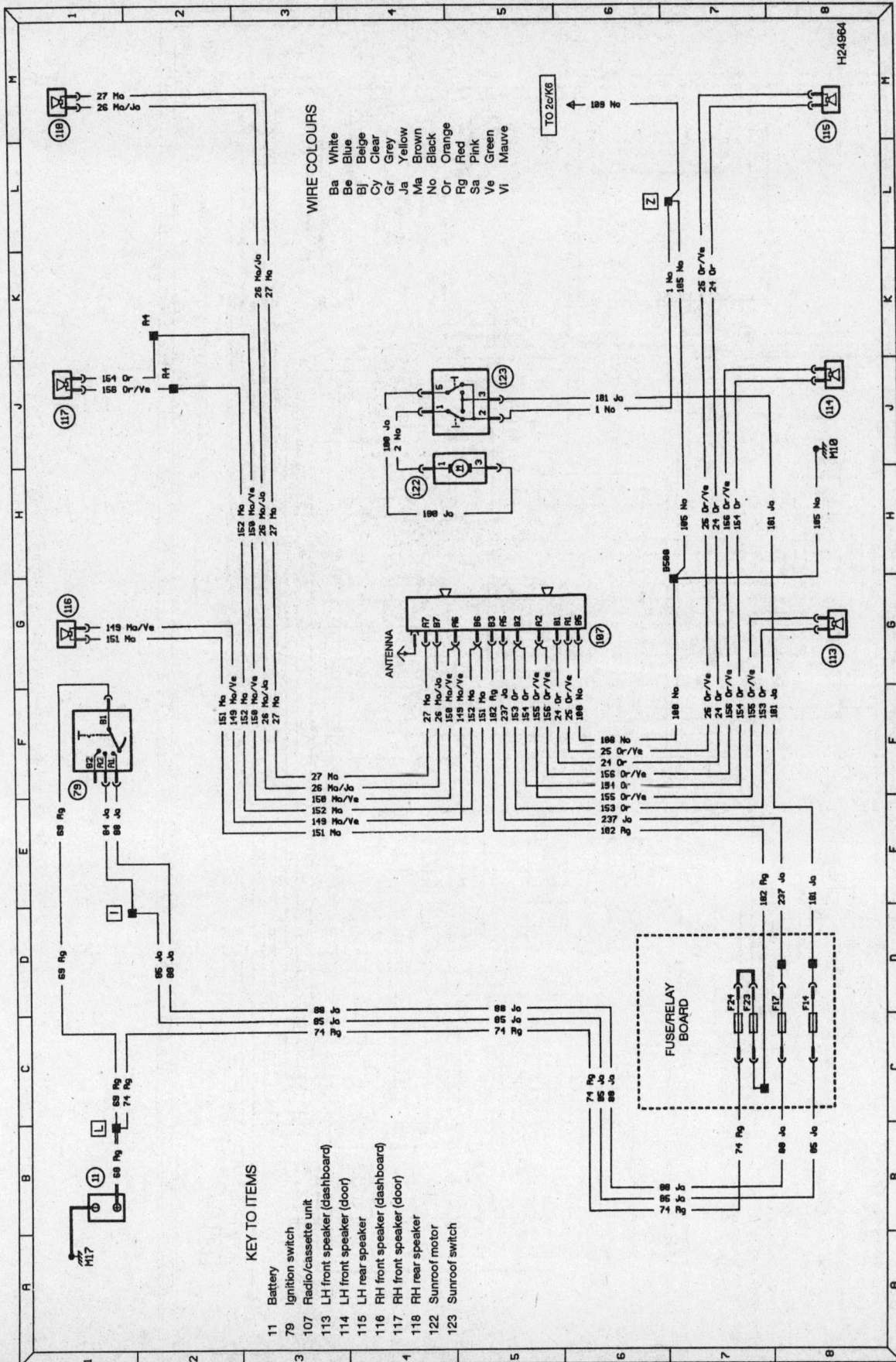

Diagram 4: Typical sunroof and radio

12

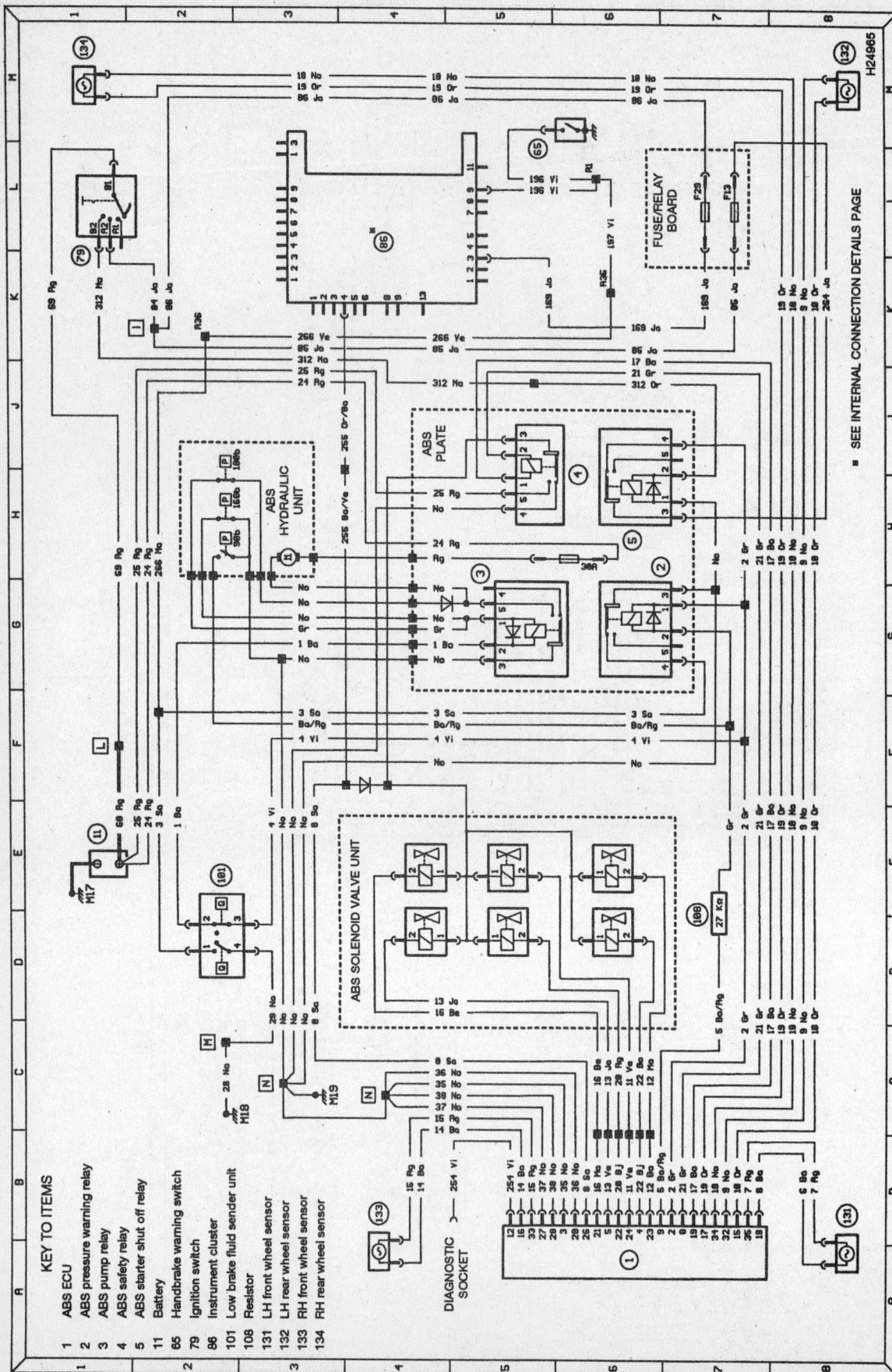

Diagram 4a: Anti-lock braking system (ABS)

KEY TO ITEMS

1	ABS ECU
2	ABS pressure warning relay
3	ABS pump relay
4	ABS safety relay
5	ABS starter shut off relay
11	Battery
65	Handbrake warning switch
79	Ignition switch
86	Instrument cluster
101	Low brake fluid sender unit
108	Resistor
131	LH front wheel sensor
132	LH rear wheel sensor
133	RH front wheel sensor
134	RH rear wheel sensor

Dimensions and Weights

Note: *All figures are approximate, and may vary according to model. Refer to manufacturer's data for exact figures.*

Dimensions

Overall length:	
Hatchback models	4150 to 4160 mm
Saloon models	4250 to 4260 mm
Overall width	1680 to 1700 mm
Overall height (unladen)	1400 to 1410 mm
Wheelbase	2540 mm
Front and rear track	1400 to 1430 mm

Weights

Kerb weight:	
"Phase 1" models:	
3-door Hatchback	985 to 1040 kg
5-door Hatchback and 4-door Saloon	1005 to 1060 kg
"Phase 2" models:	
3-door Hatchback	1025 to 1065 kg
5-door Hatchback and 4-door Saloon	1045 to 1085 kg
Maximum gross vehicle weight:	
"Phase 1" models:	
3-door Hatchback	1460 to 1510 kg
5-door Hatchback and 4-door Saloon	1480 to 1530 kg
"Phase 2" models:	
3-door Hatchback	1520 to 1540 kg
5-door Hatchback and 4-door Hatchback	1540 to 1560 kg
Maximum roof rack load	70 kg
Maximum towing weight:	
Braked trailer	900 to 1000 kg
Unbraked trailer:	490 to 540 kg

Conversion Factors

Length (distance)

Inches (in)	x 25.4	=	Millimetres (mm)	x 0.0394	= Inches (in)
Feet (ft)	x 0.305	=	Metres (m)	x 3.281	= Feet (ft)
Miles	x 1.609	=	Kilometres (km)	x 0.621	= Miles

Volume (capacity)

Cubic inches (cu in; in³)	x 16.387	=	Cubic centimetres (cc; cm³)	x 0.061	= Cubic inches (cu in; in³)
Imperial pints (Imp pt)	x 0.568	=	Litres (l)	x 1.76	= Imperial pints (Imp pt)
Imperial quarts (Imp qt)	x 1.137	=	Litres (l)	x 0.88	= Imperial quarts (Imp qt)
Imperial quarts (Imp qt)	x 1.201	=	US quarts (US qt)	x 0.833	= Imperial quarts (Imp qt)
US quarts (US qt)	x 0.946	=	Litres (l)	x 1.057	= US quarts (US qt)
Imperial gallons (Imp gal)	x 4.546	=	Litres (l)	x 0.22	= Imperial gallons (Imp gal)
Imperial gallons (Imp gal)	x 1.201	=	US gallons (US gal)	x 0.833	= Imperial gallons (Imp gal)
US gallons (US gal)	x 3.785	=	Litres (l)	x 0.264	= US gallons (US gal)

Mass (weight)

Ounces (oz)	x 28.35	=	Grams (g)	x 0.035	= Ounces (oz)
Pounds (lb)	x 0.454	=	Kilograms (kg)	x 2.205	= Pounds (lb)

Force

Ounces-force (ozf; oz)	x 0.278	=	Newtons (N)	x 3.6	= Ounces-force (ozf; oz)
Pounds-force (lbf; lb)	x 4.448	=	Newtons (N)	x 0.225	= Pounds-force (lbf; lb)
Newtons (N)	x 0.1	=	Kilograms-force (kgf; kg)	x 9.81	= Newtons (N)

Pressure

Pounds-force per square inch (psi; lbf/in²; lb/in²)	x 0.070	=	Kilograms-force per square centimetre (kgf/cm²; kg/cm²)	x 14.223	= Pounds-force per square inch (psi; lbf/in²; lb/in²)
Pounds-force per square inch (psi; lbf/in²; lb/in²)	x 0.068	=	Atmospheres (atm)	x 14.696	= Pounds-force per square inch (psi; lbf/in²; lb/in²)
Pounds-force per square inch (psi; lbf/in²; lb/in²)	x 0.069	=	Bars	x 14.5	= Pounds-force per square inch (psi; lbf/in²; lb/in²)
Pounds-force per square inch (psi; lbf/in²; lb/in²)	x 6.895	=	Kilopascals (kPa)	x 0.145	= Pounds-force per square inch (psi; lbf/in²; lb/in²)
Kilopascals (kPa)	x 0.01	=	Kilograms-force per square centimetre (kgf/cm²; kg/cm²)	x 98.1	= Kilopascals (kPa)
Millibar (mbar)	x 100	=	Pascals (Pa)	x 0.01	= Millibar (mbar)
Millibar (mbar)	x 0.0145	=	Pounds-force per square inch (psi; lbf/in²; lb/in²)	x 68.947	= Millibar (mbar)
Millibar (mbar)	x 0.75	=	Millimetres of mercury (mmHg)	x 1.333	= Millibar (mbar)
Millibar (mbar)	x 0.401	=	Inches of water (inH₂O)	x 2.491	= Millibar (mbar)
Millimetres of mercury (mmHg)	x 0.535	=	Inches of water (inH₂O)	x 1.868	= Millimetres of mercury (mmHg)
Inches of water (inH₂O)	x 0.036	=	Pounds-force per square inch (psi; lbf/in²; lb/in²)	x 27.68	= Inches of water (inH₂O)

Torque (moment of force)

Pounds-force inches (lbf in; lb in)	x 1.152	=	Kilograms-force centimetre (kgf cm; kg cm)	x 0.868	= Pounds-force inches (lbf in; lb in)
Pounds-force inches (lbf in; lb in)	x 0.113	=	Newton metres (Nm)	x 8.85	= Pounds-force inches (lbf in; lb in)
Pounds-force inches (lbf in; lb in)	x 0.083	=	Pounds-force feet (lbf ft; lb ft)	x 12	= Pounds-force inches (lbf in; lb in)
Pounds-force feet (lbf ft; lb ft)	x 0.138	=	Kilograms-force metres (kgf m; kg m)	x 7.233	= Pounds-force feet (lbf ft; lb ft)
Pounds-force feet (lbf ft; lb ft)	x 1.356	=	Newton metres (Nm)	x 0.738	= Pounds-force feet (lbf ft; lb ft)
Newton metres (Nm)	x 0.102	=	Kilograms-force metres (kgf m; kg m)	x 9.804	= Newton metres (Nm)

Power

Horsepower (hp)	x 745.7	=	Watts (W)	x 0.0013	= Horsepower (hp)

Velocity (speed)

Miles per hour (miles/hr; mph)	x 1.609	=	Kilometres per hour (km/hr; kph)	x 0.621	= Miles per hour (miles/hr; mph)

Fuel consumption*

Miles per gallon (mpg)	x 0.354	=	Kilometres per litre (km/l)	x 2.825	= Miles per gallon (mpg)

It is common practice to convert from miles per gallon (mpg) to litres/100 kilometres (l/100km), where mpg x l/100 km = 282

Temperature

Degrees Fahrenheit = (°C x 1.8) + 32   Degrees Celsius (Degrees Centigrade; °C) = (°F - 32) x 0.56

Spare parts are available from many sources; for example, Renault garages, other garages and accessory shops, and motor factors. Our advice regarding spare part sources is as follows.

Officially appointed Renault garages - This is the best source for parts which are peculiar to your car, and are not generally available (eg complete cylinder heads, internal gearbox components, badges, interior trim etc). It is also the only place at which you should buy parts if the vehicle is still under warranty. To be sure of obtaining the correct parts, it will be necessary to give the storeman your car's vehicle identification number, and if possible, take the old parts along for positive identification. Many parts are available under a factory exchange scheme - any parts returned should always be clean. It obviously makes good sense to go straight to the specialists on your car for this type of part, as they are best equipped to supply you.

Other garages and accessory shops - These are often very good places to buy materials and components needed for the maintenance of your car (eg oil filters, spark plugs, bulbs, drivebelts, oils and greases, touch-up paint, filler paste, etc). They also sell general accessories, usually have convenient opening hours, charge lower prices and can often be found not far from home.

Motor factors - Good factors will stock all the more important components which wear out comparatively quickly (eg exhaust systems, brake pads, seals and hydraulic parts, clutch components, bearing shells, pistons, valves etc). Motor factors will often provide new or reconditioned components on a part exchange basis - this can save a considerable amount of money.

Vehicle Identification

Modifications are a continuing and unpublicised process in vehicle manufacture, quite apart from major model changes. Spare parts manuals and lists are compiled upon a numerical basis, the individual vehicle identification numbers being essential to correct identification of the component concerned.

When ordering spare parts, always give as much information as possible. Quote the car model, year of manufacture, body and engine numbers as appropriate.

The *vehicle identification number (VIN)* is stamped on the VIN plate located under the bonnet, and is also stamped into the top of the right-hand front suspension strut turret. On early models, the VIN plate is located on the right-hand suspension turret - two separate plates may be fitted, or all the information may be incorporated on a single plate. On later models, the VIN plate is located on the body front panel, at the front right-hand side of the engine compartment - all information is incorporated on a single plate **(see illustrations)**.

VIN plate - early models

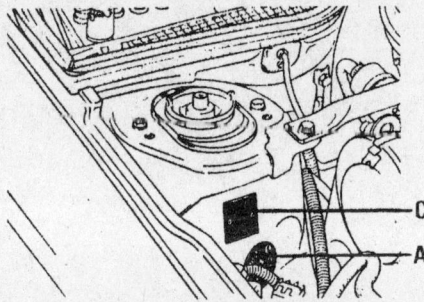

VIN plate (A - oval plate and C - manufacturer's plate) (alternative type) - early models

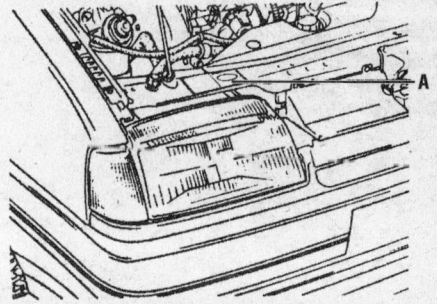

VIN plate (A) - later models

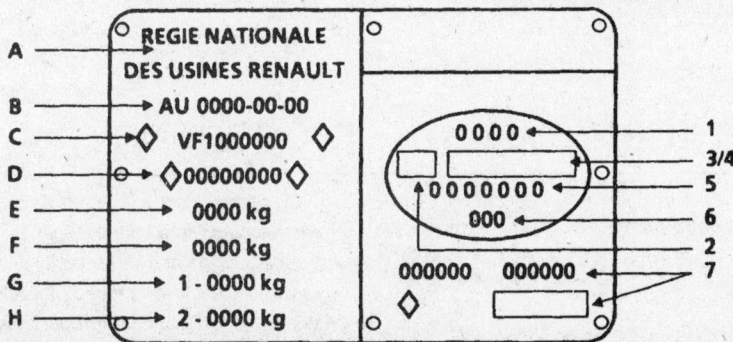

VIN plate codes

A Manufacturer's name
B EEC official approval number
C VIN number
D Chassis number
E Gross vehicle weight
F Gross train weight
G Maximum permissible front axle weight
H Maximum permissible rear axle weight
1 Vehicle model code
2 Special features of vehicle
3 Country of origin
4 Equipment number and options
5 Factory and fabrication number
6 Paint code
7 Additional marking

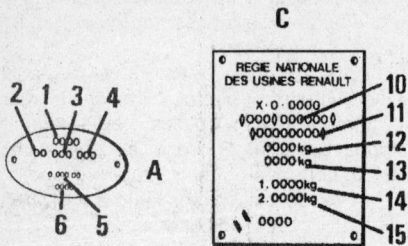

Alternative VIN plate codes

A Oval plate
C Manufacturer's plate
1 Vehicle model code
2 Special features of vehicle
3 Country of origin
4 Equipment number and options
5 Factory and fabrication number
6 Paint code
10 VIN number
11 Chassis number
12 Gross vehicle weight
13 Gross train weight
14 Maximum permissible front axle weight
15 Maximum permissible rear axle weight

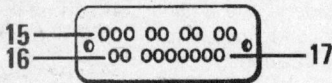

Engine plate codes

15 Engine type
16 Engine type suffix
17 Engine number

VIN and chassis number stamped on suspension turret

The *chassis number* appears on the VIN plate (as described previously), and is also stamped into the top of the right-hand front suspension strut turret, directly after the VIN number **(see illustration)**.

The *paint code number* is stamped on the VIN plate.

The *engine number* is stamped on a plate riveted to the front flywheel end of the engine cylinder block **(see illustrations)**.

Engine identification

The engine type can be identified from the engine number, located on a plate, as described previously ("Vehicle identification numbers").

Full details of engine codes can be found in the Specifications Section of Chapter 2A.

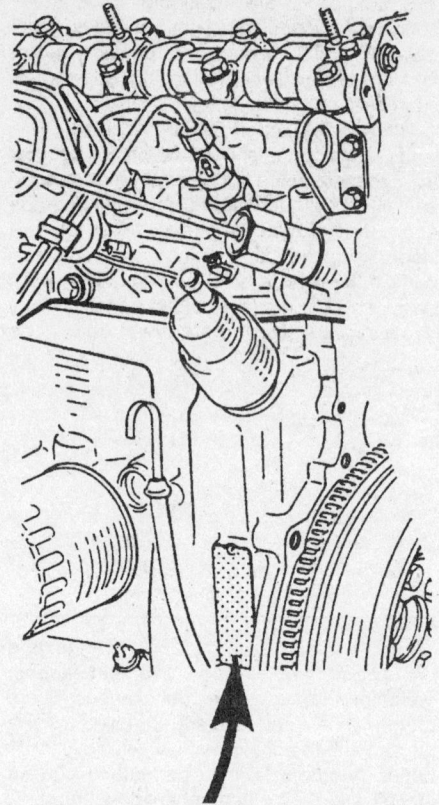

Engine number location (arrowed)

Radio/cassette unit anti-theft system - precaution

The radio/cassette unit fitted as standard equipment by Renault may be equipped with a built-in security code to deter thieves. If the power source to the unit is cut, the anti-theft system will activate. Even if the power source is immediately reconnected, the radio/cassette unit will not function until the correct security code has been entered.

Therefore, if you do not know the correct security code for the radio/cassette unit **do not** disconnect the battery negative terminal of the battery or remove the radio/cassette unit from the vehicle.

To enter the correct security code, follow the instructions provided with the radio/cassette player handbook.

If an incorrect code is entered, the unit will become locked, and cannot be operated.

If this happens or if the security code is lost or forgotten, seek the advice of your Renault dealer. On presentation of proof of ownership, a Renault dealer will be able to unlock the unit and provide you with a new security code.

Whenever servicing, repair or overhaul work is carried out on the car or its components, observe the following procedures and instructions. This will assist in carrying out the operation efficiently and to a professional standard of workmanship.

Joint mating faces and gaskets

When separating components at their mating faces, never insert screwdrivers or similar implements into the joint between the faces in order to prise them apart. This can cause severe damage which results in oil leaks, coolant leaks, etc upon reassembly. Separation is usually achieved by tapping along the joint with a soft-faced hammer in order to break the seal. However, note that this method may not be suitable where dowels are used for component location.

Where a gasket is used between the mating faces of two components, a new one must be fitted on reassembly; fit it dry unless otherwise stated in the repair procedure. Make sure that the mating faces are clean and dry, with all traces of old gasket removed. When cleaning a joint face, use a tool which is unlikely to score or damage the face, and remove any burrs or nicks with an oilstone or fine file.

Make sure that tapped holes are cleaned with a pipe cleaner, and keep them free of jointing compound, if this is being used, unless specifically instructed otherwise.

Ensure that all orifices, channels or pipes are clear, and blow through them, preferably using compressed air.

Oil seals

Oil seals can be removed by levering them out with a wide flat-bladed screwdriver or similar implement. Alternatively, a number of self-tapping screws may be screwed into the seal, and these used as a purchase for pliers or some similar device in order to pull the seal free.

Whenever an oil seal is removed from its working location, either individually or as part of an assembly, it should be renewed.

The very fine sealing lip of the seal is easily damaged, and will not seal if the surface it contacts is not completely clean and free from scratches, nicks or grooves. If the original sealing surface of the component cannot be restored, and the manufacturer has not made provision for slight relocation of the seal relative to the sealing surface, the component should be renewed.

Protect the lips of the seal from any surface which may damage them in the course of fitting. Use tape or a conical sleeve where possible. Lubricate the seal lips with oil before fitting and, on dual-lipped seals, fill the space between the lips with grease.

Unless otherwise stated, oil seals must be fitted with their sealing lips toward the lubricant to be sealed.

Use a tubular drift or block of wood of the appropriate size to install the seal and, if the seal housing is shouldered, drive the seal down to the shoulder. If the seal housing is unshouldered, the seal should be fitted with its face flush with the housing top face (unless otherwise instructed).

Screw threads and fastenings

Seized nuts, bolts and screws are quite a common occurrence where corrosion has set in, and the use of penetrating oil or releasing fluid will often overcome this problem if the offending item is soaked for a while before attempting to release it. The use of an impact driver may also provide a means of releasing such stubborn fastening devices, when used in conjunction with the appropriate screwdriver bit or socket. If none of these methods works, it may be necessary to resort to the careful application of heat, or the use of a hacksaw or nut splitter device.

Studs are usually removed by locking two nuts together on the threaded part, and then using a spanner on the lower nut to unscrew the stud. Studs or bolts which have broken off below the surface of the component in which they are mounted can sometimes be removed using a stud extractor. Always ensure that a blind tapped hole is completely free from oil, grease, water or other fluid before installing the bolt or stud. Failure to do this could cause the housing to crack due to the hydraulic action of the bolt or stud as it is screwed in.

When tightening a castellated nut to accept a split pin, tighten the nut to the specified torque, where applicable, and then tighten further to the next split pin hole. Never slacken the nut to align the split pin hole, unless stated in the repair procedure.

When checking or retightening a nut or bolt to a specified torque setting, slacken the nut or bolt by a quarter of a turn, and then retighten to the specified setting. However, this should not be attempted where angular tightening has been used.

For some screw fastenings, notably cylinder head bolts or nuts, torque wrench settings are no longer specified for the latter stages of tightening, "angle-tightening" being called up instead. Typically, a fairly low torque wrench setting will be applied to the bolts/nuts in the correct sequence, followed by one or more stages of tightening through specified angles.

Locknuts, locktabs and washers

Any fastening which will rotate against a component or housing during tightening should always have a washer between it and the relevant component or housing.

Spring or split washers should always be renewed when they are used to lock a critical component such as a big-end bearing retaining bolt or nut. Locktabs which are folded over to retain a nut or bolt should always be renewed.

Self-locking nuts can be re-used in non-critical areas, providing resistance can be felt when the locking portion passes over the bolt or stud thread. However, it should be noted that self-locking stiffnuts tend to lose their effectiveness after long periods of use, and should then be renewed as a matter of course.

Split pins must always be replaced with new ones of the correct size for the hole.

When thread-locking compound is found on the threads of a fastener which is to be re-used, it should be cleaned off with a wire brush and solvent, and fresh compound applied on reassembly.

Special tools

Some repair procedures in this manual entail the use of special tools such as a press, two or three-legged pullers, spring compressors, etc. Wherever possible, suitable readily-available alternatives to the manufacturer's special tools are described, and are shown in use. In some instances, where no alternative is possible, it has been necessary to resort to the use of a manufacturer's tool, and this has been done for reasons of safety as well as the efficient completion of the repair operation. Unless you are highly-skilled and have a thorough understanding of the procedures described, never attempt to bypass the use of any special tool when the procedure described specifies its use. Not only is there a very great risk of personal injury, but expensive damage could be caused to the components involved.

Environmental considerations

When disposing of used engine oil, brake fluid, antifreeze, etc, give due consideration to any detrimental environmental effects. Do not, for instance, pour any of the above liquids down drains into the general sewage system, or onto the ground to soak away. Many local council refuse tips provide a facility for waste oil disposal, as do some garages. If none of these facilities are available, consult your local Environmental Health Department, or the National Rivers Authority, for further advice.

With the universal tightening-up of legislation regarding the emission of environmentally-harmful substances from motor vehicles, most vehicles have tamperproof devices fitted to the main adjustment points of the fuel system. These devices are primarily designed to prevent unqualified persons from adjusting the fuel/air mixture, with the chance of a consequent increase in toxic emissions. If such devices are found during servicing or overhaul, they should, wherever possible, be renewed or refitted in accordance with the manufacturer's requirements or current legislation.

OIL CARE
FOLLOW THE CODE

OIL BANK LINE
0800 66 33 66

Note: It is antisocial and illegal to dump oil down the drain. To find the location of your local oil recycling bank, call this number free.

The jack supplied with the vehicle tool kit should only be used for changing the roadwheels - see *"Wheel changing"* later in this Section. When carrying out any other kind of work, raise the vehicle using a hydraulic jack, and always supplement the jack with axle stands positioned under the vehicle jacking points.

When using a hydraulic jack or axle stands, always position the jack head or axle stand head under one of the relevant jacking points (note that the jacking points for use with a hydraulic jack are different to those for use with the vehicle jack and axle stands) **(see illustrations). Do not** jack the vehicle under the sump or any of the steering or suspension components. **Never** *work under, around, or near a raised vehicle, unless it is adequately supported in at least two places.*

Note the following when using a hydraulic jack:

a)   *When raising the side of the vehicle, ensure that the load is taken by the raised jacking plates on the sill panels (refer to the accompanying illustration) - do not*

jack under the body panel behind the sill panels.

b)   *When raising the front of the vehicle, use a suitable metal or strong wooden bar and wooden spacer blocks under the front suspension subframe (refer to the accompanying illustration).*

c)   *When raising the rear of the vehicle, position the jack or axle stands under the rear jacking plates on the sill panels.* **DO NOT** *place a jack or axle stands under the rear axle components.*

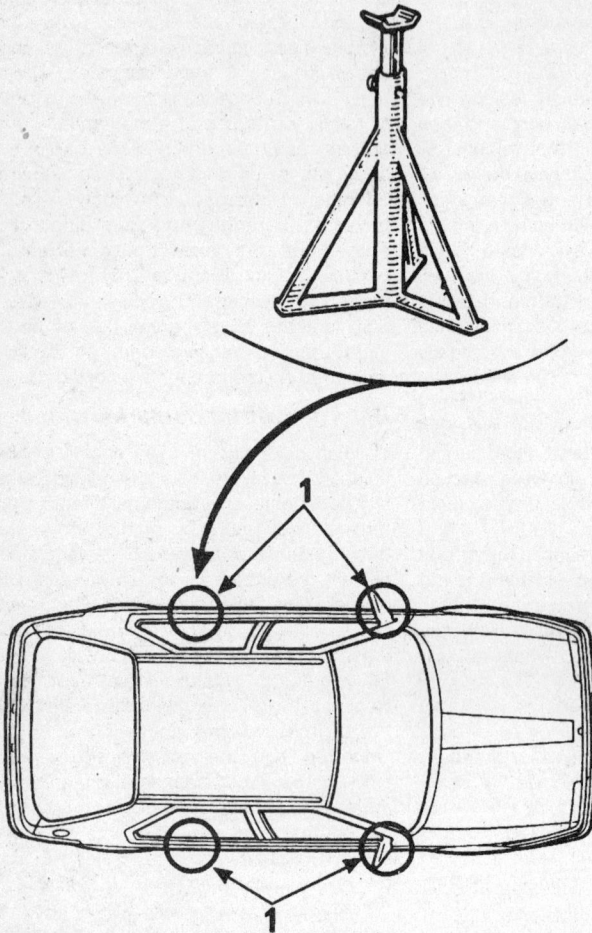

Jacking points (1) for use with vehicle jack and axle stands

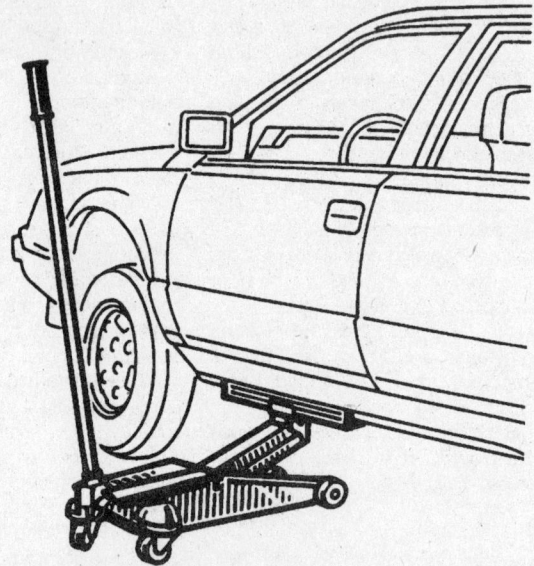

Jacking up the side of the car using a hydraulic jack

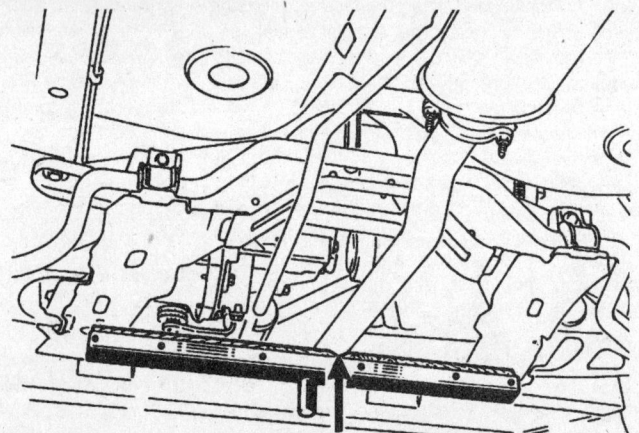

Beam for raising the front of the car - cut where shown (arrowed) if necessary to clear exhaust system

Introduction

A selection of good tools is a fundamental requirement for anyone contemplating the maintenance and repair of a motor vehicle. For the owner who does not possess any, their purchase will prove a considerable expense, offsetting some of the savings made by doing-it-yourself. However, provided that the tools purchased meet the relevant national safety standards and are of good quality, they will last for many years and prove an extremely worthwhile investment.

To help the average owner to decide which tools are needed to carry out the various tasks detailed in this manual, we have compiled three lists of tools under the following headings: *Maintenance and minor repair, Repair and overhaul*, and *Special*. Newcomers to practical mechanics should start off with the *Maintenance and minor repair* tool kit, and confine themselves to the simpler jobs around the vehicle. Then, as confidence and experience grow, more difficult tasks can be undertaken, with extra tools being purchased as, and when, they are needed. In this way, a *Maintenance and minor repair* tool kit can be built up into a *Repair and overhaul* tool kit over a considerable period of time, without any major cash outlays. The experienced do-it-yourselfer will have a tool kit good enough for most repair and overhaul procedures, and will add tools from the *Special* category when it is felt that the expense is justified by the amount of use to which these tools will be put.

Maintenance and minor repair tool kit

The tools given in this list should be considered as a minimum requirement if routine maintenance, servicing and minor repair operations are to be undertaken. We recommend the purchase of combination spanners (ring one end, open-ended the other); although more expensive than open-ended ones, they do give the advantages of both types of spanner.

□ *Combination spanners:*
  Metric - 8 to 19 mm inclusive
□ *Adjustable spanner - 35 mm jaw (approx.)*
□ *Spark plug spanner (with rubber insert) - petrol models*
□ *Spark plug gap adjustment tool - petrol models*
□ *Set of feeler gauges*
□ *Brake bleed nipple spanner*
□ *Screwdrivers:*
  Flat blade - 100 mm long x 6 mm dia
  Cross blade - 100 mm long x 6 mm dia
□ *Combination pliers*
□ *Hacksaw (junior)*
□ *Tyre pump*
□ *Tyre pressure gauge*
□ *Oil can*
□ *Oil filter removal tool*
□ *Fine emery cloth*
□ *Wire brush (small)*
□ *Funnel (medium size)*

Repair and overhaul tool kit

These tools are virtually essential for anyone undertaking any major repairs to a motor vehicle, and are additional to those given in the *Maintenance and minor repair* list. Included in this list is a comprehensive set of sockets. Although these are expensive, they will be found invaluable as they are so versatile - particularly if various drives are included in the set. We recommend the half-inch square-drive type, as this can be used with most proprietary torque wrenches.

The tools in this list will sometimes need to be supplemented by tools from the *Special* list:

□ *Sockets (or box spanners) to cover range in previous list (including Torx sockets)*
□ *Reversible ratchet drive (for use with sockets)*
□ *Extension piece, 250 mm (for use with sockets)*
□ *Universal joint (for use with sockets)*
□ *Torque wrench (for use with sockets)*
□ *Self-locking grips*
□ *Ball pein hammer*
□ *Soft-faced mallet (plastic/aluminium or rubber)*
□ *Screwdrivers:*
  Flat blade - long & sturdy, short (chubby), and narrow (electrician's) types
  Cross blade – Long & sturdy, and short (chubby) types
□ *Pliers:*
  Long-nosed
  Side cutters (electrician's)
  Circlip (internal and external)
□ *Cold chisel - 25 mm*
□ *Scriber*
□ *Scraper*
□ *Centre-punch*
□ *Pin punch*
□ *Hacksaw*
□ *Brake hose clamp*
□ *Brake/clutch bleeding kit*
□ *Selection of twist drills*
□ *Steel rule/straight-edge*
□ *Allen keys (inc. splined/Torx type)*
□ *Selection of files*
□ *Wire brush*
□ *Axle stands*
□ *Jack (strong trolley or hydraulic type)*
□ *Light with extension lead*

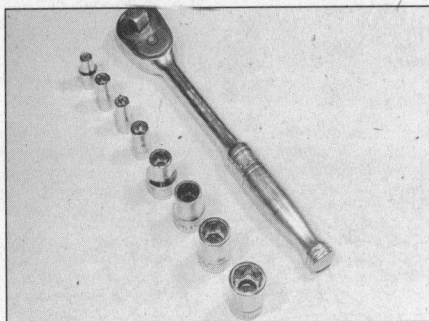
Sockets and reversible ratchet drive

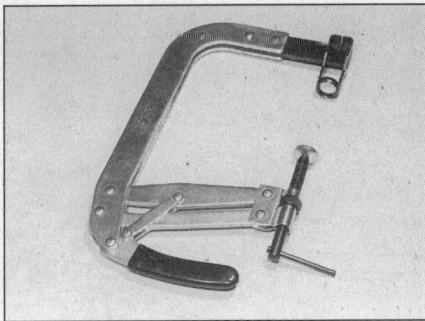
Valve spring compressor

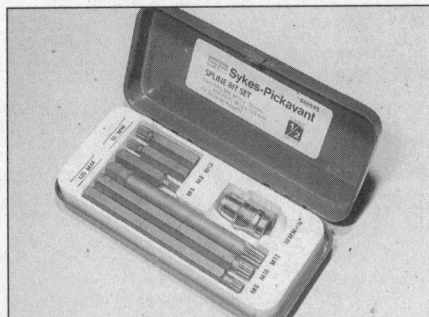
Spline bit set

Piston ring compressor

Clutch plate alignment set

Special tools

The tools in this list are those which are not used regularly, are expensive to buy, or which need to be used in accordance with their manufacturers' instructions. Unless relatively difficult mechanical jobs are undertaken frequently, it will not be economic to buy many of these tools. Where this is the case, you could consider clubbing together with friends (or joining a motorists' club) to make a joint purchase, or borrowing the tools against a deposit from a local garage or tool hire specialist. It is worth noting that many of the larger DIY superstores now carry a large range of special tools for hire at modest rates.

The following list contains only those tools and instruments freely available to the public, and not those special tools produced by the vehicle manufacturer specifically for its dealer network. You will find occasional references to these manufacturers' special tools in the text of this manual. Generally, an alternative method of doing the job without the vehicle manufacturers' special tool is given. However, sometimes there is no alternative to using them. Where this is the case and the relevant tool cannot be bought or borrowed, you will have to entrust the work to a dealer.

☐ Valve spring compressor
☐ Valve grinding tool
☐ Piston ring compressor
☐ Piston ring removal/installation tool
☐ Cylinder bore hone
☐ Balljoint separator
☐ Coil spring compressors (where applicable)
☐ Two/three-legged hub and bearing puller
☐ Impact screwdriver
☐ Micrometer and/or vernier calipers
☐ Dial gauge
☐ Stroboscopic timing light
☐ Dwell angle meter/tachometer
☐ Universal electrical multi-meter
☐ Cylinder compression gauge
☐ Hand-operated vacuum pump and gauge
☐ Clutch plate alignment set
☐ Brake shoe steady spring cup removal tool
☐ Bush and bearing removal/installation set
☐ Stud extractors
☐ Tap and die set
☐ Lifting tackle
☐ Trolley jack

Buying tools

Reputable motor accessory shops and superstores often offer excellent quality tools at discount prices, so it pays to shop around.

Remember, you don't have to buy the most expensive items on the shelf, but it is always advisable to steer clear of the very cheap tools. Beware of 'bargains' offered on market stalls or at car boot sales. There are plenty of good tools around at reasonable prices, but always aim to purchase items which meet the relevant national safety standards. If in doubt, ask the proprietor or manager of the shop for advice before making a purchase.

Care and maintenance of tools

Having purchased a reasonable tool kit, it is necessary to keep the tools in a clean and serviceable condition. After use, always wipe off any dirt, grease and metal particles using a clean, dry cloth, before putting the tools away. Never leave them lying around after they have been used. A simple tool rack on the garage or workshop wall for items such as screwdrivers and pliers is a good idea. Store all normal spanners and sockets in a metal box. Any measuring instruments, gauges, meters, etc, must be carefully stored where they cannot be damaged or become rusty.

Take a little care when tools are used. Hammer heads inevitably become marked, and screwdrivers lose the keen edge on their blades from time to time. A little timely attention with emery cloth or a file will soon restore items like this to a good finish.

Working facilities

Not to be forgotten when discussing tools is the workshop itself. If anything more than routine maintenance is to be carried out, a suitable working area becomes essential.

It is appreciated that many an owner-mechanic is forced by circumstances to remove an engine or similar item without the benefit of a garage or workshop. Having done this, any repairs should always be done under the cover of a roof.

Wherever possible, any dismantling should be done on a clean, flat workbench or table at a suitable working height.

Any workbench needs a vice; one with a jaw opening of 100 mm is suitable for most jobs. As mentioned previously, some clean dry storage space is also required for tools, as well as for any lubricants, cleaning fluids, touch-up paints etc, which become necessary.

Another item which may be required, and which has a much more general usage, is an electric drill with a chuck capacity of at least 8 mm. This, together with a good range of twist drills, is virtually essential for fitting accessories.

Last, but not least, always keep a supply of old newspapers and clean, lint-free rags available, and try to keep any working area as clean as possible.

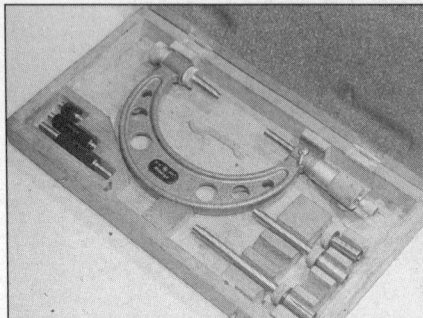
Micrometer set

Dial test indicator ("dial gauge")

Stroboscopic timing light

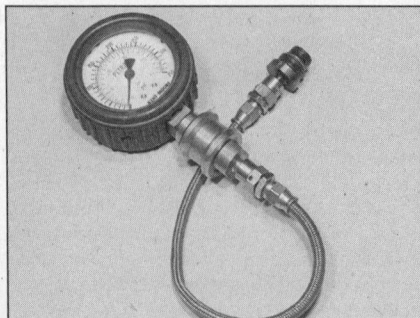
Compression tester

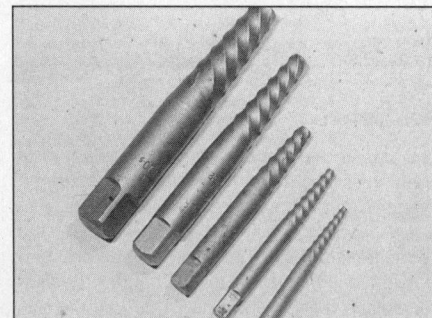
Stud extractor set

This is a guide to getting your vehicle through the MOT test. Obviously it will not be possible to examine the vehicle to the same standard as the professional MOT tester. However, working through the following checks will enable you to identify any problem areas before submitting the vehicle for the test.

Where a testable component is in borderline condition, the tester has discretion in deciding whether to pass or fail it. The basis of such discretion is whether the tester would be happy for a close relative or friend to use the vehicle with the component in that condition. If the vehicle presented is clean and evidently well cared for, the tester may be more inclined to pass a borderline component than if the vehicle is scruffy and apparently neglected.

It has only been possible to summarise the test requirements here, based on the regulations in force at the time of printing. Test standards are becoming increasingly stringent, although there are some exemptions for older vehicles. For full details obtain a copy of the Haynes publication Pass the MOT! (available from stockists of Haynes manuals).

An assistant will be needed to help carry out some of these checks.

The checks have been sub-divided into four categories, as follows:

1 Checks carried out **FROM THE DRIVER'S SEAT**

2 Checks carried out **WITH THE VEHICLE ON THE GROUND**

3 Checks carried out **WITH THE VEHICLE RAISED AND THE WHEELS FREE TO TURN**

4 Checks carried out on **YOUR VEHICLE'S EXHAUST EMISSION SYSTEM**

1 Checks carried out **FROM THE DRIVER'S SEAT**

Handbrake

☐ Test the operation of the handbrake. Excessive travel (too many clicks) indicates incorrect brake or cable adjustment.

☐ Check that the handbrake cannot be released by tapping the lever sideways. Check the security of the lever mountings.

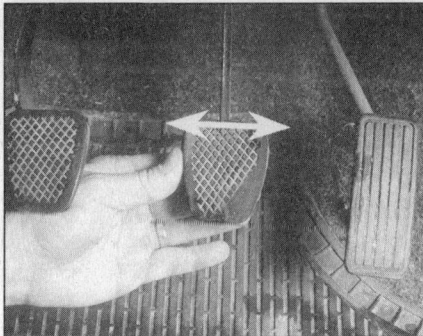

Footbrake

☐ Depress the brake pedal and check that it does not creep down to the floor, indicating a master cylinder fault. Release the pedal, wait a few seconds, then depress it again. If the pedal travels nearly to the floor before firm resistance is felt, brake adjustment or repair is necessary. If the pedal feels spongy, there is air in the hydraulic system which must be removed by bleeding.

☐ Check that the brake pedal is secure and in good condition. Check also for signs of fluid leaks on the pedal, floor or carpets, which would indicate failed seals in the brake master cylinder.

☐ Check the servo unit (when applicable) by operating the brake pedal several times, then keeping the pedal depressed and starting the engine. As the engine starts, the pedal will move down slightly. If not, the vacuum hose or the servo itself may be faulty.

Steering wheel and column

☐ Examine the steering wheel for fractures or looseness of the hub, spokes or rim.

☐ Move the steering wheel from side to side and then up and down. Check that the steering wheel is not loose on the column, indicating wear or a loose retaining nut. Continue moving the steering wheel as before, but also turn it slightly from left to right.

☐ Check that the steering wheel is not loose on the column, and that there is no abnormal movement of the steering wheel, indicating wear in the column support bearings or couplings.

Windscreen and mirrors

☐ The windscreen must be free of cracks or other significant damage within the driver's field of view. (Small stone chips are acceptable.) Rear view mirrors must be secure, intact, and capable of being adjusted.

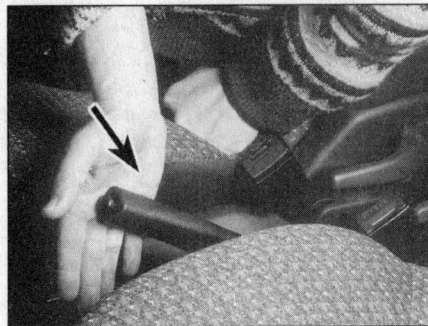

290mm

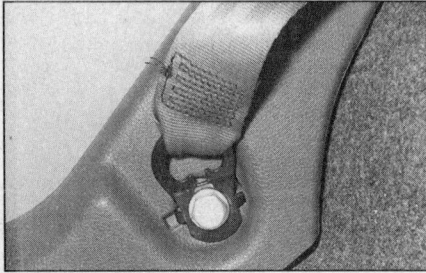

Seat belts and seats

Note: *The following checks are applicable to all seat belts, front and rear.*

☐ Examine the webbing of all the belts (including rear belts if fitted) for cuts, serious fraying or deterioration. Fasten and unfasten each belt to check the buckles. If applicable, check the retracting mechanism. Check the security of all seat belt mountings accessible from inside the vehicle.

☐ The front seats themselves must be securely attached and the backrests must lock in the upright position.

Doors

☐ Both front doors must be able to be opened and closed from outside and inside, and must latch securely when closed.

2 Checks carried out WITH THE VEHICLE ON THE GROUND

Vehicle identification

☐ Number plates must be in good condition, secure and legible, with letters and numbers correctly spaced – spacing at (A) should be twice that at (B).

☐ The VIN plate and/or homologation plate must be legible.

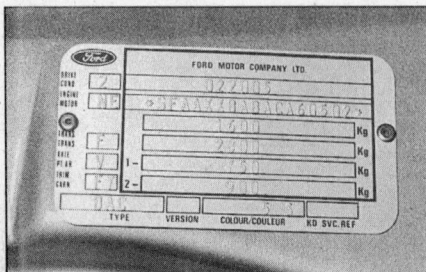

Electrical equipment

☐ Switch on the ignition and check the operation of the horn.

☐ Check the windscreen washers and wipers, examining the wiper blades; renew damaged or perished blades. Also check the operation of the stop-lights.

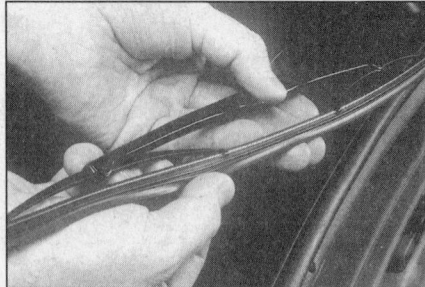

☐ Check the operation of the sidelights and number plate lights. The lenses and reflectors must be secure, clean and undamaged.

☐ Check the operation and alignment of the headlights. The headlight reflectors must not be tarnished and the lenses must be undamaged.

☐ Switch on the ignition and check the operation of the direction indicators (including the instrument panel tell-tale) and the hazard warning lights. Operation of the sidelights and stop-lights must not affect the indicators - if it does, the cause is usually a bad earth at the rear light cluster.

☐ Check the operation of the rear foglight(s), including the warning light on the instrument panel or in the switch.

Footbrake

☐ Examine the master cylinder, brake pipes and servo unit for leaks, loose mountings, corrosion or other damage.

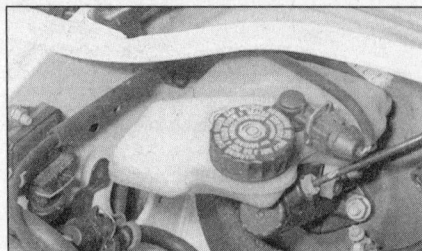

☐ The fluid reservoir must be secure and the fluid level must be between the upper (**A**) and lower (**B**) markings.

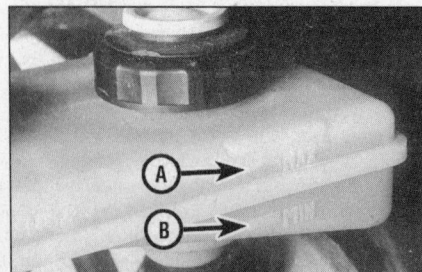

☐ Inspect both front brake flexible hoses for cracks or deterioration of the rubber. Turn the steering from lock to lock, and ensure that the hoses do not contact the wheel, tyre, or any part of the steering or suspension mechanism. With the brake pedal firmly depressed, check the hoses for bulges or leaks under pressure.

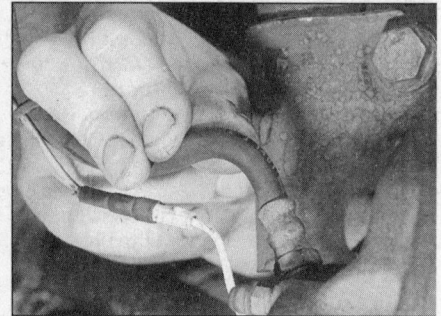

Steering and suspension

☐ Have your assistant turn the steering wheel from side to side slightly, up to the point where the steering gear just begins to transmit this movement to the roadwheels. Check for excessive free play between the steering wheel and the steering gear, indicating wear or insecurity of the steering column joints, the column-to-steering gear coupling, or the steering gear itself.

☐ Have your assistant turn the steering wheel more vigorously in each direction, so that the roadwheels just begin to turn. As this is done, examine all the steering joints, linkages, fittings and attachments. Renew any component that shows signs of wear or damage. On vehicles with power steering, check the security and condition of the steering pump, drivebelt and hoses.

☐ Check that the vehicle is standing level, and at approximately the correct ride height.

Shock absorbers

☐ Depress each corner of the vehicle in turn, then release it. The vehicle should rise and then settle in its normal position. If the vehicle continues to rise and fall, the shock absorber is defective. A shock absorber which has seized will also cause the vehicle to fail.

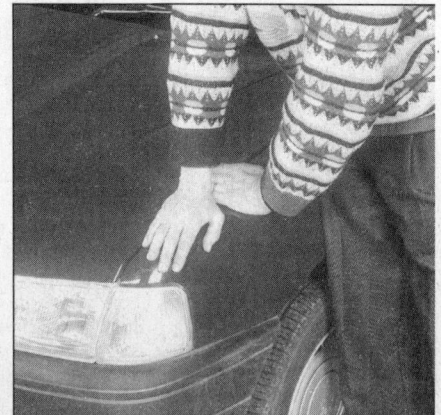

Exhaust system

☐ Start the engine. With your assistant holding a rag over the tailpipe, check the entire system for leaks. Repair or renew leaking sections.

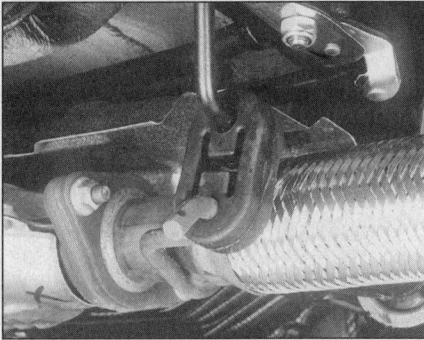

3 Checks carried out **WITH THE VEHICLE RAISED AND THE WHEELS FREE TO TURN**

Jack up the front and rear of the vehicle, and securely support it on axle stands. Position the stands clear of the suspension assemblies. Ensure that the wheels are clear of the ground and that the steering can be turned from lock to lock.

Steering mechanism

☐ Have your assistant turn the steering from lock to lock. Check that the steering turns smoothly, and that no part of the steering mechanism, including a wheel or tyre, fouls any brake hose or pipe or any part of the body structure.
☐ Examine the steering rack rubber gaiters for damage or insecurity of the retaining clips. If power steering is fitted, check for signs of damage or leakage of the fluid hoses, pipes or connections. Also check for excessive stiffness or binding of the steering, a missing split pin or locking device, or severe corrosion of the body structure within 30 cm of any steering component attachment point.

Front and rear suspension and wheel bearings

☐ Starting at the front right-hand side, grasp the roadwheel at the 3 o'clock and 9 o'clock positions and shake it vigorously. Check for free play or insecurity at the wheel bearings, suspension balljoints, or suspension mountings, pivots and attachments.
☐ Now grasp the wheel at the 12 o'clock and 6 o'clock positions and repeat the previous inspection. Spin the wheel, and check for roughness or tightness of the front wheel bearing.

☐ If excess free play is suspected at a component pivot point, this can be confirmed by using a large screwdriver or similar tool and levering between the mounting and the component attachment. This will confirm whether the wear is in the pivot bush, its retaining bolt, or in the mounting itself (the bolt holes can often become elongated).

☐ Carry out all the above checks at the other front wheel, and then at both rear wheels.

Springs and shock absorbers

☐ Examine the suspension struts (when applicable) for serious fluid leakage, corrosion, or damage to the casing. Also check the security of the mounting points.
☐ If coil springs are fitted, check that the spring ends locate in their seats, and that the spring is not corroded, cracked or broken.
☐ If leaf springs are fitted, check that all leaves are intact, that the axle is securely attached to each spring, and that there is no deterioration of the spring eye mountings, bushes, and shackles.

☐ The same general checks apply to vehicles fitted with other suspension types, such as torsion bars, hydraulic displacer units, etc. Ensure that all mountings and attachments are secure, that there are no signs of excessive wear, corrosion or damage, and (on hydraulic types) that there are no fluid leaks or damaged pipes.
☐ Inspect the shock absorbers for signs of serious fluid leakage. Check for wear of the mounting bushes or attachments, or damage to the body of the unit.

Driveshafts (fwd vehicles only)

☐ Rotate each front wheel in turn and inspect the constant velocity joint gaiters for splits or damage. Also check that each driveshaft is straight and undamaged.

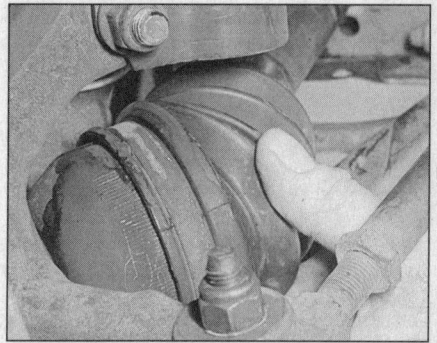

Braking system

☐ If possible without dismantling, check brake pad wear and disc condition. Ensure that the friction lining material has not worn excessively, (A) and that the discs are not fractured, pitted, scored or badly worn (B).

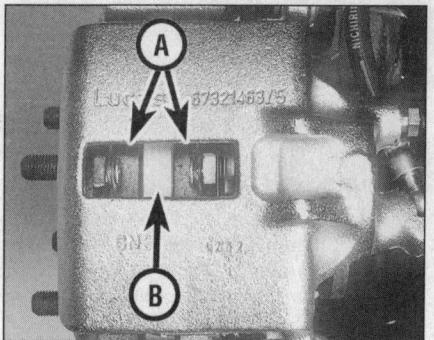

☐ Examine all the rigid brake pipes underneath the vehicle, and the flexible hose(s) at the rear. Look for corrosion, chafing or insecurity of the pipes, and for signs of bulging under pressure, chafing, splits or deterioration of the flexible hoses.
☐ Look for signs of fluid leaks at the brake calipers or on the brake backplates. Repair or renew leaking components.
☐ Slowly spin each wheel, while your assistant depresses and releases the footbrake. Ensure that each brake is operating and does not bind when the pedal is released.

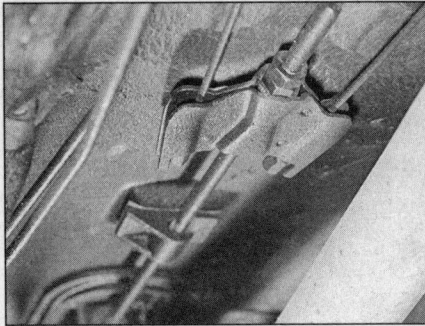

☐ Examine the handbrake mechanism, checking for frayed or broken cables, excessive corrosion, or wear or insecurity of the linkage. Check that the mechanism works on each relevant wheel, and releases fully, without binding.

☐ It is not possible to test brake efficiency without special equipment, but a road test can be carried out later to check that the vehicle pulls up in a straight line.

Fuel and exhaust systems

☐ Inspect the fuel tank (including the filler cap), fuel pipes, hoses and unions. All components must be secure and free from leaks.

☐ Examine the exhaust system over its entire length, checking for any damaged, broken or missing mountings, security of the retaining clamps and rust or corrosion.

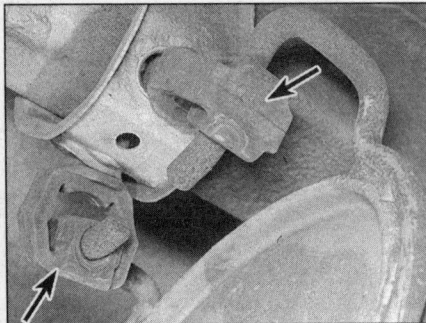

Wheels and tyres

☐ Examine the sidewalls and tread area of each tyre in turn. Check for cuts, tears, lumps, bulges, separation of the tread, and exposure of the ply or cord due to wear or damage. Check that the tyre bead is correctly seated on the wheel rim, that the valve is sound and properly seated, and that the wheel is not distorted or damaged.

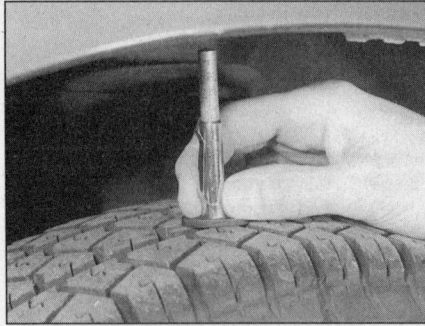

☐ Check that the tyres are of the correct size for the vehicle, that they are of the same size and type on each axle, and that the pressures are correct.

☐ Check the tyre tread depth. The legal minimum at the time of writing is 1.6 mm over at least three-quarters of the tread width. Abnormal tread wear may indicate incorrect front wheel alignment.

Body corrosion

☐ Check the condition of the entire vehicle structure for signs of corrosion in load-bearing areas. (These include chassis box sections, side sills, cross-members, pillars, and all suspension, steering, braking system and seat belt mountings and anchorages.) Any corrosion which has seriously reduced the thickness of a load-bearing area is likely to cause the vehicle to fail. In this case professional repairs are likely to be needed.

☐ Damage or corrosion which causes sharp or otherwise dangerous edges to be exposed will also cause the vehicle to fail.

4 Checks carried out on YOUR VEHICLE'S EXHAUST EMISSION SYSTEM

Petrol models

☐ Have the engine at normal operating temperature, and make sure that it is in good tune (ignition system in good order, air filter element clean, etc).

☐ Before any measurements are carried out, raise the engine speed to around 2500 rpm, and hold it at this speed for 20 seconds. Allow the engine speed to return to idle, and watch for smoke emissions from the exhaust tailpipe. If the idle speed is obviously much too high, or if dense blue or clearly-visible black smoke comes from the tailpipe for more than 5 seconds, the vehicle will fail. As a rule of thumb, blue smoke signifies oil being burnt (engine wear) while black smoke signifies unburnt fuel (dirty air cleaner element, or other carburettor or fuel system fault).

☐ An exhaust gas analyser capable of measuring carbon monoxide (CO) and hydrocarbons (HC) is now needed. If such an instrument cannot be hired or borrowed, a local garage may agree to perform the check for a small fee.

CO emissions (mixture)

☐ At the time of writing, the maximum CO level at idle is 3.5% for vehicles first used after August 1986 and 4.5% for older vehicles. From January 1996 a much tighter limit (around 0.5%) applies to catalyst-equipped vehicles first used from August 1992. If the CO level cannot be reduced far enough to pass the test (and the fuel and ignition systems are otherwise in good condition) then the carburettor is badly worn, or there is some problem in the fuel injection system or catalytic converter (as applicable).

HC emissions

☐ With the CO emissions within limits, HC emissions must be no more than 1200 ppm (parts per million). If the vehicle fails this test at idle, it can be re-tested at around 2000 rpm; if the HC level is then 1200 ppm or less, this counts as a pass.

☐ Excessive HC emissions can be caused by oil being burnt, but they are more likely to be due to unburnt fuel.

Diesel models

☐ The only emission test applicable to Diesel engines is the measuring of exhaust smoke density. The test involves accelerating the engine several times to its maximum unloaded speed.

Note: *It is of the utmost importance that the engine timing belt is in good condition before the test is carried out.*

☐ Excessive smoke can be caused by a dirty air cleaner element. Otherwise, professional advice may be needed to find the cause.

Introduction

The vehicle owner who does his or her own maintenance according to the recommended service schedules should not have to use this section of the manual very often. Modern component reliability is such that, provided those items subject to wear or deterioration are inspected or renewed at the specified intervals, sudden failure is comparatively rare. Faults do not usually just happen as a result of sudden failure, but develop over a period of time. Major mechanical failures in particular are usually preceded by characteristic symptoms over hundreds or even thousands of miles. Those components which do occasionally fail without warning are often small and easily carried in the vehicle.

With any fault finding, the first step is to decide where to begin investigations. Sometimes this is obvious, but on other occasions a little detective work will be necessary. The owner who makes half a dozen haphazard adjustments or replacements may be successful in curing a fault (or its symptoms), but will be none the wiser if the fault recurs and ultimately may have spent more time and money than was

necessary. A calm and logical approach will be found to be more satisfactory in the long run. Always take into account any warning signs or abnormalities that may have been noticed in the period preceding the fault - power loss, high or low gauge readings, unusual smells, etc - and remember that failure of components such as fuses or relays may only be pointers to some underlying fault.

The pages which follow provide an easy reference guide to the more common problems which may occur during the operation of the vehicle. These problems and their possible causes are grouped under headings denoting various components or systems, such as Engine, Cooling system, etc. The Chapter and/or Section which deals with the problem is also shown in brackets. Whatever the fault, certain basic principles apply. These are as follows:

Verify the fault. This is simply a matter of being sure that you know what the symptoms are before starting work. This is particularly important if you are investigating a fault for someone else who may not have described it very accurately.

Don't overlook the obvious. For example, if the vehicle won't start, is there fuel in the tank? (Don't take anyone else's word on this particular point, and don't trust the fuel gauge either!) If an electrical fault is indicated, look for loose or broken wires before digging out the test gear.

Cure the disease, not the symptom. Substituting a flat battery with a fully charged one will get you off the hard shoulder, but if the underlying cause is not fixed, the new battery will go the same way.

Don't take anything for granted. Particularly, don't forget that a "new" component may itself be defective (especially if it's been rattling around in the boot for months), and don't leave components out of a fault diagnosis sequence just because they are new or recently fitted. When you do finally diagnose a difficult fault, you'll probably realise that all the evidence was there from the start.

1 Engine

Engine fails to rotate when attempting to start

☐ Battery terminal connections loose or corroded (Chapter 1).
☐ Battery discharged or faulty (Chapter 5).
☐ Broken, loose or disconnected wiring in the starting circuit (Chapter 5).
☐ Defective starter solenoid or switch (Chapter 5).
☐ Defective starter motor (Chapter 5).
☐ Starter pinion or flywheel ring gear teeth loose or broken (Chapter 5 and Chapter 2A).
☐ Engine earth strap broken or disconnected (Chapter 5).

Starter motor turns engine slowly

☐ Partially discharged battery (recharge, use jump leads, or push start) (Chapter 5).
☐ Battery terminals loose or corroded (Chapter 1).
☐ Battery earth to body defective (Chapter 5).
☐ Engine earth strap loose (Chapter 5).
☐ Starter motor (or solenoid) wiring loose (Chapter 5).
☐ Starter motor internal fault (Chapter 5).

Starter motor spins without turning engine

☐ Starter motor reduction gears stripped (Chapter 5).
☐ Starter motor mounting bolts loose (Chapter 5).

Starter motor noisy or excessively rough in engagement

☐ Starter pinion or flywheel ring gear teeth loose or broken (Chapter 5 and Chapter 2A).
☐ Starter motor mounting bolts loose or missing (Chapter 5).
☐ Starter motor internal components worn or damaged (Chapter 5).

Engine rotates but will not start

☐ Fuel tank empty.
☐ Battery discharged (engine rotates slowly) (Chapter 5).
☐ Battery terminal connections loose or corroded (Chapter 1).
☐ Air in fuel (Chapter 4).
☐ Wax formed in fuel (in very cold weather).
☐ Faulty stop solenoid (Chapter 4).
☐ Low cylinder compressions (Chapter 2A).
☐ Fuel system or preheating system fault (Chapters 4 and 5).
☐ Major mechanical failure (eg camshaft drive) (Chapter 2A).

Engine fires but will not run

☐ Preheating system fault (Chapter 5).
☐ Air in fuel (Chapter 4).
☐ Wax formed in fuel (in very cold weather).
☐ Other fuel system fault (Chapter 4).

Engine difficult to start when cold

☐ Battery discharged (Chapter 5).
☐ Battery terminal connections loose or corroded (Chapter 1).
☐ Air in fuel (Chapter 4).
☐ Air filter element dirty or clogged (Chapter 1).
☐ Wax formed in fuel (in very cold weather).
☐ Preheating system fault (Chapter 5).
☐ Other fuel system fault (Chapter 4).
☐ Low cylinder compressions (Chapter 2A).

Engine difficult to start when hot

☐ Battery discharged (Chapter 5).
☐ Battery terminal connections loose or corroded (Chapter 1).
☐ Air filter element dirty or clogged (Chapter 1).
☐ Air in fuel (Chapter 4).
☐ Low cylinder compressions (Chapter 2A).

Engine idles erratically

☐ Incorrectly adjusted idle speed (Chapter 1).
☐ Air filter element clogged (Chapter 1).
☐ Incorrectly adjusted valve clearances (Chapter 2A).
☐ Uneven or low cylinder compressions (Chapter 2A).
☐ Camshaft lobes worn (Chapter 2A).
☐ Timing belt incorrectly tensioned (Chapter 2A).
☐ Incorrect fuel injection pump timing (Chapter 4).

Engine misfires at idle speed

☐ Air in fuel (Chapter 4).
☐ Wax formed in fuel (in very cold weather).
☐ Other fuel system fault (Chapter 4).
☐ Incorrectly adjusted valve clearances (Chapter 2A).
☐ Uneven or low cylinder compressions (Chapter 2A).
☐ Disconnected, leaking or perished crankcase ventilation hoses (Chapters 1 and 3).
☐ Incorrect fuel injection pump timing (Chapter 4).

Engine misfires throughout the driving speed range

☐ Fuel filter choked (Chapter 1).
☐ Fuel tank vent blocked or fuel pipes restricted (Chapter 4).
☐ Uneven or low cylinder compressions (Chapter 2A).
☐ Incorrect fuel injection pump timing (Chapter 4).

Engine stalls

☐ Incorrectly adjusted idle speed (Chapter 1).
☐ Fuel filter choked (Chapter 1).
☐ Fuel tank vent blocked or fuel pipes restricted (Chapter 4).

Engine lacks power

☐ Air in fuel (Chapter 4).
☐ Incorrect fuel injection pump timing (Chapter 4).
☐ Timing belt incorrectly fitted or tensioned (Chapter 2A).
☐ Fuel filter choked (Chapter 1).
☐ Uneven or low cylinder compressions (Chapter 2A).
☐ Brakes binding (Chapters 1 and 9).
☐ Clutch slipping (Chapter 6).

Oil pressure warning light illuminated with engine running

☐ Low oil level or incorrect grade (Chapter 1).
☐ Faulty oil pressure switch (Chapter 5).
☐ Worn engine bearings and/or oil pump (Chapters 2A and 2B).
☐ High engine operating temperature (Chapter 3).
☐ Oil pressure relief valve defective (Chapter 2A).
☐ Oil pick-up strainer clogged (Chapter 2A).

Note: *Low oil pressure in a high-mileage engine at tickover is not necessarily a cause for concern. Sudden pressure loss at speed is far more significant. In any event, check the gauge or warning light sender before condemning the engine.*

Engine runs-on after switching off

☐ Faulty stop solenoid (Chapter 4).

Engine noises

Note: *To inexperienced ears, the diesel engine can sound alarming even when there is nothing wrong with it, so it may be prudent to have an unusual noise expertly diagnosed before making renewals or repairs.*

Whistling or wheezing noises

☐ Leaking manifold gasket (Chapter 4).
☐ Leaking vacuum hose (Chapters 1 and 4).
☐ Blowing cylinder head gasket (Chapter 2A).

Tapping or rattling noises

☐ Incorrect valve clearances (Chapter 2A).
☐ Worn valve gear or camshaft (Chapter 2A).
☐ Broken piston ring (ticking noise) (Chapter 2B).
☐ Ancillary component fault (water pump, alternator etc) (Chapters 3 and 5).

Knocking or thumping noises

☐ Air in fuel (Chapter 4).
☐ Worn drivebelt (Chapter 1 and Chapter 2A).
☐ Fuel injector(s) leaking or sticking (Chapter 4).
☐ Worn big-end bearings (regular heavy knocking, perhaps less under load) (Chapter 2B).
☐ Worn main bearings (rumbling and knocking, perhaps worsening under load) (Chapter 2B).
☐ Piston slap (most noticeable when cold) (Chapter 2B).
☐ Ancillary component fault (alternator, water pump etc) (Chapters 3 and 5).

2 Cooling system

Overheating

☐ Insufficient coolant in system (Chapter 1).
☐ Thermostat faulty (Chapter 3).
☐ Radiator core blocked or grille restricted (Chapter 3).
☐ Electric cooling fan or thermoswitch faulty (Chapter 3).
☐ Pressure cap faulty (Chapter 3).
☐ Timing belt worn, or incorrectly adjusted (Chapter 2A).
☐ Inaccurate temperature gauge sender unit (Chapter 3).
☐ Air lock in cooling system (Chapter 1).

Overcooling

☐ Thermostat faulty (Chapter 3).
☐ Inaccurate temperature gauge sender unit (Chapter 3).

External coolant leakage

☐ Deteriorated or damaged hoses or hose clips (Chapter 1).
☐ Radiator core or heater matrix leaking (Chapter 3).
☐ Pressure cap faulty (Chapter 3).
☐ Water pump seal leaking (Chapter 3).
☐ Boiling due to overheating (Chapter 3).
☐ Core plug leaking (Chapter 2B).

Internal coolant leakage

☐ Leaking cylinder head gasket (Chapter 2A).
☐ Cracked cylinder head or cylinder bore (Chapters 2A and 2B).

Corrosion

☐ Infrequent draining and flushing (Chapter 1).
☐ Incorrect antifreeze mixture or inappropriate type (Chapter 1).

3 Fuel and exhaust system

Excessive fuel consumption

☐ Air filter element dirty or clogged (Chapter 1).
☐ Preheating system fault (Chapter 5).
☐ Incorrect idle speed (Chapter 1).
☐ Incorrect fuel injection pump timing (Chapter 4).
☐ Brakes binding (Chapter 9).
☐ Tyres underinflated (Chapter 1).

Fuel leakage and/or fuel odour

☐ Damaged or corroded fuel tank, pipes or connections (Chapters 1 and 4).

Excessive noise or fumes from exhaust system

☐ Leaking exhaust system or manifold joints (Chapter 4).
☐ Leaking, corroded or damaged silencers or pipe (Chapter 4).
☐ Broken mountings giving body or suspension contact (Chapter 4).

4 Clutch

Pedal travels to floor - no pressure or very little resistance

☐ Broken clutch cable (Chapter 6).
☐ Incorrect clutch adjustment (Chapter 6).
☐ Broken clutch release bearing or fork (Chapter 6).
☐ Broken diaphragm spring in clutch pressure plate (Chapter 6).

Clutch fails to disengage (unable to select gears)

☐ Incorrect clutch adjustment (Chapter 6).
☐ Friction plate sticking on gearbox input shaft splines (Chapter 6).
☐ Friction plate sticking to flywheel or pressure plate (Chapter 6).
☐ Faulty pressure plate assembly (Chapter 6).
☐ Clutch release mechanism worn or incorrectly assembled (Chapter 6).

Clutch slips (engine speed increases with no increase in vehicle speed)

☐ Incorrect clutch adjustment (Chapter 6).
☐ Friction plate linings excessively worn (Chapter 6).
☐ Friction plate linings contaminated with oil or grease (Chapter 6).
☐ Faulty pressure plate or weak diaphragm spring (Chapter 6).

Judder as clutch is engaged

☐ Friction plate linings contaminated with oil or grease (Chapter 6).
☐ Friction plate linings excessively worn (Chapter 6).
☐ Clutch cable sticking or frayed (Chapter 6).
☐ Faulty or distorted pressure plate or diaphragm spring (Chapter 6).
☐ Worn or loose engine or gearbox mountings (Chapter 2A).
☐ Friction plate hub or gearbox input shaft splines worn (Chapter 6).

4 Clutch (continued)

Noise when depressing or releasing clutch pedal

☐ Worn clutch release bearing (Chapter 6).
☐ Worn or dry clutch pedal bushes (Chapter 6).
☐ Faulty pressure plate assembly (Chapter 6).
☐ Pressure plate diaphragm spring broken (Chapter 6).
☐ Broken friction plate cushioning springs (Chapter 6).

5 Manual gearbox

Noisy in neutral with engine running

☐ Input shaft bearings worn (noise apparent with clutch pedal released but not when depressed) (Chapter 7).*
☐ Clutch release bearing worn (noise apparent with clutch pedal depressed, possibly less when released) (Chapter 6).

Noisy in one particular gear

☐ Worn, damaged or chipped gear teeth (Chapter 7).*

Difficulty engaging gears

☐ Clutch fault (Chapter 6).
☐ Worn or damaged gear linkage (Chapter 7).
☐ Incorrectly adjusted gear linkage (Chapter 7).
☐ Worn synchroniser units (Chapter 7).*

Jumps out of gear

☐ Worn or damaged gear linkage (Chapter 7).
☐ Incorrectly adjusted gear linkage (Chapter 7).
☐ Worn synchroniser units (Chapter 7).*
☐ Worn selector forks (Chapter 7).*

Vibration

☐ Lack of oil (Chapter 1).
☐ Worn bearings (Chapter 7).*

Lubricant leaks

☐ Leaking oil seal (Chapter 7).
☐ Leaking housing joint (Chapter 7).*

*Although the corrective action necessary to remedy the symptoms described is beyond the scope of the home mechanic, the above information should be helpful in isolating the cause of the condition so that the owner can communicate clearly with a professional mechanic.

6 Driveshafts

Clicking or knocking noise on turns (at slow speed on full lock)

☐ Lack of constant velocity joint lubricant (Chapter 8).
☐ Worn outer constant velocity joint (Chapter 8).

Vibration when accelerating or decelerating

☐ Worn inner constant velocity joint (Chapter 8).
☐ Bent or distorted driveshaft (Chapter 8).

7 Braking system

Note: *Before assuming that a brake problem exists, make sure that the tyres are in good condition and correctly inflated, the front wheel alignment is correct and the vehicle is not loaded with weight in an unequal manner. Apart from checking the condition of all pipe and hose connections, any faults occurring on the anti-lock braking system should be referred to a Renault dealer for diagnosis.*

Vehicle pulls to one side under braking

☐ Worn, defective, damaged or contaminated front or rear brake pads/shoes on one side (Chapter 9).
☐ Seized or partially seized front or rear brake caliper/wheel cylinder piston (Chapter 9).
☐ A mixture of brake pad/shoe lining materials fitted between sides (Chapter 9).
☐ Brake caliper mounting bolts loose (Chapter 9).
☐ Rear brake backplate mounting bolts loose (Chapter 9).
☐ Worn or damaged steering or suspension parts (Chapter 10).

Noise (grinding or high-pitched squeal) when brakes applied

☐ Brake pad or shoe friction lining material worn down to metal backing (Chapter 9).
☐ Excessive corrosion of brake disc or drum. (May be apparent after the vehicle has been standing for some time (Chapter 9).

Excessive brake pedal travel

☐ Inoperative rear brake self-adjust mechanism (Chapter 9).
☐ Faulty master cylinder (Chapter 9).
☐ Air in hydraulic system (Chapter 9).
☐ Faulty vacuum servo unit (Chapter 9).
☐ Faulty brake vacuum pump (Chapter 9).

Brake pedal feels spongy when depressed

☐ Air in hydraulic system (Chapter 9).
☐ Deteriorated flexible rubber brake hoses (Chapter 9).
☐ Master cylinder mountings loose (Chapter 9).
☐ Faulty master cylinder (Chapter 9).

Excessive brake pedal effort required to stop car

☐ Faulty vacuum servo unit (Chapter 9).
☐ Disconnected, damaged or insecure brake servo vacuum hose (Chapters 1 and 9).
☐ Faulty brake vacuum pump (Chapter 9).
☐ Primary or secondary hydraulic circuit failure (Chapter 9).
☐ Seized brake caliper or wheel cylinder piston(s) (Chapter 9).
☐ Brake pads or brake shoes incorrectly fitted (Chapter 9).
☐ Incorrect grade of brake pads or brake shoes fitted (Chapter 9).
☐ Brake pads or brake shoe linings contaminated (Chapter 9).

7 Braking system (continued)

Judder felt through brake pedal or steering wheel when braking

☐ Excessive run-out or distortion of front discs or rear drums (Chapter 9).
☐ Brake pad or brake shoe linings worn (Chapter 9).
☐ Brake caliper or rear brake backplate mounting bolts loose (Chapter 9).
☐ Wear in suspension or steering parts or mountings (Chapter 10).

Brakes binding

☐ Seized brake caliper or wheel cylinder piston(s) (Chapter 9).
☐ Incorrectly adjusted handbrake mechanism or linkage (Chapter 9).
☐ Faulty master cylinder (Chapter 9).

Rear wheels locking under normal braking

☐ Rear brake shoe linings contaminated (Chapter 9).
☐ Faulty brake pressure regulator (Chapter 9).

8 Suspension and steering systems

Note: *Before diagnosing suspension or steering faults, be sure that the trouble is not due to incorrect tyre pressures, mixtures of tyre types or binding brakes.*

Vehicle pulls to one side

☐ Defective tyre (Chapter 1).
☐ Excessive wear in suspension or steering parts (Chapter 10).
☐ Incorrect front wheel alignment (Chapter 10).
☐ Accident damage to steering or suspension components (Chapter 10).

Wheel wobble and vibration

☐ Front roadwheels out of balance (vibration felt mainly through the steering wheel) (Chapter 10).
☐ Rear roadwheels out of balance (vibration felt throughout the vehicle) (Chapter 10).
☐ Roadwheels damaged or distorted (Chapter 1).
☐ Faulty or damaged tyre (Chapter 1).
☐ Worn steering or suspension joints, bushes or components (Chapter 10).
☐ Wheel bolts loose (Chapter 10).

Excessive pitching and/or rolling around corners or during braking

☐ Defective shock absorbers (Chapter 10).
☐ Broken or weak coil spring and/or suspension component (Chapter 10).
☐ Worn or damaged anti-roll bar or mountings (Chapter 10).

Wandering or general instability

☐ Incorrect front wheel alignment (Chapter 10).
☐ Worn steering or suspension joints, bushes or components (Chapter 10).
☐ Roadwheels out of balance (Chapter 10).
☐ Faulty or damaged tyre (Chapter 1).
☐ Wheel bolts loose (Chapter 10).
☐ Defective shock absorbers (Chapter 10).

Excessively stiff steering

☐ Lack of steering gear lubricant (Chapter 10).
☐ Seized track-rod end balljoint or suspension balljoint (Chapter 10).
☐ Broken or incorrectly adjusted power steering pump drivebelt (Chapter 1).

☐ Incorrect front wheel alignment (Chapter 10).
☐ Steering rack or column bent or damaged (Chapter 10).

Excessive play in steering

☐ Worn steering column universal joint(s) or intermediate coupling (Chapter 10).
☐ Worn steering track-rod end balljoints (Chapter 10).
☐ Worn rack and pinion steering gear (Chapter 10).
☐ Worn steering or suspension joints, bushes or components (Chapter 10).

Lack of power assistance

☐ Broken or incorrectly adjusted power steering pump drivebelt (Chapter 1).
☐ Incorrect power steering fluid level (Chapter 1).
☐ Restriction in power steering fluid hoses (Chapter 1).
☐ Faulty power steering pump (Chapter 10).
☐ Faulty rack and pinion steering gear (Chapter 10).

Tyre wear excessive

Tyres worn on inside or outside edges

☐ Tyres underinflated (wear on both edges) (Chapter 1).
☐ Incorrect camber or castor angles (wear on one edge only) (Chapter 10).
☐ Worn steering or suspension joints, bushes or components (Chapter 10).
☐ Excessively hard cornering.
☐ Accident damage.

Tyre treads exhibit feathered edges

☐ Incorrect toe setting (Chapter 10).

Tyres worn in centre of tread

☐ Tyres overinflated (Chapter 1).

Tyres worn on inside and outside edges

☐ Tyres underinflated (Chapter 1).

Tyres worn unevenly

☐ Tyres out of balance (Chapter 1).
☐ Excessive wheel or tyre run-out (Chapter 1).
☐ Worn shock absorbers (Chapter 10).
☐ Faulty tyre (Chapter 1).

9 Electrical system

Note: *For problems associated with the starting system, refer to the faults listed under "Engine" earlier in this Section.*

Battery will only hold a charge for a few days

☐ Battery defective internally (Chapter 5).
☐ Battery electrolyte level low - where applicable (Chapter 1).

☐ Battery terminal connections loose or corroded (Chapter 1).
☐ Alternator drivebelt worn or incorrectly adjusted (Chapter 1).
☐ Alternator not charging at correct output (Chapter 5).
☐ Alternator or voltage regulator faulty (Chapter 5).
☐ Short-circuit causing continual battery drain (Chapter 5).

9 Electrical system (continued)

Ignition warning light remains illuminated with engine running

- ☐ Alternator drivebelt broken, worn, or incorrectly adjusted (Chapter 1).
- ☐ Alternator brushes worn, sticking, or dirty (Chapter 5).
- ☐ Alternator brush springs weak or broken (Chapter 5).
- ☐ Internal fault in alternator or voltage regulator (Chapter 5).
- ☐ Broken, disconnected, or loose wiring in charging circuit (Chapter 5).

Ignition warning light fails to come on

- ☐ Warning light bulb blown (Chapter 12).
- ☐ Broken, disconnected, or loose wiring in warning light circuit (Chapter 12).
- ☐ Alternator faulty (Chapter 5).

Lights inoperative

- ☐ Bulb blown (Chapter 12).
- ☐ Corrosion of bulb or bulbholder contacts (Chapter 12).
- ☐ Blown fuse (Chapter 12).
- ☐ Faulty relay (Chapter 12).
- ☐ Broken, loose, or disconnected wiring (Chapter 12).
- ☐ Faulty switch (Chapter 12).

Instrument readings inaccurate or erratic

Instrument readings increase with engine speed

- ☐ Faulty voltage regulator (Chapter 12).

Fuel or temperature gauge give no reading

- ☐ Faulty gauge sender unit (Chapters 3 or 4).
- ☐ Wiring open-circuit (Chapter 5).
- ☐ Faulty gauge (Chapter 12).

Fuel or temperature gauges give continuous maximum reading

- ☐ Faulty gauge sender unit (Chapters 3 or 4).
- ☐ Wiring short-circuit (Chapter 5).
- ☐ Faulty gauge (Chapter 12).

Horn inoperative or unsatisfactory in operation

Horn operates all the time

- ☐ Horn push either earthed or stuck down (Chapter 12).
- ☐ Horn cable to horn push earthed (Chapter 12).

Horn fails to operate

- ☐ Blown fuse (Chapter 12).
- ☐ Cable or cable connections loose, broken or disconnected (Chapter 12).
- ☐ Faulty horn (Chapter 12).

Horn emits intermittent or unsatisfactory sound

- ☐ Cable connections loose (Chapter 12).
- ☐ Horn mountings loose (Chapter 12).
- ☐ Faulty horn (Chapter 12).

Windscreen/tailgate wipers inoperative or unsatisfactory in operation

Wipers fail to operate or operate very slowly

- ☐ Wiper blades stuck to screen or linkage seized or binding (Chapters 1 and 12).
- ☐ Blown fuse (Chapter 12).
- ☐ Cable or cable connections loose, broken or disconnected (Chapter 12).
- ☐ Faulty relay (Chapter 12).
- ☐ Faulty wiper motor (Chapter 12).

Wiper blades sweep over too large or too small an area of the glass

- ☐ Wiper arms incorrectly positioned on spindles (Chapter 12).
- ☐ Excessive wear of wiper linkage (Chapter 12).
- ☐ Wiper motor or linkage mountings loose or insecure (Chapter 12).

Wiper blades fail to clean the glass effectively

- ☐ Wiper blade rubbers worn or perished (Chapter 1).
- ☐ Wiper arm tension springs broken or arm pivots seized (Chapter 12).
- ☐ Insufficient windscreen washer additive to adequately remove road film (Chapter 1).

Windscreen/tailgate washers inoperative or unsatisfactory in operation

One or more washer jets inoperative

- ☐ Blocked washer jet (Chapter 12).
- ☐ Disconnected, kinked or restricted fluid hose (Chapter 12).
- ☐ Insufficient fluid in washer reservoir (Chapter 1).

Washer pump fails to operate

- ☐ Broken or disconnected wiring or connections (Chapter 12).
- ☐ Blown fuse (Chapter 12).
- ☐ Faulty washer switch (Chapter 12).
- ☐ Faulty washer pump (Chapter 12).

Washer pump runs for some time before fluid is emitted from jets

- ☐ Faulty one-way valve in fluid supply hose (Chapter 12).

Electric windows inoperative or unsatisfactory in operation

Window glass will only move in one direction

- ☐ Faulty switch (Chapter 11).

Window glass slow to move

- ☐ Regulator seized or damaged, or in need of lubrication (Chapter 11).
- ☐ Door internal components or trim fouling regulator (Chapter 11).
- ☐ Faulty motor (Chapter 11).

Window glass fails to move

- ☐ Blown fuse (Chapter 12).
- ☐ Faulty relay (Chapter 12).
- ☐ Broken or disconnected wiring or connections (Chapter 12).
- ☐ Faulty motor (Chapter 11).

Central locking system inoperative or unsatisfactory in operation

Complete system failure

- ☐ Blown fuse (Chapter 12).
- ☐ Faulty relay (Chapter 12).
- ☐ Broken or disconnected wiring or connections (Chapter 12).

Latch locks but will not unlock, or unlocks but will not lock

- ☐ Faulty switch (Chapter 12).
- ☐ Broken or disconnected latch operating rods or levers (Chapter 11).
- ☐ Faulty relay (Chapter 12).

One solenoid/motor fails to operate

- ☐ Broken or disconnected wiring or connections (Chapter 12).
- ☐ Faulty solenoid/motor (Chapter 11).
- ☐ Broken, binding or disconnected latch operating rods or levers (Chapter 11).
- ☐ Fault in door latch (Chapter 11).

A

ABS (Anti-lock brake system) A system, usually electronically controlled, that senses incipient wheel lockup during braking and relieves hydraulic pressure at wheels that are about to skid.

Air bag An inflatable bag hidden in the steering wheel (driver's side) or the dash or glovebox (passenger side). In a head-on collision, the bags inflate, preventing the driver and front passenger from being thrown forward into the steering wheel or windscreen.

Air cleaner A metal or plastic housing, containing a filter element, which removes dust and dirt from the air being drawn into the engine.

Air filter element The actual filter in an air cleaner system, usually manufactured from pleated paper and requiring renewal at regular intervals.

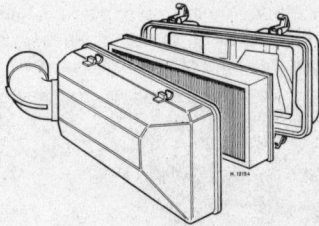

Air filter

Allen key A hexagonal wrench which fits into a recessed hexagonal hole.

Alligator clip A long-nosed spring-loaded metal clip with meshing teeth. Used to make temporary electrical connections.

Alternator A component in the electrical system which converts mechanical energy from a drivebelt into electrical energy to charge the battery and to operate the starting system, ignition system and electrical accessories.

Ampere (amp) A unit of measurement for the flow of electric current. One amp is the amount of current produced by one volt acting through a resistance of one ohm.

Anaerobic sealer A substance used to prevent bolts and screws from loosening. Anaerobic means that it does not require oxygen for activation. The Loctite brand is widely used.

Antifreeze A substance (usually ethylene glycol) mixed with water, and added to a vehicle's cooling system, to prevent freezing of the coolant in winter. Antifreeze also contains chemicals to inhibit corrosion and the formation of rust and other deposits that would tend to clog the radiator and coolant passages and reduce cooling efficiency.

Anti-seize compound A coating that reduces the risk of seizing on fasteners that are subjected to high temperatures, such as exhaust manifold bolts and nuts.

Asbestos A natural fibrous mineral with great heat resistance, commonly used in the composition of brake friction materials.

Asbestos is a health hazard and the dust created by brake systems should never be inhaled or ingested.

Axle A shaft on which a wheel revolves, or which revolves with a wheel. Also, a solid beam that connects the two wheels at one end of the vehicle. An axle which also transmits power to the wheels is known as a live axle.

Axleshaft A single rotating shaft, on either side of the differential, which delivers power from the final drive assembly to the drive wheels. Also called a driveshaft or a halfshaft.

B

Ball bearing An anti-friction bearing consisting of a hardened inner and outer race with hardened steel balls between two races.

Bearing The curved surface on a shaft or in a bore, or the part assembled into either, that permits relative motion between them with minimum wear and friction.

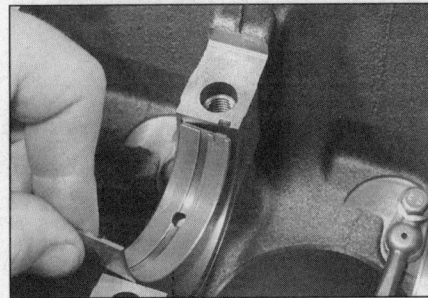

Bearing

Big-end bearing The bearing in the end of the connecting rod that's attached to the crankshaft.

Bleed nipple A valve on a brake wheel cylinder, caliper or other hydraulic component that is opened to purge the hydraulic system of air. Also called a bleed screw.

Brake bleeding Procedure for removing air from lines of a hydraulic brake system.

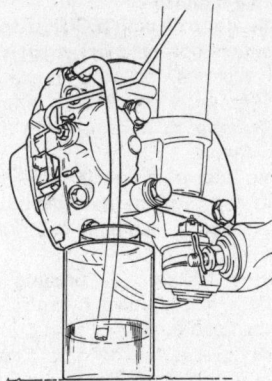

Brake bleeding

Brake disc The component of a disc brake that rotates with the wheels.

Brake drum The component of a drum brake that rotates with the wheels.

Brake linings The friction material which contacts the brake disc or drum to retard the vehicle's speed. The linings are bonded or riveted to the brake pads or shoes.

Brake pads The replaceable friction pads that pinch the brake disc when the brakes are applied. Brake pads consist of a friction material bonded or riveted to a rigid backing plate.

Brake shoe The crescent-shaped carrier to which the brake linings are mounted and which forces the lining against the rotating drum during braking.

Braking systems For more information on braking systems, consult the *Haynes Automotive Brake Manual*.

Breaker bar A long socket wrench handle providing greater leverage.

Bulkhead The insulated partition between the engine and the passenger compartment.

C

Caliper The non-rotating part of a disc-brake assembly that straddles the disc and carries the brake pads. The caliper also contains the hydraulic components that cause the pads to pinch the disc when the brakes are applied. A caliper is also a measuring tool that can be set to measure inside or outside dimensions of an object.

Camshaft A rotating shaft on which a series of cam lobes operate the valve mechanisms. The camshaft may be driven by gears, by sprockets and chain or by sprockets and a belt.

Canister A container in an evaporative emission control system; contains activated charcoal granules to trap vapours from the fuel system.

Canister

Carburettor A device which mixes fuel with air in the proper proportions to provide a desired power output from a spark ignition internal combustion engine.

Castellated Resembling the parapets along the top of a castle wall. For example, a castellated balljoint stud nut.

Castor In wheel alignment, the backward or forward tilt of the steering axis. Castor is positive when the steering axis is inclined rearward at the top.

Catalytic converter A silencer-like device in the exhaust system which converts certain pollutants in the exhaust gases into less harmful substances.

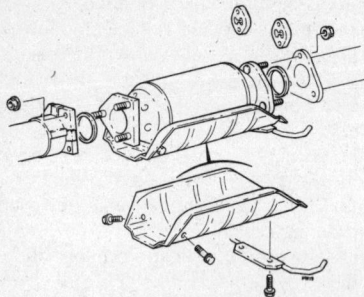

Catalytic converter

Circlip A ring-shaped clip used to prevent endwise movement of cylindrical parts and shafts. An internal circlip is installed in a groove in a housing; an external circlip fits into a groove on the outside of a cylindrical piece such as a shaft.

Clearance The amount of space between two parts. For example, between a piston and a cylinder, between a bearing and a journal, etc.

Coil spring A spiral of elastic steel found in various sizes throughout a vehicle, for example as a springing medium in the suspension and in the valve train.

Compression Reduction in volume, and increase in pressure and temperature, of a gas, caused by squeezing it into a smaller space.

Compression ratio The relationship between cylinder volume when the piston is at top dead centre and cylinder volume when the piston is at bottom dead centre.

Constant velocity (CV) joint A type of universal joint that cancels out vibrations caused by driving power being transmitted through an angle.

Core plug A disc or cup-shaped metal device inserted in a hole in a casting through which core was removed when the casting was formed. Also known as a freeze plug or expansion plug.

Crankcase The lower part of the engine block in which the crankshaft rotates.

Crankshaft The main rotating member, or shaft, running the length of the crankcase, with offset "throws" to which the connecting rods are attached.

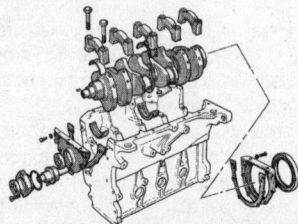

Crankshaft assembly

Crocodile clip See Alligator clip

D

Diagnostic code Code numbers obtained by accessing the diagnostic mode of an engine management computer. This code can be used to determine the area in the system where a malfunction may be located.

Disc brake A brake design incorporating a rotating disc onto which brake pads are squeezed. The resulting friction converts the energy of a moving vehicle into heat.

Double-overhead cam (DOHC) An engine that uses two overhead camshafts, usually one for the intake valves and one for the exhaust valves.

Drivebelt(s) The belt(s) used to drive accessories such as the alternator, water pump, power steering pump, air conditioning compressor, etc. off the crankshaft pulley.

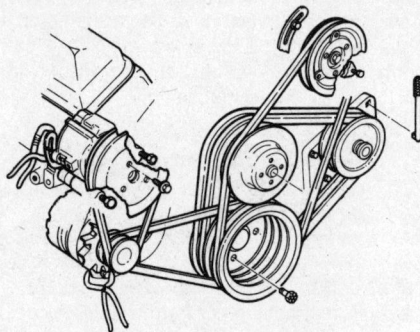

Accessory drivebelts

Driveshaft Any shaft used to transmit motion. Commonly used when referring to the axleshafts on a front wheel drive vehicle.

Drum brake A type of brake using a drum-shaped metal cylinder attached to the inner surface of the wheel. When the brake pedal is pressed, curved brake shoes with friction linings press against the inside of the drum to slow or stop the vehicle.

E

EGR valve A valve used to introduce exhaust gases into the intake air stream.

Electronic control unit (ECU) A computer which controls (for instance) ignition and fuel injection systems, or an anti-lock braking system. For more information refer to the *Haynes Automotive Electrical and Electronic Systems Manual*.

Electronic Fuel Injection (EFI) A computer controlled fuel system that distributes fuel through an injector located in each intake port of the engine.

Emergency brake A braking system, independent of the main hydraulic system, that can be used to slow or stop the vehicle if the primary brakes fail, or to hold the vehicle stationary even though the brake pedal isn't depressed. It usually consists of a hand lever that actuates either front or rear brakes mechanically through a series of cables and linkages. Also known as a handbrake or parking brake.

Endfloat The amount of lengthwise movement between two parts. As applied to a crankshaft, the distance that the crankshaft can move forward and back in the cylinder block.

Engine management system (EMS) A computer controlled system which manages the fuel injection and the ignition systems in an integrated fashion.

Exhaust manifold A part with several passages through which exhaust gases leave the engine combustion chambers and enter the exhaust pipe.

F

Fan clutch A viscous (fluid) drive coupling device which permits variable engine fan speeds in relation to engine speeds.

Feeler blade A thin strip or blade of hardened steel, ground to an exact thickness, used to check or measure clearances between parts.

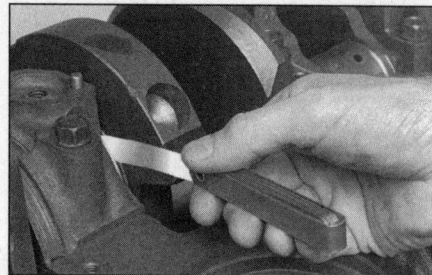

Feeler blade

Firing order The order in which the engine cylinders fire, or deliver their power strokes, beginning with the number one cylinder.

Flywheel A heavy spinning wheel in which energy is absorbed and stored by means of momentum. On cars, the flywheel is attached to the crankshaft to smooth out firing impulses.

Free play The amount of travel before any action takes place. The "looseness" in a linkage, or an assembly of parts, between the initial application of force and actual movement. For example, the distance the brake pedal moves before the pistons in the master cylinder are actuated.

Fuse An electrical device which protects a circuit against accidental overload. The typical fuse contains a soft piece of metal which is calibrated to melt at a predetermined current flow (expressed as amps) and break the circuit.

Fusible link A circuit protection device consisting of a conductor surrounded by heat-resistant insulation. The conductor is smaller than the wire it protects, so it acts as the weakest link in the circuit. Unlike a blown fuse, a failed fusible link must frequently be cut from the wire for replacement.

G

Gap The distance the spark must travel in jumping from the centre electrode to the side electrode in a spark plug. Also refers to the spacing between the points in a contact breaker assembly in a conventional points-type ignition, or to the distance between the reluctor or rotor and the pickup coil in an electronic ignition.

Adjusting spark plug gap

Gasket Any thin, soft material - usually cork, cardboard, asbestos or soft metal - installed between two metal surfaces to ensure a good seal. For instance, the cylinder head gasket seals the joint between the block and the cylinder head.

Gasket

Gauge An instrument panel display used to monitor engine conditions. A gauge with a movable pointer on a dial or a fixed scale is an analogue gauge. A gauge with a numerical readout is called a digital gauge.

H

Halfshaft A rotating shaft that transmits power from the final drive unit to a drive wheel, usually when referring to a live rear axle.

Harmonic balancer A device designed to reduce torsion or twisting vibration in the crankshaft. May be incorporated in the crankshaft pulley. Also known as a vibration damper.

Hone An abrasive tool for correcting small irregularities or differences in diameter in an engine cylinder, brake cylinder, etc.

Hydraulic tappet A tappet that utilises hydraulic pressure from the engine's lubrication system to maintain zero clearance (constant contact with both camshaft and valve stem). Automatically adjusts to variation in valve stem length. Hydraulic tappets also reduce valve noise.

I

Ignition timing The moment at which the spark plug fires, usually expressed in the number of crankshaft degrees before the piston reaches the top of its stroke.

Inlet manifold A tube or housing with passages through which flows the air-fuel mixture (carburettor vehicles and vehicles with throttle body injection) or air only (port fuel-injected vehicles) to the port openings in the cylinder head.

J

Jump start Starting the engine of a vehicle with a discharged or weak battery by attaching jump leads from the weak battery to a charged or helper battery.

L

Load Sensing Proportioning Valve (LSPV) A brake hydraulic system control valve that works like a proportioning valve, but also takes into consideration the amount of weight carried by the rear axle.

Locknut A nut used to lock an adjustment nut, or other threaded component, in place. For example, a locknut is employed to keep the adjusting nut on the rocker arm in position.

Lockwasher A form of washer designed to prevent an attaching nut from working loose.

M

MacPherson strut A type of front suspension system devised by Earle MacPherson at Ford of England. In its original form, a simple lateral link with the anti-roll bar creates the lower control arm. A long strut - an integral coil spring and shock absorber - is mounted between the body and the steering knuckle. Many modern so-called MacPherson strut systems use a conventional lower A-arm and don't rely on the anti-roll bar for location.

Multimeter An electrical test instrument with the capability to measure voltage, current and resistance.

N

NOx Oxides of Nitrogen. A common toxic pollutant emitted by petrol and diesel engines at higher temperatures.

O

Ohm The unit of electrical resistance. One volt applied to a resistance of one ohm will produce a current of one amp.

Ohmmeter An instrument for measuring electrical resistance.

O-ring A type of sealing ring made of a special rubber-like material; in use, the O-ring is compressed into a groove to provide the sealing action.

Overhead cam (ohc) engine An engine with the camshaft(s) located on top of the cylinder head(s).

Overhead valve (ohv) engine An engine with the valves located in the cylinder head, but with the camshaft located in the engine block.

Oxygen sensor A device installed in the engine exhaust manifold, which senses the oxygen content in the exhaust and converts this information into an electric current. Also called a Lambda sensor.

P

Phillips screw A type of screw head having a cross instead of a slot for a corresponding type of screwdriver.

Plastigage A thin strip of plastic thread, available in different sizes, used for measuring clearances. For example, a strip of Plastigage is laid across a bearing journal. The parts are assembled and dismantled; the width of the crushed strip indicates the clearance between journal and bearing.

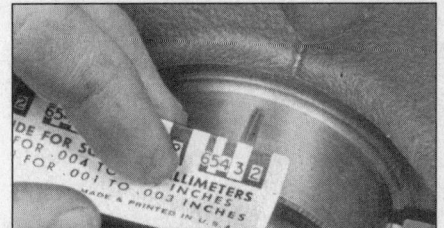

Plastigage

Propeller shaft The long hollow tube with universal joints at both ends that carries power from the transmission to the differential on front-engined rear wheel drive vehicles.

Proportioning valve A hydraulic control valve which limits the amount of pressure to the rear brakes during panic stops to prevent wheel lock-up.

R

Rack-and-pinion steering A steering system with a pinion gear on the end of the steering shaft that mates with a rack (think of a geared wheel opened up and laid flat). When the steering wheel is turned, the pinion turns, moving the rack to the left or right. This movement is transmitted through the track rods to the steering arms at the wheels.

Radiator A liquid-to-air heat transfer device designed to reduce the temperature of the coolant in an internal combustion engine cooling system.

Refrigerant Any substance used as a heat transfer agent in an air-conditioning system. R-12 has been the principle refrigerant for many years; recently, however, manufacturers have begun using R-134a, a non-CFC substance that is considered less harmful to the ozone in the upper atmosphere.

Rocker arm A lever arm that rocks on a shaft or pivots on a stud. In an overhead valve engine, the rocker arm converts the upward movement of the pushrod into a downward movement to open a valve.

Rotor In a distributor, the rotating device inside the cap that connects the centre electrode and the outer terminals as it turns, distributing the high voltage from the coil secondary winding to the proper spark plug. Also, that part of an alternator which rotates inside the stator. Also, the rotating assembly of a turbocharger, including the compressor wheel, shaft and turbine wheel.

Runout The amount of wobble (in-and-out movement) of a gear or wheel as it's rotated. The amount a shaft rotates "out-of-true." The out-of-round condition of a rotating part.

S

Sealant A liquid or paste used to prevent leakage at a joint. Sometimes used in conjunction with a gasket.

Sealed beam lamp An older headlight design which integrates the reflector, lens and filaments into a hermetically-sealed one-piece unit. When a filament burns out or the lens cracks, the entire unit is simply replaced.

Serpentine drivebelt A single, long, wide accessory drivebelt that's used on some newer vehicles to drive all the accessories, instead of a series of smaller, shorter belts. Serpentine drivebelts are usually tensioned by an automatic tensioner.

Serpentine drivebelt

Shim Thin spacer, commonly used to adjust the clearance or relative positions between two parts. For example, shims inserted into or under bucket tappets control valve clearances. Clearance is adjusted by changing the thickness of the shim.

Slide hammer A special puller that screws into or hooks onto a component such as a shaft or bearing; a heavy sliding handle on the shaft bottoms against the end of the shaft to knock the component free.

Sprocket A tooth or projection on the periphery of a wheel, shaped to engage with a chain or drivebelt. Commonly used to refer to the sprocket wheel itself.

Starter inhibitor switch On vehicles with an automatic transmission, a switch that prevents starting if the vehicle is not in Neutral or Park.

Strut See MacPherson strut.

T

Tappet A cylindrical component which transmits motion from the cam to the valve stem, either directly or via a pushrod and rocker arm. Also called a cam follower.

Thermostat A heat-controlled valve that regulates the flow of coolant between the cylinder block and the radiator, so maintaining optimum engine operating temperature. A thermostat is also used in some air cleaners in which the temperature is regulated.

Thrust bearing The bearing in the clutch assembly that is moved in to the release levers by clutch pedal action to disengage the clutch. Also referred to as a release bearing.

Timing belt A toothed belt which drives the camshaft. Serious engine damage may result if it breaks in service.

Timing chain A chain which drives the camshaft.

Toe-in The amount the front wheels are closer together at the front than at the rear. On rear wheel drive vehicles, a slight amount of toe-in is usually specified to keep the front wheels running parallel on the road by offsetting other forces that tend to spread the wheels apart.

Toe-out The amount the front wheels are closer together at the rear than at the front. On front wheel drive vehicles, a slight amount of toe-out is usually specified.

Tools For full information on choosing and using tools, refer to the *Haynes Automotive Tools Manual*.

Tracer A stripe of a second colour applied to a wire insulator to distinguish that wire from another one with the same colour insulator.

Tune-up A process of accurate and careful adjustments and parts replacement to obtain the best possible engine performance.

Turbocharger A centrifugal device, driven by exhaust gases, that pressurises the intake air. Normally used to increase the power output from a given engine displacement, but can also be used primarily to reduce exhaust emissions (as on VW's "Umwelt" Diesel engine).

U

Universal joint or U-joint A double-pivoted connection for transmitting power from a driving to a driven shaft through an angle. A U-joint consists of two Y-shaped yokes and a cross-shaped member called the spider.

V

Valve A device through which the flow of liquid, gas, vacuum, or loose material in bulk may be started, stopped, or regulated by a movable part that opens, shuts, or partially obstructs one or more ports or passageways. A valve is also the movable part of such a device.

Valve clearance The clearance between the valve tip (the end of the valve stem) and the rocker arm or tappet. The valve clearance is measured when the valve is closed.

Vernier caliper A precision measuring instrument that measures inside and outside dimensions. Not quite as accurate as a micrometer, but more convenient.

Viscosity The thickness of a liquid or its resistance to flow.

Volt A unit for expressing electrical "pressure" in a circuit. One volt that will produce a current of one ampere through a resistance of one ohm.

W

Welding Various processes used to join metal items by heating the areas to be joined to a molten state and fusing them together. For more information refer to the *Haynes Automotive Welding Manual*.

Wiring diagram A drawing portraying the components and wires in a vehicle's electrical system, using standardised symbols. For more information refer to the *Haynes Automotive Electrical and Electronic Systems Manual*.

Note: *References throughout this index are in the form - "Chapter number" • "page number"*

Preserving Our Motoring Heritage

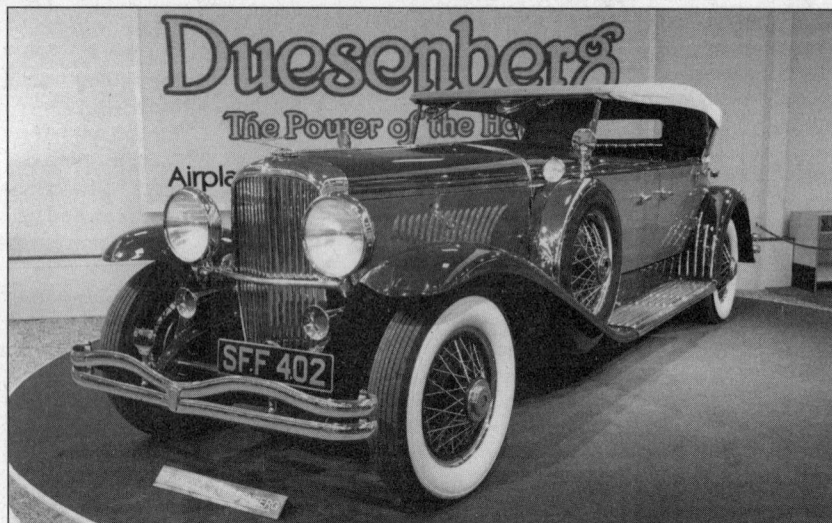

< The Model J Duesenberg
Derham Tourster.
Only eight of these
magnificent cars were
ever built – this is the
only example to be found
outside the United
States of America

Almost every car you've ever loved, loathed or desired is gathered under one roof at the Haynes Motor Museum. Over 300 immaculately presented cars and motorbikes represent every aspect of our motoring heritage, from elegant reminders of bygone days, such as the superb Model J Duesenberg to curiosities like the bug-eyed BMW Isetta. There are also many old friends and flames. Perhaps you remember the 1959 Ford Popular that you did your courting in? The magnificent 'Red Collection' is a spectacle of classic sports cars including AC, Alfa Romeo, Austin Healey, Ferrari, Lamborghini, Maserati, MG, Riley, Porsche and Triumph.

A Perfect Day Out

Each and every vehicle at the Haynes Motor Museum has played its part in the history and culture of Motoring. Today, they make a wonderful spectacle and a great day out for all the family. Bring the kids, bring Mum and Dad, but above all bring your camera to capture those golden memories for ever. You will also find an impressive array of motoring memorabilia, a comfortable 70 seat video cinema and one of the most extensive transport book shops in Britain. The Pit Stop Cafe serves everything from a cup of tea to wholesome, home-made meals or, if you prefer, you can enjoy the large picnic area nestled in the beautiful rural surroundings of Somerset.

> John Haynes O.B.E.,
Founder and
Chairman of the
museum at the wheel
of a Haynes Light 12.

< Graham Hill's Lola
Cosworth Formula 1
car next to a 1934
Riley Sports.

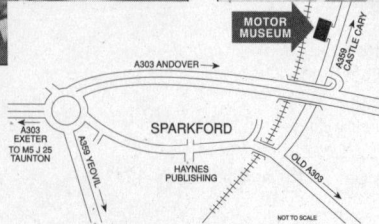

The Museum is situated on the A359 Yeovil to Frome road at Sparkford, just off the A303 in Somerset. It is about 40 miles south of Bristol, and 25 minutes drive from the M5 intersection at Taunton.

Open 9.30am - 5.30pm (10.00am - 4.00pm Winter) 7 days a week, *except Christmas Day, Boxing Day and New Years Day*
Special rates available for schools, coach parties and outings Charitable Trust No. 292048